ISBN 978-0-656-35756-7
PIBN 10068778

This book is a reproduction of an important historical work. Forgotten Books uses
state-of-the-art technology to digitally reconstruct the work, preserving the original format
whilst repairing imperfections present in the aged copy. In rare cases, an imperfection in
the original, such as a blemish or missing page, may be replicated in our edition. We do,
however, repair the vast majority of imperfections successfully; any imperfections that
remain are intentionally left to preserve the state of such historical works.

THE

NEW SOUTH WALES

LAW REPORTS.

REPORTERS:

COMMON LAW AND DIVORCE ... { H. M. COCKSHOTT,
S. E. LAMB.

EQUITY ... ... J. M. HARVEY.

BANKRUPTCY AND PROBATE ... R. K. MANNING.

BARRISTERS-AT-LAW.

VOL. XIX.

1898.

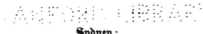

Sydney:

C. F. MAXWELL (HAYES BROS.), LTD.,

161 KING STREET.

294547

F. CUNNINGHAME & CO. PRINTERS, 146 PITT STREET, SYDNEY.

THE

SUPREME COURT OF NEW SOUTH WALES.

JUDGES AND LAW OFFICERS

DURING THE PERIOD COMPRISED IN THIS VOLUME.

The Hon. SIR FREDERICK DARLEY, K.C.M.G., CHIEF JUSTICE.

The Hon. MATTHEW HENRY STEPHEN
The Hon. WILLIAM OWEN
The Hon. CHARLES JAMES MANNING
The Hon. GEORGE BOWEN SIMPSON
The Hon. HENRY EMANUEL COHEN
The Hon. ARCHIBALD HENRY SIMPSON
The Hon. WILLIAM GREGORY WALKER
The Hon. RICHARD EDWARD O'CONNOR (Acting)

} PUISNE JUDGES.

JUDGES IN EQUITY:

The Hon. CHARLES JAMES MANNING, CHIEF JUDGE.
The Hon. ARCHIBALD HENRY SIMPSON, CHIEF JUDGE.
The Hon. WILLIAM GREGORY WALKER.

JUDGE IN VICE-ADMIRALTY:

The Hon. SIR FREDERICK DARLEY, K.C.M.G., JUDGE COMMISSARY.

JUDGE IN DIVORCE:

The Hon. GEORGE BOWEN SIMPSON.

JUDGES IN BANKRUPTCY AND PROBATE:

The Hon. ARCHIBALD HENRY SIMPSON.
The Hon. WILLIAM GREGORY WALKER.

ATTORNEY-GENERAL:

The Hon. JOHN H WANT, Q.C.

SOLICITOR-GENERAL:

The Right Hon. GEORGE H. REID, Q.C.

MEMORANDA.

On Monday, the 8th of August, the Hon. CHARLES JAMES MANNING, Chief Judge in Equity, died.

On Tuesday, the 9th of August, when the Court sat :—

The Chief Justice said : When the sad news reached me yesterday that the Almighty had seen fit take our dear friend Mr. Justice Manning to Himself I was too stunned to do more than announce the fact to the Bar. I fancy I saw my own feelings reflected on the faces of all those in Court. It is not possible to meet now without saying a few words which may express our feeling of deep sorrow at the loss of so dear and valuable a colleague. Mr. Justice Manning was a refined, courteous, and kindly gentleman, a learned, able, hardworking, and conscientious Judge ; one who, having a keen insight into human nature, among many other noble characteristics, knew how to temper justice with mercy. Rarely do we find in any one man such a combination of qualities fitting him for the position of a Judge as Mr. Justice Manning possessed. An exceedingly ably Equity lawyer, he was perfectly at home when sitting on the Common Law side of the Court, and this whether in the exercise of its civil or its criminal jurisdiction. It may with truth be said that he formed and established the practice which now prevails in the Bankruptcy Court and which has proved so satisfactory to the public. Consequently the loss the public sustain by his too early death is well nigh irreparable. Having practised for some 24 years at our Bar with great success, he was in 1889 raised to the Bench, which he has adorned for the past nine years. Although more or less an invalid for some years past, his indomitable courage, a prevailing sense of duty, and a total abnegation of self sustained and enabled him to fulfil his onerous work to the entire satisfaction of the public, his colleagues on the Bench, and the Bar, who now mourn their loss. He was at all times a genial companion, possessed of a most lovable nature, and was a true and loyal colleague, always ready to afford his valuable assistance to any branch of our varied jurisdictions which required his aid. Only on Friday last, at my request, he was sitting in this Court, with his mind so bright and his perception so clear as to lead one to hope that we might have the benefit of his services for some years yet to come. For myself, I may say I have lost one of my oldest and dearest friends. He leaves behind him an example for us all to follow. The nearer we approach the end he aimed at—a high standard of judicial excellence—the more useful we will be in the discharge of our high duty to the public. Nothing now remains but to express our deep and heartfelt sympathy with Mrs. Manning and the other members of his family, and to pray that the Almighty may see fit in His own good time to assuage the inevitable and bitter grief which flows from the irreparable loss they have sustained.

Sir Julian Salomons, Q.C., said : If your Honours please, may I be allowed to inform the Court that as the Honourable the Attorney-General is unfortunately kept at home to-day by illness, he has sent a request that I think I shall best fulfil by reading with your Honours' permission the letter I have received. Mr. Want writes :

Sydney, August 8.

"My dear Sir Julian,—I have just heard of the sad death of my dear friend Mr. Justice Manning. I am confined to my room through illness, and therefore prevented from paying (as the official head of the Bar) my tribute of respect and esteem to his memory. Will you as senior member of the profession undertake the painful duty which would otherwise have fallen upon me ? I feel that the Bench has suffered an almost irreparable loss by the death of Mr.

Justice Manning. His great patience and common sense, combined with his acknowledged high legal attainments, made Mr. Justice Manning a conspicuous judicial figure, and I am much afraid that his devotion to duty unduly hastened his end. Both branches of the profession will ever remember his great courtesy and impartiality, and the people of the colony will soon realise that they have seen a truly faithful and loyal servant called away. It was my privilege to number Mr. Justice Manning amongst my dearest personal friends, and his death has caused me a great sense of sorrow and grief, which cannot be effaced. I am sincerely grieved that I cannot attend personally to give expression to my recognition of our great loss; but I am sure that I can depend upon you conveying to the Court our universal sorrow and our sympathy with those who, near and dear to him, are left to mourn their loss.

"Yours sincerely, J. H. WANT."

But the wish of the Attorney-General I need not carry out literally. The Bar has heard with sympathetic accord and sorrowful appreciation what has been so well and aptly said by his Honour the Chief Justice and in the letter I have read; so I think I ought only to add on behalf of the Bar our full and heartfelt concurrence in the tributes of admiration, regret, and affection so perfectly and sincerely expressed. I had the friendship of Mr. Justice Manning without a ripple of misunderstanding throughout the whole of his career from the time he left college till the day—only last Friday—when he sat here and gave judgment in a case I had then argued. I am naturally somewhat unnerved by his sudden going from amongst us. But I must not refer to myself alone. All of us at the Bar can testify not only to his legal knowledge and ability, but also to his never-failing patience and unvarying urbanity—qualities as much needed as great learning for the smooth and efficient discharge of the difficult duties of the judicial office. We at the Bar have to deplore the sudden parting with a dear and true friend, the Supreme Court Bench has lost a most valued colleague, and the whole colony cannot but mourn the untimely death of one of her best sons, who, to the last, served his country faithfully and well. As to this world it is too true that he is no longer living; but we may hope that as long as the lives of sorely tried and much to be pitied mankind need the aid of human laws to guide, control, and coerce them, the spirit of his wise and beneficent influence may live and be entwined in the traditions of the Court of which he was so honoured and distinguished a member.

On the 25th of August, The Hon. ARCHIBALD HENRY SIMPSON, Judge in Bankruptcy and Probate, was appointed Chief Judge in Equity.

On the 25th of August, WILLIAM GREGORY WALKER, Esquire, Q.C., was appointed Judge in Bankruptcy and Probate.

On the same day in the Banco Court, Mr. Justice WALKER was sworn in.

THE ATTORNEY-GENERAL (Mr. J. H. Want, Q.C.) said : On behalf of the members of the Bar, of which I have the honour to be the official head, and on behalf of and at the request of the members of the other branch of the profession—the solicitors of the Court—I desire to offer to you, Mr. Justice Gregory Walker, our hearty and sincere congratulations upon your elevation to the distinguished position which you now occupy. Our pleasure in offering these congratulations and words of welcome is necessarily tinged with some feeling of regret that the vacancy on the Bench which has been filled by your appointment was caused by the death of one who endeared himself to the hearts of all of us ; but we feel perfectly certain that it must be an incentive to all those who follow in the late Mr. Justice Manning's footsteps to endeavour to emulate the example of one who won for himself the commendation, not only of the legal profession, but of the public generally. We on this side of the Court—the common law jurisdiction—have not had the distinguished privilege of close acquaintanceship with your Honour which my brethren of the Equity Bar have had, who practise in what I may call the more peaceful atmosphere of its equitable jurisdiction, but we know sufficient of your many good qualities and of your high legal attainments to feel perfectly certain that you will be a worthy successor of Mr. Justice Manning, who previously presided there. So far as our welcome is concerned we will not yield one jot to those who have had that distinguished privilege. We offer, and I am sure your Honour will accept, our promise of that loyal assistance which we know tends to make the duties of a Judge easier. On behalf of the other branch of the legal profession I am also asked to say for those who stand as guardians between the public and litigation that they will also endeavour to render your Honour's duties as light as possible. In conclusion, I ask your Honour to accept the congratulations of both branches of the profession, and I am sure I may add, the public. We feel certain that your Honour will occupy your new position with credit to yourself and with satisfaction to the people of New South Wales.

Mr. Justice WALKER said : I thank you, Mr. Attorney, for the kind words of congratulation addressed to me on behalf of yourself and the Bar. It is with unfeigned pleasure that I join my brethren of the Bench. Yet pain is mingled with the pleasure. Our regret is yet poignant for that good man and good Judge whose lamented death occasioned the vacancy which I have been invited to fill. Nor can I with equanimity regard the cessation of that life of friendly contest in which I have so long lived happily. Certainly I carry with me into this serener atmosphere keen memories of the delights of battle, but I shall be satisfied if, with the help of God, whose aid I humbly invoke, I am enabled to do my duty in this new sphere of activity. New South Wales has been very good to me ; and to her, the land of my adoption, my best services are due, and shall be rendered. I recall with gratification the cordial relations that I have always enjoyed with my comrades of the Bar and also with the solicitors of the Court, and I hope that the coming years will cement, not weaken, the many personal friendships I have formed with members of both branches of the profession. It shall be my endeavour, Mr. Attorney, to acquit myself worthily of the high position in which I have been placed, always remembering the serious responsibilities of my office and studying to discharge them in the spirit of the aphorism "Quanto quis scit, tanto se scit nescire."

On the 28th of September, The Right Honourable GEORGE HOUSTON REID was appointed Queen's Counsel.

On the 1st of November, The Hon. RICHARD EDWARD O'CONNOR, Q.C., M.L.C., was appointed an Acting Judge of the Supreme Court.

On the 4th of November, BERNARD RINGROSE WISE, Esquire, was appointed Queen's Counsel.

A TABLE

OF THE

NAMES OF THE CASES REPORTED

IN THIS VOLUME.

COMMON LAW.

TABLE OF CASES REPORTED.

EQUITY.

BANKRUPTCY AND PROBATE.

TABLE OF CASES REPORTED.

DIVORCE.

CASES

DETERMINED BY THE

SUPREME COURT OF NEW SOUTH WALES

IN ITS

Common Law Jurisdiction,

AND BY THE

PRIVY COUNCIL ON APPEAL THEREFROM DURING 1898.

KELLY *v.* CALÉDONIAN COAL CO.

Contract—Statute of Frauds, s. 4.

1898.

Feb. 16.
March 1.

The C.J.
Stephen J.
and
Cohen J.

The plaintiff, being about to tender for the supply of coal to the Harbours and Rivers Department for 18 months, saw the defendants' manager, and had certain conversations with him as to the price they would supply him with coal in the event of his being the successful tenderer ; and the following letter was written to him, "I beg to confirm verbal arrangements made with reference to the prices for the contract to the Harbours and Rivers Department," and then followed the prices. The plaintiff was the successful tenderer, and entered into a contract with the department to supply such coal as should be required up to 6,500 tons. But under that contract the department was not bound to take any quantity of coal from the plaintiff. The plaintiff brought an action for breach of contract against the defendants, alleging that they had entered into an agreement to supply him with coal for the purpose of his carrying out his contract with the department. The defendants pleaded the Statute of Frauds. *Held*, that the letter above referred to, even when read with the contract between the plaintiff and the department, did not contain a promise to supply the coal he might require to fulfil that contract.

NEW TRIAL MOTION.

DECLARATION. For that before the grievances hereinafter alleged, the plaintiff was carrying on the business of a coal merchant, and the Public Works Department had advertised for tenders for the supply of coal to the Harbours and Rivers Branch of the said department for a period of 18 months from the 1st January, 1896, and the plaintiff was about to send in a tender for the supply of the said coal ; all of which things the defendants well knew, and it was agreed by and between the plaintiff and defendants that, in the event of the plaintiff being the successful tenderer, the defendants would supply the plaintiff with all the coal required by the plaintiff under such contract as the plaintiff should enter into with the said Public Works Department for the supply of coal to the said Harbours and Rivers Branch during the said period of 18 months at the price, etc.; and the plaintiff became and was the successful tenderer, and entered into a contract with the said Public Works Department to supply to the said Harbours and Rivers Branch such coal as might be required during the period aforesaid, all of which things the defendants well knew, and all conditions were fulfilled, etc.; yet the defendants supplied portion only of the said coal at the said prices, and refused to supply a large part thereof at all, etc.

PLEA (*inter alia*). Statute of Frauds.

It appeared that the plaintiff, being about to tender for the supply of coal to the Public Works Department, saw Dr. Robertson, the manager of the defendant company, and told him that that department was calling for tenders, and that he was about to tender, and wanted a list of prices at which his company would supply him with coal. He got a letter from the company in these terms:

"Dear Sir,

I beg to confirm verbal arrangements made with reference to the prices for the contract to Harbours and Rivers Department, viz., best Waratah at shoots, 6*s.* 4*d.* per ton F.O.B.; small Waratah at shoots, 3*s.* 6*d.* per ton F.O.B. These prices refer to this contract alone. Payment by p/n. due at a month from date of shipment.

I am, yours truly,
F. W. TANN,
Secretary."

After receipt of this letter the plaintiff tendered for the supply of coal to the Public Works Department, and his tender was accepted. Under the contract entered into with the department, the plaintiff was to supply whatever coal the department wanted for a period of 18 months from the 1st January, 1896, up to the amount of 6500 tons at certain prices, but there was nothing in the contract which in any way bound the department to take any quantity of coal from the plaintiff. The plaintiff got coal regularly from January to March from the company at the prices

quoted in the letter, but after March they refused to supply coal
to the plaintiff on those terms.

1898.

KELLY
v.
CALEDONIAN
COAL Co.

In order to prove the contract declared on the plaintiff put in
the letter above referred to and the contract between himself and
the Public Works Department.

The jury found a verdict for the plaintiff.

The jury specially found in answer to questions put to them
by *Stephen*, J., that there was an agreement between the plaintiff
and defendants that, in the event of the plaintiff being the successful tenderer, the defendants should supply all such coal as
the plaintiff should require, and that there was a breach of such
agreement. His Honour formally ruled that that agreement was
in writing, and leave was reserved to the defendants to move to
enter a nonsuit.

A rule *nisi* was granted calling upon the plaintiff to shew cause
why the verdict should not be set aside, and a nonsuit entered on
the ground (*inter alia*) that there was no evidence in writing of
the alleged contract sued upon sufficient to satisfy the requirements of the Statute of Frauds.

Scholes and *Pickburn*, for the defendants. The contract
declared on being one which was not to be performed within the
space of one year had to be in writing under the Statute of
Frauds. All the terms of the contract must be in writing. Here
the letter from the defendants to Kelly did not contain all the
terms of the contract: *Wain* v. *Warlters*(1); *Munday* v. *Asprey* (2).

Shand and *James*, for the plaintiff. The letter from the
defendants to Kelly refers to the contract entered into between
him and the Public Works Department. That contract can,
therefore, be looked at to explain the agreement entered into
between the parties. It is not necessary in order to satisfy the
Statute of Frauds that the whole agreement should be written on
one piece of paper. If the signed paper refers to other written
papers, then the separate documents can be looked at to see what
the agreement is between the parties. Here the contract between

(1) 5 East 10.   (2) 13 Ch. D. 855.

A 2

1898.

Kelly and the Public Works Department was to supply the coal

KELLY
v.
CALEDONIAN
COAL CO.

required by the department, and the agreement between Kelly and the company was that the latter should supply the coal required by him to carry out that contract.

They referred to *Benjamin on Sales*, 3rd Ed. 185 ; *Macdonald* v. *Longbottom* (1) ; *Long* v. *Millar* (2) ; *Reuss* v. *Picksley* (3) ; *Horsey* v. *Graham* (4).

Scholes in reply. I admit that a number of papers may be looked at where they contain the whole bargain between the parties. This letter contains no promise on the part of the defendants to supply any quantity of coal. This letter is nothing more than a schedule of prices. Kelly, in giving evidence, said that the defendants had promised to supply him with what coal he wanted for the department, but that term is not in the letter.

[COHEN, J., referred to *Harvey* v. *Facey* (5) ; *Pearce* v. *Gardner* (6).

James referred to *Newell* v. *Radford* (7).]

Harvey v. *Facey* (5) is in my favour, and shews that here there was no concluded agreement.

THE CHIEF JUSTICE. In this case the plaintiff brought an action against the defendants, who are colliery proprietors, and in the declaration he alleged that the Public Works Department had advertised for tenders for the supply of coal for a period of 18 months, and he was about to send in a tender for the supply of the coal, and it was agreed that, in the event of the plaintiff being the successful tenderer, the defendants would supply the plaintiff with all the coal required by the plaintiff under such contract as the plaintiff should enter into with the Public Works Department at the price of so much per ton, and then the declaration goes on to allege that the plaintiff was the successful tenderer, and did enter into a contract with the Public Works

(1) 29 L.J.Q.B. 256.   (4) L.R. 5 C.P. 9.
(2) 4 C.P.D. 450.   (5) [1893] A.C. 552.
(3) L.R. 1 Ex. 342.   (6) [1897] 1 Q.B. 688.
                    (7) L.R. 3 C.P. 52.

Department, and then alleges the breach that the defendants refused to supply a large part of the coal, &c.

The question now is, whether a certain letter written by the secretary of the company can in any way be said to be a contract which can be supported under the Statute of Frauds, this being a contract extending over a period of more than a year. The case no doubt presents some difficulty, but after giving this letter the utmost consideration I fail to see that there is in it any promise on the part of the defendants to supply coal. It appears that the Government had issued an invitation for tenders for the supply of coal to the Harbours and Rivers Department, and that the plaintiff had some conversation with Dr. Robertson, the manager of the defendant company, about the prices of their coal in order that he might base his tender on those prices. The letter in question was thereupon handed to him. It is in these terms, " I beg to confirm verbal arrangements made with reference to the prices for the contract to Harbours and Rivers Department." At that time there was no contract with the department, nor had he made any tender. What is there referred to is the contract which might be obtained—the contract in contemplation. On the authority of *Horsey* v. *Graham* (1) I think, in construing this letter, we should be entitled to look at the contract which was subsequently entered into. But when we do look at it, we find that there is no contract on the part of the department to take one ounce of coal. The plaintiff no doubt is bound to supply the coal whether the department required 1,000 tons or 6,000 tons, but there is no contract on their part to take any quantity of coal. The letter then continues, " Best Waratah at shoots, 6s. 4d. per ton F.O.B. ; small Waratah at shoots, 3s. 6d. per ton F.O.B. These prices refer to this contract alone. Payment by p/n. due at one month from date of shipment." Now it is perfectly clear that in the letter there is no promise to the plaintiff to supply the coal which the department required, and I can quite see that it would have been very foolish on their part to have entered into such a contract, for whilst they would have been bound to supply any quantity of coal at a moment's notice, and for that purpose bound

1898.

KELLY
v.
CALEDONIAN
COAL CO.

The C.J.

(1) L.R. 5 C.P. 9.

1898.

KELLY

v.

CALEDONIAN

COAL Co.

The C.J.

to keep a large supply of coal on hand; yet they might never have had to supply a single ounce of coal. There are really no words of promise in this letter, and no words from which a promise could be implied. The position seems to me just the same as if I having a contract for fencing, and wanting some fencing wire I went into an ironmonger's shop, and asked the proprietor of the establishment to give me a list of his prices, and he said the price of No. 6 wire is such and such, and the price of No. 8 such and such. Would that be a contract to supply any quantity of wire I required? Suppose I afterwards went to him, and said "I want 1000 tons." Surely it would be open to him to say "I cannot supply that amount, I have not got it in stock. I never promised to supply you with one ton or 1000 tons." That is exactly the position of the defendants here. This letter simply gives the plaintiff a list of prices. There is no promise to supply any quantity of coal, nor are there any words in the letter from which a promise can be implied. This case falls within the authority of *Harvey* v. *Facey* (1) referred to by Mr. Justice *Cohen.*

For these reasons I am of opinion that a nonsuit ought to be entered, and that the rule should be made absolute with costs.

STEPHEN, J. I agree. I only wish to add one word as to the case of *Newell* v. *Radford* (2). In that case the quantity of flour purchased was specified, whereas in the letter in this case there is nothing to shew the quantity of coal to be delivered, and yet we are asked to read into the contract a promise on the part of the defendants to supply any quantity of coal that the plaintiff might require. It seems to me quite clear that we cannot read that term into the letter.

COHEN, J. I think that the case of *Harvey* v. *Facey* (1) exactly covers this case. It is clear that there is no promise in writing either express or implied that the defendants would sell to the plaintiff such coal as he should require for the purpose of fulfilling his agreement with the Government.

Rule absolute with costs.

Attorneys for the plaintiff: *White & Wolstenholme.*

Attorney for the defendants : *C. J. Bull.*

(1) [1893] A.C. 552.   (2) L.R. 3 C.P. 52.

Ex parte MYLECHARANE.

Justices—Detention of property—19 Vic. No. 24, s. 10—Residence of defendant.

Sect. 10 of 19 Vic. No. 24 is of general application, and a Justice has jurisdiction under that section irrespective of where the defendant resides or where the goods are detained.

1898.

February 24.

The C.J.
Stephen J.
and
Cohen J.

THIS was an application for a mandamus to E. A. L. Sharp, P.M., Forbes, directing him to hear and determine a certain cause in the Court of Petty Sessions.

An information was issued by the applicant that on the 1st of October, "without any just cause, and after demand made by this complainant, and due notice in writing of that demand, one Michael Coffey, at Forbes, did detain from and refuse to deliver up to this complainant certain property belonging to this complainant to wit one dark creamy pony," etc.

A demand was made on Coffey for the pony in Forbes, and he refused to deliver it up. When the matter came before the Police Magistrate it appeared that Coffey was resident at Nyngan, nearly 300 miles from Forbes, and that the horse was there.

The adjudication of the Magistrate was "no jurisdiction," but in an affidavit filed by him he stated: "On the 2nd November I gave my decision that as the defendant resided near Nyngan, where also the horse alleged to be detained was, which is about 300 miles from Forbes, he should not be harassed by being brought to Forbes when Nyngan was the nearest Court of Petty Sessions. I openly stated in Court that, although I had jurisdiction, I did not intend to exercise it, and quoted the late Sir *James Martin's* opinion (*Wilk. Aust. Mag.*, 4th Ed. 338) in support of my decision. The entry in the police book 'no jurisdiction' is simply a clerical error, as I did not hold that I had no jurisdiction."

Garland, for the applicant. 19 Vic. No. 24 has been extended to all parts of the colony by 32 Vic. No. 7, and therefore the Magistrate had jurisdiction and was bound to exercise it.

Ferguson, for the respondent (Coffey), referred to *Ex parte Clarke* (1) ; *Ex parte Skinner* (2) ; *Ex parte Austen* (3).

THE CHIEF JUSTICE.   In this case Mylecharane claimed a certain horse, which he alleged was in the possession of Coffey. It may be taken that Coffey's residence was in Nyngan, and that the horse was there.   It appears that Mylecharane met Coffey in Forbes and demanded the horse from him, and that he refused to deliver it up.   A summons was then taken out under s. 10 of 19 Vic. No. 24, and served upon him in Forbes, and the matter came before Mr. Sharp, Police Magistrate at Forbes.   Objection was taken that he had no jurisdiction because Coffey was resident at Nyngan.   Sect. 10 of 19 Vic. No. 24 is of general application, and the jurisdiction given by that section does not depend on where the respondent resides or where the goods are detained.   But even if the jurisdiction depended upon where the goods were detained, the demand and refusal took place at Forbes, and therefore the detention took place there.   The records shew that the Magistrate decided that he had no jurisdiction.   It is clear that he had jurisdiction.   No doubt, in an affidavit, he says that he had jurisdiction, but declined to exercise it.   A Magistrate has no right to decline to exercise jurisdiction.   If he has jurisdiction he is bound to exercise it, just as this Court in any matter which comes before it, if it has jurisdiction, must exercise it.

I am, therefore, of opinion that the rule should be made absolute, and with costs.

STEPHEN, J., and COHEN, J., concurred.

Rule absolute, with costs.

Attorneys for the applicant : *Chenhall & Eddie*, agents for *Robinson* (Forbes).

Attorney for the respondent : *H. A. Lyons*, agent for *Lamrock* (Forbes).

(1) 7 S.C.R. 146.   (2) 5 W.N. 38.
                    (3) 13 W.N. 193.

MINISTER FOR LANDS *v.* CHAPMAN.

Crown Lands Act of 1884, *s.* 20—*Crown Lands Act of* 1895, *s.* 59—*Reference by Minister*—"*Rights, interests, or revenues of the Crown.*"

1898.
_____
March 4.

The Minister referred a question of forfeiture to the Land Board, under s. 20 of the Crown Lands Act of 1884, and the Board decided against the Crown, and there was no appeal against its decision. Subsequently he referred the Board's decision to the Land Appeal Court, purporting to act under s. 59 of the Crown Lands Act of 1895. *Held*, that the decision being by s. 20 final, he had no power to refer it under s. 59.

The C.J.
Stephen J.
and
Cohen J.

Under s. 59, the Minister may refer to the Land Appeal Court any decision of a Land Board "whereby the rights, interests, or revenues of the Crown may have been affected." The Board having given a decision on the question of the forfeiture of a selection, held that its decision did not affect the "rights, interests, or revenues" of the Crown within the meaning of those words in that section.

SPECIAL CASE stated by the Land Appeal Court.

"1. On the 27th November, 1890, William Chapman applied for an original conditional purchase, and his application was confirmed by the Local Land Board on the 21st January, 1892.

2. In pursuance of s. 20 of the Crown Lands Act of 1884, the Minister for Lands, on the 17th April, 1896, referred to the Local Land Board at Armidale the question whether any statement or statements in the declaration of W. Chapman, lodged with his application, were false within the meaning of s. 26 of the Crown Lands Act of 1884, and in particular, whether the statement in the declaration as to the respective answers or as to any such answer to the following questions was false within the meaning of the said section :—

1. Do you intend to use the land now applied for solely for your own use and benefit ?

2. Is there any agreement or arrangement by which any person other than yourself can acquire any interest in or obtain the use of the land now applied for ?

3. Is there any understanding between you and any person that will tend to defeat or evade the provisions of the law as to conditional purchases ?

3. On the 15th May, 1896, the Local Land Board held an enquiry at Armidale and found (the chairman dissenting) that the answer, "Yes," in the declaration of W. Chapman, to the first question set out above in paragraph 2, was true; that the answer, "No," in the declaration of W. Chapman, to the second question set out as aforesaid, was true; and that the answer, "No," in the declaration of W. Chapman, to the third question set out as aforesaid, was true.

4. On the 18th August, 1896, the Minister for Lands, by a reference purporting to be made in pursuance of the provisions of s. 59 of the Crown Lands Act of 1895, referred the decision of the said Local Land Board to the Land Appeal Court, on the ground that the Local Land Board in its finding and decision had failed or neglected to discharge its duty according to law.

5. The said reference was heard before the Land Appeal Court sitting at Sydney on the 3rd November, 1896, and their reserved decision was given on the 16th November, 1896. The Land Appeal Court ordered the case to be remitted to the Local Land Board for rehearing.

6. On the 9th April, 1897, the Local Land Board, after hearing further evidence, gave their decision in accordance with their previous decision, as set forth above in paragraph 3. The chairman again dissented from the decision of the Board.

7. Being of opinion that the rights or interests of the Crown were injuriously affected by the said decision of the Local Land Board, the Minister for Lands, by a reference purporting to be made in pursuance of the provisions of s. 59 of the Crown Lands Act of 1895, referred the same on the 7th May, 1897, to the Land Appeal Court.

8. The said reference in the preceding paragraph mentioned was heard before the Land Appeal Court sitting at Tamworth, on the 25th June, 1897, and the present respondent's agent agreed that the evidence taken before the Local Land Board at their inquiry, held on the 9th April, 1897, should be taken as evidence before the said Land Appeal Court, and the reference was heard in accordance with such agreement.

9. The Land Appeal Court gave its decision at Sydney on the 14th July, 1897, and dismissed the said reference of the 7th

May, 1897, holding that the Minister for Lands had no power to
make the same.

The question for decision by the Supreme Court is, whether,
under the circumstances hereinbefore set forth, the Land Appeal
Court was right in holding that the Minister for Lands had no
power to make the said reference of the 7th May, 1897.

Sir *Julian Salomons*, Q.C., and *Hanbury Davies*, for the
appellant (the Minister for Lands). Sect. 26 of the Crown
Lands Act of 1884 provides that if the applicant makes any
false statement in the declaration lodged with his application he
shall forfeit his land. In this case the Minister referred to the
Local Land Board, under s. 20, the question whether Chapman
had made a false statement in his declaration. They decided
against the Minister. The Minister did not appeal against their
decision, but referred it to the Land Appeal Court, under s. 59
of the Act of 1895. That power was given to the Minister so that
in cases where the rights of the Crown were affected, and where
he had not the opportunity of appealing, he might, nevertheless,
refer the matter to the Land Appeal Court. In cases heard in
remote parts of the country the matter might not come to the
knowledge of the Minister until after the time for appealing was
passed, and, therefore, he was given the power under s. 59.

[THE CHIEF JUSTICE. How often do you say that the Minister
may refer the decision of the Land Board to the Land Court?]

As often as he likes.

[THE CHIEF JUSTICE. The first reference was under s. 20 of
the Act of 1884, and under that section the decision of the Land
Board, unless appealed against, is final. How could the Minister
refer to the Land Court a decision which is declared to be final?]

Under s. 59, *any decision* of the Land Board can be referred
to the Land Court. But the decision of the Land Court did not
turn upon that point. The matter was first referred to the Land
Court, on the ground that the Land Board had failed to do its
duty. In the case of *Gardiner* v. *Minister for Lands* (1) it was

(1) 18 N.S.W.L.R. 182 ; 13 W.N. 190.

held, under similar circumstances, that the Land Board had not
failed to do its duty.   That being so, what was there to prevent
the Minister afterwards referring the matter to the Land Court,
on the ground that the rights or interests of the Crown had been
injuriously affected ?

[STEPHEN, J.   It was really the same matter which was
referred to the Land Court on the second occasion.

THE CHIEF JUSTICE.   It seems to me that you have to go
further back and shew that once the matter had been decided by
the Land Board under s. 20 of the Act of 1884, the Land Court
had any power to deal with the case on the first reference.]

If the rights or interests of the Crown were affected by the
decision, then the Minister had power to refer it to the Land
Court under s. 59 of the Act of 1895.

[STEPHEN, J.   How is it shewn that the "rights, interests, or
revenues" of the Crown have been affected by this decision ?]

The rights of the Crown are always affected by the alienation
of Crown lands.   No doubt there is this difficulty in the case if
the Minister can refer this decision under that section ; then
there would be no case which comes before the Land Board to
which this section would not apply.   This was a question of forfeiture of a conditional purchase, and if the land had been
forfeited it would have reverted to the Crown, and, therefore,
we say that the rights of the Crown are affected.

. [STEPHEN, J.   I do not think that those words in that section
can bear so wide a meaning; and I am prepared to rest my judgment on that point.]

It may be that though, in a popular sense this being a forfeiture, it would be said to affect the rights of the Crown,
possibly it does not come within the meaning of the words in
that section.

There was no appearance for the respondent.

THE CHIEF JUSTICE.   I am of opinion that the Minister had
no power to make the reference to the Land Appeal Court of the
7th May, 1897, nor the reference of the 18th Aug., 1896.   It

appears that one Chapman applied for a conditional purchase on
the 26th Nov., 1890, and that his application was confirmed by
the Local Land Board on the 21st Jan., 1892, more than six years
ago.   After the time had elapsed within which he had to comply
with all the conditions, some person must have put the Minister
in motion to have an enquiry held as to whether, when he made
his application, he had returned certain false answers to the
questions then put to him.   I would point out that the proper
time for raising the question of the bona fides of a conditional
purchaser is when the application comes before the Local Land
Board for confirmation.   Sect. 13 of the Act of 1889 provides for
the confirmation of the application.   Under that section it is
open to any person, who is aware that the applicant has not
applied for the land for his own use and benefit, to come forward
and say so, and so have the matter determined in open Court.
In this case it appears that the application was confirmed on the
21st Jan., 1892.   On the 17th April, 1896—more than four years
after the confirmation of the application—the Minister referred
the matter to the Local Land Board under s. 20 of the Act of
1884, as to whether a forfeiture had not been incurred by reason
of Chapman having made a false statement in the declaration
lodged with his application.   However inadvisable and in many
cases unjust such a reference may be, the Minister clearly had the
power to make it.   A man might have witnesses in 1892,
whom, in 1896, he might find difficult to bring together; but
still it is the duty of the Minister, if it comes to his ears that
there has been anything wrong in the taking up of the land,
to have the matter sifted, and for that purpose to refer it to
the Local Land Board under s. 20.   That section is as follows:—
" Any question of lapse, voidance or forfeiture whether arising
under this Act or any of the said repealed Acts may be by the
Minister referred to the Local Land Board and the decision
· thereon of the said Board after due investigation in open Court
shall unless appealed from in the prescribed manner be final."

I have no hesitation in saying, and I so lay it down, that once
a decision has been given under that section, there is no section
in any Act of Parliament which gives the Minister the right to
re-open the matter.   This point has indeed been already decided in

1898.

MINISTER FOR
LANDS
v.
CHAPMAN.

The C.J.

1898.

MINISTER FOR LANDS
v.
CHAPMAN.

The C.J.

two cases which have been before this Court. By s. 14 (6) of the Act of 1884, it was provided that "the Minister may return to the Local Land Board for revision, rehearing, or further consideration, any case which, to such Minister, shall appear to have been improperly or insufficiently considered or determined by such Board." That section is just as strong as s. 59 of the Act of 1895, under which this matter was referred to the Land Appeal Court. In 1890, the case of *Ex parte Robinson* (1) was decided. In that case the matter had been referred to the Local Land Board under s. 20, and had been determined by them, and subsequently the Minister, purporting to act under s. 14 (6), sent the matter back again to them. Robinson then moved for a prohibition to restrain the Board from dealing with the matter, on the ground that under s. 20 the decision of the Board was final. The rule came on for argument before Mr. Justice *Windeyer*, Mr. Justice *Foster*, and myself. In delivering the judgment of the Court I said—" It has been argued that the Minister has power, as often as he is dissatisfied with their decision, to refer the case to the Land Board under s. 14, sub-s. 6, of the Crown Lands Act, which provides that 'the Minister may return to the Local Land Board for revision, rehearing, or further consideration any case or matter which to such Minister shall appear to have been improperly or insufficiently considered or determined by such Board;' but that section does not, and cannot govern a case where it is provided by another section of the Act that the determination of the Board shall be final. Sect. 20 provides that in certain cases the decision of the Board, after due investigation, shall be final, and that being so, although by s. 14 (6) the Minister has power to send any matter back for further consideration which he regards as not having been sufficiently considered, such sending back can only be in reference to a matter upon which the Legislature has not provided that the decision of the Board shall be final."

In August last year this point again came before this Court in the case of the *Minister for Lands* v. *Thorley* (2). There a matter had been referred to the Local Land Board under s. 20, as to whether any statements in the declaration lodged with the

(1) 11 N.S.W. L.R. 57 ; 6 W.N. 164.   (2) 18 N.S.W. L.R. 328 ; 14 W.N. 42.

application were false, and the Board there came to a conclusion
which amounted to a finding of "not proven." The Minister
again attempted to send the matter back to the Board. The
case came before Mr. Justice *Owen*, Mr. Justice *Manning* and
myself. Mr. Justice *Owen*, though agreeing with us on the
general principles laid down by us, dissented on the ground that
the decision, in the form in which it was given, amounted to no
decision at all, and thought that the matter could be referred
back to the Board. Mr. Justice *Manning* and I held that
the matter could not be re-opened after the first decision of
the Board. I there said, after referring to *Ex parte Robinson* :
" Applying the principle of that case to the construction
of s. 135, I am of opinion that that section must apply to
statements or evidence made or given upon enquiries other
than references under s. 20 which have been the subject of
a final decision. The Minister might, in 1893, have referred the
case for enquiry under s. 135, but inasmuch as he saw fit to
refer it under s. 20, he is bound by the decision at which the
Board arrived. The effect of the present reference is that the
enquiry of 1893 will be re-opened by way of new trial to try the
truth of statements made in the declaration nearly seven years
ago. I think that the maxim *Nemo bis vexari debet pro una et
eadem causa* is applicable." I then referred to the case of
Marriott v. *Hampton*, and continued, " I think it would be far
less harmful that Crown land should occasionally be taken up
fraudulently than that every selector should be liable after enquiry
duly made by the proper tribunal to have his title re-opened
after an indefinite lapse of time. If it can be done after three
years it can be done after twenty. In 1893 a man might be
ready with an absolute answer to a charge brought against him,
but if, in 1897, the matter is to be tried over again it may be
impossible for him to produce the witnesses who gave, or could
have given, evidence for him upon the former enquiry. Enquiries
of the kind we are considering should not, and I have no doubt
are not, lightly instituted by the Minister. He doubtless had
information before him which he believed he could support by
evidence, but I am most strongly of opinion that once an enquiry
has been duly held and all the evidence which the parties are

1898.

MINISTER FOR
LANDS
v.
CHAPMAN.

The C.J.

1898.

MINISTER FOR
LANDS
v.
CHAPMAN.

The C.J.

prepared with has been brought forward and a decision arrived at, it would be most dangerous to allow the whole matter to be re-opened years afterwards."

That is the last case on the subject, and now we are asked to say that the Minister has the right by force of s. 59 of the Act of 1895 to remit this matter to the Land Appeal Court, although the decision of the Board is declared to be final. I am of opinion that once this matter was decided by the Local Land Board on a reference under s. 20 of the Act of 1884, the Minister had no power to refer it to the Land Appeal Court. The Minister pursued a wrong course in referring the case to the Land Appeal Court, and that Court pursued a wrong course originally in entertaining the matter and referring it back to the Local Land Board. However, the question for us now is whether the Land Appeal Court was right in refusing to entertain the reference to them by the Minister of the 7th May, 1897. We are of opinion that it was right, and that the Minister had no power to make the reference of the 7th May, 1897.

STEPHEN, J. I quite agree with all that *The Chief Justice* has said, but I prefer to rest my judgment on the point that this was not a case in which the "rights, interests, or revenues may have been injuriously affected " within the meaning of those words in s. 59 of the Act of 1895.

COHEN, J. I agree with *The Chief Justice*. I also agree with Mr. Justice *Stephen* in thinking that the words in s. 59 do not bear the meaning attributed to them by the Minister for Lands.

With regard to the meaning of s. 20 of the Act of 1884, and of s. 59 of the Act of 1895, it seems to me that they can stand together, and that s. 59 of the latter Act does not impliedly repeal s. 20, nor is there in it any implied qualification of s. 20.

Appeal dismissed.

MINISTER FOR LANDS *v.* NELSON.

Crown Lands Act of 1889, *s.* 39—*Crown Lands Act of* 1895, *ss.* 11, 47—*Conditional purchase.*

Under s. 11 of the Crown Lands Act of 1895, a person cannot apply for an additional conditional purchase of land which is not otherwise open for conditional purchase.

That section does not give an applicant for an additional conditional purchase a preferent right as against an applicant for a settlement lease.

A reservation made by notification under s. 39 of the Crown Lands Act of 1889, which "temporarily reserved and exempted from sale or lease other than settlement lease" certain land; *held,* a good reservation.

1898.

February 25.

The C.J.
Stephen J.
and
Cohen J.

SPECIAL CASE stated by the Land Appeal Court.

"1. Before the date of the *Gazette* next hereinafter mentioned a tract of land, situated within the external boundaries of the leasehold area of Milkengowrie Pastoral Holding, and containing 3025½ acres, had been measured into two farms to be let by way of settlement lease. More than half of the said tract consisted of lands which had been surrendered to the Crown by the then owner thereof in exchange for other lands, and the residue consisted of ordinary Crown lands forming part of the said leasehold area.

2. The *Gazette* of the 21st August, 1896, contained three notifications having reference to the said tract of 3025½ acres or to some part thereof that is to say :—

(*a*) A proclamation by the Governor that the said surrendered lands were to be Crown lands for the purposes of the Crown Lands Act.

(*b*) A notification that the lands theretofore subject to the pastoral lease of Milkengowrie were to be a resumed area, and to cease to be a leasehold within the meaning of the Crown Lands Acts.

(*c*) A notification that the said tract of 3025½ acres was temporarily reserved and exempted from sale or lease other than settlement lease. That notification was as follows :—

"Department of Lands,
Sydney, 21st August, 1896.
RESERVE FROM SALE OR LEASE OTHER THAN SETTLEMENT LEASE.

His Excellency the Governor, with the advice of the Executive Council, directs it to be notified that, in pursuance of the provisions of the 39th section of the Crown Lands Act of 1889, the land hereunder described shall be and is hereby temporarily reserved and exempted from sale or lease other than settlement lease.
J. H. CARRUTHERS."

. 3. On the 22nd August, 1896, the Crown lands comprised within the two farms into which the said 3025½ acres had been measured were by notification in the *Gazette* set apart for settlement leases, and it was thereby also notified that applications for settlement leases of the said farms might be made on or after the 17th September, 1896.

4. One of the said farms contained an area of 1745½ acres, and on the 17th September, 1896, twenty-eight applications for a settlement lease thereof were lodged with the land agent. Amongst the persons lodging such applications were James Nelson and Richard Lumby.

5. Upon a ballot being had to determine the priority of the said applications, the application of Richard Lumby came out first, and the application of James Nelson came out twenty-second in the ballot; and James Nelson thereupon withdrew his said application.

6. The said James Nelson was the holder by transfer of an original conditional purchase of 610 acres which adjoined the said farm of 1745½ acres, and more especially that part thereof which consisted of surrendered lands, and for six months and upwards the said James Nelson had been in bona fide residence upon the said conditional purchase.

7. After withdrawing his application for a settlement lease of the aforesaid farm, the said James Nelson lodged an application for an additional conditional purchase of 437½ acres in virtue of the said original conditional purchase, and an application for a conditional lease of 1308 acres in virtue of the said additional conditional purchase. The land so applied for was identical with the said farm, and the land included in the application for the additional conditional purchase consisted of the surrendered land comprised in the said farm. The said applications were received by the land agent under protest.

8. When the aforesaid applications of Richard Lumby for a settlement lease and of James Nelson for an additional conditional purchase and for a conditional lease came before the Local Land Board, it was agreed that the said applications should be heard and dealt with together, and the Local Land Board thereupon confirmed Lumby's application, and disallowed Nelson's application.

9. James Nelson appealed to the Land Appeal Court; and upon the hearing of the appeal the Minister for Lands appeared by counsel as a party thereto.

10. The Land Appeal Court, on the 8th day of June, 1897, decided that the aforesaid applications by James Nelson ought to be confirmed, and that the aforesaid application by Richard Lumby ought to be disallowed, and directed the Local Land Board accordingly.

11. The Minister for Lands has duly required the Land Appeal Court to state and submit a case for decision by the Supreme Court upon the questions of law hereunder specified.

The questions for decision by the Supreme Court are :—

1. Whether under the circumstances hereinbefore set forth the said James Nelson was entitled to apply for the aforesaid additional conditional purchase and conditional lease ?

If so, 2. Whether the reservation of the land from sale and lease other than settlement lease notified on August 21st, 1896, was void as against the right of the said James Nelson to apply for the said additional conditional purchase and conditional lease?

If so, 3. Whether the said applications of James Nelson were entitled to priority over the application of the said Richard Lumby ?

4. Whether under the circumstances hereinbefore set forth the said James Nelson has waived as against the said Richard Lumby any right he might have had to make such application."

Sir *Julian Salomons*, Q.C., and *Canaway*, for the appellant (the Minister for Lands). This case is governed by the case of *Minister for Lands* v. *Colless* (1), which decided that a conditional purchaser under s. 11 of the Act of 1895 had no preferent right

(1) 18 N.S.W. L.R. 91 ; 13 W.N. 225.

as against an applicant for a settlement lease. This case was
decided by the Land Appeal Court previously to the decision of
the Full Court in that case. There is this difference between the
two cases : in *Colless' Case*, the land was not open for settlement
lease at the time that Colless applied for a conditional lease,
whereas in this case at the time Nelson applied for the land as
an additional conditional purchase it was open for settlement
lease. But that difference does not affect the applicability of that
case to this case on the question of whether an applicant under
s. 11 has a preferent right. Nelson's application was made after
Lumby had applied for the land as a settlement lease, and, therefore, his application was no good, that is even assuming the land
was open for conditional sale. But the land applied for by
Nelson as an additional conditional purchase was not open for
conditional purchase, first because it was land which had been
exchanged under s. 47 of the Act of 1895. That section says
that "lands so surrendered shall become Crown lands for the
purpose of the Crown Lands Acts, but shall not be available
until a notification to that effect has been published in the
Gazette." There was no notification in the *Gazette*, making this
land available for conditional purchase, and, therefore, it never
was open for conditional purchase.

[THE CHIEF JUSTICE. I have looked through the judgment
of the Land Court, and I cannot find any reference to that section
which seems to me to have a very significant bearing on the case.]

That section does not appear to have been referred to in the
Court below. Secondly, this land was not open for conditional
purchase because it had been expressly exempted from sale or
lease other than settlement lease by the notification of the 21st
August, 1896. That notification was made under s. 39 of the
Act of 1889. That section provides that "the Minister may by
notification in the *Gazette* reserve any land therein described from
being sold or let upon lease or license in such particular manner
as may be specified in such notification." There is no doubt a
difficulty with regard to that section as to whether, in view of
the words "as may be specified," it is not necessary in a notification under that section to specify the particular form of tenure

from which the land is to be reserved. We feel it our duty as
appearing for the Crown to point out that difficulty. There is
also the case of *Harrington* v. *Minister for Lands* (1), which is
a decision on s. 11 of the Act of 1895.

1898.

MINISTER FOR
LANDS
v.
NELSON.

[THE CHIEF JUSTICE. I do not think that that case has any
bearing upon the case now before the Court.]

There was no appearance for the respondent.

THE CHIEF JUSTICE. This was a special case stated by the Land
Appeal Court for the opinion of the Supreme Court at the request of the Minister for Lands, and like many other cases which
are stated for this Court by inferior Courts, it is very difficult
from the case to arrive at the particular points on which this
Court is asked to give a decision. To see what is the duty of the
Land Appeal Court in stating these cases, it is only necessary to
look at s. 8 of the Crown Lands Act of 1889, which, in point of
fact, creates that Court. Sub-s. 6 of that section shews what
that Court ought to do, and if they attended to that sub-section
there ought to be no difficulty in the statement of the case.
That sub-section is in these terms, " Whenever any question of
law shall arise in a case before the Land Court, the Land Court
shall, if required in writing by any of the parties . . . or
may of its own motion, state and *submit a case* for decision by
the Supreme Court thereon." "Thereon" means the question of
law which arises. Instead of stating the specific point of law
which arises, we generally have a number of facts set forth, and
a decision thereon, and we are asked to say which party is right
and are left to discover the points of law for ourselves.

In this case it appears that, within the boundaries of the leasehold area of Milkengowrie Pastoral Holding there was a tract of
land containing 3025½ acres. Half of this land had been surrendered to the Crown under s. 47 of the Land Act of 1895, and
so had become Crown lands. Now s. 47 provides (amongst other
things) that " Lands so surrendered shall become Crown lands,
but shall not be available for the purposes of any application until
a notification to that effect has been published in the *Gazette*."

(1) 18 N.S.W. L.R. 418.

1898.

MINISTER FOR
LANDS
v.
NELSON.

The C.J.

That means that it is to be available on notification for such and
such a purpose, but that it shall not be available for any purpose
until notification. That section applies to about half this land.
Now it appears from para. 7 of the special case that the land
applied for by Nelson as an additional conditional purchase
was a portion of the land included in the half which
had been exchanged under s. 47. If the additional conditional purchase could not be made, then it follows that the
conditional lease made by virtue of the additional conditional
purchase must also fall to the ground. Now if there was no
notification under s. 47 declaring that this land was open for
conditional purchase, it is quite clear that under the section the
land did not become open for conditional purchase. There was
no such notification, and, therefore, on that ground it is clear
under s. 47 that this land was not open for conditional purchase.
But the matter does not rest there. It appears that, on the 21st
August, 1896, there was a proclamation declaring these lands to
be Crown lands; and in the same *Gazette* there was a notification
that these lands were to be a resumed area, and also a notification
that these lands were exempted from sale or lease other than
settlement lease. That reservation was made under s. 39 of the
Act of 1889, which provides, "The Governor may, by notification
in the *Gazette*, reserve any land therein described from being sold
or let upon lease or license in such particular manner as may be
specified in such notification." No doubt there is at first sight a
difficulty raised on the wording of that section by the words,
"as may be specified," but the section continues, "and the land
shall thereupon be temporarily reserved and exempt from sale or
lease or license accordingly, and unless expressly otherwise
declared shall not be reserved or exempt from sale or lease
generally." Here it has been otherwise declared. These lands
are, by this notification, expressly declared to be reserved from
sale or lease other than settlement lease. On the 22nd of August
there appeared another notification which set apart this land for
settlement lease. Now it seems to me that there were two
reasons why this land was not available for conditional purchase.
First, because it was land which had been exchanged under s. 47,
and there was no notification declaring it to be open for conditional

purchase; and secondly, because there was a notification under
s. 39 expressly reserving it from sale or lease other than settlement lease.

    On the 17th September, Nelson applied for this land as a
settlement lease. There were many other applications, and
amongst them was Lumby's application. There was a ballot, and
the lot fell to Lumby. Thereupon Nelson, purporting to act
under s. 11 of the Act of 1895, applied for this land as an
additional conditional purchase and as a conditional lease. The
matter then came before the Land Board, and they decided that
he had not the preferent right claimed by him, and that Lumby's
application being before Nelson's application Lumby was entitled
to the land as a settlement lease. Then there was an appeal to
the Land Appeal Court. That Court upheld the appeal, Mr.
Commissioner Brandis dissenting from the other members of the
Court. His judgment is clear and precise, and correctly lays
down the law, and I might content myself by adopting his
judgment. In the first place Nelson was entitled to apply for
a settlement lease just as much as the other applicant, but
unfortunately for him he was not successful in the ballot.
But it is quite clear that he was not entitled to apply for
the land as a conditional purchase, as it was not open for
conditional purchase, being land which had been surrendered
under s. 47. And being such land it could only become available
after notification, and there was no notification except the
notification which made it available for settlement lease. Therefore, Nelson could have no preferent right, and I deny that a
conditional purchaser has a preferent right under s. 11. It may
be that his right under that section would act preferentially in
this way. The land, if otherwise open for conditional purchase,
is open for 40 days after the date of notification, whereas it is
not open for settlement lease until the date mentioned in the
notification as the date when it is to be open for settlement lease.
Here the date of notification was the 22nd August, but the date
when it was available for settlement lease as declared in the
notification, was the 17th September. Therefore, in this case, if
the land had been open for conditional purchase, an application
could have been made between those dates, whilst a person

1898.

MINISTER FOR
LANDS
v.
NELSON.

The C.J.

1898.

MINISTER FOR
LANDS
v.
NELSON.

The C.J.

wishing to take up the land as a settlement lease could make no application until the 17th September. But this land never was open for conditional purchase, and, therefore, the decision of the Land Appeal Court was wrong.

The first question submitted to us will, therefore, be answered in the negative. Questions 2 and 3 are contingent on the first question being answered in the affirmative, and as we answer that question in the negative we are not called upon to answer questions 2 and 3. It also becomes unnecessary to give any decision on the fourth question.

STEPHEN, J. I do not wish to add anything to the judgment which has been delivered by *The Chief Justice*, but I wish to say one word about the way in which these cases are brought before us. This case does not tell the Court what the specific point of law was that was decided by the Land Appeal Court, and had we not been assisted by counsel we should not have known what were the points we were called upon to decide. The first question submitted to us does not set out a point of law for our decision. What the Court should have before it is the specific point of law which it has to decide. I will never sit again in an appeal from the Land Appeal Court unless the special case sets out specifically the points of law which we are called upon to decide.

COHEN, J. I agree.

Appeal upheld.

Ex parte JORDAN.

District Court—Ca. sa.—Summons—Evidence of means.

An order for the issue of *ca. sa.* in the District Court may be made without summoning the judgment debtor to shew cause why the order should not be made. Evidence on which the Judge is justified in making the order considered.

On an application for a prohibition to restrain further proceedings on an order directing a *ca. sa.* to issue, the only evidence which can be considered as before the Judge is that contained in the affidavits recited in the order.

1898.

March 4.

The C.J.
Stephen J.
and
Cohen J.

THIS was a motion to make absolute a rule *nisi* calling upon *Docker*, D.C.J., and R. Parker to shew cause why a prohibition should not issue to restrain them from proceeding upon an order made by *Docker*, D.C.J., directing a writ of *ca. sa.* to issue against the applicant.

Parker sued the applicant in the District Court, and recovered a judgment against him for the sum of 23*l.* 3*s.* 11*d.* on the 10th February. On the 14th February, at 10 o'clock, the plaintiff issued execution against the defendant. At noon on the same day the defendant transferred his interest in an hotel which he had bought from Parker in December to one Purcell, and Purcell went into possession before any levy was made.

On the 15th February, on an application *ex parte* for a writ of *ca. sa.*, *Docker*, D.C.J., made the following order:—" Upon reading the affidavit of R. Parker, and upon hearing his attorney, and being satisfied that the above-named defendant has means whereby he can satisfy the amount of the judgment and costs herein, I do hereby authorise the Registrar of the said Court to issue a writ of *capias ad satisfaciendum* to arrest the above-named defendant for 23*l.* 3*s.* 11*d.* . . . . ."

The only evidence as to the means of the defendant in Parker's affidavit was that he had transferred a certain hotel and stock to the defendant in December last, which the defendant subsequently transferred to Purcell.

1898.
Ex parte
JORDAN.

The rule *nisi* for a prohibition was granted upon the grounds: —1. That the said order was against natural justice, inasmuch as the applicant was entitled to be summoned to appear. 2. That there was no evidence to support the order.

Jamieson, for the applicant. The applicant should have been summoned to shew cause why the writ of *ca. sa.* should not be issued. It is contrary to natural justice to imprison a man without giving him the opportunity of being heard: *Ex parte Kinning* (1); *Abley* v. *Dale* (2).

[THE CHIEF JUSTICE. A form of summons is provided for by the rules; see F. 81.

Ferguson. This very point has been decided by Mr. Justice *Windeyer: Ex parte Gunn* (3).

STEPHEN, J. I see that Sir *Julian Salomons* in that case uses the argument which occurred to me that it would be absurd to suppose that the Legislature contemplated serving a summons on a man who was about to abscond.]

That case is only a decision in Chambers. The case of *Abley* v. *Dale* (2) was not there cited. This Court ought to follow a decision of the Court of Common Pleas rather than a decision of a Judge in Chambers.

On the second point. There was no evidence before the Judge that the applicant had any means with which he could satisfy the judgment. The only evidence before the Judge was Parker's affidavit : *In re Karett* (4).

[THE CHIEF JUSTICE. There are several cases where this Court has granted a prohibition to Courts of Petty Sessions on the ground that there was no evidence to support their finding.]

The ground of the decision in those cases is that the finding when there is no evidence to support it is contrary to natural justice.

THE COURT called upon *Ferguson* on the second point only.

(1) 16 L.J.Q.B. 257.   (3) T.T.R. 29.
(2) 20 L.J.C.P. 33.   (4) 7 W.N. 5.

1898.

Ex parte
JORDAN.

Ferguson, for the respondent. Where a person comes to the Court, and complains that an order is against natural justice, he must shew that it is unjust, and that he has suffered some wrong. The applicant has not shewn that in this case. There were other facts before the Judge than on Parker's affidavit. His Honour had tried the case, and he was entitled to take into his consideration all the facts which appeared before him on the trial. But taking the facts as they appear on Parker's affidavit, there is sufficient evidence of means. It appears from that that the applicant was possessed of an hotel at the time that execution was issued, although it was sold before the levy was made. If it was a bona fide sale, then the Judge was entitled to infer that the applicant had the purchase money ; or if the sale was a bogus one, then the hotel still remained his, and, therefore, he had means.

Jamieson in reply.

THE CHIEF JUSTICE. The rule must be discharged. It appears that the applicant became possessed of a public-house. We need not stop to enquire how he became possessed of it. In fact, we may assume that he came honestly in possession by transfer from Parker. There was an agreement between them that the applicant should take the stock in trade in the public-house at a valuation. The stock was accordingly valued, but the applicant refused to pay the amount of the valuation. Parker thereupon sued him in the District Court. The applicant entered a defence. That was a dishonest thing to do in respect of a debt for which there was no question that he was liable. The case came on for trial on the 10th February before *Docker*, D.C.J., and on that day his Honour pronounced judgment against the applicant for the amount claimed and costs. At that time he was in possession of the public-house and stock purchased from Parker, having been in possession since December. On the 14th February the amount of the judgment not having been paid, Parker issued execution. At noon of that day and before levy, the applicant transferred his interest in the public-house and stock to one Purcell. Now the position is this. This was either a bona fide transfer or it was not. If it was bona fide, then presumably the applicant was paid the purchase-money, and, therefore, he had means to satisfy the judgment; or if it was not bona fide, then the transaction was fraudulent and void, and the property was still his, and, therefore, he had means. It appears to me that the Judge was entitled to be satisfied from the facts before him that the applicant had means, and from the order made it appears that he was satisfied. That being the case, the judgment creditor did shew to the satisfaction of the Judge that the applicant had means to satisfy the debt. The applicant, therefore, fails upon that ground.

Another point has been taken that the applicant should have been summoned to shew cause before the *ca. sa.* issued. At first sight it appeared to me, especially taking into consideration that the rules provide a form of summons, that before the writ is issued the judgment debtor should be summoned to shew cause. But on more careful consideration, I am of opinion that it is not necessary to summon the defendant. The order is not punitive, it is merely a means of enforcing a civil right. In the Supreme Court, before the Judge makes an order for a writ of *ca. sa.* to issue, he has to be satisfied on certain facts; the defendant, however, is not called upon to shew cause why the writ should not issue. One of the grounds upon which a writ of *ca. sa* is issued is that the judgment debtor is about to abscond, and as was pointed out by Sir *Julian Salomons* in argument in the case of *Ex parte Gunn* (1), it would be absurd to call upon a man to shew cause when he was about to abscond, because it would only have the effect of making him abscond a little faster. In that case Mr. Justice *Windeyer* said : " It is clear that a person proceeding under s. 87 is not required to summon a judgment debtor against whom he is about to get a writ. The words in s. 87—' Shewn to the satisfaction of a Judge '—are the same as in 3 Vic. No. 15, s. 2. This section in our District Court Act was passed to prevent the debtor defeating the creditor's judgment. Whether the District Court Act is defective in not going on to provide a remedy for a wrong decision of the Judge, it is not necessary to decide. I simply decide that to summon the defendant was not necessary." That decides the very point before us. It is a decision in Chambers, and of course not binding upon us. But looking at the nature of the

(1) Tarl. Term. Rep. 29.

1898.

Ex parte
JORDAN.

The C.J.

proceedings, and seeing that they are not punitive but simply a means of enforcing a civil right, I think that that decision is right. It appears to me, therefore, that the Judge had jurisdiction to entertain the application, although no summons had been issued, and further that his Honour had evidence before him which justified him in coming to the conclusion that the applicant had means. This rule must, therefore, be discharged with costs.

STEPHEN, J. I agree. I should like to say one word as to my decision in the case of *In re Karett* (1). The point there taken was that the Judge had no jurisdiction to make the order for the issue of the writ of *ca. sa.*, if there was no evidence before him on which to found the order. It seems to have been assumed by counsel on both sides that the Judge had no jurisdiction if there was no evidence before him, and I seem to have decided the case on that point. I should, however, be more satisfied if it had been decided on the ground that it was contrary to natural justice for the Judge to make the order without evidence before him.

COHEN, J. I concur in the discharge of the rule. The point has been taken that the only evidence which this Court can now consider is the evidence in the affidavit recited in the order. I think that is a good point. The only convenient and safe rule is that the only affidavits which can be considered as being before the Judge are those affidavits which are recited in the order.

THE CHIEF JUSTICE. I quite agree with Mr. Justice *Cohen* on that point.

Rule discharged with costs.

Attorneys for the applicant: *Ellis & Button.*
Attorney for the respondent: *Fealey.*

(1) 7 W.N. 5.

JOSEPH AND OTHERS v. BRIGGS AND OTHERS.

1898.
February 15.

The C.J.
Stephen J.
and
Cohen J.

Contract—Written contract—Parol evidence—Condition to suspend operation—Performance of consideration.

The plaintiffs and defendants were owners of different collieries, and the defendants agreed in writing to pay the plaintiffs £00l. if they would tender at a certain price for a certain coal contract. The plaintiffs tendered at the price agreed upon, thereby performing their part of the agreement, and sued the defendants for the 500l. Defendants pleaded a contemporaneous agreement that the contract was not to take effect unless the defendants' tender was accepted, whereas it had been rejected. The agreement pleaded not being in writing, *held*, that evidence in support of it was inadmissible.

NEW TRIAL MOTION.

The plaintiffs were a firm of colliery proprietors owning the Cullen Bullen Coal Mine, and the defendants were the representatives of an Association of the Coal Mines at Lithgow. The Railway Commissioners had called for tenders for the supply of coal for the year July, 1897, to June, 1898. The plaintiffs and defendants were owners of the only collieries on the Western Line, and on the 25th May, 1897, the following agreement was signed:—Memorandum of Agreement made between the Cullen Bullen Coal Proprietary of the one part and the Lithgow Coal Association of the other part, whereby it is mutually agreed that the Cullen Bullen Coal Proprietary shall tender to supply the Commissioners for Railways with engine coal for the Western Districts for the year ending the 30th June, 1898, at the price of three pence per ton less than the price the Lithgow Coal Association shall tender for, in consideration of which the Lithgow Coal Association will pay the Cullen Bullen Proprietors the sum of 500l. per annum, payable by equal monthly instalments.

Owing to the Cullen Bullen Mine being some 20 miles further from Sydney than the Lithgow Collieries, it was apparently considered that this agreement would ensure the acceptance by the Commissioners of the tender of the Lithgow Association, as the extra haulage would more than cover the difference in price.

The plaintiffs carried out the agreement, and sent in tenders in accordance with the agreement. In the result the tender of neither party was accepted by the Commissioners.

1898.

JOSEPH
v.
BRIGGS.

The plaintiffs now sued to recover 41*l*. 13*s*. 4*d*., the first monthly instalment payable to them under the contract.

The defendants pleaded *non assumpsit*, and (2), that at the time of the making of the said agreement it was agreed by and between the plaintiffs and defendants that the said agreement was made subject to the condition that it should be null and void if the Commissioners for Railways should not accept the tender of the defendants for the supply of coal, and the defendants say that the Commissioners did not accept the said tender, but the same was refused and rejected, whereby the agreement became and is null and void, and the defendants are discharged therefrom.

At the trial before *Owen*, J., the plaintiffs proved the contract, and it was admitted that the plaintiffs had performed the agreement on their part. The defendants tendered evidence to shew that the agreement was subject to the parol condition stated in the second plea. His Honour rejected the evidence, and a verdict was found for the plaintiffs.

Coghlan now moved for a rule *nisi* for a new trial on the ground that the evidence should have been admitted. It is clear from the nature of the agreement and the circumstances of the case, that it was only intended to operate if the defendants' tender was successful. There was no reason for the existence of the arrangement otherwise.

THE CHIEF JUSTICE. Suppose the Cullen Bullen tender had been accepted notwithstanding their efforts to get it refused?

Coghlan. Our case is that it was never contemplated that the agreement should operate unless we got the tender. It is not a case of altering or varying a contract, but of suspending it until a certain event happened. Till our tender was accepted there was no contract.

THE CHIEF JUSTICE. How can that be when the plaintiffs performed the whole of their part of the contract?

Coghlan. The performance of their part necessarily took place before it could be known whether the defendants' tender was accepted or not. If it was accepted, the plaintiffs got the benefit; if not, both parties were in the same position as if no tenders had ever been called for. As it stands the plaintiffs will get 500*l.* for nothing. He referred to *Pym* v. *Campbell* (1); *Wallis* v. *Littell* (2); *Clever* v. *Kirkman* (3); *Pattle* v. *Hornibrook* (4); *Keith* v. *McEdwards* (5).

THE CHIEF JUSTICE. I am of opinion that this rule should be refused. The agreement was that in consideration of 500*l.*, the plaintiffs should tender in such a way, that if any tender was accepted, it would, in all probability, be that of the defendants. The plaintiffs accordingly sent in their tender in compliance with the agreement, that is to say, they carried out their part of the agreement to its conclusion. Then, when the plaintiffs ask for their money, the defendants endeavour to set up a contemporaneous parol agreement that the contract was not to bind the defendants unless they were the successful tenderers. The cases cited to us have no application to the present case. If the plaintiffs had not tendered in accordance with the agreement, they could have been sued for not carrying out their part of it. They have carried out their part of the agreement; they put themselves in such a position that their tender could not be accepted, when, but for this agreement, they might, for all we know, have been able to secure a contract with the Railway Commissioners. I think that the evidence was properly rejected upon the ground that the evidence sought to be adduced was an attempt to add a term by parol to a complete written agreement.

STEPHEN and COHEN, JJ., concurred.

Rule refused.

Attorney for the defendants: *H. L. Tress.*

(1) 6 E. & B. 370.   (3) 33 L.T. N.S. 672.
(2) 11 C.B. N.S. 369.   (4) [1897] 1 Ch. 25.
              (5) 16 N.S.W. L.R. 182.

DIXON v. ROGERS.

Coal Mines Regulation Act, 1896 (60 *Vic. No.* 12), *ss.* 38, 40—*Miner's wages—Payment by weight—Actual weight—Average weight.*

1898.

February 28.

The C.J.
Stephen J.
and
Cohen J.

Sect. 38 of the Coal Mines Regulation Act, 1896, provides that miners who are paid by weight shall be paid according to the actual weight of mineral gotten by them, and such mineral shall be truly weighed as near to the pit mouth as practicable. *Held*, that all the mineral must be weighed, and that it is an offence to weigh a limited number of skips and arrive at the gross amount by averaging, even though the weighing machinery of the mine, by continuous use, is not capable of weighing the whole output.

JUSTICES' APPEAL.

The information, which was laid by Dixon, an inspector of collieries, charged that the defendant Rogers, on the 29th September, 1897, then being the manager of a certain mine, to wit the Mount Kembla Coal and Oil Company's Collieries, situate at Mt. Kembla, near Wollongong, and in which mine the amount of wages paid to persons employed therein did, on the said date, depend on the amount of mineral gotten by them, did unlawfully fail to comply with the provisions of s. 38 (1) of the Coal Mines Regulation Act, 1896, in that the mineral gotten on the said date by the persons employed in the mine was not truly weighed at a place as near to the pit mouth as was reasonably practical, or at all.

The case was heard at Wollongong on the 11th October before H. J. Chisholm, Esq., P.M., and two Justices. The evidence amounted to this, that the men were paid according to the weight of clean coal obtained by them; that with the appliances at present in use at the mine it was impossible to weigh more than about 30 skips of coal, although the weighing was carried on continuously during working hours, except whilst the weighmen were checking their accounts, which it was customary for them to do in working hours; that the output of the mine in full work was about 1,500 skips per day; that as, therefore, every skip could not be weighed, and the actual true weight of all the coal sent out ascertained, a certain number of the skips were weighed, and the average taken by multiplication; and that if the mine owners were compelled to weigh every skip, the output of the mine must be reduced. The defendant contended that the only practical way to work the mine was to ascertain the weight by average, and it was not suggested by the prosecution that there was any unfairness in respect of the system in use.

The Magistrates convicted the defendant, and fined him 2*l.* and costs. The defendant appealed.

The Court objected to the way in which the case was stated, inasmuch as there was no statement of the points of law which were referred for decision, but counsel agreed that the only point for argument was whether the defendant was bound under s. 38 of the Coal Mines Regulation Act to weigh all the coal, or whether, under the circumstances, he was at liberty to average the weight.

The Coal Mines Regulation Act, 1896, s. 38 (1), provides that:

" Where the amount of wages paid to any of the persons employed in a mine depends on the amount of mineral gotten by them, those persons shall be paid according to the *actual weight* gotten by them of the mineral contracted to be gotten, and the mineral gotten by them shall be *truly weighed* at a place as near to the pit mouth as is reasonably practicable."

Walker, Q.C. (*Garland* with him), in support of the appeal. The Act must be construed by the light of the custom of practical mining as it is to-day carried on in New South Wales, and must be taken to apply to existing circumstances and possibilities. At no mine of any importance in the colony is it possible to weigh the whole output; it has never been the practice, and the mines are not provided with the necessary machinery. It would take six or nine months to import and set up the weighing machines necessary to do so. The Act cannot be literally complied with without a re-arrangement of the works at the pit mouth, which would entail great expense. To shew that the Act was never intended to insist upon the actual weighing of every skip of coal, I refer the Court to the report of the Royal Commission upon whose recommendations the Act was drafted.

Sir *Julian Salomons*, Q.C., objected.

1898.

DIXON
v.
ROGERS.

THE CHIEF JUSTICE. We cannot look at that. It could only be admissible if there were any ambiguity in the Act. Here the words of the Act are as clear as words can be, and need no explanation.

Walker, Q.C. It is true that s. 38 says that the mineral is to be *truly weighed*, but the true weight is sufficiently ascertained by the method of averaging, and the real intention of the Act is discoverable from s. 40 (1), which says that the check-weigher may require that the process of weighing shall be carried on *continuously* throughout the working hours. All that is required is that the weighing should be continuous, up to the capacity of the appliances available, and that condition was complied with here.

Sir *Julian Salomons*, Q.C., and *Wallace*, for the respondent, were not called upon.

THE CHIEF JUSTICE. I am unable to see any ambiguity in s. 38, or any difficulty in its construction. There is no possibility of doubt as to what the Legislature has said, or as to the meaning of the words used. The section provides that the miners are to be paid according to the actual weight of mineral gotten by them, and such mineral is to be truly weighed at a certain place. There is only one meaning, so far as I know, attaching to the word "weigh," and when a thing is to be paid for according to its actual weight, it must be actually weighed.

As to the proviso to s. 38 it appears from *Kearney* v. *Whitehaven Colliery Co.* (1) that the deduction there mentioned must be a deduction from the ascertained weight of the tub or skip, and not from any average weight.

It is said that it will be a hardship upon colliery owners, if, with their present appliances, they are forced to weigh every skip of coal. It may be that it will, and it is to be remarked that there is no power given here, as there is in England, to suspend the operation of the section. Mr. *Walker* endeavoured to refer us to a report by a Royal Commission, containing recommendations as to the provisions to be incorporated in the Act,

(1) [1893] 1 Q.B. 700.

but seeing how explicit the words used are, the report could throw no light on the construction of the section under consideration. It may be that the Legislature determined not to give effect to the recommendations relied upon. I am, therefore, of opinion that the decision of the Magistrates should be affirmed.

STEPHEN, J. I am of the same opinion. If actual weight is equivalent to the real ascertained weight, I do not see how it can be equivalent to average weight.

COHEN, J. I agree with their Honours. The language of the Act clearly points to the real weight being ascertained, and not the average weight. The words "actual weight" seem to have been expressly used to obviate any possibility of any doubt attaching to the meaning of the word "weight."

Appeal dismissed with costs.

Attorneys for the appellant: *Norton, Smith & Co.*
Attorneys for the informant: *The Crown Solicitor.*

ADAMS v. YOUNG.

Public Service Act, 1895, s. 58—Civil Service Act, 1884—Dismissal of Civil servants.

Held by the Privy Council affirming the decision of the Full Court, that s 58 of the Public Service Act, 1895, which provides that " nothing in this Act, or in the Civil Service Act, 1884, shall be construed or held to abrogate or restrict the right or power of the Crown, as it existed before the passing of the said Civil Service Act, to dispense with the services of any person employed in the public service," does not apply to the case of a Civil servant who entered the service after the Civil Service Act, 1884, and was dismissed before the passing of the Public Service Act, 1895.

1898.
———
April 29.

Privy Council. *

THIS was an appeal by the defendant from the judgment of the Full Court (reported *ante*, Vol. XVIII., p. 73).

On the 29th April, the judgment of their Lordships was delivered by

April 29.

LORD WATSON. The respondent entered the service of the Government of New South Wales in the year 1885, as a road surveyor, at a yearly salary. He continued in their employment, in that capacity, until the 30th June, 1895, when he was summarily dismissed without compensation.

During the period between the original engagement of the respondent and his dismissal, the rights of Civil servants in the colony of New South Wales were governed by the Colonial Act, 48 Vic. No. 24. In the appeal *Gould* v. *Stuart* (1), it was held by this Board, affirming the judgment of the Supreme Court of New South Wales, that the power generally possessed by the Crown to dismiss a Civil officer at pleasure was restricted by the provisions of the Civil Service Act, 1884, and that the Government had no power to dismiss a Civil servant, except upon the grounds and after the enquiry, which that statute prescribes.

Upon the 14th July, 1896, the present suit was brought by the respondent against the appellant, who had been duly appointed to

* Present: LORD WATSON, LORD MACNAGHTEN, LORD MORRIS, and SIR RICHARD COUCH.

(1) [1896] A.C. 577 ; 17 N.S.W. L.R. 331.

be sued as nominal defendant on behalf of the Government of the
colony. The declaration sets forth the employment of the
respondent as a Civil servant, and the fact that he was not
dismissed in the manner and on the terms prescribed by the
Civil Service Act of 1884; and it concludes with a claim for the
sum of 6,160*l.* as damages.

By his third plea in defence, the appellant maintained that the
services and employment of the respondent in the declaration
mentioned, " were the services of a person employed in the public
service, within the meaning of the Act 59 Vic. No. 25, s. 58, and
the alleged grievances in the declaration mentioned were the
exercise by the said Government of the right and power of the
Crown, in the said section of the said Act mentioned, to dispense
with the services of any person employed in the said public
service, and not otherwise."

The statute upon which the plea is founded, the short title of
which is the Public Service Act of 1895, was passed upon the
23rd December, 1895, five months after the summary dismissal of
the respondent. Sect. 58 enacts that, " Nothing in this Act, or in
the Civil Service Act of 1884, shall be construed or held to
abrogate or restrict the right or power of the Crown as it
existed before the passing of the said Civil Service Act, to
dispense with the services of any person employed in the public
service."

The respondent demurred to the third plea, and the appellant
joined in the demurrer, which was then heard before the Supreme
Court of the colony. On the 26th April, 1897, the majority of the
Court, consisting of *Darley,* C.J., and *Owen,* J., gave judgment for
the respondent, *dissentiente, Stephen,* J. Their Lordships have
come to the conclusion that the decision of the majority was
right, and they approve of the reasons which were assigned for
it in the opinion delivered by *Darley,* C.J.

It was argued for the appellant, that the provisions of s. 58,
being declaratory, must of necessity be enforced by the Courts of
the colony in every case, whether arising before or after the date
of their enactment; and, consequently, that the present case
having been brought before the Supreme Court after the 23rd
December, 1895, when the Public Service Act, 1895, became law,

the summary dismissal of respondent must be held to have been
within the power of the Government, although on the 30th June,
1895, when it took place, such act of dismissal may have been
illegal, and might then have given the respondent a good cause
of action. It may be true that the enactments are declaratory in
form; but it does not necessarily follow that they are therefore
retrospective in their operation, and were meant to apply to acts
which had been completed, or to interests which had vested before
they became law. Neither the context of the statute, nor the
terms of the clause itself, appear to their Lordships to favour
that result.

Sect. 58 is the last of a group of ten clauses which are collected
under the statutory heading, "Dismissals, Removals, &c.," which
is part of the statute and must be taken into account in construing
its provisions. Leaving s. 58 out of view in the meantime, the
other clauses of the group deal exclusively with the dismissal,
removal or punishment of officers permanently employed in the
public service, in consequence of misconduct committed after the
commencement of the Act of 1895. Sect. 58 is complementary
of these provisions, and restores the power of the Crown, which
was taken away by the Act of 1894, to dismiss at pleasure, and
without cause assigned. The right or power which it restores is
"to dispense with the services of any person employed in the
public service." Can these words be reasonably construed so as
to include persons who are not employed in the public service,
and who, like the respondent, had ceased to be so before its power
of summary dismissal was given back to the Crown? In the
opinion of their Lordships, the words of the clause, as they stand,
do not admit of that construction. Counsel for the appellant
were, by the exigencies of their case, driven to maintain the
contrary, and they accordingly argued that the clause ought to
be read in the same way as if after "any person employed in the
public service," there had been inserted, "or who, before the
passing of this Act, had been dismissed from the public service."
The words of the clause, according to their ordinary and natural
meaning, refer to persons who are employed in the public service;
and neither in s. 58, nor in the context of the Act, is there to be

1898.

ADAMS
v.
YOUNG.

Lord Watson.

found any expression which can qualify that meaning, and make
them refer to persons who had been, but had ceased to be
employed, before the Act came into existence.

Their Lordships are unable to discover the least analogy
between the enactments which require to be construed in this
appeal, and those which were under the consideration of the
Court in *The King* v. *Inhabitants of Dursley* (1), and in *Attorney-
General* v. *Theobald* (2), which were much relied on in appellant's
argument. It does not seem to be very probable that the Legislature should intend to extinguish, by means of retrospective
enactment, rights and interests which might have already vested
in a very limited class of persons, consisting, so far as appears,
of one individual, namely, the respondent. In such cases, their
Lordships are of opinion that the rule laid down by *Erle*, C.J., in
Midland Railway Company v. *Pye* (3) ought to apply. They
think that in a case like the present, the learned *Chief Justice*
was right in saying that a retrospective operation ought not to
be given to the statute, "unless the intention of the Legislature
that it should be so construed is expressed in clear, plain, and
unambiguous language, because it manifestly shocks one's sense of
justice that an act legal at the time of doing it should be made
unlawful by some new enactment." The *ratio* is equally
apparent when a new enactment is said to convert an act,
wrongfully done at the time, into a legal act, and to deprive the
person injured of the remedy which the law then gave him.

Their Lordships do not suggest that the language of s. 58 is, in
any sense, ambiguous. On the contrary, its enactments appear
to them to have plain reference to persons who are actually
employed in the public service at and after the date of the Act
of 1895, and to those persons only. In their opinion, no construction is possible, which would extend the enactments to persons
who had ceased to be employed in the public service before the
date of the Act, without reading into the clause words which are
not implied, and are not to be found there.

Their Lordships will, therefore, humbly advise Her Majesty to
affirm the judgment appealed from. The appellant must pay to
the respondent his costs of this appeal.

(1) 3 B. & Ad. 465.   (2) 24 Q.B.D. 557.
              (3) 10 C.B. N.S. 191.

MUNICIPAL COUNCIL OF SYDNEY v. YOUNG.

Public Works Act, 1888 (51 *Vic. No.* 37), *ss.* 24, 30, 34—*Sydney Corporation Act*
(43 *Vic. No.* 3), *s.* 67—48 *Vic. No.* 5—*Resumption of land—Compensation—
Street.*

1898.

March 10,

Certain land was resumed for tramway purposes under the Public Works Act,
1888, being portion of a street in the city of Sydney which was vested in the
plaintiff council under s. 67 of the Sydney Corporation Act. *Held*, by the Privy
Council, affirming the decision of the Full Court, that the plaintiffs were not
entitled to claim compensation for the value of the land as owners, or for improvements and materials thereon, such as kerbing and guttering.

*Privy
Council.**

Sect. 67 of the Sydney Corporation Act vests in the municipal authority no
property in a street or public way beyond the surface of it, and such portion as
may be absolutely necessarily incidental to the repairing and proper management
of the street; it does not vest the soil or the land in the municipal council as
owners.

THIS was an appeal by the plaintiffs from the judgment of the
Supreme Court (reported 18 N.S.W. L.R. 44; 13 W.N. 157).

On the 10th March, the judgment of their Lordships was
delivered by

March 10.

LORD MORRIS. In this case their Lordships feel no difficulty. A
local Act (51 Vic. No. 37) enabled the Secretary for Public Works of
Sydney, who is called the constructing authority, to form a
tramway.

It became necessary in the making of the tramway to take some
12 perches of a street leading from a particular named place to a
public park. The municipal authority of Sydney alleged that by
the taking of those 12 perches of this street they were entitled
to compensation under the Act, which, of course, entitles the
owner of the property to compensation. That, of course, depends
on whether the municipal authority of Sydney are the owners of
the street in any sense that would give them a claim for compensation. The provision by which the property in the street in any
respect rests in them is under the Sydney Corporation Act of
1879 (43 Vic. No. 3), which states that "All public ways in the city

* Present: The LORD CHANCELLOR, Lord HERSCHELL, Lord MACNAGHTEN, Lord
MORRIS, and Sir RICHARD COUCH.

1898.
MUNICIPAL
COUNCIL OF
SYDNEY
v.
YOUNG.

Lord Morris.

of Sydney, now or hereafter formed, shall be vested in the council, who shall have full power," and so on.

. Now, it has been settled by repeated authorities which were referred to by the learned *Chief Justice* that the vesting of a street or public way vests no property in the municipal authority beyond the surface of the street, and such portion as may be absolutely necessarily incidental to the repairing and proper management of the street, but that it does not vest the soil or the land in them as the owners. If that be so, the only claim that they could make would be for the surface of the street as being merely property vested in them, *qua* street, and not as general property. Their Lordships are of opinion that that is not the subject matter of compensation, but the street being diverted into a tramway is in no way a taking of property within the meaning of the compensation to be assessed under the Public Works Act of Sydney. In point of fact, it is rather the opposite, because the municipal authority, by getting rid of the street, *pro tanto* have less expense, and it is in that respect a relief to the ratepayers.

Then it has been said that the construction should not be given to the words " shall be vested in the council " in the Sydney Corporation Act of 1879, which has been given to similar Acts in England, because there has been an amending Act passed which seems, as is suggested, to widen that interpretation as to what is vested in them. Their Lordships are of opinion that the amending Act does not do so. It provides that " It shall be lawful for the Municipal Council of Sydney, for the purpose of opening, altering, and widening," &c., to purchase land, to exchange land, or to sell land. That must mean to which they are really entitled as land, and which, as a matter of law, they have acquired, and can sell like any ordinary individual.

Their Lordships are of opinion, therefore, that the judgment of the Supreme Court ought to be affirmed, and they will accordingly humbly advise Her Majesty to that effect. The appellant must pay the costs of this appeal.

Appeal dismissed.

JONES v. JONES.

1898.

May 12, 17.

The C.J.
Stephen J.
and
Cohen J.

Practice—4 Vic. No. 22, *s.* 27—*Confirmation of rule nisi—Appeal—Attachment for contempt of Court—Contempts of criminal and civil nature—Affidavits sworn before J.P.—Matter pending—37 Vic. No.* 10.

Where a rule *nisi* has been granted by a Judge in Chambers under 4 Vic. No. 22, s. 27, the respondent may not oppose the confirmation of the rule *nisi* by the Court.

An application by one party to a suit or action to attach another for contempt of Court in interfering with the due administration of justice, is an application in respect of a criminal offence, and is not a proceeding in the suit, and therefore, although the suit is still proceeding, there is no matter pending within the meaning of 37 Vic. No. 10, s. 1, so as to permit of the affidavits upon which the application is founded being sworn before a Justice of the Peace.

MOTION for attachment for contempt.

The petitioner sued for a dissolution of marriage on the ground of the respondent's adultery, and at the trial before *G. B. Simpson*, J., on the 3rd March, the jury found all the issues in favour of the petitioner, and awarded him 400*l.* damages against the co-respondent. A decree *nisi* was accordingly pronounced. On the 17th March a notice of appeal and of a motion for a new trial was lodged.

On the 25th March, being out of Term, a rule *nisi* was granted by *Stephen*, J., on the application of the petitioner, calling on the co-respondent Higgins to shew cause, on the first day of next Term, why he should not be attached or otherwise punished for contempt of Court in interfering with the due course of justice, upon certain affidavits which alleged that, after the date of the decree *nisi*, he had endeavoured to induce one of the petitioner's witnesses to confess that she had committed perjury at the trial.

The affidavits were sworn before a Justice of the Peace, and were intituled in the divorce suit; but on the 1st April, after the making of the rule *nisi*, an order was obtained from *Cohen*, J., amending the title, by striking out the words "In Divorce," and substituting the heading "In the matter of the suit between, etc., and in the matter of the application of A. B. Jones for a writ of attachment, etc."; and it was further ordered that the said affidavits be transferred from the divorce jurisdiction to the common law office of the Court.

On the first day of the second Term, *Kelynack*, for the petitioner, moved to confirm the order of *Stephen*, J., granting the rule *nisi*. *Ralston*, for the co-respondent, opposed, and the case was, in the usual way, ordered to take its place on the list.

On the 12th May, the case was called on, and

Kelynack moved to confirm the rule *nisi*.

Ralston and *Whitfeld* appeared to oppose.

Kelynack objected that the other side could not be heard. The application is only to confirm a rule *nisi*, and as the other party could not oppose the granting of the rule, it being an *ex parte* application, so he cannot be heard to object to the confirmation of the order granting the rule. He will be heard on the application to make the rule absolute. There is no appeal from a rule *nisi*.

Ralston. In *Ex parte Fergusson* (1), which originated the present practice, the motion was to confirm both the rule *nisi* and the rule absolute. The rule *nisi* was made by a Judge for the Court, and was served upon us; therefore we are entitled to appeal against it.

THE CHIEF JUSTICE. The party who has been refused a rule may appeal, but where the rule is granted the other party must wait until the motion to make the rule absolute comes on for hearing. I do not think Mr. *Ralston* can be heard. We confirm the rule *nisi*.

STEPHEN and COHEN, JJ., concurred.

Kelynack then moved to make the rule *nisi* absolute.

Ralston took the preliminary objection that the affidavits on which the rule was granted were sworn before a Justice of the Peace. There was no matter pending in this Court when they were sworn. The fact that the application is in connection with a suit now in progress, does not enable the affidavits to be sworn in this way. This is not a step or stage in the suit; it is an

(1) 6 W.N. 1.

entirely independent proceeding, and may be directed against a
person not a party to the suit. If there is a matter pending, it
is pending in the Divorce Court, or in the divorce appellate
jurisdiction of the Supreme Court; but this application is made
to the common law side of the Court. Further, the contempt, if
any, is of the Divorce Court, and, therefore, this application
should have been made to that Court.

Kelynack. The Act 37 Vic. No. 10 says that Justices may
' take affidavits in all matters pending in the Supreme Court, or
in any Court or Courts." This application is made in a suit
which is now pending in the Divorce Court, and the Divorce
Court is the Supreme Court; see the title of the Divorce Act,
and ss. 2 and 3. The suit is pending till the decree is made
absolute: *Foden* v. *Foden* (1). Further, the notice of appeal was
lodged before the affidavits were sworn, and, therefore, there was
a matter pending before the Court to which this application is
now made. A matter pending is defined in *In re Clagett* (2) to
be one in which any proceeding can, by any possibility, be taken.
The affidavits in support of a rule *nisi* for an attachment must
be entitled on the civil side of the Court in the cause out of which
the motion arises; after the rule is granted they are entitled
on the Crown side: *Whitehead* v. *Firth* (3); *Wood* v. *Webb* (4);
Brown v. *Edwards* (5); shewing that the application is, at all
events until the rule is granted, a proceeding in the cause, and a
civil, not a criminal proceeding.

THE CHIEF JUSTICE. I think this point is concluded by the
case of *O'Shea* v. *O'Shea* (6). In that case an application was
made by a party in a divorce suit for an attachment against one
Tuohy, a person not a party to the action, for contempt of Court
in the publication of comments calculated to prejudice the fair
trial of the action, and *Butt*, J., ordered a writ of attachment to
issue, unless a fine of 100*l.* was paid by the person guilty of the
contempt. It was held that from this order there was no appeal,
on the ground that the application was a "criminal cause or

(1) [1894] P. at 312.   (4) 3 T.R. 253.
(2) 20 Ch. D. at 653.   (5) 2 D. & L. 520.
(3) 12 East 165.   (6) 15 P.D. 59.

matter" within the meaning of s. 47 of the Judicature Act, 1873.
Lord Justice *Cotton* says, "Of course there are many contempts
of Court that are not of a criminal nature; for instance, when a
man does not obey an order of the Court made in some civil proceedings to do or to abstain from doing something, that is really
only a procedure to get something done in the action, and has
nothing of a criminal nature in it. But is that so here? No doubt
the notice of motion is so entitled in the divorce suit, but it is also
entitled in the matter of an application against Tuohy (the
appellant), and the essential part of the motion is the application
to commit Tuohy for contempt. It is convenient that the notice
should be intituled in the cause to shew to what matter the
motion to commit refers; but what gives the Court the power to
act is the fact that the appellant has done something to prevent
the course of justice, by preventing the divorce suit from being
properly tried. That is clearly a contempt of Court of a criminal
nature. It is argued by the appellant that the act is complained
of, not by the Attorney-General as a public wrong, but by the
petitioner, who complains of it as a personal injury; but that
makes no difference. It is conceded that it was a wrongful act,
otherwise there could be no fine or imprisonment. And when
you concede that it is a wrongful act, you find that, although it
is headed in the divorce action, it is not a proceeding in the
action—not a proceeding for the purpose of obtaining anything
in the action, but an application to punish an attempt to induce
the jury not to try the case properly, which is as much a criminal
act as an attack upon the Judge himself." And *Lindley*, L.J.,
says: "There are, obviously, contempts and contempts; there is
an ambiguity in the word; and an attachment may sometimes
be regarded as a civil proceeding. We must not, therefore, be
misled by the words contempt and attachment, but we must look
at the substance of the thing."

So in the present case we are asked to punish a criminal
offence, for it is a misdemeanour to do anything to interfere with
the administration of justice. That being so, the matter is
clearly altogether outside the divorce suit. It follows, therefore,
that these affidavits were not sworn in a "pending" matter, and

the only course open to the applicant is to re-swear his affidavits before a commissioner, and make a fresh application for a rule *nisi.*

STEPHEN and COHEN, JJ., concurred.

Rule discharged with costs.

Attorneys for the petitioner : *Newman & Son* (Tamworth).

Attorneys for the co-respondent : *Abbott, Vindin, & Littlejohn.*

1898.

JONES
v.
JONES.

The C.J.

RUSSELL v. REID.

1898.
———
May 13.

The C J.
Stephen J.
and
Cohen J.

Public Service Act, 1895, ss. 12, 59, 60, 62— Voluntary retirement—Superannuation Fund—Refund—Gratuity.

A voluntary resignation accepted by the Public Service Board is not a retirement from the Public Service for any cause other than an offence within the meaning of s. 62 of the Public Service Act, and does not entitle the officer retiring to the refund and gratuity provided for by that section.

DEMURRER.

Declaration against the Hon. G. H. Reid, as nominal defendant, for that the plaintiff before and at the time of the commencement of the Public Service Act of 1895, had been and then was an officer in the public service within the meaning of the said Act, employed by the said Government as a clerk in the office of the Crown Solicitor, and was a contributor to the superannuation account under the Civil Service Act of 1884, and had, as such contributor, and in pursuance of the provisions of the said Act, paid divers large sums of money to the said account, and the plaintiff, within twelve months after the commencement of the Public Service Act of 1895, to wit on or about the 1st October, 1896, duly elected to discontinue contributing to the said account, and duly notified the said Government of such election, and from and after the time of the commencement of the Public Service Act of 1895 the plaintiff remained in his said employment, and continued therein as such officer as aforesaid, until the 31st October, 1897, and then retired from the said service for a cause other than an offence, and thereupon the plaintiff, by virtue of the provisions of the Civil Service Act of 1884, and of the Public Service Act of 1895, and of the premises, became and was entitled to receive from the said account and to be paid by the Government a refund of the sums so paid by him to the account as aforesaid, with interest on the said sums at the rate of 3 per centum per annum, and also a further sum by way of gratuity of one month's pay for each year of his service, calculated at the average rate of his salary during the whole term of his service, from the date of his appointment to the date of the commence-

ment of the Public Service Act of 1895, and a further sum by
way of gratuity at the rate of one fortnight's pay in respect of
each year of temporary service, and by virtue of the provisions
of the said Act, and of the premises, the said sums became and
were eventually due and owing by the Government to the
plaintiff, and all conditions were performed and all times
elapsed, and all things happened necessary to entitle the
plaintiff to receive from and be paid by the Government the
said several sums and each of them respectively, and to maintain
this action for the breaches hereinafter alleged. Yet the said
Government did not nor would pay the said sums nor any part
thereof, and the said several sums remain wholly due and unpaid
to the plaintiff.

Pleas—1. As to the first count of the declaration, that the said
retirement of the plaintiff from the said service was not a retirement or removal within the meaning of the said Public Service
Act, but was the plaintiff's voluntary act by resigning his said
office and voluntarily retiring from the said service, and not
otherwise.

Demurrer to the first plea upon the grounds—

1. That voluntary retirement, as alleged in the plea, is retirement within the meaning of the Act.

2. That the said plea, admitting plaintiff's voluntary retirement, discloses no reason good in law why payment of the amount
should be withheld.

Sect. 62 of the Public Service Act, 1895, provides that :—

"Any officer who at the commencement of this Act, shall be a contributor to
the superannuation account, under the Civil Service Act of 1884, may, within
twelve months thereafter, elect to discontinue contributing thereto, in which
event he shall be entitled to receive from the said account *on his retirement from
the public service for any cause other than an offence* (or in the event of his death
before retirement, his representative shall be entitled to receive), a refund of the
amount paid thereto up to the date of his so electing, together with interest
thereon at the rate of three per centum per annum from the date of his ceasing to
contribute ; and every officer who shall, under the provisions of this section,
cease to contribute to the said account shall thereupon cease to be entitled to any
right in or benefit from such account except such refund and interest aforesaid ;
but every such officer shall, on retirement, in addition to such refund and interest,
be entitled to claim under sub-s. (2) of s. 60.   Provided, &c."

Garland and *Russell,* for the plaintiff.   Sect. 62 clearly confers
the right to a refund and gratuity on retirement for any cause

other than an offence; that is to say, unless the retirement is caused by dismissal for an offence. The word retirement, in its ordinary meaning, signifies a voluntary resignation.

STEPHEN, J. Is not the word used with an active rather than a passive meaning, that is, does it not mean on his retirement *by the Board?*

Garland. It is not so used in other sections: see ss. 12 and 68. In the second part of the section, the expression used is "retirement or removal otherwise than for an offence," and the word removal has, apparently, been omitted by mistake in the first part. But if retirement in the first portion of s. 62 does not necessarily include a voluntary resignation, then I say that a person who retires, and whose resignation has been accepted by the Board, is a person whose "services have been dispensed with" within the meaning of s. 60. Those words as used in s. 67 cover all removals, dismissals and retirements. Except in cases where the right to retire is conferred by the Act, as in s. 68, an officer of the public service is not at liberty to resign; he is bound to serve, unless the Crown relieves him of his obligation, and, therefore, if the Board accept the resignation and permit him to retire, they "dispense with his services," and so the plaintiff is brought within the terms of s. 60.

An officer may retire at sixty years of age, under ss. 68, 69, but he is not bound to retire till 65, and if he retires at 60 his retirement is therefore voluntary, yet he is clearly entitled to a refund. But s. 69 makes no provision for this refund or gratuity in cases of officers retiring for age who have elected to discontinue their contributions to the fund, and, therefore, they can only claim it under s. 62, as read with s. 60, and it is, therefore, plain that one form of retirement, and to a certain extent *voluntary* retirement, is looked upon as a "dispensing with services" within the meaning of s. 60. The phrase "dispensing with the services" really is used to include *all* legal means of leaving the service; it is not a happy phrase, because in ordinary parlance it implies dismissal, but it is the only sense in which it can be construed in s. 60, and that section merely provides the rate at which the gratuity is to be calculated.

Further, by s. 62 the refund is payable, on the death of the
officer before retirement, to his representatives. All right to a
pension is usually lost by death or retirement before a certain
period of service, but the words of the section seem to imply that
the right to the refund attaches upon the election to cease
contributing, though not actually payable till death or retirement,
and this would naturally be expected from the special nature of
this particular pension fund, which is formed of the officers' own
contributions. The object of retaining it till retirement, and not
paying it at once, is to ensure the officer being in possession of a
substantial sum when he leaves the service and his salary ceases.
Lastly, the evident object of the Act is to put an end to the
Superannuation Fund as soon as possible, and to induce officers
to cease contributing to it, and as each officer only receives back
what he puts into the fund it cannot matter, so far as the solvency
of the fund is concerned, when it is paid, or how many claims
are made.

Sir *Julian Salomons*, Q.C., and *Pring*, for the defendant.

THE CHIEF JUSTICE. The plaintiff in this case was an officer
in the public service, and having, under the provisions of s. 62 of
the Public Service Act of 1895, elected to discontinue contributing
to the superannuation account, afterwards resigned his position
in the public service. His resignation having been accepted,
he thereupon considered that he came within the provisions
of s. 62, and claimed a refund of the amount paid by him to
the superannuation account, as also the gratuities provided for
by s. 60, sub-s. 2, of the Act. The question for the consideration
of the Court is: Is such resignation a "retirement" from the
public service within the meaning of s. 62? The plaintiff contends that it is; the defendant maintains the contrary position.

I am clearly of opinion that the voluntary resignation of an
officer in the public service, unless such resignation is expressly
provided for by the Act itself, is not a retirement within the
meaning of this section.

Sect. 12 of the Act provides for voluntary resignation under
prescribed conditions. The second sub-clause provides that if, in
the opinion of the Board, an officer is unfitted for, or incapable of

1898.

RUSSELL
v.
REID.

performing work of a class equivalent to the amount of his salary, or if such work shall not be available, the Board shall reduce the salary of such officer, and he shall have the option of continuing in the service at such reduced salary or retiring therefrom. The third sub-clause provides for the reduction of salary upon the ground, only, that no work equivalent to the salary previously received by the officer affected is, at the time of reduction, available. In such case, the officer has the right to elect whether he will stay in the service or retire. The fourth sub-section provides that if the reduction contemplated by sub-s. 3 exceeds one-fourth of the salary, the officer "shall be entitled to retire," and if a contributor to the superannuation account shall receive the payment and gratuity mentioned in s. 60, sub-s. 1; and if not a contributor, shall be entitled to receive the payment and gratuity mentioned in s. 60, sub-s. 2. If the reduction of salary is in consequence of the unfitness or incapacity of the officer, and shall exceed one-fourth, and the officer, being a contributor to the superannuation fund, shall elect to retire, he shall be entitled to retire from the service and receive the payment or gratuity provided for by s. 60, sub-s. 1. If the reduction do not exceed one-fourth, the officer electing to retire shall only recover such capital sum as he shall have paid to the superannuation account, together with interest thereon at $4\frac{1}{2}\%$.

I refer to this section to establish that where the Act provides for resignation, it expressly provides for the claim of officers arising upon such resignation. Sects. 68 and 69 provide for both voluntary and compulsory retirements of officers on account of age; s. 69 providing for the case of such officers, not being contributors to the superannuation account, receiving, on retirement, the gratuity or allowance specified in s. 60, sub-s. 2.

Sect. 56 provides for the compulsory retirement of an officer on account of unfitness or incapacity, not arising from actual misconduct or from causes within his own control; here, again, compensation may be made under the provisions of s. 60. So also, if, for any cause other than an offence, the Board shall dispense with the services of any person, the claim of such person as against the superannuation account, or for a gratuity, is regulated by s. 60.

The Act accordingly provides:—First : For voluntary retirement under certain conditions.   Second : For compulsory retirement in certain cases.   Third : For dispensation under the
provisions of the Act with the services of any officer otherwise
than for an offence.   No provision, however, is made for the
voluntary resignation of an officer, except he fall within the
provisions of s. 12, or of ss. 68 and 69.   From this it may fairly
be contended that the maxim *expressio unius est exclusio alterius*
applies.

It is, however, contended on behalf of the plaintiff, that s. 62
stands by itself, and that the words therein, " on his retirement
from the public service for any cause other than an offence,"
include the case of resignation immediately following the election
to cease contributing to the superannuation account.   Were this
so, I would expect to find some such words as are contained in s.
12, sub-s. 4, " and such officer shall be entitled to retire and shall
be entitled to receive, &c.," following the words " elect to discontinue contributing thereto."   In my opinion, the " retirement "
there mentioned includes the retirement provided for by ss. 68
and 69, which, on account of age, may be either voluntary or
compulsory, and also refers to any other species of retirement
which may take place under the provisions of the Act, such as
the dispensation with the services of an officer.

The words, " for any cause other than an offence," conclusively
prove to my mind that the retirement in question cannot be on
the initiative of the officer himself, but must be for some cause
brought about, either in consequence of the express provisions of
the Act, as, for instance, on account of age ; or by the Board
taking action within the provisions of the Act ; or outside the
Act, as by the abolition of an office causing dispensation with
services.   See *Waller* v. *Young* (1).

I am, accordingly, of opinion that the plaintiff, having voluntarily retired from the service, and not having retired or been
retired under its provisions, or his services dispensed with in
consequence of the abolition of his office, does not come within

1898.

RUSSELL
v.
REID.

The C.J.

_____

(1) 18 N.S.W. L. R. 200 ; 13 W.N. 208.

s. 62, and is not entitled to the benefit of its provisions.   Judgment upon this demurrer must, accordingly, pass for the defendant.

STEPHEN, J.   I am of the same opinion.   I cannot get over the
words in s. 62, "for any cause other than an offence."   Mere
disinclination to remain in the service leading to a voluntary
retirement cannot be a *cause* within the meaning of the section.
We are asked in effect to read those words as if they were
equivalent to "unless dismissed for an offence," and that in my
opinion is not their meaning.   They must mean some cause other
than the officer's own motive for retiring.

COHEN, J., concurred.

Judgment for the defendant.

Attorney for the plaintiff: *C. T. Russell.*

Attorney for the defendant : *The Crown Solicitor.*

DOWLING AND ANOTHER v. BURT.

Costs—Taxation—Scales of costs—Certificate for costs—20 Vic. No. 8, s. 3—Reg. Gen. of 6th September, 1872—District Courts Act, s. 101.

1898.

May 19.

The C.J.
Stephen J.
and
Cohen J.

When granting a certificate for costs under s. 101 of the District Courts Act, a Judge has no power to direct that the costs shall be taxed upon any particular one of the scales provided by the Reg. Gen. of the 6th September, 1872. Rule 4 of those rules is *ultra vires* of 20 Vic. No. 8, s 3. If the Judge certifies for costs, it becomes the duty of the taxing officer to tax under the scale indicated by s. 3 of 20 Vic. No. 8, having regard to the amount sued for, or the value of the matter sought to be recovered.

A Judge has no power to grant a] certificate for costs upon terms, or to assess the costs except by consent.

MOTION to vary an order.

The action was one for a libel published in the defendant's newspaper, and the plaintiffs claimed 1,000*l.* The case was heard before Mr. Acting-Justice *Heydon* at the Grafton Circuit Court in April last, and the jury found a verdict for the plaintiffs for 5*l.* On an application for a certificate for costs, the defendant's counsel contended that, if granted, the order should be that the costs be taxed on the lowest or on the second scale provided by the Reg. Gen. of September, 1872 (*Pilcher* 634), and not on the ordinary scale. His Honour doubted whether he had power to make such an order, but, on the defendant's counsel undertaking to accept the risk of the order being set aside, he ordered the costs to be taxed on the second or two-thirds scale, and leave . was reserved to the plaintiffs by consent to appeal against that part of the order.

The certificate was accordingly granted in the following terms : "I do certify that it appears to me that there was a sufficient reason for bringing this action in this Court, and I do order that the plaintiffs do recover their costs of action against the defendant, and I do further order that such costs be taxed and allowed on the two-thirds or lower scale as provided in R. 3 of the Rules of the 6th September, 1872, or any other rule (if any) thereunto me enabling, and by consent I do further order that the plaintiffs be at liberty to move this Honourable Court to set this order aside so far as relates to the costs being taxed on the lower scale."

Pilcher, Q.C., and *E. M. Stephen*, for the plaintiffs, now moved to vary the certificate in accordance with the leave reserved. The rules of the 6th September, 1872 (*Pilcher* 634), are made in pursuance of the Act 20 Vic. No. 8 (*Pilcher* 1554).

THE CHIEF JUSTICE. I am not clear that the Judges had any power to make rules under that Act. The only power is to establish scales of costs. In any case the 4th Rule (*Pilcher* 637) seems to me to be *ultra vires.*

Pilcher, Q.C. I am not concerned to argue that the rules are *ultra vires*, because, even if they are not, the learned Judge was wrong in ordering the two-thirds scale to be adopted. By s. 3 of the Act that scale is only allowed to apply to cases where the amount sought to be recovered is over 50*l.* and under 100*l.* Here the claim was 1,000*l.*

COHEN, J. In some actions the "amount sued for" might be held to be the amount actually recovered.

Pilcher, Q.C. It would be so no doubt in actions on promissory notes, where the amount claimed, if it exceeds the amount of the note and interest, is mere surplusage, but in an action of libel, as this is, the amount sued for is the amount claimed in the declaration.

Gannon (*Pickburn* with him), for the defendant. It has been the practice to make orders such as the one now appealed against. It is within my personal knowledge that your Honour *The Chief Justice* made a similar order in a trespass case in which 500*l.* was sued for, and several members of the Bar have mentioned to me instances of similar orders made by various Judges. He referred to *Friend* v. *Dykes* (1).

THE CHIEF JUSTICE. As to that case there is no doubt that it is the every-day practice in Chambers for a Judge to assess the costs when granting a certificate. But I think he has no power either to grant a certificate on terms, or to assess the costs unless by consent.

(1) 5 W.N. 80.

Pilcher, Q.C., in reply. No doubt these orders have, by an
oversight as to the effect of 20 Vic. No. 8, been made in the past,
but the question of what scale should be applied is one for the
Prothonotary, and not for the Judge.

THE CHIEF JUSTICE. I am of opinion that a Judge has no
power to direct that costs shall be taxed under any particular
scale. The Act 20 Vic. No. 8 is the one which gave rise to separate
scales of costs. Sect. 3 enacts that it shall be lawful for the
Judges to establish three separate scales of costs in actions, having
regard severally to the amount sued for, or the value of the
matter sought to be recovered ; provided that the lowest scale
shall extend to all cases not exceeding 50*l.*, the second to all cases
above 50*l.* and not exceeding 100*l.*, and the highest to all other
cases. It is not perfectly clear what that means, because if
the "amount sued for" is to be taken to be the amount claimed
at the foot of the declaration, plaintiffs would invariably insert a
claim for over 1,000*l.*, however small the amount might be which
they sought to recover, and so would always be entitled to taxation
upon the highest scale if they obtained a certificate for costs.
Nevertheless the words of the Act are, "amount sued for."

That Act was passed in 1857, and no separate scales were established under it until 1872, when the Judges made certain rules providing for separate scales of costs (*Pilcher* 634). The first three rules
provide the lowest and second scales, and the fourth goes on to
provide that "whenever a Judge shall grant a certificate for costs
under s. 101 of the District Courts Act without directing such
costs to be taxed on any particular scale, or shall not in any case
direct the costs to be taxed under the second or third of these
rules, the costs shall be taxed on the now existing scale." With
all respect to the Judges who framed that rule, I think they had
no power to make it. Under s. 101 of the District Courts Act,
it is the duty of the Judge simply to certify that there was a
sufficient reason for bringing or trying the action in the Supreme
Court, and neither the District Courts Act nor the 20 Vic. No. 8
gives power to the Judge to order that the costs shall be taxed
on any particular scale. That is a matter purely for the taxing
officer, and depends upon the provisions of the two Acts I have

1898.

DOWLING
v.
BURT.

The C.J.

mentioned. If the amount sued for exceeds 100*l.*, the costs should be taxed upon the highest scale ; if the amount is over 50*l.* and under 100*l.*, upon the second scale ; and if under 50*l.*, upon the lowest scale. His Honour should, therefore, have confined himself to certifying that the action was one proper to bring in the Supreme Court, and the order must be amended in the manner asked ; but seeing that similar orders have from time to time been made, the application will be granted without costs.

STEPHEN, J. I am of the same opinion. Our decision will apparently create a revolution in the present practice as to taxation, because, unless an order such as the one before us has been made, it has been hitherto the invariable practice to tax on the highest scale. Now it appears that the Prothonotary will have to ascertain what is the amount sued for, and tax accordingly upon the appropriate scale.

COHEN, J. I have nothing to add.

Order accordingly.

Attorneys for the plaintiffs : *Dowling & Taylor.*
Attorneys for the defendant : *Lobban & Lobban.*

THE EXCELSIOR LAND INVESTMENT AND BUILDING COMPANY AND BANK, LIMITED *v.* PHELAN.

Company—Scheme of arrangement—Distinct class—Separate meetings—Joint Stock Companies Arrangement Act, 1891 (55 *Vic. No.* 9), *s.* 3—*Principles.*

1898.
May 6, 20.

Stephen J.
G. B. Simpson J.
and
Cohen J.

In an action by a company against a member for calls, the defendant set up a special agreement with the company that his calls were to be paid out of deposits with the company ; to this the company replied that a scheme of arrangement between the company and its depositors had been duly sanctioned ; the defendant rejoined that there was no separate meeting held of depositors who had a special agreement as to calls ; to this the plaintiff company demurred.

Held, by the Court (G. B. SIMPSON, J., *dissentiente*) that the mere fact of there being no such separate meeting, no prejudice to the defendant being alleged or proved, was not a fatal objection to the scheme sanctioned ; in any case the point should have been raised before the Judge who sanctioned the scheme. *In re Madras Irrigation and Canal Company* (1) ; *In re Alabama, &c., Company* (2) ; *In re English, Scottish, and Australian Chartered Bank* (3) ; *Metropolitan Mutual Permanent, &c. Association* (4), discussed and applied ; *Sovereign Life Assurance Company* v. *Dodd* (5) distinguished.

Per G. B. SIMPSON, J. The depositors with the special agreement are in a distinct class from the ordinary depositors, and the fact of no separate meeting having been held is fatal to the scheme   The case is governed by *Sovereign Life Assurance Company* v. *Dodd* (5).

DEMURRER.

The plaintiff company sued the defendant, as a member of the company, for the sum of 285*l.* in respect of two calls of ten shillings each on 285 shares in the company held by him. The defendant pleaded " on equitable grounds " that " before the time of the making of the said calls or either of them it was agreed by and between the plaintiffs and the defendant, that in consideration that the defendant would pay the plaintiffs a certain sum, exceeding the amount of the plaintiffs' claim herein, the plaintiffs would accept the said sum and place the same to the credit of the defendant in the books of the plaintiffs, and, in the event of any call or calls being thereafter made in respect of the said shares,

(1) W.N. [1881] 172.   (3) [1893] 3 Ch. 385.
(2) [1891] 1 Ch. 213.   (4) 8 B.C. 11.
                    (5) [1892] 2 Q.B. 573.

1898.

EXCELSIOR
LAND
INVESTMENT
AND
BUILDING Co.
AND BANK,
LTD.
v.
PHELAN.

would appropriate and accept so much of the said sum as would
be sufficient to pay such call or calls in payment and discharge
thereof ; and in pursuance of the said agreement, and before the
making of the said calls or either of them, the defendant paid the
said sum to the plaintiffs, and the plaintiffs accepted and retained
and still retain the same, and . . . . after the making of each
of the said calls, the plaintiffs appropriated so much of the said
sum as was sufficient to pay and discharge the said call."

To this plea the plaintiffs replied on equitable grounds, that the
money alleged to have been paid by the defendant to the plaintiff
company was a deposit with them, and that after the said agreement and deposit, and before the making of the calls, an arrangement between the company and its depositors in respect of all
obligations in connection with the deposits was duly made and
sanctioned by an order of the Court, dated May 2nd, 1893,
according to the provisions of s. 3 of the Joint Stock Companies
Arrangement Act, 1891, and thereupon became binding upon the
defendant as a shareholder, and also as a depositor; and that under
this arrangement all deposits of over fifty pounds, among which
was the defendant's deposit, were to be re-deposited for three
years with the company, and were, at the expiration of that
period, to be repayable by five equal annual instalments; so that
any appropriation to calls of the deposit, under the first-mentioned
agreement between the plaintiffs and the defendant, was null and
void.

To this replication the defendant rejoined on equitable grounds,
that from the time of the proposal of the arrangement, up to the
date of the same being sanctioned by the Court, part of the
depositors in the plaintiff company, including the defendant,
were also shareholders therein, and that part of such depositors,
who were also shareholders, including the defendant, at the time
of making such deposit, and in consideration thereof, agreed with
the plaintiff company, that, in the event of any call being thereafter made in respect of their shares, the plaintiff company would
appropriate and accept so much of the said deposit as would be
sufficient to pay such call or calls in payment and discharge
thereof, although the due date of the said deposit might not
have arrived ; and the defendant further said that separate

meetings of depositors, depositor shareholders, and depositor shareholders who had agreed as to calls made on their shares as above-mentioned, were not summoned and held to consider the proposed arrangement.

The defendant further rejoined that the terms of the arrangement were as follows :—

"1. That all depositors whose individual claims do not exceed twenty-five pounds be paid in two equal quarterly instalments, the first of such payments to be made within three calendar months from the confirmation by the Court of this arrangement.

2. That all depositors whose individual claims exceed twenty-five pounds and do not exceed fifty pounds be paid in four equal quarterly instalments, the first of such payments to be made as provided in clause one herein.

3. That all deposits at present with the company not included under clauses one and two be re-deposited from the due dates thereof for a period of three years, and that interest shall accrue thereon at the rate of four per cent. per annum, payable half-yearly.

4. That the sum so redeposited shall, at the expiration of the said period of three years, be repayable thereafter by five equal annual instalments, and that interest shall accrue thereon at the rate of four per cent. per annum, payable half-yearly.

5. The company's deposit receipts may at the directors' discretion be accepted in whole or in part payment for any land or property held, purchased, or which may be hereafter purchased from the company, or in the purchase of any mortgage, or other security held by the company.

6. That the directors of the company shall have power to pay any deposit, or portion thereof, prior to its due date, should the funds of the company permit thereof, on such terms as may be mutually arranged."

The defendant further rejoined upon equitable grounds that it was a term of the arrangement or compromise that the directors should have power to pay any deposit, or portion thereof, prior to its due date should the funds of the plaintiff company permit thereof, upon such terms as might be mutually arranged, and the defendant said that, at the time of the appropriation referred

1898.

EXCELSIOR
LAND
INVESTMENT
AND
BUILDING CO.
AND BANK,
LTD.
v.
PHELAN.

1898.

EXCELSIOR
LAND
INVESTMENT
AND
BUILDING Co.
AND BANK,
LTD.
v.
PHELAN.

to in his plea, the funds of the plaintiff company did permit of the said appropriation being made, and that the directors debited the defendant in his capacity as depositor in the company with the amount of the said appropriations, and the defendant accepted the same in payment of a portion of the said deposits.

To this the plaintiff company demurred, saying that the rejoinders were bad in substance.

The matters of law intended to be argued were stated as follows :—

1. That the rejoinder first above set out was no answer to the replication inasmuch as the said arrangement or compromise was binding on the defendant notwithstanding that separate meetings as therein set out were not summoned and held.

2. As to the rejoinder secondly above set out that there was nothing in the terms of the said arrangement or compromise as set out in such rejoinder, or any other matter alleged in such rejoinder disentitling the plaintiff company to succeed by reason of the matters alleged in the replication set out.

3. As to the rejoinder thirdly above set out that the same was a departure from the defence raised by the defendant's plea above set out to which the replication above set out was pleaded, inasmuch as it set up an agreement with the directors of the plaintiff company by virtue of a term in the said arrangement or compromise, which alleged agreement is of later date and distinct from the agreement alleged in the said plea.

To this the defendant said that the rejoinders were good in substance, and that he intended, upon the argument of the demurrer, to object to the plaintiffs' replication as above set out upon the following grounds :—

1. That the said replication does not state that no order had been made or resolution passed for winding-up of the plaintiff company at the time when the Supreme Court is alleged to have ordered a meeting of the depositors to be summoned.

2. That notwithstanding the said compromise or scheme of arrangement as set out in the said replication the said appropriations were not *ultra vires* the plaintiff company or the directors thereof.

The defendant's deposit was one for 508*l.* 6*s.* 10*d.* for three years, repayable on November 3rd, 1894, with interest at six per cent., and the deposit slip and certificate both contained these words:—"This deposit to be available to pay any calls that may be at any time made upon me as a shareholder."

On September 21st, 1892, the defendant agreed to renew the deposit for a further period of four years from the date it became due and payable, conditionally that interest be paid by the company thereon half-yearly at the rate of 7 per cent. per annum and subject to any calls upon his shares in the company, if made, being paid out of such deposits.

Sir *Julian Salomons*, Q.C. (*Cullen* with him), for the plaintiff company. Separate meetings were not necessary, but in any case the votes could be taken together: *In re Madras Irrigation Company* (1); *Metropolitan Mutual Permanent, &c., Association* (2); *In re Alabama, New Orleans, &c., Railway Company* (3).

The rejoinder should set up the original plea in its entirety, but sets up entirely new matter.

Sly (*Rich* with him). Payment can be made by the writing off in the books of a set off. There is no winding-up, and the rights of creditors did not arise: *Ferrao's Case* (4); *Black and Co.'s Case* (5).

The defendant was in a distinct class from the other depositors, and separate meetings of these distinct classes should have been held: *Sovereign Life Assurance Co.* v. *Dodd* (6); *St. Joseph's Investment and Building Society* (7).

The rejoinder is no departure from the defendant's plea.

Sir *Julian Salomons*, Q.C, in reply.

[The Court only required argument on the point as to whether separate meetings ought to have been held.]

The defendant was in a different position from the depositors who had no special agreement, but was not in a distinct class from them within the meaning of the cases.

1898.

EXCELSIOR LAND INVESTMENT AND BUILDING CO. AND BANK, LTD.
v.
PHELAN.

(1) W.N. [1881] 172.
(2) 8 B.C. 11.
(3) [1891] 1 Ch. 213, at p. 239.
(4) L.R. 9 Ch. 355.
(5) L.R. 8 Ch. 254.
(6) [1892] 2 Q.B. 573.
(7) 6 B.C. 45.

1898.
EXCELSIOR
LAND
INVESTMENT
AND
BUILDING Co.
AND BANK,
LTD.
v.
PHELAN.

The question of the validity of the scheme could only be raised on appeal from the Judge who sanctioned it.

[G. B. SIMPSON, J. The Judge can only give validity to a scheme where the Act has been complied with]

The Court must assume that when the sanction was given all the conditions of the Act had been complied with.

[STEPHEN, J. Does it not appear in *Sovereign Life Assurance Co.* v. *Dodd* (6), that the Court went behind the sanction of the Judge ?]

In that case a matured policy was set off before winding-up against a debt due by the policy-holder to the company.

The decision in that case did not turn on the point raised here. [He referred to the report of the case in the Court below ([1892] 1 Q.B., pp. 408, 409)].

There is no winding-up here, but s. 3 of the Act brings about conditions analogous to a winding-up, that is a restriction of the ordinary rights of creditors.

Sly. There is no such section in the English Act as our s. 3.

Sir *Julian Salomons*, Q.C. Under the English section the winding-up is vacated ; there is no real difference for the purposes of the point at issue here.

STEPHEN, J. This case will be better understood by a consideration of the pleadings as they stand. By the declaration the plaintiff company sued the defendant as a member of the company for calls in respect of the shares held by him. The plea on equitable grounds does not exactly set forth the state of facts as they appear from the subsequent pleadings, its effect being that the defendant had paid the calls by anticipation. The replication on equitable grounds shews the true facts, namely, that the defendant was a creditor of the company in respect of a deposit made by him with the company, so that it is strictly a case of set off rather than of payment. The replication then sets up an arrangement between the company and its depositors made under s. 3 of the Joint Stock Companies Arrangement Act, 1891.

It further shews that the provisions of section 3 in respect of the calling of a meeting of depositors, and otherwise with respect to the making of the arrangement, were duly complied with, and that was duly sanctioned by the Court. The replication then alleges that by virtue of the arrangement the alleged agreement as to the set off of deposits against calls was void, as all payments of deposits were postponed under the arrangement.

The replication was not demurred to, but the defendant in his joinder in demurrer appended certain objections to the replication.

We hold the replication good on the grounds:—First, that as by the agreement sanctioned the payments under the deposits were to be postponed to a date beyond that at which they were at first made payable, the plaintiff could not insist, when a call was made, that the bank should pay it prior to the postponed date. In short, we hold that the new agreement impliedly abrogated the original one.

Further, it would be a fraud on the other creditors if this set off were allowed, because under paragraph 6 of the arrangement the directors have power to pay off any deposits or portion of deposits should the funds of the company permit, and, if the agreement were allowed to stand in face of the arrangement, those funds might be materially diminished.

Prima facie, therefore, the replication sets up an arrangement binding on all the depositors under which the defendant cannot evade payment of his calls.

The rejoinder seeks to displace that arrangement, and the main question to be decided is whether it does so, thereby rendering the arrangement null and void against the defendant and all the parties to it.

The rejoinder alleges that separate meetings of depositors, depositor shareholders, and depositor shareholders who had agreed as to any calls made on their shares, were not held to consider the arrangement.

I am of opinion that this Court is bound, in the first place, to assume that all the provisions of the Joint Stock Companies Arrangement Act were complied with, and that the Judge who sanctioned the arrangement did so on proper and just grounds.

In *In re Alabama, &c., Company* (1), *Lindley*, L.J., at pp. 238, 239, says, with regard to the sanctioning of arrangements under

(1) [1891] 1 Ch. 213.

(marginal notes:)

1898.

EXCELSIOR LAND INVESTMENT AND BUILDING CO. AND BANK, LTD.
v.
PHELAN.

Stephen J.

1898.

EXCELSIOR
LAND
INVESTMENT
AND
BUILDING CO.
AND BANK,
LTD.
v.
PHELAN.

Stephen J.

the Act :—" What the Court has to do is to see, first of all, that the provisions of that statute have been complied with ; and secondly, that the majority has been acting *bona fide*. The Court also has to see that the minority is not being overridden by a majority having interests of its own, clashing with those of the minority whom they seek to coerce. Further than that, the Court has to look at the scheme and see whether it is one as to which persons acting honestly, and viewing the scheme laid before them in the interests of those whom they represent, take a view which can be reasonably taken by business men. The Court must look at the scheme, and see whether the Act has been complied with, whether the majority are acting *bona fide*, and whether they are coercing the minority in order to promote interests adverse to those of the class whom they purport to represent ; and then see whether the scheme is a reasonable one, or whether there is any reasonable objection to it, or such an objection to it as that any reasonable man might say that he could not approve of it."

I say that this Court is bound to suppose that the Judge who sanctioned the arrangement had those principles present to his mind, and that the arrangement he sanctioned was arrived at fairly, and was in itself fair and just.

It is contended on behalf of the defendant that, because there were no separate meetings of what he alleges to be separate classes of depositors, the Act was not complied with. I am of opinion that it cannot be necessary in all cases that separate meetings should be held.

With regard to this particular case let us consider that the bare fact only is stated in the rejoinder that such a meeting was not held. It is consistent with it that the defendant was an assenting party, summoned to and present at the meeting at which the arrangement was discussed. It is not shewn even that it was ever brought to the attention of the Judge that there were separate classes of depositors. No absolute necessity for separate meetings is shewn, nor was the point raised before the Judge, but on the contrary the facts are consistent with all classes having had an opportunity to object to the scheme.

It would, it seems to me, be most dangerous to hold that the arrangement could now be set aside on the ground urged by the defendant. Otherwise he might lie by designedly and upset the whole scheme by alleging afterwards the bare omission, by which, in his rejoinder, he seeks to displace the replication. Once it is admitted that a meeting was held, it is incumbent on the defendant to displace the replication, and it is argued that it is displaced by the bare omission to hold separate meetings.

1898.

EXCELSIOR
LAND
INVESTMENT
AND
BUILDING Co.
AND BANK,
LTD.
v.
PHELAN.

Stephen J.

The only authority cited in support of this contention was *Sovereign Life Assurance Company* v. *Dodd* (1).

That case brought forward prominently the fact that the defendant there was dissentient, and to my mind that makes all the difference, and I am content to rest my decision upon that point. In that case *Bowen*, L.J., says, at p. 582 :—" I feel grave doubt whether the term 'policy-holder' includes those persons who have been policy-holders, but whose policies have matured not by death, but by the happening of the stipulated event; but it is unnecessary to decide that question if we think that under the Act of 1870 the deed of arrangement did not bind dissentient creditors. What is the proper constuction of that statute? It makes the majority of the creditors, or of a class of creditors, bind the minority; it exercises a most formidable compulsion upon dissentient, or would-be dissentient creditors, and it therefore requires to be construed with care, so as not to place in the hands of some of the creditors the means and opportunity of forcing dissentients to do that which it is unreasonable to require them to do, or of making a mere jest of the interests of the minority."

If a meeting was called at which all these depositors were present, I do not see how the case cited, which refers only to the case of a dissentient, can apply.

The point as to the necessity for separate meetings was not fully discussed in that case, as there the policy had matured and there was no reason that a set off should not be allowed in the winding-up.

I am not now deciding, as it is not necessary for me to decide, that, if the pleadings were amended by adding an allegation that the defendant was a dissentient from the scheme, the case might

(1) [1892] 2 Q.B. 573.

1896.
EXCELSIOR
LAND
INVESTMENT
AND
BUILDING Co.
AND BANK,
LTD.

v.

PHELAN.

Stephen J.

not be different, and possibly governed by *Sovereign Life Assurance Company* v. *Dodd* (1). In that case the question as to what constitutes a " class " would have first to be decided. On that point I am at present in favour of the plaintiff company.

Bowen, L.J., in the case last cited, says, at p. 583 :—" It seems plain that we must give such a meaning to the term 'class' as will prevent the section being so worked as to result in confiscation and injustice, and that it must be confined to those persons whose rights are not so dissimilar as to make it impossible for them to consult together with a view to their common interest." My present impression is that the classes here were not so dissimilar.

For these reasons I think the rejoinder mentioned is bad.

With regard to the other rejoinders we are all agreed that they are bad. The first simply sets out the terms of the arrangement, and, among them, clause 6, which cannot have any bearing on the replication. The next we hold bad as a departure. They both set up rights under the new arrangement. Judgment must, therefore, pass for the plaintiffs on the record.

G. B. SIMPSON, J. I am of opinion that the objection of the defendant to the replication cannot be sustained ; the replication amounts to an answer to the plea, and is a good one. I am also of opinion that the defendant's rejoinders are bad, other than the rejoinder as to separate meetings, and for the same reasons as those given by *Stephen, J.* I cannot, however, agree with *Stephen, J.,* as to the rejoinder I have specially mentioned. Were it not for the view he has expressed, I should have no doubt at all on the point, but I now give my opinion with some doubt.

The question on which a difference of opinion has arisen among the members of the Court is this : the defendant was a shareholder in the plaintiff company, and was also a person who had deposited money with the company ; he deposited that money upon a special agreement that, if any calls were made upon the shares held by him, he was not to be liable to pay them except in one way, that is by the appropriation of money deposited in satisfaction of the calls. A man in that position is, in my opinion, in a totally different position from an ordinary depositor without any

(1) [1892] 2 Q.B. 573.

such agreement, and also from one who is a mere depositor share- holder, and who must pay any calls made upon his shares out of his own pocket.

I am, therefore, of opinion that such first-mentioned depositor is in a different class from a mere depositor shareholder, or a depositor without the special agreement, by reason of his having inconsistent and possibly antagonistic rights.

The Joint Stock Companies Arrangement Act is one which requires most careful consideration in construing, as it is an Act which interferes with people's rights, and capable of working great injustice unless carefully administered. It contains pro- visions by which a majority can bind a minority, under which a hostile majority may have the opportunity of inflicting irreparable injustice on the minority. The Legislature, therefore, wisely provided that, in order that a majority should bind a minority, it must be a majority of the same class as the minority.

Upon this point I will refer to the judgment of *Bowen*, L.J., in *In re Alabama, &c., Company* (1). At p. 243, he says:— "The object of this section is not confiscation. It is not that one person should be a victim, and that the rest of the body should feast upon his rights. Its object is to enable compromises to be made, which are for the common benefit of the creditors as creditors, or for the common benefit of some class of creditors as such. Now, it is very important to observe that creditors of the company may have other interests besides those of creditors, and that there may be a class of creditors composed of many individuals, some of whom have only interests as members of that class, but others of whom may have interests of a predomi- nant kind which they hold, not as members of that class, but because they belong also to some other class of creditors, or because they also belong to the body of shareholders of the company. Therefore, although in a meeting that is to be held under this section, it is perfectly fair for every man to do that which is best for himself, yet the Court, which has to see what is reasonable and just as regards the interests of the whole class,

1898.

EXCELSIOR LAND INVESTMENT AND BUILDING CO. AND BANK, LTD.

v.

PHELAN.

G. B. Simpson J.

(1) [1891] 1 Ch. 213.

1898.

EXCELSIOR
LAND
INVESTMENT
AND
BUILDING CO.
AND BANK,
LTD.
v.
PHELAN.

G. B. Simpson J.
would certainly be very much influenced in its decision, if it
turned out that the majority was composed of persons who had
not really the interests of that class at stake."

The same learned Judge, in *Sovereign Life Assurance Company* v. *Dodd* (1), says, at p. 583 :—" The word ' class ' is vague.
and to find out what is meant by it we must look at the scope of
the section, which is a section enabling the Court to order a
meeting of a class of creditors to be called.   It seems plain that
we must give such a meaning to the term ' class ' as will prevent
the section being so worked as to result in confiscation and
injustice, and that it must be confined to those persons whose
rights are not so dissimilar as to make it impossible for them to
consult together with a view to their common interest."

That language is very distinct, and the learned Judge seems to
have had the same idea present to his mind as he had in the case
I have just before cited.

In this case we have depositors, who are also shareholders, and
who have a special agreement under which they have a right to
have the amount of their deposits applied towards payment of
calls.   Are not their interests different to those of shareholder
depositors who have no such agreement, and different again to
those of mere depositors ?

Bowen, L.J., then proceeds to point out the difference between
policy-holders whose policies had ripened into debts, and those
whose policies might not ripen into debts for years to come, and
continues :—" It was, therefore, not right to summon as members
of one and the same class those who had an absolute bar against
any claim of the company, and those who had not.   I think,
therefore, that there was no release of the defendant's claim
against the plaintiffs, and that the appeal must be dismissed."

So here, I think it was not right to summon the three classes
I have mentioned to one meeting.

No doubt, in that case, it appears that the defendant was a
dissenting creditor, but, as shewn by the marginal note to the
report of the case, the decision was based on grounds other than
the question of set-off.

(1) [1892] 2 Q.B. 573.

The case is, in my opinion, parallel to that now before us, and
the principle laid down by it is that separate meetings should
have been held.   I think that a separate meeting of the class to
which the defendant here belonged should have been held in order
to bind him.   If it is once admitted that a different class exists,
there must be a separate meeting of that class.

I may point out that the plaintiff company is not trying to bind
this defendant by an agreement to which he was an assenting
party; they are trying to bind him by a majority of persons not
belonging to the same class as himself ; therefore I see no necessity
for an allegation that the defendant was a dissenting, or not
assenting creditor.   Further, the replication assumes that the
defendant was a dissenting creditor.   The defendant can, in my
opinion, only be bound by a majority at a properly called meeting.

It was contended by Sir *Julian Salomons* that the Court
cannot go behind the arrangement after it has been sanctioned,
but I am of opinion that the sanction of the Court does not give
validity to an arrangement which was not come to in accordance
with the provisions of the Act.

[His Honour referred to the words of s. 3.]

Before sanction can be given, a proper meeting must have been
called.

This Court will always pay respect to a decision of the English
Court of Appeal, as it is in fact bound to do, and, in my opinion,
we are bound by the principle laid down in *Sovereign Life
Assurance Company* v. *Dodd* (1), which is to the effect that no
person is bound by an arrangement under the Act unless a meeting
is summoned of the class to which such person belongs.

I therefore think that the rejoinder is in that respect good, and
the demurrer to it bad.

COHEN, J.   I concur with their Honours that the replication is
good, and the second and third rejoinders are bad.

With regard to the fourth rejoinder, I concur with *Stephen*, J.
It is set up as an answer to the second replication of the plaintiff
company, which sets out that, "after the making of the said

(1) [1892] 2 Q.B. 573.

H 2

EXCELSIOR
LAND
INVESTMENT
AND
BUILDING CO.
AND BANK,
LTD.
v.
PHELAN.

Cohen J.

agreement" (that is the agreement that deposits should be utilised
in payment of calls) "and the said deposit and before the making
of the said calls . . . . a compromise or arrangement was
proposed between the plaintiff company and the depositors of
money in the said bank in respect of all obligations of the plaintiff company in respect of such deposits. . ."

That replication is so far a complete answer to the plea; but
the fourth rejoinder sets up that separate meetings of depositors,
depositor shareholders, and depositor shareholders who had agreed
for the payment of calls on their shares as above-mentioned, were
not summoned.

The fair interpretation of the replication is that the defendant
was summoned to the meeting which was held, and had an
opportunity of attending; and, inasmuch as there is no assertion
to the contrary, or that he was dissentient, I think the Court may
fairly conclude that the defendant was an assenting party to the
scheme of arrangement.

It was suggested by Dr. *Sly* that, because it is stated in the
replication that the arrangement was agreed to by a majority,
therefore it follows that the defendant formed one of the minority,
but I am unable to take that view.

I agree with Sir *Julian Salomons* that we must presume that,
when the Judge sanctioned the scheme of arrangement, the provisions of the Act had been duly complied with; and, further, I
am of opinion that, if the defendant wants to shew that he was
not an assenting party, the burden of proof is upon him.

It may be stated, as a general rule, that the Court will be strict
in not allowing vested rights to be taken away except by clear
words; but in a matter of this kind, where a compromise of
rights and liabilities is sought, and the general benefit rather than
the individual interest is contemplated, I do not think that the
Act of Parliament should be construed with rigid strictness.
Upon this it is instructive to read a passage in the judgment of
Vaughan Williams, J., in *In re English, Scottish and Australian
Chartered Bank* (1): "When I came to consider whether I had
jurisdiction to make the order, I could not, it seemed to me, but

(1) [1893] 3 Ch. 385, at p. 392.

take into consideration what I may call the tide of authority.
The decisions of twenty years or a quarter of a century ago shew
the strongest possible feeling that one ought never to deprive any
creditor of his common law right, and ought never to require him
to give up anything, to which he is by law entitled, at the will of
the majority of the creditors, unless all the steps, which are provided by the statute, have been most carefully followed, and the
tendency was to construe in the strictest possible manner any
statute which gave to the majority of creditors the right to impose their will upon the minority. But I do not think that
anyone who has followed the subsequent decisions—whether under
the Companies Acts or the Bankruptcy Acts—will hesitate to say
that the tendency of late has been rather to favour the power of
the majority of creditors to impose their will upon the minority,
and to construe the legislation upon the subject with some freedom.
In fact, whatever the subject matter of legislation, the tendency
of the Courts, rightly or wrongly, has been to construe Acts of
Parliament with freedom, and to approach nearer to legislation
by construction than the Judges in former days used to consider
themselves entitled to do. I, therefore, feel that I ought to construe this Act of Parliament freely, and to try, as far as I can, to
adapt it to the particular necessity which has arisen in this case."

I need hardly say that *Vaughan Williams*, J., was a Judge who
had vast experience in this branch of the law; and his judgment
in the case was affirmed on appeal.

The passage I have quoted shews the tendency of the Courts
in modern days towards a liberal construction of the statute. In
order, however, to prevent a majority from unfairly affecting the
minority, the scheme of arrangement must be brought before a
Judge for sanction.

I now consider whether or not the defendant is legally justified
in setting up that separate meetings of classes alleged by him to
be distinct should have been held. So far as I can see there were,
in this case, no distinct classes within the meaning of the cases.

A meeting of depositors was called, and, in my opinion, the
depositors having the special agreement above referred to are not
a distinct class from the depositors who had no such agreement,
so as to make it impossible for them to consult together in their

1898.

EXCELSIOR
LAND
INVESTMENT
AND
BUILDING Co.
AND BANK,
LTD.
v.
PHELAN.

Cohen J.

1898.

EXCELSIOR
LAND
INVESTMENT
AND
BUILDING Co.
AND BANK,
LTD.
v.
PHELAN.

Cohen J.

common interest as to the scheme. But, even if I am wrong in this, the defendant should have brought the matter before the Judge who sanctioned the scheme, and should not have lain by and set up the point at this stage.

It should be borne in mind that, whilst the defendant had his vested rights, so had the other depositors, and if they were induced to abandon or qualify those rights by the knowledge, as is probable, that they could rely on the uncalled capital of the company, free from restrictions, as a fund from which the liabilities of the company could at any rate in part be met, it is, to say the least, manifestly inequitable that the defendant should then have remained silent as to the agreement which he alleges he had with the directors, and now seek to enforce it as against the other depositors, when the uncalled capital is being resorted to, to liquidate the company's liabilities.

In 1881, *In re Madras Irrigation and Canal Company* (1) was decided. In that case a meeting of creditors was called to consider a compromise between the liquidator and the creditors of the company ; at this meeting creditors, who were also shareholders, attended and voted at the meeting, yet it was held that their votes could be taken into consideration, so as to make the vote of the majority binding on the minority ; though it might well have been argued that the interests of shareholder creditors were opposed to those of the other creditors. That case was followed in our own Courts in *The Metropolitan Mutual Permanent Building and Investment Association, Limited* (2).

In that case there were two classes, debenture holders, who were also shareholders, and debenture holders, who were not shareholders ; taking each of these classes separately there was not a statutory majority, but counting the votes of the two classes together there was a sufficient majority. *A. H. Simpson*, J., held that the votes could be taken together as being those of one class of creditors.

The next case which I shall refer to, is *Sovereign Life Assurance Company* v. *Dodd* (3). The real decision in that case does not seem to me to apply to the present There the real question

(1) W.N. [1881] 172.   (2) 8 B.C. 11.
                 (3) [1892] 2 Q.B. 573.

was as to the right of Dodd to a set off against the company, and the real decision was as to that set off.

The next case is *In re Alabama, &c., Company* (1). There a meeting of "first debenture-holders" was called, the debentures representing a liability of 1,500,000*l.*; at the meeting there were present 72 first debenture-holders, 8 first debenture-holders who were also holders of second debentures, and 21 first debenture-holders who were also shareholders, but representing only about 500,000*l.*; now that may be considered a fairly mixed meeting, and one containing antagonistic elements, and yet the scheme was sanctioned.   The point that there had not been separate meetings of the different classes of first debenture-holders was not definitely raised, though, if it had been a tenable one, it might not unreasonably be assumed it would have been taken, for the scheme was actively opposed both out of and in Court by two of the 21 debenture-holders.

In his judgment *North*, J., at p. 229, says:—"In the present case it was suggested that some of the persons who had voted as first debenture-holders might have been influenced by their being also holders of second debentures. But there is no evidence before me upon which I can give any weight to that argument. There is nothing in the slightest degree impugning the good faith and honest intention of all the first debenture-holders who support the resolution."

In the report of the case on appeal, at p. 234, counsel for the liquidator said in argument:—"It is said that many of the class are not looking at the matter only as first-class debenture-holders, but as having other interests. That would not be conclusive."

To this *Lindley*, L.J., says:—"No; but it is a matter to be considered by the Court as to confirming the scheme."

Counsel for the liquidator then submitted:—"The Court, though it may think the scheme not advantageous, will not refuse to confirm it unless it can see that the scheme cannot possibly be for the benefit of the first-class debenture-holders."

To this *Lindley*, L.J., says:—"Unless we see that, all we have to do is to see that a minority is not overborne by a majority composed of persons who have adverse interests."

(1) [1891] 1 Ch. 213.

1898.

EXCELSIOR LAND INVESTMENT AND BUILDING Co. AND BANK, LTD. *v.* PHELAN.

Cohen J.

1898.

EXCELSIOR
LAND
INVESTMENT
AND
BUILDING Co.
AND BANK,
LTD.
v.
PHELAN.

Cohen J.

In his judgment, at p. 239, *Lindley*, L.J., says:—" Now, it is said, and said with truth, that some of the majority held second debentures, and it is also said that some of the majority were shareholders holding a considerable amount of shares, and it is urged that they voted not simply as first debenture-holders, and were not looking at the matter from the point of view of first debenture-holders, but from the point of view of second debenture-holders and of interested shareholders. That state of complicated interest would not prevent them from voting, but it would necessarily induce the Court to look with caution and care at the effect of what was done at that meeting. Now, I could understand that a dissentient might say that, in consequence of the shortness of the notice convening the meeting, in consequence of the complex interests of some of the majority, that meeting did not really represent the views of the debenture-holders. I can understand that, and I can understand that it might be reasonable to convene another meeting to ascertain whether the real bulk of the first debenture-holders were in favour of the scheme, but no such application has been made; and Mr. *Rigby*, thinking probably, I suppose, that, if another meeting were convened, there would still be three-fourths against him, has naturally not desired to have another meeting called."

If the defendant here thought that he was being unduly over-ridden by the majority, it was his duty to bring that fact to the notice of the Judge at the time of the application for the sanctioning of the scheme; to hold otherwise would lead to the gravest uncertainty, and to perhaps a greater danger and disaster than if there had been no scheme of arrangement sanctioned.

In *In re London Chartered Bank of Australia* (1), *Vaughan Williams*, J., at p. 545, says (after referring to the judgment of *Lindley*, L.J., in *In re English, Scottish and Australian Chartered Bank*) (2):—" It seems, therefore, that I ought to sanction the present scheme unless there is something *ex facie* wrong about it, or unless something is brought to my attention shewing that there has been some material oversight or miscarriage."

In this case there is no such thing as oversight or miscarriage suggested, and, if there had been, the defendant should have

(1) [1893] 3 Ch. 540.   (2) [1893] 3 Ch. 385.

brought it before the Judge who sanctioned the scheme. It is too late now to raise the point. The fact remains he was a depositor at a depositors' meeting.

For these reasons, I am of opinion that the rejoinder is bad in law, and there must be judgment for the plaintiff company.

Judgment for the plaintiffs.

Attorneys for the plaintiffs: *A. Rofe & Son.*

Attorneys for the defendant: *Fitzhardinge, Son & Houston.*

1898.

EXCELSIOR LAND INVESTMENT AND BUILDING Co. AND BANK, LTD.

v.

PHELAN.

Cohen J.

WRENCH v. RICHARDSON & WRENCH, LIMITED.

1898.

Feb. 18.
June 24.

Moore Street Improvement Act, 54 Vic. No. 30—Assessment—Nature of liability—
Landlord and tenant—Covenant to pay rates, taxes, assessments, impositions and
charges.

The plaintiff, the owner of freehold property within the improvement area
contemplated by the Moore Street Improvement Act, 54 Vic. No. 30, let to the
defendants for ten years by a lease containing a covenant by the lessee to pay
"all taxes, rates, assessments, impositions and charges, whether municipal, parochial or otherwise, now and hereafter to be imposed, etc., excepting a Government
property tax." The Moore Street Improvement Act came into force about two
years after the date of the lease, and the plaintiff, having paid certain annual
instalments of the amount thereby assessed in respect of the premises, now sued
the defendants under the covenant to recover the amount.

Held, that the liability imposed upon owners of property by the Moore Street
Improvement Act is a personal liability upon such owners, and not a charge upon
the land.

Held, further (COHEN, J., *dissentiente*), that the liability imposed by the Act was
not contemplated by the parties when executing the lease, and was not covered
by the terms of the covenant.

The C.J.
Stephen J.
and
Cohen J.

THIS was a special case stated under the Common Law Procedure Act for the opinion of the Supreme Court. The facts are
fully stated in the judgments.

Cullen, for the plaintiff.

Gordon, for the defendants.

Cur. adv. vult.

June 24. On the 24th June judgment was delivered.

THE CHIEF JUSTICE. The plaintiff in this case is the owner of
certain freehold property, situate in Pitt-street, Sydney. By an
indenture of lease, dated the 17th of April, 1889, the plaintiff
leased the premises in question to the defendants for a term of
ten years from the 1st of April, 1889. This lease contained
amongst others a covenant in the words following: "And shall
and will well and truly pay, or cause to be paid, all taxes, rates,
assessments, impositions and charges, whether municipal, parochial
or otherwise, now and hereafter to be imposed, assessed, levied

or made payable on or in respect of the premises, excepting nevertheless a Government property tax."

1898.

WRENCH
v.
RICHARDSON
& WRENCH,
LTD.

The C.J.

After the date of this lease, the Moore Street Improvement Act of 1890 (54 Vic. No. 30) and the Moore Street Improvement Act Amendment Act of 1892 (55 Vic. No. 13) came into force. The premises in question, although not situate in Moore-street, are within the "improvement area" mentioned in s. 4 of the 54th Vic. No. 30.

The Legislature have assumed that all lands within this "improvement area" will be permanently improved, both as to the capital and annual value, by the improvement of Moore-street, and accordingly have provided that all owners of land within this "improvement area" shall pay a certain specified sum as a contribution towards the sum necessary for the carrying out of the improvement in question. This contribution may either be paid in one sum by the owner, or the payments may be spread over a period of years not exceeding 100 or less than 50. The amount of the plaintiff's contribution has been assessed at 1,560l., which spread over 100 years at 4 per cent. amounts to 63l. 13s. 2d. per annum. The Municipal Council of Sydney has called upon the plaintiff to pay, and she has paid the sum of 318l. 5s. 10d., being five annual instalments at the rate of 63l. 13s. 2d.

The plaintiff now seeks to recover this amount as against the defendants, contending that under the covenant in the lease the defendants are liable. On the other hand, the defendants contend that the covenant does not include a payment of this description. The question for the determination of the Court, is, whether this contribution falls within the terms of the covenant in the lease so as to render the defendants liable for its repayment to the plaintiff?

Now, two matters have to be considered : first, the construction of the Act of Parliament ; and secondly, the construction of the covenant.

The Act provides that the funds necessary for the carrying out of the improvement shall be ascertained, and when ascertained shall be raised in two ways. As to a sum not less than one-half of the whole amount the owners of the lands within the improvement area are to be liable to pay, and as to the balance s. 25

1898.

WRENCH
v.
RICHARDSON
& WRENCH,
LTD.

The C.J.

of the Act provides that this is to be paid out of a " special street improvement rate," to be raised as therein mentioned. Upon appeal the Court may reduce the contribution of the owner to one-fourth of the whole, thus casting three-fourths upon the " Special Street Improvement Rate." The 55 Vic. No. 13 repeals s. 25 of the 54 Vic. No. 30, and provides that in place of a " Special Street Improvement Rate " being provided for, " The City Fund" should defray that which the " Special Street Improvement Rate " was intended to meet. As to how the " City Fund " is constituted, see the 43 Vic. No. 3, s. 217.

Now it appears to me that the 54 Vic. No. 30 imposes upon the owners of the land a personal liability to pay the contribution in question. Sects. 4, 5, 6, 7 and 26 have reference to "owners only." Sect. 4 provides for an initiatory notification which is to contain a large number of details, amongst others it is to state the respective proportion in which the owners of property within the improvement area, and the City Fund shall defray the cost. Sect. 5 provides that the proportion which the owners have to pay shall not be less than one-half of the whole; this may be on appeal reduced to a sum not less than one-fourth of the whole. Sect. 6 provides for the deposit at the Town Hall of an assessment-book in which shall be specified the amount which every owner of property within the improvement area shall be required to pay in respect of his property as his share of the aggregate amount of the contribution of all such owners. In the determination of this share, the council have to regard the position of every such property and the degree of permanent enhancement in its capital or annual value which the said improvement may reasonably be expected to produce. Sect. 7 provides for appeals by owners only. No right of appeal is reserved to occupiers. Sect. 26 provides the means of enforcing payment of any sum payable by way of contribution for any owner, and this must be either by distress of his goods if any upon the property, see s. 118, or by action or suit, see s. 238 of the 43 Vic. No. 3. It is manifest that this Act creates no charge upon the land, nor, as in some Acts of this nature, is the tenant, if there be one, made liable either primarily or at all, payment cannot be demanded from him, nor has

he any right of appeal.   Again, it will be observed that this Act
does not contain the provision to be found in most Acts of this
class that its provisions are not to affect any contract as to the
payment of rates, etc., which may have been made between the
landlord and tenant.

1898.

WRENCH
v.
RICHARDSON
& WRENCH,
LTD.

The C.J.

All this leads me to the conclusion that, for this improvement
which was supposed to enhance the capital or annual value of
the property, the owner has to submit to a charge, which is not
imposed upon the land, but is one of a personal nature only.

Now having considered the effect of the Act for the purpose
of ascertaining the nature of the charge, I turn to the covenant,
and I am of opinion that this annual payment, which may at any
time be commuted at the plaintiff's pleasure is not a tax, a rate,
an assessment, an imposition or a charge within the meaning of
the covenant.

A large number of authorities were cited before us. I have
carefully considered these and many others, some decided in
favour of the landlord, some in favour of the tenant. It was
said by Mr. Justice *Grove*, in *Aldridge* v. *Ferne* (1): "It is difficult
to extract any very distinct rule from the numerous cases upon
this subject." I think, however, it is safe to lay this down, that
in the first place the Act imposing payment should be considered,
to ascertain the nature of the charge, whether it be a charge upon
the land or one of a personal nature upon the owner.   Whether
the charge is one for the permanent improvement of the property,
or whether the Act creates a rate or a tax; and then looking at
the lease to consider, whether this charge is one which falls
within the words of the covenant. So far as I know the 54 Vic.
No. 30 was the first attempt by the Legislature to apply what is
known as the "betterment principle" to improvements made
within the city of Sydney. It can scarcely be supposed, therefore, that, when the lease of the 17th April, 1889, was entered
into, that it was within the intention of any of the parties to that
document that such a charge as this should be embraced in the
covenant. That, however, is not conclusive if the words used
are large enough to embrace it.

It appears to me, however, that a charge which is one personal
to the owner made for the improvement of the property, and

(1) 17 Q.B.D. 214.

1898.

Wrench
v.
Richardson
& Wrench,
Ltd.

The C.J.

which can only be demanded from him, is not a tax, rate, assessment, imposition or charge which the tenant is bound under this covenant to pay to the landlord. In *Wilkinson* v. *Collyer* (1), the tenant agreed to pay all rates, taxes and assessments payable in respect of the premises. It was held that a sum assessed upon the owners as their proportion of the expense of paving the street upon which the premises abutted was not a rate, tax or assessment within the meaning of the agreement, but a charge imposed upon the owner for the permanent improvement of his property. In that case the Act contemplated a payment by the occupier to be deducted from the rent. It also provided for non-interference between landlord and tenant as to any contract as to the payment of rates. *Manisty, J.,* at p. 4, says : " That raises the question, whether the expenses of paving the street in question, which were payable by the owners, though recoverable from the occupier, were a sum payable in respect of the premises from which the tenant had agreed to indemnify his landlords. It certainly is not a ' rate ' or a ' tax,' but a sum incurred by the vestry for improving the property of the owners of the premises ; and unless there is some authority to the contrary, I should hold the words here used to apply to rates and assessments of a temporary or recurring nature, and not to a sum which is a charge upon the property giving it an increased permanent value. But the question is, whether the defendant has by his covenant taken upon himself this extraordinary liability. The cases seem to shew the desire of the Courts not to impose such a liability upon the tenant unless compelled by express words, or necessary implication to do so." *Grove, J.,* in *Aldridge* v. *Ferne* (2) speaks of the above statement as the only broad principle to be found laid down in these cases. *Allum* v. *Dickinson* (3) is a case very much to the same effect as *Wilkinson* v. *Collyer* (1). There the *Master of the Rolls* says, at p. 635 : " The tenant is not usually made liable to any charges for the permanent improvement of the property."

It may be said that the charge in *Allum* v. *Dickinson,* and in *Wilkinson* v. *Collyer,* was not a recurring charge, as the charge

(1) 13 Q.B.D. 1.   (2) 17 Q.B.D. 214.
                    (3) 9 Q.B.D. 632.

in this case now is, but it must be borne in mind that the owner may discharge the whole amount at once, and that the amount is spread over a period of years apparently for the convenience of those who do not desire to pay at once. Accordingly it being made recurring for the sake of convenience, cannot affect the question, or afford any real ground of distinction between this case and those cited. If the gross sum charged be not a "rate" or a "tax" neither can its separate portions constituting the annual payment become such. It is, therefore, obvious that if the plaintiff so elect she can discharge the whole of the liability by making one payment, in which case it is impossible to suppose that she could recover the whole or any part of the payment so made from the tenant.

· 1898.

WRENCH
v.
RICHARDSON
& WRENCH,
LTD.

The C.J.

I have accordingly come to the conclusion that the charge in this case is a distinctly personal charge upon plaintiff, and was not contemplated by, neither is it included within, the defendants' covenant. This being so the defendants are entitled to judgment with the costs of suit.

STEPHEN, J.   I need not refer to the facts of this case, nor, in detail, to the authorities cited upon one side or the other. They are referred to and fully commented on in the judgments of *The Chief Justice* and Mr. Justice *Cohen*, which I have had the advantage of reading before I had an opportunity of preparing my own judgment. As far as the authorities are concerned, they are so numerous and depend upon such nice shades of distinction, that, with the exception of one or two, to which I shall more particularly refer, they have scarcely afforded me any guide to a conclusion. In *Budd* v. *Marshall* (1), *Bramwell*, L.J., says, "As to the cases it is extremely difficult to take them into account." Another Judge in *Wilkinson* v. *Collyer* (2), contents himself with putting a construction upon certain terms, "without regard to the seemingly conflicting authorities which have been cited." In *Aldridge* v. *Ferne* (3), *Grove*, J., says, "It is difficult to extract any very distinct rule from the numerous cases upon this subject." A reference to pages 490 and 491 of *Budd* v. *Marshall*, in which the cases of *Tidswell* v. *Whitworth* (4),

(1) 5 C.P.D. 487.   (3) 17 Q.B.D. 214.
(2) 13 Q.B.D. 1.   (4) L.R. 2 C.P. 326.

1898.   and *Thompson* v. *Lapworth* (1), are commented on by *Buggallay*,
WRENCH   L.J., will sufficiently verify the difficulty of distinguishing between
v.   decided cases. The liability of tenants has turned very much
RICHARDSON
& WRENCH, upon the exact expressions used. I will name a few of them,
LTD.   upon combinations of which decisions have turned, *e.g.*, rates,
Stephen J. taxes, impositions, assessments, burthens, duties, services,
           outgoings,—these again being accompanied by other phrases
           more or less indicating the intent of the parties. So again with
           regard to the intent of the parties, one Judge says in *Budd* v.
           Marshall, "Landlords always endeavour to extend the liability
           of tenants by putting in additional words, and in this they
           generally succeed, for tenants have not the same persistency."

               In *Allum* v. *Dickinson* (2), the *Master of the Rolls* says, "The
           tenant is not usually made liable to any charges for the permanent
           improvement of the property, though " he adds, "this is not
           conclusive."

               Now with regard to the terms used in this covenant, it is
           clear that the liability of the tenant is not created by the words,
           "rates and taxes." With regard to the word "impositions,"
           Keatinge, J., says, in *Tidswell* v. *Whitworth*, referring to that
           expression, "Looking at the words with which it is associated in
           this covenant," (which were ' taxes, rates, assessments ')," it seems
           to me that that word is not to be taken in the widest sense of which
           it is susceptible, but that it must be limited to impositions in the
           nature of taxes, rates, and assessments." I find that the latest
           decision but one of those that have been cited, *i.e.*, *Wilkinson* v.
           Collyer (3), gives a construction to those words in favour of the
           tenant. *Manisty*, J., seems to have reviewed very many of the
           conflicting cases to which I have referred. He says, "the cases
           seem to shew the desire of the Courts not to impose such a
           liability upon the tenant unless compelled by express words, or
           by necessary implication to do so." He says also, "unless there
           is some authority to the contrary, I should hold the words here
           used to apply to rates and assessments of a temporary or recur-
           ring nature, and not to a sum which is a charge upon the property
           giving it an increased permanent value." He further characterises

           (1) L.R. 3 C.P. 149.   (2) 9 Q.B.D. p. 635.
                          (3) 13 Q.B.D. 1.

the liability sought to be imposed upon the tenant as extraordinary. This was a liability to pay a sum assessed upon the
owners as their proportion of the cost of paving a street upon
which the premises abutted. In *Aldridge* v. *Ferne, Grove, J.,*
says that the only broad principle is that laid down by *Manisty,*
J., in *Wilkinson* v. *Collyer,* in the passage I have just quoted. The
judgment in the case of *Aldridge* v. *Ferne,* the latest of the cases
cited on this subject, was against the tenant, the word "outgoing"
being principally relied upon, together with the words, "for the
time being payable by the landlord or the tenant in respect of
the premises." In relying upon these two cases I feel that I
should be standing upon safe ground, inasmuch as the decisions
were made in full view and consideration of all past ones. The
only word in the covenant before us to which I have not alluded
is the word "charges," and I cannot see that its introduction can
make any difference. No charge is imposed upon the land.

I will only add that, were it not for the two cases upon which
I have based my judgment, I might have considered that the
tenant intended to run all risks, and used words fairly capable
of carrying out that intention. If it had entered into his mind
that the risk he ran was so wide, I can hardly think that he
would have consented to a covenant that included the liability
in question. It is some satisfaction, therefore, that the tenant is
not mulcted in a sum that could scarcely have been in the contemplation either of himself or his landlord.

COHEN, J. The plaintiffs in this action, by indenture of
April 17th, 1889, let to the defendants certain premises in Pitt-
street, Sydney, for a term of ten years, from April 1st, 1889, at a
clear yearly rental of 2,000*l.*, "without any deduction or abatement whatsoever"; and after covenanting for payment of that
rent, the defendants further covenanted that "they would pay or
cause to be paid all taxes, rates, assessments, impositions, and
charges, whether municipal, parochial, or otherwise, then or
thereafter to be imposed, assessed, levied, or made payable on, or
in respect of, the premises, excepting a Government property
tax." In the year 1890 the Moore Street Improvement Act of

N.S.W.R., Vol. XIX., Law.

1898.

WRENCH
v.
RICHARDSON
& WRENCH,
LTD.

Stephen J.

1898.

Wrench
v.
Richardson
& Wrench,
Ltd.

Cohen J.

1890 was passed for the purpose of widening and improving Moore-street, the Municipal Council of Sydney having the necessary powers conferred upon it for that purpose. By s. 4 of the Act a list of the owners of property within the improvement area had to be included in a notification therein mentioned, and the notification had also to contain a detailed estimate of the cost of the improvement, including the cost of the acquisition of land, and the amounts and dates of making the repayments necessary to defray the whole cost, together with interest at a rate not exceeding four pounds per centum per annum, and the period, in any case, over which such repayments would spread was not to exceed 100 years, nor be less than 50 years ; but any owner might within such period make any repayment for which he was liable, with interest at 4 per cent. per annum to the date of repayment.

By s. 5 the proportion in which the owners of property within the improvement area should contribute to the entire cost, together with interest, was not to be less than one-half of such entire cost and interest, leave, however, being reserved to the Supreme Court on appeal to fix the liability of the owners to contribute at not less than one-fourth of the costs and interest. By s. 6, within 30 days after the publication of the notification referred to in s. 4, the council had to have made and deposited at the Town Hall an "*assessment-book,*" in which was specified the amount which every owner of property within the improvement area would be required to pay *in respect of his property,* as his share of the aggregate amount of the contributions of all such owners. In determining such share regard was to be had to the position of the property, and the degree of its enhancement in its capital or annual value, which the improvement might reasonably be expected to produce. And the council was required during three successive weeks to publish in the *Gazette* and two newspapers a notice stating that such *assessment*-book · had been deposited and was open to the inspection of all persons ·interested therein.

By s. 7, within 30 days after the last publication of the notices referred to in s. 6, any owner of property *assessed* in such *assessment*-book, might give notice in writing to the town clerk of his

intention to appeal to the Supreme Court against (1) The
inclusion of his property within the improvement area; (2) The
proportions in which the cost of such improvement, with interest
thereon, had been notified as *chargeable on the property owners*
within the said area . . . ; (3) The amount or share of the
contribution at which such owner had been *assessed* towards the
aggregate contributions of the whole of such owners.

1898.

WRENCH
v.
RICHARDSON
& WRENCH,
LTD.

Cohen J.

From the express language of this Act the payments, or as
they are termed in it, the "repayments," which the plaintiff was
required to make were "assessments" which the owner of the
property was "assessed" at, and if one literally and strictly
applies the language of s. 7, the cost might also be regarded as a
"charge," for it speaks of the cost as *chargeable* on the property
owners. It is clear that the cost is not a charge on the property,
and is a purely personal obligation imposed upon the owner;
but imposed upon him clearly "in respect of" the property.
Apart from the words of s. 6, which speak of the amount which
every property owner is required to *pay in respect of his property,* and what one's intelligence would dictate, if legal authority
were required for the meaning of the words "in respect of," it is
to be found in *Brett* v. *Rogers* (1), where *Bruce,* J., says : "The
words '*in respect of the premises*' are used in contradistinction to
the words '*on the premises,*' and an assessment or duty made or
imposed, not on the premises, but in respect of the premises,
must be made or imposed upon some person in respect of the
premises, and an assessment duly made upon any person in
respect of the premises seems to us to come within the meaning
of the covenant." See also *Thompson* v. *Lapworth* (2). The
assessed amount of the plaintiff's contribution as owner appearing in the assessment book is 1560*l.*, and the annual repayment
thereof, if extended over 100 years at 4 per cent., is 63*l.* 13*s.* 2*d.*
The plaintiff has paid five of these instalments, amounting to
318*l.* 5*s.* 10*d.*, and now seeks to recover that amount from the
defendants.

It may at once be conceded that the repayments sought to be
recovered are not "rates or taxes" within the covenant. But

(1) [1897] 1 Q.B. at p. 529.   (2) L.R. 3 C.P. 149,

1898.
WRENCH
v.
RICHARDSON
& WRENCH,
LTD.

Cohen J.

beyond these expressions, and with the view of extending the
scope of the covenant, there are the words " assessments,
impositions, and charges," and connected with the entire preceding parts of the covenant, whether "*municipal, parochial, or
otherwise, excepting a Government property tax.*" That the contributions by property owners are municipal is apparent, seeing
that they are devoted to municipal improvement, and are raised
and disbursed by the municipal council; and, although, at the
date of the covenant, the Government property tax was not in
the contemplation of Parliament any more than was the raising
of money for the improvement of Moore-street under the Act
now in review, yet provision was made to protect the lessees from
the burden of the property tax, whilst the *exception* from the
covenant of any such charge as that we are now considering, is
not made. It may, however, be urged in answer that whilst a
property tax was a thing generally known, and might, therefore,
be thought of in framing the covenant, such a charge as that in
the Moore Street Improvement Act was then not known as an
existent thing, and would not, therefore, be thought of. Still
there remains the question, do the moneys sought to be recovered
come within the meaning of the language of the covenant.

In *Payne* v. *Burridge* (1) by a local Act commissioners were
authorised to pave and flag footways, and the costs thereof were
to be paid by the tenants or occupiers of the houses next adjoining, in default they were to be recovered by distress. Another
clause empowered the tenant to deduct the costs so paid by him
out of his rent. The tenant subsequently covenanted to pay all
" taxes, rates, duties, levies, assessments, and payments whatsoever, which were, or during the term might be, rated, levied,
assessed, or imposed on the premises." The tenant was held
liable, *Pollock*, C.B., observing: "The language of the defendant's
covenant leaves no doubt . . . This covenant was entered
into since the passing of the local Act, although if it had been
made before, I think it must have operated in the same manner
. . . . It cannot be doubted that the charge in question is an
assessment or *payment*, which, according to the terms of his contract, is to be borne by the tenant." *Parke*, B., says: "I am of

(1) 12 M. & W. 727.

the same opinion. The words of the covenant must be construed according to their natural and ordinary sense, and it seems to me that they are too strong to be got over." And *Alderson*, B., states: " I entirely agree. If the parties had been desirous of imposing this particular burden on the tenant, I do not see what other terms they could have used than those which are contained in this lease." *Rolfe*, B., concurred.

In *Sweet* v. *Seager* (1) there was a covenant by which the covenantor covenanted to " pay, bear, and discharge all . . . such Parliamentary, parochial, and county, district, and occasional levies, rates, assessments, taxes, charges, impositions, contributions, burthens, duties, and services whatsover as during the term should be taxed, assessed, or imposed upon or in respect of the premises, or any part thereof." It was held that the expense of drainage works done upon the premises under the authority of the Metropolis Local Management Act, 1855 (18 & 19 Vic. c. 120), was within the covenant. *Cockburn*, C.J., in his judgment says : "It was clearly the intention of the original landlord, and also of Seager, that the tenant should bear the landlord harmless against all charges of a general local character imposed upon or in respect of the premises. The words used are very large, and quite large enough, in my opionion, to include the imposition or duty in question . . . As to the supposed distinction between ordinary rates and occasional particular assessments for permanent improvements, it is to be observed that the same suggestion was made in *Payne* v. *Burridge* (2) and the Court of Exchequer held that, although the charge was in respect of a permanent improvement, it fell within the terms of a lease subsequently made, whereby the tenant covenanted to bear and pay all taxes, rates, duties, levies, assessments, and payments whatsoever, which were, or during the term might be, rated, levied, assessed, or imposed on the premises. Words even less comprehensive than those of the covenant in the present case." *Cresswell*, *Crowder*, and *Willes*, JJ., agreed with the judgment of the learned *Chief Justice*.

Thompson v. *Lapworth* (3) was a case in which the tenant covenanted to pay " all taxes, rates, duties, and assessments what-

1898.

WRENCH
v.
RICHARDSON
& WRENCH,
LTD.

Cohen J.

(1) 2 C.B.N.S. 119.   (2) 12 M. & W. 727.
(3) L.R. 3 C.P. 149.

1898.

WRENCH
v.
RICHARDSON
& WRENCH,
LTD.

Cohen J.

soever, which, during the continuance of the demise, should be
taxed, assessed, or imposed on the tenant or landlord of the
premises thereby demised in respect thereof." The vestry of the
parish under s. 96 of the Metropolis Management Act (25 & 26
Vic. c. 102) paved the street upon which the premises abutted,
assessed the sum payable by the owner at 49l. 2s. 6d. It was
held that this was a *duty* or *assessment* within the covenant.
Willes, J., at p. 156 says : " And it (the Act of Parliament) gives
the vestry or board power to receive payment of the sums charged
or assessed on the respective owners by instalments spread over
a period not exceeding 20 years, the remedy for the recovery of
the money being still confined to the owner." And at p. 157 : " I
come back then to the terms of the contract itself, and to the
question whether the money which the landlord was bound to
pay, and did pay, was a money payment falling within the
terms of the defendants' covenant. It appears to me that it was.
I think it was clearly a duty in the sense of a money payment
imposed upon the landlord of the premises demised in respect thereof.
Our attention has very properly been called by the defendants'
counsel to other provisions of the statute, and to the familiar
rule according to which general words following special words in
deeds or acts of Parliament are to be restricted to the particular
genus; and that the words 'duties and assessments' in this
covenant are to be referred to matters *ejusdem generis* with
those before referred to, viz., 'taxes and rates,' and it was said
that it was not likely that the parties in framing the covenant,
would contemplate that the tenant, whose term peradventure
might last only five years, should pay an assessment which was
imposed, not as an ordinary rate or tax, but for the permanent
improvement of the premises. The substance of the argument is
this, that the duties intended by this covenant are not occasional
or exceptional expenses incurred once for all in respect of permanent and substantial improvements, but duties or assessments
accruing from year to year, or occasionally, like the old sewer
rate in the out districts—matters of a recurring character. The
argument is a strong and captivating one, and one to which I
might have yielded if it had not been excluded by decisions
which ought to bind us. I think it is excluded by the case of

Payne v. *Burridge* (1).   I cannot, without carping at words, point
out any distinction between that case and the case now before us."

Mr. Justice *Keating* says: "It was urged by Mr. Holker that
this could not have been intended to be a charge on the tenant,
inasmuch as it was a charge incurred in the permanent improvement of the premises, and it might be that the tenant's interest
in them would enure only for five years.   But the argument is
much weakened by the consideration that the twenty-one years
term was determinable at the option of the tenant only, and not
at that of the landlord."

Lord Chief Justice *Bovill* says: "I cannot distinguish this
case upon any principle of law or fact from *Payne* v. *Burridge*.
In *Crosse* v. *Raw* (2) the defendant covenanted with the plaintiff to bear, pay, and discharge the sewer rate, tythes, rent, charge
in lieu of tythes, and 'all other taxes, rates, assessments, and
outgoings whatsoever,' which at any time or times during the
said demise should be taxed, rated, charged, assessed, or imposed
upon the said demised premises, or upon the landlord or tenant
in respect thereof, and under it he was held liable for the
expenses of making a drain, which, under 29 & 30 Vic. c. 90, s.
10, the landlord, as 'owner,' might have been required to make
'as an outgoing.'"   *Bramwell*, B., in his judgment says, in speaking of the nature of the expense: "It would certainly be something which had gone out, an expense which he had been at in
respect of the premises, and it would have been an expense
imposed upon him."   *Pollock*, B., observes: "That a charge paid
in consequence of the making of a sewer was an outgoing charged in
respect of the premises, or on the landlord or tenant in respect
thereof."   And further says: "It is certain that the general
scope and intention of the covenant and the reservation was that
the landlord should get the rent clear of all charges."

In *Hartley* v. *Hudson* (3), the cost of sewering, levelling, and
paving the street, in which a house was situate, under the Public
Health Act, 1848, was held to be within a covenant in a lease to
"pay all rates, taxes, charges, and assessments whatever," which
now are, or may be, charged or assessed upon the premises, or any

(1) 12 M. & W. 727.   (2) L.R. 9 Ex. 209.
          (3) 4 C.P.D. 367.

1898.

WRENCH
v.
RICHARDSON
& WRENCH,
LTD.

Cohen J.

1898.

WRENCH
v.
RICHARDSON
& WRENCH,
LTD.

Cohen J.

part thereof, or upon any person or persons in respect thereof, or a "charge upon the premises," "or upon a person in respect thereof."

Again in *Budd* v. *Marshall* (1), the defendant was held liable for the cost of repairing defective drainage, under the Public Health Act of 1875 ; under his covenant to " bear, pay, and discharge . . . . all other taxes, rates, duties, and assessments whatsoever, whether Parliamentary, parochial, or otherwise." Though certainly the judgment turned mainly, if not altogether, upon the word "duties," a word which is not in the covenant now *sub judice.* But as to the question whether covenants of this class apply only to recurrent charges, and do not apply to permanent improvements, *Bramwell,* L.J., says :—" It is said that the covenant is applicable only to charges which are recurrent in their nature ; but it extends to improvement rates, which are not of that description. It has been said, why should not this expense be borne by the landlord ? But the question is, whether words sufficiently wide have been used to cast the burden upon the tenant ? I am at loss to see what other words can be put in. It seems to me that the parties intended to specify every kind of disbursement which they could think of. Suppose that the local authority were to do the work in the first instance, could it be contended that in that case there would not be a ' duty ' cast upon the landlord, which the tenant would be bound to discharge by force of this covenant ? Will it not be strange if the landlord cannot recover it from the tenant because he has himself done what was necessary ? In other words, will it not be unreasonable if the liability depends upon the circumstance whether the local authority itself has done the work ? *Willes,* J., in *Thompson* v. *Lapworth,* spoke of the argument as captivating, that it was an injustice to the tenant, who has only a limited interest, to be compelled to bear the whole expense for his landlord's benefit ; but the answer is, that under a lease for ninety-nine years the tenant would gain substantially the whole benefit. Landlords always endeavour to extend the liability of the tenants by putting in additional words, and in this they generally succeed, for tenants have not the same persistency. I am of opinion that the con-

(1) 5 C.P.D. 481.

struction of the lease is in favour of the plaintiffs; the lessors
wanted to get as rent a certain fixed sum without any abatement."

Lord Justice *Baggallay* says:—" Before concluding I must say
a few words with reference to an argument which has been
somewhat strongly pressed upon us; it has been urged on behalf
of the defendant that it would be inequitable to charge upon the
tenant an expenditure which is made for the permanent improvement of a property in which he has only a temporary interest,
and that a construction which would have that effect, should not
be put upon the covenant in question, if the language will fairly
admit of any other.   Now with reference to this argument it
must be borne in mind that a tenant for a term of years derives
a benefit, greater or less, according to the unexpired portion of
his term, from any expenditure for the permanent improvement
of the property, and that it would be equally inequitable to
impose upon the landlord the whole burden of an expenditure,
from which he can derive no benefit during the remaining portion
of his tenant's term; in the present case at least half of the
defendant's term was unexpired at the time when the drainage
works were executed.   Again, the defendant has, by the terms of
the covenant which we are now considering, clearly taken upon
himself, and must be presumed to have done so knowingly and
willingly, some burdens which may result in a benefit to the
demised premises beyond the period of his tenancy; as for
instance, 'improvement rates,' which under ordinary circumstances
are imposed in respect of an expenditure for permanent improvements; and, inasmuch as, at the date of the lease a Public Health
Act was in force, under which burdens might have been imposed
upon the plaintiffs similar to that which they have been called
upon to bear under the existing Act, it is difficult to suppose that
such a burden was not in the contemplation of the parties at the
time when the covenant was entered into.   But even if the
argument has force to the extent of supporting the view, that
expenditure of a like character should primarily be thrown upon
the landlord, as it has been by the Public Health Act, I can well
understand that for the purpose of obtaining what he might deem
in other respects an eligible lease an intending tenant would
willingly subject himself to obligations, to which, but for his

1898.

WRENCH
v.
RICHARDSON
& WRENCH,
LTD.

Cohen J.

1898.

WRENCH
v.
RICHARDSON
& WRENCH,
LTD.

Cohen J.

covenant, he would not be made liable. Again, it is common knowledge that, generally speaking, the object of a landlord is to secure during the term a rent of certain amount, as free from all deductions as the law will permit, and to effectuate this object the amount of rent is fixed with reference to all the obligations which the tenant may be willing to take upon himself, and I can see nothing inequitable in holding the tenant to the terms of his bargain."

In *Batchelor* v. *Bigger* (1), the expense of paving a road abutting on a house under the Metropolis Local Management Act was held to come within the tenant's covenant to pay, *inter alia*, all "outgoings" of every description in respect of the premises, and it was further held that the meaning could not be regarded as altered because the agreement was only for three years. *Kay, J.,* who heard the action, says :—" Of course naturally a covenant like this refers, *prima facie*, to recurring payments, and if this had been in the form of a recurring payment, as it might have been if it had been assessed to be paid by instalments spread over a number of years, it would have been impossible for the occupier to maintain that the instalments during his tenancy would not be payable by him. But I agree that that would be a different state of things, because then it would be made more like the ordinary rate or tax, which is a recurring payment," and a like decision was come to in *Aldridge* v. *Ferne* (2). In *Brett* v. *Rogers* (3), the expense of taking up a defective drain and laying a new drain throughout the premises, under the Public Health (London) Act, 1891, was held to be payable by a lessee under his covenant to pay, *inter alia*, all ' duties ' imposed on in respect of the premises."

There are two cases, *Allum* v. *Dickinson* (4) and *Wilkinson* v. *Collyer* (5), in which the lessees were not held liable ; but the former case is decided upon grounds which in no way trench upon the authorities already cited, and the latter, if inconsistent with them, should, in my opinion, not prevail against the line of decisions outside it.

(1) 60 L.T.N.S. 416.   (3) [1897] 1 Q.B. 525.
(2) 17 Q.B.D. 212.   (4) 9 Q.B.D. 633.
                (5) 13 Q.B.D. 1.

Allum v. *Dickinson* (1) decided that a covenant to pay all
rates and assessments charged, assessed, or imposed upon the
demised premises, or upon, or payable by the occupier, or tenant
in respect thereof, did not cover the expense of paving a new
street assessed upon the demised house under 25 & 26 Vic. c.
102, s. 96. At p. 635 *Jessel*, M.R., says :—" If we look at the
section of the Act of Parliament, namely, s. 96 of 25 & 26 Vic.
c. 102, it is certainly not charged or imposed on the
premises. It is imposed on the owner in respect of the premises.
It is a personal demand on the owner which may be enforced on
his premises." It was thus clearly shewn that it did not come
within the covenant as a rate or assessment upon the demised
premises, or upon or payable by the *occupier or tenant* in respect
thereof.

Wilkinson v. *Collyer* (2) determined that the expense of
paving a street abutting on the leased premises did not come
within the meaning of a covenant to pay all "rates, taxes, and
assessments," but from the observations of *Manisty*, J., it is not
unreasonable to assume that the word "charges," if in the covenant,
would have been held to cover the expenditure.

To summarise these decisions we see that the cost of "paving and
flagging footways" is an "assessment or payment:" *Payne* v.
Burridge ; "drainage " is an "imposition," " duty," or " outgoing:"
Sweet v. *Seager, Crosse* v. *Raw, Budd* v. *Marshall, Rogers* v.
Bretts; "paving " is a " duty," " assessment," or " outgoing:"
Thompson v. *Lapworth, Batchelor* v. *Betts, Aldridge* v. *Ferne ;*
"sewerage, levelling, and paving " is a "charge and assessment:"
Hartley v. *Hudson.*

In my opinion the payments made by the plaintiff came
naturally and etymologically within the words of the covenant
"assessments, impositions, and charges," and I cannot see any
sufficient reason why they should not be held to do so legally.
Conceding, as is the fact, that this particular obligation was not
at the date of the covenant created by Parliament, and, therefore,
was not as a definite existent thing in the minds of the plaintiff
and the defendants when the lease was executed, yet the covenant
contemplates, in very wide language, the future imposition of rates,

(1) 9 Q.B.D. 633.

1898.

WRENCH
v.
RICHARDSON
& WRENCH,
LTD.

Cohen J.

1898.

WRENCH
r.
RICHARDSON
& WRENCH,
LTD

Cohen J.

taxes, &c. If then the language naturally covers the obligation, may it not be reasonably said that the defendants willingly undertook a risk, uncertain in its range though it then was, but within which this disputed liability may now fairly come, in consideration of procuring a lease which they considered advantageous.

Although the Moore Street Improvement Act embodies what is known as the " betterment " principle for the first time, as far as I remember, in our municipal legislation, yet the obligation imposed by the Act was so imposed because it was considered that the work contemplated by it would improve the property of the owners, and, therefore, its value to them, and it is obviously this element of improvement which also lies at the base of the English Acts, and likewise forms the foundation of the obligation created by them. The betterment principle is the principle by which the extent of the obligation is measured, the Legislature seeking by its adoption to make the individual obligation co-extensive with the estimated enhancement in value in each individual property, affected by the improvements, but not measured by the mere cost of the works so far as it could be exclusively attributed to each property. A rule different, however, from the betterment rule is applied to measure the extent of the obligation of the property owner under the English Acts : the measure of that obligation apparently being the actual cost of the works, apart altogether from any independent estimate of enhancement in the value of the property to or in connection with which the improvements have been made. But this cannot make any difference as to the existence of the liability, though it may as to its extent. It has been contended that if the plaintiff can succeed as to these particular payments she could enforce the payment of the aggregate amount of her contributions if she should exercise the option of at once paying their full amount. But that is not a necessary sequitur, for in my opinion the only burden that the lessor could fairly and justly pass on to the lessees is that which is compulsory under the Act, and as it only enforces payment by instalments, it is only for the instalments falling due during the currency of the lease that the lessees can be held liable under the covenant. The obligation is thus made co-extensive with the enjoy-

ment of the advantages. If the lessor for her own benefit and
advantage should exercise the option of at once liquidating her full
liability to the council, that should not be done to the prejudice
of the lessees.   Upon reason and authority, therefore, I am of
opinion that a verdict should be entered for the plaintiff for the
amount claimed.

1898.

WRENCH
v.
RICHARDSON
& WRENCH,
LTD.

Cohen J.

Verdict entered for defendants.

Attorneys for the plaintiff: *Holdsworth & Son.*

Attorneys for the defendants: *Johnson, Minter, Simpson &
Co.*

HILL, CLARK & Co. *v.* DALGETY & Co.

1897.
———————
December 15.

Rabbit Act of 1890 (54 *Vic. No.* 29), *s.* 5—*Crown Lands Act of* 1889 (53 *Vic. No.* 21), *s.* 8, *sub-s.* 6—*Appeal from Land Appeal Court.*

*Privy
Council.* *

Held (reversing the decision of the Full Court), that the Land Appeal Court, sitting under the Rabbit Act of 1890, has power at the request of a party to state a case for the opinion of the Supreme Court.

. THIS was an appeal from a decision of the Full Court, reported in 17 N.S.W. L R. 282, where the facts fully appear.

Sir *R. Reid*, Q.C., and *V. Hawkins*, for the appellants.

Swinfen Eady, Q.C., and *Upjohn*, Q.C., for the respondents.

The judgment was delivered by

Sir RICHARD COUCH. This is an appeal from an order of the Supreme Court of New South Wales of the 12th August, 1896, dismissing a special case which had been stated for its opinion by the Land Appeal Court of New South Wales, and refusing to answer the question asked therein on the ground that the Land Appeal Court had no jurisdiction to state the special case. By s. 4 of the Rabbit Act of 1890, it is enacted that "The Land Court and the Local Land Boards shall perform the duties respectively imposed upon it and them under this Act, and the respective jurisdictions of the said Court and of the said Boards are hereby extended accordingly." And s. 5 (ii) enacts, "The provisions of the said Acts" (Crown Lands Acts) "in regulation of the procedure before a Board, and upon appeals and references to the Land Court thereunder shall, so far as possible, be applied." One of these provisions is in s. 8 (vi) of the Crown Lands Act of 1889, and is as follows:—

"Whenever any question of law shall arise in a case before the Land Court the Land Court shall if required in writing by any of the parties within the prescribed time and upon the prescribed conditions or may of its own motion state and submit a case for decision by the Supreme Court thereon which decision shall be conclusive," etc.

* Present: Lord WATSON, Lord HOBHOUSE, Lord DAVEY, and Sir RICHARD COUCH.

In an appeal in the Land Appeal Court by the respondents against the dismissal by the Local Land Board of Cobar of an application by them against the appellants for a contribution of the half cost of the erection of a rabbit proof fence, a case was stated by the Land Appeal Court at the request of the appellants in pursuance of the above sub-section of s. 8. This is the case which was dismissed by the Supreme Court.

It appears to their Lordships to be clear that the stating this case is part of the procedure of the Land Court in the appeal to it, and that it is also clear that it was the duty of the Supreme Court under sub-s. 6 of s. 8 of the Crown Lands Act to hear the case, and return it to the Land Court with a decision on the question submitted. In the opinion of their Lordships, the Supreme Court was in error in holding that the Land Appeal Court had no jurisdiction to state the case. In the 14th paragraph of the case, it appears that there was a question of law, viz., whether there having been no assessment by the Land Board under proceedings which, as stated in the case, had been taken against former owners of the same property, such proceedings were a bar to proceedings against the appellants. In paragraph 15 of the case, it is said that the question for consideration of the Supreme Court is, " Whether the Land Appeal Court was right in sustaining the appeal upon the grounds set forth in paragraph 14 hereof, and directing the said Board as therein expressed." It may be that this is too general, and does not state the question of law so precisely as it might have been stated, but the Supreme Court could have returned the case to the Land Court to have this amended. It did not affect the power of the Supreme Court to hear it, or make the proceeding an appeal generally upon the whole case which, apparently in the reasons given by the learned Judges, they considered it to be. Their Lordships will, therefore, humbly advise Her Majesty to reverse the order of the Supreme Court, and direct it to hear the case, and return it with the decision of the Court thereon to the Land Court. The respondents will pay the costs of this appeal.

Appeal upheld.

1897.

HILL, CLARK
& Co.
v.
DALGETY
& Co.

*Sir Richard
Couch.*

HOLLAND v. STOCKTON COAL CO.

1898.

May 3.
June 24.

The C.J.
Cohen J.
and
A.H. Simpson J.

Employers Liability Act (50 Vic. No. 8), *s.* 9—*Workman—Miner—Manual labour
—Work incidental to ordinary employment.*

M. was a miner employed in the defendants' coal mine, and ordinarily engaged
as a hewer. The mine having been laid idle owing to the occurrence in the
workings of a poisonous gas, the manager organised an exploring party, consisting
partly of officials and partly of miners, to enter the mine and locate the origin of
the gas. M. was sent for by the manager to make one of the party, and whilst
down the mine died from the effects of the gas. The plaintiff, his administratrix,
sued the defendants under the Employers Liability Act, alleging that his death
was caused by the negligence of the manager in taking the exploring party into
the mine without proper precautions. *Held*, that M. was a workman in the
employment of the defendants within the meaning of the Employers Liability Act.

If the real and substantial business of a person whose avocation is mentioned
in the Act involves manual labour, and such workman is injured while carrying
out some duty or work incidental to his real and substantial avocation, although
it does not involve immediate manual labour, nevertheless he is within the
purview of the Act.

MOTION to set aside a nonsuit.

This was an action brought by the administratrix of Thomas
M'Alpine against the Stockton Coal Co., Ltd., in whose mine
M'Alpine was killed in December, 1896. The declaration was
drawn under the Employers Liability Act, 50 Vic. No. 8, and
contained counts framed under the first four sub-sections of s. 1 of
that Act. The defendants pleaded, amongst other pleas, that
M'Alpine was not a workman in the employment of the defendants within the meaning of the Act. The action was tried at
Maitland in October, 1897, before his honour Mr. Justice *G. B.
Simpson* and a jury of four, and at the close of the plaintiff's
case the defendants applied for a nonsuit. The argument upon
this point was adjourned to Sydney, and on the 26th October his
Honour granted a nonsuit, holding that there was no evidence
that M'Alpine was a workman within the meaning of the Act.
It appeared from the evidence that on the 2nd December, 1896,
the dead bodies of two miners were found in the workings. An
examination was thereupon made by Mr. Humble, a Government
inspector, who discovered the existence in the mine of carbon
monoxide, commonly known as fire-stink, a highly dangerous gas,

of which the presence of one-fifth of one per cent. in the air is
speedily fatal.   On the 4th December the manager, M'Auliffe,
organised a search party, consisting of officials and miners, to
explore the mine and locate the fires, known as "gob-fires," which
caused the fire-stink, with the object of sealing them up and so
putting them out by means of excluding the air.   A message was
sent by the manager to M'Alpine, telling him to come to work
at half-past six that night.   M'Alpine accordingly attended,
and went down with the exploring party, and was killed by
inhaling the poisonous gas.   The plaintiff then brought the
present action, alleging that his death was caused by the negligence of the mine manager in taking the exploring party into
the mine without using proper precautions.

Further facts, and the evidence bearing on the case, are stated
in the judgment of *The Chief Justice.*

Mr. Justice *Simpson* found that there was no evidence on
which the jury could reasonably come to the conclusion that
M'Alpine was engaged to perform manual labour, and unless he
was engaged to perform manual labour, and unless he actually
worked at manual labour, his representative could not recover.
When the exploring party went in they took no tools, as there
was no work to be done.   It was simply an exploring party to
find out the position of the gob-fires.   The men had been withdrawn from the mine, and no coal was being got, and his Honour,
under these circumstances, held that M'Alpine was not, at the
time of the accident, a workman within the meaning of the
Employers Liability Act.

The plaintiff now moved to set aside the nonsuit upon the
ground that his Honour was wrong in holding that there was
no evidence to go to the jury that M'Alpine was a workman
within the meaning of the Employers Liability Act.

Sir *Julian Salomons*, Q.C., *Edmunds* and *Tighe*, for the
plaintiff.   The Employers Liability Act, s. 9, defines a workman
to be "a railway servant, and any other person who, being a
labourer, servant in husbandry, journeyman artificer, handicrafts-
man, miner, *or otherwise engaged in manual labour* . . . .

1898.

HOLLAND
v.
STOCKTON
COAL CO.

1898.

HOLLAND
v.
STOCKTON
COAL CO.

works under a contract with an employer . . . . express or
implied." There is nothing in that section to imply, as the
learned Judge held, that the person injured must be actually
engaged in manual labour at the time the injury is sustained.
The section refers to the general nature of the employment necessary to constitute a person a workman; it shuts out the higher
classes of labour, and confines the benefit of the Act to the classes
comprised under the head of "manual labour." Miners and the
other persons specifically mentioned are assumed to belong to the
manual labour class, and with regard to them the Court is relieved
from enquiring whether their occupations involve manual labour.
As to persons not mentioned, the standard created is, are they
engaged in occupations primarily and mainly involving manual
labour? Once, then, it is shewn that a person is a member, either
of one of the classes specified in the section, or of a trade
involving manual labour, and that he is employed as such by the
defendant, he is to be considered a "workman" under the Act,
and it is immaterial whether he was actually engaged at the
time of injury in the performance of manual labour. Otherwise
a miner, who has perhaps to walk through miles of tunnel to get
to his work, could not recover if injured while doing so: *Roebuck*
v. *Norwegian Titanic Co.* (1); *Leach* v. *Gartside* (2); *Cowler* v.
Moresby Coal Co. (3). In the present case M'Alpine was still
working under his contract with his employer, not as a hewer of
coal, which was his general occupation. but as a *miner*, and as
long as he was working as a miner it does not matter what was
the precise nature of the work that his employer called upon him
to perform. When the mine was laid idle the employer could,
no doubt, have put an end to the contract, but instead he chose
still to employ him as a miner, to explore the mine. And there
was evidence that it is customary to call on miners to do such
work, and that it is part of their contract that miners are liable to
be called upon to perform it. He referred to *Yarmouth* v. *France*
(4); *Cook* v. *Metropolitan Tramway Co.* (5); *Smith* v. *Baker* (6);
Thomas v. *Quartermaine* (7).

(1) 1 T.L.R. 117	(4) 19 Q.B.D. 647.
(2) 1 T.L.R. 391.	(5) 18 Q.B.D. 683.
(3) 1 T.L.R. 575.	(6) [1891] A.C. 325.
	(7) 18 Q.B.D. 685.

J. L. Campbell, for the defendants. I never contended that the person injured should be actually engaged in the performance of manual labour at the time of the injury, and his Honour never decided any such point. My contention was, and is now, that the contract of service which made the injured person a workman within the Act must be actually subsisting at the time of the injury. Here M'Alpine was a miner, a hewer of coal employed by the defendants, and paid every fortnight according to the amount of coal hewn by him. The moment the first deaths occurred in the mine on December 2nd, the mine was, by the Coal Mines Regulation Act, laid idle, and there was either an actual end, or a putting in abeyance of the contract under which M'Alpine was working. The company could neither order him to work, nor could he demand it while the gas remained in the mine. It was to the interest of all parties, both employers and employed, to get the mine to work again, and an exploring party was formed, as the evidence shewed, merely to find out the location of the " gob fires." The party could do no work because they only had tea bottles and lamps with them. Sealing up the fires was bricklayers' work, and several bricklayers were kept at the mine for that purpose. The plaintiffs proved no contract by which any duty could be implied on M'Alpine's part to go into the mine if anything unusual or dangerous occurred, and the Court cannot imply a contract under which the miner was to go into danger. It was a purely voluntary service on M'Alpine's part, and the work of exploration was not a work necessitating manual labour—the explorer merely being required to use his eyes and nose—and, therefore, was not within the Employers Liability Act. It cannot be held that the original contract to work as a miner still subsisted, and that the nature of the work merely was changed as a matter of convenience, because the whole foundation of the original contract *i.e.*, the measure of wages, was put an end to while the mine was idle. He referred to the cases of *Grainger* v. *Aynsley* (1); *Lobb* v. *Amos* (2); *Morgan* v. *General Omnibus Co.* (3); *Jackson* v. *Hill* (4); *Bound* v. *Lawrence* (5).

1898.

HOLLAND
v.
STOCKTON
COAL CO.

(1) 6 Q.B.D. 182.   (3) 13 Q.B.D. 832.
(2) 7 N.S.W. L.R. 92.   (4) 13 Q.B.D. 618.
            (5) [1892] 1 Q.B. 226.

Cur. adv. vult.

K 2

On June 24th, judgment was delivered.

THE CHIEF JUSTICE. In this case the deceased was a miner who was employed by the defendants as a coal-hewer, being paid at the rate of so much per ton on the coal won by him. Upon December 2nd, 1896, a large quantity of poisonous gas was emitted from some old workings in the defendants' mine, the result of which was that two men, who were attending the ventilating furnace, were killed. This was discovered on the morning of December 2nd before work commenced, and the bodies of the deceased men were brought to the surface. On the same morning Mr. Humble, one of the Government inspectors of collieries in New South Wales, went down the mine to the place where the bodies of the two men were found, and by smell detected the presence of this poisonous gas known by the various names of "fire stink," "gob stink," "white damp," its proper name being "carbon monoxide gas." The mine was accordingly laid idle on December 2, 3 and 4. On the evening of the 4th Daniel M'Auliffe, who was the manager of the mine, being anxious to discover from what portion of the mine this poisonous gas was proceeding, and with the object of sealing that portion of the mine off when discovered, sent a message to the deceased man M'Alpine by one Bayley to come back to work with him at half-past 6 that evening. The plaintiff stated she heard the message given. She said, "I heard Bayley tell M'Alpine to come to work at half-past 6 to-night." He said, "Tom, you and Syd. have to come to-night at half-past 6." The deceased having received this message went to the mine at the time stated, and in company with some ten or eleven other persons went below for the purpose of looking for "gob fires," which fires give off the poisonous gas in question. While looking for the fires, the deceased and some other of the men with him succumbed to the action of this gas, and were killed. It was admitted that they died from the effect of the gas. The declaration in the action was framed under the provisions of the Employers Liability Act. This declaration contained, amongst other counts, a count alleging that the death of the deceased was caused by the negligence of a person in the service of the defendants, to whose

orders the deceased was at the time of the injury bound to
conform, and did conform. There was also a count alleging
defect in the state of the ways, &c. At the trial it was proved
that, when the party of whom the deceased was one was sent
below, a current of air was caused to flow through the passages
of the mine, and that the men were sent against this current in
place of being sent with the current, and this was alleged as
shewing ignorance and want of skill and negligence on the part
of the manager. It was also alleged that the quantity of air
sent down before the men entered the mine was wholly insufficient to dissipate the gas, and this should have been known to
the manager.

At the close of the plaintiff's case the defendants' counsel moved
for a nonsuit upon various grounds, one of which was that there
was no evidence to go to the jury of negligence. His Honour
refused to grant a nonsuit upon this ground, and I am clearly of
opinion he was right. Without expressing any opinion upon the
value of the evidence, I think it is obvious that the opinion of
such an expert as Mr. Humble, to the effect that sending the
men into the mine against, in place of sending them with the
current of air evinced a want of skill, and shewed negligence and
carelessness, and further that the amount of air sent in was
insufficient, precluded the possibility of taking the case from the
jury upon this ground.

It was also contended as a ground of nonsuit that the deceased
was purely a volunteer, and that the maxim "Volenti non fit
injuria" applied. This contention his Honour, I think, rightly
rejected. In the first place the contention raised a question of
fact and not one of law, and the question for the jury would be:
Did the deceased know the danger he incurred in proceeding in
the mine against the current of air? Did he with this knowledge consent to this being done and consent to take the risk
upon himself? There must in such a case be a thorough comprehension of the risk and a voluntary undertaking with a full
knowledge of the risk: see *Smith* v. *Baker* (1); *Donaldson* v.
The Stockton Coal Company (2).

(1) [1891] A.C. 325.　　　　　　(2) 16 N.S.W.L.R. 69.

1898.

HOLLAND
v.
STOCKTON
COAL CO.

The C.J.

The point was then taken that the deceased was not shewn to be a " workman " within the meaning of the Employers Liability Act, and the learned Judge being of this opinion nonsuited the plaintiff. The plaintiff now moves to set aside this nonsuit and for a new trial upon the ground that this ruling of the learned Judge was erroneous, and contends that there was evidence to go to the jury that the deceased was a " workman " within the meaning of the Act.

It was contended on the part of the defendants that inasmuch as the deceased, although by occupation a miner, was not at the time of his death engaged in manual labour, he could not recover. This contention was supported by the argument that the deceased being by occupation a coal-hewer at so much a ton when the mine was thrown idle by the accident of December 2nd, all privity between him and the defendants ceased, so that when he undertook to enter the mine on the evening of December 4th, he did not do so as a miner or as a person about to be engaged in manual labour, but as an explorer who had merely to use his eyes and thus locate the place of danger. The evidence, however, shewed that miners do other work besides coal-hewing. The witness Bayley, who was deputy overman underneath the ground, stated : " When no mining is going on there is sometimes stone-work and sometimes timbering going on, and sometimes miners are engaged." Again he said : " Miners, when there is any extra thing to be done connected with the mine, are sent for, and the deputy takes them to the work and shews them what has to be done. It is a common occurrence for miners to be sent for when-ever anything goes wrong in the pit to put it right." A juror then asked, " Was the deceased sent for on this occasion in the ordinary way ?" Bayley answered, " Yes ; I mean by being sent for in the ordinary way that the manager would send a deputy or my son to tell the men he wanted to come to the pit." Before considering the effect of this evidence, or the evidence that the deceased was sent for by the manager to come to work, it will be necessary to consider the 9th section of the Employers' Liability Act (50 Vic. No. 8), which enacts that " the expression workman means a railway servant, and any other person who, being a labourer, &c., a miner, or otherwise engaged in manual labour, has entered into or

1898.

HOLLAND
v.
STOCKTON
COAL CO.

The C.J.

works under a contract with an employer, whether the contract be express or implied, oral or in writing, and be a contract of service or a contract personally to execute any work or labour." Now, here the deceased was a miner, which is one of the avocations mentioned in the Act. It appears to me, therefore, that although there was no express yet there was an implied contract entered into by him with the defendants through the manager to enter the mine and endeavour to locate the point of danger, and for the rendering of which service, if he chose to demand it, he would have been entitled to remuneration, this being one of those cases where, as the witness Bayley said, "It is a common occurrence for miners to be sent for whenever anything goes wrong in the pit to put it right." No doubt it is understood by all miners that this is part of their duty as such miners. *Prima facie*, therefore, the deceased falls within the definition of "workman"; but it is said that at the time of his death he was not engaged in manual labour, and therefore, although a miner and working under a contract, he cannot recover. If the contract of a coal-miner is not merely to hew coal, but to do such other work about a mine as he may be directed to do, particularly if directed to put any matter right which goes wrong in the mine, the case falls within the principle laid down in *Yarmouth* v. *France*, and *Leach* v. *Gartside*, to which cases I will presently refer. In any event the nature and extent of the deceased's employment was a question for the jury, and if they had found that it was part of the deceased's contract with the defendants to do other work in the mine besides hewing, including setting matters right which had gone wrong, then I do not think this case can be distinguished from the cases just referred to. It appears to me that it might with equal force be contended that a miner, injured through the negligence of a person to whose orders he was bound to conform, while walking in the mine to or from his work, or during his meal time, or while resting, not being at this time engaged in manual labour, would be outside the protection contemplated by the Act.

I am of opinion that this contention cannot be supported, and that as the deceased when killed was a miner and was then engaged in the avocation of a miner, engaged in a work of necessity in

1898.

HOLLAND
v.
STOCKTON
COAL CO.

The C.J.

the mine, viz., the location of the seat of danger so that it might
be sealed up, he is within the purview of the Act. Here the
real and substantial employment of the deceased was that of a
miner; incident to this employment he was engaged as a miner
to do something in the mine which, although not involving at
the moment of death manual labour, was incidental to it. The
case, therefore, differs widely from such cases as *Morgan* v. *The
London Omnibus Company* (1), the case of an omnibus conductor, *Hunt* v. *The Great Northern Railway Company* (2), the
case of a railway guard, *Bound* v. *Lawrence* (3), the case of a
grocer's assistant. The Act does not refer to the avocations of
any of these persons, and their real and substantial business did
not involve manual labour. The case rather resembles *Yarmouth*
v. *France* (4). There the plaintiff was engaged in a dual capacity
—to drive a trolly, and to load and unload it. While driving
the trolly, and therefore not engaged in manual labour (see *Cook*
v. *The North Metropolitan Tramways Company* [5]) he was
injured ; nevertheless as part of his real and substantial business
(the loading and unloading of the trolly) was manual labour, he
was held to be a " workman " within the meaning of the Act.
So in *Cowler* v. *The Moresby Coal Company* (6), a miner who was
working in the defendants' mine was discharged. Before he
could receive his wages he had to deliver up his tools. On a day
subsequent to his discharge he went down the mine for the
purpose of getting his tools, and for no other purpose. While
there he was injured through the negligence of the defendant's
servants. He was held entitled to recover inasmuch as he was
still under contract. Although several points were raised it was
not contended that he was not entitled to recover because not
engaged in manual labour at the time of the accident. Again, in
Roebuck v. *The Norwegian Titanic Company* (7) it was clear
quite clear that the deceased, a miner, was not engaged in manual
labour at the time of his death. He was in fact going to and
struggling to assist a fellow workman overcome by gas, and find-

(1) 13 Q.B.D. 832.   (4) 19 Q.B.D. 647.
(2) [1891] 1 Q.B. 601.   (5) 18 Q.B.D. 683.
(3) [1892] 1 Q.B. 226.   (6) 1 T.L.R. 575.
                (7) 1 T.L.R. 117.

1898.

HOLLAND
v.
STOCKTON
COAL Co.

The C.J.

ing him dead was endeavouring to recover his body, yet his administratrix was held entitled to recover. So in *Leach* v. *Gartside* (1) the plaintiff was engaged in a dual capacity, one involving manual labour, the other not. While not engaged in manual labour he was injured, yet he was held entitled to recover. When I say that the deceased was working under a contract I do not mean it to be implied that the contract was such as to bind the deceased to go into any danger. No ordinary contract of service can bind a man to risk his life by going into a position of danger, but if he does elect to do this he does so under a contract, is entitled to be paid for his services, and is entitled to demand that the danger be not enhanced by any negligence on the part of his employer or on the part of those to whose orders he conforms.

I am of opinion, therefore, that if the real and substantial business of a person whose avocation is mentioned in the Act involves manual labour, and such workman is injured while carrying out some duty or work incidental to his real and substantial avocation, although the latter does not involve immediate manual labour, nevertheless he is within the purview of the Act. It is obvious that the deceased when killed was as a miner engaged in making this exploration. It was because he was a miner (probably one of considerable experience) that his services were sought. This being established, I think a broad view should be taken of the circumstances, and that the beneficial and remedial provisions of this Act should be given their full effect. I am of opinion, therefore, that the plaintiff should not have been nonsuited, that the nonsuit should be set aside, and a new trial granted.

COHEN, J. Having read and considered the judgment delivered by his Honour *The Chief Justice*, I have to express my concurrence in it, except where his Honour lays down as a matter of law that, apart from the general employment of the deceased by the defendants, the deceased, had he lived, would have been entitled to remuneration for his services as one of the exploring party. I think that apart from the contract of general employment, which

(1) 1 T.L.R. 391.

a jury might hold to cover these services, the deceased could not
have claimed such remuneration, upon the principle that a
voluntary courtesy will not support a subsequent promise, though
such courtesy moved by a previous request will, and there is no
evidence of any subsequent promise of remuneration to the
deceased in respect of these services. Putting it most in favour
of the plaintiff, it should be a question of fact for the jury,
whether, having regard to all the circumstances, there was any
implied promise by the defendants to pay for the exploring
services of the deceased.

A. H. SIMPSON, J.   Thomas M'Alpine had been for two years
previous to the 2nd December, 1896, employed by the defendant
company as a hewer in their mine.   On the 2nd December
poisonous gas found its way into the mine from some old workings, and two furnacemen died from the effects of it.   Work
was thereupon suspended, and all the men were withdrawn from
the mine.   On the 4th December an exploring party was formed,
comprising among other persons the deceased Thos. M'Alpine
and another miner, and there is evidence that the deceased was
requested by the defendant company's officers to join the party.
The object of the exploring party was to look for gob fires, so
that they might be sealed off.   The party did not take any tools
with them.   According to the evidence of Mr. Humble, it is very
seldom that miners form part of an exploring party ; it is usually
made up of officials.   While exploring the deceased was killed
by poisonous gas, and there is clear evidence from which a jury
might hold that his death was caused by the defendants' negligence.   The action was brought by M'Alpine's representative
for compensation for his death, and the plaintiff was nonsuited
by the learned Judge who tried the case on the ground that there
was no evidence that M'Alpine was a workman within the
Employers' Liability Act of 1886.   The question turns mainly
on the true meaning and effect of s. 9, which defines " workman "
as meaning " a railway servant and any other person, who, being
a labourer, servant in husbandry, journeyman artificer, handi-
craftsman, miner, or otherwise engaged in manual labour, whether
under the age of 21 years or above that age, has entered into or

works under a contract with an employer, whether the contract
be made before or after the passing of this Act, be express or
implied, oral or in writing, and be a contract of service or a
contract personally to execute any work or labour." A "railway
servant" is apparently within the protection of the Act, whether
engaged to perform manual labour or not, but as regards the
other persons specified, the words "or otherwise engaged in
manual labour" imply, in my opinion, that the persons so specified
are regarded by the Act as engaged in manual labour. Whether
one of the persons specified, *e.g.*, a miner, not engaged in manual
labour (if such a case should occur), would be within the Act, it
is not necessary to determine, as it is clear that the deceased was
engaged in manual labour, viz., hewing, but I imagine he would
be within the Act. See *Cook* v. *North Metropolitan Tramways
Co.* (1), where *A. L. Smith*, J., says:—"Had the Legislature
intended to include coachmen, they would have included them
among the specific instances." Did, then, the deceased, being
one of the persons specified, enter into a work under a contract
with the defendant company, either express or implied, and was
such contract "a contract of service or a contract personally to
execute any work or labour?"

It will be observed that the concluding words of the definition
are not limited to contracts for the performance of manual
labour, and indeed the words "work or labour" seem expressly
to point to "work" as a different thing from "labour": see *Cook*
v. *North Metropolitan Tramways Company* (1).

It is clear that a person engaged to perform manual labour is
not taken out of the provisions of the Act, because he may have
to perform other work as well, if his main employment is manual
labour (*Leach* v. *Gartside* [2], and other cases cited), nor need he
be actually engaged in manual labour at the time the injury
occurs: *Cowler* v. *Moresby Coal Co.* (3). If, then, the original
contract with the deceased had been that he should hew coal and
do any other work about the mine that might be required,
including exploring when necessary, it would seem clear that he
was within the Act, and could recover for any injury sustained,

1898.

HOLLAND
v.
STOCKTON
COAL CO.

A.H. Simpson J.

(1) 18 Q.B.D. 683, 684.   (2) 1 T.L.R. 391.
(3) 1 T.L.R. 575.

while exploring, through the defendants' negligence. Does it make any difference that his original contract was to hew only, and that while this contract was still in force, he entered into an additional contract to explore? If the additional contract had been entirely outside the scope of a miner's employment, e.g., to steer a steamboat, or drive a pair of horses, it may well be that he could. not sue for an injury sustained during such employment, but in this case the additional contract was made with a person who was in the defendants' employ at the time as a miner, and was for work in the defendants' mine, which the evidence shews to be within the scope of a miner's employment, or from which a jury might at any rate infer it to be so. In my opinion there is nothing in the Act or the decided cases to shew that the concluding words of s. 9 are to be limited to contracts for manual labour.

It was contended that the additional contract was confined to "exploring," and that exploring did not involve manual labour. Even if I am wrong in the view expressed above, it seems to me there was evidence from which a jury might infer—(1) that the additional contract was not confined to exploring; and (2) that exploring involved manual labour.

For these reasons I think the rule should be made absolute, and a new trial granted.

Attorney for the plaintiff: *W. H. Mahoney* (agent for *Sparke & Millard*, Newcastle).

Attorneys for the defendants: *Johnson, Minter, Simpson & Co.*

1898.

May 26.

The C.J.
G. B. Simpson J.
and
Cohen J.

Ex parte CAULFIELD, In re JOHN NORTON.

Contempt of Court—Publication calculated to prejudice the fair trial of an action.

The plaintiff commenced an action against the defendant to recover damages for an alleged libel published in the defendant's newspaper. After the writ had been issued the defendant published an article in which it was stated that an action had been commenced against him, etc., and then followed this passage, "meanwhile *Truth*," the defendant's newspaper, "is preparing to do its duty by this Jay Pay Tay Jackanapes," the plaintiff, "and his personal, political, social, and philanthropic career, in such a manner as to facilitate the task of a Judge and jury in estimating the real damage done to the true character of such a man." *Held*, that the article was calculated to interfere with the due administration of justice, and, therefore, amounted to a contempt of Court.

THIS was a motion to make absolute a rule *nisi* calling upon John Norton, the proprietor of *Truth*, to shew cause why he should not be attached for contempt of Court, on the ground that he had published certain articles in *Truth*, in the issues of the 1st May, and of the 8th May, commenting on an action pending, in which the applicant is the plaintiff, and the respondent the defendant, such comments being calculated to prejudice the fair trial of the action.

On the 24th April, an article appeared in *Truth*, in respect of which the applicant instituted a libel action, the writ being issued on the 27th April.

The applicant was the representative of and lecturer for the Hagey Institute, which was formed for the purpose of treating persons afflicted with the disease of alcoholism. It was in reference to that institution that the article of the 24th April appeared. On the 1st May, in the following issue of *Truth*, which is a weekly paper, this article appeared :—

"'TRUTH'S TROUBLES.'
MORE LIBEL ACTIONS.
'JAY PAY TAY' CAULFIELD,
'THE BOY POLITICIAN '--' ALCOHOL, & I.'
SUES OUT A WRIT FOR 2,000*l.*

Truth has received another little blue *billet doux*, in the form of a Supreme Court writ, which sets out that the ex-boy politician and stump stirrer, J. P. T. Caulfield, of Melbourne, Sydney, Perth, and Hagey Institute notoriety, desires the small sum of 2,000*l.* as compensation for alleged shock to his sensitive soul, and damage to his sublime character, caused by certain strictures in the article which appeared in the last issue of *Truth*. This reverend-looking, be-barnacled, erstwhile bibulous, bar-polishing, single-tax barracker intends to conduct the suit in person, as he names himself as his own solicitor. There are few instances wherein the old proverb, about the man who is his own solicitor, etc., fails, and it is somewhat interesting to speculate upon the motives that have induced this leather-lunged, brazen-faced, *soi-disant* reformed boozer and boozer reformer, to lay his client under the laughable suspicion inferred. He, no doubt, thinks to paralyse the puny intellects of their Honours of the Supreme Court with his foaming high falutin; and anticipates no little political kudos from the very obvious move. . . . . Meanwhile *Truth* is preparing to do its duty by this Jay Pay Tay Jackanapes, and his personal, political, social, and philanthropic career, in such a manner as to facilitate the task of a Judge and jury in estimating the real damage done to the *true* character of such a man. Meanwhile, *Truth* is mum, mutely inviting Caulfield and the whole Hagey Host to come on before they, or *Truth*, go bung, both in character and in cash, which must now be the inevitable fate of one of the parties—which one, *Truth* neither desires, nor dares to say, or even surmise "

In the next issue of *Truth* there appeared the following letter:

"THE HAGEY HOCUS.

Sir,—The Hagey Institute deserve all they got from you, and I hope you will come out in the impending action on top. In Auckland, N.Z., they came, they saw, and they conquered. Two plausible 'Murkan' men worked it for all it was worth, and then sold it as a going concern to a company, mostly composed of the goody-goody element, who wanted to make money out of the spec, at the expense of the poor drunks. . . . ."

There then followed a description of how the drunkards were supposed to be treated in the institute, and the letter was signed " Anti Humbug."

The applicant appeared in person.

Pilcher, Q.C., and *P. K. White*, appeared for the respondent.

After the affidavits had been read,

THE CHIEF JUSTICE. We think we ought to call upon you, Mr. *Pilcher*, with reference to the article which appeared in *Truth* on the 1st May.

Pilcher, Q.C. In the first place, we submit that this article is not a contempt at all; and secondly, if it be a technical contempt, it is not one that the Court will deal with. The Court will not interfere unless it is necessary that it should do so, to secure the due administration of justice: *In re The Evening News* (1).

(1) 1 N.S.W. L.R. 211.

[THE CHIEF JUSTICE. No one disputes that proposition.]

There are also the cases of *Troughton* v. *MacIntosh* (1) and *Ex parte Abigail* (2), where the same law is laid down.

[THE CHIEF JUSTICE. In the latter case the pictures alluded to the past and not the future.]

It was not on that point that the judgment of the Court proceeded. The Court there held that the publications were not likely to affect the minds of reasonable men. It could make no difference whether they alluded to the past or future, the effect would be just the same. Suppose a man was committed to take his trial for an offence, and a paper were to publish that he was a man of bad character, and had frequently been convicted of similar offences. That would clearly be a contempt, although it alluded to the past. The question is this: Is the publication calculated so to interfere with the administration of justice as to compel the Court to deal with it ? *Hunt* v. *Clarke* (3); *In re Clements* (4); *R.* v. *Payne* (5).

[COHEN, J., referred to *Greenwood* v. *Leathershod Wheel Co.* (6).]

The respondent did not intend to interfere with the administration of justice.

[THE CHIEF JUSTICE. Has the respondent filed an affidavit to that effect ?]

No; but an affidavit could be filed.

[THE CHIEF JUSTICE. It must not be lost sight of that the publisher of this paper is the defendant in the action.]

That cannot affect the question whether this article is calculated to interfere with the administration of justice.

[THE CHIEF JUSTICE. But it would shew the intention with which it was published.]

In the article there is nothing more than idle abuse, and nothing that would be likely to interfere with the administration of justice. Before the Court will take upon itself to exercise this summary jurisdiction, the Court must see that there has been something more than a mere technical contempt, and that

1898.

Ex parte CAULFIELD, *In re* JOHN NORTON

(1) 17 N.S.W. L.R. 334 ; 13 W.N. 125.   (4) 46 L.J. Ch. 375
(2) 13 N.S.W. L.R. 183 ; 9 W.N. 22.   (5) [1896] 1 Q.B. 577.
(3) 37 W.R. 724.   (6) 14 T.L.R. 141.

1898.

Ex parte
CAULFIELD,
In re
JOHN NORTON

unless it exercises it the plaintiff will be unable to get a fair trial of the action.

The applicant, in reply, referred to *In re Crossley* (1) and *Ex parte Butler* (2).

THE CHIEF JUSTICE.   In this case Caulfield, who is plaintiff in an action against Norton, has moved this Court for a rule absolute to pronounce Norton guilty of contempt of Court for publishing an article which appeared in *Truth* on the 1st May.   It is conceded that Norton is the proprietor of that paper, and, therefore, responsible for what may appear in its columns.

At the outset I fully endorse the observations made by *Jessel*, M.R., in *In re Clements* (3), where he says "that this jurisdiction of committing for contempt being practically arbitrary and unlimited should be most jealously and carefully watched, and exercised with the greatest reluctance and the greatest anxiety on the part of Judges to see whether there is no other mode which is not open to the objection of arbitrariness, and which can be brought to bear on the subject."   I also feel that this jurisdiction is an extraordinary one.   The matter charged is in the nature of a criminal offence, but nevertheless the law imposes on Judges the duty of saying whether a person charged with this criminal offence is guilty or not.   I say, therefore, that it is an extraordinary jurisdiction, and the Court sits as a jury for determining whether the person is guilty of this offence.   The Judges should, therefore, be careful how they exercise this jurisdiction, and should only exercise it where they are convinced that the matter complained of is likely to prejudice the due trial of the action.   The law on this point is aptly laid down in the case of *Ex parte Abigail* (4).   I said during the argument that "contempt of Court" was an unfortunate term to use.   The offence is the interference with the due administration of justice, though there is no doubt that the person in the event of the Court finding him guilty is punished as if it were a contempt of Court.   But it will be found in the judgment of the Court which I delivered in *Ex parte Abigail* (4) I did not use the term "contempt of Court."

(1) 15 N.S.W.L.R. 154; 10 W.N. 186.   (3) 46 L.J. Ch. 375.
(2) 18 N.S.W.L.R. 132; 13 W.N. 200.   (4) 13 N.S.W. L.R. 183; 9 W.N. 22.

1898.

Ex parte
CAULFIELD,
In re
JOHN NORTON

The C.J.

I there said :—" There is no doubt that any publication, whether
pictorial or otherwise affecting any person before the Court,
whether as a suitor or committed to take his trial upon a criminal
charge, and which publication is calculated to interfere with the
due course of justice, or intended to prejudice the public against
or in favour of the suitor or person committed, is a serious
criminal offence.   The summary power which this Court possesses
of promptly and summarily awarding punishment for the commission of such offences is possessed by the Court for the sole
purpose of securing the due administration of justice.   Every
publication which may tend to interfere with the due course of
justice, or made with a view of influencing the ultimate result
is a contempt of the Court.   So far back as the year 1742, Lord
Hardwick stated in apt words what was the duty of the Court,
and this statement has been echoed in every case where the
matter has come on for consideration since.   He says (2 Atkyns,
at p. 469): ' Nothing is more incumbent upon Courts of justice
than to preserve their proceedings from being misrepresented,
nor is there anything of more pernicious consequence than to
prejudice the minds of the public against persons concerned as
parties in causes before the cause is finally heard.'   It makes no
difference whether the publication is in reference to a trial in
course of proceeding or with respect to one about to take place :
in all such cases the Court is bound to punish, and in some cases
to punish with severity, any attempt to interfere with the due
course of justice."   I apprehend that that passage contains the
law on the subject.

A number of cases have been cited to shew that the Court is
very reluctant to deal with matters of this description.   That is
very true.   The Courts always require that a case of this kind
should be clearly made out.   Where it is apparent that an article
was published, and the only object of that article was to prejudge
the case or prejudice the parties concerned in it, then inasmuch
as this jurisdiction is cast upon the Judges it is their duty to see
that it is exercised.

Now in this case it appears that a letter appeared in *Truth* on
the 24th April, and the plaintiff alleges that certain matters con-

1898.
Ex parte
CAULFIELD,
In re
JOHN NORTON

The C.J.
.

tained in it are defamatory. As to whether they are defamatory or not I offer no opinion. That will be a matter for the jury. Having brought his action, and the writ having been served, an article appeared in the very next issue of *Truth*, on the 1st May, manifestly referring to the action which was then pending. No doubt, as Mr. *Pilcher* pointed out, there was no declaration then filed, and it was impossible for Norton to know what portion of the article was alleged to be defamatory, or whether the whole of it was alleged to be defamatory. But however that may be, Norton knew that it was in respect of what appeared in *Truth* in the issue of the 24th April that the action was brought, because the article of 1st May begins :—"*Truth* has received another little blue *billet doux* in the form of a Supreme Court writ, which sets out that the ex-boy politician and stump stirrer, J. P. T. Caulfield, of Melbourne, Sydney, Perth and Hagey Institute notoriety, desires the small sum of 2,000*l.* as compensation for alleged shock to his sensitive soul and damage to his sublime character caused by certain· strictures in the article which appeared in the last issue of *Truth.*" Then come some passages of abuse, to which it is not necessary to refer, and then follows this passage :—" Meanwhile *Truth* is preparing to do its duty by this Jay Pay Tay Jackanapes and his personal, political, social and philanthropic career in such a manner *as to facilitate the task of a Judge and jury in estimating the real damage done to the true character of such a man.*" It is my duty to give the accused the benefit of every reasonable doubt, but sitting as a juryman I entertain no reasonable doubt that the paragraph I have quoted was calculated to prejudice the fair trial of the action in the minds of those who would have to try it. It may be that if the matter were for a Judge to decide that he would not be affected by such a statement as this, and it may be that an intelligent juryman would not be influenced by it. But that is not the question. The question is : is it calculated to interfere with the course of justice ? It appears to me that this statement is calculated to interfere with the due course of justice. In the case of *In re Crown Bank* (1) *North*, J., uses words which are very applicable to this case. He says :—" So far, however, as the

(1) 44 Ch. D. 649.

earlier paragraphs published before the petition was presented are
concerned, their publication might be the subject of an action for
libel, but could be no contempt of Court.   But when with notice
that the petition had been presented the newspaper deliberately
took one side in the controversy and took on itself to foretell
what the result would be, in my opinion there was a gross
contempt of Court.   It was doing what might interfere with the
course of justice.   Whether it actually would so interfere in any
case, I do not know.   Whether there is any person with a mind
so constituted that he would be influenced by such a paragraph
in a newspaper of this sort I cannot tell.   The only object for
which such a paragraph could be inserted must be to influence
persons who might read it, and induce them to take one side."
Now if in this case it was intended by this article to acquaint
the public with the fact that an action had been brought in
reference to the article in the previous issue, the mere announcement of the fact would have been sufficient, and would have
injured no one.   But what was the object of saying that " *Truth*
is preparing to do its duty in such a manner as to facilitate the
task of Judge and jury in estimating the real damage done to
the true character of such a man ?"   The object was something
more than merely to announce that an action had been commenced, and was in my opinion inserted for the purpose of
prejudicing the fair trial of the action.   I am, therefore, of
opinion that the case has been established, and that Norton is
guilty of attempting to interfere with the due administration of
justice.

As to the article in the issue of the 8th May, I think it would
have been far better if it had not been written; once an action
has been begun there should be absolute silence as to it, and it is
the duty of journalists to abstain from comments of any sort
about a matter which is before the Court.   But though this article
was an undesirable one to write, I do not think that Caulfield
was so identified with the Hagey Institute that I can see that
anything in it would be likely to prejudice him or prejudge the
case.

The only question which remains is what the punishment is to
be. I stopped Caulfield during the argument saying anything

1898.

Ex parte
CAULFIELD,
In re
JOHN NORTON

The C.J.

1898.

Ex parte
CAULFIELD,
In re
JOHN NORTON

The C.J.

about Norton having been formerly convicted of this offence, but now that we are considering what the punishment is to be we cannot lose sight of the fact that Norton has been twice previously convicted of the very same offence. On one occasion he was fined 50*l.*, and on another 100*l.* Seeing that these warnings have not been sufficient, it appears to me that the penalty in this case must be larger. The order of the Court is that Norton must pay a fine of 150*l.* We do not order that Norton be imprisoned till the fine be paid, but we make the same order as was made in *Ex parte Butler* (1). It must be borne in mind that if we find that this sentence, which is a severe one, prove unavailing, and if at some future time Norton allows matters of this kind to appear in his paper in reference to cases pending, it may be the duty of the Court to award imprisonment.

G. B. SIMPSON, J. In this matter I am of opinion that the article published was seriously calculated to interfere with the administration of justice and therefore amounts to a contempt of Court. All the cases which have been cited to the Court were before us in the case of *Ex parte Freeman*, decided by the Court on the 6th August last, and Mr. Justice *Stephen* in giving judgment referred to the last case quoted by *The Chief Justice* in 44 Ch.D. That was an application against the present respondent. Having a knowledge of the principles of law as they are to be gathered from the cases cited and the case decided by this Court, Norton thought fit to publish this article and to publish it in reference to an action in which he was the defendant. I had some hesitation as to whether it would not, in the face of this warning which he disregarded, be incumbent upon us to exercise our summary power of ordering a term of imprisonment as a punishment for this offence. I am glad, however, to be able to come to the conclusion that it is not necessary to take that extreme step.

[His Honour then referred to *Troughton* v. *MacIntosh* (2) ; *Lee* v. *Evans* (3); and *Ex parte Butler* (4).]

(1) 18 N.S.W. L.R. 132 ; 13 W.N. 200.　(3) 12 N.S.W.L.R. 7.
(2) 17 N.S.W.L.R. 334.　(4) 18 N.S.W.L.R. 132.

The article in question contains the following passage [his Honour read the same passage as *The Chief Justice*]. What does that mean? It appears to me to mean that *Truth* will be in a position to shew the true character of the plaintiff in the action with respect to his social and political career in such a way that when the matter comes on for trial he will get no damages at the hands of the jury. I feel very reluctant to exercise this arbitrary jurisdiction, but it is our duty to the public to see that nothing is published in respect of proceedings pending which is calculated to influence the administration of justice. It is to be hoped that the punishment which we now impose will have the effect of restraining Norton from ever publishing any matter of this kind again. If it have not that effect and he be so indiscreet as to bring himself again within the law, I for my part will have no hesitation in adopting the course of sentencing him to imprisonment.

1897.

Ex parte
CAULVIELD,
In re
JOHN NORTON

G. B. Simpson J.

COHEN, J. Apart from the text of this article, I cannot shut my eyes to the way in which it is headed. I can see no reason for giving prominence to this article except for the purpose of attracting readers to it, and that clearly indicates, to my mind, the object and purpose for which it was written—to prejudice Caulfield in the trial of the action. As to whether it was likely to prejudice him, I have not the slightest doubt. Various cases have been referred to, and at first I was much struck with the case of *Hunt* v. *Clarke* (1). But when that is looked at it appears that there is only one line and a half in the whole paragraph which could be considered objectionable. The rest of the article contains a plain statement of the proceedings then pending. That case and the case *R.* v *Payne* (2) are clearly distinguishable from this. In deciding this case against the respondent we are acting entirely in accordance with the authorities both here and in England. In the case of *In re Crown Bank* (3) the Court awarded punishment in a case in which the article in question was not so strong as the article now under consideration. I agree with *The Chief Justice* that so far

---

(1) 37 W.R. 724.   (2) [1896] 1 Q.B 577.
                    (3) 44 Ch.D. 649.

1898.

Ex parte
CAULFIELD,
In re
JOHN NORTON

Cohen J.

as the second article is concerned, it does not rest on so strong a foundation, and that if this application were based on that article alone it would not have justified our making any order against the respondent. I also agree as to the punishment which should be awarded, and hope that it will act as a warning to prevent any repetition of the offence. In *Skipworth's Case* (1) the respondent had on two occasions been guilty of contempt of Court, and on the second occasion the Court fined him 500*l.* and ordered him to be imprisoned for three months.

Rule absolute.

Attorney for the respondent : *A. W. Nathan.*

(1) 9 L.R. Q.B. 230.

VAUGHAN v. CHENHALL (LESLIE, GARNISHEE).

Attachment of debts—Garnishee order—Attachment of money due on a judgment—
Attorney's lien for costs.

The judgment creditor attached money due from the garnishee to the judgment
debtor under a judgment recovered against him, and the garnishee paid the money
into Court. The attorney who acted for the judgment debtor claimed a lien on
the fund for costs incurred in the action after the order for attachment had been
made. *Held*, that though the attorney would have been entitled to a lien for
costs properly incurred, as the costs were improperly and erroneously incurred,
he had no lien.

1897.

May 2, 6, 23.

The C.J.
Stephen J.
and
G. B. Simpson J.

APPEAL from *Cohen*, J., in Chambers.

The facts of the case fully appear in his Honour's judgment.

The matter came on before his Honour on the 2nd May, and
after hearing argument he reserved his judgment, which was
delivered on the 6th May.

COHEN, J. The facts of this case are as follows : Vaughan
obtained a judgment against Chenhall for 41*l*. 6*s*. 5*d*., and Chenhall, in an action brought by him, afterwards obtained a verdict
against Leslie, for which, together with costs, judgment was
signed for 341*l*. 6*s*. 5*d*. In this latter action Chenhall & Eddie
acted as attorneys for the plaintiff. On the 11th August, 1897,
a garnishee order directed to Leslie for the sum of 41*l*. 6*s*. 5*d*.,
part of the 341*l*. 6*s*. 5*d*., was made at the instance of Vaughan ;
and Chenhall & Eddie, when it was made, gave notice of their
lien for costs, and on the 16th August this sum was paid into
Court by Mr. Davenport, acting as town agent for Nicholson,
Leslie's attorney. On the same date he gave to Chenhall & Eddie
written notice of his having done so. But prior to that Chenhall
had given notice to Davenport of his firm's lien. On the 17th
August Davenport received Nicholson's cheque for 300*l*., which he
enclosed in a letter to Chenhall & Eddie, but they refused it,
asserting their right to 341*l*. 6*s*. 5*d*. Davenport apparently saw
Chenhall after the refusal to accept Nicholson's cheque, and he
again, by letter on the 17th August, forwarded his own cheque

1898.

VAUGHAN
v.
CHENHALL
(LESLIE,
Garnishee).

Cohen J.

for 300*l.*, and suggested to Chenhall & Eddie that they should arrange with Thompson, who was Vaughan's attorney, for a consent order to take the money out of Court to be paid to Davenport, he undertaking to withdraw and pay it over to Chenhall & Eddie free of cost. On that date Chenhall & Eddie refused to accept the cheque on the terms proposed, and intimated to Davenport that unless the full amount of the judgment was paid by 10 a.m. the next day, execution would be issued. Later in the same day Davenport wrote in reply that he would attend at Chenhall & Eddie's office the next morning at 10.30, and would tender the full amount due by Leslie. Later still on the same date Chenhall seems to have had an interview with Davenport, and to have again informed Davenport that unless the full amount of the judgment was paid by 10 o'clock the following morning execution would issue. Afterwards, and still on the same date, Chenhall & Eddie wrote to Davenport a letter, which was received by Davenport at 10.5 a.m. of the 18th, and in that letter they say : " Being assured of this (referring to an earlier portion of the letter, which is immaterial) we think it only necessary to say that the definite notice we gave you of the firm's lien precludes any claim on behalf of Vaughan We have simply asked for a recognition of that lien, and we are advised that our position in maintaining that lien against third parties is clear. We, therefore, have to say again that we cannot accept a less amount than the full amount of judgment and interest to date . . . and unless the amount above stated is paid by 10 a.m. on Wednesday (18th inst.), execution will issue." At 10.20 a.m. of the 18th August, Davenport attended at the office of Chenhall & Eddie, and made a formal tender of 300*l.* in sovereigns, but the money was refused as execution had been issued that morning. Application was, therefore, made on behalf of Leslie to have the writ of *fi. fa.* set aside, and it was set aside with costs to be paid by Chenhall, it being made a condition of the order that Leslie might retain his costs out of the 300*l.* Leslie's attorney afterwards paid to Chenhall & Eddie the sum of 283*l.* 4*s.* 6*d.*, this representing the 300*l.* less the costs, 16*l.* 15*s.* 6*d.*

On the 16th October a summons was taken out by Chenhall & Eddie for payment out to them of the 41*l.* 6*s.* 5*d.*, when, by an

order made by myself on 20th October, it was referred to the
Prothonotary to tax Chenhall & Eddie's costs against Chenhall,
as between attorney and client in *Chenhall* v. *Leslie*, and to ascertain if Chenhall & Eddie had a lien over the 41*l.* 6*s.* 5*d.* paid into
Court under the garnishee order.

1898.

VAUGHAN
v.
CHENHALL
(LESLIE,
Garnishee).

The Prothonotary taxed and allowed the bill at 360*l.* 19*s.* 4*d.*,
and after deducting the 283*l.* 4*s.* 6*d.* paid to Chenhall & Eddie
by Leslie's attorney, and 40*l.* paid to them by their client, Chenhall, he found there was a balance of 37*l.* 14*s.* 10*d.* due to
Chenhall & Eddie from Chenhall, of which balance 15*l.* 16*s.* 10*d.*
was for their costs in connection with the issue of the *fi. fa.*
against Leslie, which had been set aside. He further found that
the 15*l.* 16*s.* 10*d.* was for costs properly and bona fide incurred
under the instructions of their client, and were incurred, as is the
obvious fact, after Chenhall & Eddie had notice of the garnishee
order. And he also found that Chenhall & Eddie were entitled
to a lien for the whole of their costs, and, therefore, to a lien on
the 41*l.* 6*s.* 5*d.* to the extent of 37*l.* 14*s.* 10*d.*, the balance due to
to them.

Cohen J.

The present summons is by Vaughan, calling on Chenhall &
Eddie to shew cause why the decision of the Prothonotary, or so
much thereof as declared that their lien extends as against
Vaughan to costs incurred after the garnishee attachment order,
should not be set aside, and why the sum of 41*l.* 6*s.* 5*d.*, or so
much thereof as remains after satisfying the proper lien of Chenhall & Eddie, should not be paid out of Court to Vaughan, upon
the grounds that the lien could not arise against him in respect
of the costs incurred after the date of the attachment order.
Although the right of Chenhall & Eddie has been referred to as a
lien, it is not a lien in strictness, but it is a right to the equitable
interference of the Court to have the judgment held as security
for the debt: *In re Suttor* (1).

Dealing with the figures first, inasmuch as Chenhall & Eddie's
right extends to 37*l.* 14*s.* 10*d.* only, the difference between it and
the 41*l.* 6*s.* 5*d.*, viz., 3*l.* 11*s.* 7*d.*, must be paid to Vaughan, and
inasmuch as the two sums of 16*l.* 15*s.* 6*d.* and 15*l.* 16*s.* 10*d.*,
totalling 32*l.* 14*s.* 4*d.*, represent the costs, after the attachment

(1) [1890] 11 N.S.W.R. 401.

1898.

VAUGHAN
v.
CHENHALL
(LESLIE,
Garnishee).

Cohen J.

order was made, the difference between that sum and 37*l.* 14*s.*
10*d.*, viz., 5*l.* 2*s.* 6*d.*, represents Chenhall & Eddie's costs before
that order was made, which stand unaffected by the subsequent
steps.   And as to that 5*l.* 2*s.* 6*d.*, there can be no question of
Chenhall & Eddie's claim.

It is perfectly plain from *Sympson* v. *Prothero* (1); *Eisdell* v.
Conyngham (2); *Lyons* v. *Castle* (3); and *Lynch* v. *Levinge* (4);
that as a general rule an attorney's right to the equitable interference of the Court to protect his costs properly incurred in
recovering judgment, will prevail over a garnishee order attaching
the judgment.   This right, however, will not extend to costs
otherwise incurred : *Hough* v. *Edwards* (5).   But in considering
the rights of the attorney, the Court should have regard to the
equities on both sides : *Wilson* v. *Smith* (6)   I cannot assent to
the broad principle submitted by Mr. *Mann*, that as against an
attachment order no costs incurred after it was made will be protected.   If this were the law a judgment creditor immediately
upon his judgment debtor recovering a judgment against a third
person, might attach that judgment, though the time for issuing
execution thereon may not have arrived, and with this result, that
if thereafter, and as soon as he could, the judgment debtor's
attorney properly issued execution against that third person, and
the *fi. fa.* were returned " *nulla bona*," the attorney would be deprived of his right to protection for his costs incurred in so issuing
execution, if the amount of the judgment was subsequently
recovered.

It was also contended by Mr. *Mann* that the 41*l.* 6*s.* 5*d.* having
been paid into Court upon the application of Vaughan to attach
that amount, the payment so made was equivalent to a payment
to Vaughan himself, and that he, therefore, was absolutely entitled
to the money, and for this position he cited *Culverhouse* v.
Wickens (7).   I do not think that case applies, for there the contention was not between an attorney asserting his right to the
interference of the Court, and a judgment creditor, who had

(1) [1857] 26 L.J. Ch. 671.   (4) *Idem* 169.
(2) [1859] 28 L.J. Ex. 213.   (5) [1857] 1 H.N. 171.
(3) [1893] 14 N.S.W. L.R. Eq. 135.   (6) [1880] 1 N.S W.L.R. 310
                    (7) [1868] L.R. 3 C.P. 295.

obtained a garnishee order, but between the judgment creditor and the garnishee, under somewhat peculiar circumstances, and the expressions of the Court in dealing with the merits must be viewed in the light of the facts *sub judice*.

On the other hand, Mr. *Garland* has contended that the attorney has a right to the security of the judgment for all costs which may be properly incurred by him until the final winding-up of the action, even although a garnishee order attaching the judgment may be obtained before the final winding-up. That may perhaps be so, and I am inclined to yield to it as a general principle; but I think when a contention arises between the attorney and a judgment creditor who has attached the judgment debt, this further element should be considered, viz., what are the then existing equities of the contestants? If the proceedings in an action are taking their proper course after judgment, and the attorney has done nothing to establish an equity against himself, I can well understand the Court protecting him in respect of costs to be incurred in the action, after the attachment order has been made; but to accept the proposition as a hard and fast one, and to so apply it to the present case, I find impossible, even though nothing in the shape of misconduct on the part of Chenhall & Eddie is suggested. But what do we find to be the facts here? On August 16th Leslie, through Davenport, paid into Court 41*l.* 6*s.* 5*d.*, as he had a right to do under the attachment, notice of this payment being given to Chenhall & Eddie on the same day, and it is clear that that payment discharged Leslie *pro tanto* from his liability under the judgment [s. 31 of the C.L.P. Act, 1857, and *Culverhouse* v. *Wickens*], as I have already decided on the application to set aside the *fi. fa.* We thus have Chenhall, or Chenhall & Eddie, as his attorneys as from that date, entitled to issue execution against Leslie for 300*l.*, and no more. On 17th August Davenport successively tendered to Chenhall & Eddie, first Nicholson's, and then his own cheque for 300*l.*, in liquidation of the balance due upon the judgment, but Chenhall & Eddie declined to accept these payments, asserting their right to be paid 341*l.* 6*s.* 5*d.*, and continuing to emphatically insist on their lien for full costs in the action *Chenhall* v. *Leslie*, which no one then controverted in principle. On that same day they informed

1898.

VAUGHAN
v.
CHENHALL
(LESLIE,
Garnishee).

Cohen J.

1898.

VAUGHAN
v.
CHENHALL
(LESLIE,
Garnishee).

Cohen J.

Davenport very definitely that unless the full amount of the
judgment was paid by 10 o'clock the next morning, execution
would be issued; and Davenport, with equal confidence in his
position, intimated that he would attend at Chenhall & Eddie's office
at 10.30 the next morning (the 18th), and tender the full amount
due by Leslie, meaning the 300*l.* At 10.20 of that morning
Davenport kept his appointment, tendered to Chenhall & Eddie
300 sovereigns, which they declined, as they had already issued
execution. Now, Chenhall & Eddie should have accepted the
300*l.* offered to them on the 17th, for the sufficiency of the
cheques tendered to them was not questioned, and if questioned
no doubt the sovereigns would have been substituted promptly.
And as to the 41*l.* 6*s.* 5*d.* they could have and should have then
invoked the equitable interference of the Court as they are doing now,
and have abstained from issuing execution, as they did. And why
this proper and, apart altogether from its legality, reasonable
course was not adopted, I cannot understand, except the cause be
that spirit of combativeness which often inspires opposing
attorneys, and a desire to prove the cleverer of the two, the
cleverness being indicated by the success. They say they were
acting under the instructions of their client, and were, therefore,
bound to carry out those instructions; but there cannot be a
reasonable doubt but that in a matter of this kind, which turns
mainly, if not altogether, upon legal considerations, the client
would be guided by the advice of his attorneys. It is plainly to
be seen, too, that Chenhall & Eddie were acting with an equal, if
not a larger, eye to their own interests, for which, of course, they
are not to be blamed, but rather to be commended; but if the
result of their action is that the rights of Vaughan are prejudiced,
then to the extent of that prejudice Chenhall & Eddie should
suffer. That Vaughan had some right in this 41*l.* 6*s.* 5*d.* is apparent, not alone to one's own intelligence, but may be gathered
from the spirit of the precedents I have alluded to, and from the
judgment of *Willes,* J., in *Culverhouse* v. *Wickens,* in which he
says: " If there be any cases in which, after money has been paid
into Court by the garnishee, the creditor may prove not to be
entitled to it, it must be treated as a conditional payment to the
creditor, and liable to be discharged if it should so turn out; and

1898.

VAUGHAN
v.
CHENHALL
(LESLIE,
Garnishee).

Cohen J.

the payment of money into Court is subject to the equitable
jurisdiction of the Court." I must not be supposed to be laying
down the naked proposition that an attorney's right to the equitable aid of the Court is cut away in respect of all costs incurred
in proceedings which are not based upon legal grounds, for such
a proposition would be quite inconsistent with law. But I do
think that the legality of the proceedings, out of which costs in
question arise, may be considered as an element in the general
circumstances, when the Court is called upon to act in protection
of the attorney, and to exercise an equitable jurisdiction.

The result then is this—that if the *fi. fa.* had not been issued
and Chenhall & Eddie had, without issuing it, accepted from
Davenport, as they should have done, the 300*l.*, they would have
had in hand 16*l.* 15*s.* 6*d.* more than reached them in payment of
their costs, and they would not have incurred the 15*l.* 16*s.* 10*d.*
costs in connection with issuing the *fi. fa.*, which costs they have
not received from their client, Chenhall. The 41*l.* 6*s.* 5*d.* paid
into Court would then have been relieved of the burden of these
two sums—32*l.* 12*s.* 4*d.*—which they now seek to cast upon it to
the prejudice of Vaughan. I therefore decide that as to 5*l.* 2*s.* 6*d.*
costs incurred before the issue of the *fi. fa.* Chenhall & Eddie are
entitled to payment out of the 41*l.* 6*s.* 5*d.*; but as to the balance,
36*l.* 3*s.* 11*d.*, they have no claim, and this I direct to be paid to
Vaughan or his attorney. The costs of this application will be
paid by Chenhall & Eddie. I have gone very fully into this case,
which is one of much importance, though the amount involved is
comparatively small, and whilst deciding as I have in accordance
with what I believe to be the substantial merits of the case, I
must state that it is not without its difficulties.

Order accordingly.

From this order Messrs. Chenhall & Eddie now appealed on the
ground that his Honour was in error in declaring that they had
not a lien for costs upon the sum of 36*l.* 3*s.* 11*d.* ordered by him
to be paid to the judgment creditor.

Garland, for the appellants. The whole question in dispute
between the parties is whether the appellants are entitled to a

lien on the fund in Court for the costs incurred after the garnishee order, *i.e.*, 32*l.* 12*s.* 4*d.*

[THE CHIEF JUSTICE. These costs appear to have been improperly incurred after the order, and if that be so, it would be a strange thing if the attorneys were entitled to a lien for them.]

If an attorney makes a mistake that will not deprive him of his lien. The Prothonotary here found that the costs were properly and bona fide incurred by the attorneys under the instructions of their client.

[THE CHIEF JUSTICE. If an attorney is to be entitled to a lien for all costs incurred in the action after a garnishee order, then an unscrupulous attorney might eat up all the money attached by making useless applications.]

If the application was not made bona fide and honestly, then, no doubt, he would be deprived of his lien. But he should not be deprived of his lien merely because the application was not successful. The only cases where the Court has refused to uphold the attorney's lien are in cases like *Wilson* v. *Smith* (1), where the attorney acted improperly. In *Faithful* v. *Ewen* (2) the Court says that the attorney ought not to be deprived of his lien because "he misstated nothing, he concealed nothing; no one can be heard effectually to say that he was misled by him." It is only where an attorney conceals the fact of his lien or makes a misrepresentation that the Court will deprive him of his lien. When the judgment creditor attaches a fund, he knows that the attachment is subject to the attorney's lien. Where there has been a mere error of judgment on the part of the attorney, he should not be deprived of his costs.

[THE CHIEF JUSTICE. There was more than a mere error of judgment in this case; there was gross ignorance.]

But the Prothonotary and *Cohen*, J., found that the attorneys acted honestly and bona fide. An attorney has an absolute right to a lien on a fund recovered by his exertions. The only ground for depriving him of that right is misconduct or concealment of his right. He also referred to *Cole* v. *Eley* (3); *Lyons* v. *Castle* (4); *Shippey* v. *Grey* (5).

(1) 1 N.S.W.L.R. 310.   (3) [1894] 2 Q.B. 180.
(2) 7 Ch. D. 495.   (4) 14 N.S.W.L.R. 135.
                    (5) 49 L.J. C.L. 524.

Mann, for the respondent, was not heard.

1898.

VAUGHAN
v.
CHENHALL
(LESLIE,
Garnishee).

THE CHIEF JUSTICE. I am of opinion that the order made by Mr. Justice *Cohen* is correct. The facts are simply these :— Vaughan recovered a judgment against Chenhall for 41*l.* 6*s.* 5*d.*, and Chenhall recovered a judgment against Leslie for 341*l.* 6*s.* 5*d.* Vaughan having this judgment against Chenhall, attached Chenhall's judgment against Leslie. Leslie thereupon paid the sum of 41*l.* 6*s.* 5*d.* into Court, as he had a right to do. After this he was asked by Chenhall to pay the full amount of the judgment. He refused, saying that he had already paid 41*l.* 6*s.* 5*d.* into Court, and he tendered a cheque for the balance. This Chenhall refused to accept, and he then tendered 300*l.* in sovereigns. This was also refused. Thereupon a writ of *fi. fa.* was issued for the whole amount of the judgment. One does not like to use hard words against the attorneys who advised the issue of the *fi. fa.*, but to say the least of it, it was an ignorant course to pursue. It was such an erroneous course that one can scarcely conceive an attorney making such a mistake. That writ of *fi. fa.* was set aside with costs. The costs amounted to the sum of 16*l.* 15*s.* 6*d.* paid to Leslie, and there was the further sum of 15*l.* 16*s.* 10*d.*, being Chenhall's own costs in the matter, making in all the sum of 32*l.* 12*s.* 4*d.*, the amount now in dispute. Chenhall & Eddie, who acted as Chenhall's attorneys in the action, now claim a lien on the amount in Court to the extent of 32*l.* 12*s.* 4*d.*, in payment for costs which never ought to have been incurred. Mr. Justice *Cohen*, while admitting that they would have had a lien for costs properly incurred after the garnishee order, said that it was impossible do hold that they had a lien for costs improperly and erroneously incurred. I am clearly of opinion that his Honour was right. In the case of *Wilson* v. *Smith* (1), Mr. Justice *Faucett* says : "Now he" (the attorney) "insists upon his lien. Is this a course of proceeding which we should sanction ? is it to be tolerated that an attorney should put the other party to costs merely for his own purposes, without doing any service to his client at all ;" and later on in his judgment he says : "I think the rule is intended for the protection of an attorney in fair, regular,

(1) 1 N.S.W.L.R. 310.

1898.

VAUGHAN
v.
CHENHALL
(LESLIE,
Garnishee).

The C.J.

and proper practice." In my opinion the principle established by the Rule referred to by Mr. Justice *Faucett* applies to such a case as this. The Court will give its protection to an attorney so long as he is acting in fair, regular and proper practice, but not in a case of this kind, where the costs should never have been incurred.

This application must be dismissed with costs.

STEPHEN, J., and G. B. SIMPSON, J., concurred.

Appeal dismissed with costs.

Attorney for the respondent: *Joseph Thompson.*

Ex parte FREDERICK HARPER.

1898.

May 26.

The C.J.
G. B. Simpson J.
and
Cohen J.

Crown Lands Act of 1884, *ss.* 20, 26—*Crown Lands Act of* 1889, *s.* 13—*Conditional purchase—Bona fides—Form of declaration of applicant.*

Although the question, whether the applicant for a conditional purchase has applied for the land solely for his own use and benefit, is determined by the Local Land Board on the confirmation of the application, that does not prevent the Minister afterwards referring that question again to the Land Board.

The form of declaration by the applicant for a conditional purchase (Form 8) prescribed by the Regulations of the 2nd December, 1889, which requires an answer to the question " do you intend to use the land now applied for solely for your own use and benefit? " is not *ultra vires.*

PROHIBITION.

This was a motion to make absolute a rule *nisi,* calling upon the members of the Local Land Board at Warren and J. H. Carruthers, Minister for Lands, to shew cause why a writ of prohibition should not issue to prohibit any further proceedings upon a reference made by the Minister for Lands to the Local Land Board.

The reference was as follows :—

" Department of Lands,
Sydney, 19th May, 1897.

In pursuance of s. 20 of the Crown Lands Act of 1884, the Minister for Lands refers to the Local Land Board at Warren the question whether any statement or statements in the declaration lodged with the application for the C P. noted in the margin are false within the meaning of s. 26 of the said Crown Lands Act of 1884, and in particular whether the statements in the said declaration as to the respective answers or as to any such answers to the following questions are false within the meaning of the said section :—

' Do you intend to use the land now applied for solely for your own use and benefit?

Is there any agreement or arrangement by which any person other than yourself can acquire any interest in, or obtain the use of the land now applied for?

Is there any understanding between you and any person that will tend to defeat or evade the provisions of the law as to conditional purchases?'

And the Local Land Board is hereby required to specify in its decision the statement or statements if any which it may find to be false as aforesaid.

> J. H. CARRUTHERS,
> Minister for Lands."

The conditional purchase in question was Frederick Harper's (the applicant).

The matter came before the Board on the 4th December, and was adjourned until the 7th February; in the meantime (*i.e.*, on the 21st December) this rule was granted.

The conditional purchase application of F. Harper had been duly confirmed under s. 13 of the Crown Lands Act of 1889 long before this reference was made.

The ground upon which the rule *nisi* was granted was that the said application having been duly confirmed under s. 13 of the Crown Lands Act of 1889, it was not open to the Minister or the Land Board to reopen the question of bona fides, which was *res judicata*.

Pilcher, Q.C., and *P. K. White*, for the applicant.

Sir *Julian Salomons*, Q.C., and *Cunaway*, for the respondents, took the preliminary objection that the ground upon which the rule was granted was not a ground upon which a prohibition would go. The applicant says that the matter is *res judicata*. If so, that is a matter which should be raised before the Board, but it does not oust the jurisdiction of the Board. It is a matter which must be pleaded in that Court. If it is pleaded, then that Court can enquire into the truth of the plea; but it in no way prevents the Board from giving its decision, nor does it oust its jurisdiction. The plea of *res judicata* in the District Court does not oust the jurisdiction of that Court: *Ex parte Rayner* (1).

THE CHIEF JUSTICE. You cannot take this point by way of preliminary objection.

(1) 17 L.J.C.P. 16.

Pilcher, Q.C. Before the Land Board confirms an application,
it must be satisfied that "the applicant has bona fide applied for the
question having been, therefore, enquired into and determined on
the application for confirmation by a Court of competent jurisdiction, it became *res judicata*, and it was not open to the
Minister to afterwards refer that same question to the Board.

[THE CHIEF JUSTICE.   Under s. 26 the applicant for a conditional purchase must lodge with his application a declaration
in the prescribed form, and then the section says "and if any
person shall make a false statement in such declaration as to
any of the matters contained therein, he shall forfeit .   .   .   .
all right and title to such land ; " what does the word " forfeit "
mean ?]

The question of bona fides must be gone into on the application, and if he does not make the application bona fide he forfeits his right to the land.

[THE CHIEF JUSTICE.   How can he forfeit what does not
exist ?]

If the Court thinks that that section gives the Minister the
right to forfeit after confirmation, then I am driven to argue
that the form of declaration (Form 8) prescribed by R. 45 of the
Regulations of the 2nd December, 1889, is *ultra vires.*

[THE CHIEF JUSTICE.   Sect. 26 requires the declaration to be
in the " prescribed form," and under s. 145 a regulation has been
passed and the form prescribed.]

Sect. 26 contemplates that the form should give effect to the
provisions in the Act.   There is nothing in the Act of 1884 which
provides that the land shall be taken up for the applicant's sole
use and benefit, and, therefore, the form so far as it requires an
answer to the question " Do you intend to use the land now
applied for solely for your own use and benefit ? " is *ultra vires.*
It is the Act of 1889 (s. 13) that provides that the land is to be
taken up for his sole use and benefit.

[THE CHIEF JUSTICE. But the Act of 1884 and the Act of 1889 are to be read together, and inasmuch as the latter Act does require that the land shall be taken up for the applicant's sole use and benefit, what is there to prevent this question being in the form prescribed? These regulations were made after the Act of 1889 came into force.]

The applicant only forfeits his land for a false statement made in the declaration referred to in s. 26 of the Act of 1884, and under that Act this question in the declaration would be *ultra vires*.

[G. B. SIMPSON, J. The reference by the Minister was not limited to the enquiry as to whether the answer to that question was false. If the Board had jurisdiction to enquire into the other answers to the questions which were not *ultra vires*, how could we grant a prohibition?]

If the Board had not jurisdiction to enquire into the question of bona fides it would have no jurisdiction as to part of the reference, and, therefore, a prohibition should go. But apart from that point these questions submitted to the Board all related to the one question of bona fides, and my contention is that, inasmuch as that has already been adjudicated upon under s. 13, it cannot be reopened.

Sir *Julian Salomons*, Q.C., was not heard.

THE CHIEF JUSTICE. I have no doubt that if we were confined to the Act of 1884, these questions, which are said to be *ultra vires*, are fully justified. It was clearly the intention of the Legislature under that Act that the selector should take up the land for his sole use and benefit. But it appears to me that we need not consider that point, because the Act of 1884 and the Act of 1889 form one code, and must be read together. Sect. 1 of the Act of 1889 provides that "This Act . . . shall be read with, and forms part of the Crown Lands Act of 1884." These regulations and forms, which we are now considering. were made by the Governor under s. 145 of the Act of 1884, if indeed they were not made under the last section of the Act of 1889, and were made on the 2nd December, 1889, after the Act of 1889 came into force. Under the Acts of 1884 and 1889 and the regulations made thereunder, it was necessary for the applicant for a conditional purchase to make a certain declaration. One question in the form prescribed is " Do you intend to use the land now applied for solely for your own use and benefit ?" There is no doubt that that question is not *ultra vires.* Taking the land up for your own use and benefit does not mean that you are bound to run your own cattle on the land ; you may no doubt let it, provided you do so for your own use and benefit. Sect. 26 of the Act of 1884 provides that the applicant for a conditional purchase must lodge with his application a declaration in the prescribed form, " and if any person shall make a false statement in such declaration as to any matters contained therein he shall forfeit . . . all right and title to such land."

Mr. *Pilcher* argues that under s. 13 of the Act of 1889 it is the duty of the Land Board to be satisfied as to the bona fides of the applicant, and that the land is taken up for his sole use and benefit, and that once the Board is satisfied on that point their decision is final. No doubt their finding is final as against everybody except the Crown ; but in case it should turn out that the confirmation was brought about by any false statement in the declaration, then the Minister can after due enquiry forfeit the land. In this case the Minister has referred under s. 20 to the Land Board the question whether a false statement was made by the applicant Harper in his declaration. That reference the Minister clearly had power to make, and the Board has jurisdiction to hear the matter.

I may say that I think it would be better as a matter of policy that the question of bona fides should be enquired into when the application is before the Board for confirmation, and that once they have given their decision there should be an end of the matter, and that the confirmation should be good against the world. But that, of course, is a matter for the Legislature.

I am, however, clearly of opinion that as the law now is the Minister had power to make this reference to the Land Board, and that, therefore, this rule should be discharged with costs.

G. B. SIMPSON, J. The declaration has to be in the prescribed form. The form has been prescribed, and the statements to be

1898.

Ex parte
FREDERICK
HARPER.

The C.J.

made in the declaration are not limited to the question of bona fides. The reference made by the Minister is as to whether there are *any* false statements in the declaration. It is quite clear that the Board would have jurisdiction as to some of those statements, and, therefore, on that ground alone we could not prohibit the Board from entertaining the reference.

COHEN, J. I concur.

Rule discharged with costs.

Attorney for the applicant: *W. P. Crick.*

Ex parte JAMES BENNETT.

Prohibition—Crown Lands Act—Local Land Board—Minister for Lands.

1898.

May 23, 25.

The C.J.
G. B. *Simpson* J.
and
Cohen J.

The Land Board held an enquiry on the reference of the Minister for Lands as to whether any evidence given on oath by a selector in connection with his conditional purchase had, within the meaning of s. 135 of the Crown Lands Act of 1884, been given for the purpose of misleading any officer, etc., or had wilfully misrepresented facts, and the Board found against the selector. *Held,* on an application for a prohibition to the Board and to the Minister, that a prohibition would not lie to the Board, because, so far as its functions were concerned, they were at an end, and there was nothing to prohibit; nor would it lie to the Minister, as he was not a Court.

PROHIBITION.

This was a motion to make absolute a rule *nisi* calling upon W. C. Cardew and John Reddan, members of the Local Land Board, Warren, and J. H. Carruthers, Minister for Lands, to shew cause why a writ of prohibition should not issue to prohibit any further proceedings upon a certain reference by the said Minister to the said Board, and to restrain the said Minister from acting upon or giving effect to the decision thereon.

On the 27th April, 1897, the Minister for Lands, in pursuance of s. 20 of the Crown Lands Act of 1884, referred to the Land Board at Warren the question whether any statements in the declaration lodged by James Bennett on the 14th May, 1891, with his application for a certain conditional purchase, were false within the meaning of s. 26 of the Crown Lands Act of 1884 ; and the Minister further referred to the Land Board for decision, after due investigation in open Court, the question whether any evidence given on oath in connection with the said conditional purchase had, within the meaning of s. 135, been given for the purpose of misleading any officer, etc., or had wilfully misrepresented facts.

The Board after enquiry found by a majority that a certain statement made by Bennett did wilfully misrepresent facts.

The rule was granted on various grounds.

Pilcher, Q.C., and *White* appeared for the applicant.

[THE CHIEF JUSTICE. What is there to prohibit? A prohibition will not lie against the Minister, and, as far as the Land

Board is concerned, there is nothing to prohibit. The functions of the Board are at an end.]

It may be that the Board, having dealt with the matter, they have nothing further to do, but a prohibition would go to prevent the Minister acting upon the decision of the Board.

[THE CHIEF JUSTICE referred to *Grant* v. *Gould* (1); *Ex parte Poe* (2).

G. B. SIMPSON, J., referred to *Ex parte Medlyn* (3), decided on the authority of *Denton* v. *Marshall* (4); and *Ex parte Foster* (5).

Sir *Julian Salomons*, Q.C. There is also the case of *Ex parte McInnes* (6)].

We should like to have an opportunity of considering the point whether a prohibition would not lie to the Minister. We did not come prepared to argue this point, because, on a previous application by the applicant in this case, a prohibition was issued against the Minister under similar circumstances, the Crown consenting.

[THE CHIEF JUSTICE. The matter was not then considered by the Court, as the Crown consented to the prohibition going. The Minister is not a Court, and how can a prohibition lie against him ?]

A prohibition will lie to prevent him acting on the decision of the Court.

Sir *Julian Salomons*, Q.C., and *Canaway*, for the respondents, were not heard.

THE CHIEF JUSTICE. The rule must be discharged on the ground that it manifestly appears that there is nothing to prohibit.

G. B. SIMPSON, J., and COHEN, J., concurred.

Rule discharged with costs.

Attorney for the applicant: *W. P. Crick.*

(1) 2 H. Bl. 69 ; 3 R. R. 342.   (4) 1 H. & C. 654.
(2) 5 B. & Ad. 681.   (5) 11 S.C.R. 195.
(3) 14 N.S.W.R. 276 ; 9 W.N. 185.   (6) 4 N.S.W.L.R. 143.

Ex parte GLASHEEN.

Justices—Jurisdiction—42 Vic. No. 23, s. 8 — "Wilfully causing animals to trespass"
—Conviction.

1898.

March 3.
May 18.

The C.J.
Stephen J.
and
Cohen J.

The information charged the applicant with wilfully causing horses, the property of the respondent, to trespass. The evidence shewed that the alleged trespass was upon the applicant's own land. The Justices convicted him. *Held*, that the evidence did not support the charge.

If a person appears before Justices on an information for a certain offence and he is then charged with a different offence within their jurisdiction he has a good ground for asking for an adjournment, but if he waives that and answers the latter charge he may be convicted of it notwithstanding that no information or summons has been previously issued in respect of it; but the Justices have no power, after hearing a case, to convict him of an offence with which he has not been charged.

The information charged the applicant, under s. 8 of 42 Vic. No. 23, with wilfully causing horses, the property of the respondent, to trespass. There was no evidence to support that charge, but there was evidence to support a charge for a different offence under that section. *Held*, that not having been charged with the latter the applicant could not be convicted of it.

PROHIBITION.

The information alleged that on the 20th December, 1897, "at Pioneer Farm, near North Bourke, one Edward Glasheen did wilfully cause 16 horses, the property of H. W. King, to trespass contrary," etc. From the evidence tendered for the prosecution it appeared that Glasheen was seen cutting the wires of a fence between his own land and the land of one James, and driving King's horses on to his own land, where they were subsequently found. When Glasheen was asked to deliver up the horses he demanded 8*l.* 15*s.*, being 5*l.* for a stallion, and 5*s.* a head for the other 15 horses. Subsequently on payment of 16*s.* he delivered up the horses.

The Justices convicted Glasheen. There was no formal conviction drawn up, but the minute of the order made was as follows :—" Case considered proved, and the defendant fined 5*l.* and costs, in default immediate payment levy and distress."

The applicant (Glasheen) now moved to make absolute a rule *nisi* for a prohibition, on the ground that under the information as laid he could not be convicted of wilfully causing horses to trespass on his own land.

Sect. 8 of 42 Vic. No. 23 provides that "any person unlawfully and wilfully leaving open any gate or slip panel, or making any gap in any fence, thereby permitting or causing any animal to trespass, or otherwise wilfully causing any animal to trespass, or who shall illegally impound any cattle, or shall drive any cattle without proper authority on or from the land of any other person, shall in each case be liable to a penalty not exceeding five pounds."

J. L. Campbell, for the applicant. The information is laid under s. 8 of 42 Vic. No. 23, and alleges that the applicant " did wilfully cause 16 horses, the property of H. W. King, to trespass." The evidence shews that he drove King's horses on to his own land. If a man takes another's horses on to his own land, how can it be said that he wilfully caused them to trespass ? Trespass is an act done against the will of the owner.

C. B. Stephen, for the respondent The word " trespass " in s. 8 should not be strictly construed. Whether a person is owner of the land or not, he can cause animals to trespass upon it. The applicant took the horses on to his own land with a view to taking proceedings against the owner for trespass ; that was sufficient to shew that he wilfully caused the horses to trespass.

Apart from that question the evidence clearly shews that the applicant was guilty of illegally impounding the horses and also of driving them without proper authority from the land of another person. If the Justices convicted him of either of those offences, then the Court should allow the conviction to be drawn up to that effect.

[THE CHIEF JUSTICE. Could the Justices have convicted him of illegally impounding on this information ?]

The Justices had jurisdiction to convict him of any offence within their jurisdiction, no matter what the information was:

Ex parte Ah Yee (1). The Court should now send the matter back to the Justices to have the conviction drawn up (s. 9 of 17 Vic. No. 39).

J. L. Campbell in reply.

[THE CHIEF JUSTICE. Our impression at present is that the case should go back to the Justices to allow the Justices to draw up the conviction.]

It would be useless to send the case back, because if they were to draw up the conviction for the offence charged, then it would clearly be bad because the evidence does not support it. If, on the other hand, they drew it up for any other offence, it would be bad because they could not convict him of an offence with which he had not been charged: *Martin* v. *Pridgeon* (2). In *Ex parte Hopkins* (3), *Smith*, J., says: "Nor can any person exercising criminal jurisdiction in this country, try anyone unless they first charge the person, and give the person charged the opportunity of pleading to the charge upon which he is to be tried." The charge made here was that he "wilfully caused horses to trespass," and that was the only charge made, and, therefore, they could not have convicted the applicant of any other offence, even if the evidence warranted it.

[COHEN, J., referred to *Ralph* v. *Hurrell* (4).]

In that case there was merely a variance between the information and the evidence adduced in support of it.

C.A.V.

On the 18th May, the judgment of the Court was delivered.

May 18.

THE CHIEF JUSTICE. I much regret that in this case I am compelled to come to the conclusion that the rule for a prohibition must be made absolute; I say I regret this, for I am of opinion that the evidence clearly established that Glasheen was guilty of one of the offences included within 42 Vic. No. 23, s. 8.

There is no doubt in my mind but that Glasheen, finding the prosecutor's horses on land adjoining his own, cut down his own

1898.

Ex parte
GLASHEEN.

The C.J.

fence, and drove the horses on to his own land, and then impounded them. For doing this an information might have gone
for illegally impounding horses under s. 8 of the above mentioned
Act, or he might have been tried for illegally using horses: See
Ex parte Fox (1). In that case *Manning, J.*, seemed to think
that a man who drove cattle off lands where they lawfully were
for the purpose of illegally impounding them, might be indicted
for larceny. Again, in this case, Glasheen took money from the
prosecutor in respect to the impounding. I think he obtained
that money by a false pretence, and that for this he might have
been made amenable. Indeed, I am of opinion that Glasheen
should now be proceeded against either for illegally using these
horses, or for obtaining money under false pretences, to wit, by
falsely pretending that he had legally impounded these horses.
I say this because I agree with *Manning, J.*, when he states in
Ex parte Fox (1) that this is " a question of immense importance,
as it applies to great numbers of our country population." I also
look upon the offence of deliberately taking cattle and horses
from where they lawfully are, and driving them on to land, from
which, if trespassing, they might be lawfully impounded, and
then impounding them, to be a very serious offence indeed, and
one which demands severe punishment.

   In this case, however, the information was " for wilfully causing horses, the property of H. W. King, to trespass." To this
charge Glasheen appeared, and was called upon to plead. To
this charge he pleaded. This was the only charge heard before
the Justices, and the evidence in support of it was simply that
Glasheen, finding the horses in question in the vicinity of his
land, cut his fence and drove the horses in upon his land, and
then impounded them for trespassing. Now these horses having
been driven by Glasheen on to his own land, could not be trespassing, for trespass *quare clausum fregit* is " an unwarrantable
entry upon the land of another," and, however illegally Glasheen
was acting, still he was entering his own land, and the horses he
drove in were there with his consent, and not against his will.
Upon the only charge heard before the Justices, " wilfully causing
horses to trespass," he should have been acquitted.

(1) 2 S.C.R. N.S. 47.

1898.

Ex parte
GLASHEEN.

The C.J.

It was argued that at most there was only a variance, and *Ralph* v. *Hurrell* (1) was relied upon, or, if not, that there was a defect in substance, in which case *Rodgers* v. *Richards* (2) was relied on as bringing the case within s. 1 of 11 & 12 Vic. cap. 43. But rightly looked at, there was no variance or defect in substance. It was simply a case of there being no evidence to support the charge, or rather, that the evidence adduced disproved the charge. If, indeed, the Justices had, during the hearing, seen the mistake which had been made in making this particular charge, and called upon Glasheen to plead to a charge of illegally impounding, and convicted him of that charge, this would have been within their power. They would, of course, have given Glasheen time, had he asked for it, to meet the then new charge : see *R.* v. *Hughes* (3), a case which was heard before ten Judges, where *Blake* v. *Beech* (4) is explained. *Hawkins*, J., at p. 626 says :—" A flood of authorities might be cited in support of the proposition that no process at all is necessary where the accused being bodily before the Justices, the charge is made in his presence and he appears and answers it "; and he cited *Erle*, C.J., in the case of *R.* v. *Shaw* (5), where that learned Judge says: "In my opinion, if a party is before a Magistrate, and he is then charged with the commission of an offence within the jurisdiction of that Magistrate, the latter has jurisdiction to proceed with that charge without any information or summons having been previously issued, unless the statute creating the offence imposes the necessity of taking some such step." *Blackburn*, J., in the same case, says :—" I think when a man appears before Justices, and a charge is then made against him, if he has not been summoned he has a good ground for asking for an adjournment; if he waives that and answers the charge, a conviction would be perfectly good against him." In *R.* v. *Hughes* (3), *Huddlestone*, B., in the course of his judgment, gives a lucid explanation of the course pursued before Justices. He says, at p. 632 :—" The jurisdiction to try arises on the appearance of the party charged, the nature of the charges, and the charging of the defendant ";

(1) 44 L.J. M.C. 145.   (3) 4 Q.B.D. 614.
(2) [1892] 1 Q.B. 555.   (4) 1 Ex. D. 320.
                (5) 34 L.J. M.C. 169.

and again at p. 633, "principle and the authorities seem to shew that objection and defect in the form of procuring the appearance of a party charged, will be cured by appearance. The principle is that a party charged should have an opportunity of knowing the charge against him, and be fully heard before being condemned If he has the opportunity, the method by which he is brought before the Justices cannot take away the jurisdiction to hear and determine when he is before them."

In this case Glasheen was not called upon to answer a charge of illegally impounding, or any other charge which upon the evidence he could have been adjudged guilty. The only charge made against him was that contained in the summons, and that charge the evidence disproved. I am, therefore, of opinion that the rule for a prohibition must be made absolute, but under the peculiar circumstances of the case without costs.

STEPHEN, J. I concur in thinking that the rule should be made absolute, but I offer no opinion as to the offence with which the applicant might have been charged, as I have not considered the question.

COHEN, J. In this case the applicant was charged under 42 Vic. No. 23, s. 8, by information "for that he did wilfully cause 16 horses, the property of H. W. King, to trespass," and he was convicted and fined.

Against this conviction the applicant has applied for a prohibition, on the ground that he could not be convicted of a wilful trespass on his own land. The evidence, in my opinion, shewed that the alleged trespass was upon the applicant's own land and not elsewhere. It is beyond doubt that there was evidence to justify the conclusion that the applicant " wilfully " caused the horses to go upon his land, but that still leaves open the question whether the applicant could cause a trespass upon it. I am of opinion that he could not. The very idea of trespass suggests the wrongful act of one person, which violates the right of another. In *Pollock on Torts* (1), under the heading of trespass it is said, " Trespass may be committed by various kinds of acts. of which the most obvious are entry on another man's land (trespass *quare*

(1) 1897 Ed., p. 321.

clausum fregit), and taking another man's goods (trespass *de bonis* asportatis). . . . Every invasion of private property, be it ever so minute, is a trespass." In *Addison on Torts*, ch. VI., in defining what constitutes trespass, it is stated, "Every entry upon land in the occupation or possession of another constitutes trespass." Of course it is an elementary proposition that any entry upon the land of another or any taking of another's goods would be justified, if the authority of that other man for the entry or the taking were given ; in other words, in neither of such cases would there be a trespass. How it is possible for a man to trespass or to cause a trespass upon his own land, that is his land in his own possession, as is the case here, I cannot conceive. This entry in such circumstances would not be an entry upon another man's land, and would not be the "invasion of private property" ; "invasion" obviously meaning, and is interpreted in the Imperial Dictionary as "an attack on the rights of another; infringement; violation."

In answer to the contention, supposing it to be valid that a man cannot wilfully cause a trespass upon his own land, and in support of the conviction, it was argued that nevertheless there was evidence which would justify the Magistrates in convicting the applicant of "illegally impounding," an offence which is also created by the same s. 8 of 42 Vic. No. 23, and that, therefore, the conviction should stand. In support of this view the Court was referred to 11 & 12 Vic., c. 43, s. 1 (adopted in New South Wales by 14 Vic. No. 23), the proviso to which is as follows : "No objection shall be taken or allowed to any information, complaint or summons for any alleged defect therein in substance or in form, or for any variance between such information, complaint or summons, and the evidence adduced on the part of the informant or complainant at the hearing of such information or complaint as hereinafter mentioned ; but if any such variance shall appear to the Justice or Justices present and acting at such hearing to be such that the party so summoned and appearing has been thereby deceived or misled, it shall be lawful for such Justice or Justices, upon such terms as he or they shall think fit, to adjourn the hearing of the case to some future day."

The rejoinder to this argument was that the "variance" mentioned in that section can only have relation to evidence in

1898.

Ex parte
GLASHEEN.

Cohen J.

reference to the charge which the person charged is actually called upon to answer, and cannot be construed so as to make a person charged with one offence amenable to conviction for an entirely distinct offence, which he has not been called upon to answer, when the evidence fails to support the one, but is sufficient to maintain the other. The authorities bearing upon the point, in my opinion, favour the position assumed by counsel for the applicant. In *Martin* v. *Pridgeon* (1), the appellant appeared in answer to a summons charging him with having " been in a public street drunk and guilty of riotous behaviour," an offence punishable by a fine not exceeding 40s. or imprisonment not exceeding 7 days, under 10 & 11 Vic., c. 89. The charge of drunkenness only was proved to the satisfaction of the Magistrates, who convicted the appellant thereof under 21 Jac. 1, c. 7, which made him liable to a fine of 5s., which was imposed. The conviction was set aside; *Crompton, J.*, at p. 779, observing : " Sect. 1 of Stat. 11 & 12 Vic., c. 43, was framed to meet the case of a variance between the summons and the evidence adduced in support of it. But the appellant has been summoned for an offence under one Act, and convicted of another and a different offence under another Act. The section in question does not permit that." And Lord *Campbell*, C.J., says : " But he was convicted under one Act which imposes for this offence a different punishment from that imposed by the Act under which he was summoned. He was convicted of a distinct statutory offence." *Soden* v. *Cray* (2) expressly follows *Martin* v. *Pridgeon* (1) under precisely similar circumstances. In *Whittle* v. *Frankland* (3), Whittle was charged by information with having absented himself from service under a contract entered into by him with T. B. and others. At the hearing it appeared that the agreement had been made with T. B. on behalf of himself and partners forming a company with limited liability. The Magistrates disregarded the variance and convicted Whittle, and it was held they were right; *Cockburn, C.J.*, and *Crompton, J.*, stating, " That that was the class of variance contemplated by the statute." It will be seen that the variance there was merely

(1) [1859] 1 E. & E. 778.   (2) [1862] 7 L.T.N.S. 324.
(3) [1862] 31 L.J.M.C. 81.

between the description of the employers in the information and
their description as disclosed by the evidence. There was no
variance between the essential nature of the offence as laid and
that proved.   The next case to which I shall refer is *Ex parte
Cunliffe* (1).   There Cunliffe was charged by information with
having assaulted the prosecutor, he being a bailiff of a Court of
Requests at Newcastle, in the discharge of a public duty." There
being no such Court the Magistrates allowed the information to
be amended by striking out the words " of the Court of Requests."
The Court held that the Magistrates were wrong in making the
amendment, and granted a prohibition.   The then Chief Justice,
the late Sir *Alfred Stephen*, in his judgment, points out that the
Act 11 & 12 Vic., c. 43, s. 1, whilst giving the Magistrates power
to disregard a variance, does not authorise them to make amendments, and then proceeds as follows : " The course that ought to
have been pursued here was either to dismiss the case (on which
a fresh information might have been laid), or to proceed with it,
disregarding the variance, or to adjourn the hearing on terms, in
case it appeared that the accused had been deceived or
misled by the mistake." He then referred to *Whittle* v. *Frankland* (2) evidently with approval as indicating the class of
variances contemplated by s. 1 of 11 & 12 Vic., c. 43, and I
infer from his judgment, which was concurred in by the other
members of the Court, that, if the Magistrates had convicted
without amending, the conviction would have been upheld because
the variance between the information and the evidence in support
of it was such as was within the purview of that section.

In *Ralph* v. *Hurrell* (3) an information was laid against the
appellant, charging him with damaging a lamp alleged to be the
property of A., B. and C., the trustees of a club house. The
evidence shewed that B. was the lessee of the club house, but
that he had declared himself a trustee of it for the trustees.
The information was dismissed, the Magistrates stating that they
were of opinion, *inter alia*, "that the evidence given was not
sufficient to shew that the trustees were the owners of the lamp,
or whether B. was not the sole owner thereof." On a case stated

1898.

Ex parte
GLASHEEN.

Cohen J.

(1) [1871] 10 S.C.R. 250.   (2) [1862] 31 L.J.M.C. 81.
          (3) [1872] 44 L.J.M.C. 145.

it was decided that the Magistrates were wrong. *Blackburn*, J.,
in his judgment, says: "Then it was objected that the property
was laid in three persons, while the evidence did not shew that
those three persons were the owners. The declaration of trust
was put in, from which it appeared that Bentall was the owner;
but the other two were, at any rate, equitable owners. This is a
variance which would be fatal at common law; but when we
come to Jervis' Act (11 & 12 Vic. c. 43, s. 1) we find" (here the
section is cited). "I can put no other construction on these
words than this—that if there be a variance, they should either
go on and decide the case, notwithstanding such variance, or
should adjourn to a future day, if they think that the person
summoned has been deceived or misled   .   .   .   This is just such
a variance as the 11 & 12 Vic. c. 43 was intended to cure, and
the Justices should either have gone on to convict, or should have
adjourned the hearing." *Lush* and *Field*, JJ., were of the same
opinion.

In *Blake* v. *Beech* (1) the respondent laid an information before
a Justice that a house was "kept or used as a common gaming
house" within the meaning of the "Act to Amend the Law
concerning Games and Wagers" (8 & 9 Vic. c. 109), and thereupon the Justice granted a warrant, under which the appellant
was arrested at the house in question. He was brought before
two Justices, and charged under the "Act for the Suppression of
Betting Houses" (16 and 17 Vic. c. 119), s. 3, as "the person"
who, "having the management of a room" in the house, used it
"for the purpose of betting with persons resorting thereto." No
information was laid, nor was any summons issued under the
last-named statute; and the appellant did not waive this omission.
The charge having been heard, he was convicted, and a penalty
was imposed; but the conviction was held to be wrong, and was
quashed. At p. 333, *Cleasby*, B., observes: "If this Court has
any control over summary jurisdictions, it cannot be better
exercised than by insisting that there shall not be such a
departure from the first principles of criminal justice as that a
man shall not be heard in his defence before he is convicted, as
would be the result of allowing a man, who happened to be in

(1) [1876] 1 Ex. D. 320.

custody, to be at once upon his trial for any offence of which he could have had no notice before . . .   But it is not a matter within the discretion of the Magistrates whether a man shall be put upon his trial without any proper preliminary proceedings, and when such a question is brought before this Court, I can consider only one answer can be given.   A proper exercise of the Magistrates' discretion in granting delay, if applied for, would, no doubt, correct the erroneous conclusion of the Magistrates in entertaining the case; but no one would contend that a man should be at the mercy of the Magistrates, in granting delay, where he has a right not to be put upon his trial, or that this Court would allow it."

In *Ex parte Ah Yee* (1) the applicants were charged on information with assaulting in company with others one Ah Chuck, with intent to do him grievous bodily harm, and were convicted and sentenced to four months' imprisonment; but it did not appear on the depositions for what offence they were convicted.   A formal order was afterwards drawn up, convicting them of an assault in company with several others.   On an application for a prohibition, the Court, consisting of the late Chief Justice, Sir *James Martin*, and the late Sir *George Innes*, discharged the rule, and in the judgment, as reported, it is stated : ' A Magistrate might convict of an offence within his jurisdiction, whatever the information, or even if there were no information filed   Here the Magistrate had jurisdiction to make the order which he did, and it is immaterial that the information charged an offence which the Magistrate could not have dealt with summarily."

All the foregoing authorities, except *Ex parte Ah Yee*, exhibit a clearly defined line between the class of cases represented by *Martin* v. *Pridgeon*, in which the Magistrates cannot convict, and that class represented by *Whittle* v. *Frankland*, in which they may convict.   The test appears to be, does the evidence adduced support in substance the charge the accused is called upon to answer, there being a variance only as to some matter which is not an essential ingredient in the nature of the offence ?

(1) 1 W.N. 62.

1898.

Ex parte
GLASHEEN.

Cohen J.

1898.

Ex parte
GLASHEEN.

Cohen J.

Now, *Martin* v. *Pridgeon* and *Soden* v. *Cray* decide that a man charged with an offence composed of two essential elements, cannot be convicted of an offence which is complete with one only of those elements, at least where the two offences are created by different statutes, and are liable to different punishments; and this, although having been called upon to answer the larger offence, he knows he will have to meet that part of it, which alone constitutes the smaller one. These considerations, so far as knowledge of the charge is concerned, are applicable to *Ex parte Ah Yee.* Whether the offence which the applicants in that case were called upon to answer, and that of which they were convicted, were created by the same statute, does not appear; it is clear, however, that different punishments must be attached to them. On the argument to make the rule absolute the applicants were not represented, and the pertinent authorities seemingly were not cited. With the deepest respect for the judgment of so eminent a criminal lawyer as Sir *James Martin*, and for the experience and ability of Sir *George Innes*, I am not, after serious consideration, able to reconcile the decision in *Ex parte Ah Yee* with the decisions which preceded or follow it. Had those precedent authorities been cited, I may venture to say, with all deference, that the decision would have been the other way, though I do not question that part of the judgment which declares the general power of Magistrates to entertain a charge, notwithstanding no formal information has been laid, provided the accused is informed of the charge, and has reasonable opportunity for refuting it. In principle, I can discern no difference between the legal inability of Magistrates to convict of an offence not charged, and which is created by a different Act from that creating the offence charged, and their inability to convict of an offence not charged, but created by the same Act as creates the offence charged, and even though in this latter case the punishments are the same. To my mind the substance of the objection to Magistrates so acting is, that the offences are distinct, though the objection may be rendered still stronger where the punishments are different. And if, as has been decided in the English Courts, the Magistrates have no power to convict of an offence not charged, though its ingredients be contained and are

stated in the information as part of the wider offence which is
charged, and though it is liable to a smaller punishment, it must,
a fortiori, be out of their power to convict of an offence not
charged which is altogether distinct in its nature from and is not
stated in the information even as an ingredient in that charged.
In the facts with which we are now dealing the offence laid in
the information, viz., " wilfully causing the horses to trespass,"
and that for which it is said the evidence will support, the
conviction, viz., " illegally impounding," are created by the same
section, and carry the same punishment; but as I have already
said, that, in my opinion, makes no difference ; the offence charged
is distinct in its nature from that which it is said, and it may be so
taken, the evidence will support. and that it would require
altogether different evidence on the one hand to prove and on the
other to meet it, is too palpable to need illustration.

In *R.* v. *Laird* (1), the prisoner was indicted for horse stealing,
and at the close of the case for the prosecution the prisoner gave
evidence on his own behalf, which involved a confession, and
whilst so giving evidence the Crown Prosecutor applied for leave
to add a count for receiving, to which there was no objection, and
the Judge permitted it. On the application of the prisoner's
attorney the Judge reserved, *inter alia*, the point whether the
addition of the count was legal, and, although the conviction was
quashed on another ground, the late Mr. Justice *Windeyer*, as to
the point here referred to, says : " With reference to the addition
of the count for receiving, I am of opinion that what was done
was wrong, and that the Judge had no power to add the count.
The evidence necessary to support a charge of feloniously
receiving, is entirely different to that required to support a charge
of larceny, and the Judge might just as well have added a count
for murder." The late Mr. Justice *Innes* observes : " I am also of
opinion that the learned Judge was in error in adding the count
for receiving." Mr. Justice *Foster*, the remaining member of the
Court, did not state his views upon the point. Assuming,
however, that the opinion of *Windeyer* and *Innes*, JJ., was
correct, and I quite concur in it, it would be strikingly strange
that in the Supreme Court *with* power of amendment, but *without*

(1) 14 N.S.W.L.R. 354 ; 10 W.N. 74.

1898.

Ex parte
GLASHEEN.

Cohen J.

power to amend in the manner adverted to, a prisoner would not be liable to conviction for an offence distinct from that laid against him, and yet in the inferior Courts, without any power of amendment, an accused person should be liable to be convicted upon a distinct charge not expressly preferred against him, when the evidence was sufficient to support that charge, but was insufficient to support that to which he had pleaded.

To my mind it would be virtually toying with justice, if a man called upon to answer one charge, and without being called upon in due course of law to answer another, could be convicted of that other because the evidence failed to support the one, but happened to justify a conviction upon the other. The traps and pitfalls that might be laid by spiteful or unscrupulous prosecutors to ensnare accused persons, were such a proceeding sanctioned, too readily suggest themselves, and indicate a grave and far-reaching danger. It is indeed requisite for public freedom, and essential to a healthy and trustful administration of justice, that the rule *audi alteram partem*, sacred by its age and its equity, should be actively and sedulously enforced in the unabated fulness of its wisdom and its fairness, and as to allow the present conviction to stand upon the ground I have thus lengthily discussed, would be to openly violate that rule, I am of opinion that the prohibition should be granted.

Rule absolute without costs.

Attorneys for the applicant : *Clayton & Pratt*, agents for *L. E. Serisier* (Bourke).

Attorney for the respondent : *G. E. Russell Jones*, agent for *Biddulph* (Bourke).

REGINA *v.* WALLACE (formerly CLEAVE).

1898.

April 28.

The C.J.
G. B. Simpson J
and
Cohen J.

Criminal law—Evidence—Dying declaration—Evidence of the commission of other crimes.

A dying declaration reduced into writing and signed is admissible in evidence.

On the trial of a prisoner for manslaughter, death being caused by the use of instruments for the purpose of procuring abortion, evidence that on a former occasion the prisoner had procured abortion on the deceased is admissible.

After a witness has been cross-examined by the counsel for the prisoner, the Judge may allow questions to be put to such witness by the Crown which do not arise out of such cross-examination.

CROWN CASE RESERVED.

SPECIAL CASE stated by *Rogers*, acting Supreme Court Judge: "The above-named accused was tried before me at the Central Criminal Court on the 3rd and 4th of March for manslaughter on the 7th of October last, it being alleged that the accused, by the use of certain instruments and appliances for the purpose of procuring miscarriage, had caused the death of a young girl called Mabel Lila Roberts.

The counsel for the Crown, Mr. *Gannon*, tendered in evidence a statement of the deceased made under the following circumstances. Mr. *William Bryce Simpson*, a Magistrate, was asked to go to the Balmain Cottage Hospital on the evening of the 16th of October last, and went there about 9 p.m. The following is a copy of my notes of his evidence. 'I saw a young woman since deceased called Mabel Lila Roberts She was in bed. I had some conversation with her. I administered an oath to her, and she gave me a statement which I wrote down. (Cross-examined at this stage by leave.) I did not question her. I don't think I questioned her at all. Sergeant Taylor may have asked her some questions which I put down. I don't think Sergeant Blackburn questioned her. It was not like the examination of a witness. I don't think Blackburn asked her one question. (Examination in chief continued). I remember obtaining from deceased a statement, and committing it to writing. She was dying. Her

mind was very clear. The accused came in when the statement
was about half finished.   This is the deceased's signature (looking
at statement).   At the conclusion of the first page, the deceased
got very bad, and I got her to sign at the foot of the first page.
She recovered after, and went on to make a further statement.
I put down word for word what she stated.   She got ill again.
I got her to sign again in the middle of the second page.   All I
had so far written I read over to her before she signed.   Mrs.
Cleave (the accused) had come in, and heard all I read from the
beginning.   The deceased again recovered and made a further
statement which I also took down.   That finished the statement
I then read all the statement over again from the beginning in
the hearing of the accused.   Deceased, when I read it over the
last time, said 'That's all true.'   Before deceased made any statement, she said in answer to my question, 'I know I am going to
die, for the doctor has told me so.'   When the statement was
read out as far as the second signature, and before it was signed,
I said to the accused, 'Have you any questions to ask?'   The
accused Cleave said, I believe, 'No! I never saw her in my life
before.   I was ill in bed all that day under Dr. Hall's attention.'
After this I saw her dead.   Cross-examined: I did not take this
as a deposition.   I have always spoken of it as a dying declaration.   I can distinguish between what was given in answer to
questions and what was given spontaneously.'

I admitted the statement, or rather dying declaration, in
evidence.

A witness named Alice White, who had, I understand, been
called by the police at an inquest held on the deceased girl,
Mabel Lila Roberts, was called by the counsel for the Crown and
sworn, but was not then examined by him.   She was cross-
examined by the counsel for the defence, and after such cross-
examination I gave the counsel for the Crown leave to ask her
questions which did not arise out of the cross-examination, at
the same time intimating that the counsel for the defence could
further cross-examine her if he so desired.

Mr. *Edmunds,* who appeared as counsel for the accused, asked
me to reserve the following points for the consideration of their

Honours the Judges of the Supreme Court which I have copied from a paper handed by him to me :—

1. That I was in error in admitting, in evidence for the prosecution, the document purporting to be the dying declaration of the deceased.

2. That I was in error in permitting the witness White to be questioned for the prosecution, such questions being after the cross-examination of the said witness by the counsel for the accused, and not relating to the matter of such cross-examination."

1898.

R.

v.

WALLACE (formerly CLEAVE).

DYING DECLARATION.

October 16th, 1897.

"I, Mabel Lila Roberts, will be twenty years of age upon the fourteenth day of April next. I know a person of the name of Mrs. Cleave, of number 10 High Holborn-street, Surry Hills. I went to see her upon last Thursday week, the seventh day of October instant. She is a tall, stout person of dark complexion, and stout, near her confinement. I went to see her upon last Thursday week to ask her to do me a favour. I asked her to treat me, as I was three months gone in the family way. She said, 'Yes, I will charge you three pounds.' I gave her that amount. She said, 'Good God, I think it little enough.' James Baker gave me the money, amounting to four pounds ten shillings ; he said, 'Will you take the responsibility upon your own shoulders ?" I here now identify James Baker just now brought before me as the person I have kept company with, and he is the father of my child, and it was he that gave me the four pounds ten shillings. I told him I was in trouble, and wanted the money to see a woman about it. Mrs. Cleave put a carved instrument up my person into my womb, when it was over she put another article up also, and afterwards gave me a draught. I know that I am about to die, as the doctor has informed me so, and what I state now is the absolute truth, and nothing but the truth.

Sworn on the above date before me   M. L. ROBERTS.

WILLIAM B. SIMPSON,
A Justice of the Peace.

October 16th, 1897.

Mabel Lila Roberts also states that I now identify Mrs. Cleave as the person who performed the operation upon me. I bear her no malice. I saw her thirteen months previously when she performed a similar operation upon me, and procured an abortion upon me for which I then paid her three pounds. I know her perfectly well, and she is the person who performed both operations upon me for abortion.

M. ROBERTS.

11.15 P.M.

And when Mr. Baker gave me the money in Darling-street, Balmain, I told him that I was going to have an abortion procured ; that was about a week before the abortion was procured. Emily Smith went with me to Mrs. Cleave's to have the operation performed. She lives in Goodsir-street, Balmain. She went into the same room in Mrs. Cleave's house as I did. She was present when the operation was performed. She went twice. She called one day, and was present when the

operation was performed. I now identify Emily Smith as the lady that was
with me when the operation was performed.

Sworn before me upon the above date,   M. ROBERTS."
                WILLIAM B. SIMPSON,
                     A Justice of the Peace.

Edmunds, for the petitioner. The Judge was in error in
admitting this document, which purported to be a dying declaration.

[THE CHIEF JUSTICE. Suppose the prisoner had not been
present, would not this have been a declaration under s. 344 of
the Criminal Law Amendment Act ?]

It was not a declaration under that section. Before such a
declaration is admissible, it must be in the form required and
certain conditions have to be complied with.

[*Wade*. It is not contended that it was admissible under that
section, but that it is admissible as a dying declaration at common
law.]

The person who took the declaration might have been called
to give evidence of what was said by the deceased, but the
document itself which contained the declaration was not
admissible. That very distinction is pointed out in *R.* v. *Solari*
(1).

[COHEN, J., referred to *R.* v. *Gay* (2), where *Coleridge*, J.,
refused to admit parol evidence, or a copy of a dying declaration
signed by the deceased.]

That case has been questioned. It is, however, based on the
assumption that the document itself was admissible. No point
was raised in that case as to the admissibility of the document if
it had been produced.

[G. B. SIMPSON, J. Secondary evidence was shut out because
the document was admissible.]

But the point was not taken that the document would have
been inadmissible.

[COHEN, J. Apart from the technical point, it seems to me
that it would be much better in the interests of justice, that the
declaration should be reduced into writing.]

(1) 12 N.S.W. L.R. 18.   (2) 7 C. & P. 230.

If it be reduced into writing, the formalities required by ss. 344 and 345 should be complied with. In *Russell on Crimes* (5th Ed., Vol. III. p. 360), he says, after referring to *R. v. Gay*, "But the decisions on this point are altogether unsatisfactory, for there is no authority by Act of Parliament, or otherwise, for taking a dying declaration in writing, and the words uttered by the deceased are just as much primary evidence as any writing in which they may be incorporated;" and see *Taylor on Evidence* 721. In *R. v. Solari* the statement made by the deceased was reduced into writing. *The Chief Justice* says, "I know of no principle which could make such a document admissible. What the woman said was of course admissible. The whole of the contents of this document could have been given orally by the person to whom the statement was made, and I am at a loss to know why that course was not adopted."

[THE CHIEF JUSTICE. That was not the case of a dying declaration.]

But it would have been admissible as such, if this document is.

[THE CHIEF JUSTICE. It was not tendered as a dying declaration.]

That case shews that where a statement is made, parol evidence of it can be given, though the document itself cannot be admitted.

[THE CHIEF JUSTICE. Why is it less a declaration because it is in writing? Suppose the case of a person who was unable to speak writing out a statement, would not that be admissible?]

That no doubt would be admissible, because it would be her own writing.

[THE CHIEF JUSTICE. It is the same as if it were her own writing, because she signed it.]

The mere signature can make no difference.

[THE CHIEF JUSTICE. Surely it makes all the difference, because it makes the declaration her own just as much as if she had written it herself.]

[COHEN, J., referred to *R. v. Woodcock* (1).]

(1) 1 Leach 500.

O 2

1898.

R.
v.
WALLACE
(formerly
CLEAVE).

1898.

R.
v.
WALLACE
(formerly
CLEAVE).

No objection was there taken to the document as a document. The question there raised was, whether the person who made the declaration apprehended that she was about to die.

[THE CHIEF JUSTICE. You admit that if a person writes out the declaration it would be admissible; where is the difference between that case and the case where the words are taken down by a third person, and then signed ?]

Where a statement is written out by a person herself, those are her very words. Where the statement is written out by some- body else, it is not an exact record of what takes place. It does not shew what questions were put to her. It only gives the substance of what she says, and does not give the questions and answers : *R. v. Mitchell* (1).

Secondly, this document was objectionable, in that it contained evidence which was not admissible, where she says that the prisoner had on a former occasion used an instrument upon her for the purpose of procuring abortion. *R. v. Makin* (2) is no authority for the admission of this evidence. In that case the evidence was admitted because the case for the Crown was con- sistent with the fact that the child might have died from natural causes. Such evidence was admitted to prove criminal agency. Here the question was—was the prisoner the person who used the instruments ?

[THE CHIEF JUSTICE. The defence might have been raised that the instrument was used for a lawful purpose.]

The case for the Crown here was that the prisoner had been asked to procure abortion, and did use the instrument for the purpose of procuring abortion. The only defence open to the prisoner was that she was not the woman who had done it. Where the facts proved by the Crown are consistent with the innocence, or guilt, of the accused, then this kind of evidence is admissible. But where the facts proved by the Crown are only consistent with the guilt of some person, and the question is who is that person, then this kind of evidence is not admissible.

[*Wade* referred to *R. v. Dale* (3).]

(1) 17 Cox 503.   (2) 14 N.S.W. L.R. 1, 548.
(3 16 Cox 703.

The second point taken was that the Judge should not have allowed the Crown Prosecutor to ask the witness White any questions which did not arise out of the cross-examination.

1898.

R.
v.
WALLACE
(formerly
CLEAVE).

[THE CHIEF JUSTICE. Surely you are not going to argue that point? That was a matter entirely for the discretion of the Judge.]

Here the witness was put in the box by the Crown, and not asked any questions; after she had been cross-examined the Judge should not have allowed questions to be put to her which did not arise out of the cross-examination: *Arch. Crim. Cas.* (19th Ed. 332): *R. v. Beezley* (1).

[G. B. SIMPSON, J. That case only shews that the questions cannot be asked without the leave of the Judge.]

Wade, for the Crown, was not called upon.

THE CHIEF JUSTICE. In this case the prisoner (a woman) was tried at the Central Criminal Court for manslaughter. It is alleged that she brought about the death of the deceased by the use of an instrument for the purpose of procuring a miscarriage. The deceased was seen by a Magistrate just before her death. It appears that she made a statement in the first person, and that it was taken down as she stated it by the Magistrate. After part of the statement had been made, she became very ill, and the Magistrate read it over to her, and she signed it. She slightly recovered and made a further statement, which the Magistrate read over to her, and got her to sign. She then made a further statement which he read over to her, and which she signed. The Magistrate then read the whole statement over to her. Deceased said, " That is all true." The objection has been taken (assuming on this part of the case that the evidence in the document is not objectionable) that, though the Magistrate might have given in evidence what the deceased said, the document itself was not admissible in evidence. The first case cited in support of that proposition was *R. v. Solari* (2). That was quite a different case. That was not the case of a dying declaration. The declaration there was made some three weeks before the death of the person in question. It was not shewn in that case that the woman was

(1) 4 C. & P. 220.   (2) 12 N.S.W. L.R. 18; 7 W.N. 102.

dying when she made the declaration. The elements to make it a dying declaration were absent, and it was not a declaration made under the provisions of the Criminal Law Amendment Act. It was, therefore, held inadmissible.

Then it was contended that this point had never been decided, and that although in the case of *R. v. Gay* (1), *Coleridge,* J., held that parol evidence was not admissible because the statement had been reduced to writing, it was not there decided that the declaration itself would have been admissible, but the earlier cases shew that, if the declaration had been tendered, it would have been admissible; and, therefore, the parol evidence of it was inadmissible. In the case of *R. v. Woodcock* (2), a document was tendered as a deposition made under the statute, but it was not admissible as a deposition. It was there held, however, that, as it was a declaration signed by the deceased when she was aware that she was dying, it was admissible as a dying declaration. In that case *Eyre,* C.B., says, " Although we must strip this examination of the sanction to which it would have been entitled if it had been taken pursuant to the directions of the Legislature; yet still it is the declaration of the deceased, signed by herself, and it may be classed with all those other confirmatory declarations which she made after she had received the mortal wounds, and before she died. Now the general principle on which this species of evidence is admitted is, that they are declarations made in extremity when the party is at the point of death, and when every hope of this world is gone; when every motive to falsehood is silenced, and the mind is induced by the most powerful considerations to speak the truth, a situation so solemn and so awful, is considered by the law as creating an obligation equal to that which is imposed by a positive oath administered in a Court of justice." Accordingly the declaration was received in evidence. The prisoner was found guilty and executed. That case followed *Trowter's Case,* which is referred to in *Viner's Abridgment.* I am, therefore, clearly of opinion, both on authority and on principle, that this document was admissible in evidence. It is just as much admissible as if, having been deprived of speech, she had written out the document herself. In such a case Mr.

(1) 7 C. & P. 230.   (2) 1 Leach 500.

1898.

R.
v.
WALLACE
(formerly
CLEAVE).

The C.J.

Edmunds admitted that it would be admissible. She knew that she was dying, and she knew that what she said was being taken down, and it was afterwards read over to her, and she signed it, and it was, therefore, just the same as if she had herself written out the document.

Then Mr. *Edmunds* has taken another point. He contends that, even if the document was not inadmissible on that ground, a certain portion of the document was not admissible, and that the jury ought to have been told that, whilst the first and third portions of the document were admissible, they should not consider the second portion. That objection does not appear to have been taken. The objection taken was as to the document as a whole. However, I am of opinion that the objection now raised to that part cannot be sustained. This is the statement objected to—" I now identify Mrs. Cleave as the person who performed the operation upon me. I bear her no malice. I saw her thirteen months previously when she performed a similar operation on me, and procured an abortion upon me for which I then paid her three pounds. I know her perfectly well, and she is the person who performed both operations upon me for abortion."

Mr. *Edmunds* contends that this statement relating to a former offence ought not to have been before the jury, because it has no relevancy to the matter which the jury were then trying, and it was as if this woman was being tried for this former offence. When I first heard the evidence read, it struck me that it was admissible on the authority of the case of *R.* v. *Makin* (1), and having heard the argument on the point, I am still of the same opinion. If this woman had recovered from the operation, she might have given evidence in respect to this former operation in order to anticipate the case which the prisoner might very naturally have set up that she had used this instrument for a natural purpose. She might have raised the defence that this young woman had come to her to consult her for some complaint, and believing what she told her that she had used this instrument for an innocent and natural purpose. If the Crown could shew that this young woman had been to the prisoner before, and that she had previously procured abortion, what stronger evidence

(1) 14 N.S.W. L.R. 1, 548 ; 9 W.N. 129 ; 10 W.N. 134.

could the Crown produce to anticipate the case which might be made by the prisoner ? In the case of *R.* v. *Dale* (1), the very same evidence was admitted, and that is a stronger case than this, because there the evidence of previously procuring abortion related to another woman. All the cases on the question of the admission of evidence of this kind are very fully gone into in *R.* v. *Makin.* Mr. Justice *Windeyer*, after referring to them, says : " All these cases go to shew that, though the evidence of other crimes was in the earlier cases only admitted on the narrower ground of merely rebutting the defence of accident, in the later cases the tendency has been to allow evidence of other cases to be admitted if they are connected with the transaction in question in such a manner as to throw light upon it by shewing that the criminal agent in the one case was the criminal agent in the other." He then quotes from the judgment of Lord *Coleridge* in *Blake* v. *Albion Life Assurance Society* (2), where he says, "' With a few exceptions on the ground of public policy, the law now is, that all which can throw light on the disputed transaction is admittted, not of course matters of mere prejudice, nor anything open to real moral or sensible objection, but all things which fairly throw light on the case, and,' to apply his further words to this case, ' in any but an English Court and to the mind of any but an English lawyer, the controversy whether this evidence is or is not evidence which a Court of justice should receive, would seem, I think, supremely ridiculous, because everyone would say that the evidence was most cogent and material.' " That case was upheld on appeal to the Privy Council, and in the judgment given by the *Lord Chancellor* he says that the evidence is admissible to rebut a defence which would be otherwise open to the accused.

Another point has been taken to which it is scarcely necessary to refer, and which was not very seriously argued. The point is that the Judge was in error in allowing a Crown witness to be questioned for the prosecution after the witness had been cross-examined, the questions not relating to the matter of such cross-examination. That was a matter clearly for the discretion of the Judge. I think that the Judge was perfectly right in the course

(1) 16 Cox 703.   (2) 4 C.P.D. 109.

which he adopted, seeing that he reserved to the counsel for the prisoner the right to cross-examine the witness upon any of those questions.

The conviction must be sustained.

G. B. SIMPSON, J., and COHEN, J., concurred.

Conviction sustained.

Attorney for the prisoner : *J. A. Doyle.*

1898.

R.
v.
WALLACE
(formerly
CLEAVE).

The C.J.

REGINA v. CULGAN.

1898.

April 28.

The C.J.
G. B. Simpson J.
and
Cohen J.

Criminal law—Indecent assault—Evidence—Direction of Judge—·Point appearing in case stated, though not taken in the Court below.

An assault committed with an indecent motive is not an indecent assault.

The prisoner used indecent language to a woman and shortly afterwards assaulted her. *Held* (*per* THE CHIEF JUSTICE and G. B. SIMPSON, J.), not an indecent assault.

Quære (*per* COHEN, J.), whether an assault accompanied with indecent language is not an indecent assault?

A point not taken in the Court below, if it appear in the case stated, can be entertained by the Full Court.

CROWN CASE RESERVED.

SPECIAL CASE stated by *Rogers*, D. C. J.: " This prisoner was tried before me at the last Gundagai General Sessions. The information contained two counts—1. Assault with intent to commit a rape on one Mary Rae. 2. Indecent assault on the said Mary Rae.

The evidence shewed that Mrs. Rae was a married woman living with her husband in a tent on a river flat near Gundagai, and that on the afternoon of the 18th of November last, the prisoner, knowing that Mrs. Rae's husband had gone to town, went to the door of her tent and said to her, ' I've come to go with you.' She was lying down at the time, but she got up, rushed out of the tent, and said to prisoner, ' Go away, like a good man, and don't insult an old woman old enough to be your grandmother.' The prisoner caught hold of her by the shoulder and dragged her along, saying, ' It's no use your singing out, as your husband is away in town;' he then caught her by the hair and tried to drag her towards the river. She made all the resistance she could, and eventually assistance came, and the prisoner was compelled to let her go.

The prisoner was found guilty on the second count only. At the close of the Crown case, Mr. *Griffin*, the prisoner's solicitor, asked me to withdraw the second count from the jury on the ground that there was no evidence of *indecent* assault.

I declined to do so, and told the jury that if, looking at all the circumstances, they came to the conclusion that the assault was committed with an indecent motive, the second count would be sustained.

The question (reserved at Mr. *Griffin's* request) for the consideration of their Honours the Judges of the Supreme Court is, whether I was right?"

There was no appearance for the prisoner.

H. Harris, for the Crown.

[THE CHIEF JUSTICE. To constitute an indecent assault, must not the assault be of an indecent nature?]

Archbold at p. 770 says that to prove an indecent assault you must prove an assault "accompanied with circumstances of indecency."

[THE CHIEF JUSTICE. The Judge seems to have told the jury that though the assault was not accompanied with indecent acts, it was an indecent assault if it was made with an indecent motive.]

The Judge was not asked to withdraw the case from the jury on the first count, and so it was admitted that there was some evidence to go to the jury on that count, that is that there was some evidence of an assault with intent to commit a rape, and yet it was contended that there was no evidence of an indecent assault. If there was evidence of an assault with intent to commit a rape, surely there was evidence to support a count for an indecent assault.

[THE CHIEF JUSTICE. I gather from what the Judge says that there was no act of indecency. He seems to have thought that it was an indecent assault if made with an indecent motive.]

There was some evidence of indecent acts, and therefore it would be better if the case were referred back to the Judge to state exactly what the evidence was.

1898.
———
R.
v.
CULGAN.

[THE CHIEF JUSTICE. If the Judge's summing up was wrong, what use would there be in referring the case back to him ?]

No objection was taken to the Judge's summing up.

[THE CHIEF JUSTICE. I think there are cases which shew that where the Court sees on the case stated there has been a manifest defect, although the point is not taken, the Court will not allow the conviction to stand.*]

The Judge has only given a small part of his summing up. It would be better for the case to go back so that he could set out exactly what his direction was.

[G. B. SIMPSON, J. I am inclined to think that the Judge should have withdrawn the case from the jury. Where is there any evidence of circumstances of indecency ?]

The prisoner went into this woman's tent when she was lying down and said, " I have come to go with you." Surely that was a circumstance of indecency ? Indecency is defined as something offensive to modesty and delicacy.

THE CHIEF JUSTICE. In this case the prisoner was indicted on two counts. The first count charged him with an assault with intent to commit a rape, and the second with an indecent assault. The prisoner was convicted on the second count. [His Honour referred to the evidence in the special case] There do not appear to be any circumstances of indecency connected with the assault. At the close of the Crown case the prisoner's advocate asked the Judge to withdraw the second count from the jury. His Honour refused, and in summing up told the jury that if, looking at all the circumstances, they came to the conclusion that the assault was committed with an indecent motive it was an indecent assault. That was a wrong direction. The conviction must be quashed.

G. B. SIMPSON, J. I agree.

COHEN, J. As far as the direction given by *Rogers*, D.C.J., to the jury is concerned, I am of the same opinion. I am, however,

* See on this point *R.* v. *O'Keefe* (10 W.N. at p. 74), *R.* v. *Dean* (17 N.S.W.L.R., at p. 39), *R.* v. *Powell* (13 W.N. 44).

not prepared to say that there were no circumstances of indecency connected with the assault. I do not give a definite opinion on this point. Indecent words accompanying an assault might constitute an indecent assault. The words used in this case prior to the assault suggested indecency. I only wish to point that out without saying that I dissent.

Conviction quashed.

POTTER *v.* THOMAS.

1898.

April 29.
May 2.

The C.J.
Stephen J.
and
Cohen J.

Gaming and wagering—Betting Houses Suppression Act (39 *Vic. No.* 28), *s.* 3—
" *Place.*"

The appellant used, for the purpose of betting with persons who resorted thereto, a lane, or private right of way, opening from a street, and from which there was access to certain bookmakers' shops, which fronted an adjoining street. *Held,* that the lane was a " place " within the meaning of s. 3 of the Betting Houses Suppression Act.

SPECIAL CASE STATED UNDER THE JUSTICES' APPEAL ACT.

The information alleged that on the 14th July, one John Thomas "did use a certain place, to wit, a right of way off Market-street, giving access to premises No. 241 Pitt-street, Sydney . . . . for the purpose of money being received by him as or for the consideration for the promise to give thereafter certain money on a contingency relating to certain horse races, called the 'Flying Handicap' and 'Rosehill Handicap,' thereafter to be run at the Rosehill racecourse," etc.

On this information Thomas, the appellant, was convicted before *Isaacs,* S.M., and ordered to pay the sum of 25*l.*

From the evidence it appeared that the appellant was in a lane making bets with people. The lane led from Market-street to shops fronting Pitt-street on one side, and stores on the other. At the end of the lane opening into Market-street were gates. which were closed at night. The appellant was standing just outside No. 241 Pitt-street, in which there were posted up lists shewing the odds that could be obtained against certain horses for certain races. There were about 100 people in the lane. The appellant was seen on three occasions on the same day betting with people.

It was contended on behalf of Thomas that the place referred to in the information and evidence was not a place within the meaning of the Betting Houses Suppression Act. The Magistrate held that it was, and convicted the defendant. The ques-

1898.

POTTER
v.
THOMAS.

tion for the opinion of the Court was, whether the Magistrate's determination was erroneous in point of law.

The Court previously held in *Potter* v. *Moss* (1) that this very lane was a " place " within the meaning of the Act. ·

Heydon, Q.C., and *G. H. Simpson*, for the appellant. This case raises exactly the same point as was raised in *Potter* v. *Moss*. That case was, however, decided on the authority of *Hawke* v. *Dunn* (2), which has since been overruled by *Powell* v. *Kempton Park Racecourse Co.* (3).

The question to be determined in this case is whether this lane was used by the appellant as if it were his house, office, or room, and that depends upon whether he had, or claimed to have, any right peculiar to himself, and exclusive of the rights of other persons (see judgment of Lord *Esher* at p. 257). He had no more right to any particular spot in this lane than he would have to a .part of any public street. He had merely a right of way over this lane, and had no right to prevent any other person from using that lane.

[THE CHIEF JUSTICE. It seems to me that the question we have to determine is the first question stated by Lord *Esher*, "Is such an enclosure such a place as can come within the meaning of the statute ?"]

We submit not. The question is not whether the lane can be a " place "; but whether it was used as a place.

[THE CHIEF JUSTICE. Was not that a question of fact to be determined by the Magistrate ?]

The question whether the appellant used this lane as if it were a " house, room or office " is a question of law. It is the user that makes it a " place " and not the mere description of it. In the *Kempton Park Case* Lord *Esher* held that the inclosure was capable of being a " place," but that used in the way in which it was, it was not a place. ·   ·

They also referred to *Gleeson* v. *Adams* (4); *Davis* v. *Stephenson* (5); *Bradford* v. *Dawson* (6).

(1) 18 N.S.W.L.R. 165 ; 13 W.N. 206.   (4) 15 Aust. L.T. 250 ; 20 V.L.R. 229.
(2) [1897] 1 Q.B. 579.   (5) 24 Q.B.D. 529.
(3) [1897] 2 Q.B. 242.   (6) [1897] 1 Q.B 307.

1898.

POTTER
v.
THOMAS.

Sir *Julian Salomons*, Q.C., and *J. L. Campbell*, for the respondent. We submit that there was evidence here which justified
the finding of the Magistrate, that this lane was a "place." If
that be so, then it follows that the Court cannot disturb the finding of the Magistrate any more than it could disturb the verdict
of the jury in a civil case.

[THE CHIEF JUSTICE. The Magistrate is in a stronger position,
because, if the finding of the jury is demonstrably wrong, we can
upset it, but the Court cannot interfere with the finding of the
Magistrate on the ground that he was wrong on the facts. On
an appeal under the Justices Appeal Act the only point we have
to consider is whether he was wrong as a matter of law.]

The distinction between this case and the *Kempton Park Case*
is that this lane was a private right of way, to which the public
had not access. Suppose two persons have a right of way leading to their houses, and one of them used it for the purpose of
betting, it would be a place. If that be so it can make no difference that a number of people had a right of way over this lane.
If this lane was capable of being a place, the Court cannot say
that the Magistrate was wrong in holding that it was a place.
In the *Kempton Park Case* there were certain facts admitted,
and it is on those facts that the judgment proceeds. One of
those facts was that the bookmakers were admitted to the
inclosure as members of the general public, and that they had no
rights, interests, or control in or over the enclosure (see p. 245).
Here the appellant had a right over this lane. It was a private
right of way, and only open to a certain class of persons. The
admitted facts in the *Kempton Park Case* made it impossible
for the Court to hold it was a "place." The preamble of the
English Act says, "Whereas a kind of gaming has of late sprung
up by the opening of places called betting houses . . ." That
shews the kind of betting aimed at, and yet in the statement of
facts it was admitted that this form of betting had been openly
and habitually carried on since the beginning of the century. In
that case it was admitted that the bookmakers only had a right
to enter the enclosure as members of the public, and had no right
peculiar to themselves. In this case this man had a right
peculiar to himself over this lane.

1898.

POTTER
v.
THOMAS.

[COHEN, J. (after referring to Lord *Esher's* judgment at p. 258). Assuming that the appellant had a right of way, what right would he have to exclude other persons from the lane ?]

This was a private right of way. The appellant and the other persons in whom the right was vested could have excluded any person who had not such a right from using this lane.

[STEPHEN, J. Did you ever hear of a person who had a right of way bringing an action against another person for using the right of way ?

THE CHIEF JUSTICE. The argument based on that passage in Lord *Esher's* judgment does not arise here, because the question is whether this lane is capable of being a " place."]

In *Liddell* v. *Lofthouse* (1) the respondent had no right at all to be on the land where he was betting, and yet it was held a "place." The question whether a man has a right to be in the "place" does not make any difference: *McInaney* v. *Hildreth* (2). The case of *R.* v. *Preedy* (3) shews that the decision of Sir James Martin in *Waters* v. *Cox* was based on a misconception of *Doggett* v. *Catterns* (4).

Heydon, Q.C., in reply. The case of *Potter* v. *Moss* was decided on *Hawke* v. *Dunn*, which was expressly overruled in the *Kempton Park Case*. That case really reviews all the previous authorities. It is useless to refer to cases like *R.* v. *Preedy* and *McInaney* v. *Hildreth*, which are decisions of *Hawkins*, J., when his view of the Act has been expressly dissented from by the Court of Appeal. The appellant here was charged with using a right of way for the purpose of betting. Now whether that was a "place" or not does not depend upon its physical character. It is the use of the place that makes it a place within the meaning of the Act.

[THE CHIEF JUSTICE. The question is, whether it was a defined place ?]

That cannot be regarded as the test, because in the *Kempton Park Case* the enclosure was clearly a defined place. The

(1) [1896] 1 Q.B. 295.　　　　(3) 17 Cox 433.
(2) [1897] 1 Q.B. 600.　　　　(4) 19 C.B.N.S. 765.

question, whether it is a "place" or not, depends upon the manner in which it is used, that is to say, is it used as if it were a "house, room or office?" Suppose two clerks coming out of one of these warehouses into this lane were to make a bet, it clearly would not be a "place."

In Lord *Esher's* judgment, p. 255, he says, in considering whether the enclosure was a place that you first have to consider, "Is such an enclosure such a place as can come within the meaning of the statute." And he held that it was, but he held that, though it might be a "place," still seeing the way it was used, it was not a "place." At p. 258, he points out the fallacy of *Hawke* v. *Dunn* (1); he says: "Their judgment is open to this criticism, that according to it if a bookmaker makes what the judgment calls a ready money bet in a place, which it is possible to use so as to make it a prohibited place within the statute, the mere fact of his so doing makes it a prohibited place." Before you can say that a particular spot is a "place," you have got to see how it is used. At p. 276, *Smith,* L.J., points out that it is the user which makes it a "place," and again at p. 281. And at p. 302, *Chitty,* L.J., says: "The question is, whether they use the enclosure as a betting-house, room or office? . . . I think they do not." To get rid of that case it has been contended that the appellant had a right of way over this lane. In the first place, there is nothing in the special case to shew that he had; and secondly, even if he had it would give him no exclusive right of user.

[COHEN, J. Suppose six bookmakers had the right to use the lane, would not the user by one of them for the purpose of betting be using it as a "place"? would he not have a right of user peculiar to himself?]

Giving a person a right of way does not give him the right to exclude other persons from the land. The question is not whether he had the right to use it, but did he use it as if it were his room or office? Did he claim to use, or did he use this lane or part of it exclusively as against anyone else? It is quite clear he did not, and, therefore, his user did not make it a "place."

In *Liddell* v. *Lofthouse* (2), the respondent appropriated a piece of ground for the purpose of carrying on the business of betting,

(1) [1897] 1 Q.B. 579.   (2) [1896] 1 Q.B. 295.

and, therefore, was rightly held to be using a "place." That case has no application to the present case.

1898.
POTTER
v.
THOMAS.

THE CHIEF JUSTICE. If I felt any doubt about this case, I should take time to consider my judgment, but the matter seems to me to be clear beyond all question. I think the conviction was right, and that the appeal should be dismissed. In my opinion the case does not fall within the decision of *Powell* v. *Kempton Park Racecourse Co.* (1).

The section under consideration is s. 3 of the Betting Houses Suppression Act, which provides that "any person who shall open, keep, or use any house, office, room, or other place for the purposes aforesaid . . . shall on summary conviction be liable," etc. "For the purposes aforesaid" mean for the purpose of betting as defined in s. 1. Now the difficulty in the construction of this section arises from the fact that the word "place" is not defined in the Act; and yet it could not be defined. It is far better that it should be left exactly as it is. It is clear that the words "other place" must mean something *ejusdem generis* with "house, room or office," and yet they must refer to something different, otherwise there would be no use introducing those words into the section. In what respect is the word "place" to be *ejusdem generis* with "house, room or office"? Inasmuch as a "house, room or office" is a defined place, so must the "place" be a defined place, to which the public may go, knowing that if they go there they will find a person ready to bet with them. Once you arrive at the conclusion that the word "place" must be read *ejusdem generis* with the words "house, room or office" in the sense that it must be a defined place, then each case must be determined on its own facts.

Now, what are the facts in this case? It appears from the evidence before the Magistrate that there is a private lane opening out of Market-street. There are gates to it, which are open during the day, but are closed at night to vehicles, though persons can get in through a wicket gate. The lane at first is twelve feet wide, but gets wider as you proceed from Market-street.

(1) [1897] 2 Q.B. 242.

P 2

Here there are five houses, three of which, at the time of the prosecution, were used by betting men. These houses front Pitt-street, the backs of the houses opening into the lane. On the other side there are certain stores, open during the daytime. It appears that on three occasions on one day a sergeant of police went to this lane, and on each occasion found the appellant betting there outside the door of No. 241 Pitt-street, which was his house. He was standing about 2 feet from his door. There was also another man in the lane, standing near his own door, betting in the same way. They had at night electric lamps over their heads, and their clerks were recording the bets as they were made. Looking at all these circumstances, and that it was habitually used for this purpose, there can be no doubt that this was a "place" within the meaning of s. 3 of the Betting Act. In *Powell* v. *Kempton Park Racecourse Co.* (1), there was an enclosure of a quarter of an acre on a racecourse, to which, when race meetings were held, the public were admitted on payment, among them being a number of bookmakers, who laid wagers with any of the public who desired to bet. That enclosure used in such a manner was there held not to be a "place" within the Act. In so holding the Court upheld the opinion of Sir *James Martin* in *Waters* v. *Cox* (2). In that case it was held that the St. Leger enclosure at Randwick, which was used for the purpose of betting, was not a "place" within the meaning of the Act. That case, though properly decided, seems to have been decided on a mis-conception of the case of *Doggett* v. *Catterns* (3). In the latter case a man went under a tree in Hyde Park, and made bets there. He was not prosecuted under s. 3 of the Act. If he had been, and had been convicted under that section, the conviction would have been right. It was a civil action brought against the man to recover money which had been paid to him by way of a wager. It was a decision under ss. 4 and 5 of the Act, and turned on the question that the place was not capable of occupation. That is clearly pointed out in the case of *Liddell* v. *Lofthouse* (4). There-fore, so far as the judgment in *Waters* v. *Cox* (2) proceeded upon that case, it was a mistake. This was not a case of that kind,

(1) [1897] 2 Q.B. 242.   (3) 17 C.B.N.S. 669.
(2) 6 N.S.W.L.R. 113   (4) [1896] 1 Q.B. 295.

for here the place could be easily defined. Suppose a stranger to
Sydney were to ask where he could find a person with whom he
could bet, he would be told, "if you go to this lane, you will find
a bookmaker ready to bet with you." There would be a defined
place just as much as a house, room or office is a defined place.
What Mr. *Heydon* says is quite true, that if two clerks coming
out of a warehouse into this lane made a bet, it would not be a
place so far as they were concerned, but, nevertheless, it is a
"place" so far as the bookmakers are concerned who use it, just
as they would use a house, office or room for the purpose of
carrying on their business of betting.

The *Kempton Park Case* should be carefully considered to see
what it really decides. That was not a case under s. 3 of the
Betting Act. It was an application for an injunction in equity
by a shareholder of the company to restrain the company from
allowing betting on the racecourse. The Court there held that
the injunction could not be granted. That case, when examined,
shews that each case must depend very much upon its own facts.
Lord *Esher* says, at p. 257 : "It seems to me that the place must
be a place used for betting, which can, for the purpose of betting,
be not unreasonably deemed to be a place of the same kind as a
house, office or room used for the purpose of betting. It need
not be a building built like a house, room or office; it need not
be a covered place; it need not be railed off, or boarded off, so as
to prevent physical access to it except through a particular part
of the railing or boarding ; but it must be a defined space capable
from its condition of being used by a person who desires so to
use it as if it were his house, room or office, used by him as such
for his betting business." Can there be the slightest doubt that
the appellant was using this lane for his betting business? Here
were three houses used by three men, who knew that if they
used the rooms for betting they could be prosecuted under the
Act. So they say, "We have this right of way ; we can't go and
use the street, because we might be treated as vagrants ; but this
lane is not a street, and we will go into this lane, just outside
our doors, and use it as a betting place." Can there be the
slightest doubt that the appellant was carrying on his business
of betting in this lane, and that he was using it (adopting the

1898.

POTTER
v.
THOMAS.

The C.J.

language of Lord *Esher*) " as if it were his house, room or office "?
And further on in his judgment Lord *Esher* says, at p. 258 : " As
matter of law, there is no legal evidence to bring it within the
statute. If any other circumstance is added and relied upon in
any other case, the whole case must then be considered subject
to the rule I have laid down."   Well, here there are circumstances
which clearly distinguish this case from *Waters* v. *Cox* (1) and
the *Kempton Park Case.*

   This case is governed by *Liddell* v. *Lofthouse* (2) and *McInaney*
v. *Hildreth* (3).   In the former case the respondent was charged
with using a certain piece of ground, which was bounded on one
side by a hoarding, and on two other sides by stays supporting
the hoarding.   The Justices held that this was not a place.   The
Court there, consisting of *Lindley*, L.J., and *Kay*, L.J., held that
the decision of the Justices was wrong.   *Lindley*, L.J., says,
" As has been said, the Act is directed not against betting itself,
but against bookmakers and those who make a trade of betting.
We are asked whether the respondent, in what he did, 'was
using a place for the purpose of betting with persons resorting
thereto.'   I am of opinion that he was, and, therefore, that he
ought to have been convicted.   Then it is said that the place was
not sufficiently defined in the information.   I do not think that
that point is left to us by the case, but if it is I am of opinion
that the place was sufficiently defined for all purposes.   As to its
being partly undefined, I think that there are many places which,
though in some sense undefined, can yet be described with
sufficient clearness for the purpose of identification.   I have no
doubt that this appeal ought to be allowed."   And *Kay*, L.J.,
says : " It is contended that the place was not sufficiently defined
in the information.   I cannot find anything in the Act requiring
the place to be defined by metes and bounds.   In my opinion,
the fact that the expression is not defined in the Act shews that
it was intended that Justices should have a discretion to say
whether the ground in question was 'a place' or not.   As it
seems to me, if a man were to use the ground at the foot of the
statue at Charing Cross for the purpose of habitually betting

(1) 6 N.S.W. L.R. 113.   (2) [1896] 1 Q.B. 295.
                    (3) [1897] 1 Q.B. 600.

with persons resorting to him there, that, although the space used was entirely undefined, would be 'a place' within the meaning of the statute." That case was approved of in the *Kempton Park Case* (1). In *McInaney* v. *Hildreth* (2) the appellant was charged with using a certain place called "The Pit Heap" for the purpose of betting with persons resorting thereto. The Pit Heap was a piece of ground about ⅛-acre, bounded by various buildings and hoardings, and a row of posts and a road. The Justices found that the spot where the appellant stood was a "place," and on appeal five Judges held that the Justices were right. If that was a "place," how can it possibly be contended that this lane was not a "place" within the meaning of the Act?

For these reasons I think that the decision of the Magistrate was right, and that the decision of this Court in *Potter* v. *Moss* (3) was also right. That case was decided, not only on the authority of *Hawke* v. *Dunn*, but also on the authority of *Liddell* v. *Lofthouse* (4).

I am also of opinion that *Ex parte Westbrook* (5) was rightly decided. In that case it appeared that Westbrook occupied a piece of ground under a particular tree in the saddling paddock at Randwick racecourse, and there carried on his business of betting.

The appeal must be dismissed with costs.

STEPHEN, J. I agree, though not without some doubt, for I think that this is just one of those cases in which a Judge might be justified in expressing his opinion with some hesitation, because there has been extreme difference of opinion amongst Judges on this very point. The words in s. 3 of the Betting Act are, "any person who shall open, keep, or use any house, office, room, *or other place* for the purposes aforesaid," etc. I cannot see, if you were to exclude a lane of this kind from the operation of the Act, how you could ever give any meaning to the words "or other place," and the Act would be perfectly useless, unless the person charged was found betting in a "house, office, or room." We have not now to determine whether, in our opinion, the

(1) [1897] 2 Q.B. 242.   (3) 18 N.S.W. L.R. 165.
(2) [1897] 1 Q.B. 600.   (4) [1896] 1 Q.B. 295.
(5) 18 N.S.W.L.R. 169; 13 W.N 207.

1898.

POTTER
v.
THOMAS.

Stephen J.

Magistrate was wrong, as a matter of fact, when he found that
this lane was a "place"; but what we have to determine is
whether he was wrong as a matter of law [see judgment of
Lindley, L.J., in *Powell* v. *Kempton Park Racecourse Co.* (1).]
It seems to me that we might base our decision on that lower
ground.

Another ground I take is this. This Court has already decided
this very point in *Potter* v. *Moss*, and I should not think of overruling that decision unless bound to do so by reason of some
English case on all fours with it. *The Chief Justice* has already
pointed out why the *Kempton Park Case* is not so, and until I
see a case which overrules *Potter* v. *Moss* I shall maintain that
decision.

I quite agree with Mr. *Heydon* when he says that " if I went
into this lane, and saw no one there, I could not say that it was
a 'place' within the meaning of the Act," and with him I agree
that it can only be made so by user. If a person makes bets
there, and is guilty of the conduct described in the special case,
how could it, in common sense, be said that he was not using a
place for the purpose of betting?

The Magistrate seems to have decided that the appellant,
without appropriating any particular spot in the lane, was using
this lane as a place. It does not follow that a person may not be
rightly said to use a given area as a place for betting, though
while doing so he may only have stood on a particular portion
of it. So the lane may be said to have been used, although the
appellant transacted his business only on one portion, immediately in front of his own door.

If this lane had been a public place, then I must say that I
think our decision would be governed by the *Kempton Park
Case*, the lane being similar in that respect to a racecourse. This
lane was a defined place. It was enclosed on two sides by houses,
and there was a gate at the end of it. The appellant had a right
to use this lane as a private right of way, and availed himself of
it. This, in my opinion, constitutes a material distinction.

I give my decision very much on the ground that the appellant had a right of way, and had that right as against the whole,

(1) [1897] 2 Q.B. at p. 263.

public, except as against persons who had an equal right with
himself [see the remarks of Lord *Esher* in *Powell* v. *Kempton
Park Racecourse Co* (1).]

For these reasons I cannot say that the Magistrate was wrong,
and I therefore think that the conviction should be sustained.

COHEN, J. I am of the same opinion. As to what is a place,
as far as the principle of law underlying the cases of *Hawks* v.
Dunn (2) and *Powell* v. *Kempton Park Racecourse Co.* (3) is
concerned, there is no difference. The difference of opinion in
those two cases seems to have arisen from the application of the
principles as to its being "used" as a place to the different sets of
facts in each. In the former case at p. 598 Mr. Justice *Hawkins*
says : "It is not possible to give so precise a definition of what
is an 'other place' as shall be applicable to every imaginable state
of facts. Each case must of necessity depend and be decided
upon its own particular circumstances. But after very careful
consideration, I have arrived at the conclusion that any area of
enclosed ground (expressing no opinion as to unenclosed areas),
covered or uncovered, which is known by a name, or is capable
of reasonably accurate description, to which persons from time to
time, or upon any particular occasions or occasion resort, and
who may very properly be described as resorting thereto, used
by a professional betting man for the purpose of exercising his
calling, and betting with such persons, or for the purpose of
carrying on a ready money betting business, may be a place
within the meaning of the statute. Metes and bounds are not
essential, and it matters not, in my opinion, whether for his own
convenience the bookmaker chooses to remain during his hours
of attendance, upon one particular spot within that area, or
whether he prefers to move about within that area from one spot
to another, as he is minded. The Act speaks of an other 'place,'
not a 'spot' in a place. If, to make it a place, the bookmaker
must fix himself on and use only one spot, he would always have
it in his power to evade the Act by wandering over the whole
area." If you read the judgment of Lord *Esher* in the *Kempton*

(1) [1996] 2 Q.B. at p. 257.   (2) [1897] 1 Q.B. 579.
                     (3) [1897] 2 Q.B. 242.

Park Case at p. 257, you find that he lays down substantially the same principles. It appears that the appellant occupies a house in Pitt-street, and that at the back of this house there is a lane opening into Market-street, and that at the end of the lane there are gates, which are shut at night. Here then is an enclosed and defined place. If he had conducted the business of betting in the house itself, he would of course have come within the Act; but he appears to have been standing in this lane, near the door of his house, and to have been betting there. There was another person also standing in the lane making bets, and there were about one hundred other persons there for the purpose of betting, who evidently knew that by so resorting they could take part in the business of betting with the appellant; was it not then a fair inference for the Magistrate to draw that the appellant was using a "place" for the purpose of betting? It seems to me that when you take all these circumstances into consideration, there cannot be any doubt. If the appellant had used the back yard of his house, I do not suppose that anyone would contend that it was not a "place," and if, instead of doing that, he goes out of the yard into the adjoining lane, enclosed as it was, and over which he has a right of way—a right peculiar to himself—I cannot see why in all justice and common sense it could be said that he was not using a "place" for the purpose of betting. The case of *Liddell* v. *Lofthouse* was expressly approved by *Smith*, L.J., in the *Kempton Park Case*, and it may perhaps be assumed that the other Lords Justice who took part in that judgment by their silence acquiesced in it, and it was also approved by all the Judges who decided *Hawke* v. *Dunn*, for the judgment delivered in it by *Hawkins*, J., was the judgment of the Court. The case now before us is a stronger case for a conviction than *Liddell* v. *Lofthouse*. There the person using the place had not a shadow of right to it, whereas in this case the appellant was using a place over which he had a right of way. I have no difficulty in coming to the conclusion that this conviction should be upheld.

Appeal dismissed with costs.[*]

Attorney for the appellant: *T. M. Slattery.*

[*] [See *R.* v. *Humphrey*, (1898) 1 Q.B. 875, decided 2nd April, 1898.]

THE COMMISSIONERS OF TAXATION *v.* ST. JOSEPH'S INVESTMENT
AND BUILDING SOCIETY

1898.

August 5.

The C.J.
Manning J.
and
A.H. Simpson J.

Land & Income Tax Assessment Act, 1895, *s.* 10—*Mortgagee in possession—Aggregate value of several parcels—Bare trustee—Mortgagor and mortgagee.*

The respondent society were the mortgagees in possession of a large number of parcels of land mortgaged to them by different mortgagors. *Held,* that the society, being mortgagee in possession and not a bare trustee of different estates for the benefit of different *cestuis que trustent,* was only entitled to one deduction upon the aggregate value of all the said parcels of land.

SPECIAL CASE stated by the Court of Review under the Land and Income Tax Assessment Act of 1895.

The St. Joseph's Investment and Building Society is mortgagee in possession of 205 separate estates or parcels of land mortgaged to the society by different mortgagors under different legal mortgages.

For the year 1896 the society made and sent in to the Commissioners of Taxation 205 separate returns, that is:—one return in respect of each separate estate or parcel of land held by the society as mortgagee in possession, the society in each case by its return alleging itself to be mortgagee in possession and joint owner with the mortgagor; and claiming under s. 10 (1) a deduction of 240*l.* in each return in respect of the estate or parcel of land included in such return, making a total deduction claimed in the 205 returns of 49,200*l.*

Of the 205 returns only 17 returns shewed a taxable balance of unimproved value over and above the deductions of 240*l.* claimed.

The Commissioners of Taxation refused to allow the deductions claimed, and in the assessment of the lands of the said society aggregated the whole of the said 205 estates or parcels and the unimproved value thereof, and allowed only one deduction of 240*l.* from the aggregate.

The society appealed to the Court of Review. For the purposes of the appeal it was admitted that each separate mortgagor had

1898.

COMMISSION-
ERS OF
TAXATION
v.
ST. JOSEPH'S
I. & B.
SOCIETY.

no other property entitling him to, or on which he had obtained, any exemption.

On the hearing of the appeal it was contended by the said society that, being mortgagee in possession under mortgages from different mortgagors, it was entitled to a separate deduction of 240*l.* in respect of each mortgaged property in every case where the mortgagor had not claimed and received the benefit of the deduction of 240*l.* in another assessment.

The contention of the Commissioners of Taxation, on the other hand, was that the aggregate of the unimproved values of the several estates or parcels of land held by the said society as mortgagee in possession, must be regarded for the purposes of taxation as if such aggregate represented the unimproved value of a single estate or parcel, and that only one deduction of 240*l.* from such aggregate value was allowable.

The Judge decided in favour of the contention of the society and against that of the Commissioners of Taxation, and upheld the appeal. The question for the determination of the honorable the Supreme Court was whether he was right in so deciding.

Sir *Julian Salomons*, Q.C. (*J. L. Campbell* with him), for the Commissioners, appellants. The mortgagee in possession is defined to be an "owner" by s. 68; all these properties of which he is in possession must be included in one return, and he is only entitled to one deduction by s. 10 (1); whatever else he may be he is not a "bare trustee of different estates for the benefit of different *cestuis que trustent*."

Heydon, Q.C. (*Harvey* with him). It is very hard on the mortgagor if, when the mortgagee goes into possession, the mortgagor loses the deduction which he obtained while he remained in possession; the mortgagor, when he comes to redeem, will have to recoup the mortgagee what the latter has paid by way of land tax; the mortgagee can add the land tax to the debt: *Knowles* v. *Chapman* (1). The Legislature cannot have intended this hardship.

A mortgagee in possession comes within the definition of trustee in s. 68. He is "a person acting in a fiduciary capacity"; he is not

(1) Seton on Dec., 5th Edit., 1639.

a trustee in the strict sense, no doubt, but in the popular use of the term he is: *Dobson* v. *Land* (1); he is fettered in his ownership by the rights of the mortgagor. Compare the definition of the term "trust" in the Trustee Act (16 Vic. No. 19), where mortgagees are expressly excepted from the definition.

1898.

COMMISSION-
ERS OF
TAXATION
v.
MT. JOSEPH'S
I. & B.
SOCIETY.

A. H. SIMPSON, J. Admitting that, for the sake of argument, s. 10 only allows one deduction of 240*l.* unless the owner is a "bare trustee," surely a mortgagee in possession cannot be a bare trustee.

MANNING, J. The mortgagee's right is to look after his own interests and obtain repayment of his money, the only duty lying on him being that he is not to sacrifice the mortgagor's property : see *Kennedy* v. *de Trafford* (2). That position seems hardly compatible with his being a bare trustee.

Heydon, Q.C. That expression has been variously interpreted: *Morgan* v. *Swansea Sanitary Authority* (3) ; *In re Cunningham* (4). In s. 10 it is submitted the word "bare" has no meaning. Every separate trust estate must be entitled to its own deduction, although the same person is trustee of two estates and beneficially interested in both as well. Suppose A is absolutely entitled in fee to Whiteacre, and entitled in fee to Blackacre upon trust for himself and four other persons ; would there not be two assessments, although A is not a bare trustee; and would not each assessment obtain the deduction ? For the deduction is in respect of the assessment, not the individual: *Coveny's Case* (5).

THE CHIEF JUSTICE. No doubt that may be so in the case of trustees, but in s. 68 both trustees and mortgagees in possession are mentioned as "owners" ; if your argument is correct, the reference to mortgagees in possession is superfluous.

Heydon, Q.C. Mortgagees in possession are there mentioned for precaution ; the definition of trustee in s. 68 is wide enough to include a mortgagee in possession.

(1) 8 Ha. 216.　　　　　　(3) 9 Ch. D. 582.
(2) [1896] 1 Ch. at 772.　　(4) [1891] 2 Ch. 567.
(5) *Infra.*

1898.

COMMISSION-
ERS OF
TAXATION
v.
ST. JOSEPH'S
I. & B.
SOCIETY.

THE CHIEF JUSTICE.   In this case the St. Joseph's Investment Society are the mortgagees in possession of some 205 separate parcels of land mortgaged to them by different persons, and the society claims to be entitled to a separate assessment and deduction in respect of each different piece of land.   No doubt, the land being in various parts of the colony, separate valuations would have to be made, but the valuations having been made, it is clear from s. 10 (1) that the aggregate of the values of the various estates or parcels of land are to be regarded for the purposes of taxation as if such aggregate represented the unimproved value of a single estate or parcel.   The question, therefore, is whether the society have the right of placing themselves in the position of their mortgagors and making a separate deduction in each case.

The term owner includes, under s. 68, a mortgagee in possession, so that we may read the words " mortgagee in possession " into s. 10 wherever the word " owner " occurs, and thus we see that it is provided that a mortgagee in possession of several estates or parcels of land is to be entitled to but one deduction.   It is, however, argued that the society, being mortgagees in possession, fall within the saving words of the section " not being a bare trustee of different estates for the benefit of different *cestuis que trustent*."   It is said that the appellants are bare trustees for their *cestuis que trustent*, the mortgagors.   I confess that until to-day I never heard the expressions trustee and *cestui que trust* used with regard to a mortgagee in possession and his mortgagor.   When a mortgagee in possession has sold the land, and after paying himself, has a balance left in his hands he holds that balance in trust for the mortgagor, but that is the first time he becomes a trustee during the transaction, and he is then a trustee of the money, not of the land.   In some sense perhaps the positions of mortgagor and mortgagee resemble those of trustee and *cestui que trust*, but the former relationship is really one which stands by itself, and the well known rights and duties that it involves can hardly be expressed by any other terms than those of mortgagor and mortgagee.*

*See the judgment of *Kekewich, J., In re Brooke and Fremlin's Contract* (1898, 1 Ch. at p. 651).

In my opinion, therefore, once we see that a mortgagee in possession comes within the definition of the word owner, there is no answer to the appellants' contention. *Coveny's Case* was cited to us, but has no bearing upon the point in this case. The principles involved in the two cases are entirely different, and the only resemblance is that in each case it was sought to obtain a double deduction.

1898.

COMMISSION-
ERS OF
TAXATION
v.
ST. JOSEPH'S
I. & B.
SOCIETY.

The C.J.

MANNING, J. Upon the definition of owner as contained in s. 68, it seems to be quite clear that the contention of the Commissioners is the right one, unless it is possible to bring a mortgagee in possession within the words enclosed in brackets in s. 10. I do not see how he can come within those words. The case of a trustee is specifically dealt with in s. 14, but no mention is there made of a mortgagee in possession ; nor do the terms in which a trustee is there spoken of seem at all applicable to the position of a mortgagee in possession. Sect. 10 clearly differentiates the position of a bare trustee of different estates from that of other owners, including in that term a mortgagee in possession of the land of different mortgagors, but having regard to the provisions of s. 14, I confess that I do not see that any particular meaning can be attached to the word "bare" in the parenthesis in s. 10. Sect. 14 appears to contemplate separate assessments in the case of a person who is a trustee for different estates, and, therefore, although a trustee is an owner within the interpretation clause, a trustee for a number of different estates is not in the same position as the owner of several estates or parcels of land. The introduction of the expression *cestui que trust* in s. 10 makes it clear to me that trustee was not intended to include mortgagees in possession, but to refer to another well-known and defined relationship.

I am, therefore, of opinion that a mortgagee in possession must be treated as the owner of all the properties of which he is in possession. It is hard, no doubt, upon the mortgagors when they come to redeem, but they have put themselves in that position by giving the mortgagee the right to take possession, and, most probably, the Legislature thought that the case of a mortgagor redeeming after the mortgagee has taken possession is of com-

1898.

COMMISSION-
ERS OF
TAXATION
v.
ST. JOSEPH'S
I. & B.
SOCIETY.

Manning J.

paratively rare occurrence, and that the mortgagee seldom goes into possession, except as a last resource, when, in all probability, he will remain in possession as owner, and will not be likely to be redeemed by the mortgagor; therefore, in practice, no great hardship would result.

A. H. SIMPSON, J., concurred.

Appeal sustained.

Attorneys for the respondents: *Makinson & Plunkett.*

MORAN *v.* THE COMMISSIONERS OF TAXATION.

Land and Income Tax Assessment Act, ss. 11 (5), 45, 68—*Lands held upon trust—*
Unimproved value — Assessment — Appeal—Question of fact — Exemption—
Church land.

Lands held upon trust without power of sale are assessable notwithstanding that whilst subject to the trust they are unsaleable.

The Judge of the Court of Review, having held that certain land was not exclusively occupied for or in connection with a church, and, therefore, not exempt under s. 11 (5)—*Held*, that his decision was upon a question of fact, and that no appeal lay to the Supreme Court.

1898.

July 29.

The C.J.
Owen J.
and
A. H. Simpson J.

SPECIAL CASE stated by the Court of Review under the Land and Income Tax Assessment Act, 1895.

The following facts were admitted or proved at the hearing before the Court of Review :—

A parcel of land at Manly, containing fifty-eight acres three roods thirteen perches, was, and is by grant from the Crown, vested in trustees " upon trust for the erection thereon of an episcopal residence for the Roman Catholic Archbishop of Sydney, in the said colony, for the time being, and of such buildings, if any, for educational purposes as the said Roman Catholic Archbishop of Sydney for the time being shall authorise and permit to be erected thereon." The appellant, as Roman Catholic Archbishop of Sydney and head of the Roman Catholic Church in this colony, was on and before the 31st of December, 1895, and now is in exclusive possession of the said land for the purposes for which it is granted. On the southern portion is erected an episcopal residence occupied by the appellant as such Archbishop, in respect of his Cathedral Church of St. Mary, in the city of Sydney, he being the head of the clergy serving such Cathedral Church. On the northern portion is erected St. Patrick's seminary, used under the authority and by direction of the appellant, for the residence and education of students for holy orders in the Roman Catholic Church intended to serve the Roman Catholic Churches in this colony.

The appellant returned the said land as of the value of 10,500l., if assessable, but contended that being granted and occupied as aforesaid, it was exempt from taxation, and had no assessable value. It was admitted that if the fee simple estate in the said land could be sold, that the capital sum for which it would have sold under such reasonable conditions of sale as a bona fide seller would require (assuming the improvements had not been made), would be the said sum of 10,500l.

The Commissioners for Taxation assessed the said land for taxation at the value of 10,500l. The appellant duly lodged in the Court of Review a notice of appeal, contending that the said land being granted and occupied as aforesaid, was exempt from taxation under s. 11 of the said Act, and had no assessable value.

The Judge of the Court of Review dismissed the appeal, holding that the land assessed had an assessable value, and that the unimproved value thereof was 10,500l, and that it was not exempt under s. 11 of the said Act.

The questions for the determination of the Honourable the Supreme Court were :—1. Whether under the circumstances the land assessed had an assessable value. 2. Whether the land assessed was exempt from taxation under s. 11.

Sir *Julian Salomons*, Q.C., for the Commissioners, took the preliminary objection that the Court could not deal with the second question submitted by the case. It is a question of fact whether the land was occupied or used exclusively for or in connection with a church under s. 11 (v), and the Judge, after a personal inspection, held that it was not. Sect. 45 provides an appeal from the Court of Review on questions of law only.

THE CHIEF JUSTICE. You shall have the advantage of the point when we have heard the case.

Heydon, Q.C., and *Blacket*, for the appellant. While burdened with this trust the land is valueless, and if put up for sale to-morrow would not fetch a shilling.

OWEN, J. Are all lands which are subject to trusts exempt from tax where there is no power of sale ?

Heydon, Q.C. The trusts to which the land is subject must have some effect upon its value. "Unimproved value," by s. 68, means the sum for which the land would sell. This would not bring anything while it is saddled with such a trust. Again, how is the tax to be paid, since the trustee has no money in his hands, and he is not personally liable ?

OWEN, J. It is a charge upon the land imposed by an Act of Parliament, and I do not think the Court of Equity would allow the trust to override a charge of that nature.

Heydon, Q.C. As to the other ground, the land is occupied in connection with St. Mary's Cathedral, and the work of the diocese.

Sir *Julian Salomons*, Q.C., and *J. L. Campbell* were not called upon.

THE CHIEF JUSTICE. Two questions are submitted for our consideration. The first is whether under the circumstances the land assessed had an assessable value, and that may be a question of law for our determination. It appears that many years ago the land in question was by grant from the Crown vested in trustees, to be used in connection with the Roman Catholic Church. The land is now valued for the purposes of taxation at the sum of 10,500*l.* But it is contended that, inasmuch as under the deed of trust the land cannot be sold, it has no assessable value, or no such value as falls within the meaning of the words "unimproved value," as used in the Act. In s. 68 an attempt has been made to define the meaning of the expression " unimproved value," by stating the way in which the value of the land is to be assessed. The assessors have simply to say what the fee simple of the land, if it could be sold, would realise under reasonable conditions of sale, leaving improvements out of con-sideration. But they have not to consider whether the land can or cannot be sold, they have merely to say what the land ought to fetch if it were sold. It frequently happens that land, the subject of wills and settlements, cannot be sold for a certain time, and if it could be successfully contended that because land could not be sold, it could not be assessed, a very large quantity of

1898.

MORAN
v.
COMMISSION-
ERS OF
TAXATION.

The C.J.

land would be withdrawn from the operation of the Act, and I venture to think that it would shortly be found that nearly all the land in the colony would be the subject of a trust. I am, therefore, of opinion as to the first point that the decision of the Judge of the Court of Review was right.

The second question is whether the land is exempt. This appears to me to be a question of fact, and the Judge below has decided it. His Honour has satisfied himself that the land is not used exclusively for the purposes of a church, and we are told that he personally visited and inspected the land. Having decided the matter as a question of fact, this Court has no power to review his decision.

OWEN and A. H. SIMPSON, JJ., concurred.

Appeal dismissed.

Attorneys for the appellant : *Makinson & Plunkett.*

THE COMMISSIONERS OF TAXATION *v.* JENNINGS.

1898.

—————

August 5.

—————

The C.J.
Manning J.
and
A.H. Simpson J.

Land and Income Tax Assessment Act, 1895, *s.* 10—*Land tax—Mortgagor's deduction—Debt collaterally secured on land in another colony.*

A mortgage debt was secured upon lands in New South Wales, and collaterally by a further mortgage on land in Queensland. '*Held*, that the source of the interest being the covenant in the N.S.W. mortgage and not the land, the mortgagor was entitled to a deduction under s. 10 of a sum equal to the income tax leviable for that year upon the interest derivable from the whole mortgage debt, and that such interest could not be apportioned to the several securities.

SPECIAL CASE stated by the Court of Review under the Land and Income Tax Assessment Act, 1895. '

Sir P. A. Jennings, on behalf of himself and as executor of his deceased co-owner Martin Shanahan, made, in March, 1896, for land tax purposes, a return of lands in New South Wales of which he was owner, being a run called Garrawilla, the total unimproved value of which was stated to be 58,622*l.*

The said lands were subject to a first mortgage to the A.M.P. Society securing 50,000*l.* at 5½ per cent. and to a second mortgage to the London Bank of Australia securing 135,968*l.* at 7 per cent., the total interest for the year 1895 on the two mortgages being 12,633*l.* From further particulars supplied to the Commissioners at their request, it appeared that the first mortgage was confined to the lands comprised in Garrawilla. The second mortgage was effected by three several memoranda of mortgage under the Real Property Act, over the Garrawilla estate only, and the sums so secured, viz., 135,968*l.*, were further and collaterally secured by a separate mortgage over certain freehold land, known as the Westbrook estate, in Queensland, which, together with a stock mortgage over the stock thereon, was stated to be worth 92,220*l.* ; also by a mortgage over a Government leasehold area in N.S.W., valued at 1070*l.*; and by a stock mortgage over the stock depastured on Garrawilla. These mortgages by way of collateral security were stated and referred to in the memoranda of mortgage relating to Garrawilla. The bank valued its interest under the said second mortgage on Garrawilla at 25,000*l.*, the stock thereon at 25,000*l.*, and upon its mortgage over Westbrook and the stock thereon at 99,600*l.*

Sir P. A. Jennings claimed a deduction from the land tax chargeable in respect of Garrawilla a sum equal to the income tax leviable on the total interest, viz., 12,633*l.* The Commissioners disallowed the deduction claimed in respect of the second mortgage, and allowed only a proportion thereof equal to that proportion of the whole mortgage debt (135,968*l.*) which, on the appellant's valuations of the properties covered by the mortgages collateral to the said second mortgage, and referred to therein as security for the said mortgage debt, was appropriable to the security represented by the lands of Garrawilla, with the improvements thereon.

Sir P. A. Jennings appealed to the Court of Review, contending that no tax was payable in respect of the lands at Garrawilla, inasmuch as the deductions in respect of the said mortgages exceeded the amount of the land tax chargeable, and that the Commissioners had no right to apportion the mortgage debt to the different securities covered by the collateral mortgages, so as to reduce the deduction claimed.

It was contended by the Commissioners that where a debt secured on a mortgage of taxable lands is also secured (by the same or other instruments collateral thereto) on other properties and the improvements thereon, and where such other properties so charged are of separate and independent values, then the mortgage could be regarded, for the purpose of determining the deductions provided in s. 10, as a mortgage of the taxable lands and improvements thereon to secure the proportion only of the whole debt fairly apportionable on the valuations of the mortgagor and mortgagee, to the security of the said taxable lands and the improvements thereon.

The Judge upheld the appeal, holding that the Commissioners had no such right of apportionment. The Commissioners of Taxation appealed, and the question stated for the determination of the Supreme Court was :—

Where lands liable to land tax are subject to a mortgage securing a debt also secured by charges on other properties in the manner appearing in this case, does the right of deduction under the first proviso to sub-s. 1 of s. 10 of the Land and Income Tax Assessment Act of 1895 exist to the extent of the income tax leviable on the interest payable on the whole mortgage debt, or is it limited to a sum equal to the tax leviable on the interest derivable only from that proportion of the whole mortgage debt which equals the proportion of the value of the taxable land, with improvements, to the total value of all the properties on which the debt is secured ?

Sir P. A. Jennings died in June, 1897, whilst his appeal to the Court of Review was pending, but the appeal was continued on behalf of the estate.

Sir *Julian Salomons*, Q.C., and *J. L. Campbell*, for the appellants, the Commissioners of Taxation.

Lingen and *G. R. Campbell*, for the respondents, the executors of Sir P. A. Jennings.

THE CHIEF JUSTICE. I am of opinion that the executors of the estate of Sir P. A. Jennings are entitled to a deduction from the land tax payable by them equal to the income tax leviable for the year upon the interest derivable from the whole mortgage. It would have been better, no doubt, if this matter had been specifically provided for in the Act, but when we remember that the source of the income of the mortgagee is the covenant to pay interest, and not the land, it really becomes too clear for argument that the deduction must be allowed upon the whole amount payable under the covenant. The covenant in the New South Wales mortgage is to pay the whole of the interest upon the total debt, and although that is secured as well upon certain lands in Queensland, the covenant is to pay the whole amount in New South Wales, and the matter comes therefore within the express words of the proviso to s. 10. The learned Judge of the Court of Review was right in the conclusion at which he arrived.

MANNING, J. I am of the same opinion. It seems to me that the matter is settled when you look at the source from which the interest is derived. The interest is not derivable from the land, but is payable on the whole amount of the mortgage by virtue

1898.

COMMISSION-
ERS OF
TAXATION
v.
JENNINGS.

Manning J.

of the covenant in the mortgage.   It does not arise wholly or partly from any property outside the colony, but upon a covenant to pay upon a mortgage in the colony.

A. H. SIMPSON, J.   I agree.   If the mortgage debt was charge-able only on land in New South Wales there could be no question as to the mortgagor's right to make the deduction claimed, and I am unable to see how it can make any difference that it is secured *collaterally* on land in Queensland.

> *Appeal dismissed with costs of and incidental to the appeal.*

Attorney for the respondents : *P. W. Creagh.*

FOREMAN *v.* THE COMMISSIONERS OF TAXATION.

Land and Income Tax Assessment Act, 1895, *ss.* 15, 28 (1), 28 (7)—*Deductions—Total income—Losses incurred in the production of income—Two businesses—Employment or vocation.*

A professional man who speculates in shares is not entitled to set off losses incurred in such speculations against the tax on his total income, such losses being losses of capital, and not incurred in the production of income.

A professional man who speculates in shares is not carrying on two businesses within the meaning of s. 28 (7).

1898.

August 26.

The C.J.
Stephen J.
and
Cohen J.

SPECIAL CASE stated by the Court of Review under the Land and Income Tax Assessment Act, 1895.

The appellant duly made a return of his income for the year ending the 31st December, 1897, wherein he deducted from the taxable amount sums amounting to 1922*l.*, whereof 1332*l.* was loss sustained by the appellant on his dealings in shares in public companies and concerns, and 590*l.* was for sums paid by the appellant as a contributor to the debts and liabilities of a company in liquidation.

The Commissioners disallowed the whole of the said deductions, and the appellant appealed to the Court of Review. On the hearing of the appeal before the Court of Review it was admitted that the appellant, in addition to carrying on the profession of a surgeon in Sydney, also speculated in the buying and selling of shares in mines and public companies, and concerns of a like nature. It was proved that the sum of 1332*l.* had in fact been lost by the appellant in the course of buying and selling shares in New South Wales during the year 1897, and that sum represented the difference between the price at which he had purchased the shares, including the amount of calls paid, and the price for which he had sold them. Some of the shares so realised at a loss had been purchased in previous years. The said sum of 590*l.* was made up of sums for which the appellant was liable, and which he had paid, during the said year as a con-

tributor to the debts and liabilities of a company then and for
some time before the commencement of the said year in course of
liquidation.

The Judge of the Court of Review dismissed the appeal, holding that the appellant had no right to the deduction claimed
under s. 28 (1), and secondly that the appellant did not carry on
(with regard to his dealings in shares) a "business" within the
meaning of s. 28 (7).

The appellant appealed to the Supreme Court, and the questions for determination were:—Is the appellant entitled to the
deduction claimed or any part thereof under s. 28 (1) or under
s. 28 (7).

Pilcher, Q.C., and *Salusbury*, for the appellant. The deductions claimed by the appellant are losses incurred in the production of his income within the meaning of s. 28 (1), which
specifies the deductions allowable from the taxable amount. In
the first place it is clearly a "loss."

[THE CHIEF JUSTICE. But a loss of capital. Once you
separate portion of your income and invest it, it becomes capital,
and you only pay tax on what it earns.]

Pilcher, Q.C. But if when you realise that capital you receive
less than you originally invested, that is a loss, and the section
does not say what kind of loss. It says any loss incurred in the
production of income, and can only refer to a loss of capital. It
cannot refer to a loss of income or diminution of profits, because
that cannot in any way be the subject of a deduction. If you
have less income, you pay less tax. The only qualification of the
loss is that it must be incurred in the production of income.
If I buy a share, or any other chattel, with the object of producing income, and subsequently sell at a loss, that is a loss
incurred in the production of income. If I make a profit I pay
tax on that profit; if I lose I am entitled to deduct the loss,
because it is a loss incurred in an operation undertaken with a
view of producing income.

[THE CHIEF JUSTICE. If you invest 100*l*. in 3 per cent. con-
sols, and sell at the end of the year for 90*l*., is not that purely a
loss of capital?]

Pilcher, Q.C. I think it is; but if I sell for 110*l.*, I am charged income tax on the 10*l.*, as well as on the interest I have received, and I say that if in the one case I have to pay the tax, in the other I am entitled to the deduction. The English Act contains a special provision that losses of capital are not deductible.

1898.

FOREMAN
v.
COMMISSION-
ERS OF
TAXATION.

[THE CHIEF JUSTICE. If your bank shares decline this year in value by one-half, but still pay you the same dividend as before, can you deduct the amount you have lost by the fall in the market ?]

Pilcher, Q.C. You must realise first. As to the second point, the investing of money and looking after it is a vocation or business within s. 28 (7). Some persons have no other vocation or business than nursing and investing their capital.

[COHEN, J. There were five separate speculations, and not all of them were commenced in the year in question. · Is that sufficient to constitute a vocation ?]

Pilcher, Q.C. The words of the section were not intended to have too narrow a construction placed upon them; but were intended to include any recognised method of earning an income: see *Partridge* v. *Mallandaine* (1). Even if the appellant does not carry on two businesses, income means total income, and under s. 15 includes income from all sources whatever.

Sir *Julian Salomons*, Q.C. Then s. 28 (7) was unnecessary.

THE CHIEF JUSTICE. I confess that I am entirely at a loss to know what exact meaning to put upon the words of s. 28 (1)— "Losses actually incurred by the taxpayer in the production of his income." In the present case, however, we are not called upon to define these words; it suffices to say that they do not mean what the appellant contends they do, viz., a loss of capital.

It appears that Dr. Foreman is by profession a surgeon, and invested certain money, which I may assume to be portion of his income or savings, in the shares of certain companies. When

(1) 18 Q.B.D. 276.

1898.

FOREMAN
v.
COMMISSION-
ERS OF
TAXATION.

The C.J.

so invested that money became capital. During the year 1897 he realised a portion of his capital so invested, with the result that his capital suffered a considerable diminution for that year. He now seeks to set off that diminution as against the income-tax payable upon his whole income for 1897. In other words he asks the Court to say that s. 28 (1) should be construed as if it read : " From the taxable amount so ascertained every taxpayer shall be entitled to deductions in respect of the annual amount of *losses of capital* actually incurred by the taxpayer in the production of his income." As I have already stated, I am not prepared to say exactly what the words of the section do mean ; but I can see nothing to warrant us in reading the word *capital* into the section. Mr. *Pilcher* argues that " in the production of income " means " in the course of an operation, the object of which is to produce income " ; but I do not see how we can put that meaning upon the words of the section, or how a man can be entitled to deduct a loss of capital from his professional income, or from the reduced income produced by his diminished capital.

The other point arises upon the construction of the seventh sub-clause of s. 28, and I am of opinion that this gentleman cannot be said to be carrying on two businesses within the meaning of the sub-section. He is a medical man, and is able to use a portion of the money derived as income from his profession as capital by investing it in company shares. He may or may not derive income from those investments, and may sell them at a profit or a loss ; but, in my opinion, that is not the carrying on of a business, nor a profession, employment, or vocation within the meaning of s. 28 (7). The case is simply that of a man carrying on one profession, and investing his savings, and in my opinion the section does not apply to such a case. It was argued upon this point for the appellant that income means the whole actual taxable income from whatever source derived. If it does, then the appellant is not entitled to the deduction, for the reasons which I have given in answering the first of the questions submitted to us.

STEPHEN and COHEN, JJ., concurred.

Appeal dismissed with costs.

Attorneys for the appellant : *Norton, Smith & Co.*

1898.

Aug. 16.

The C.J.
Owen J.
and
A.H.Simpson J

Ex parte KELLY.

Mining Act, 1874, s. 70—Reg. 3 of Practice Regulations—Warden's Court—Summons - Personal service—Substituted service—Discretion of Warden.

Where a summons under s. 70 of the Mining Act, 1874, has not been personally served, the Warden may proceed with the case in the absence of the defendant if, in his opinion, there has been sufficient substituted service, either in the manner prescribed by R. 3 of the Rules of 21st July, 1874, or otherwise.

PROHIBITION.

On the 30th November, 1897, a summons under s. 70 of the Mining Act, 1874, was taken out at Grafton by John Hansen calling upon Kelly, Pumfrey and Jonsen to appear before the Warden at the Warden's Court at Grafton on the 20th December. The object of the summons was to have it determined that Hansen was, as against the respondents, in lawful possession of a certain claim at Upper Bucca Bucca, and that the respondents had abandoned the said claim, and to prevent the respondents from further trespassing upon it. The summons was served personally upon Pumfrey and Jonsen more than eight days before the return day. Kelly was not personally served, but on the 11th December it was served at his business premises upon one Popkin, who was in charge of the said premises during Kelly's absence, and who was a person "apparently fourteen years of age." Popkin, on being served with the summons, handed it to Pumfrey, one of the respondents and Kelly's partner, and who attended to the business in Kelly's absence. Pumfrey immediately communicated with Kelly by telegraph at Murwillumbah, and informed him of the service of the summons, and Kelly replied that he would be in Grafton on the 18th December.

Mr. *A. Nicholson*, the attorney for the respondents, who was to appear for them at the Warden's Court on the 20th December, was anxious, to suit his professional engagements at other Courts, to obtain a postponement of the case till after Christmas, and he applied by letter to the complainant's attorney in Grafton and to

the Warden to have the case postponed. After a considerable
amount of correspondence Mr. *Nicholson* was finally informed by
telegram on the 17th December that the complainant would not
consent to a postponement, and that the case must come on
upon the day fixed.

On the 18th December, *Nicholson* wired to Grafton to Hansen's
attorney and to the Warden that he had been instructed that
Kelly had not been personally served, and that, under those circumstances, the case could not be proceeded with. He also sent
a wire to Kelly instructing him not to attend the Court, and
Kelly, who was then at Chatsworth on his way from Murwillumbah to Grafton, turned back on the receipt of the telegram, and
did not attend the Court.

The case came on in the Warden's Court on the 21st December,
Pumfrey being the only one of the respondents present. An
affidavit was put in by the person who had served the summons
for Kelly upon Popkin, and the Warden had this person called,
and examined him orally as to the service. Pumfrey was also
called and stated that he was a partner of Kelly's, and that he had
informed Kelly of the service of the summons. The Warden,
being satisfied upon this evidence as to the service of the summons,
proceeded to hear the case in the absence of Kelly and Jonsen, and
gave his decision in favour of the complainant.

Rule 3 of the Rules for the regulation of the practice in
Wardens' Courts (21st July, 1874) provides that—

Any summons under the 70th section of the said Act may be served personally
or at the dwelling or place of business of the defendant, upon any person apparently fourteen years of age, eight days before the return day, or such other time
as the Warden shall direct ; and in the event of the Warden giving any such
direction the time mentioned in such direction shall be noted at the foot of the
summons.

Kelly obtained a rule *nisi* for a prohibition to restrain further
proceedings upon the said order upon the ground that the
Warden had no jurisdiction to hear and determine the complaint
in the absence of Kelly, who had not been duly served with the
summons, and (2) that the order was against natural justice.
There was a strong conflict of evidence upon the affidavits as to
whether the place where the summons for Kelly was served upon
Popkin was at that time occupied by Kelly as his place of business.

Wise and *Ralston*, for the applicant. It was necessary that all the defendants in the Warden's Court should be served with the summons: *R.* v. *Heron, Ex parte Bryer* (1); *R.* v. *Belcher, Ex parte Gilbee* (2). The Warden had no power to make any order as to substituted service until the case came on for hearing, when he might, if personal service had not been effected, have directed that some other form of service be substituted: *Taylor* v. *Stubbs* (3); *R.* v. *Akehurst* (4). Rule 3 is *ultra vires* of s. 70, and, if the Warden followed the rule in holding the service sufficient, he has not exercised the discretion which s. 70 renders it incumbent on him to exercise as to whether the substituted service was sufficient.

Pilcher, Q.C., and *Kelynack*, for the respondent Hansen, were not called upon,

THE CHIEF JUSTICE. It seems to me that s. 70 of the Mining Act is very clear in its provisions. It provides that every·proceeding in a Warden's Court shall be commenced by a summons, which, since it has to contain a statement of the facts constituting the cause of complaint, is somewhat in the nature of a declaration. The defendant is summoned to appear before the Warden's Court upon a day named in the summons, when "upon proof of such service or substituted service of the said summons as the Warden shall think sufficient, the Court shall proceed to investigate the matter of such complaint, and in the presence of all the parties interested or of such of them as shall appear to him sufficiently to represent all the parties interested, or in the absence of any of the parties interested who having been duly served with such summons shall not appear, shall hear, receive and examine evidence, and determine such complaint in a summary way."

That gives the Warden an absolute discretion to act upon what he considers is sufficient proof of service, *i.e.*, personal service, or upon what he considers is sufficient substituted service. In the present case personal service had not been effected upon Kelly, and the Warden had, therefore, to consider whether what had

(1) 2 V.L.R. 155.   (3) 6 W.W. & A'B. [M] 19.
(2) 4 A.J.R. 80, 110.   (4) 6 W.W. & A'B. 84, 244.

taken place was sufficient substituted service to entitle him to proceed with the case in Kelly's absence. He held that the service was sufficient, and, in my opinion, he was perfectly right in so doing. Whether he was aware or not of the fact that Kelly was stopped by *Nicholson* when actually on his way to the Court, he had before him the evidence of Pumfrey, of the communication to Kelly of the intelligence that the summons had been served, and of Kelly's reply thereto, and in view of that evidence I do not think we need concern ourselves with the question whether the place where the summons was left with Popkin was Kelly's place of business or not.

It is said, however, that the third regulation governs this case, that that rule relates to personal service only, and that, if for any reason it is desired to effect substituted service, an application must be made to the Warden under s. 70 for his leave and directions as to the form such service shall take. It seems to me, however, that Rule 3 is merely intended, for the convenience of the public, and points out what may be held to be sufficient service. It points out a way in which service *may* be effected, not the way in which it must be effected. That is left to the discretion of the Warden under s. 70.

The true construction of s. 70 appears to me to be that the Legislature has seen fit to throw upon the person who undertakes the service of a summons the responsibility of serving it either personally or in such a manner as the Warden will consider sufficient. If the service has been personal, there is no more to be said ; if it has not been personal, then, when the case comes on, the Warden has to say whether he considers there has been sufficient substituted service. If he thinks there has, he may proceed with the case. If he thinks there has not, he must adjourn the matter, and it may be that he may then give directions as to what form of substituted service will satisfy him.

For these reasons I am unable to say that the Warden was wrong in the course he took, nor, looking at the facts of the case, can it be said that the applicant suffered from any failure of natural justice.

OWEN and A. H. SIMPSON, JJ., concurred.

Rule discharged, with costs.

Attorney for the applicant : *A. Nicholson.*
Attorneys for the respondent : *Norrie & M'Guren.*

THE ATTORNEY-GENERAL *v.* LOVE.

Nullum Tempus Act, 9 *Geo. III. c.* 16—*Construction of* 9 *Geo. IV. c.* 83, *s.* 24—
Application of English Statutes to New South Wales.

Held, confirming the judgment of the Supreme Court, that the Imperial Nullum
Tempus Act, 9 Geo. III. c. 16, is in force in New South Wales, and that it applies
to lands which have never been dealt with by the Crown.

The Act 9 Geo. IV. c. 83, s. 24, *prima facie* on its true construction applies the
Nullum Tempus Act to the colony. Its operation to that effect cannot be
restricted by confining the laws and statutes thereby applied to those relating to
procedure, or by shewing that a specific exception in the applied Act preserving
the Crown's right could not operate in the circumstances of the colony.

1898.

May 14.

*Privy
Council.* [*]

THIS was an appeal to the Privy Council from the judgment of
the Supreme Court, reported 17 N.S.W.L.R. 16, where the facts and
pleadings are fully stated.

Cohen, Q.C., *Vaughan Hawkins,* and *Butterworth,* for appellant,
contended that the Crown was entitled by its prerogative to all
lands in the colony which had never been granted by the Crown,
and that its right thereto cannot be barred by adverse possession
or any lapse of time in the absence of express statutory provision.
Reference was made to *Théberge* v. *Laudry* (1); *Cushing* v. *Dupuy*
(2). This prerogative was taken away to a certain and very
limited extent in England and Wales by the Nullum Tempus Act
(9 Geo. III., c. 16). The Court below did not hold that that Act was
part of the law which the first settlers in the colony in 1788
brought with them, but that it was made applicable by s. 24 of
9 Geo. IV. c. 83 : *Whicker* v. *Hume* (3) decided that that section
referred not to laws generally, but only to laws as to modes of
procedure. But the Nullum Tempus Act does not merely deal
with procedure ; it in effect transfers title from the Crown to a
subject. See also *Attorney-General* v. *Stewart* (4). Sect. 24

[*] Present : THE LORD CHANCELLOR, Lord MACNAGHTEN, Lord MORRIS, Mr.
WAY.

(1) 2 App. Cas. 102.	(3) 7 H.L. 124.
(2) 5 App. Cas. 409, 419.	(4) 2 Mer. 143.

does not shew any intention to affect the Crown or oust it or its prerogative. The Nullum Tempus Act is not suited to the colony; it grew out of circumstances peculiar to English history. It continued 21 Jac. 1 c. 2. The object of those Acts was to protect the subject against "pretences of concealment" growing out of the circumstances subsequent to the suppression of monasteries, where lands forfeited to the Crown never came to the Crown, but were by secret devices transferred elsewhere. In the colony the evil was not that of "concealers" attacking the title of the subject, but that of squatters evading the authority of the Crown.

Neither of those Acts affected the possessions of the Crown generally or enabled mere possession to prevail against the Crown's title. 24 & 25 Vic. c. 62 was the first Act which subjected the Crown in England to a law of limitation similar to that between subject and subject. Reference was made to *Attorney-General for British Honduras* v. *Bristowe* (1), to the admission of counsel therein, and the assumption in the judgment that 60 years' adverse possession barred the Crown. As to the reconsideration of a point, see *Reg.* v. *Hughes* (2). Reference was also made to *Mayor of Hull* v. *Horner* (3). Further, on the assumption that the Nullum Tempus Act applied there had been local legislation inconsistent therewith which had the effect of repealing it. See Crown Lands Acts of 1842, 1861, and 1884, namely, 5 & 6 Vic. c. 36, 25 Vic. No. 1, and 48 Vic. No. 18. It was contended that it would be inconsistent with the provisions of those Acts that a process should have been at work as from the commencement of the colony giving to unlawful occupiers for 60 years absolute titles against the Crown free from all reservations and conditions. Lastly, the exception in the Acts in favour of the Crown of lands "duly in charge or standing in super of record" within 60 years is an essential part thereof and is inapplicable to the colony. Nothing similar to the revenue system and records of the Court of Exchequer exists or could have existed in the colony. There is no record or survey of ungranted lands. Whatever is ungranted belongs to the Crown. As for receipt of revenue, the lands originally had no pecuniary value.

(1) 6 App. Cas. 143.   (2) L. R. 1 P.C. 81, 92.
                    (3) 1 Cowp. 102, 215.

The respondent did not appear.

On the 14th May judgment was delivered by

THE LORD CHANCELLOR.   This is an appeal by the Attorney-General for New South Wales against the judgment of the Supreme Court of the colony pronounced on the 18th of February, 1896, overruling a demurrer to the defendant's plea to an information of intrusion to recover certain lands in the parish of Concord and county of Cumberland in the said colony. The question involved is whether the English Nullum Tempus Act (9 Geo. III. c. 16) is in force in the colony and applies to land which has never been granted out or dealt with by the Crown.

It does not appear to be denied that the lands in question (described by their abuttals and containing 13¼ acres), were and had ever since the original settlement of the territory of New South Wales been waste lands belonging to and vested in the Crown.

The defendant by his plea dated 10th April, 1895, averred that one Edward J. Keith more than 60 years before the filing of the information entered on and thenceforward held possession of the lands as his own property, that he conveyed his interest therein to William Love, who settled the same in trust for himself and his wife Susannah Love and the survivor of them for life, and after the decease of the survivor on the defendant, Emily Susannah Love absolutely; that the foregoing persons had from the entry of Edward J. Keith to the present time held continuous possession of the lands adversely to Her Majesty, and without payment of rent to her, and had themselves since the said entry taken and enjoyed the rents, revenues, issues, and profits of the land, and that Her Majesty's title to the land did not first accrue within 60 years next before the filing of the information. The plea did not aver that the lands had not been in charge of the Crown within the said 60 years.

On 20th May, 1895, the applicant replied traversing the allegations of the plea and also demurred thereto on the grounds: (1) that the Act 9 Geo. III. c. 16 is not in force in New South Wales. (2) That assuming it to be in force it does not apply to lands which have never been dealt with by the Crown. (3) That

1898.

ATTORNEY
GENERAL
v.
LOVE.

Lord
Chancellor.

the period of 60 years was not alleged to have run out before the date of the Constitution Act, 1855. (4) That the plea shewed no title in the defendant.

Joinder in demurrer having been delivered the demurrer came on for hearing before the Full Court (consisting of Chief Justice *Darley* and Justices *Windeyer* and *Simpson*), by whom judgment was pronounced on the 18th February, 1896, in favour of the defendant, overruling the demurrer, *Simpson*, J., stating that he felt very considerable doubt about the matter.

Their Lordships have no doubt that the judgment accurately describes the importance of the question here raised to the colony. The learned Judges say " the earlier grants issued by the Crown were vague in the extreme, and that it would be in the present day impossible to ascertain from the description in the grants to what lands they applied." And it is clear that the inference which the learned Judges draw from that state of facts is accurate " that the holders would not be able to show upon the face of the instrument a title, and have to rely upon possession."

Their Lordships do not think that the learned Judges at all exaggerate the mischief and confusion which would arise in the transfer of property if the holders could not depend upon the operation of the statute in question.

Two arguments appear to have been suggested against the application of the Act to the particular colony under 9 Geo. IV. c. 83, which *prima facie* applied the Nullum Tempus Act to the colony in question as much as if it had in terms re-enacted it for that colony.

Sect. 24 of that Act provides " that all laws and statutes in force within the realm of England at the passing of this Act" (that is to say in the year 1828) " shall be applied in the administration of justice in the Courts of New South Wales," and it is sought by construction to limit the words "all laws and 'statutes' " by introducing into the section the words " having relation to procedure" or some equivalent expression. At least that is the only intelligible mode in which the argument can be supported, because the words which do occur in the section " in the

administration of justice " would certainly include a limitation of
the time within which actions can be brought, and their Lordships are of opinion that the language of the section cannot be
limited so as to exclude the statute, which for the reasons pointed
out by the learned Judges were and are so important in the
administration of justice in the colony.

The second argument is not very intelligible since the words
upon which reliance is placed are words which in the statute
thus applied (9 Geo. III. c. 16) except from the operation of
the statute lands in respect of which the Crown has been
answered by rents, revenues, issues, or profits thereof within
the space of 60 years next before the issuing or commencing
of such action, information, &c., as shall at any times have been
duly in charge or stood *in super* of record within the space of
60 years.

The provision is intelligible enough and what in substance it
means is that if the Crown is not actually in possession but that in
the Crown's accounts some person is charged with the rent which
they had not paid and still stand as a Crown debtor in the Crown
books, and that condition of things has existed within the 60
years the title by that condition of things, although the possession
may have been for 60 years, was not adverse, because during that
period something was payable to the Crown which had not been
paid.

It is not suggested here that the person in possession filled that
character, but the argument appears to be that because there is
no such administration in the colony as involves the peculiar form
of Crown accounting thus described the remedial operation of the
statute cannot apply.

Their Lordships are unable to accept any such suggestion.
There is no allegation here of any equivalent record against the
person who held possession for 60 years, and if no modification or
limitation such as s. 24 of the Act authorises has been made so as
to apply such a mode of accounting to the Crown as might have
an equivalent effect the only result would be that there is nothing
upon which the exception preserving the Crown's right could
operate but certainly would not cut down the enacting part of

1898.

ATTORNEY
GENERAL
v.
LOVE.

*Lord
Chancellor.*

1898.

ATTORNEY
GENERAL
v.
LOVE.

*Lord
Chancellor.*

the statute or establish that it was inconsistent with the laws of England.

For these reasons their Lordships are of opinion that the judgment of the Supreme Court was right, and they will humbly advise Her Majesty that this appeal should be dismissed accordingly.

Attorneys for appellant : *Light & Galbraith.*

WALLER *v.* YOUNG.

Civil Service Act, 1884, *ss.* 10, 46—*Abolition of office—Dismissal of officer.*

The Government has power to abolish an office at will, and, if the services of the officer be dispensed with in consequence of the abolition of his office, he cannot maintain an action against the Government for wrongful dismissal.

1898.

March 23.
April 29.

Privy Council. *

APPEAL and cross appeal from the judgment of the Full Court, reported 18 N.S.W.L.R. 200, where the facts fully appear.

Cozens Hardy, Q.C., and *Corrie Grant* appeared for the plaintiff.

Sir *R. Reid*, Q.C., and *Vaughan Hawkins* appeared for the defendant.

On the 29th April the judgment of their Lordships was delivered by

April 29.

LORD WATSON. The plaintiff in this suit, who is respondent in the leading appeal, obtained employment in the public service of the Government of New South Wales, after the passing of the "Civil Service Act, 1884." Before the "Public Service Act of 1895" was passed, the office which he held was abolished by the Government. After the Act of 1895 became law the suit in which these appeals are taken was brought by the plaintiff against the Government, as represented by the appellant, who had been duly appointed to act as nominal defendant. He claims 7,500*l.* as damages for wrongful dismissal and deprivation of office.

By his defence the defendant, who is the leading appellant, pleaded (2) "that the services and employment of the plaintiff in the declaration mentioned were the services of a person employed in the public service within the meaning of the Act 59 Vic. No. 25, s. 58, and the alleged grievances in the declaration mentioned were the exercise by the said Government of the right and power of the Crown in the said section mentioned to dispense

Present : Lord WATSON, Lord MACNAGHTEN, Lord MORRIS, and Sir RICHARD COUCH.

with the services of any person employed in the said public service, and not otherwise." He pleaded (3) "that whilst the plaintiff was in the said service and employment the said Government abolished the plaintiff's said office, and thereupon dispensed with the services of the plaintiff as such officer, as in the declaration mentioned, in consequence of the said abolition of his said office under and in accordance with the said Civil Service Act, and the grievances in the declaration mentioned are the said dispensing with the services of the plaintiff in consequence of the said abolition of his office, and not otherwise."

These two pleas were heard, on demurrer, before *Darley*, C.J., with *Stephen* and *Cohen*, JJ., who, on the 6th May, 1897, unanimously entered judgment for the plaintiff on his demurrer to the defendant's second plea, and overruled his demurrer to the defendant's third plea, with costs.

The opinion of the Court was delivered by *Darley*, C.J., with the concurrence of the two learned Judges who sat with him. Their judgment upon the demurrer to the second plea was rested, without discussion, upon the decision of the Supreme Court in the case of *Adams* v. *Young* (1). In that case, however, the plaintiff's office was not abolished, and the loss of which he complained was solely due to his summary dismissal by the Government. In this case the plaintiff's loss of his office and its emoluments has not been due to his summary dismissal, but to the abolition by the Government of the office which he held. Now, although it was decided by this Board in *Stuart* v. *Gould* (2) that the effect of the "Civil Service Act, 1884," was to deprive the Crown of its right to dismiss its civil servants summarily, without following the procedure prescribed by the Act, it was certainly not suggested that the provisions of the Act do, either directly or by implication, take away the right of the Crown to abolish a civil office. In the argument addressed to us for the plaintiff it was not disputed that the Crown's power of abolition is recognised by the Act of 1884, which makes special provision, in the event of its exercise, for the compensation to be made to the civil servant who is thereby deprived of his office and its emoluments. The substance of the defendant's third plea, to

(1) 13 W.N. 175 ; 14 W.N 213.   (2) 17 N.S.W. L.R. 331 ; 13 W.N. 89.

which the plaintiff demurs, is that the plaintiff is not entitled to any compensation under the Act of 1884. If that can be shewn, it follows that the plaintiff has no title to insist on his claim of damages at common law, as for breach of contract.

There are only two clauses in the Act of 1884 which bear upon this question. Sect. 10 provides :—"If the services of any officer be dispensed with, in consequence of the abolition of his office, or of any departmental change, and not from any fault on his part, such officer may be required, at the rate of salary last received by him, to perform any duty for which he is considered competent in any public department, and should he refuse such change of duty, he shall not be entitled to receive any compensation." Sect. 46 enacts :—"When the services of any officer are dispensed with in consequence of the abolition of his office, and no office can be offered to him at the same salary as hereinbefore provided, or at a salary of not less than five-sixths of the same, he shall be entitled to retire upon the superannuation allowance hereinafter provided."

It was admitted in the argument for the plaintiff that at the date when his office was abolished he had not been a civil servant for such a period of time as would entitle him to a superannuation allowance. He therefore rested his claim for damages or compensation upon the failure of the Government to fulfil their statutory obligation, by offering him employment as a civil servant in some public department, at the rate of salary received by him before the abolition of his office, or at a salary of not less than five-sixths of the same.

The argument of the plaintiff was rested entirely upon the contention that, by ss. 10 and 46 of the Civil Service Act, 1884, an imperative duty is imposed upon the Government of the colony, in the event of their abolishing a civil office, to make compensation to the holder of it, by offering to him an office in some public department, at the same salary which he had received before the abolition, or at a salary not less than five-sixths of the same. For that contention, in their Lordships' opinion, there is no warrant to be found in the language of the Act, which places it entirely within the option of the Government to re-engage the civil servant whose office has been abolished, or not, as they shall see fit. Sect. 10 merely provides that the displaced official may be required to perform any duty for which he is considered competent in any public department, at the rate of salary last received by him; and the penalty of his declining to accept the duty when required is, that he shall not be entitled to any compensation. But it is clear that all questions relating to his competency, and to the propriety of requiring him to accept another situation, are left to the discretion of the Government.

In like manner, s. 46 enacts that a civil servant, displaced by the abolition of his office, shall be entitled " to retire upon the superannuation allowance hereinafter provided," if no other office can be offered to him at the same salary as hereinbefore provided, or at a salary of not less than five sixths of the same. These enactments, in so far as they relate to the offer of another office, refer back to the provisions of s. 10, and leave the right of judging whether such an offer ought to be made to the Government.

Their Lordships will therefore humbly advise Her Majesty to dismiss both the original and the cross appeals. The parties will each bear their own costs.

Appeals dismissed.

PLOMLEY *v.* T. K. STEANES, LIMITED.

1898.

July 26, 28.

The C.J.
Owen J.
and
Cohen J.

*Companies Act (37 Vic. No. 19), s. 68 (2)—Contract—Formalities—Seal—Managing
Director—Implied authority to contract on behalf of company—Part performance.*

The plaintiffs, by what purported to be a deed under the Leases Facilitation Act,
let certain premises to the defendants, a trading corporation, on whose behalf a
lease was signed by their managing director, but without affixing to it the seal of
the company. The defendants entered under the lease and paid rent for part of
the term, but ceased to occupy before it expired, and, in answer to an action on
the covenant for the rent due for the remainder of the term, set up that the lease
was not sealed with the company's seal, or signed by two directors as required by
the articles of association.

Held, that since, under the articles of association, the directors had power to
take a lease, and to delegate their powers to the managing director, who, in fact,
signed it, the plaintiff was entitled to assume that the managing director had the
authority of the company to sign it, and that the lease was binding on the company.

MOTION to set aside a verdict.

On the 27th December, 1894, the plaintiff by a deed in the
form provided by the Leases Facilitation Act, 11 Vic. No. 28, let
certain premises in George-street to the defendants for three years,
from the 1st February, 1895, to the 1st February, 1898, the
defendants to pay rates and taxes. The counterpart delivered to
the plaintiff was signed as follows :—

Signed, sealed, and delivered
by the above-named

    T. K. Steanes, Ltd.

T. K. STEANES,
    LIMITED.

Thos. K. Steanes,
    Managing Director. (L.S.)

Countersigned,
E. K. Forster,
    Secretary. (L.S.)

The "T. K. Steanes, Limited," of the signature was printed
with a rubber stamp, and the seals opposite the names of the

managing director and secretary were the ordinary red wafer
seals. The lease did not bear the seal of the company.
The company occupied the premises, having their registered
office therein, from 1st February, 1895, till 30th April, 1897, and
during that time they paid the rent reserved by the lease, and
the city rates up to the end of 1896, and the water and sewerage
rates up to the 30th June, 1896. By a lease in the same form
the defendants sublet part of the premises to one Lovell for one
year, from the 1st February, 1895.

The plaintiff now sued, under the covenants in the lease, to
recover a quarter's rent accrued due since the defendants ceased
to occupy, and certain rates and taxes which had become due and
payable before the defendants went out of occupation. There
was also a count for use and occupation. The defendants,
amongst other pleas, pleaded *non est factum*. When the case
came on for trial it was agreed, the above facts being admitted,
that a verdict for the amount claimed should be entered for the
plaintiff, with leave to the defendants to move the Court to set
it aside and enter a verdict for the defendants.

The defendants were a limited company registered under the
Companies Act under a memorandum of association which stated
(amongst many others) the objects of the company to be :—

(b) To carry on in Australia and all other parts of the world all or any of the
following trades and businesses namely : Importers Exporters Shipowners
Charterers of Ships or other vessels Warehousemen wholesale and retail
Merchants Manufacturers Ship and Insurance Brokers Carriers Forwarding
Agents Manufacturers' Agents Contractors Mechanical Engineers Electrical
Engineers Water Supply Engineers Gas Engineers and Gas Makers News-
paper Proprietors Printers Publishers Booksellers Stationers and Advertising
Agents Lithographers Electrotypers Engravers Chemists Druggists Oil and
Color Men Importers and Manufacturers of and Dealers in Pharmaceutical
Medicinal Chemical Industrial and other Preparations and Articles Compounds
Oils Paints Pigments and Varnishes Makers and Dealers in Proprietary
Articles of all kinds and any other trades or businesses incidental or auxiliary
to the above.

(f) To purchase lease or otherwise acquire land buildings plant machinery goods
patent and other rights and property of every description so far as deemed
necessary or expedient for any business for the time being or for the prospec-
tive business or requirements of the company.

The articles of association referred to during the case were:—

104. The Directors may from time to time appoint one or more of their body to
be Managing Director or Directors of the Company. . . . . .

1898.

PLOMLEY
v.
STEANES, LTD

107. The Directors may from time to time entrust to and confer upon a Managing Director, for the time being, such of the powers exercisable under these presents by the Directors as they may think fit, and may confer such powers for such time, and to be exercised for such objects and purposes and upon such terms and conditions, and with such restrictions as they think expedient; and they may confer such powers either collaterally with or to the exclusion of and in substitution for all or any of the powers of the Directors in that behalf, and may from time to time revoke, withdraw, alter, or vary, all or any of such powers.

118. The management of the business and the control of the Company shall be vested in the Directors, who, in addition to the powers and authorities by these presents expressly conferred upon them, may exercise all such powers and do all such acts and things as may be exercised or done by the Company, and are not hereby or by statute expressly directed or required to be exercised or done by the Company in General Meeting ; but subject nevertheless to any regulations from time to time made by the Company in General Meeting.

119. Without prejudice to the general powers conferred by the last preceding clause, and to the other powers conferred by these presents, it is hereby expressly declared that the Directors shall have the following powers, that is to say—power

(5) To purchase, or otherwise acquire for the Company, any property, rights, or privileges which the Company is authorised to acquire, at such price, and generally on such terms and conditions as they think fit.

(18) To enter into all such negotiations and contracts, and rescind and vary all such contracts, and execute and do all such acts, deeds, and things in the name and on behalf of the Company as they may consider expedient for or in relation to any of the matters aforesaid, or otherwise, for the purposes of the Company.

123. The Directors shall provide for the safe custody of the seal, and the seal shall never be used except by the authority of the Directors previously given, and in the presence of two Directors at the least, who shall sign every instrument to which the seal is affixed, and every such instrument to which the seal is affixed shall be countersigned by the Secretary, or some other person appointed by the Directors.

Mr. T. K. Steanes was appointed the first managing director of the company.

Davies, for the defendants, moved to set the verdict aside. The defendants, being a company, can only execute a deed by affixing the corporate seal with the formalities provided by Art. 123 of the articles of association. This lease is not sealed, nor is it signed by two of the directors. It is, therefore, inoperative to bind the company. The defendants paid rent whilst they were in occupation, but no tenancy can be inferred from the fact that they occupied and paid rent, inasmuch as they can only contract under seal, and no binding contract was executed by them. This very point is decided by *Finlay* v. *Bristol and Exeter Railway Co.* (1), which I submit concludes this present case. The way to

(1) 7 Ex. 409.

test the matter is this : Suppose the case had been tried in
the usual way, the lease would have been tendered. I should
have objected to it as not being under seal and properly
executed, and it must have been rejected. Then the deed being
informal and inadmissible, no other evidence of the tenancy
could be given : *Brewer* v. *Palmer* (1) ; and the plaintiff must
have been nonsuited. A person who contracts with a company
is taken to have notice of the articles of association, and is bound
to protect himself by obtaining a properly executed agreement.
It is only in matters of a trivial nature, of frequent occurrence,
or necessity that a corporation can be sued upon a simple
contract.

Heydon, Q.C., and *Rich*, for the plaintiff. The lease is properly
executed. By s. 68 (2) of the Companies Act, any contract
which, if made between private persons, would have to be in
writing and signed by the party to be charged, may be made
on behalf of the company in writing, signed by any person
acting under the express or implied authority of the company.
This lease, if made in England, would require to be by deed
under 8 & 9 Vic. c. 106, s. 3, but that statute not having been
adopted here, the lease is sufficient under s. 4 of the Statute of
Frauds, even though it be not that which it purports to be, *i.e.*, a
deed. This lease, therefore, comes within the words of s. 68 of
the Companies Act, and it is signed by the managing director on
behalf of the company. The question therefore is if he had
express or implied authority to sign it. The articles of association
shew that the directors have power to enter into such a contract,
and to appoint a managing director who may exercise the
directors' powers. The plaintiff was therefore entitled to assume,
when the managing director made the contract, that he was
authorised to do so. All the plaintiff was bound to enquire into
was whether the managing director *could* be authorised to sign
for the company, and that being clear under the articles of
association, the fact that he *did* sign was sufficient to imply that
he had authority : *Smith* v. *Hull Glass Co.* (2) ; *Biggerstaff* v.
Rowatt's Wharf (3).

(1) 3 Esp. 213.   (2) 11 C.B. 897.
            (3) [1896] 2 Ch. 93.

COHEN, J., referred to *South of Ireland Colliery Co. v. Waddle* (1).

Heydon, Q.C. That case treats *Finlay v. Bristol and Exeter Railway Co.* as overruled, and it is so referred to in *Pollock on Contracts,* 148. Further, the entry and occupation by the defendants is evidence of the ratification and adoption of the managing director's act, and the company are estopped from denying the contract.

THE CHIEF JUSTICE. The plaintiff is the owner of certain houses in Sydney, and in 1894, by what purported to be a deed under the Leases Facilitation Act, he leased certain premises to the defendant company for three years. The lease having been executed, the defendants entered and occupied the premises as offices for about two years, during which time they paid rent and taxes in accordance with the terms of the lease, but after that they left the place. The plaintiff now sues upon the covenant in the lease to recover rent and taxes and for use and occupation, and is met by the defence that as the lease was not properly executed by the company under their common seal, they were only liable for the time during which they were in actual occupation of the premises. When the case came on for trial it was agreed, upon certain admissions, to refer it to the Court, and the question now for our decision is whether the lease was executed by the defendants in such a way as to bind them.

It was argued, mainly on the authority of *Finlay v. The Bristol and Exeter Railway Co.* (2), that inasmuch as the defendant company did not execute the deed with the formalities which are required by their articles of association, it is so much waste paper, and the defendants were entitled to walk out of the premises leased when they chose; in other words, that the lease not having been sealed with the company's seal, the company was only a tenant so long as it chose to occupy the premises.

The lease was signed in this way: " T. K. Steanes, Limited ; Thos. K. Steanes, managing director," and then followed the usual wafer seal opposite the name of the managing director. Underneath was written "Countersigned: E. K. Forster, secretary,"

(1) L.R. 3 C.P. 463 ; 4 C.P. 617.   (2) 7 Ex. 409.

1898.   followed by another wafer seal.   Now I read that signature as

PLOMLEY   exactly equivalent to what it would have been if the word "per"
  v.
STEANES,LTD. had been inserted before " Thos. K. Steanes."   It is not necessary,

          to enable the plaintiff to succeed, to uphold this document as a
The C.J. deed.   It is true it purports to be a lease by deed under the
          provisions of the Leases Facilitation Act.   If a party wishes to
          gain the benefits conferred by the Leases Facilitation Act, he can
          only do so if he contracts by deed, but if he is not seeking these
          benefits, and if the document itself contains all that is necessary,
          or is sufficient in law without being a deed, then there is no
          necessity that the document relied upon should be effectual as a
          deed.   Here the plaintiff is in no way whatever calling in the
          assistance of the Act in question ; he sues for rent and relies
          upon a document which is a good lease in writing under the
          Statute of Frauds, and if held to be informal as a deed under
          seal, the words " the said lessee covenants with the said lessor"
          may be read "the said lessee agrees," &c., and will so be perfectly
          effectual.   This document, therefore, if made between two
          individuals, would be a perfectly good and sufficient lease, so long
          as it was not sought to gain under it any of the advantages con-
          ferred by the Leases Facilitation Act.   As to *Finlay* v. *Bristol
          and Exeter Railway Co.*, the defendants in that case were subject
          to the provisions of their own Act of Parliament only, and not
          to any provision such as is contained in s. 68 of our Companies
          Act, and, not having contracted in the manner prescribed by the
          Act under which they were incorporated, it was held that they
          could not bind themselves by their conduct.   That was the
          ground upon which that action failed.

              The defendant company in this case, however, is registered
          under the Companies Act, and in my opinion the case falls
          within s. 68 (2) of that Act, which provides that " any contract
          which if made between private persons would be by law required
          to be in writing and signed by the party to be charged therewith
          may be made on behalf of the company in writing signed by any
          person acting under the express or implied authority of the
          company."   What we have to consider, therefore, is if the
          managing director who signed the lease was acting under the
          express or implied authority of the company.   We find that the

company, by its memorandum of association, is a trading company, being formed to carry on the business of importing,
exporting, and dealing in all kinds of articles, and with power
"to purchase, lease, or otherwise acquire land, buildings, and
other property of every description so far as deemed necessary
for any business of the company." That being so, Mr. Steanes,
the managing director, takes a lease of these premises for three
years. The company enter and occupy under that lease and pay
rent in accordance with its provisions, and they carry on their
business there, and further, they sublet during part of the term·
Under these circumstances, the only conclusion I can come to is
that the managing director had express, or at the least implied,
authority to enter into the agreement, and that being so, his signature is sufficient to bind the defendants.

In *Wilson* v. *West Hurtlepool Railway Co.* (1), Lord Justice
Gurner says: "The case, however, does not rest here, for it cannot be denied that the acts which I have mentioned above had
reference to the contract, and they must, I think, be taken to
have been done in part performance of it. There was not merely
a ratification of the contract, but it was in part performed. . .
The Court proceeds in such cases on the ground of fraud, and I
cannot hold that acts which if done by an individual would
amount to a fraud, ought not to be so considered if done by a
company. . . . There is authority for saying that in the eye
of this Court it is a fraud to set up the absence of agreement
when possession has been given upon the faith of it. Apart
therefore from any question as to the terms of the agreement, and
as to the statutory provisions with respect to contracts with
companies, I can see no ground on which a specific performance
of this contract could have been refused by the Court."

So here possession was given upon the faith of the agreement,
and the defendants paid rent and taxes under the terms of that
agreement and otherwise adopted and ratified it, and it is now too
late after such performance for them to turn round and say there
was no contract at all. I am therefore of opinion that the
managing director is shewn to have had authority to enter into
the agreement within the meaning of the Companies Act, s. 68 (2),

(1) 2 De G. J. & S. at p. 491.

1898.

PLOMLEY
v.
STEANES, LTD.

The C.J.

and the verdict was therefore rightly entered for the plaintiff. The rule must be discharged.

OWEN, J.   I also am clearly of opinion that the lease is binding on the defendant company.   It purports to be signed, sealed and delivered by the company; it bears the signature of the managing director and the stamp of the company; and it appears to me that a lease so executed is good under s. 68 (2) of the Companies Act.   The lease is one which does not, in this colony, require to be by deed, but is sufficient if in writing and signed by the parties to be charged.   It therefore comes within the terms of the section I have mentioned, and the only question is whether the managing director who signed it was expressly or impliedly authorised to do so for the company.

Under the articles of association the power of the directors is very wide.   They may, by one article, exercise all such powers and do all such acts and things as may be exercised or done by the company, except those acts which by the articles or by statute may only be done by a general meeting, and by another article they may enter into, rescind, and vary all such contracts in the name and on behalf of the company as they may consider expedient.   The directors therefore have the full powers of the company and may delegate those full powers to the managing director, who may exercise them so as to bind the company.   If these powers were so delegated to the managing director he would have had express authority to enter into this lease.   There is, however, no actual evidence before us that this was so and that he had actually been authorised to make this contract on behalf of the company, but it is well settled law that where directors put themselves forward as authorised to act on behalf of a company, persons who deal with those directors are entitled to assume that everything has been done that ought to have been done.   In *Smith* v. *The Hull Glass Co.* (1), which was a case where goods were supplied to a company upon orders given by the manager, *Maule*, J., says :—" This is the simple case of a body corporate carrying on business in the ordinary way by the agency of persons apparently authorised by them and acting with their

(1) 11 C.B. at p. 928.

knowledge. The case differs in no respect from the ordinary one 1898.
of dealing at a shop or counting house : the customer is not called PLOMLEY
upon to prove the character or the authority of the shopman or *v.*
STEANES,LTD.
clerk with whom he deals; if he is acting without or contrary to
the authority conferred upon him by his employers, it is their own *Owen* J.
fault. . . . Every presumption here is to be made in favour
of the plaintiff, that the goods were ordered, as well as received
and enjoyed, by the company. The plaintiffs could only know
that the directors had power to appoint persons to perform the
duties they appeared to be doing; and they had a right to
assume that they were duly and properly appointed." And again
in *Biggerstaff* v. *Rowatt's Wharf* (1) it is laid down that persons
dealing bona fide with a managing director are entitled to assume
that he has all such powers as he purports to exercise, if they are
powers which according to the constitution of the company a
managing director can have.

In the present case, as I have already pointed out, the articles
of association provide for the delegation to the managing director
of power to enter into contracts of the kind in question, and it
therefore appears to me, on the authority of the cases I have
cited, that the plaintiff was entitled to assume that the managing
director was expressly authorised to sign the lease and to bind
the company by his signature. Beyond this it seems to me that
there is clear evidence from which his authority might be implied
in the action of the company in occupying the premises, paying
rent, and other acts of ratification.

As to *Finlay* v. *The Exeter and Bristol Railway Co.*, it
seems to me that the principles laid down in that case cannot be
adopted as law in the present day. When that case was decided
in 1852, it was held that, following the ancient common law, a
corporation could not, except in small matters such as the hiring
of a servant, contract unless they did so under seal or in the
manner directed by their Act of Parliament. But in the last
forty or fifty years there has been an enormous expansion in the
numbers of trading companies, and it has been found in practice
impossible for them to carry on their business if hampered by
the old conditions. The law has accordingly been brought into

(1) [1896] 2 Ch. at p. 102.

line with the practical requirements of the new order of things, and the power of companies to contract has been extended and simplified. In *South of Ireland Colliery Co.* v. *Waddle* (1) the law is thus laid down by *Bovill*, C.J. :—" A company can only carry on business by agents—managers and others ; and if the contracts made by these persons are contracts which relate to the objects and purposes of the company, and are not inconsistent with the rules and regulations which govern their acts, they are valid and binding on the company, though not under seal."

For these reasons I am of opinion that the rule ought to be discharged.

COHEN, J., concurred.

Rule discharged with costs.

Attorney for the plaintiff: *L. F. Dixon.*

Attorney for the defendant: *F. A. Davenport.*

(1) L.R. 3 C.P. at 469.

THE LIQUIDATOR OF THE NORTH SYDNEY INVESTMENT, &c., Co,
LTD. *v.* THE COMMISSIONERS OF TAXATION.

1898.
———
August 12.
———
The C.J.
Stephen J.
and
Owen J.

Land and Income Tax Assessment Act, 1895, *ss.* 10, 15, 28, 29—*Land tax—Mortgagor—Deduction—Interest not paid—Income tax leviable—Accumulation.*

A mortgagor who had paid no interest to the mortgagee, claimed to deduct from the land tax a sum equal to the income tax leviable for that year upon the interest derivable from the mortgage. *Held*, that he was not entitled to the deduction, because, since no interest had been paid to the mortgagee, no income tax was leviable upon it within the meaning of the proviso to s. 10 (1).

Held, further, that the interest due to the mortgagee not having been paid because there were no funds to pay it with, such interest had not accumulated or been credited within the meaning of s. 15. That section contemplates an actual existing sum capable of being paid over, and not a bad debt.

SPECIAL CASE stated by the Court of Review under the Land and Income Tax Assessment Act, 1895.

The official liquidator of the North Sydney Investment and Tramway Co., Ltd., duly lodged his land tax return, relating to 1,010 acres of land at North Sydney, and in such return it appeared that the said land was subject to a mortgage of 300,000*l.*, with interest at $4\frac{1}{2}\%$ payable half yearly, to the Perpetual Trustee Company, as trustees for the debenture holders of the said company in liquidation, who had purchased 300,000*l.* worth of debentures from the said company.

It was agreed between the appellant and respondents that 30,000*l.* should be taken as the unimproved value of the said land. The appellant, however, claimed that he was entitled to deduct from the amount of land tax chargeable on the said land for the year 1896, the amount of income tax alleged to be payable during the same year in respect of the interest accruing during the preceding year on the said mortgage; that is to say, the amount of income tax which would be chargeable on an income equal to $4\frac{1}{2}\%$ on 300,000*l.* The respondents refused to allow the deduction, and the appellant appealed to the Court of Review.

On the hearing of the appeal the following admissions were made :—(1) The property assessed, together with the uncalled capital of the company in liquidation (which together represent

1898.

LIQUIDATOR
OF THE
N. SYDNEY
INVESTMENT,
&c., Co., LTD.
v.
COMMISSION-
ERS OF
TAXATION.

the whole assets of the said company) is mortgaged for 300,000l., to the Perpetual Trustee Company, as trustees for the said debenture holders, to secure the amount of the debentures, the mortgage bearing interest at $4\frac{1}{2}\%$. (2) No interest has been paid by the company to the debenture holders or the Perpetual Trustee Company from the date of the winding up of the company in liquidation. (3) The company in liquidation has no assets producing income. (4) The company was ordered to be wound up under an ordinary compulsory winding up order in August, 1893. Mr. Giblin was appointed official liquidator, with the usual incidents of that office. It was agreed that a copy of the decree or decrees should be lodged if it should become necessary. (5) There was no assessment made by the Commissioners in respect of interest derivable by the debenture holders from the debentures; and no return or assessment of the Perpetual Trustee Company in respect of interest derivable from the mortgage. (6) The official liquidator is in possession of the land. (7) The unimproved value is agreed to be taken at 30,000l.

The Judge dismissed the appeal, holding that the liquidator was not entitled to the deduction claimed. The liquidator appealed, and the present case was stated, the question for the decision of the Supreme Court being whether or not on the evidence or admissions the appellant is entitled, under s. 10 (1) of the Land and Income Tax Assessment Act of 1895, to deduct from the amount of the land tax a sum equal to the income tax leviable on an income of 13,500l. (namely $4\frac{1}{2}\%$ on 300,000l.).

Pilcher, Q.C., and *Scarvell*, for the appellant. The liquidator claims to make a deduction in respect of interest due under the covenant, but which has not been paid. In the first place, whether paid or not, the interest due by the mortgagor is *derivable* from the mortgage within the proviso to s. 10. It may not be "derived," because it has not been paid, but it is "derivable" because its source is the covenant in the mortgage, and the fact that the mortgagor cannot pay does not alter that fact. In the second place, income tax is *leviable* upon the interest on a mortgage, whether that interest is paid or not. Income accruing to mortgagees is taxable whether it is paid or not. If not paid it may be the subject of a deduction, but it must be returned as

income, and income tax is therefore clearly *leviable* upon it. If
it is not paid, the [mortgagee can only escape liability in one of
two ways, *i.e.*, by obtaining a deduction for it under s. 28 (1) as
a loss incurred in the production of income.

OWEN, J. I do not see how it can be a loss incurred in the
production of income.

THE CHIEF JUSTICE. Income is what comes in, and if nothing
comes in there is no income. The failure to earn income is not a
loss within that section.

Pilcher, Q.C. If it is not a loss the mortgagee can only escape
paying tax under s. 29 (9) by proving to the Commissioners that
it is a bad debt.

THE CHIEF JUSTICE. Surely if my sole source of income is a
mortgage, and for one year I receive no interest, I return my
income for that year as *nil*. If it is paid next year it is taxable
as part of the income for next year; if it is never paid it is never
taxable. My income is what does actually come in to me from
the 1st January to the 31st December, and money that I *ought*
to receive, but do not, cannot possibly be looked upon as "income,"
or made the subject of a return as such.

Pilcher, Q.C. I submit that in cases like the present it must
be returned as income, and then made the subject of deduction
as a loss or bad debt. It is the practice to require such returns;
see the form of return. My argument is shortly this, that a
covenant in a mortgage to pay interest is property, and a source
of income within the meaning of the Act. Money due under it
is income accruing within the meaning of s. 15 (4). Income tax
is *leviable* upon that income whether the income be received or
not, because if the tax be evaded it can only be by way of
deduction as a loss or bad debt, and to get a deduction the
income must be made the subject of a return.

Lastly, we say that the interest, not having been paid, has
accumulated within the meaning of s. 15. Every year the
unpaid interest is added to the principal. Interest accumulates
whether there are funds available to pay it with or not. Any
other construction will lead to this difficulty, that if all arrears

1898.

LIQUIDATOR
OF THE
N. SYDNEY
INVESTMENT,
&c., CO., LTD.
v.
COMMISSION-
ERS OF
TAXATION.

1898.

LIQUIDATOR
OF THE
N. SYDNEY
INVESTMENT,
&c., Co., LTD.
v.
COMMISSION-
ERS OF
TAXATION.

of interest are paid, say at the end of five years, tax will be paid
for that year on the whole amount.   But in the meantime the
mortgagor has been paying the whole land tax without any
deduction, so that the Government will get the tax twice over,
and, moreover, there is no provision in the Act for adjusting the
account as between the mortgagor and mortgagee.

Sir *Julian Salomons* and *J. L. Campbell*, for the respondents.
Let us state the question from another point of view, *i.e.*, can the
Commissioners compel the Perpetual Trustee Co. to pay income
tax on this 13,500*l.*, which has not been paid ?   If the mortgagor
may deduct it, it necessarily follows that the mortgagee must
pay it.   It is true there is a covenant to pay it, but it has not
been paid, and therefore no income tax is leviable in respect of it.
"Income tax leviable" means that which can actually be assessed
and collected for that year.   A tax cannot be leviable on an
income which does not exist.

THE CHIEF JUSTICE.   The Act provides for a double tax, a
tax on land and a tax on income, and by the express provisions
of ss. 15 (4) and 17 (7), income derived from the ownership
of land is specially excepted, so that where income arises from
land which is subject to taxation, the person who derives that
income pays no tax upon it.   In order to meet the case where two
persons have an interest in land, as for instance a mortgagor and
a mortgagee, the mortgagee, who derives his income, not from
the land, but from his covenant, has to pay tax on the interest
which he receives.   At the same time the mortgagor being in
possession of the land, and in point of fact its owner, has to pay
land tax on its unimproved value.   In order, however, that the
tax shall not be paid twice it is provided that where the mortgagee pays income tax on the interest he receives from the
mortgagor, the mortgagor is entitled to deduct from his land tax a
sum equal to the income tax so paid by the mortgagee.   It seems
then to be clear that the Legislature intended to treat the mortgagor and the mortgagee as if they were joint owners of the
land.

Accordingly s. 10 provides that "with regard to any such lands
as are subject to any mortgage, there shall be deducted each year

from the tax upon such unimproved value a sum equal in amount to the income tax leviable for that year upon the interest derivable from the whole mortgage of the land; and this annual deduction shall not be diminished by reason of any exemptions or deductions from payment of income tax provided for in ss. 15, 16, 17." In my opinion the word "leviable" in that section must be read as if it were "assessed" for that year upon the interest derivable from the mortgage. If no interest is paid there can be no assessment. In the present case no interest has been paid, and, therefore, no income tax can be assessed in respect of it. No doubt the word "derivable" causes some difficulty in the construction of the proviso, but in my opinion it can only be read as equivalent to "paid."

Then the question arises, whether, although no interest has in point of fact been paid by the mortgagor, and though there is nothing in the estate which can produce interest, it must nevertheless be taken that the interest has been accumulating from year to year. Sect. 15 enacts that a tax shall be levied upon all incomes above a certain amount, arising or accruing to any person from any kind of property, except from land subject to land tax, and the same section further provides that "income shall be deemed to have accrued to a person within the meaning of this section, although the same be not actually paid over to such person, but be credited in account, or reinvested, or accumulated, or capitalized, or otherwise dealt with in his name or interest or on his behalf." That, in my opinion, means that there must be some actual, tangible sum of money which, being actually income, has come, or been coming to the taxpayer, and which, if not actually paid over to him, has been credited, reinvested, accumulated, or capitalized on his behalf. It cannot possibly be said that debts which have not been paid as they become due, are "accumulating" within the meaning of this section.

I am, therefore, of opinion that inasmuch as the mortgagor in this case has paid no interest he is not entitled to deduct from his land tax a sum equal to the income tax upon the interest which he ought to have paid, but has not.

1898.

Liquidator
of the
N. Sydney
Investment,
&c., Co., Ltd.
v.
Commission-
ers of
Taxation.

The C.J.

1898.

LIQUIDATOR
OF THE
N. SYDNEY
INVESTMENT,
&c., Co., LTD
v.
COMMISSION-
ERS OF
TAXATION.

STEPHEN, J.　I agree upon the whole because I feel my-self constrained to adopt Sir *Julian Salomon's* interpretation of the phrase "income tax leviable" as meaning income tax which can be assessed and collected for that year.　I may be wrong, but I think it will come as a sort of revelation to mort-gagees to find that they need not return interest payable to them under their mortgages, but not paid.

OWEN, J.　I confess that I had some difficulty over the con-struction of the proviso to s. 10, but it appears to me that the word "derivable" can only refer to the source from which the interest is to be derived.　It does not contemplate the question of whether the interest may or may not be paid, but merely refers to interest which, whether paid or not, has a mortgage for its source.　I think the construction put upon the proviso to s. 10 by the respondents' counsel is the only fair and right one. Income tax is only payable on income actually received, except in the cases provided for in s. 15, where, though not actually received, it is credited, invested, or otherwise dealt with on behalf of the person entitled.

Appeal dismissed with costs.

Attorneys for appellants: *Johnson, Minter, Simpson & Co.*

THE COMMISSIONERS OF TAXATION *v.* COVENY.

Land and Income Tax Assessment Act, ss. 10, 36, 68—*Land tax—Joint owners—Deduction.*

Joint owners of land are not entitled to a deduction of 240*l.* in respect of each such owner. There is one assessment of land owned jointly, and only one deduction is allowable from that assessment.

1898.

July 29.

The C.J.
Owen J.
and
Cohen J.

CASE stated by the Judge of the Court of Review under the Land and Income Tax Assessment Act, 1895.

The following facts were proved or admitted at the hearing before the Court of Review :—On the 10th of April, 1896, Constance May Coveny and Jane Frances Coveny furnished to the Commissioners of Taxation a joint return of three several parcels of land, of which they declared they were the mortgagees in possession under three separate mortgages. The said mortgages were to the said C. M. Coveny and J. F. Coveny jointly ; and they had contributed the moneys advanced upon the security of the said mortgages respectively in equal proportions. After the mortgagees had entered into possession and before the date to which the assessment referred, no division of the said parcels of land between the mortgagees had taken place. The mortgagees were and are not owners of any other land. In the said return the mortgagees claimed that there should be deducted, in the assessment of the returned land, two sums of 240*l.* each ; *i.e.,* one deduction in respect of each mortgagee. The Commissioners disallowed this claim, and allowed only one deduction of 240*l.* in the joint assessment.

The said C. M. Coveny and J. F. Coveny appealed to the Court of Review against the assessment of the Commissioners, and the Judge upheld the appeal, holding that the exemption or deduction referred to in s. 10 (1) was a personal right to the benefit of which each individual owner was entitled ; and that, in the circumstances of the case, the Commissioners ought to have allowed deductions of 240*l.* in respect to each of the mortgagees. The Commissioners appealed.

U 2

The question for the determination of the Supreme Court, was, whether, under the circumstances, an allowance of 240*l.* should be made to each of the said mortgagees.

Sir *Julian Salomons*, Q.C., and *J. L. Campbell*, for the Commissioners of Taxation, in support of the appeal. Joint tenants are in law one single owner: *Williams' Real Property*, ch. 6, p. 136; and the word "owner" in s. 10 (1) includes the plural. Sect. 68 defines "owner" to mean a person jointly entitled to land as mortgagee in possession, which is the present case, and by s. 36 joint owners are to be assessed jointly. In the case of joint owners, therefore, there can be only one assessment, and one deduction from such assessment. Otherwise by conveying to a number of persons, the tax could always be evaded.

Heydon, Q.C., for the respondents. I do not deny the general law as to the nature of a joint tenancy, but, in considering the incidence of a tax on land, the fact and common sense of the matter is that if two persons are joint owners of land worth 1000*l.*, each is the owner of land worth 500*l.* The policy of the Act is to entitle every owner of land to deduct his 240*l.* Sect. 10 expressly says that the tax is payable by *every* owner, *i.e.*, every several owner. The tax is, therefore, a tax on each and every land owner, not a tax upon the land itself, and the 240*l.* is not an exemption, but a deduction to which each owner is entitled.

THE CHIEF JUSTICE. I am of opinion that the Judge of the Court of Review was wrong, and that only one deduction of 240*l.* should be allowed. Sect. 36 of the Land and Income Tax Assessment Act provides that joint owners of land are to be assessed jointly, *i.e.*, that there is only to be one assessment in respect of the land of which they are joint owners, although each is responsible for making the returns and for payment of the tax. Then, by s. 68, owner is defined to include every person who is jointly or severally entitled to any land whether as beneficial owner, mortgagee in possession or otherwise. If then we read the words of the definition clause, so far as it applies to this case, into s. 10 in place of the word "owner," that section will run as follows:— " And such tax shall be levied and paid as follows :—By every person who is jointly or severally, whether at law or in equity, entitled to receive, or in actual receipt, or if the land were let to a tenant would be entitled to receive the rents and profits thereof, whether as beneficial owner, trustee, mortgagee in possession or otherwise, in respect of all land of which he is such owner for every pound of the unimproved value thereof as assessed under the provisions of this Act, after deducting the sum of 240*l*." It appears to me to be clear, therefore, that in respect of land held jointly there is to be but one assessment, and from that one assessment there can only be one deduction of 240*l*. The right to have the deduction made is not a personal right to which each individual owner is entitled, but a right to have the specified amount deducted once in respect of each assessment.

OWEN, J. I am of the same opinion and for the same reasons. To give effect to Mr. *Heydon's* contention, you would have to read into s. 10 (1) the words "in respect of each of the interests of the several owners" after the first sentence. These words are not in the sub-section, and I see nothing to shew that they are intended to be implied. On the contrary, the various sections of the Act seem conclusively to shew that the deduction is to be made from the same assessment once, and once only.

COHEN, J., concurred.

Appeal sustained.

Attorneys for the respondents : *Makinson & Plunkett.*

1898.

COMMISSION-
ERS OF
TAXATION
v.,
COVENY.

The C.J.

KING v. HENDERSON.

1898.

June 23.

Privy
Council.*

*Bankruptcy Act, 1887 (51 Vic. No. 19), s. 4 (2) ; R. 80—Reasonable and pro-
bable cause—Motive—Abuse of process of the Court—Bankruptcy notice.*

Proceedings which are an abuse of the process of the Court are instituted
" without reasonable and probable cause," but the mere motive with which such
proceedings are instituted, not amounting to fraud, will not make them an abuse
of the process of the Court ; it must be shewn that in the circumstances the
remedy sought would be unsuitable.

Rule 80 (which is the same as Rule 51 of the General Rules of 1887) enabling
a Judge to declare that no act of bankruptcy has been committed, is *ultra vires*.

The decision of the Registrar on a bankruptcy petition does not constitute *res
judicata* with respect to the sufficiency of the petitioning creditor's debt, and his
reasons for such decision are immaterial upon any issue as to the same. *King* v.
Henderson (1) affirmed ; *In re Vitoria* (2) approved.

The following is the judgment of the Lords of the Judicial
Committee of the Privy Council on the appeal from the judgment
of the Supreme Court, reported 18 N.S.W. L.R. 1.

The facts of the case and the nature of the appeal appear in
the judgment of their Lordships and in the report of the case in
the Court below.

June 23,

On June 23rd, judgment was delivered by

LORD WATSON. The appellant, in August, 1896, brought the
present action for damages against the respondent, before the
Supreme Court of New South Wales. The declaration sets
forth that the respondent falsely and maliciously, and without
reasonable or probable cause, presented a petition to the Judge
in Bankruptcy, praying that a sequestration order might be
made in respect of the estate of the appellant, according to the
provisions of the New South Wales Bankruptcy Act of 1887,
upon the allegation that the appellant had committed an act of
bankruptcy, inasmuch as he did not comply with the requirements of a bankruptcy notice procured at the instigation of the

(1) 18 N.S.W. L.R. 1.   (2) [1894] 2 Q.B. 387 ; 1 Man. 236.

* Present: Lord WATSON, Lord HOBHOUSE, Lord DAVEY, Sir RICHARD COUCH.

1898.

KING
v.
HENDERSON.

Lord Watson.

respondent to be issued by one Alexander Hallen against the appellant; that the appellant shewed cause against the said petition, and disputed the commission of the said act of bankruptcy, and that the said petition was dismissed; that it was afterwards ordered by the Judge in Bankruptcy that the said bankruptcy notice should be set aside, and that it was thereupon declared by the Judge that the said act of bankruptcy had not been committed by the appellant; that all proceedings in respect of said petition were, upon such dismissal and order and declaration as aforesaid, determined; and that the appellant had, by reason of the premises, been damaged in his business and otherwise. The declaration was met by a note of pleas and demurrer for the respondent, the terms of which it is unnecessary to recite.

Upon these pleadings the parties joined issue, and the case went to trial before *Cohen*, J., and a jury, on the 14th December, 1896, when three witnesses, including himself, were examined for the appellant. At the close of the appellant's evidence, the respondent moved for a nonsuit, which was allowed by the presiding Judge. On the 29th December, 1896, the appellant filed a rule *nisi*, calling upon the respondent to shew cause why the nonsuit should not be set aside, and a new trial granted. After hearing counsel for the appellant, the Court by a majority, consisting of *Darley*, C.J., and *Owen*, J., refused the rule. *Stephen*, J., was of opinion that the rule should be allowed to go on, in order that the points raised might be more fully argued.

It appears from the evidence that the appellant, who had previously carried on business as a stevedore and wool presser, on the 2nd August, 1893, entered into partnership, for the term of five years, with one William Collins, under the firm name of H. J. King & Co., for the purpose of carrying on the business of wool pressers, stevedores, and shipping agents, at Sydney and elsewhere. By the contract of co-partnery it was stipulated that Collins should, if he thought fit, be at liberty to remain in his employment of shipping clerk in the office of the German Australian Steam Ship Company, and to accept any other similar position during the continuance of the partnership; and also that the appellant should have the active conduct of the business of the firm, and should receive a salary of 400*l.* per annum,

Lordships are of opinion that the order of the learned Judge, in so far as it declares that no act of bankruptcy had been committed by the appellant, went beyond his jurisdiction, and was unwarranted by the Bankruptcy Act of the colony. These Acts define, with great minuteness, the various ways in which an act of bankruptcy may be constituted, one of them being by a bankruptcy notice under s. 4 (2) of the principal Act. When an application is made for a sequestration order, which complies with the requirements of ss. 6, 7 and 8 of the same Act, ample discretion is vested in the Judge either to grant or refuse the petition; and, if a sequestration order be made, it may subsequently (s. 5 [II.]) be discharged or annulled. But whilst the Judge may, in his discretion, competently refuse to follow up an act of bankruptcy by issuing a sequestration order, the statutes give him no jurisdiction to annul an act of bankruptcy, or to declare that it never was committed. There is no authority to be found for the procedure of the learned Judge, save in the 51st of the General Rules framed by the Court, which provides that " When the Judge makes an order setting aside the bankruptcy notice, he may at the same time declare that no act of bankruptcy has been committed by the debtor under such notice." Now the only power which the Court has to frame rules is conferred by s. 119 of the principal Act, and it is strictly limited to rules " for the purpose of regulating any matter under this Act." In the opinion of their Lordships, a rule empowering the Judge to make a declaration that no act of bankruptcy had been committed under the notice, is in no sense a regulation either framed or calculated to carry out the objects of the Act. It is, in their opinion, the new creation of a jurisdiction which the Legislature withheld, it is inconsistent with and so far repeals the plain enactments of the statute, and it takes away from creditors the absolute right which the statute gave them of founding a petition for a sequestration order upon the bankruptcy notice.

Upon the hearing of this appeal, it was maintained for the appellant that the orders of the Court below ought to be reversed, and the action remitted for new trial, upon two separate grounds; the first of these being that certain documentary evidence had been unduly rejected by the presiding Judge; and the second, that the learned Judge, instead of directing a nonsuit, ought to have submitted to the jury certain issues which were only fitted for their consideration. Their Lordships do not think that either of these objections, which they will notice in their order, is well-founded.

At the trial the decision of the Registrar, dated the 3rd July, 1896, dismissing the respondent's petition for an order seques-trating the appellant's estate was admitted without objection. But an objection was taken when the appellant's counsel tendered in evidence "the full written judgment" delivered by the Registrar on that occasion. The document thus tendered was, in their Lordships' opinion, rightly rejected by the presiding Judge. Sect. 8, sub-ss. (2) and (4) of the New South Wales Act of 1887, give the Registrar no jurisdiction, except to grant or to dismiss a creditor's petition for sequestration. The terms of that clause and of these sub-sections are substantially the same with those of s. 7, sub-ss. (2) and (3) of the English Bankruptcy Act, 1883 ; and it was held by the Court of Appeal in *Ex parte Vitoria* (1) that the decision of the Registrar, affirming the insufficiency of the petitioning creditor's debt, did not constitute *res judicata*. Lord *Esher*, M.R., observed, "all that he (*i.e.*, the Registrar) can do is to refuse to make a receiving order in respect of the judgment debt. That is the limit of his discretion. That being so, the case does not come within' the doctrine of *res judicata* at all." In their Lordships' opinion, these observations are equally applicable to the statute of New South Wales. The order made by the Registrar on the 3rd July, 1896, is very properly confined to a simple dismissal of the respondent's petition. The reasons by which he was influenced, or which he may have thought fit to assign in delivering judgment, are immaterial, because they could not raise an estoppel against the respondent ; and the document tendered, if it had been admitted, would have amounted to nothing more than hearsay evidence of the opinion of an individual upon points which he had no juris-diction to determine.

In support of his other and more serious objection to the conduct and result of the trial, the appellant's counsel mainly

(1) [1894] 2 Q.B. 387 ; 1 Man. 236.

1896.
KING
v.
HENDERSON.

Lord Watson.

CASES AT LAW.

relied upon the evidence, as shewing or tending to shew that, in presenting his petition for a sequestration order, the respondent was actuated, not by an honest wish to secure payment of the debt which the appellant owed him, but by a desire to effect the exclusion of the appellant from the firm of H. J. King & Co. He maintained that the respondent's resort to sequestration in bankruptcy with that motive and with that object constituted an abuse of the process of the Court, and a fraud ; and that the Judge ought, in some form, to have remitted to the jury the question whether the respondent had been guilty of such abuse and fraud, with the direction that, in the event of their answering the question in the affirmative, they ought to return a verdict for the appellant.

Their Lordships do not dispute the soundness of the proposition that a plaintiff or petitioner, who institutes and insists in a process before the Bankruptcy or any other Court, in circumstances which make it an abuse of the remedy sought, or a fraud upon the Court, cannot be said to have acted in that proceeding either with reasonable or probable cause. But, in using that language, it becomes necessary to consider what will, in the proper legal sense of the words, be sufficient to constitute what is generally known as an abuse of process or as fraud upon the Court. In the opinion of their Lordships, mere motive, however reprehensible, will not be sufficient for that purpose ; it must be shewn that, in the circumstances in which the interposition of the Court is sought, the remedy would be unsuitable, and would enable the person obtaining it fraudulently to defeat the rights of others, whether legal or equitable.

In *Ex parte Gallimore* (1) a tenant moved to set aside a commission of bankruptcy, issued at the instance of his landlord upon two grounds, (1) that he was not a trader within the meaning of the statutes then in force, and (2) that the commission had been taken out by his landlord, contrary to the good faith of their mutual contract, with the object of determining his mineral lease. The Lord Chancellor (Lord *Eldon*) directed issues to try the question whether the applicant was a trader. With regard to the second ground upon which the motion was based, the

(1) 2 Rose 424.

noble and learned Lord, in giving judgment, observed :—"I see
no reason why the process in bankruptcy should not be affected
by the same species of fraud which would affect and set aside
any other process in any other Court." In the subsequent case
of *Ex parte Wilbran* (1), which depended before the Vice-
Chancellor (Sir *John Leach*), a mercantile firm who were creditors
of another firm arrested its individual partners, all of whom put
in bail, with the exception of Wilbran, who remained in prison
for two months, when he was made bankrupt by the incarcera-
ting creditors. Wilbran then petitioned to supersede the commission, on the ground that it had been unfairly used for the
purpose of dissolving the partnership in so far as he was
concerned. The petition was opposed by the creditor firm, who
did not, apparently, dispute the fact that they desired and
intended to put an end to Wilbran's connection with his firm,
but pleaded that such motive was not a ground of interference,
either on general equity, or as an abuse of the commission. Sir
John Leach, after conferring with the *Lord Chancellor*, dismissed
the petition. His Honour said : "That a commission was, in a
qualified sense, a legal right, like an action, and that Courts of
justice had no concern with the motives of parties who asserted
a legal right. In *Ex parte Harcourt* (2) the bankrupt himself,
with a view to dissolve the partnership, procured a commission
to be issued against him. Being the bankrupt's commission it
could not stand. In *Ex parte Gallimore* (3) the commission was
used for a fraudulent purpose. He fully adopted the principle
of these cases. Here it appeared that the petitioning creditors,
having no concert with the other partners, desired to operate a
dissolution, considering it an advantageous measure for them
that the bankrupt should not continue in a firm with which they
had large dealings. There was, in this, no fraud, and it is not
enough that there be a bye motive, unless there be fraud."

The very intelligible principle which was recognised in *Ex
parte Wilbran*, does not appear to their Lordships to have been
departed from in any of the subsequent decisions which were
brought under their notice by the industry of the appellant's

1898.

KING
v.
HENDERSON.

Lord Watson.

(1) 5 Maddock 1.   (2) 2 Rose 203.
                  (3) 2 Rose 424.

counsel. Motive cannot in itself constitute fraud, although it may incite the person who entertains it to adopt proceedings which, if successful, would necessarily lead to a fraudulent result: and it is not the motive, but the course of procedure which leads to that result, which the law regards as constituting fraud. In *Ex parte Davies* (1) the Court of Appeal refused to make an adjudication in bankruptcy, where it was clearly shewn that the proceeding had been used and was meant to be used for the illegitimate and fraudulent purpose of extorting money from the debtor. And, again, in *Ex parte Griffin* (2) the same Court, although there was a good petitioning creditor's debt, and an act of bankruptcy had been committed, refused to make an adjudication. The ratio of the decision was thus explained by Lord Justice *James*:—"I think I never knew a case so transparent as to the fraud with which the whole thing was conceived, and the oppression which it was intended to exercise. It would, I think, be a shocking thing for any Court of justice in a civilised country to be made the instrument of proceedings like these."

Counsel for the appellant argued, with great plausibility, that on the trial of a case like the present, involving the inquiry whether the proceedings complained of were taken without reasonable and probable cause, it is within the province of the jury and not of the Judge, to find the facts upon which the question of probable cause depends, and that it is for the Judge, upon these facts, to determine the question of law. The rule was so laid down by the House of Lords in *Lister* v. *Perryman* (3). Their Lordships admit the propriety and cogency of the rule in any and every case where the facts admit of its application. But it appears to them that the circumstances of the present case, as these are disclosed in the evidence of the appellant, are very different in their character from the facts, as appearing in the evidence, with which the noble and learned Lords had to deal in *Lister* v. *Perryman*. It certainly is not the duty of the presiding Judge to submit any issue of fact to the jury which is not fairly raised by the evidence. There is, no doubt, evidence by the appellant tending to shew that the respondent, in petitioning for a sequestration order, was influenced by a

(1) 3 Ch. Div. 461.   (2) 12 Ch. Div. 480.
(3) L. R. 4 H.L. 521.

desire to get the appellant out of the firm of H. J. King & Co. But their Lordships have been unable to find in the evidence any fact or circumstance calculated to raise the question whether, in petitioning for sequestration of the appellant's estate, the respondent had committed a fraud upon the law or upon the Court; and, in their opinion, the learned Judge would not have been justified in raising such an issue, even if he had been invited to do so.

1898.

King
v.
Henderson.

Lord Watson.

Their Lordships are satisfied that, in point of fact, no such issue was raised by the appellant in either of the Courts below. There is no reference to it in the note made by the presiding Judge of the argument of the appellant's counsel against the respondent's motion for a nonsuit; and, what is of more importance, it is not raised in the memorandum for a rule *nisi* which was filed by the appellant. In that document it is pleaded (Art. 7) that the learned Judge ought to have ascertained by the verdict of the jury whether the respondent presented his bankruptcy petition for the concealed purpose of forcing the appellant out of the partnership of H. J. King & Co.; and also (Art. 11) ought to have directed the jury that "the presentation of a petition for an ulterior private purpose other than the equal distribution of a debtor's assets is a fraud upon the Court of Bankruptcy." A direction in these terms would, according to their Lordships' opinion, have been clearly erroneous. A desire and intention, on the part of the petitioning creditor, to terminate a partnership connection between the debtor and a firm which owed money to him and to Mr. Wood whom he represented as agent, is simply a bye-motive, which would not taint his procedure, unless there were proof of positive fraud, which is absent in this case. It was not necessary for the learned Judge to submit any question to the jury as to the alleged motive of the respondent; because, on the assumption that it did exist, which has never been seriously disputed, there are no legal grounds for coming to the conclusion that the respondent had acted without reasonable and probable cause.

Their Lordships will, therefore, humbly advise Her Majesty to affirm the judgment appealed from. The appellant must pay to the respondent his costs of this appeal.

Order accordingly.

Attorneys for the plaintiff: *White & Wolstenholme.*
Attorneys for the defendant: *Sly & Russell.*

HEATH v. COMMERCIAL BUILDING AND INVESTMENT CO.

1898.

August 9.

The C.J.
Stephen J.
and
Cohen J.

Registration of Deeds Act (7 Vic. No. 16), s. 16—Married woman—Acknowledg-
ment—Power of appointment.

It is not necessary for a deed made by a married woman executing a power of
appointment to be acknowledged under s 16 of the Registration of Deeds Act.

NEW TRIAL MOTION.

This was an action brought under s. 117 of the Real Property
Act. The plaintiff alleged that she was the owner in fee simple
of certain land, and that the defendants, without any title thereto, had obtained a certificate of title to the said land under the
provisions of the said Act.

It appeared that the plaintiff had been married to one G. B.
Barton, and that he had by his will devised to her all his real
estate "to and for such uses and trusts, intents, and purposes as
the said Mary Ann Barton" (the plaintiff), "notwithstanding
coverture, shall by any deed or deeds . . . . or by her last
will and testament direct, limit and appoint, and in default of
and until such appointment . . . . to the use of the said
Mary Ann Barton, her heirs and assigns, free from the debts, control, and engagements of any husband with whom she shall or
may hereafter intermarry."

On the 14th November, 1870, Barton died.

On the 11th June, 1880, the plaintiff married Richard Heath,
her present husband.

On the 7th July, 1881, the plaintiff mortgaged the land
devised to her by Mr. Barton to certain persons, who subsequently
conveyed the land to the defendants.

The defendants afterwards applied for and obtained a certificate
of title for this land under the provisions of the Real Property
Act.

The mortgage of the 7th July, 1881, was not acknowledged
under s. 16 of the Registration of Deeds Act (7 Vic. No. 16).
The mortgage recited the will of G. B. Barton, the death of
Barton, that the plaintiff had married, and was the wife of

1898.

HEATH
v.
COMMERCIAL
BUILDING &
INVESTMENT
Co.

Richard Heath, and that the said Richard Heath had occasion for the sum of 2,500*l.*, and had applied to the said mortgagees to advance such sum to him, which they had agreed to do, and it was witnessed, "that in consideration of 2,500*l.* by the said mortgagees to the said R. Heath, paid at the request of the said M. A. Heath, she, the said M. A. Heath, in exercise of the power in the said will contained, and of all other powers her thereunto enabling, did direct and appoint that the lands hereinafter described should thenceforth go, remain, and be to the use of the said mortgagees, their heirs and assigns." And there was a proviso for redemption on payment of the said mortgage moneys.

At the trial it was agreed that the deeds and documents relating to the case should be put in evidence, and that the land should be valued at 1,400*l.*, and that a verdict should be entered for the defendants, and leave was reserved to the plaintiff to move to set aside that verdict, and enter the verdict for her for the sum of 1,400*l.*

The rule was granted upon the grounds—

(1) That upon the documents put in evidence, and the various admissions made, the plaintiff was entitled to have the verdict entered for her for the sum of 1,400*l.* (2) That the mortgage of the 7th July, 1881, from the plaintiff to the mortgagees, mentioned therein, not being acknowledged by her apart from her husband, was ineffectual to transfer any interest to the said mortgagees, or any person claiming through them.

Ralston and *Windeyer*, for the plaintiff. Although under the English law it is unnecessary that a power of appointment executed by a married woman should be acknowledged, we submit that it is necessary under our Act (7 Vic. No. 16). In the English Act (3 & 4 Will. IV. c. 74) there is a proviso (see s. 78) which renders an acknowledgment in such a case unnecessary; but in our Act there is no such proviso. Sect. 16 refers to "*any deed,*" and, therefore, any deed conveying land made by a married woman must be acknowledged. Secondly, the substance of the deed must be considered. It was not intended that the mortgage should operate as a power of appointment. Under the will the

V 2

1898.

HEATH
v.
COMMERCIAL
BUILDING &
INVESTMENT
Co.

plaintiff had an estate in fee simple until appointment, and the
mortgage was a conveyance of the fee, and, therefore, should
have been acknowledged.

[THE CHIEF JUSTICE. She could only divest herself by
appointment, and in the mortgage there is the express provision
that she "in exercise of the power in the will contained did
direct and appoint," &c.]

But the mortgage in substance is a conveyance of the fee.

They referred to *A.J.S. Bank* v. *Bradley* (1); *Palmer* v.
Payne (2); *Farwell on Powers*, 116, 117; *Wynne* v. *Griffith* (3);
Nicholl v. *Jones* (4); *Lassence* v. *Tierney* (5).

J. L. Campbell and *Leibius*, for the defendants. This mortgage was not a conveyance. It was merely the exercise of the
power of appointment, and, therefore, s. 16 does not apply. No
interest was conveyed by the deed exercising the power. Where
a power of appointment is exercised, the conveyance is by the
instrument creating the power, and not by the deed exercising
the power. Sect. 16 was only passed to provide for cases where
before the Act it would have been necessary to levy a fine and
suffer a recovery; but in the exercise of a power of appointment
fines and recoveries were not necessary.

Sugden on Powers (8th Ed.), 153, 470; *Maundrell* v. *Maundrell* (6); *Skeeles* v. *Shearly* (7); *Ray* v. *Pung* (8).

They were stopped.

THE CHIEF JUSTICE. In this case it appears that the plaintiff
Mrs. Heath had, previously to her marriage with her present
husband, been married to Mr. Barton. Before Mr. Barton died
he made a will by which he devised the whole of his real estate
to his wife to such uses and trusts as she should by deed or will
appoint, and in default of, and until appointment, to her in fee.
Mr. Barton died, and after his death she married Mr Heath.
Wanting to raise some money for her husband she executed a
mortgage in which the will of Mr. Barton was recited, and the
death of Mr. Barton, and her marriage with Mr. Heath were also

(1) 17 N.S.W. L.R. 208; 13 W.N. 61.   (5) 1 McN. & G. 551.
(2) 17 N.S.W. L.R. Eq. 50; 12W.N. 129.   (6) 10 Ves. 254.
(3) 1 Russell 283.   (7) 8 Sim. 153.
(4) 36 L.J. Ch. 554.   (8) 5 B. & Ald. 561.

recited, and she appointed this property to the mortgagee in fee simple with a power of redemption on payment of the money lent. This deed was not acknowledged under s. 16 of the Registration Act, 7 Vic. No. 16. It appears that subsequently the mortgagees applied for and got a certificate of title under the Real Property Act for this land. That certificate having been obtained, Mrs. Heath was advised that she ought to have acknowledged the deed, and that, therefore, she was not bound by it, and that it was a mistake on the part of the mortgagees having brought the land under the Act, and a mistake on the part of the Registrar-General having issued the certificate, and accordingly she brought this action under the Act against the mortgagees, and it was arranged at the trial that if she was entitled to succeed the verdict should be entered for her for the sum of 1,400l., and by consent the verdict was entered for the defendant. The plaintiff now moves to set aside that verdict and to have the verdict entered for her for the sum of 1,400l. The whole question turns upon whether the mortgage should have been acknowledged by her under s. 16. After hearing argument I have come to the conclusion that it should not have been acknowledged. This mortgage was merely the exercise by her of the power of appointment contained in the will, and was not the execution by her of a deed by which she conveyed any interest of her own. It is quite clear that a person in executing a power of appointment contained in a will merely carries out the intention of the testator and does not execute any conveyance of his own: see *Maundrell* v. *Maundrell* (1). In this case, when executing the mortgage, she was not conveying any interest of her own, but was merely acting as the donee of the power of appointment She therefore does not come within the terms of the section.

STEPHEN, J., and COHEN, J., concurred.

Rule discharged with costs.

Attorneys for the plaintiff: *White & Wolstenholme.*
Attorneys for the defendant: *Johnson, Minter, Simpson & Co.*

(1) 10 Ves. Jun. 246.

1898.

HEATH
v.
COMMERCIAL
BUILDING &
INVESTMENT
Co.

The C.J.

·POY *v.* DARCEY.

District Courts Act, s. 71—New trial—Grounds for granting.

1898.
May 27.
July 28.

The C.J.
G. B. Simpson J.
and
Cohen J.

The power of granting a new trial conferred by s. 71 is not an absolute power to be exercised upon any grounds which the Judge may think fit, but is subject to the same limitation as to the grounds on which a new trial may be granted by the Supreme Court.

An appeal lies from the decision of a District Court Judge granting a new trial.

DISTRICT COURT APPEAL.

This was an appeal by the defendant against the decision of *Murray*, D.C.J., by which he set aside a judgment in favour of the defendant and granted a new trial.

The plaintiff brought an action to recover damages caused by the bite of a dog. The defence was that the dog did not belong to the defendant. The plaintiff having failed to prove this fact to his Honour's satisfaction, his Honour found a verdict for the defendant. The plaintiff applied for a new trial on two grounds:—

(1) That the plaintiff was taken by surprise owing to the evidence given by the defendant that he was not the owner of the dog which bit the plaintiff, after the defendant had obtained an order from the plaintiff to allow a medical practitioner (Dr. Wright) to inspect the plaintiff, and the fact of the defendant calling Dr. Wright to swear as to the extent and nature of the injury sustained by the plaintiff.

(2) That the plaintiff's attorney, since the date of the trial of this action, has obtained further evidence which, in his opinion, will prove conclusively that the defendant is the owner of the dog which bit the plaintiff.

An affidavit was filed by the managing clerk of the plaintiff's attorney, which stated " the evidence given by the defendant on the trial of the said action that he was not the owner of the dog which bit the plaintiff caused the plaintiff great surprise, as the defendant's attorney applied to the plaintiff's attorney for an order to allow a medical practitioner to inspect the plaintiff, and such order was accordingly given and such inspection was made

by Dr. Wright, and on the trial Dr. Wright was called as a witness
for the defendant and gave evidence as to the nature and extent
of the injury sustained by the plaintiff.   Since the date of the
trial I have obtained further evidence which, in my opinion, will
prove conclusively that the defendant is the owner of the dog
which bit the plaintiff."

1898.

Poy
v.
Darcey.

The above-mentioned affidavit was the only affidavit recited in
the order granting a new trial.   On the application for a new
trial the only point taken by the defendant's attorney was that
"there was no evidence before his Honour of surprise so as to
entitle the plaintiff to a new trial."

The rule *nisi* called upon the plaintiff to shew cause why that
order should not be set aside on the ground that there was no
evidence of surprise before his Honour entitling the plaintiff to
an order for a new trial.

Teece, for the applicant.

Garland, for the respondent, took the preliminary objection that
as there were two grounds on which the plaintiff moved for a new
trial, and as the only objection taken before his Honour was that
there was no evidence as to one of them, and his Honour granted
a new trial generally, no matter how wrong his Honour may have
been in granting the new trial, no objection having been taken as
to the other no appeal lies to this Court.   No note was taken as
to the latter point: *Saxton* v. *Stuart* (1).

Teece. The two grounds really resolve themselves into one
ground, and therefore the point was sufficiently taken before his
Honour.   On an application for a new trial on the ground of
surprise a party must shew not only that he was taken by surprise,
but that he is prepared with evidence on the point which, if given
on the first trial, would have entitled him to a verdict.

Garland in reply.

THE COURT (THE CHIEF JUSTICE and COHEN, J., G. B. SIMPSON,
J., *dissentiente*) held that, though ostensibly there were the
two grounds in the notice of motion before *Murray*, D.C.J., the
two grounds taken together only amounted to the one ground of

(1) 13 W.N. 239.

1898.

Poy

v.

Darcey.

surprise, and that therefore the point was sufficiently taken before his Honour.

[THE CHIEF JUSTICE. You will first of all have to satisfy us that there is an appeal from an order of a District Court Judge granting a new trial.]

Teece. The case of *Murray* v. *Weaver* (1), in which it was decided that there was no appeal from the order of a District Court Judge granting a new trial, has been overruled : *Murtagh* v. *Barry* (2) ; *Ewan* v. *Waddell* (3). In *Murdoch* v. *Durning* (4), an appeal from a District Court Judge granting a new trial was entertained. He also referred to *Wilson* v. *Sunlight G.M. Co.*(5); *How* v. *London and North Western Ry. Co.* (6) ; *Pole* v. *Bright* (7).

He was stopped on that point.

[THE CHIEF JUSTICE. The next point you have to satisfy us upon is that the Judge was wrong in granting a new trial.]

Teece. A District Court Judge is bound by the same rules as this Court in granting a new trial. In *Dillon* v. *City of Cork S.P. Co.* (8), it is laid down that to constitute surprise a case must have been made at the trial which the opposite party could not reasonably have been expected to meet. Here the very first thing the plaintiff would have to prove would be the ownership of the dog. How then can he be said to have been taken by surprise on that point ?

He was stopped.

Garland. There is no appeal from an order of a District Court Judge granting a new trial : *Murray* v. *Weaver* (9). That case was decided under s. 94 of the District Courts Act, but is still applicable, because s. 1 of the amending Act gives no new right of appeal. It is merely a procedure section substituting appeal by way of rule *nisi* for the old appeal by way of special case:

(1) 1 S.C.R. 166.	(5) 12 N.S.W.L.R. 237.
(2) 24 Q.B.D. 632.	(6) [1891] 2 Q.B. 496.
(3) 12 N.S.W.L.R. 98 ; 8 W.N. 40.	(7) [1892] 1 Q.B. 603.
(4) 14 N.S.W.L.R. 303; 9 W.N. 168.	(8) 9 Ir. R.C.L. 118.
(9) 1 S.C.R. 166.	

Phillips v. *Oakley* (1); *Rhodes* v. *Liverpool Commercial Invest-* 1898.
ment Co. (2). The question before the Judge was one of fact
and not of law. He decided as a matter of fact that there was
some evidence of surprise, and therefore this Court cannot
interfere. There is no appeal from a Judge refusing to grant a
new trial on the ground that the verdict is against evidence, as
he is sole judge of the fact whether the verdict is against evidence :
Wilton v. *Leeds Forge Valley Co.* (3). Similarly, I submit, he is
sole judge of whether there was evidence of surprise before him.
There was further evidence than appeared in the affidavit. The
Judge had before him the certificate of registration of the dog in
the defendant's name.

Poy
v.
Darcey.

C.A.V.

On the 26th July,

July 26.

THE CHIEF JUSTICE. This was an appeal by the defendant
against a decision of his Honour Mr. District Court Judge *Murray*,
by which he set aside a judgment he had given in favour of the
defendant and granted a new trial.

The action was to recover damages for an injury caused by the
bite of a dog. The defence was that the dog in question did not
belong to the defendant, and the plaintiff having failed to prove
this fact to his Honour's satisfaction, judgment passed for the
defendant. Thereupon the plaintiff moved for a new trial upon
the ground of surprise and new evidence. The motion was
supported by the affidavit of the clerk of the plaintiff's attorney,
in which he stated that the evidence of the defendant at the trial
that the dog in question did not belong to him caused the
plaintiff great surprise, and further stated that since the trial he,
the clerk, had obtained further evidence which, in his opinion,
would prove that the dog did belong to the defendant. After
argument and upon reading this affidavit, his Honour set aside
the judgment in favour of the defendant, and granted a new
trial. I am clearly of opinion that his Honour, with no other
facts before him, ought not to have set aside this judgment. The
sole issue in dispute between the parties was as to the ownership
of the dog. Plaintiffs not infrequently are surprised at a verdict

(1) 6 N.S.W.L.R. 105.   (2) 4 C.P.D. 425.
(3) 32 W.R. 461.

passing against them, and on the point of fresh evidence his
Honour had nothing before him except the opinion of the clerk
of the attorney that he would be able to obtain further evidence.
To grant a new trial upon such material is opposed to every rule
which binds the Courts in considering the question of surprise and
fresh evidence. I rather think the learned Judge has probably
been misled by the case of *Murray* v. *Weaver* (1). That case,
however, which was the opinion of a single Judge, has long since
been dissented from, and must be considered as overruled. The
law now is that the power to grant new trials conferred by s. 71
of the District Courts Act is not an absolute power to be
exercised upon any ground which the Judge may think fit, but
is subject to the same limitations as to the grounds on which a
new trial may be granted as are imposed upon the Judges of
the Supreme Court: *Murtagh* v. *Barry* (2); *How* v. *London and
North-Western Ry. Co.* (3). It has been well said, "New trials
are in themselves an enormous evil, though there are cases in
which justice demands them. No element in the administration
of justice is so destructive of its efficiency as uncertainty, and no
grievance is more sorely felt by suitors than that which snatches
success away at the moment of its accomplishment, and sets all
abroad and in doubt again after one complete hearing and
decision. Nothing shatters so much the confidence in the law
which it is the first duty of all tribunals to uphold," *per* Sir
James Wilde (33 L.J. Mat. Cas. 2). There is no jurisdiction
exercised by a Judge in which greater care is necessary, none in
which judicial discretion should be more carefully guided by
clearly laid down rules.

It has, however, been argued that no appeal will lie to this
Court from a decision of a Judge of a District Court granting a
new trial, and for this *Murray* v. *Weaver* is relied upon. The
decision in that case proceeded principally upon the supposed
absolute discretion vested in the Judges by s. 71 of the District
Courts Act.

It was also contended that this Court had no power to entertain
an appeal in an interlocutory matter, and *Carr* v. *Stringer* (4)

(1) 1 S.C.R. 166.   (3) [1891] 2 Q.B. 496.
(2) 24 Q.B.D. 632.   (4) El. Bl. & El. 123.

was referred to, where it was held that an appeal did not lie upon an interlocutory proceeding, such as the taxation of costs. It is true that the proceedings touching a new trial are also interlocutory, but in a vastly different sense from a question of taxation of costs. Here the defendant has had judgment in the cause. That judgment has been set aside, and we are now asked to order judgment to be again entered for the defendant. I can see no ground for argument that the defendant is not within the express provisions of s. 94 of the District Courts Act, and he, therefore, necessarily falls within the provisions of s. 1 of the Amending Act of 1881. This was the opinion of *Innes*, J., in *Ewan* v. *Waddell* (1). See also *Wilson* v. *Sunlight G.M. Co.* (2); *Murdoch* v. *Durning* (3). In none of these cases was the right to entertain such an appeal questioned. The true ground of appeal is that a judgment in the defendant's favour was properly entered for him, that the judgment has been set aside upon insufficient grounds, and he appeals to this Court against the setting aside of that judgment.

I am accordingly of opinion that this appeal should be allowed, that judgment should again be entered for the defendant, and that the defendant is entitled to all the costs of the proceedings in the Court below and in this Court.

G. B. SIMPSON, J., concurred.

' COHEN, J. This was an action tried in the District Court in which Poy, the respondent, sued Darcey, the appellant, for injuries caused to Poy by the bite of a dog, alleged to have been the property of Darcey, and a verdict was returned for Darcey, obviously on the ground that Darcey was not proved to be the owner of the dog, the fact of the biting not being in dispute.

The plaintiff then moved before the District Court Judge, who tried the case, for a new trial upon the following grounds:—(1) That the plaintiff was taken by surprise owing to the evidence given by the defendant that he was not the owner of the dog which bit the plaintiff after the defendant had obtained an order from the plaintiff to allow a medical practitioner to inspect the

(1) 12 N.S.W.L.R. 96 ; 8 W.N. 40.　　(2) 12 N.S.W.L.R. 237 ; 8 W.N. 75.
(3) 14 N.S.W.L.R. 303 ; 9 W.N. 168.

1898.

POY
v.
DARCEY.

The C.J.

plaintiff, and the fact of the defendant calling that practitioner to swear to the extent and nature of the injury sustained by the defendant; and (2) That the plaintiff's attorney since the date of the trial had obtained further evidence which, in his opinion, would 'prove conclusively that the defendant was the owner of the dog; and an affidavit by A. W. Gardner, a clerk to the plaintiff's attorney, was filed in support of these.

The learned Judge granted a new trial, and an order was thereupon drawn up and signed by the Judge, which so far as it is material is as follows: " Upon reading the notice of application for a new trial herein, and the affidavit of Archibald Walter Gardner sworn and filed in support thereof, and upon hearing Mr. E. G. M. Cohen, the attorney for the plaintiff, and Mr. G. F. R. Burcher, the attorney for the defendant, I do order a new trial of this action."

The defendant thereafter obtained a rule *nisi* under s 1 of 44 Vic. No. 30, calling upon the plaintiff to shew cause why the order granting the new trial should not be set aside, upon the ground "that there was no evidence of surprise before his Honour entitling the plaintiff to an order for a new trial." Upon the argument, it was contended on behalf of the plaintiff that the rule should be discharged, because the District Court Judge granted the new trial upon two distinct grounds, that objection was taken before his Honour as to one only, viz., that of surprise, whilst as to the other, which set up the discovery of fresh evidence, no objection was taken. It was, on the other hand, urged on behalf of the defendant that in fact and law the new trial was granted on one ground only, that of surprise, the ground setting up the discovery of fresh evidence being part of and essential to the maintenance of that setting up surprise, and that, therefore, the point to justify an appeal was well taken: *Anderson* v. *Titmas* (1); *Dillon* v. *The City of Cork St. P. Co.* (2). The Court, by a majority, consisting of his Honour *The Chief Justice* and myself, took the view contended for by the counsel for the defendant, Mr. Justice *G. B. Simpson* dissenting, and the argument of the ground taken on the rule *nisi* then proceeded.

(1) 36 L.T.N.S. 711.   (2) 9 Ir. R.C L. 118.

In order to shew what material was in fact before the Judge when he granted the new trial, it was stated by counsel for the plaintiff that, amongst other things, the Judge had had shewn to him by the plaintiff's attorney in the presence of the defendant's attorney a certificate of the registration of the ownership of the dog, but the Court decided that it could not consider any evidence except that recited in the order: see *In re Kurett* (1), *Ex parte Jordan* (2), and that the statement in Gardner's affidavit that "since the date of the said action I have obtained further evidence which, in my opinion, will prove conclusively that the said defendant was the owner of the dog, which bit the said plaintiff," was not such evidence as the Judge was justified in acting upon, it being a mere statement of the deponent's opinion formed upon material not before the Judge. The plaintiff's counsel then submitted that there could not be an appeal from an order of a District Court Judge granting a new trial, and this is the point finally for determination. I am of opinion, upon the authority of *How* v. *London and North Western Railway Co.* (3), affirmed on appeal (4) ; *Pole* v. *Bright* (5) ; and *Ewan* v. *Waddell* (6), per *Innes*, J., that such appeal does lie, and as the new trial was granted without any legal evidence to support the order—see *Murtagh* v. *Barry* (7)—this appeal should be allowed, and the order granting the new trial be set aside.

Rule absolute with costs.

Attorney for the appellant: *G. F. R. Burcher.*

Attorney for the respondent : *E. G. Maddocks Cohen.*

(1) 7 W.N. 5.   (4) [1892] 1 Q.B. 391.
(2) 14 W.N. 126.   (5) [1891] 1 Q B. 603.
(3) [1891] 2 Q.B 496.   (6) 12 N.S.W.R. 98 ; 8 W.N. 40
          (7) 24 Q.B. 632.

1898.

August 22.

Tho C.J.
Cohen J.
and
A.H.Simpson J.

MINISTER FOR LANDS *v.* WATT ᴀɴᴅ GILCHRIST.

Crown Lands Act of 1895, *s.* 59—*Reference by the Minister—Jurisdiction of the Land Appeal Court.*

The Local Land Board decided that certain improvements on land which had been withdrawn from a pastoral holding belonged to the pastoral lessees, and the Minister, under s. 59, referred their decision to the Land Appeal Court on the ground that the interests of the Crown were injuriously affected by their decision. When the matter came before the Land Appeal Court, they held that, as the Crown had called no evidence to shew that the interests of the Crown were injuriously affected by that decision, they had no jurisdiction to entertain the reference. *Held*, that the Land Appeal Court had jurisdiction to entertain the reference.

APPEAL FROM THE LAND APPEAL COURT.

SPEÇIAL CASE.

1. On the 3rd December, 1896, James Willmott applied for a homestead selection.

2. A ballot having been held on the same day to determine priority among the applicants for the said homestead selection, the said James Willmott was successful at the ballot in obtaining priority for his application, and all other applications were withdrawn after the said ballot.

3. On the 10th February, 1897, the said application came before the Local Land Board at Dubbo for investigation whether it should be confirmed, when the said Board having taken evidence and inquired into the said matter confirmed the said application, and further found as follows:—" Seeing that the lands were withdrawn from Genanagie Holding under s. 3 of the Act of 1895, we find the improvements are the property of the pastoral lessees."

4. On the 27th April, 1897, the Minister for Lands, purporting to act in pursuance of the provisions of s. 59 of the Crown Lands Act of 1895, referred the said decision of the said Local Land Board to the Land Appeal Court for determination of the owner-ship of the improvements on the grounds that the rights and

interests of the Crown were injuriously affected by the said

decision of the said Local Land Board, and that the said Board
had failed to discharge its duty according to law.

5. The said reference was heard by the Land Appeal Court
sitting at Sydney on the 6th July, 1897, and on the 14th of the
same month the said Court held that it had no jurisdiction to
entertain the said reference under s. 59, inasmuch as the Minister
had offered no evidence in support of either of the allegations in
the said reference, viz., that the rights and interests of the Crown
were injuriously affected by the said Board's decision, and that
the Board had failed to discharge its duty according to law.   The
said Court also held that there was no evidence before the Board
or the Court that the Crown is entitled to the improvements in
question; and, further, held that the mere fact (if it were a fact)
that a Board had arrived at an erroneous conclusion in no way
sustains a charge of default in the performance of judicial duty.

The question for the decision of the Supreme Court, is whether,
under the circumstances hereinbefore set forth, the Land Appeal
Court was right in holding that it had no jurisdiction to entertain
the said reference ?

Sir *Julian Salomons*, Q.C., and *H. Davies*, for the appellant
(the Minister for Lands).   The real matter in dispute between
the parties is as to the ownership of the improvements.   Do they
belong to the Crown, or do they belong to the pastoral lessees ?
It would be to the interest of both parties for the Court to decide
that question.

[THE CHIEF JUSTICE.   I do not think that that question is
before us on this case.]

The lessees claimed that these improvements belonged to them,
and the Board decided in their favour.   The Crown claimed the
improvements, and, therefore, the decision was one " whereby the
interests of the Crown may have been injuriously affected."   The
Land Appeal Court, therefore, had jurisdiction to hear the
reference under s. 59 of the Act of 1895.   Under that section the
reference is heard as if it were an appeal.   The Land Appeal
Court had before it the evidence which was before the Board,
and should have determined the matter one way or the other,

and it was unnecessary to adduce any further evidence before
them; but, instead of deciding the case, they held that they had
no jurisdiction, and were, therefore, clearly wrong.

P. K. White (*Pike* with him), for the respondents. Before
this reference could be heard, it was necessary for the Crown to
shew that the interests of the Crown had been injuriously affected.
Until that fact was established, the Land Appeal Court had no
jurisdiction to entertain the reference. As there was no evidence
upon that point, the Land Appeal Court were right in saying
that they had no jurisdiction.

Sir *Julian Salomons*, Q.C., was not heard in reply.

THE CHIEF JUSTICE. It appears in this case that a question
arose as to the ownership of certain improvements on a homestead selection, which was taken out of a pastoral holding. The
lessees of the pastoral holding claimed that these improvements
were their property, and called upon the Land Board to appraise
their value. Accordingly the Land Board appraised their value
at 33*l*. 2*s*., and found that the improvements belonged to the
pastoral lessees. The Minister seems to have thought that the
improvements did not belong to the lessees, but to the Crown.
If they belonged to the Crown, the ruling of the Land Board was
erroneous. That being the state of things the Minister, under s.
59 of the Act of 1895, referred the matter to the Land Appeal
Court, and the Land Appeal Court, as I understand the case,
simply held that they had no jurisdiction to entertain the matter,
inasmuch as the Minister offered no evidence. It may be that
as the Minister offered no evidence before that Court, their
finding should have been in favour of the pastoral lessees, and
that they should have confirmed the finding of the Land Board;
but however that may be, the Minister claims that he was entitled
to have a decision of the Land Appeal Court, one way or the
other. What he complains of is that the Land Appeal Court
have given no decision, and have declined jurisdiction. Mr.
White has contended that, before this reference can be heard, and
that as a condition precedent to their hearing the reference the
Minister must offer some evidence to shew that the rights or
interests of the Crown may have been injuriously affected by the

decision of the Land Board. There are no words in s. 59 which
make that necessary. That section is in these terms, "The
Minister may refer to the Land Court any decision of a Local
Land Board whereby the rights, interests or revenues of the
Crown may have been injuriously affected." That is a matter to
be determined on the reference. The only question we have to
determine is, whether the Land Appeal Court had jurisdiction to
entertain the reference ? They say that the Crown offered no
evidence "that the rights and interests of the Crown were
injuriously affected." If that be so, they should have affirmed
the decision of the Land Board. They also say that "there was
no evidence before the Board or the Court that the Crown is
entitled to the improvements in question." If they found that,
they should have decided the matter in favour of the pastoral
lessees. But they did not decide the matter, they simply decided
that they had no jurisdiction. I am clearly of opinion that they
had jurisdiction, and should have decided whether or not the
Land Board was right in its finding that the improvements
belonged to the pastoral lessees. The question submitted to us
must be answered in the negative.

COHEN, J. I am of the same opinion. On the wording of the
question submitted to us, I think that the Land Appeal Court
declined to exercise jurisdiction. It appears to me that if the
Land Appeal Court entertained the matter, and came to the conclusion that there was no evidence to shew that the interests of
the Crown had been injuriously affected by the decision of the
Land Board, they should have found for the respondents; but
instead of doing that, they say that they had no jurisdiction
to entertain the reference.

A. H. SIMPSON, J. My doubt in the matter arises from the
difficulty in understanding exactly what the finding of the Land
Appeal Court was. The Minister had power to refer the question
to the Land Appeal Court as to whether the improvements
belonged to the Crown, and the Land Court had jurisdiction to
entertain that reference, and as I read the case they did entertain

_1898._

MINISTER FOR
LANDS
_v._
WATT AND
GILCHRIST.

The C.J.

1898.

MINISTER FOR
LANDS
v.
WATT AND
GILCHRIST.

A.H. Simpson J.

that reference   But they say when the Minister offered no evidence to shew that the rights of the Crown had been injuriously
affected, they find that, under the circumstances of the case, they
had no jurisdiction.   They did not decide that they had no jurisdiction in the first place to entertain the reference.   I do not
differ from *The Chief Justice* and Mr. Justice *Cohen* in the
least as to the law laid down by them.   The only difficulty I
feel is as what really was the decision of the Land Appeal Court

Appeal upheld.

Attorneys for the respondents: *Ellis & Button.*

BOROUGH OF WALLSEND *v.* NEWCASTLE WALLSEND COAL CO.

1898.

Aug. 10,

The C.J.
Stephen J.
and
Cohen J.

Municipalities Act, s. 165 — *Rates* — *Lighting* — "*Property deriving benefit or advantage.*"

If any portion of a property derives benefit or advantage from lighting the whole property is benefited, and lighting rates are payable in respect of the whole property [*per* THE CHIEF JUSTICE and COHEN, J.]

Quære [*per* STEPHEN, J.], whether if in an action to recover lighting rates it be found that some portion of the property is not benefited lighting rates can be recovered in respect of the whole property.

DISTRICT COURT APPEAL.

The plaintiff borough brought an action in the District Court, Newcastle, holden before *Murray*, D.C.J., to recover from the defendants the sum of 98*l.* 10*s.* 2*d.*, alleged to be due as lighting rates under the Municipalities Act.

The defendants paid into Court the sum of 24*l.* 12*s.* 6*d.* in full satisfaction of the plaintiffs' claim, and pleaded never indebted as to the balance, the ground of defence being that the defendants derived no benefit from the lighting beyond the amount paid into Court.

The lighting rate sought to be recovered was 3*d.* in the pound upon 7,880*l.* 18*s.* 0*d.*, the assessed annual value of the property of the defendants.

At the trial it was admitted that a portion of the defendants' property was benefited by the lights of the municipality, but evidence was called by the defendants to shew that only one-fourth of their property derived any benefit from the lighting.

It was contended on behalf of the plaintiffs that the verdict should be entered for the full amount claimed on the grounds:—

1. That the decision of the Appeal Court is final under s. 175 of the Municipalities Act in respect of the amount to be assessed for lighting rates.

W 2

1898.

BOROUGH OF
WALLSEND
v.
NEWCASTLE
WALLSEND
COAL CO.

2. That if there be any benefit or advantage to the defendants in respect of the property assessed the whole amount of the lighting rate is payable.

3. That as the property of the defendants was all included in one assessment the lighting rate must be assessed and paid in respect of the whole property and cannot be assessed in respect of a portion only.

4. That as advantage and benefit to the defendants' property were admitted and proved the plaintiffs are entitled to recover the amount sued for.

His Honour's decision was as follows:—" I find verdict for the defendant on the ground that I find the amount paid into Court is sufficient."

A rule *nisi* to set aside this verdict was granted upon the same grounds as those taken in the District Court.

Sly and *Blacket*, for the appellants (plaintiffs). The Judge was in error in entering a verdict for the defendants. The Judge could not go into the question as to how much of the defendants' property was benefited. If any portion of the property was benefited then he was bound to find a verdict for the full amount claimed. The only question the Judge could go into was whether or not the property derived any benefit or advantage. It it derived any benefit or advantage then he was bound to find a verdict for the plaintiffs for the amount claimed. Under s. 165 the lighting rate is levied on the annual value of the rated property assessed. Sect. 164 shews how the property is to be assessed. The municipality has no power to assess part of a property, but must assess the property as a whole. They referred to *Borough of Alexandria* v. *Cooper* (1); *Borough of Kiama* v. *Charles* (2); *Knight* v. *Langport District Drainage Board* (3).

Sir *Julian Salomons*, Q.C., and *G. H. Simpson*, for the respondents (defendants). The lighting rate is only payable in respect of property deriving benefit and advantage from the lighting, and, therefore, if portion of the property derives no benefit no rates have to be paid in respect of it.

(1) 11 N.S.W.L.R. 166.   (2) 15 N.S.W.L.R. 497 ; 11 W.N. 120.
(3) [1898] 1 Q.B. 568.

1898.

BOROUGH OF
WALLSEND
v.
NEWCASTLE
WALLSEND
COAL CO.

[THE CHIEF JUSTICE. Where there is one indivisible property, what power has a municipality to make separate assessments as to portions of it ?]

The municipality could make an assessment of that portion which derives a benefit from the lighting just as if it belonged to a different owner. If a person has a large property a municipality could not put one lamp on a corner of it and then compel him to pay a lighting rate for the whole when only a small portion of it derived any benefit from the lighting. In the case of *Hunter District Water Supply and Sewerage Board* v. *Newcastle Wallsend Co.* (1), the Board sued the defendants for rates for the whole of the land where only a portion of it was within 60 yards of a main, and the Court held that it was only that portion of the land which was within 60 yards which could be rated, and that decision was affirmed on appeal to the Privy Council. So in this case it is only that portion which derives any benefit which is liable to be rated. They also referred to *Municipal District of Yass* v. *Barbour* (2).

Sly in reply. The only rate which can be levied is on the property assessed. The property assessed is the whole property, and, therefore, if any portion of the property is benefited the lighting rate must be paid on the whole property. What the Judge did in this case was to strike a rate, a thing which he clearly had no power to do : *Grand Junction Waterworks Co.* v. *Davies* (3); *Borough of North Sydney* v. *Milson* (4); *Municipal Council of Sydney* v. *Hurst* (5).

THE CHIEF JUSTICE. I am of opinion that a verdict should have been found for the plaintiff for the full amount claimed, and that a verdict for that amount should now be entered for the plaintiff. If we look not merely at the sections of the Act referred to during the argument, but at other sections in the Act, we find three things :— First, that there is one property; secondly, one assessment; and thirdly, one rate. The first section to which I shall refer is s. 172, which provides that " the council in each munici-

(1) 17 N.S.W.L.R. 1 ; 12 W.N. 69.   (3) [1897] 2 Q.B. 209.
(2) 13 W.N. 101.   (4) 15 N.S.W.L.R. 55 ; 10 W.N. 173.
                    (5) 18 N.S.W.L.R. 193 ; 13 W.N. 192.

1898.

BOROUGH OF
WALLSEND
v.
NEWCASTLE
WALLSEND
COAL CO.

The C.J.

pality shall cause a valuation to be made in each year of all
ratable property within such municipality by two competent
persons to be styled valuers." Under that section every inch of
property in the municipality must be valued. Sect. 163 defines
ratable property. Then s. 164 provides that the council shall
annually cause an estimate to be made of the probable amount
required for the then current year for the expenses of the municipality, and raise the amount so estimated "by an assessment and
rate upon all ratable property within such municipality, assessing
the same at nine-tenths of the fair average annual rental of all
building and cultivated lands," etc. So that the assessment has
to be made on the value of the property. The proviso to that
section throws some light on the question, and shews that each
property is subject to a separate and distinct assessment. The
next question to be determined is:—how is the rate to be
ascertained ? That is provided for in the same section, which
says "that no such rate shall exceed one shilling in the pound on
the assessed value of all such ratable property calculated and
determined as hereinbefore directed." That is the provision as to
the general rate, and it is clear that there must be one rate upon
one assessment upon one property. Looking back into the Act
it will be found that the voting power of the voters is calculated
upon the amount at which their properties are assessed (see s. 52).
It may be that an individual has several properties in a municipality, and if so, a separate assessment has to be made on each
property, each standing as a unit or entity in itself. Then we
come to s. 165, which seems to have given rise to some difficulty.
That section is as follows :—" For the purpose of constructing and
maintaining any works for, or relating to, the draining of lands,
water supply, sewerage, or lighting with gas or otherwise, the
council of any municipality may establish special rates, and may
levy the same upon the owners or occupiers of any property
within the municipality deriving any benefit or advantage from
such works." Suppose the section had stopped there and we
were asked upon what were these rates to be levied. The answer
would be that the rates must be levied upon the assessed value of the
property. The case of *Municipal Council of Sydney* v. *Hurst*
(1) shews the principles upon which Taxing Acts should be con-

(1) 18 N.S.W. L.R. 193.

strued. However, the section does not stop there, but continues: ⋅ 1898.
"Provided that such special rates so levied shall not in the aggre- BOROUGH OF
WALLSEND
gate in any one year exceed one shilling in the pound on the v.
annual value of the rated property assessed as aforesaid." It NEWCASTLE
WALLSEND
appears to me that it is perfectly clear that there could only be COAL CO.
one assessment upon one property, and that, when the rate is The C.J.
struck, we must look upon the property as one entity. If
any portion of the property is improved by the works carried
out by the council, then it must be taken that the whole
property is improved. There is no doubt that if a municipality put up one lamp at a particular place for the purpose
of levying a rate over a large property it would work great
injustice, but we cannot assume for one moment that these
public bodies elected by the ratepayers will act unjustly in
these matters. On the contrary, we must assume that while
discharging the duties cast upon them by the Act, they will
act justly to all the ratepayers.

I am therefore clearly of opinion that if any portion of the
property in question derived any benefit or advantage from the
lighting, the whole property derived a benefit or advantage within
the meaning of s. 165, and the property being assessed as one
entity, the rate was payable upon that assessment.

I might stop there, but there are other sections which make the
matter still more clear. Sect. 175 provides that any person feeling
himself aggrieved by the value at which his property has been
assessed, may appeal against such assessment to the Court of
Petty Sessions. Then comes s. 176, which provides for the
enforcement of rates, and provides, amongst other things, that
any overdue rates shall remain a charge upon the property in
respect of which the same is payable, that is, upon the whole
property.

But apart from that point, I cannot see what power the Judge
had to say what was the proper assessment to be made on any
particular piece of land. No such duty is thrown on the Judge
by the Act; on the contrary, s. 172 places that duty upon the valuers.
It is quite clear that no Judge or jury has any power to make
any assessment or strike any rate, and yet that is exactly what
the Judge has done in this case.

1898.

BOROUGH OF
WALLSEND
v.
NEWCASTLE
WALLSEND
COAL Co.

For these reasons I am of opinion that the verdict was wrong, and ought now to be entered for the plaintiffs for the full amount claimed.

STEPHEN, J. If the Judge had found that any distinct portion of the land did not derive any benefit or advantage from the lighting, notwithstanding that it had been assessed, I should have liked to consider the matter more carefully. I think that as the case is presented to us it must be taken that the Judge found that the property was benefited as a whole, but that it was not benefited to the full extent at which it was assessed, and he, therefore, found a sort of *quantum meruit*. That he had no power to do. The Judge having found that the property was benefited he should have found a verdict for the full amount claimed. I must not, however, be taken to give any opinion as to whether if in any case it be shewn that some distinct portion is not benefited the whole property can be rated.

COHEN, J., agreed with *The Chief Justice.*

Appeal upheld with costs.

Attorneys for the appellants : *McKenzie & McKenzie,* agents for *W. H. Baker* (Newcastle).

Attorneys for the respondents : *Dawson & Son.*

In re IRVING.

1898.

August 18.

The C.J.
Stephen J.
and
Cohen J.

Stamps Duties Act of 1880, *ss.* 2, 53—*Settlement*—*Pecuniary consideration*—
Amount of duty payable.

I. settled certain property which was mortgaged for 10,000*l.* upon trustees in consideration of their entering into a covenant to personally pay any balance that might be due to the mortgagees, if, upon the sale of the property, which was estimated to be worth 40,000*l.*, it did not realise 10,000*l.* *Held*, that the settlement was not made for bona fide pecuniary consideration within the meaning of s. 2.

Semble, that the duty payable under s. 53 was on the full value of the property (40,000*l.*), and not the value of the property less the amount due under the mortgage.

The settlement had been stamped as a conveyance on sale, the consideration being taken as the amount due under the mortgage. *Semble*, that that duty was properly payable in addition to the duty payable on it as a settlement under s. 53.

THIS was an application by the Commissioner of Stamp Duties, under s. 53 of the Stamp Duties Act of 1880, for an order to be made against the trustees under a settlement executed by Adelaide Irving, deceased, on the 30th January, 1896, directing that a sufficient part of the property included in such settlement should be sold, and the proceeds of such sale applied in payment of the stamp duty payable in respect of the settlement, and the costs of the sale and of this application.

The settlement of the 30th January, 1896, was made between Adelaide Irving of the one part, and A. S. M. Irving, F. E. Irving and S. R. Irving, the trustees, of the other part, and after reciting that Adelaide Irving was possessed of certain land and horses and stock subject to a certain mortgage to the Commercial Banking Co. of Sydney, to secure the sum of 10,000*l.*, and after reciting that, in consideration of the covenant and indemnity on the part of the trustees thereinafter contained, Adelaide Irving had agreed to make a settlement of the said land and other property to the uses and trusts thereinafter contained. It was witnessed that, in pursuance of the said agreement and in consideration of the covenant and indemnity thereinafter contained, Adelaide Irving granted, bargained, sold and assigned unto the trustees

all the land. horses and stock, to have and to hold the same upon
the trusts thereinafter declared, that is to say, upon trust to carry
on the business of a grazier then carried on by Adelaide Irving
until her death, and subject to the directions thereinbefore contained in relation to the carrying on of the said business, and to
the covenant and indemnity thereinafter contained, and the payment of debts, the trustees should, during the lifetime of Adelaide
Irving, apply the net annual income in the following manner : to
pay one-half to her during her life, an annuity of 100*l.* to J. C.
Irving, and to divide the residue into 9 equal parts, to pay two-
ninths to each of four of her children, and one-ninth to the other
child.   The deed then provided that upon her death the trustees
were to sell the land, horses and stock, and to stand possessed of
the purchase money in trust to pay off the mortgage and costs,
and to divide the balance into 9 parts, and to pay two-ninths to
each of four of her children, and one-ninth to the other child ;
and the deed contained the following covenant :—" In further
pursuance of the said agreement and in consideration of the
grant, release, conveyance and assignment hereinbefore contained,
they, the said A. S. M. Irving, F. E. Irving and S. R. Irving, do
hereby for themselves . . . . and as separate covenants,
each of them doth for herself and himself . . . covenant
with the said Adelaide Irving . . . . that they, the said
covenanting parties, or some or one of them, will duly pay and
discharge out of the proceeds of the said land . . . if the
same shall suffice therefor, and in so far as the same may not
suffice therefor, then out of their own proper moneys the hereinbefore cited mortgage debt to the Commercial Banking Co. of
Sydney, and also all other debts and liabilities whatsoever
incurred up to the date of these presents but not further, as and
when payment of the same may be required or be thought desirable, and until such payment will hold the said Adelaide Irving
. . . harmless and indemnified against the said debts."

On the 21st May, 1896, Adelaide Irving died.

The deed was stamped as a conveyance on sale, the consideration being estimated at 10,200*l.*, the amount due to the Commercial Banking Co. under the mortgage, and the sum of 51*l.* was
paid for that duty. Subsequently the Commissioner claimed

duty under s. 53 of the Stamp Duties Act of 1880, on the ground
that the deed was a settlement containing a trust to take effect
after the settlor's death, and also under sub-s. E of s. 2 of the
Stamp Duties Act of 1894. The trustees refused to pay the
duty, contending that it was not such a settlement. In order to
enable the Commissioner to make an assessment of the amount
due, the trustees lodged a declaration shewing that the value of
the lands and stock included in the settlement was 40,071*l.*, but
it was agreed that the lodging of the declaration should not be
taken as an admission that the settlement came within s. 53.
The Commissioner at first claimed 4 per cent. on the value of the
property less the mortgage debt, but now claimed 4 per cent. on
the whole value of the property, or 1,603*l.* The trustees paid to
the Commercial Banking Co. of Sydney the amount due under
the mortgage, viz., 10,200*l.*

Sir *Julian Salomons*, Q.C., and *G. H. Simpson*, for the Commissioner of Stamp Duties. Under s. 53 of the Stamp Act of
1880, a settlement containing a trust to take effect after the
death of the settlor is liable to stamp duty. This deed clearly
contains a trust to take effect after death, and, therefore, the only
question is whether it was made for " bona fide pecuniary consideration." In s. 2 "settlement" is defined as "any contract or
agreement (whether voluntary or upon any good or valuable
consideration other than a bona fide pecuniary consideration)
whereby any property shall be settled," etc. Here there was no
pecuniary consideration for this deed : *Cumberland* v. *Kelley* (1).

W. Gregory Walker, Q.C., and *Lamb*, for the trustees. This
deed is not a settlement under s. 53. There was bona fide pecuniary consideration for it. Here there was a covenant to pay
10,000*l.*; a promissory note has been held to be pecuniary consideration : *Rumball* v. *Murray* (2). If a promissory note be
pecuniary consideration, surely a promise under seal to pay money
is pecuniary consideration. Suppose that instead of entering into
this covenant the trustees had handed Mrs. Irving the money
with which to pay off the mortgage, or suppose that they had
themselves paid off the mortgage, there clearly would have been

(1) 3 B. & Ad. 602.   (2) 3 T.R. 298.

pecuniary consideration. Here they entered into this covenant, and they subsequently paid off the amount due to the bank. Pecuniary consideration does not mean that cash must actually pass at the time the deed is executed, but it means anything which may result in the payment of money. The Commissioner claimed duty on this deed as on a conveyance on sale as if the consideration were 10,200l., and the trustees paid 51l., and now his contention is that there was no pecuniary consideration for it.

If this be a settlement under s. 53, then we submit that it is quite clear that the Commissioner can only claim the duty on the property settled, *i.e.*, the equity of redemption. The value of the property free from the mortgage is 40,071l., and the Commissioner claims the duty upon that sum. But that was not the property settled. The property settled was the equity of redemption, and, therefore, the debt due to the bank under the mortgage (10,200l.) must be deducted from 40,071l., in order to ascertain the amount on which the duty is payable.

[THE CHIEF JUSTICE. On this application we have not to determine the amount of duty payable. How then can we go into this question?]

Under s. 53 the Court makes an order that a sufficient part of the property be sold to pay the duty, and, therefore, we submit that the Court must determine the amount of the duty.

Secondly, it is only as to half of the property that the trust is to take effect after her death. Under this deed one-half of the property is absolutely disposed of during her life, and, therefore, we submit that duty is payable only on one-half of the property; and in any event the duty already paid, 51l., would have to be deducted from the amount now demanded, because, if this is a settlement under s. 53, it is not a conveyance on sale, and, therefore, that amount was improperly paid.

Sir *Julian Salomons*, Q.C., in reply. The whole property is liable to duty under s. 53, and, therefore, duty is properly payable on 40,071l. There is in this deed a trust to take effect after Mrs. Irving's death as to the whole property, and not as to one-half only. It is only the income that is provided for during her life, and after her death there is a trust for sale as to the whole property.

THE CHIEF JUSTICE. In this case it appears that Mrs. Irving, being entitled to considerable property said to be worth 40,000*l.*, made a settlement. By that settlement she vested that property in three trustees. It was provided in the deed that they were to work the property, and after paying interest on a mortgage of 10,000*l.* over the property, they were to hand to her one-half of the net profits. The other half, after deducting an annuity of 100*l.*, which was to be paid to J. C. Irving, was to be divided into nine equal parts, and to each of four of her children two-ninths were to be paid, and one-ninth to the other child. In the deed the trustees covenant to pay off the mortgage out of the proceeds of the property, and if the proceeds should be insufficient, they covenant to pay out of their own moneys the balance due. After her death there was a trust to sell the property and pay off the mortgage, and divide the property into ninths, and to pay to four of her children two-ninths and one-ninth to one of her children. It is clear that this was a settlement containing a trust to take effect after her death, and, therefore, the only question is whether this was a settlement made for "bona fide pecuniary consideration." It is said that because of this covenant, which is to this effect : [His Honour read the covenant above set out.] it is not a settlement within the definition of the word settlement in s. 2 of the Stamp Duties Act as it was made for "bona fide pecuniary consideration." In my opinion by no stretch of the law, can it be said that it was made for bona fide pecuniary consideration. No doubt it has been held that cheques and promissory notes may be pecuniary consideration. but to constitute pecuniary consideration there must be something in the nature of money and taken at the time as money. This covenant, however, is nothing more than an undertaking to pay the balance due under the mortgage if this property which is worth 40,000*l.* does not sell for 10,000*l.* This was not something taken in lieu of money, and in no sense of the term can it be said to be pecuniary consideration. The probability is that the trustees would never have to pay one single sixpence under the covenant. I am clearly of opinion that this was a settlement made other than for pecuniary consideration.

I might stop there, and anything further that I say must be taken as *obiter dictum.* We must assume that the Commissioner for Stamp Duties will not demand more duty than he is entitled to. I may, however, say that, in my opinion, the stamp duty on this deed was properly payable during the lifetime of the settlor, and that the further duty demanded is properly payable now. This was a deed which it might be necessary to put into force during her lifetime, and it would have to be stamped according to the consideration, and the consideration in one sense was 10,000*l.* The stamp duty already paid was properly paid. It would also have to be stamped as a settlement taking effect after her death There is nothing wrong in the Commissioner requiring both duties to be paid.

Another point has been taken that the Commissioner should have deducted 10,000*l.* in estimating the value of the property on which the duty had to be paid, and that duty only should be paid on the value of the equity of redemption. One answer to that contention is this, that this is a succession duty, and that the executors in paying duty on the estate would not have had to pay the duty on the 10,000*l.*, but would have been entitled to deduct that amount from the assets and only pay probate duty on the balance. Another answer to that contention is, that under s. 53 duty has to be paid on the value of the property settled. The property settled was the whole property, and, therefore, the value of the property settled was the whole value of the property. I repeat that these last two matters are not properly before us, and, therefore, whatever I have said in respect of them is *obiter dictum.* What I decide is that this was a settlement under s. 53, as there was no pecuniary consideration for it.

STEPHEN, J. As to the parts of the judgment which are *obiter dicta*, my impression is in accordance with the view expressed by *The Chief Justice.* As to the main question I entirely agree with his Honour, and think the matter is too clear for argument.

COHEN, J. I agree.

> *Application granted with costs of sale (if necessary) and costs of this application. Order to lie in the office for one month.*

Attorneys for the trustees: *Macnamara & Smith.*

BOLGER *v.* MINISTER FOR LANDS.

Crown Lands Act of 1895, *s.* 14—*Reg.* 49—*Homestead selection—Application.*

An application for a homestead selection may include two or more blocks. Such application need not be accompanied by a deposit of one half year's rent on each block, but only the half year's rent on the block requiring the largest deposit. Reg. 49 is not *ultra vires.*

1898.

Aug. 22, 23.

The C.J.
Cohen J.
and
A.H.Simpson J.

APPEAL FROM THE LAND APPEAL COURT.

SPECIAL CASE.

1. On the 18th September, 1897, certain blocks of land were by notification in the Gazette duly set apart for disposal by way of homestead selection.

2. On the 18th November, James Bairstow lodged one application which embraced twenty-one of the said blocks, and with his application lodged one deposit only by way of rent and survey fee, such deposit being sufficient to cover rent and survey fee of the block requiring the largest deposit.

3. Amongst the blocks so applied for was a block of 515 acres, being portion 125 parish of Bama.

4. On the 18th November, Martin Bolger also lodged an application for the last-mentioned block, such application embracing only the said block and being accompanied by the prescribed rent and survey fee.

5. Ballots were held to determine the priority of application for the said twenty-one blocks, and James Bairstow was unsuccessful at all of such ballots except at that for portion 125, at which he came out first.

6. The Local Land Board confirmed the application of James Bairstow as for portion 125, and disallowed the application of Martin Bolger, on the ground that the land was not available.

7. Martin Bolger duly appealed to the Land Appeal Court against the decisions of the Local Land Board on the following grounds:—(1) That the application of James Bairstow was invalid, he having included more than one homestead block on one form, and lodged only one deposit and survey fee. (2) That the applica-

tion of James Bairstow was in contravention of s. 14 of the Crown Lands Act of 1895. (3) That Regulations 49 and 50 are *ultra vires* so far as they provide for the inclusion of two or more homestead blocks on one form and only one deposit and survey fee to be lodged in connection therewith. (4) That the Board was wrong in confirming James Bairstow's application, and the area in question was available for the purpose of Bolger's application.

8. The Land Appeal Court dismissed the appeals.

The questions for the decision of the Supreme Court are :—(1) Whether the Land Appeal Court was right in holding that the application lodged by James Bairstow for portion 125 was a valid application notwithstanding the facts that he lodged only one application form which embraced twenty-one blocks, and lodged therewith an amount sufficient only to cover rent and survey fee for the block requiring the largest deposit. (2) Whether the Land Appeal Court was right in holding that Reg. 49 is not *ultra vires*.

Pike and *Rose* for the appellant. Sect. 13 of the Act of 1895 provides that certain lands may be set apart for disposal by way of homestead selection. Sect. 14 says that "Any person who is not disqualified, may apply for any block so notified as a homestead selection." That means that he can apply for one block. He can only hold one block, and, therefore, he can only apply for one block. If an application for more than one block is valid, it is valid not only as to one block, but as to all the blocks applied for. Sect. 14 provides that "the application shall be accompanied by a half year's rent in advance and a survey fee." If, therefore, a man can apply for more than one block, his application must be accompanied by a half year's rent and survey fee for each block. Under s. 2 of 59 Vic. No. 26 the title to a homestead selection commences from the date of the application, if valid. If, therefore, the application for more than one block is valid, he gets a title to each block applied for immediately on application, and has a right to the possession of all the blocks applied for. The validity of an application cannot depend upon whether the applicant is successful in the ballot. "If valid," in s. 2, means that the land

applied for is available, and that the person applying is competent
to apply. Reg. 49 is *ultra vires* so far as it is inconsistent with
the Act. Sect. 14 of the Act of 1895 provides that the application must be accompanied by a half year's rent in advance, and,
therefore, if several blocks are applied for, the Act provides that
a half year's rent for each must be deposited. Reg. 49, in
providing that where there are a number of blocks applied for
only the half year's rent on the block requiring the largest
deposit need be deposited, is clearly inconsistent with the Act:
Blackwood v. *London Chartered Bank* (1).

Sir *Julian Salomons*, Q.C., and *H. Davies*, for the respondent
(the Minister for Lands). In making this application, the applicant (Bairstow) did not apply for more than one block ; he only
applied for one block. Where a number of blocks were set
apart for homestead selection, there would be nothing to prevent
a person applying for one block, and, if unsuccessful in the
ballot, withdrawing his deposit money and applying for the next
lot, and so on. But for the sake of convenience, and inasmuch as
through departmental arrangements the money would not be
returned in time to make the deposit on the second block, the
regulation has provided that if a person makes a deposit of a
half year's rent on the largest block he can then include in the
one application two or more blocks. That is not in any way
inconsistent with the Act. Sect. 14 says that " the application
shall be made and lodged in the prescribed form." Reg. 49 provides that it shall be in Form 7, and that form includes an application for more than one block.

Pike in reply. 59 Vic. No. 26 was passed to enable the applicant to take possession after making his application (see the
preamble).

[THE CHIEF JUSTICE. If he applies for twenty blocks, can he
take possession of all ?]

I submit he cannot, and that shews that he cannot apply for
twenty blocks.

(1) 5 L.R. P.C. 92.

1898.

BOLGER
v.
MINISTER FOR
LANDS.

1898.

BOLGER
v.
MINISTER FOR
LANDS.

[THE CHIEF JUSTICE.   There is nothing in s. 2 which gives the applicant the right to take possession of the land on making his application.]

That section says the title shall commence from the date of application, and the object of the Act, as set out in the preamble, is that "applicants for homestead selections should be enabled to *take possession* of the land applied for by them without delay."

[THE CHIEF JUSTICE.   There is nothing in the enacting part of the Act which carries out the preamble.]

Before this Act the title did not commence until the confirmation of the application, but under this Act the title commences from the application, and, therefore, enables the applicant to take possession immediately on application.

THE CHIEF JUSTICE.   In this case it appears that under s. 13 of the Act of 1895 the Governor set apart certain blocks of land for homestead selection.   Bairstow, acting in conformity with regulation 49, sent in an application in the form prescribed by that regulation, and in that form he mentions twenty-one blocks, any one of which he was willing to take.   Under that regulation he deposited a sum of money equal to the deposit on the largest block mentioned in his application, and he also lodged the survey fee.   There is no question that he complied with that regulation.   The only question is whether that regulation is so inconsistent with the Act as to enable us to say that it was not framed for the purpose of carrying the Act into effect, or possibly that it did not carry the Act into effect.   The course of procedure in applying for these homestead selections seems to be this: A certain day is appointed when persons may apply for the land, and, assuming that that regulation is *intra vires*, any number of persons may apply for each block of land, though each person cannot get more than one block.   Take the case where there are ten blocks and twelve persons applying for them. There is a ballot as to the first block, and the person who is successful stands out of the next ballot, and so on until all the blocks are disposed of.   In what way does that work any mischief or evil, and how can we say that it does not carry the Act into effect ?   It is a convenient course.   On the other hand, if a person applying for a number of blocks had to pay a deposit and survey fee on each block, it would be an inconvenient course. I do not see anything inconvenient in the regulation, or anything in it inconsistent with the Act, and, therefore, the case of *Blackwood* v. *London Chartered Bank of Australia* (1) applies. The *Lord Chancellor*, in speaking of regulations made under a former Crown Lands Act, says this: "If these regulations, properly construed, are found to be reasonable and convenient regulations for carrying the Act into full effect, though they may govern, not only the form, but the effect of instruments of transfer of those rights which precede the grant of leases; if they are found to relate to matters arising under the provisions of the Act, which they unquestionably do; if they are found to be consistent with the provisions of the Act, which they unquestionably are; and if they are not in the Act expressly provided for, then their Lordships cannot do otherwise than come to the conclusion that they are valid in law, and that there is no ground for the objection that they are *ultra vires*." Apply that principle and it is clear. that this regulation is not *ultra vires*.

It is said that very great inconvenience might arise, because by the Act of 1896 where a man applies for twenty blocks, they would be taken out of the holding of the lessee or licensee, and that he would be entitled to go into possession of all of them, when eventually he would only be entitled to one block. That Act was passed to amend s. 40 of the Act of 1895, which provided that the title to a homestead lease should commence from the date of confirmation. It merely provides that the title shall commence from the date of the application; but it does not give the applicant the right to go into possession on that date; although the preamble to that Act speaks of the applicant taking possession there is nothing in the enacting part of the Act which says that the applicant can take possession on the date of the application. The Act simply provides that the title to the land is to date back to the application.

(1) 5 L.R.P.C. 92.

X 2

1898.
—————
BOLGER
v.
MINISTER FOR
LANDS.

I am, therefore, of opinion that the appeal should be dismissed with costs, and that both questions should be answered in the affirmative.

COHEN, J. I am of the same opinion. It appears to me that Regulation 49 is one framed for promoting public convenience and the expeditious settlement on Crown lands. and framed for the purpose of carrying out the Crown Lands Acts, and is therefore *intra vires.*

A. H. SIMPSON, J., concurred.

Appeal dismissed with costs.

Attorneys for the appellant: *Ellis & Button.*

THE MINISTER FOR LANDS *v.* RICKETSON AND THE AUSTRALIAN
MORTGAGE, LAND AND FINANCE CO.

1898.
───
Nov. 17, 18.
December 13.
───
The C.J.
Owen J.
and
Walker J.

Crown lands—Pastoral lessee—Crown Lands Act of 1884, *s.* 78—*Withdrawal from
lease—Compensation.*

Under s. 78 (7) of the Crown Lands Act of 1884 "the Governor may withdraw
from lease any land required for any public purpose . . . and upon the publication in the *Gazette* of such withdrawal the lessee shall be entitled to compensation in respect of the land so withdrawn for the unexpired term of such lease,
and for improvements . . . upon the land so withdrawn," etc. *Held*, that
the mode of arriving at the compensation to which the lessees are entitled under
that section is to assess the value of the whole of the leasehold area with all its
improvements thereon at its value upon the day when the withdrawal was
gazetted, and then assess the value of the whole leasehold area less the area withdrawn, and the difference between the two amounts assessed is the amount of
compensation to which they are entitled.

SPECIAL CASE STATED BY THE LAND APPEAL COURT.

1. The leasehold area of Billabong pastoral holding has for some
years past been held by Henry Ricketson and The Australian
Mortgage, Land and Finance Co., Limited, under a pastoral lease
granted by the Governor under s. 78 of the Crown Lands Act of
1884. The original term of the lease expired in the year 1895,
but an extension thereof under s. 43 of the Crown Lands Act of
1889 is still current.

2. Between the years 1885 and 1891 the lessees held the leasehold area under the right to a pastoral lease created by the
Crown Lands Act of 1884, but in 1891 a lease was issued to them
in the form prescribed under the Crown Lands Act of 1889.

3. The leasehold area contains about 30,000 acres, and, together
with freeholds and other lands held by the aforesaid lessees, is
worked as one property known as Billabong station.

4. Within the leasehold area is a natural catchment area of
about 400 acres, on which a tank (known as Bartley's tank) had
been excavated, and other improvements effected during the
original term of the pastoral lease, and for the purposes of this
case it is to be taken that the said improvements had been lawfully made by the lessees of Billabong pastoral holding.

1898.

Minister for
Lands
v.
Ricketson
and the
Australian
M L and F.
Co.

5. For the purposes of this case it is to be taken as admitted that the catchment area was required for the purpose of providing the town of Wyalong with a water supply: and, on April 1st, 1896, the Governor, in exercise of the power in that behalf conferred upon him by sub-s. 7 of s. 78 of the Crown Lands Act of 1884, withdrew the said 400 acres from the pastoral lease. And upon such withdrawal the lessees became entitled to such a refund out of the rent for the year 1896, which had been paid in advance, and to such a reduction in the future rent of the leasehold area as was proportionate to the area withdrawn.

6. The Local Land Board thereafter proceeded to appraise the compensation provided for by the aforesaid sub-s. 7 of s. 78, and in so doing it limited the inquiry to the area actually withdrawn, refusing to receive evidence as to the effect of the withdrawal on Billabong leasehold area, or to consider such effect in appraising compensation.

7. The Local Land Board accordingly appraised the compensation to which the lessees were entitled under two headings, fixing one amount to represent the value of the lease of the 400 acres for the unexpired period of the extended term, and another amount to represent the value of the improvements; these values being ascertained irrespective of the effect of the aforesaid withdrawal upon the working of any other lands held by the lessees and worked in conjunction with the area so withdrawn.

8. The lessees having appealed to the Land Appeal Court, the Court (Mr. Commissioner Brandis dissenting) held that the Local Land Board had appraised the compensation in respect of the subject improvement upon a wrong basis, and that such Board should be directed to appraise such compensation on the basis of the loss or injury which the owners have sustained and will sustain by reason of the said withdrawal, not as limited to the 400 acres withdrawn, but in connection with the entire area of the pastoral lease benefited by such improvement. And for the purposes of this case it may be taken that the Court in effect held that in respect to "compensation for the unexpired term of the lease" the proper measure of compensation was the difference between the value to the lessees of the leasehold

area before the withdrawal, and the value after the withdrawal. And that in respect of "compensation for improve- MINISTER FOR
ments" the proper measure of compensation was the loss or LANDS
injury which the lessees had sustained and would sustain by reason RICKETSON
of the withdrawal, not as limited to the 400 acres, but in con- AND THE AUSTRALIAN
nection with the entire area of the pastoral lease benefited by M. L. AND F.
the improvements. Accordingly the said Court sustained the Co.
appeal, and ordered the Local Land Board to rehear the matter.

9. The Minister for Lands has duly required the Land Appeal
Court to state and submit a case for decision by the Supreme
Court upon the questions of law hereunder specified.

The questions for decision by the Supreme Court are :—

1. Whether compensation for the "unexpired term of the
lease," as provided in sub-s. 7 of s. 78 of the Crown Lands Act of
1884, is to be appraised upon the basis of the difference between
the value to the lessees of Billabong leasehold area before the
withdrawal, and its value after the withdrawal as aforesaid.

2. Whether in appraising "compensation for improvements"
under the aforesaid section and sub-section, the effects of the
withdrawal of the improvements upon the lessees' occupancy of
the residue of the leasehold area in so far as such residue was
benefited by such improvements should be taken into account.

Sir *Julian Salomons*, Q.C., and *Canaway*, for the appellant.
The question in this case is what is the proper mode to arrive at
the compensation to be allowed to a lessee on the withdrawal
of a portion of his lease under the terms of s. 78 (7)* of the
Crown Lands Act of 1884.

The view taken by the Land Board was the correct one. In
assessing the amount of compensation you cannot take into
consideration the effect of the withdrawal on the remainder of
the leasehold area. The lessee, when he took the lease, took it

---

* Sub-s. 7 of s. 78 of the Crown Lands Act of 1884 is as follows :—"The
Governor may withdraw from lease any land required for any public purpose
. . . and upon publication in the *Gazette* of such withdrawal the lessee shall
be entitled to such compensation in respect of the land so withdrawn for the
unexpired term of such lease, and for improvements lawfully made by such lessee
upon the land so withdrawn from lease as may be determined by the Minister
after appraisement by the Local Land Board."

1898.

MINISTER FOR
LANDS
v.
RICKETSON
AND THE
M. L. AND F.
Co.

subject to the right of the Crown to resume any part of it for a public purpose. The Crown should only be compelled to pay the value of the improvements and the value of the land taken, and should not have to pay any compensation for severance. Sect. 78 limits the compensation to "compensation in respect of the land so withdrawn, and for improvements." That section says nothing about compensation for the injurious effect the withdrawal may have on the rest of the land; and it is expressly limited to those two things. The cases where freehold land is taken against the will of the owner have no application to a case where land is resumed by a landlord under the terms of the lease.

[WALKER, J. You say that it must be taken as if he had only a lease for 400 acres, and that had been resumed?]

Yes. The lessees cannot saddle the Crown with the consequential damage that may ensue to the rest of the leasehold area. The Land Appeal Court were clearly wrong in their method of valuation, because, if you take that method, the lessees would get the value of the improvements twice over. Under their method in valuing the "unexpired term of the lease" the value of the improvements would be given, and the value of the improvements would be given under the "compensation for improvements." This case is just the converse case of *Deane* v. *Minister for Lands* (1). There Deane applied under s. 63 for the rescission of a reservation and the sale of the land to him contained in the reservation, and the Court held that in estimating the value of the land the Land Board could not take into consideration the value it was to him by reason of his ownership of the adjoining land, but must estimate its value apart from that.

They also referred to *Cooper* v. *Stuart* (2); *McCulloch* v. *Abbott* (3).

Pilcher, Q.C., and *Pike*, for the respondents. Under s. 78 (7) the lessee is entitled to compensation on the withdrawal of land from the lease. Giving a man "compensation" means where you take a thing from him that you put him in the same position as

(1) 17 N.S.W.L.R. 287.   (2) 10 N.S.W.L.R. Eq. 172.
          (3) 6 N.S.W.L.R. 212.

if you had not taken it. Take the case of a tank watering a
paddock of 5,000 acres, and that the tank is made in the only
place in the 5,000 acres where you could get water. Take away
the tank, and the whole 5,000 acres become valueless. Would it
be any compensation if the Crown were to resume the land on
which the tank stood if they merely paid the value of that land
and the cost of making the tank?

[THE CHIEF JUSTICE. In the mode suggested by the Land
Appeal Court would you not get the value of the improvements
twice over?]

We submit not. In valuing the "unexpired term of the lease"
they say you should value the whole of the leasehold area without
improvements, and assess the loss occasioned by the withdrawal of
the land, and then you value the loss occasioned by taking the
tank away. We do not contend that you can get the value of
the improvements twice over. The whole question is whether
the lessees are entitled to get as compensation the value of the
damage done to the rest of the leasehold area by reason of the
withdrawal of the 400 acres. If the Court thinks that the mode
which the Land Court has said is the proper mode of valuation
is not the right one, the Court should not simply uphold the
appeal, but should say what is the proper mode of valuation.

They referred to *Stebbing* v. *Metropolitan Board of Works* (1);
McBean v. *Grieve* (2); *Cafe* v. *Morrison* (3).

Sir *Julian Salomons*, Q.C., in reply.

C. A. V.

13th December,

THE CHIEF JUSTICE. In this case it appears that the respondents are the lessees from the Crown of some 30,000 acres of Crown
lands known as the Billabong pastoral holding. Upon this holding
there is a natural catchment area of about 400 acres, on which a tank
known as Bartley's tank has been excavated, and other improvements have been lawfully effected by the lessees during the
term of a pastoral lease granted under the provisions of s. 78 of

1898.

MINISTER FOR
LANDS
v.
RICKETSON
AND THE
AUSTRALIAN
M. L. AND F.
Co.

December 13.

(1) 6 L.R. Q.B. at p. 42.   (2) 2 S.C.R. N.S. 153.
                    (3) 2 S.C.R. N.S. 297.

1898.

MINISTER FOR
LANDS
v.
RICKETSON
AND THE
AUSTRALIAN
M. L. AND F.
Co.

The C.J.

the Crown Lands Act of 1884. The existing lease is an extension of the lease so granted, and takes effect under the provisions of s. 43 of the Crown Lands Act of 1889. The Governor, under the powers conferred by sub-s. 7 of s. 78 of the Act of 1884, has withdrawn from the existing lease the natural catchment area of 400 acres for the purpose of supplying the town of Wyalong with water, and it is conceded that the lessees are entitled to compensation under sub-s. 7, the question between the parties being upon what basis or principle the amount of such compensation is to be arrived at. Sub-s. 7 reads as follows:—" The Governor may withdraw from lease any land required for any public purpose, including, for the purposes of settlement for towns and villages, and upon publication in the *Gazette* of such withdrawal, the lessee shall be entitled to such compensation in respect of the land so withdrawn from lease as may be determined by the Minister after appraisement by the Local Land Board." It is evident the intention of the Legislature was that the lessee should have full compensation for the withdrawal of the land from his holding, for observe, they do not direct that he shall merely obtain compensation for his interest in the lease in respect of the land withdrawn, which is the meaning of the words "for the unexpired term of such lease," but they also direct that the improvements which may be upon the land are to be taken into consideration. In effect, the Legislature say we reserve to the Governor power to withdraw any land from the lease granted to you for public purposes, but we will make you full compensation in so far as your interest in the lease may be effected by such withdrawal, and if there happen to be any improvements upon the land so withdrawn that fact must be taken into consideration when considering the value of your interest in the lease. Accordingly, compensation is to be in respect of the land withdrawn, and is to be for the unexpired term of the lease, and for the improvements.

Now, "compensation" is defined to be "that which constitutes or is regarded as an equivalent," "that which compensates for loss," and is said to be synonymous with "indemnification." In *Stebbing* v. *The Metropolitan Board of Works* (1), *Cockburn*,

(1) 6 L. R. Q.B., at p. 42.

1898.

MINISTER FOR
LANDS
v.
RICKETSON
AND THE
AUSTRALIAN
M. L. AND F.
Co.

The C.J.

C.J., says: "When Parliament gives compulsory powers, and provides that compensation shall be made to the person from whom property is taken for the loss he sustains, it is intended that he shall be compensated to the extent of his loss, and that his loss shall be tested by what was the value of the thing to him." The lessees are therefore entitled to indemnification; they are entitled to say "we are to have compensation for our loss of this natural catchment area and the improvements thereon, and our loss is to be tested by what was the value of this to us."

Now, it appears obvious to me that there is but one mode of arriving at the compensation to which these lessees are entitled, and that is to take the two things for which compensation is to be given, the unexpired term of the lease and improvements together, as being one, and then you get at the amount of compensation or indemnification in this way. Assess the value of the whole 30,000 acres, with all its improvements thereon, at its value, upon the day when the withdrawal was gazetted, and then assess the value of the 29,600 acres, being all that is left to the lessees, the difference between the two amounts assessed will be the loss which the lessees incur, and the amount of compensation to which they are entitled. As, for instance, suppose the assessors value the lessees' interest in the whole 30,000 acres upon the day before the withdrawal at 5000*l*., and value the 29,600 acres the day after the withdrawal of the 400 acres at 3,000*l*., then the compensation to which the lessees will become entitled will be 2,000*l*. It is evident by this mode of assessment the lessee is fully compensated for all loss he suffers in respect of the land withdrawn, inasmuch as to arrive at the difference between the 5,000*l*. and the 3,000*l*., the question of the unexpired term of the lease, as also the question of the improvements, are necessarily involved. Both the unexpired term of the lease and the improvements on the 400 acres formed part of the 30,000 acres assessed at 5,000*l*., while the 400 acres and improvements were excluded from the assessment which gave the 3,000*l*. In other words, in the case I have put, the sum of 2,000*l*. is the full measure of the loss which the lessees have sustained by the withdrawal from the lease of the 400 acres in question, with the improvements which were then upon such 400 acres.

1898.

MINISTER FOR
LANDS
v.
RICKETSON
AND THE
AUSTRALIAN
M. L. AND F.
Co.

The C.J.

As to the details of assessment, or the means by which the assessors are to arrive at the value, I express no opinion; I have not facts before me which would enable me to offer any guide; of course the assessors have to bear in mind it is leasehold they are assessing, and have to take the currency of the lease into consideration, and that on its expiration all the improvements upon the 30,000 acres become the property of the Crown : see s. 44 of Crown Lands Act of 1889. This applies whether they are assessing the whole 30,000 acres or the 29,600 acres.

And now as to the question placed before the Court. If the abstract question be asked, upon what principle or basis is the compensation provided for by sub-s. 7 to be arrived at ? I would have no difficulty in answering the question as I have answered it. The difficulty in this case arises from the way in which it has been presented to the Court. Both the Land Board and the Land Court treat the two matters " unexpired term of lease " and " improvements " as being two distinct things to be valued separately. The Land Board clearly came to an erroneous conclusion. They appear to have taken the value of the improvements merely with relation to the 400 acres, overlooking the fact that the tank placed on the 400 acres was not for the use of the 400 acres only, but for the use of the 30,000 acres, and that the 29,600 acres, being deprived of the use of this tank, might render them of but little if any value. The Land Court's method of valuation is also erroneous, although not open to such grave objection as that of the Land Board. This latter method is open to the objection that in assessing compensation for the unexpired term of the lease, apart from compensation for improvements, you incur the risk of valuing the improvements twice over. I am unable to see how the value to the lessees of the leasehold area before the withdrawal, and the value after the withdrawal, can be arrived at, without taking into consideration the value of the improvements to the property as a whole.

Being of opinion that there cannot be *separate* compensation for the unexpired term of the lease, and for improvements, I am unable to answer the questions placed before the Court. I think the Land Board and Land Court were both in error, and that the only basis upon which compensation under sub-s. 7 can properly be ascertained, is that which I have stated in this judgment.

I think the matter should be remitted to the Land Board, with directions to assess compensation in the mode pointed out by me. There will be no costs of this appeal.

OWEN, J. This is a special case stated by the Land Appeal Court. The questions for the decision of the Supreme Court are :—1. Whether compensation for the "unexpired term of the lease" as provided in sub-s. 7 of s. 78 of the Crown Lands Act of 1884, is to be appraised upon the basis of the difference between the value to the lessees of Billabong leasehold area before the withdrawal, and its value after the withdrawal. 2. Whether in appraising "compensation for improvements" under the aforesaid section and sub-section, the effects of the withdrawal of the improvements upon the lessees' occupancy of the residue of the leasehold area, in so far as such residue was benefited by such improvements, should be taken into account.

The leasehold area of Billabong pastoral holding, containing about 30,000 acres, is held by Henry Ricketson and The Australian Mortgage Land and Finance Company, under a pastoral lease dated the 17th day of September, 1891, and granted under s. 78 of the Crown Lands Act of 1884, which lease expired in 1895, but had been extended under s. 43 of the Crown Lands Act of 1889, and is still current. Between the years 1885 and 1891 this leasehold area was held by the lessees under the provisions of the Crown Lands Act of 1884, and, together with freehold and other lands, is worked by the lessees as one property. Within the leasehold is a natural catchment area of about 400 acres, on which a tank has been excavated and other improvements made during the term of the original lease. This catchment area and tank were required to supply the town of Wyalong with water; and accordingly the Governor, under the powers conferred by sub-s. 7 of s. 78 of the Crown Lands Act of 1884, withdrew the whole catchment area and tank from the pastoral lease.

Sub-s. 7 provides that " The Government may withdraw from lease any land required for any public purpose . . . . and

Margin notes:

1898.

MINISTER FOR LANDS
v.
RICKETSON AND THE AUSTRALIAN M. L. AND F. Co.

The C.J.

MINISTER FOR
LANDS
v.
RICKERSON
AND THE
AUSTRALIAN
M. L. AND F.
Co.

Owen J.

upon publication in the *Gazette* of such withdrawal, the lessee shall be entitled to such compensation in respect of the land so withdrawn for the unexpired term of such lease, and for improvements lawfully made by such lessee upon the land so withdrawn from lease as may be determined by the Minister after appraisement by the Local Land Board."

The main question turns on the mode of appraising compensation for improvements, whether such compensation is to be limited to the cost of such improvements, or whether it is to include the loss and injury to the rest of the leasehold by the withdrawal of the catchment area and tank. It appears to me that if the Legislature had intended only to recoup the lessee for his expenditure on the improvements that are taken away, it would have said so expressly, and the sub-section would have run thus :—The lessee shall be entitled to compensation for the unexpired term of the lease together with the cost of improvements made on the land withdrawn. But the Legislature has used the words " compensation for improvements." Now in the new English Dictionary, by Dr. Murray, "compensation" means " that which is given in recompense, an equivalent rendered, remuneration, amends. Amends or compensation for loss or damage." I read the word " compensation," therefore, in this sub-section to mean " an equivalent rendered for loss or damage," and in using so wide a term it appears to me that the Legislature intended to give to the lessee full recompense for the loss or damage he may sustain in respect of his improvements by the withdrawal of the land from his lease.

And this accords with the spirit of British legislation everywhere, and under all circumstances :—that wherever authority is given to take away property from a person for any public purpose or in furtherance of public policy, full compensation must be given for the loss or damage sustained thereby. In England this has been done in the Lands Clauses Consolidation Act and in numerous private Acts, and the principle was recognised when liberal compensation was made to the former owners of slaves when slavery was abolished.

The same principle has always been applied by the Legislature of this colony, as in the Railway Act, and the Act 44 Vic. No. 16, relating to the acquisition of land for public purposes.

No doubt in those Acts the basis of compensation is stated in detail, whereas this Act speaks generally of compensation for improvements, but that does not, in my opinion, necessarily narrow the basis of computation, or exclude the various matters in respect of which compensation under the former Acts was given.

It was, however, contended that that principle only applied where freehold or other property was taken away *in invitum*, whereas here the lessee takes his lease expressly subject to the provisions of sub-s. 7, and must, therefore, have known when he took the lease that any portion of it might be withdrawn at any time for any public purpose.

I do not see that that affects the principle in any way, because the same sub-section provides for compensation on withdrawal, and the lessee must have known that if any portion was withdrawn he was entitled to get compensation for improvements thereon.

The question, therefore, still remains on what basis is the compensation to be calculated. I am of opinion that it ought to be on the basis of payment for all such loss or damage as may be shewn to flow reasonably from the deprivation of the land and improvements. Now some improvements may not affect in any way the remainder of the leasehold area, and in such cases the repayment of the cost of the improvement may be full compensation. Other improvements may have a very material effect on the remainder of the leasehold area, and the loss of those improvements may render the rest of the land practically useless, or, at any rate, may injuriously affect some portion of it. Where that is the case, it stands to reason that the mere repayment of the cost of the improvement would be very inadequate compensation. This applies particularly to improvements giving or adding to the water supply on a pastoral holding.

In the dry hot climate of the central and western plains of New South Wales the value of a run depends largely on the water supply, and tanks to conserve the water that comes from the scanty and intermittent rainfall in those districts are often the most valuable improvements on the land, without which for

1898.

MINISTER FOR LANDS
v.
RICKETSON AND THE AUSTRALIAN M. L. AND F. Co.

Owen J.

1898.

MINISTER FOR LANDS
v.
RICKETSON AND THE AUSTRALIAN M. L. AND F. Co.

Owen J.

many months in ordinary seasons, and sometimes for years in seasons of drought, the land could not be used to depasture sheep or cattle, or at any rate in such numbers as if the tanks were available.

It may be contended that if the cost of making the tank were paid the tenant could apply it in making another tank. But the value of a tank largely depends on the situation and the surrounding catchment, and on the level plains of the interior such catchment areas may be few and far between.

Now, in the case before the Court, the whole catchment area of 400 acres is withdrawn, as well as the tank, and it may be that the loss of such a tank so situated will render a large portion of the remainder of the leasehold practically useless for many months of the year, and in times of drought for longer periods. If that is so, then in my opinion the lessee is entitled to compensation for such injury. I think that in this case the compensation in respect of the land withdrawn for the unexpired term of the lease and the compensation for the improvements should be assessed together, and ought to be estimated on the basis of the difference between the value of the whole of the leasehold area of Billabong to the lessees before the withdrawal of the land and the improvements, and the value of the residue of the leasehold area after the withdrawal.

The Land Board and the Land Court have assessed these two matters separately, and in assessing the compensation for the unexpired term of the lease, taken separately, they appear to me to have assessed it on a basis that includes the value of the improvements, for the difference between the value to the lessees of the Billabong leasehold area before the withdrawal and its value after the withdrawal must include the value of the improvements.

As to the second question I do not see how, in this case, the effect of the withdrawal of the improvements can be ascertained apart from the withdrawal of the land—for the 400 acres form the catchment area, which gives the tank its special value. By taking the two together, and estimating the compensation for the land withdrawn for the unexpired term of the lease, along with

the compensation for improvements, on the basis I have above
indicated, the lessees will be fully and fairly compensated for
any loss or damage to the rest of the leasehold area occasioned
by the withdrawal of the land and improvements.

WALKER, J., concurred.

Order accordingly. ·

Attorney for the respondents : *C. G. W. Croaker.*

1898.

MINISTER FOR
LANDS
v.
RICKETSON
AND THE
AUSTRALIAN
M. L. AND F.
Co.

Owen J.

THE COMMISSIONERS OF TAXATION *v.* THE BROKEN HILL
PROPRIETARY CO.*

1898.

November 11.
December 13.

Owen J.
G. B. Simpson J
and
Cohen J.

*Land and Income Tax Assessment Act, 1895, ss. 15 (3), 27 (3)—Income derived
from Crown lands—Earned outside New South Wales.*

A company registered in Melbourne held lands under lease from the Crown on
which they carried on mining operations. The ore was treated partly in New
South Wales and partly outside New South Wales. Contracts for the sale of the
products of the ore were made in London and Melbourne, and the profits arising
from such sales were received there. *Held,* that the income arising from such
sales was not taxable as it was earned outside the colony [see s. 27 (3).] *Held,*
also, in a case where the facts were the same except that the ore was entirely
treated in New South Wales, that the income of the company was not taxable.

SPECIAL CASE STATED BY THE COURT OF REVIEW.

1. On the 31st March, 1898, R. N. Kirk, as the public officer
of the Broken Hill Proprietary Company, furnished to the Commissioners of Taxation an income tax return for the year 1898
on the basis of the income for the preceding year on behalf of
the company, in which it was stated that the company had no
income to return, and no income liable to taxation.

2. The Commissioners, being dissatisfied with the return, made
an assessment of income tax under s. 39 on the basis of the
return of income made for the preceding year, being the amount
on which, in their judgment, tax ought to be charged subject to
reduction on appeal.

3. The company appealed from the assessment on the following grounds:—

(*a*) That it was not liable for the tax or any part thereof.

(*b*) That the amount of the assessment was excessive.

4. When the matter came before the Court of Review, the
following admissions were made:—

(*a*) The company is a company duly registered in the colony
of Victoria, and has its head office with a board of directors at
Melbourne.

[* Since this decision the Act 1898 No. 37 has been passed. *See Stat. Pract.
Ut.*, Vol. II., p. 511.]

(b) The company has also a branch office and a local board of directors in London.

(c) The company has an office at Broken Hill in which a large staff of clerks is employed under the supervision of the manager of the mine, who is also the manager of the company's works at Port Pirie in South Australia.

(d) The company has no office in Sydney, but has an agent in Sydney at a salary, who is also agent for other companies, and provides his own office.

(e) The company carries on the business of mining on leasehold lands held from the Crown.

(f) The gross amount of ore raised or won during the year 1897 was 385,016 tons, of which 332,413 tons were treated at Broken Hill, 45,119 tons at Port Pirie, and 7,484 remained on hand.

(g) The gross amount of ore treated by the company during 1897 was 349,003 tons net weight, and was treated as follows:—

By Company's Smelting Plant at Broken Hill...			...	...	204,445
,,	,,	Chloriding ,,	,,	... ...	43,112
,,	,,	Concentrating ,,	,,	... ...	52,657
By Company's Smelting Plant at Port Pirie		...	...	37,405
,,	,,	Refinery Furnace at ,,		... ...	11,386
					349,003

The difference between the amount of ore raised and the amount of ore treated is accounted for thus:—The weights of ore raised are gross weights, which include moisture, while the weights of the ore treated are net weights, and there was on hand a certain quantity at the commencement of the year, and a certain quantity at the close of the year, the exact amounts being unknown.

(h) From the treatment at Broken Hill of the ore mentioned above, the company obtained the following products:—

17,550	tons	silver lead bullion
7,130	,,	lead concentrates
1,885	,,	zinc ,,
325	,,	leaching product
1,896	,,	first matte

and from the treatment at Port Pirie of the ore mentioned above:—

6,512	tons	silver lead bullion
2,528	,,	first matte

1898.

COMMISSION-
ERS OF
TAXATION
v.
BROKEN HILL
PROPRIETARY
Co.

1898.
COMMISSION-
ERS OF
TAXATION
v.
BROKEN HILL
PROPRIETARY
Co.

Some of the 6,512 tons was obtained from the treatment of the first matte obtained at Broken Hill.

(i) All products obtained by the company from the treatment of the ore by its smelting, chloridising and concentrating plants at Broken Hill, with the exception of the zinc concentrates, were further treated at Port Pirie, yielding fine silver, desilverized lead, sulphate of copper, etc.

(j) The gross amounts received by the company from the sales of silver, desilverized lead, and sulphate of copper mentioned above were 1,132,430l. 2s. 6d., and such amounts were received by the Company or collected by its agents at the following places:—

London	...	...	...	... £913,762	16 11
New South Wales	...	..	...	1,633	8 2
South Australia	...	...	...	59,815	6 5
Victoria	...	...	...	... 153,428	6 3
New Zealand	...	...	...	3,790	4 9
				£1,132,430	2 6

(k) The sales of the said products were made in the year 1897, either in London by the board of directors there under instructions from the directors in Melbourne, or in Melbourne by the board of directors there.

(l) The company's only other source of income during 1897 was derived from investments of the reserve funds and surplus profits outside the colony of New South Wales, from transfer fees received in Melbourne and London, from forfeited dividends retained by the company in Melbourne, and from wharfage fees received in South Australia.

(m) The net profits of the company for 1897 were 262,929l. 13s. 10d., including 13,717l. 16s. 6d. received from reserve fund, investments and other sources mentioned in the preceding paragraph, and except the latter sum the whole of such net profits were derived from sales as aforesaid.

(n) Silver lead bullion, zinc concentrates, leaching product and first matte are all saleable in New South Wales, but not at prices so profitable as under the present course of business, and they can be successfully treated for the extraction of their final products in New South Wales.

(o) The whole of the ores from another Broken Hill Mining Company (The Broken Hill Proprietary Block 10 Company) is sold in New South Wales in the form of concentrates under contracts made in Victoria.

5. It was contended on behalf of the company that the company had no income which came within the meaning and operation of ss. 15 and 27, and the contrary was contended on behalf of the Commissioners.

6. The Court of Review, on the authority of *In re Tindal* (1), upheld the contention of the company.

7. The questions submitted for the Full Court were :—

(a) Had the company any income in 1897 within the meaning and operation of the Land and Income Tax Assessment Act of 1895, and liable to taxation under the provisions of that Act?

(b). Did the judgment in *In re Tindal* (1) govern this case?

Pilcher, Q.C., asked that the case should be heard in camera. Companies do not like their affairs made public. The special case discloses a number of things which the company would not like to have published. Under s. 44 of the Act, the Court of Review can exclude the public. This Court has the same power.

OWEN, J. We have no power to exclude the public, but I am sure that if there is anything which the parties do not want published, and we request the gentlemen of the press not to publish it, they will not do so.

Sir *Julian Salomons*, Q.C., and *J. L. Campbell*, for the appellants (The Commissioners of Taxation). The Court of Review was in error in thinking that this case was governed by the decision in *In re Tindal* (1). That case was decided upon sub-ss. 1 and 4 of s. 15. This case does not turn on those sub-sections, but on sub-s. 3. That sub-section says that income "derived from lands of the Crown held under lease" shall be taxable. The income in the case of this company was derived from a mine at Broken Hill held under lease from the Crown. They contend that, because the ore is sold outside the colony, therefore

1898.

COMMISSIONERS OF TAXATION
v.
BROKEN HILL PROPRIETARY Co.

(1) 18 N.S.W. L.R. 378.

1898.

COMMISSION-
ERS OF
TAXATION
v.
BROKEN HILL
PROPRIETARY
Co.

they are not taxable. Take the case of two companies at Broken
Hill, one selling the ore in this colony and the other selling it in
Melbourne, surely it would be the grossest absurdity to say that
the latter had no taxable income, but that the former had. The
income would be derived from the mine in either case, and,
therefore, would be taxable.

[G. B. SIMPSON, J. Giving the fullest effect to your argument
under that sub-section, does not the question really turn upon
sub-s. 3 of s. 27, whether the income was earned in New South
Wales?]

We contend that the income was earned in New South Wales.

In *Tindal's Case* the Court held that Tindal carried on his
business outside New South Wales. But here the whole business
of mining was carried on in New South Wales. Suppose a
manager of a Victorian bank carrying on business in New South
Wales was paid his salary in Melbourne, could it be contended
that his income was earned outside the colony? Income "derived
from lands" means income having its origin in lands.

Pilcher, Q.C., and *Pring*, for the respondents. Under this
Act the thing which is taxed is *income*. It is not the ore raised
that is taxed. Suppose the company was to raise 50,000 tons
of ore, worth 5l. a ton, that could not be taxed. If it is refined,
then it does not become taxable. It is the profits made on the
sale which is taxable and then comes the question where are
those profits made? If made outside New South Wales, they
are not taxable. Where is the income made? It is made where
the profitable contracts are entered into, and where the profits
come home, that is in this case outside New South Wales. The
profit arises from the sale of the silver in Melbourne and London.
Is not the sale of ore a trade just as much as the sale of tinned
meat? This case is on all fours with *Tindal's Case*. There the
meat was prepared and treated for sale here, just as in this case
the ore is won and treated here, but the sale took place in England, and the profits were made there, and, therefore, they were
not taxable.

[G. B. SIMPSON, J.   In that case I pointed out that even if it
could be said that the trade was carried on in New South Wales,
still the income being earned outside the colony was not taxable,
because of the provisions of sub-s. 3 of s. 27, and in those remarks
The Chief Justice concurred.]

The Court there held that the profitable contracts being made
outside the colony, the income was earned outside the colony.
The words in sub-s. 3 of s. 15 " derived from " mean the same as
"arising or accruing to " in sub-ss. 1 and 4.   They referred to
Erichsen v. *Last* (1); *Grainger* v. *Gough* (2); *Sulley* v. *Attorney-
General* (3).

Sir *Julian Salomons*, Q.C., in reply.

C.A.V.

On the 13th December, the judgment of the Court was delivered
by

OWEN, J.   This matter came before this Court on a special case
stated by the Court of Review.

The Judge of that Court held that the case was governed by
the decision of the Supreme Court in *In re Tindal* (4), and that
the company had no income taxable under the Land and Income
Tax Assessment Act.

The questions for our decision are :—1. Had The Broken Hill
Proprietary Company, Limited, any income in 1897 within the
meaning and operation of the Land and Income Tax Assessment
Act of 1895, and liable to taxation under the provisions of that
Act and the Income Tax Act of 1895 ?   2. Did the judgment of
the Honourable the Supreme Court in *In re Tindal* (4) govern
and conclude the appeal of the company ?

It appears that the company is registered in the colony of
Victoria, and has its head office with a board of directors in
Melbourne.   It has also a branch office and local board of
directors in London.   The company has an office at Broken
Hill, and a large staff of clerks under a manager there, and has

1898.

COMMISSION-
ERS OF
TAXATION
v.
BROKEN HILL
PROPRIETARY
Co.

December 13.

(1) 8 Q.B.D. 414.   (3) 5 H. & N. 711.
(2) [1896] A.C. 325.   (4) 18 N.S.W. L.R. 378.

Z 2

1898.

COMMISSION-
ERS OF
TAXATION
v.
BROKEN HILL
PROPRIETARY
Co.

Owen J.

an agent in Sydney. The company carries on the business of mining on leasehold lands held from the Crown at Broken Hill in this colony. The ore, with a small exception, was all treated in the first instance at the company's plant at Broken Hill, only about 45,119 tons having been sent to be smelted at Port Pirie in South Australia. The products obtained by the company from the treatment of the ore by its smelting, chloridising and concentrating plants at Broken Hill were sent to the company's works at Port Pirie to be there further treated. The sales of the products were made in the year 1897, either in London by the board of directors there under instructions from the directors in Melbourne, or in Melbourne. The purchase-money for the sales made in London was received there by the directors and retained there to be disposed of for the purposes of the company, and the money for sales in Melbourne was received there, except a sum of 1,633l. 8s. 2d. received in Sydney or at Broken Hill in respect of sales made in Melbourne, and some other small sums received in other colonies and remitted to Melbourne.

It was admitted that the ores could be successfully treated for the extraction of their final products in this colony, and are all saleable here, but not at prices so profitable to the company.

It was contended by Sir *Julian Salomons* on behalf of the Commissioners that this case came within sub-s. 3 of s. 15 of the Land and Income Tax Assessment Act of 1895, and not as in *Tindal's Case* within sub-ss. 1 and 4, and he distinguished *Tindal's Case* because the income there was an income arising or accruing to a person from a trade or business, whereas the income of this company in this case is "income derived from lands of the Crown held under lease or license issued by or on behalf of the Crown," and he further contended that sub-s. 3 of s. 27 of the Act, "No tax shall be payable in respect of income earned outside the colony of New South Wales," did not apply to this case, or that, if it did, the income derived from the mine was earned in this colony.

It is clear to us that the last sub-section is the key to the meaning of the whole Act, and distinguishes it from the Acts in force in England imposing income tax in Great Britain. The intention of the Legislature here was to limit the tax to incomes

earned within the colony. This is expressly limited in sub-ss. 1,
2 and 4 of s. 15, and I am of opinion that it must be so
limited in respect of sub-s. 3 of the same section by reading, in
connection with it, sub-s. 3 of s. 27.

It is income alone which is taxed by this statute, and we must
consider how this income is earned, and where. In this case the
crude ore, when taken from the mine, is partly treated at the
company's works at Broken Hill, and is then sent to Port Pirie
in South Australia, where it is treated so as to render the ore
marketable, and when so rendered marketable it is sold by the
company in Melbourne or London, and the profits of the sale
received by the company there. It appears to us, therefore, that
this company do not limit their operations to mining, but carry
on the trade or business of preparing the ore for market and
selling such ore. The crude ore is the only thing derived from
Crown lands, and the preparing that crude ore for market is
part of the trade or business of the company, whether the ore is
so prepared in this colony or elsewhere, and the income of the
company is earned where the profits come home, in this case at
Melbourne in the colony of Victoria. The income, therefore, falls
within the exception mentioned in sub-s. 3 of s. 27.

In that respect we can see no difference in principle between
this case and *Tindal's Case*. The income in each case is earned
outside the colony. In *Tindal's Case*, the cattle were bought in
this colony, and the meat works were also here, but, because the
products of the meat works were shipped to London, and there
finished for the market and sold, and the profits received in
London, it was held that the income was earned outside the
colony, and, therefore, exempt from taxation.

We, therefore, answer the first question in the negative and
the second in the affirmative. The appeal is, therefore, dismissed
with costs.

Appeal dismissed with costs.

THE COMMISSIONERS OF TAXATION v. THE BROKEN HILL
PROPRIETARY BLOCK 10 COMPANY.

THIS case was argued together with the preceding case.

The facts were similar to those in that case, except that the
ore in this case was treated only at Broken Hill.

1898.

COMMISSION-
ERS OF
TAXATION
v.
BROKEN HILL
PROPRIETARY
BLOCK 10 Co.

December 13.

THE COURT reserved its decision in this case also.

13th December,

OWEN, J. This case differs only from the case of the Broken Hill Proprietary Company, Limited, in that the ore in this case was treated only at Broken Hill. That fact removes one point of resemblance to *Tindal's Case*, but all the sales were effected in Melbourne, and all the profits received there, and, as I read *Tindal's Case*, it decided that income is earned where the profits come home. In *Tindal's Case, The Chief Justice* points out the distinction between the source of income and the source of the commodity which produces the income. In this case the commodity is the crude ore, and that no doubt is derived from Crown lands under lease, but the source of the income is the trade or business of preparing for market and selling the refined ore, and that income is earned in the place where the profits come home.

We, therefore, think that *Tindal's Case* governs this case also. We, therefore, dismiss the appeal with costs of and incidental to the appeal.

Appeal dismissed with costs.

Attorneys for the respondents : *Fisher & Macansh.*

JOHN COOPER *v.* COMMISSIONERS OF TAXATION.

1898.

August 15, 16,
October 27.

Stephen J.
G. B. Simpson J
and
Cohen J.

Land and Income Tax Assessment Act of 1895, *s.* 10—*Land tax—Land held by one owner subdivided.*

The appellant was the holder of a large block of land (known as Thrupp's Grant) which he had subdivided and let to various tenants, and the whole had been subdivided by streets. The portions thus separated were further subdivided in allotments, and buildings were erected thereon. The Commissioners for the purposes of taxation treated Thrupp's grant as an aggregation of 422 separate and divided estates and not as one estate, and each block facing a street was treated by them as forming one estate, and each such estate was valued separately as unimproved. The Commissioners did not take into consideration any improvements actually existing upon any one of these distinct estates, but did take into consideration the benefit of streets and all other improvements of every kind existing upon all the remainder of the grant as well as upon land surrounding the same. It was argued on behalf of the appellant that, under no circumstances, while the land remained under one title could the Commissioners take into consideration any division of the land into parcels, and that Thrupp's grant should have been valued as a whole. *Held,* that the principle of valuation adopted by the Commissioners was the right one.

APPEAL FROM THE COURT OF REVIEW.

From the special case it appeared that the following were the facts of the case :—

1. The appellant is the owner within the meaning of the Land and Income Tax Assessment Act of 1895 of certain lands for the most part let on building leases partly situate in the parish of Willoughby, being the unsold residue of Thrupp's grant (hereinafter referred to as " Thrupp's Grant "), and partly situate on the Cleveland Estate in the parish of St. Lawrence, in the city of Sydney, and having frontages to Elizabeth-street, Devonshire-street, Randle-street, and Railway Place (hereinafter referred to as "Cleveland Estate ").

2. Thrupp's grant and Cleveland Estate were devised to the appellant by the will of Daniel Cooper.

3. Thrupp's grant contains an area of 563 acres, or thereabouts, and has been let on building and improving leases to tenants, by whom it has been improved. Cleveland Estate contains 2 acres

3 roods 23 perches, or thereabouts, and is let on building and improving leases.

4. On the 28th December, 1896, the appellant made a return of the said lands pursuant to the Act, wherein Thrupp's grant was returned as one estate or parcel, and the unimproved value thereof was stated at 84,450l., and Cleveland Estate was returned as one other estate or parcel, and the unimproved value thereof was stated at 11,000l.

5. By an assessment notice the Commissioners gave notice to the appellant that they had regarded and treated Thrupp's grant for the purposes of assessment as an aggregation of 422 separate and divided estates or parcels, and not as one estate or parcel, and had fixed the unimproved value of the whole at 220,000l., and had regarded and treated Cleveland Estate as being divided into separate estates or parcels, and not as one whole estate or parcel, and had assessed each of the estates or parcels separately from the others, and had fixed the aggregate of the unimproved value of all the estates or parcels at 20,697l.

6. The appellant appealed from this assessment to the Court of Review.

7. It was admitted that the Commissioners in dealing with Thrupp's grant, and in arriving at the unimproved value of 220,000l., had valued and assessed the same in the manner following, viz.—Each block facing a street had been treated as forming one estate or parcel, and had been valued as if it were itself unimproved land; but taking into consideration in estimating the unimproved value thereof, all the roads and other improvements of every description existing on the 31st December, 1895, through and upon all the remainder of Thrupp's grant and elsewhere. It was also admitted that in dealing with Cleveland Estate they had valued and assessed each of the estates or parcels, into which the land was divided by streets and lanes, as if it were itself unimproved; but taking into consideration streets and lanes, and all other improvements whatsoever on the remainder of Cleveland Estate, or elsewhere existing at the date aforesaid.

8. Upon the hearing of the appeal it was agreed between the parties thereto as follows :—(a) If, under the Act, the proper

principle of arriving at the unimproved value of Thrupp's grant 1898.
is to value and assess such land, estate or parcel of land as in a JOHN COOPER
primitive condition, without roads, streets, or any other improve- v.
COMMISSION-
ments thereon, but taking into consideration all the improve- ERS OF
TAXATION.
ments existing on the 31st December, 1895, upon lands surrounding Thrupp's grant, then the unimproved value should be
60,000l. (b) If the proper principle of arriving at the unimproved value of Thrupp's grant is to value and assess such land
as one undivided estate or parcel of land in its primitive
condition, but taking into consideration the existence of roads or
streets thereon, as well as all the improvements existing on lands
surrounding Thrupp's grant, then the unimproved value should
be 90,000l. (c) If the proper principle of arriving at the unimproved value of Thrupp's grant is to value and assess such land,
not as one undivided estate or parcel, but as an aggregation of
separate and distinct estates or parcels, each such estate being
valued separately as unimproved, but taking into consideration
the benefit of roads and streets, and all other improvements
existing upon all the remainder of Thrupp's grant, as well as
upon lands surrounding the same, then the unimproved value
should be 220,000l. (d) If the proper principle of arriving at the
unimproved value of Cleveland Estate is to value it as Thrupp's
grant is valued in (b), then the unimproved value should be
11,000l. (e) If the proper principle of arriving at the unimproved value of Cleveland Estate is to value it as Thrupp's grant
in (c), then the unimproved value should be 20,000l

9. The Court of Review held that the proper principle was as
to Thrupp's grant, that stated in (c), and as to Cleveland estate,
that stated in (e).

10. The question for the Full Court was, which was the proper
principle of arriving at the unimproved value of the respective
estates ?

Pilcher, Q.C., and *Salusbury*, for the appellants. The Court of
Review was in error on the principle on which they assessed
Thrupp's grant. That land should have been assessed as one
holding, and none of the improvements on it should have been
taken into consideration. Suppose there are a number of sub-

divisions—A. B. C. D.—of one block of land belonging to one owner. The Commissioners say in valuing portion A. they cannot take into consideration the buildings and improvements on A. itself, but they can take into consideration the buildings and improvements on B., C. and D., and so in valuing B. they can take into consideration the improvements on A., C. and D., and so the whole block is not valued apart from the improvements on it, and, therefore, they do not value it as they are bound to do under s. 68, "assuming the actual improvements had not been made." The land should, therefore, be taken as one block, apart from all improvements. That is the only way to get at the unimproved value.

[COHEN, J. Unless you take into consideration the surroundings, you must get back to the Captain Cook values.]

Where a man has a block you cannot take into consideration as against him the improvements on his own block, although improvements on the surrounding blocks, which do not belong to him, can be taken into consideration. If a man has an estate, and lets half of it, and improvements are put on it, you cannot, in valuing the half which has no improvements, take into consideration the improvements on the other half.

Sir *Julian Salomons*, Q.C., and *J. L. Campbell*, for the respondents. The principle adopted by the Commissioners was the right one. The only improvements which are disregarded in valuing the land in question are the improvements on the land itself. Suppose there are two allotments side by side, belonging to two different owners, the improvements on one must be taken into consideration in valuing the other. Why should any difference be made in the assessment if they happen to belong to the same owner. Suppose a man owns allotment A., and some one else owns allotment B. In valuing A. the improvements on B. must be taken into consideration. Suppose then that he buys allotment B., is allotment A. to be differently valued? You must either value land having regard to the surroundings, or you must value it according to the Captain Cook values. If the latter basis is the right one, the land tax would be meaningless, as the land, according to that valuation, would have no value at all.

The land must be valued irrespective of its ownership. If the land in Thrupp's grant has to be valued as one block, how could you assess what contribution has to be paid by the tenants; as against the tenant, you would have to take the allotment held by him and value it. If each allotment is valued separately, then the contribution payable by the tenant under s. 12 could be adjusted, but if the whole is valued then it would be impossible to adjust the contribution. The Judge has found that these are separate parcels. That is a question of fact, and, therefore, his decision cannot be disturbed on that point.

1898.

JOHN COOPER
v.
COMMISSION-
ERS OF
TAXATION.

[STEPHEN, J. The question is not whether they are in fact separate parcels, but whether the Commissioners can treat them as separate parcels for the purposes of assessment.]

If they are separate parcels, and it must be taken that they are, because the Judge has so found, they must be valued as separate parcels.

They referred to *R.* v. *Commissioners of Income Tax* (1).

Pilcher, Q.C., in reply. We contend that the Commissioners cannot take the land as subdivided, whether the subdivisions are real or imaginary, but must value it as a whole. Sect. 12 throws no light on the matter. The only question there to be considered is between Cooper and his tenants, and in no way shews how the land should be valued.

C.A.V.

Oct. 27th,   *October 27.*

STEPHEN, J. This is a special case stated by the Court of Review, under and by virtue of the Land and Income Tax Assessment Act of 1895, the decision of that Court being upon an appeal by John Cooper from an assessment by the Commissioners of Taxation.

It appears that the appellant is the owner of certain lands known by the name of Thrupp's grant. This land was devised to the appellant, and at the time of its devolution upon him it was (adopting the words of the Judge of the Court of Review) "physically undivided." It has been let by the owner on 99

(1) 22 Q. B. D. 296.

1898.

JOHN COOPER
v.
COMMISSION-
ERS OF
TAXATION.

Stephen J.

years' leases to various persons, and the whole has been subdivided
by streets and roads, laid out, partly by tenants, and partly by
the appellant himself. The portions thus separated have been
further subdivided into allotments. Some of the streets have
been formed and metalled, and some exist only in name. Buildings have been erected to a very considerable extent in various
parts of the estate. It has been largely subleased and re-sub-
leased.

The Commissioners, for the purposes of assessment, treated
Thrupp's grant as an aggregation of 422 separate and divided
estates or parcels, and not as one estate or parcel. Each block
facing a street was treated by them as forming one estate or
parcel, each such estate or parcel being valued separately as
unimproved. The expression " unimproved value " means (see
s. 68 of the Act) " in respect of land, the capital sum for which
the fee simple estate in such land would sell, under such
reasonable conditions of sale as a bona fide seller would require,
assuming the actual improvements, if any, had not been made."
The Commissioners did not, of course, take into consideration any
improvements actually existing upon any one of these distinct
estates or parcels as affecting its value, but they did take into
consideration the benefit of roads and streets and all other
improvements of every kind existing on the 31st December, 1896,
upon all the remainder of the grant as well as upon land
surrounding the same, and they fixed the unimproved value of
the whole number for purposes of the land tax at a sum of
220,000l.

The question which I have to decide is, whether the Commissioners were right in so doing. I am of opinion that they
were. Assuming that the Commissioners had a right to regard
the land as divided into separate and distinct estates or parcels,
it is not contended that they did so in any arbitrary or improper
manner. In the case of *Grand Junction Waterworks Co.* v.
Davies (1), the distinction between the separation of a portion of
the tenement from the residue, not contemplated by the owner,
and arbitrarily made by the Justices for the purposes of valuation, and a division made by an owner for himself, is pointed out.

(1) [1897] 2 Q. B. 209.

Here the Commissioners adopted the divisions or parcels patently 1898.
indicated on the land by the owner's own disposition of portions, JOHN COOPER
marking out others by roads and streets. Again, there is no COMMISSION-
question made as to the Commissioners' valuation being excessive. ERS OF
The amount is agreed upon, *i.e.*, if the Commissioners are right. TAXATION.

   It was not intended that the Commissioners, in ascertaining *Stephen* J.
the sum for which the fee simple would sell, were not entitled to
consider surroundings other than those upon the estate itself.
The objection is that they took into consideration improvements
on other parts of the same estate. It was argued broadly for
the appellant that under no circumstances while the land
remained under one title, could the Commissioners take into
consideration any division of the land into parcels, and that this
valuation ought to have been upon Thrupp's grant as a whole.
It was admitted that, if the owner of three estates in different
localities held under one title, were being assessed, the value of
each estate must be taken separately, and added together for the
purpose of ascertaining the taxable amount. This would seem
to me to be an admission, and I take it to be the law, that unity
of title alone cannot affect the question, so that the question for
decision seems to be reduced to this, whether an undivided piece
of land can ever be so divided into different parcels by erection of
buildings and laying-out of streets as to justify the Commissioners
of Taxation in holding, as they have done, that they were
entitled to value what they considered separate parcels of land by
taking into consideration improvements upon other parts of the
land itself.

   It appears to me that the case really depends upon the construction of s. 10 of the Act, that is whether the term parcels of land can
only refer to land separated by land intervening that does not belong
to the same owner. The word " parcel " means a " part or portion
or piece, as a certain piece of land is part and parcel of another
piece " (*vide* Webster's Dictionary). We must give a meaning to
the word " parcel " distinct from " estate." They are not synonymous. For myself I cannot conceive why an estate like this
Thrupp's grant, consisting of about 500 acres, cannot be so
parcelled off by the owner as to be no longer considered as an
undivided whole, but an aggregation of portions or divisions

1898.

JOHN COOPER
v.
COMMISSION-
ERS OF
TAXATION.

Stephen J.

which the Commissioners may consider as parcels within the section. If this is not the case, then no one of the houses erected upon the estate, owned by tenants under 99 years' leases, occupied in as distinct a manner as they could possibly be, could be considered a parcel. It has been argued that the effect of allowing the Commissioners to adopt this course, would be to tax the estate as improved estate. It may be that the appellant will have to pay a larger sum than he would have had to pay if the unimproved value of the estate as a whole had been taken as the taxable amount, but whether this is right or not, the question necessarily comes back to the point I am discussing, whether portions of the land can be regarded as separate parcels. I can see no injustice in this, as it seems evident that the owner, by selling the land in parcels, obtains for it a value highly enhanced by the other improvements on the land, and whether they were erected by the tenants or by the owner himself, does not, it seems to me, touch the case. Each parcel would, in my view, come within the term " such land " in the interpretation clause as to the meaning of "unimproved value." The word " such " has reference to the previous word "land," and that is, in my opinion, each parcel_into which the land may be fairly said to have been divided, the value of which, as I pointed out, was increased by improvements upon other parcels of the whole estate.

Our decision is, therefore, that the Court of Review was right in its determination, both as to Thrupp's grant and the Cleveland Estate.

G. B. SIMPSON, J., concurred.

COHEN, J. The appellant was the owner, in fee simple in possession, of an estate containing 563 acres, which is known and may be described as Thrupp's grant, and was a grant from the Crown, and devolved upon the appellant in its entirety, under the will of a former owner. At the time of its devolution it was of small, as compared with its present value, when all the improvements upon and around it are taken into consideration. After the appellant so became possessed of these lands, he carved out of his estate in fee several leasehold estates for 99 years, which are demised to different lessees, to whom' he parcelled out the

1898.

JOHN COOPER
v.
COMMISSION-
ERS OF
TAXATION.

Cohen J.

greater part of the 563 acres, neither the commencement of the leases nor the areas comprised in them being uniform.

The appellant in some instances, and the lessees in others, sub-divided portions of the lands, and made provision for streets and roads within their boundaries, and the lessees in all cases made improvements upon their holdings, in compliance with their leasehold obligations.

The result is that the lands as a whole, as well as each lease-hold separately, have been vastly enhanced in value, by reason of the improvements so made by the respective lessees, as well as by the general improvement in the surrounding neighbourhood.

The question submitted to the Court is whether for the purposes of the land tax the assessment should be made upon the principle *(a)*, *(b)* or *(c)*, the appellant contending that it should be upon either *(a)*, or at the most *(b)*, and the respondent that it should only be upon *(c)*. The sections of the Act 59 Vic. No. 15 directly affecting the dispute are s. 10, sub-s. 1, which provides—"Such land tax shall be levied and paid as follows—(1) by every owner of land in respect of all land of which he is such owner, for every pound of the unimproved value thereof as assessed under the provisions of this Act, after deducting the sum of two hundred and forty pounds.; such deduction shall not be made more than once in the case of an owner of several estates or parcels of land . . . but in every such case the aggregate of the values of such several estates or parcels shall be regarded for the purpose of taxation as if such aggregate represented the unimproved value of a single estate or parcel "—and s. 68, which enacts that "unimproved value" means in respect to the land, "the capital sum for which the fee simple estate in such land would sell under such reasonable conditions of sale as a bona fide seller would require, assuming the actual improvements, if any, had not been made."

It is contended, on behalf of the appellant, that as he is still owner of the fee simple of all the lands comprised in the grant, that as they came to and are still held by him as such owner in fee in their entirety, and under one instrument of title, the whole area must be regarded as undivided, and, therefore, the improvements on any part of it cannot be relied upon to heighten the

1898.
JOHN COOPER
v.
COMMISSION-
ERS OF
TAXATION.

Cohen J.

value, as it would then be the "improved" and not the "unimproved" value, as contemplated by the Act, which would be the
basis of the assessment.   The fact that the improvements were
affected by the lessees is immaterial, and it seems to me also to
be immaterial that the lands in question passed to the appellant
by one instrument of title, for it was conceded in argument by
Mr. *Pilcher*, that if there were two different blocks of land
physically separated by an intervening area, though contained in
one grant, they could be assessed separately.   On the other hand,
it was argued by Sir *Julian Salomons*, on behalf of the Commissioners, that as the appellant had, for his own purpose and
advantage, cut the land up into different parcels as between himself and his various lessees, the area comprised in each lease
became a separate parcel, and that in assessing each such parcel
the Commissioners, whilst eliminating from their calculation of
value the improvements upon it, could consider the improvements
upon all the other leasehold parcels, and thus effect would, as it
could be, properly given to the word "parcels" as distinct from
its associated word "estates."   The argument in reply to this
was, that the result would be to give the Commissioners the
advantage of all the improvements on the entire area, as no doubt
it would when each leasehold in the entire series is taken in turn
and the effect of the improvements on all the others is considered
to ascertain the value of any one.   This, it was again submitted,
would be taxing upon the improved, and not the unimproved
value, as required by the Act.

I am of opinion that the appellant should not succeed, and
that the assessment should be made upon the principle *(c)*. The
Commissioners have not adopted, and do not desire to adopt, as
they certainly could not, any arbitrary parcelling of their own,
but going upon the land they find it cut up by the appellant
into separate leasehold holdings or parcels, held through or under
him by different lessees or sub-lessees in possession, a possession
to which they are entitled as against him during the currency of
their leases or sub-leases, or so long as they comply with their
leasehold obligations, if there be conditions of forfeiture on
breach of any of them, and forfeiture should follow. If the
argument for the appellant should prevail, then, as pointed out

by Sir *Julian Salomons*, the appellant might grant leases for 99 years, for the fee simple price paid down, and a purely nominal rental, such as a peppercorn, thus create a holding in essence practically, though not technically, equivalent to an estate in fee simple, and then claim that he, as the owner of the fee simple, though in such dimly remote reversion, could only be assessed upon the value of the entire area, after excluding from considera-'tion all or any of the improvements upon it. On the other hand, it was not denied that if he had granted the fee simple of any portion of the land, that that portion would be a "parcel" within the Act. It is not unimportant to bear in mind that if the lessees were directly taxable they could not set up that the area comprised in each lease was not a separate parcel, and was not liable to be assessed, in the light of the improvements upon any of the other leasehold parcels. Now, although the owner in fee simple is the only person assessable and directly taxable, yet he is entitled to contribution from the lessees in proportion to their interests in the land (see s. 12, sub-s. 1), and they thus become indirectly taxable, and taxable according to the opinion I have expressed, upon a principle, the correctness of which, if they could be directly assessed, is not disputable. I have so far only expressly dealt with Thrupp's grant, but as it is admitted that the Cleveland Estate appeal involves exactly the same principles, my judgment will also apply to it, and the assessment of that estate should proceed upon *(e)*.

Appeal dismissed with costs.

Attorneys for the appellant: *Norton, Smith & Co.*

1898.

JOHN COOPER
v.
COMMISSION-
ERS OF
TAXATION.

Cohen J.

1898.

July 26.
October 25.

The C.J.
Owen J.
and
Cohen J.

LANDALE v. THE MINISTER FOR LANDS.

Crown Lands Act, 1884, ss. 70-81, 142, 143—Pastoral lease—Occupation license—Rent and license fee—Estimated area—Actual area—Money paid by mistake—Course of dealing.

The plaintiff, a runholder, upon the passing of the Crown Lands Act, 1884, applied for a pastoral lease and occupation license, and under s. 71 furnished a plan of his holding shewing the boundaries and area to the best of his knowledge and ability The Minister adopted the area shewn upon the plan, and upon the estimate so arrived at the rent and license fee were assessed, gazetted, and paid by the plaintiff for a number of years. It was now admitted by the defendant that the area of both the leasehold and resumed areas had been over-estimated, and the plaintiff sued to recover the rent and license fee paid in respect of the over-estimate, upon the ground of a mutual mistake. *Held*, that the plaintiff was not entitled to recover, upon the grounds (1) that the Crown Lands Acts do not require or contemplate a survey, but that rent and license fee are payable upon the estimated area ascertained as provided in ss. 71 and 72; and (2) that the case was not one of mistake, but of a contract by the parties to pay and receive rent and license fee upon an estimated, and not upon the actual area.

NEW TRIAL MOTION.

This was an action on the common money counts by the pastoral lessee of the Deniliquin run against the Minister for Lands.

On the division of the plaintiff's run, under the Crown Lands Act, 1884, the plaintiff, under s. 71, sent in a statement of his estimate of the area of the run, and also a plan. The plaintiff's estimate of the acreage was 18,000 acres. The estimate adopted by the Lands Department which was gazetted on the 12th September, 1887, and which they arrived at by scaling from the plaintiff's plan, was—leasehold area, 13,925 ; resumed area, 14,816 ; total, 28,741 acres.

It was admitted on the trial that the *Gazette* of the 12th September shewed an excess of 2,100 acres over the actual acreage of the leasehold area, and an excess of 1,300 over the actual acreage of the resumed area. It was also admitted that the difference had remained the same during the years to which the action had reference.

The plaintiff now sought to recover the sum of 378*l.* 5*s.* 5*d.*,
being the difference upon the rent actually paid by him for the
years 1885-1890, upon the estimated area of his run, ascertained
as above stated, and the amount which he ought to have paid
upon the actual acreage. Of the amount claimed, 249*l.* 7*s.* 6*d.*
was in respect of rent paid for the leasehold area, and
128*l.* 17*s.* 11*d.* in respect of the license fee of the resumed area.
By consent at the trial, before *The Chief Justice*, a verdict was
entered for the plaintiff, with leave reserved to the defendant to
move to set it aside.

The facts are fully stated in the judgment of the *Chief Justice.*

A rule *nisi* to set aside the verdict was obtained on the
grounds (1) that the several payments made to the Crown on
account of the rent of the pastoral lease and license fee of the
occupation license, were only of the amounts required or justified
by the Crown Lands Acts ; (2) that the plaintiffs having full notice
that the sums called for by the Crown had been computed on the
basis of an estimate of the areas, and having acquiesced in such
basis, and paid the said sums without protest or question, are
now precluded from opening the matter ; (3) that assuming that
the plaintiffs paid the said sums under a mistake, the said mistake was as to a matter of law, that is to say, as to the power of
the Minister to estimate and determine the said areas, or as to the
legal effect of the estimates and determination made by him ; (4)
that the evidence shews that the plaintiff, when paying the sums
called for by the Crown, waived all inquiry as to the correctness of
the said sums in relation to the actual areas, or that both parties
accepted and intended to accept the estimated areas as the basis
of calculation, and dealt together on that basis for a variety of
other purposes connected with the pastoral lease and occupation
license ; (5) that in any event the verdict ought not to stand as
to the sum of 249*l.* 7*s.* 6*d.* paid on account of rent of the pastoral
lease ; (6) that in any event the verdict ought not to stand as to
the sum of 128*l.* 17*s.* 11*d.* paid on account of the license fee.

Sir *Julian Salomons*, Q.C., and *Canaway*, for the defendant,
moved to make the rule absolute. Although by s. 78 (2) of the
Crown Lands Act, 1884, rent of a pastoral lease is payable at so

much per acre, there is nothing in the Act which requires a
survey to be made, or the exact acreage otherwise ascertained.
The rent is chargeable on the estimated acreage: see ss. 71-80.
A survey *may* be directed at the option of the Minister: ss. 142,
143. It would have been impossible to survey all the runs in the
colony before appraising the rent. In this case the plaintiff sent
in his own estimate, and the Minister adopted the area as shewn
on the plaintiff's own plan. If the plaintiff is entitled to succeed,
the Crown will be entitled to recover in all cases where the
estimate has been less than the actual acreage. Secondly, even
if rent is payable on actual area, the parties here have adopted a
certain course of dealing by which they are bound. The estimate
was mutually adopted with full knowledge of the facts, and the
plaintiff paid rent on that basis for years without protest:
McCance v. *L. & N.W.R. Co.* (1), *Blackburn's Contract of Sale* (2),
Moss v. *Mersey Docks and Harbour Board* (3), *Freeman* v.
Jeffries (4).

Pilcher, Q.C., and *Pring*, for the plaintiff. The Act provides
that rent is to be payable at so much per acre. Pending the
ascertainment of the acreage the rent is assessed upon an
estimate, but that estimate may be wrong, and must be corrected
by a subsequent survey. When that survey is made, both parties
are subject to a settlement, and if the estimate has been too
small the Crown is entitled to recover the rent that ought to have
been paid, just as the tenant is entitled to recover if he has paid
on an excessive estimate. The case was one of a mutual mistake
as to the acreage, a question of fact, and the plaintiff is entitled
to recover. He referred to *McCulloch* v. *Abbott* (5), *White* v.
Copeland (6), *Durrant* v. *Ecclesiastical Commissioners* (7).

My learned friend's second argument amounts to this, that the
Minister let Crown lands to the plaintiff under a private agree-
ment. Sect. 5 of the Act of 1884 affords a complete answer to
any such argument. The Minister has no power to deal with
Crown lands except according to the provisions of the Crown
Lands Act.

Cur. adv. vult.

(1) 3 H. & C. 343.
(2) p. 163.
(3) 26 L.T.N.S. 425.
(4) L.R. 4 Ex. 189.
(5) 6 N.S.W.L.R. 212 ; 2 W.N. 32.
(6) 15 N.S.W.L.R. 281; 11 W.N. 28.
(7) 6 Q.B.D. 234.

On October 25th, judgment was delivered.

1898.

LANDALE
v.
MINISTER FOR
LANDS.

October 25.

THE CHIEF JUSTICE. This was an action for money had and received. At the trial the plaintiff was examined, and after certain documents had been placed in evidence, certain admissions made, together with an admission on the part of the plaintiff that the defendant was in a position to prove the truth of nine several allegations contained in defendant's Exhibit No. 1, an agreement was entered into between the parties that a verdict should pass for the plaintiff for 378*l.* 5*s.* 5*d.*, with leave to the defendant to move that such verdict should be set aside, and a verdict entered for such amount as the Court might direct, or for the defendant, the Court to have power to draw inferences of fact. Last term the defendant obtained a rule *nisi* for the purpose of bringing the matter before the Court in pursuance of such leave reserved, and that rule the defendant now asks to be made absolute.

For many years previous to the coming into force of the Crown Lands Act of 1884, the plaintiff was a run-holder within the meaning of s. 71 of that Act. In other words, the plaintiff was the lessee of a certain run or runs. In ordinary cases a run consisted of not more than 25 square miles, but if this was insufficient in ordinary seasons for the pasturage of 4000 sheep or 800 head of cattle, the run might be enlarged up to 100 square miles. Rents were payable in regard to the run as a whole, not so much per acre, or so much per mile, but so much per run. No actual survey was ever made to ascertain the exact mileage in a run, nor was this of much consequence when lessees held several adjoining runs, embracing 400 or 500 square miles of country, frequently much more. As a matter of history, this mileage was often calculated according to the rate of speed of the Commissioner's horse, or in some equally rough and ready manner.

By force of the operation of the Lands Act of 1861 and subsequent Acts, any part of these runs being Crown lands was liable to be taken away from the lessee by way of conditional purchase in blocks not exceeding 640 acres, and accordingly the tenure of the runholder was extremely insecure. One object of the Crown Lands Act of 1884 was to remedy this, and while it afforded security of tenure to the lessee, still left abundant land open to permanent settlement. With this object in view, it was provided that each pastoral holding should be divided into two parts, as nearly equal in area as practicable, to be called respectively the leasehold area and the resumed area; that a lease should be granted to the runholders of the "leasehold area," which during its currency should be exempt from conditional purchase; and as to the "resumed area," the runholder might, on application, obtain an occupation license, but this portion was not exempt from conditional purchase.

Sect. 70 of the Act of 1884 brought all pastoral holdings under the provisions of that Act Sect. 71 provided that every runholder should, within 120 days after the passing of the Act, lodge with the Minister a written application for a pastoral lease of whichever portion of his run might be converted into a "leasehold area," and should with such application furnish a plan of his pastoral holding, shewing to the best of his knowledge and ability (amongst other matters) the boundaries and area of such holding, and should divide by lines the entire area of all Crown lands situate within such pastoral holding into two parts as nearly equal in area as practicable. The Minister upon being furnished with the applicant's plan, and a certain statement provided for (not material to this case), was empowered to call upon the runholder to amend or supplement the plan, or to furnish such further information as he might require. Sect. 76 provided that when the division of the run had been determined by the Minister, a notification should be published in the *Gazette*, and the runholder should thereupon become entitled to a pastoral lease of the leasehold area, and that until the rent was determined he should pay the same rent as theretofore. Sect. 78 empowered the Governor to grant pastoral leases of the leasehold area. The 2nd sub-clause of that section provided that rent should in all cases commence from the date of the notification of the division of the pastoral holding, should be determined by the Minister after appraisement, and should not be less than so much per acre. The 5th sub-clause of this section provided that so soon as the rent of a pastoral lease should be determined, notice thereof should be published in the *Gazette* and notified to the runholder,

and that if he failed to pay this rent within the prescribed time,
his right to the lease should be forfeited. So much with respect
to the leasehold area. Now as regards the resumed area. Sect.
81 empowered the Governor to issue an occupation license; sub-
clause 1 of this section provided that the runholder should be
entitled to this occupation license if he applied for it when
applying for the pastoral lease, and had deposited a sum equal to
2l. "per section of 640 acres of the estimated area." It will be
noticed from the above, that no means were provided to ascertain
actual acreage, the amount of acreage rested entirely upon the
estimate to be furnished by the runholder, acting to the best of his
knowledge and ability.

Accordingly the plaintiff within the period of 120 days, sent in
an application for a pastoral lease, also an application for an
occupation license, and paid the sum necessary in regard to the
latter; he also sent in a plan and a statement, in which he
alleged that the area within the boundaries of his pastoral
holding amounted to 24,000 acres, less a claim for about 6,000
acres, thus reducing the area to 18,000 acres. The plan, however,
he furnished shewed that the area of lands upon which he had to
pay rent within this leasehold area amounted to 13,925 acres, and
the land within the resumed area, and for which he applied under
an occupation license, amounted to 14,816 acres, together 28,741
acres.

The division of the run as proposed by the defendant was duly
determined by the Minister, as appears from the *Government
Gazette* of the 11th July, 1885, p. 4403. The annual rental of the
pastoral lease was not determined by the Minister until the 12th
of September, 1887, as appears in the *Gazette* of that date,
p. 6057, and is calculated upon the "estimated acreage of leasehold area," which is stated as 13,925 acres. Upon the same date
the Minister notified that he had determined the rate and amount
of fee upon the occupation license, as appears by the *Gazette* of
that date, p. 6038, the "estimated area" being stated as 14,816
acres, these being the same quantities as shewn upon the plan
furnished by the plaintiff in January, 1885. It was admitted
that the defendant was in a position to prove at the trial that the
acreage mentioned in these *Gazettes* were taken from the plan

1898.

LANDALE
v.
MINISTER FOR
LANDS.

The C.J.

furnished by the plaintiff. The plaintiff paid rent and occupation license fees in accordance with the Minister's determination, from 1885 to 1897.

It is now alleged by the plaintiff, and admitted by the defendant, that the acreage of the leasehold area has been over-estimated by 2,100 acres, and that the acreage of the occupation license has been over-estimated by 1,300 acres, and the plaintiff thereupon claims a refund of the rent and license fees paid in respect of this over-estimate. It would appear that the Government did make a refund to the plaintiff of the alleged overcharge from 1890 to July, 1897, a period of seven years, and this action is brought in reality to recover the amount of the alleged overcharge from 1885, when the rent, etc., commenced, to 1890. The fact that the Government have in fact repaid the alleged overcharge from 1890 goes for nothing, unless they were in law bound to make this repayment, and this is the question for our solution. The defendant has not set up, nor does he desire to set up, the Statute of Limitations.

It is contended upon the part of the plaintiff that there has been a mutual mistake as to the acreage, and that as this is a mistake of fact the alleged over-payment may now be recovered by the plaintiff. Now there is no doubt as to the law upon this subject. Money paid under a mistake of facts, even though the party paying may at the time of payment have had means of knowledge of which he has neglected to avail himself, may be recovered back. If, on the other hand, " the money is intentionally paid without reference to the truth or falsehood of the fact, the party paying meaning to waive all enquiry into it, and that the person receiving shall have the money at all events, whether the fact be true or false, the latter is certainly entitled to retain it": *per Parke*, B., in *Kelly* v. *Solari* (1). In my opinion this case falls within the law as laid down in the passage quoted from Mr. Baron *Parke's* judgment. Here there was no mistake, both parties were aware that there was no actual measurement, that it was improbable there would be an actual measurement at any time, and accordingly the plaintiff himself put forward

(1) 9 M. & W. 59.

and was content to take an estimated acreage as the basis of acreage upon which the rent was to be determined and paid.

It is quite clear that at no time was the acreage of these runs, nay even the mileage, accurately ascertained. The defendant, according to the first statement in Exhibit No. 1, knows nothing of the acreage even now being ascertained by survey. When, therefore, the plaintiff sent in a plan shewing a certain acreage of Crown lands being in his possession as a runholder, he did this from the best of his knowledge and ability, he knew it was merely approximate to truth, an estimate which might be somewhat over or somewhat under the true acreage. The Minister on his part assumed that the area shewn on the plan was approximate to truth, knew that it was an estimate, and so described it when determining the rent. In 1887 the rent was determined, and there arose, indeed there had arisen previous to that date, a contract between the plaintiff and the Crown to pay rent, not upon the actual, but the estimated acreage, the acreage as estimated by the plaintiff himself, and not upon the true acreage, the truth of which could only be discovered by a survey to be made at a very considerable expense. These facts cause the case to fall expressly within the principle of law and equity referred to in the passage from *Blackburn on Sales*, p. 163, cited by Sir *Julian Salomons*, which is as follows :—" When parties have agreed to act upon an assumed state of facts their rights as between themselves are justly made to depend on the conventional state of facts and not on the truth."

It is obvious that this acreage might have been underestimated. In very many cases this must have taken place, and bearing in mind that the estimate was to come from the runholders the tendency would be rather to under-estimate than over-estimate. If, then, the plaintiff was entitled to recover in this action, the Crown would also be entitled to recover in the case of an under-estimate.

If the rent was to be paid according to the true, and not the estimated, acreage one would expect to find in the Act some special provisions for the obtaining of accuracy, some power given to refund or surcharge whenever an error was discovered, which in the case of every run would be inevitable. To provide for the payment of rent according to the actual acreage of the Crown land within each pastoral holding would entail a survey of each holding, an impossible undertaking, one which, if commenced in 1885, would, I venture to say, be scarcely complete at the present day, leaving in the meantime the rents of these holdings unsurveyed in a state of abeyance and uncertainty.

I am, therefore, clearly of opinion that the contract between the plaintiff and the Crown was to pay rent according to the acreage, as estimated by the plaintiff when he sent in his application for the lease and occupation license, in case these estimates were accepted by the Minister. They were so accepted, and the matter was then concluded. The case is not one of mistake, but an attempt to disregard the express terms of the contract which was entered into.

Accordingly, the rule to set aside the verdict found for the plaintiff and to enter the verdict for the defendant is made absolute with costs.

OWEN, J. The Crown Lands Act of 1884 first introduced the principle of fixing the rent of pastoral leases at so much per acre (s. 78, sub-s. 11), but the Act nowhere provides that the acreage of the leasehold *shall* be ascertained by survey. The only section relating to survey is the 143rd, which provides that the Minister *may* direct a survey of the boundaries of any pastoral or homestead lease; and this power is apparently intended only to be exercised occasionally, and in order to remove difficulties or doubts as to the boundaries, for the preceding section 142 provides that " for the purposes of any lease . . . . . it shall be sufficient if the land and the boundaries thereof be defined by a general description, and no such lease . . . shall be void by reason of the imperfection of any such description if the land therein is defined with reasonable certainty." The Act of 1889, s. 52, does not appear to give any wider power of directing a survey of land held under pastoral lease.

Again, it is clear that in the first instance the application for a pastoral lease does not require a previous survey to be made.

Sect 71 provides that every runholder shall send in a written application, and with such application shall furnish a plan of his

pastoral holding on the prescribed scale, shewing *to the best of his* 1898.
knowledge and ability the boundaries and area of such LANDALE
holding, &c., and shall divide the entire area of such holding MINISTER FOR
into two parts, as nearly equal in area as practicable. One of such LANDS.
parts is to be included in the pastoral lease, and the other is to be Owen J.
the resumed area. Sect. 72 enables the Minister to accept any
application for a pastoral lease as sufficient, or he may call on the
runholder to amend or supplement any application, or plan, or
document. Sect. 81 provides that of the resumed area the
Governor may grant an occupation license to the runholder, and
the deposit for the license fee is fixed (sub-s. 1) according to the
"estimated area."

These considerations satisfy my mind that neither the Act of
1884, nor that of 1889, contemplate or require a survey of the
lands included in a pastoral lease, though reserving to the
Minister, if he should think fit, the power to direct a survey.
And this view is confirmed if we take into consideration the
enormous cost and the great delay which would be inevitable if
a survey was required of every pastoral holding in the colony,
many of them being as large as an English county.

If, then, a survey is not required, how is the acreage of the
pastoral leasehold, for the purpose of fixing the rent, to be
ascertained? It can only be by an estimated area, first submitted by the runholder in his plan on his application for a lease,
and either accepted by the Minister as sufficient in its original
form, or as amended or supplemented under s. 72. If, then, the
runholder and the Minister agree upon an estimated area, and
deal with one another for years on the basis of that estimated
area, and the rent for those years has been fixed according to that
estimated area, I am of opinion that neither the runholder nor
the Minister can, after the true area has been ascertained by
survey, open up the past transactions and readjust the rent for
the past years according to the surveyed area.

It was contended that this was a case of common mistake of
fact, but there was no mistake here on either side. Both knew
that no survey had been made of the leasehold area, and that the
acreage had been determined by an estimated area only. Now,
the expression "estimated area" *ex vi termini*, implies that it

may not be exact, and that the surveyed area may turn out to be more or less than the estimated area. Both parties therefore dealt with one another with full knowledge of the facts, and there was no common mistake.

COHEN, J., concurred.

Rule absolute.

Attorneys for the plaintiff: *Abbott & Allen.*

Attorney for the defendant: *The Crown Solicitor.*

ADAMS *v.* YOUNG.

Civil Service Act, 1884—Dismissal of civil servant—Right of Crown to dismiss at pleasure—Reorganisation of department.

Except in cases of misconduct as provided in Part III, the Civil Service Act of 1884 does not restrict the prerogative right of the Crown to dismiss its servants at pleasure.

1898.

November 17.

G. B. Simpson J.
Cohen J.
and
O'Connor J.

NEW TRIAL MOTION.

Declaration against the Minister of Public Works as nominal defendant for wrongful dismissal from the Government service. The declaration is set out in full in *Adams* v. *Young* (1). Pleas: (1) that the said Government did not promise as alleged; (2) denial of the alleged breaches.

The dismissal of the plaintiff was communicated to him by the following letter from the Under Secretary, which was put in by the plaintiff at the trial:—"18th April, 1895. Sir,—I am directed to inform you that owing to the necessity for retrenchment, and in consequence of the reorganisation of the department, Mr. Secretary Young has determined to dispense with your services on and from the 30th June next, and in view of your faithful service, purposes recommending to the Governor in Council that you be allowed leave of absence for six months on full pay, and that the deduction on account of the Superannuation Fund be met by the Government. I am to express Mr. Young's appreciation of the service you have rendered since your connection with the department, and his regret that in the reorganisation it has not been found possible to provide a position for you."

At the trial before *Owen,* J., the plaintiff was nonsuited.

The plaintiff now moved to make absolute a rule *nisi* to set aside the nonsuit upon the grounds that his Honour was wrong in holding that under the Civil Service Act of 1884 the Government had only lost the power of dispensing with the services of a civil servant at will in cases where such dispensing purported

(1) 18 N.S.W. L.R. 73; 13 W.N. 195.

to be for misconduct or incompetence and coming within the
purview of Part III of that Act.

Armstrong, for the plaintiff. *Stuart* v. *Gould* (1) decides
broadly that the Crown has, under the Civil Service Act of 1884,
lost its right to dismiss at pleasure. The judgment does not limit
the application of the case to dismissals for misconduct or incompetence. See the remarks of *The Chief Justice* in *Titterton* v.
The Railway Commissioners (2). There was no question here of
an abolition of office as in *Waller* v. *Young* (3). The reason
given for the plaintiff's dismissal, *i.e*, the reorganisation of the
department, does not affect the matter; any reason might be
given, and if the Crown can dismiss at pleasure no reason is
required. The only ground really raised by the rule is whether
the Crown has lost its right to dismiss at pleasure, and that is
decided in *Stuart* v. *Gould.* If it has not lost that power, the
declaration shews no cause of action.

Sly, for the defendant, was not heard.

G. B. SIMPSON, J. In order to entitle the plaintiff to succeed
it is incumbent upon him to shew that the right of the Crown to
dismiss him under the circumstances disclosed in this case, *i.e.*,
upon a reorganisation of the department in which the plaintiff
was employed, has been taken away by the Civil Service Act of
1884. The plaintiff relies upon the case of *Stuart* v. *Gould* (1)
to support his contention. I am, however, clearly of opinion that
the circumstances of this case do not bring it within the decision
in *Stuart* v. *Gould.* In that case the defendant pleaded that the
plaintiff was incompetent and had misconducted himself, and it
was on these pleas decided that where the Government propose
to dismiss a civil servant for incompetence or misconduct under
Part III of the Civil Service Act of 1884, the provisions of that
Part of that Act must be complied with. But there is no decision
in that case to the effect that the common law right of the Crown
to discharge its servants at its will and pleasure has been

(1) 16 N.S.W. L.R. 132; 11 W.N.   (2) 16 N.S.W. L.R. 235; 12 W.N.
175.   54.
           (3) 18 N.S.W. L.R. 200; 13 W.N. 208·

abrogated, except so far as that right has been abrogated by the 1898.
Civil Service Act, and there is nothing in that Act so far as I can ADAMS
v.
YOUNG.
see which abrogates the undoubted right of the Crown to dis-
charge any of its servants at will.   It is admitted that if the
plaintiff's office had been abolished the Crown would have been G. B. Simpson J
at liberty to dismiss him, or if his services had been dispensed
with by reason of departmental changes, but it was contended
that the onus of shewing that the dismissal was the result of a
departmental change lay on the defendant, and that he ought to
have pleaded it.   In my opinion the onus of shewing that he was
improperly dismissed lies on the plaintiff, and as he has failed to
shew that the undoubted right of the Crown to remove its
servants at pleasure has been abrogated, he cannot succeed.   The
dismissal of the plaintiff was upon his own shewing brought
about by reason of a departmental reorganisation, and the plaintiff has therefore no cause of action, but must submit to the right
of the Crown to dismiss its servants at pleasure which it possesses
even under the Civil Service Act of 1884, except so far as that
right is modified in cases of misconduct.   For these reasons I am
of opinion that the rule should be discharged.

COHEN, J.   I am of the same opinion.   This is a very different
case to *Stuart* v. *Gould.*   It comes, however, within *Waller* v.
Young, the only difference being that in that case the services of
the officer were dispensed with by reason of the abolition of his
office, whereas in the present case the cause of dismissal is a reorganisation of the department in which the plaintiff served, as is
shewn by the letter put in at the trial.   Apart from the Civil
Service Act, the power of the Crown to dismiss its servants is
unrestricted, and by that Act it is only restricted in cases coming
under Part III.

O'CONNOR, J.   The right to discharge its servants at pleasure
is one of the prerogatives of the Crown, and can only be taken
away by express statutory enactment.   It may be that the
language used by Sir *William Windeyer* in the judgment in
Stuart v. *Gould* goes somewhat beyond the necessities of that case,
but I do not think there has ever been any doubt that the Act of
1884 made one exception only to the prerogative right of the

1898.

ADAMS
v.
YOUNG.

O'Connor J.

Crown to dismiss its servants at will, and that was where the cause of dismissal was misconduct. That was a very proper exception to make, because it is only right that a civil servant should not be turned adrift upon a charge of misconduct without an opportunity being afforded him of answering the charge. *Stuart* v. *Gould* was never intended to go beyond the principle I have mentioned, and I therefore agree in thinking that the present rule must be discharged.

Rule discharged.

Attorney for the plaintiff: *A. J. Cormack.*

Attorney for the defendant: *The Crown Solicitor.*

1898.
_____
Aug. 11, 12.
December 13.
_____
The C.J.
Stephen J.
and
Owen J.

REGINA v. PRIOR.

Criminal Law Amendment Act, s. 46—Abduction—Taking away or detaining girl under 21—Possession—Lawful charge— Master and servant—Parental right of custody.

A girl, over 16 and under 21, was, with her mother's consent, engaged by the prisoner as his servant. The mother, becoming aware that the prisoner had seduced her daughter, applied to the Court for a writ of *habeas corpus*, which the Court refused to grant since the girl stated that she desired to continue living with the prisoner as his mistress. After the decision of the Court was pronounced the prisoner went to one of the ante-rooms of the Court where the mother and daughter were together, and called to the girl to come away. She left her mother and ran to the prisoner, and notwithstanding the expostulations of the mother they went away together. *Held,* that the prisoner was rightly convicted, under s. 46 of the Criminal Law Amendment Act, of detaining the girl against the will of the person having lawful charge of her with intent, &c. ; and, *per The Chief Justice,* that he was rightly convicted of taking her away under the same section.

The father, and after his death the mother, has the right to the custody and control of his child until the age of 21. This right is assumed by s. 46 of the Criminal Law Amendment Act with regard to female children, and is not affected by the fact that the Court cannot grant a writ of *habeas corpus* in the case of a boy over 14 or of a girl over 16 unless he or she is detained against his or her own will. The parent of a girl under 21 who has been, or is in danger of being, seduced by her employer may immediately terminate the contract of service, and demand the custody of his child.

CROWN CASE RESERVED.

The following case was stated by Mr Acting Justice *Sly* :—

"The accused was tried before me at the Central Criminal Court on an information framed under s. 46 of the C.L.A. Act, containing two counts. The first count charged that the accused, on the 26th of April last, did take away Jessie Stewart Macdonald, a female under the age of twenty-one years, to wit of the age of sixteen years and nine months, out of the possession and against the will of Annie Macdonald, a person then having the lawful charge of the said Jessie Stewart Macdonald with intent to carnally know the said Jessie Stewart Macdonald. And the second count charged that the accused on the above day did detain the said Jessie Stewart Macdonald, a female under twenty-one years, to wit of the age of sixteen years and nine months, out of the possession and against the will of Annie Macdonald, a person then having the lawful charge of the said Jessie Stewart Macdonald with intent to carnally know the said Jessie Stewart Macdonald.

"The accused was found guilty on both counts, and I subsequently sentenced him to three years' penal servitude on each count—the sentences to be concurrent.

" At the close of the Crown case Mr. *Pilcher*, Q.C., who appeared with Mr. *Gannon* for the defence, asked me to take the case from the jury on the ground that there was no evidence to go to the jury on either count of the information. I declined to do so. I annex the evidence, and it is to be taken as part of this case. The Crown in the conduct of the case did not rely on any offence being committed before the 26th day of April. The girl Jessie Macdonald was called as a witness for the defence, and gave evidence that illicit intercourse took place between herself and the accused about Easter last, and there was evidence that subsequently thereto the mother Annie Macdonald demanded the girl from the accused.

"In the course of my summing up I told the jury that, under the circumstances of this case, if they believed a demand was made by the mother on the accused for the girl, then, that as between the mother and the accused, and for the purposes of the section under which the accused was charged, the mother (if the father were dead) was entitled to the custody of the child and to her lawful charge. I read to the jury the following passage from the judgment of *Lindley*, L.J., in *Thomasset* v. *Thomasset* (1):— ' It must not, however, be inferred from the decisions referred to above that a father has no legal right to the custody of his child after he or she has attained the age of fourteen or sixteen. The father's right to such custody exists until the child attains twenty-one,' directing them that the mother in this case had the same right as the father in that passage. I also told the jury that if they believed the accused did take away the girl under the first count, or did detain her on the second count, that the consent of the girl was immaterial, but at the same time I told

(1) L. R. [1895] P.D., p. 298.

them, in favour of the accused, that the willingness and consent
of the girl were elements for their consideration in determining
whether the accused did really take away the girl, or detain
her as charged, and in determining whether such taking away
and detainer charged were not really the act of the girl
herself, and not of the accused. I also told the jury with
regard to the first count that there was evidence from which
they could find that the mother had possession of the child
after the *habeas corpus* proceedings were over, and that if they
came to the conclusion that the mother did have possession of
the child after the *habeas corpus* proceedings were over, then
there was evidence from which they could find that the accused
did take away the girl. But I left the whole matter to them as
a question of fact.

"The following points were handed up to me in writing by
counsel for the defence:—1. That his Honour should have
withdrawn the case from the jury. 2. That his Honour should
have held or directed that, under the circumstances appearing in
evidence, the girl Jessie was not on the 26th of April in the
possession of the mother within the meaning of s. 46. 3. That
his Honour should have held or directed that, on the 26th of
April, Mrs. Macdonald had not the lawful charge of Jessie
Macdonald. 4. That there was no evidence of any intent within
the meaning of the said section. 5. That whether Jessie
Macdonald was or was not in Prior's employment on the 26th of
April. she was not in the possession of her mother. 6. That as
Jessie was over 16 on the 26th of April, her mother was not
entitled to the lawful charge of Jessie unless Jessie was then
willing to go to her mother, and his Honour ought to have so
directed. 7. That on the question whether Jessie was in the
possession of a person having the lawful charge of her on the
26th April, the jury have to consider whether Jessie was on that
day willing to go to her mother. 8. That there was no evidence
of a taking away within the meaning of s. 46. 9. That the
mother has in law no power to determine the relationship of
master and servant between Jessie and Prior against the will of
Jessie.

"I reserve for the consideration of the Court the above points submitted in writing on behalf of the accused, and also the point, taken by counsel, that the word 'fraudulently' governs 'takes away' and 'detains' in the section under which the accused was indicted.

(Sgd). R. M. SLY."

The facts with reference to the taking and detention are set forth in the judgments.

Pilcher, Q.C. (*Gannon* with him), for the prisoner. As to the construction of s. 46 of the Criminal Law Amendment Act, I submit that the word "fraudulently" governs all the succeeding words, *i.e.,* "takes away" and "detains" as well as "allures," but in view of *R.* v. *Spooner* (1) I do not press the argument. Further, the words "out of the possession and against the will of" are governed both by "takes away" and "detains," and the second count is properly drawn in this respect.

There was no evidence either of a taking or of a detaining out of the possession of the mother by the prisoner. As to what is a taking out of the possession of the person having the lawful charge, see *R.* v. *Meadows* (2); *R.* v. *Mankletow* (3); *R.* v. *Green* (4); *Ex parte Barford* (5); *R.* v. *Burrell* (6); *R.* v. *Olifier* (7); *R.* v. *Mycock* (8); *R.* v. *Henkers* (9); *R.* v. *Hilbert* (10).

In the present case the girl went into the prisoner's service with her mother's full consent, and she continued in his service and was paid her wages up to the 26th April, when the alleged taking away occurred, and even if she became the prisoner's mistress during that time, she did not for that reason cease to be his servant. Up to the time of the mother's application for the *habeas corpus,* the girl was in the possession and lawful charge of the prisoner himself, and whilst that application was being heard, and till she left the Courthouse, she was, it seems from the evidence of the Court officials, in the custody of the Court

(1) 6 N.S.W. L.R. 191.
(2) 1 C. & K. 399.
(3) Dears. 159.
    3 F. & F. 274.
    8 Cox 405.

(6) 9 Cox 368.
(7) 10 Cox 402.
(8) 12 Cox 79.
(9) 16 Cox 257.
(10) 38 L.J. M.C. 61.

through them. The Judge should have asked the jury to say whether on the evidence, which on this point was all one way, the girl was not the servant of the prisoner upon the 26th April, and, therefore, in his possession. As to the detention, I submit that a parent cannot by a demand, or by affecting to assume physical possession of a girl, repossess himself or herself of the right to the lawful charge of that girl, where she, being over the age of sixteen, does not assent to the demand. The girl was then in Prior's service, she had refused to return to her mother, and the Court had just refused upon that very ground to grant the mother's application for a *habeas corpus*; how then could the mother by any exercise of parental authority, or by throwing her arms round the girl's neck, retake or revest in herself the right to the lawful charge of her daughter? The Court has no power to force a girl of over sixteen against her will to remain with her father or legal guardian, it can only set her free if she is illegally detained: *Thomasset* v. *Thomasset* (1). There cannot be any offence under this Act where a girl refuses to leave her employer. Lawful charge means a right that can be enforced in law, and it cannot be said that the mother had the lawful charge of the girl when she could not compel her to return to her custody, and when no process of law exists by which, if the girl is unwilling, she can enforce her right. The question of who is the person having the lawful charge must be investigated and determined altogether apart from the question of immorality. He also referred to *In re Agar Ellis* (2); *Ryder* v. *Ryder* (3); *In re O'Connor* (4).

Sir *Julian Salomons*, Q C. (*Wade* with him), for the Crown. I rely on the second count of the information, which is supported by shewing that the prisoner detained the girl against the will of her mother. Secondly, the age of the girl, if under twenty-one, is absolutely immaterial. The section simply says "a girl under the age of twenty-one." Nor is the right of the parent to the lawful custody of his child affected by the fact that the Court, on an application for a writ of *habeas corpus*, will enquire if the child, if over a certain age, consents to being where it is.

1898.

R.
v.
PRIOR.

---

(1) [1894] P. 238.   (3) 30 L.J. P.M. & A. 164.
(2) 24 Ch.   (4) 16 Ir. C.L.R. 112.

The effect of the decisions upon that point upon the right of guardianship are fully stated in *In re Agar Ellis* (1). The right to the lawful custody does depend on the question whether there is immorality or not. If a girl under age goes out to service, and her father discovers that she is in danger of being seduced by her employer, I submit that the law is that whether the girl herself be willing or not, her father may go and claim her, and may use force and even commit homicide if resisted, in order to get her back safe into his custody.

He was stopped.

THE CHIEF JUSTICE. The conviction is affirmed. We will deliver a considered judgment later on.

December 13.   On 13th December, the following judgments were delivered:—

THE CHIEF JUSTICE. The prisoner in this case was indicted under s. 46 of the Criminal Law Amendment Act. The information contained two counts. First, for taking away one Jessie Macdonald, a female under the age of 21 years, out of the possession and against the will of Annie Macdonald, a person then having the lawful charge of the said Jessie Macdonald, with intent to carnally know the said Jessie Macdonald. Secondly, for detaining the said Jessie Macdonald, etc., as in the first count.

The prisoner was tried before Mr. Acting Justice *Sly*, and being found guilty was sentenced to three years' penal servitude. Before sentence the prisoner's counsel submitted a number of points which he asked to have reserved, amounting to this, that the evidence was not sufficient to sustain the conviction, and that Annie Macdonald, who is the mother of Jessie Macdonald, was not entitled to the custody of her daughter, she being a few months over the age of 16 years, and having been engaged as a servant by the prisoner.

The facts may be shortly stated. It appears that the prisoner, requiring a nursemaid for an infant, engaged Jessie in that capacity. This engagement was with the sanction of her mother. Annie Macdonald hearing that the prisoner was a man of immoral character, and that the woman who was then living with the prisoner was not his wife (the prisoner was in fact living

(1) 24 Ch. D. 317.

1898.

R.
v.
PRIOR.

The C.J.

separate from his wife, and was living with the mother of the infant Jessie was engaged to nurse) went to the prisoner's home to take her daughter away. In the meantime the prisoner had got rid of his mistress and her infant, and had seduced Jessie, who was, when her mother first became alive to the situation, living with the prisoner as his mistress. The prisoner refused to give the daughter up to her mother, whereupon Annie Macdonald applied to this Court for a writ of *habeas corpus* in order to get her daughter out of the possession of the prisoner. However, as the daughter was over 16 years of age, and desired to live with the prisoner as his mistress, the Court was unable to grant the writ.

During the application to this Court the mother and daughter were in one of the ante-rooms, where the mother was imploring her daughter to give up the life she had entered upon with the prisoner, and return home. After the matter of the application for the *habeas corpus* had been determined, the prisoner came to this room and called to the girl to come away; she left her mother and ran to the prisoner, who put his arm round her, whereupon they ran away together, the mother pursuing, calling out "Stop that villain from running away with my child." Refuge, I regret to say, was afforded the prisoner and the girl in the office of the attorney who was acting for the prisoner, the door of which was shut in the mother's face, and when the mother left the prisoner got a cab, put the girl in, and drove with the girl to his house. This was the taking and detaining charged in the information. The case was argued before us on the 11th and 12th of August last, when we upheld the conviction, and stated that, later on, we would give our reasons in writing for so doing.

There can be no doubt that the father, and in case of his death the mother, of an infant under the age of 21 years is, according to the common law of England, entitled to the custody of the infant, and, as Lord Justice *Bowen* expresses it in the case of *In re Agar Ellis* (1), has a "natural jurisdiction over the infant till that age is reached." It is true that, after a boy has reached the age of 14 years, or a girl has reached the age of 16 years, the Court

(1) 24 Ch. D. at p. 336.

cannot grant a writ of *habeas corpus* unless the boy or girl, as
the case may be, is detained against his or her own will. This,
however, in no way affects the right of the parent to the custody
of the child. In the case to which I have referred, Lord *Esher*,
after considering the argument arising from the fact that, unless
the boy over 14 or the girl over 16 is detained against his or her
will, the Court cannot grant a writ of *habeas corpus*, says at p.
336 :—" Now I cannot accede to the argument thus put forward.
It seems to me to be directly contrary to the law of England,
which is that the father has the control over the person, education
and conduct of his children until they are 21 years of age." And
Lord Justice *Bowen*, at p. 336, says :—"The Act of 12 Car. 2
enables the father, by his will, to dispose of the custody and
tuition of his children until they attain the age of 21 years. It
seems to me to follow that, if a father can dispose of the custody
and tuition of his children by will until the age of 21 years, it
must be because the law recognises to some extent that he has
himself an authority over the children till that age is reached.
To neglect the natural jurisdiction of the father over the child
until the age of 21 would be really to set aside the whole course
and order of nature, and it seems to me it would disturb the
very foundation of family life." The very Act, on which the
information is framed, assumes that a female may be in lawful
charge till she is 21 years of age, in other words, assumes the
existence of the common law, and provides for the penalty accruing to him who takes or detains the female out of the possession
of the person having lawful charge.

A large number of cases have been referred to in argument
which have no bearing upon this case ; they were decided upon
questions arising under the 24th and 25th Vic. cap. 100, s. 55,
which section is applicable to girls under sixteen years of age,
and the offence of detaining is not provided for. The law in
force in England, upon which ss. 45 and 46 of our Criminal Law
Amendment Act have been founded, is to be found in the 24 and
25 Vic. cap. 100, s. 53, which, however, is only applicable to
heiresses, whereas s. 46 of our Act is applicable to any female
under 21 years, whether she be an heiress or not.

If then Mrs. Macdonald was entitled to the custody of her
daughter, of which I have no doubt, she had the power to put an

1898.

R.
v.
PRIOR.

The C.J.

end to the so-called service of her daughter with the prisoner at once. The prisoner, however, had previously put an end to this service by seducing his servant and making her his mistress. Then, when the mother and daughter were together in the ante-room of the Court, the mother had the right to exercise authority over her daughter, and direct her not to leave her. The prisoner then came and, disregarding and defying this authority, took the daughter out of the custody and possession of the mother, clearly with the intent of carnally knowing her, and thus committed a crime under this section. Whatever doubt may exist as to this taking out of possession, and I confess I feel none, he certainly detained the daughter out of the possession of the mother when he ran away with her, utterly disregarding the expostulations of the unfortunate mother, and made his attorney's office his shelter and the means of detaining the daughter. Our Criminal Law Amendment Act has somewhat extended the law as it exists in England. Our law most properly draws no distinction between the heiress and non-heiress, so that the sacred right of a parent to the custody of his children, which exists in all alike, is alike protected by our criminal law.

The monstrous proposition was put forward and argued that, inasmuch as the daughter had entered into a contract of service with the prisoner, that it was he who had lawful charge of her, and that, after he had committed a breach of the solemn trust reposed in him by seducing this young child, he had the right to defy the unfortunate mother, and live with her daughter as his concubine, thus ruining the daughter and bringing disgrace on her mother and family. I am thankful to think that the law is not so, and that the mother's jurisdiction over her daughter and her right to her daughter's custody did not cease. I am thankful to know that our law is strong enough to protect the parent's right, and to punish with severity so great a crime against family life and against the public. It is well that such men as the prisoner should know that acting as he did renders them liable to seven years' penal servitude.

OWEN, J. The information in this case contained two counts:-- (His Honour read the indictment). The prisoner was found guilty on both counts.

Counsel for the prisoner reserved a number points, which were submitted to the Court in a special case stated by the presiding Judge. The two points on which counsel mainly relied were, (1) that Jessie Stewart Macdonald was not in the possession of her mother on the 26th of April, the day on which the offence is alleged to have been committed, and (2) that Annie Macdonald, the mother, had not the lawful charge of Jessie Stewart Macdonald.

On the first point I feel considerable doubt. On the 26th April Jessie S. Macdonald was of the age of 16 years and 9 months, and for some time previously had been in the service of the prisoner as nurse girl. On that day a writ of *habeas corpus*, sued out by Annie Macdonald, the mother, came on for argument before the Full Court, and the prisoner and Jessie S. Macdonald appeared. While the Court was considering its judgment, Jessie S. Macdonald was removed to the witness's room, and while there the mother clasped her daughter in her arms. The prisoner then came along the passage and beckoned to her, and said, "Come away, Jessie, come away home." Thereupon Jessie went away with the prisoner and ran along the street hand in hand with the prisoner, followed by her mother shouting out " Stop that villain for running away with my child." The only evidence of possession by the mother is the fact that at one time while in the witness's room in the Court-house her mother clasped her in her arms, but the girl had been brought into Court by the prisoner in obedience to the writ, and had been for some time previously and was then living with the prisoner in his house either as his servant or mistress, and apart from her mother's residence. Under the circumstances, I entertain great doubt whether Jessie S. Macdonald was in the possession of her mother within the meaning of s. 46 of the Act.

But this objection relates only to the first count. The second count is for detaining, and on that point I entertain no doubt. The whole of the evidence is conclusive to my mind that there was a detaining within the meaning of s. 46. That section is not grammatically worded. It runs thus :—" Whosoever fraudulently allures, takes away or detains any female under the age of 21 years out of the possession and against the will of any person

having lawful charge of her with intent to . . . . carnally
know her."   The words " out of the possession " must either be
read to refer only to the words " allures " and " takes away," or
—as is probably the best construction—must be read as if the
words were " against the will of any person having lawful charge
of her, and so as to prevent such person having the possession of
that female."

1898.

R.
v.
PRIOR.

Owen J.

Whichever construction be adopted, I am satisfied that there
was a detention of the girl within the meaning of the section.
The evidence is that the prisoner called to the girl to come home,
and ran away with her from her mother, and went with her into
Mr. Abigail's office, so that the mother was unable to get possession of her daughter.

It was further contended that, as Jessie S. Macdonald was over
16 years of age and living with the prisoner with her consent, her
mother was not a person having lawful charge of her.   And the
fact that the Court had refused to grant a writ of *habeas corpus*
was urged in support of this proposition.

Now the law, in my opinion, is clear that a father in his lifetime, and after his death a mother, has the right to the custody,
control and charge of his or her child until the age of 21 ; but as
a boy over 14, and a girl over 16 can consent, if they are willing
to remain with the person detaining the child from the parents'
custody, the Court will not grant a writ of *habeas corpus*, and
restore the child to the custody of the parent.   The reason of
that is that the Court will only grant a *habeas corpus* where the
person is illegally detained *against his will*.

In *Agar Ellis' Case* (1), *Brett*, M.R., says : " It was said that
the authorities shew that where a girl over sixteen is absent from
her father and with other people, the Court upon a *habeas corpus*
sued out by the father will see the girl who is above sixteen
and ascertain her view of the position, and if she is content to
remain where she is, will not grant to the father upon the *habeas
corpus* a return of the child into his custody.   And it is said
that that shews that the law is that when a girl is over sixteen,
her father has no longer any control over her.   It was said
further that this was shewn to be the law, because the Court in

(1) 24 Ch. D. 317.

1898.

R.
v.
Prior.

Owen J.

the case of a testamentary guardian will, if necessary, interfere
with regard to his mode of exercising the control which is given
to him by law.   Now I cannot accede to the argument thus put
forward   It seems to me to be directly contrary to the law of
England, which is that the father has the control over the person,
education and conduct of his children until they are twenty-one
years of age.   That is the law.   If a child is taken away from
the father, or if a child leaves the father and is under the
control of, or with, other people, then the application for a
habeas corpus is no part of the law of equity as distinguished
from the common law of England.   It is the universal law of
England that if any one person alleges that another is under
illegal control by anybody, that person, whoever it may be, may
apply for a *habeas corpus*, and thereupon the person under whose
supposed control, or in whose custody, the person is alleged to
be illegally and without his consent, is brought before the Court.
But the question before the Court upon *habeas corpus* is whether
the person is in illegal custody *without that person's consent*.
Now up to a certain age, children cannot consent or withhold
consent . . . .   But above the age of fourteen in the case of
a boy, and above the age of sixteen in the case of a girl, the
Court will enquire whether the child consents to be where it is;
and if the Court finds that the infant, no longer a child, but
capable of consenting or not consenting, is consenting to the
place where it is, then the very ground of an application for a
habeas corpus falls away."   The latest case on the subject is
Thomasset v. *Thomasset* (1) in which the law is laid down as in
Agar Ellis' Case.   *Lindley*, L.J., after referring to the cases on
habeas corpus, says :—" It must not, however, be inferred from
the decisions referred to above that a father has no legal right
to the custody of his child after he or she has attained the age of
14 or 16.   The father's right to such custody exists till the child
attains 21.   This is clearly stated in Hargreave's note to Coke
upon Littleton, 886."

Again, this right of the parent to have the charge of a child
under 21 years appears to be recognised by the very section under
which the prisoner was tried, for it applies to the case of a

(1) [1894] P. D. 295.

female under the age of 21 years, and speaks of such female
being in the possession and allured, taken away or detained
against the will of any person having the lawful charge of her.
These latter words must, in my opinion, refer to the parents or
some one in *loco parentis* as a testamentary guardian.

Further, I hold that a parent finding that a daughter under
the age of 21 is in the service of a man of immoral character,
and has been seduced by him, or is in danger of being seduced,
can immediately terminate the contract of service, and demand
the custody of the child, and that anyone detaining such female
from the possession of the parent with intent to carnally know
her is guilty of the offence in s. 46 of the Act.

For these reasons, I am of opinion that the conviction was
good.

STEPHEN, J., concurred.

Attorney for the prisoner: *J. W. Abigail.*

1898.

R.
v.
PRIOR.

Owen J.

FLOOD v. GARNSEY & WIFE.

1898.

June 23.

Privy
Council.*

*Appeal from Land Court—Effect of decision — Determination of title of person not
represented.*

F. and G. having applied for the same land, F. appealed from the decision of
the Land Board to the Land Court. G. had notice of this appeal as a party
interested, but did not appear, but the Minister for Lands appeared and defended
the case. The Land Court held that F.'s application was bad. and F. appealed
to the Supreme Court, the Minister again being the respondent, and G. not being
a party to or represented on the appeal. The Court held that F.'s application
was good, and G.'s therefore bad. In a subsequent action of ejectment by F.
against G. to recover the same land—*Held*, by the Privy Council, affirming the
decision of the Supreme Court (13 W.N. 60), that the decision upon the appeal
from the Land Court was conclusive against G., and could not be re-opened.

THIS was an appeal by the defendants from the judgment of
the Full Court (reported 13 W.N. 60).

Warrington, Q.C., and *Daldy*, for the appellants, contended
that the Supreme Court by the decision *In re Flood* (1) did
not decide or purport to decide anything as to the rights of
the appellants. The effect of their ruling was that the general
words at the end of the Crown Lands Amendment Act,
1891, s. 3, sub-s. 2, enacting that a revocation of a provisional
reversal of an order of forfeiture shall have the same effect as if
the provisional reversal had never been made, only applied to
the relationship between the Crown and its purchaser, and did
not in any way affect the rights of third parties. It was, therefore, open to the appellants to contend that this decision was
wrong. The Court in construction inserted the words " as between the Crown and the forfeiting purchaser," and limited the
operation of the clause accordingly. That interpolation was not
justified. The sub-section on its true construction, especially
having regard to its earlier words, means that a provisional
reversal, afterwards revoked, does not actually suspend the

* Present : Lord WATSON, Lord HOBHOUSE, Lord DAVEY, and Sir RICHARD
COUCH.

(1) 15 N.S.W. L.R. 330 ; 11 W.N. 24.

operation of the forfeiture, but is during its currency to be deemed to have that effect. It was submitted that there was no evidence that the appellants were parties to or represented upon any of the proceedings in relation to the respondent's applications, either before the Local Land Board, or in the Land Court, or in the Supreme Court. It was contended that the lands in suit were Crown lands at the date of the appellant's application for them, made so by the forfeiture of them on September 21st, 1892, the operation of which was ·not suspended by a provisional reversal thereof afterwards revoked. The revocation made them Crown lands from the date of the forfeiture. Besides, the appellant's applications were continuing tenders, and took effect during the six days which elapsed between the date of revocation and the respondent's application. Reference was made to *Ricketson* v. *Barbour* (1).

Sir *R. T. Reid*, Q.C., and *Vaughan Hawkins*, for the respondent, contended that the decision of the Supreme Court was conclusive, not having been appealed from : see Crown Lands Act of 1889, s. 8, sub-s. 6. Following upon that decision the Land Appeal Court directed the Land Board to confirm the respondent's applications if there were no other objection than that dealt with by the Supreme Court, and the Land Board confirmed them accordingly. The Land Board also disallowed the appellant's application. Consequently the appellants, at the date of suit, had no title and no *locus standi* under the Crown Lands Acts. The decision of the Supreme Court to the effect that the lands in question were not Crown lands at the date of the appellant's application, could not be reopened in this suit, and if reopened was manifestly right for the reasons therein stated. Accordingly in this ejectment suit the respondent had shewn an absolute title, and the appellants had shewn no title whatever.

Daldy replied.

On the 23rd June, judgment was delivered by

Sir RICHARD COUCH. The respondent brought a suit in the Supreme Court of New South Wales against the appellants to

1898.

FLOOD
v.
GARNSEY AND
WIFE.

June 23.

(1) [1893] A.C. 194.

1898.

FLOOD
v.
GARNSEY AND
WIFE.

Sir Richard
Couch.

recover possession of 640 acres of land situate in the Central Division, Land District of Coonamble, county of Gregory, parish of Quambone, in the colony of New South Wales, and 1,920 acres of land situate in the same land district. On the 2nd September, 1886, one Edith Florence Flood made an application under the Crown Lands Acts of New South Wales for the 640 acres as a conditional purchase, and an application for the 1,920 acres as a conditional lease in virtue of the conditional purchase of the 640. These applications were confirmed by the Local Land Board on the 18th July, 1887. On the 21st September, 1892, this conditional purchase, and the conditional lease in virtue of it, were by notice in the *Government Gazette* under s. 26 of the Crown Lands Act of 1884 (45 Vic. No. 18) declared to be forfeited. The effect of the forfeiture was, by s. 136 of this Act, that the lands became Crown lands and might be dealt with as such, but no forfeiture could take effect until the expiration of 30 clear days after the notification in the *Gazette*. By s. 3 of the Crown Lands Act Amendment Act of 1891 power was given to the Minister for Lands to reverse any forfeiture whether provisionally or otherwise, subject to the provisions thereinafter contained. The provision in sub-s. 2 of the section is as follows:—
" A provisional reversal hereafter to be made of a forfeiture shall be deemed to have suspended or shall suspend, as the case may be, the operation of the forfeiture as from the date when such forfeiture has been or shall be notified, declared, or otherwise asserted or enforced ; in any case where such provisional reversal shall afterwards be revoked, such revocation shall have the same effect as if the provisional reversal so revoked had never been made."

On the 25th October, 1892, the Minister for Lands approved of the provisional reversal of the before-mentioned forfeitures of the conditional purchase and the conditional lease, and on the 28th October it was notified in the *Government Gazette*. On the 19th May, 1893, this provisional reversal was by notification in the *Government Gazette* revoked. In the meantime, on the 27th October, 1892, the appellant Isabella Garnsey, then Isabella Cambridge, lodged applications for a conditional purchase of the 640 acres, and for a conditional lease in virtue thereof of the 1,920

acres. On the 25th May, 1893, the respondent, Ida Flora Flood,   1898.
lodged similar applications. On the 20th June, 1893, the Local Land   FLOOD
Board confirmed the applications of Isabella Cambridge, and on the   GARNSEY AND
14th August it disallowed the applications of Ida Flora Flood on the   WIFE.
ground that the areas applied for were not available, the same   *Sir Richard*
having been confirmed to Isabella Cambridge on the previous   *Couch.*
20th June. Under the Crown Lands Act of 1884, 45 Vic. No.
18, there was an appeal from a decision of the Local Land Board
to the Minister for Lands. By the Crown Lands Act of 1889,
53 Vic. No. 21, s. 8, a Land Court was constituted and substituted
for the Minister, to which any decision or award of any Local
Land Board may be appealed against, and by sub-s. 3 the Land
Court has power to hear and determine all appeals, and the
Crown may, without having lodged a caveat or appeared before
the Local Land Board, appear as a party in all proceedings in
which its rights, interests, or revenues may be concerned, and all
parties may be heard by counsel, attorney, or agent. Sub-sect.
6 provides that whenever any question of law shall arise in a
case before the Land Court, it shall, if required by any of the
parties, or may of its own motion state and submit a case for
decision by the Supreme Court thereon, which decision shall be
conclusive.

Ida Flora Flood appealed to the Land Court against the order
of the 14th August, 1893, on the ground that the lands were
Crown lands at the time of her applications, but were not Crown
lands at the date of the applications of Isabella Cambridge. It
appears from Exhibit 3 of the appellants' exhibits, put in by
them at the trial of the action, that a notice of this appeal was
served on Isabella Cambridge as a party interested on the 12th
October, 1893. She did not appear at the hearing, but the
Minister for Lands appeared and defended the case. On the 8th
December, 1893, the Land Court dismissed the appeal, but Ida
Flora Flood having required a case to be stated for the opinion
of the Supreme Court a special case was stated, the question for
decision being " whether the provisional reversal of the forfeiture
(which reversal was itself subsequently reversed) prevented the
lands from being Crown lands for the purposes of Isabella Cam-

1898.

FLOOD
v.
GARNSEY AND
WIFE.

Sir Richard
Couch.

bridge's application." The special case was heard before the Supreme Court on the 16th August, 1894, and is reported in 15 N.S.W. L.R. 330. The Minister appeared by counsel, and after the case had been fully argued by him and by counsel for Ida Flora Flood, the Supreme Court held that when Isabella Cambridge applied for the land it was not Crown land, and, therefore, was not open for selection under the Crown Lands Act of 1884, and that the question submitted to the Court must be answered in the affirmative. Thereupon, on the 14th September, 1894, the Land Court made an order directing the Land Board to confirm Ida Flora Flood's applications, which was done by the Land Board on the 3rd December, 1894. On the same day the Land Board reversed the order of the 20th June, 1893, and disallowed the applications of Isabella Cambridge (who had then become the wife of the other appellant). She appealed to the Land Court against this order. That Court held that it was technically defective, as a direction from it was necessary to enable the Land Board to reverse their former order, and on the 19th March, 1895, the Court made an order directing the Land Board to re-hear the case and to disallow the application of Isabella Garnsey.

The action in which this appeal is brought was tried on the 3rd September, 1895, when a verdict was found for the plaintiff. On the 20th October, 1895, a rule was obtained by the appellants calling upon the respondent to shew cause why the verdict should not be set aside and a new trial granted. On the 26th August, 1896, this rule was ordered to be discharged with costs, the Court refusing to allow the question which was decided on the special case to be re-opened, and the present appeal is against that order.

Their Lordships are of opinion that the respondent had proved a good title to the possession of the lands in dispute. It follows from the decision of the Supreme Court that when Isabella Cambridge applied for the land it was not Crown land, and was not open for selection, and that the confirmation on the 30th June of that application by the Local Land Board could not have any effect. The Act of 1884 created a special Court in the place of the Minister for Lands to hear appeals against adjudications or decisions of a Local Land Board, and provided that upon questions of law submitted to it by the Land Court the decision of the Supreme Court should be conclusive. It would be wholly contrary to the design and purpose of the Crown land laws, and the institution of the Land Court, that the rival claimants of the land in this case should be allowed to raise the question which has been decided by the Supreme Court on the special case in an action in that Court, and have its decision reviewed. The verdict was a proper one, and there was no ground for a new trial. Their Lordships will, therefore, humbly advise Her Majesty to affirm the order of the Supreme Court discharging the rule, and to dismiss this appeal, the costs of which are to be paid by the appellants.

Attorneys for the appellants (defendants): *Laurence & McLachlan.*

Attorney for the respondent: *W. P. Crick.*

1898.

FLOOD
v.
GARNSEY AND
WIFE.

*Sir Richard
Couch.*

LINDSAY v. HANSON.

1898.
————
Nov. 10, 18.

Mining Act, 1874, *s.* 115—*Reg. Gen.* 18*th Nov.*, 1875—*Appeal—Special case—
Signature of Judge—Notice of appeal—Form of appeal.*

Owen J.
G. B. Simpson J.
and
Cohen J.

A mining appeal was heard in the District Court before an acting Judge, and on an appeal from his decision to the Supreme Court, the acting Judge's commission having expired, the special case was signed by the then Judge of the District Court in which the appeal had been heard. *Held*, that the case was properly signed.

The notice of appeal did not contain a statement of the determination or direction appealed from as required by Reg. Gen., 18th November, 1875, but contained instead a number of grounds of appeal. *Held*, that the notice of appeal was informal, but as the special case contained a statement of the final determination arrived at by the Judge below, the Court (*Cohen*, J., *dissentiente*) overruled the objection to the notice of appeal.

Semble. an appeal under the Mining Act, s. 115, from the District Court to the Supreme Court, is not intended to take the form of a special case, but to be set down for argument, upon the notice of appeal and the statement signed by the Judge whose decision is appealed from, in the same way as special cases are set down for argument.

MINING APPEAL.

Emma Lindsay issued a summons in the Warden's Court at Wyalong against William Hanson to restrain the defendant from trespassing on her registered gold mining tenement, and claiming damages. The Warden dismissed the complaint, and the complainant appealed to the District Court as the Court of Mining Appeal. The appeal was heard before Mr. Acting-Judge *Wade*, who delivered a written judgment reversing the decision of the Warden. From this decision Hanson appealed to the Supreme Court under s. 115 of the Mining Act by way of special case.

Mr. Acting-Judge *Wade's* commission having expired, the special case was signed by *Rogers*, D.C.J., the Judge of the district in which Wyalong was situated.

The notice of appeal to the Supreme Court followed the form prescribed in the Reg. Gen., 18th November, 1875 (*Pilcher*, 671), except that instead of stating "the determination or direction appealed from," it stated the appellant's intention to appeal "against the determination and direction made herein on the 21st March, 1898, upon the following grounds," and then followed fifteen grounds of appeal, some commencing "that as a matter of law his Honour should have held, etc.," and others, "that his Honour was in error in holding, etc.," and the last ground was "that the decision of his Honour was against evidence and the weight of evidence."

The special case contained the original summons, the evidence taken before the Warden and documents produced to him, the Warden's written decision, the notice of appeal to the District Court, the evidence taken before the D.C.J. and the documents produced, the written judgment of Mr. Acting-Judge *Wade*, and a copy of the notice of appeal. The judgment was a lengthy one, stating the facts and dealing with a number of points, and in conclusion his Honour stated, "I then sustain the appeal and order that the decision of the Warden be reversed. I further order that possession of the land be delivered by the respondent to the appellant, that the respondent be removed therefrom, together with his buildings, improvements, goods and chattels, and I assess damages as asked at the nominal sum of 40s."

The case was signed by the attorneys of both parties, the attorney for the respondent agreeing to its terms, "subject to the notice of appeal being in proper form" The questions stated for the determination of the Supreme Court were identical with the grounds of appeal stated in the notice of appeal.

Wise, Q.C., for the respondent (Lindsay), took the objection that the special case was signed by a Judge who did not pronounce the decision appealed from. The case should have been signed by Acting-Judge *Wade*. He could have signed it even though his commission had expired. Judge *Rogers* knew nothing about the matter, and it may be that Judge *Wade* would have refused to sign this case. The other day a Crown case reserved was sent back for amendment to an Acting-Judge whose commission had expired: *R. v. Murray Prior*.

G. B. SIMPSON, J., referred to *Ex parte Neville* (*Foster's District Court*, App. 272).

Sly, for the appellant. The Judge exercising jurisdiction at the time of the appeal must sign the case. We appeal from the order of the Court, and the Judge for the time being has power to sign the case. He referred to *Ex parte Dempsey* (1). Further, the parties agreed to the case being signed by Judge *Rogers*, so that this point is not open to the respondent.

Wise, Q.C. *Ex parte Neville* is distinguishable. Sect. 94 of the District Courts Act says that the Judge of the District Court in which the case was heard shall sign the case, whereas Rule 2 of the Mining Appeal Rules says that "such Judge" may sign the case, and that expression must refer to the Judge mentioned in R. 1, who is "the Judge whose decision is appealed from."

OWEN, J. We are all of opinion that the point is determined by *Ex parte Neville* (2), and that the special case might properly be signed by Judge *Rogers*.

G. B. SIMPSON and COHEN, JJ., concurred.

Wise, Q.C., then took the objection to the notice of appeal that it did not contain a statement of the determination or direction appealed from. This is a purely statutory jurisdiction, and the procedure must be strictly complied with. The rules of the 18th November, 1875, are made in pursuance of s. 115 of the Mining Act, and the form provided by R. 1 has not been followed. The determination appealed from is nowhere set forth. The grounds of appeal are not required, and do not supply any information as to what the determination was. The rule, though it directs certain matters to be done in the Court below, is a rule regulating the procedure of the Supreme Court, and must be complied with. The omission is matter of substance, and not of mere form.

OWEN, J. I cannot tell, from the notice of appeal, what the Judge's decision was. All the rulings stated in the grounds of appeal may have been *obiter dicta*, and the case may have really been decided upon some other ground.

Wise, Q.C. The Court has insisted on a strict compliance with the provisions of s. 70 of the Mining Act as to the contents of a Warden's summons, which is an analogous case to this: *Ex*

(1) 13 W.N. 83.   (2) Fost. D.C. 272.

parte *Long* (1); *Ex parte Pearson* (2). The fact that the judgment appealed from is contained in the special case does not
affect the informality of the notice of appeal, because even if the
Court can discover in this particular case what is the decision
appealed from, in other cases they might not be able to do so.
The so-called special case is not really a special case at all : see
the remarks of the Judges in *Saxton* v. *Stuart* (3). He also
referred to *Hardcastle*, 2nd Ed., 281; *Edwards* v. *Roberts* (4);
Hurt v. *Todd* (5); *Murphy* v. *Coman* (6).

Sly. The parties consented to the case being stated in its
present form. The grounds of appeal, taken with the judgment
set out in the case, shew fully what is the determination appealed
from. The rule does not necessarily mean the *final* determination appealed from. An informality in the notice of appeal does
not deprive this Court of jurisdiction. The object of the notice
is for the information of the District Court Judge to enable him
to state the case, and the sufficiency of the notice is purely a
matter for his consideration. If he accepts it as sufficient and
signs a case, objection to it cannot be taken in this Court:
Cannon v. *Johnson* (7); *Evans* v. *Mathews* (8); *Park Gate
Iron Co.* v. *Coates* (9).

OWEN, J. In this case the respondent has taken a preliminary
objection that the notice of appeal is defective in form, on the
ground that it does not set out the determination appealed from.

Sect. 115 of the Mining Act provides that either party, if
dissatisfied with the determination or direction of the Mining
Court of Appeal in point of law or upon the admission or
rejection of any evidence, may appeal to the Supreme Court,
"and such appeal shall be in such manner and form, and subject
to such regulations in all respects as the Judges of the Supreme
Court shall, by general rules in that behalf, prescribe." In
pursuance of the power so conferred, the rules of the 18th
November, 1875, were framed for the regulation of mining

(1) 16 N.S.W. L.R. 120; 11 W.N. 184.   (5) 11 W.N. 123.
(2) 17 N.S.W. L.R. 245; 13 W.N. 55.   (6) 2 N.S.W. L.R. 179.
(3) 13 W.N. 40, 239.   (7) 21 L.J. Q.B. 164.
(4) [1891] 1 Q.B. 302.   (8) 26 L.J. Q.B. 166.
                      (9) L.R. 5 C.P. 634.

1898.

LINDSAY
v.
HANSON.

Owen J.

appeals. The form which the notice of appeal is to take is there prescribed (his Honour read it), and the form concludes, "here set forth the determination or direction appealed from." The objection was that in the present case the determination appealed from is not set forth in the notice, which contained only the grounds upon which the appellant sought to reverse the judgment appealed from.

For a long time I was of opinion that the objection was fatal, because unless the determination is set forth no one can know with certainty what the matter appealed from is, and it was to provide for that very thing that the rule was framed. It was contended that from the grounds of appeal, of which there are in the present case a great number, the Court might discover what is the ruling or determination appealed from. I am satisfied that the course suggested is not the proper way for the Court to ascertain what is the subject matter of the appeal. The Court is not in any way bound by these grounds of appeal, and it was never intended that the Court should have to go through a number of such grounds, and spell out from them what was the determination appealed from. The grounds of appeal might all be bad and yet the decision appealed from be right, or, on the other hand, all the grounds of appeal considered in the abstract might be perfectly good, and yet the decision appealed from be wrong.

What has altered my opinion as to the decision to be come to with regard to this particular case is this, that in the special case which is before us the judgment of the Judge of the Court below is set out in full, and in the last few lines of that judgment there is set forth the real decision which he came to. (His Honour read the passage referred to). So that there, in full, is the whole of the determination from which the parties are appealing, and if the notice of appeal had been in proper form that passage would simply have been copied into it.

It therefore appears to me that, although the objection is a good one, we ought not to treat it as fatal. The Court leans as strongly in favour of appeals as possible, and is loth to allow an appeal to be defeated upon a purely technical objection. Had it not been that the exact determination appealed from was stated

in the special case, I should, I think, have felt bound to uphold
the point taken, but as it is, I feel that we should be barring the
appellant of his right of appeal upon an entirely technical point.
I am, therefore, of opinion that the preliminary objection should
be overruled.

1898.

LINDSAY
v.
HANSON.

Owen J.

In considering this matter I have looked very carefully into
the provisions respecting mining appeals to this Court, which
have hitherto come before us in the form of a special case. I do
not think that that is the proper form. It has no doubt been
the usual practice, but I think a moment's glance at the Act and
rules will shew that the practice is erroneous. In the last three
lines of s. 115 of the Mining Act it is provided that "such
appeal shall be transmitted by the appellant to the Prothonotary,
and be set down for argument in the Supreme Court in the same
manner as special cases in actions at law in that Court." That
does not say that the appeal is to be by way of special case, but
that the appeal, when ripe for argument, is to be set down in the
same manner as special cases in actions at law. Then turning to
the Reg. Gen. of the 18th Nov., 1875, Rule 1 provides that the
appeal is to be by notice in the form there provided, and Rule 2
provides that one copy of such notice is to be served on the
District Court Judge, and one on the opposite party. The
Judge then signs a statement of the case, and on such statement,
with an affidavit of service, being filed in the Supreme Court
office, "the appeal shall be entered for argument in the same
way as other appeals under the District Courts Act of 1858."
Sect. 94 of the District Courts Act provides, in the same words
as are used in s. 115 of the Mining Act, that the appeal shall be
set down for argument in the Supreme Court in the same manner
as special cases in actions in that Court.

What is required then in an appeal under the Mining Act is,
first a copy of the notice of appeal containing the determination
appealed from, then an affidavit of the service thereof, and
thirdly, a statement of the case signed by the District Court
Judge. These three documents having been filed in Court, the
case is then ready to be set down for argument *in the same way
as* special cases. The way in which special cases are set down

for argument appears from R. 22 of the Reg. Gen. of 1st March,
1856 (*Pilcher*, 386). That, I think, is what is meant by the
provisions of s. 115 of the Mining Act, and when the matter
comes before the Court in the way I have indicated the question
for decision will be, not if the grounds upon which it is sought
to appeal are good or bad, but whether the determination
appealed from is good or bad, and the Court may arrive at a
conclusion upon that question upon entirely different grounds
from those stated by the parties.

G. B. SIMPSON, J. I am of the same opinion. There can be
no doubt that the strict requirements of the rule must be complied with, but for the reasons given by his Honour Mr. Justice
Owen, I am of opinion that the objection should be overruled.

COHEN, J. I am of a different opinion, and although I
sympathise with the principle that appeals are to be favoured
where possible, and am glad for that reason that their Honours
have seen fit to allow the appeal to proceed, yet I cannot but
think that the objection is well founded and ought to be sustained.
Rule 1 appears to me to have been framed as it is for very good
reasons, and it expressly requires the notice of appeal to contain
a statement of the determination appealed from. In the case
before us not only is that statement omitted, but other matters,
not required either by the Act or rules, have been inserted, *i.e.*,
the grounds of appeal. The Court is, of course, not a slave to
its own rules, but it should see that they are fairly and properly
adhered to, and I think in the present case a plain rule has been
clearly and needlessly broken. See *Murphy* v. *Coman* (1). The
reason of the rule is that the Court may have clearly before it
what is the determination appealed from, and to prevent the
burden from being thrown upon the Court of discovering what
that determination is from a large mass of matter. I used my
best endeavours whilst considering the grounds of appeal in the
present case, but, except in one instance, I found myself entirely
unable to say what was the determination appealed from, and I
think this will be found to present great difficulty when the case

(1) 2 N.S.W. L.R. 179.

comes to be argued. On the ground, therefore, that the rule has
been very materially departed from, I am of opinion that the
objection should prevail.

1898.

LINDSAY
v.
HANSON.

Cohen J.

Preliminary objections overruled.

Attorneys for the appellant: *Coonan & Griffith.*

Attorney for the respondent: *G. P. Evans.*

W. COOPER v. THE COMMISSIONERS OF TAXATION.

1898.
November 1.

The C.J.
Owen J.
and
Cohen J.

Land and Income Tax Assessment Act, 1895, ss. 23, 27, 28—Agent—Imported goods—Taxable amount—Deductions.

An agent who sells in N.S.W. the goods of a foreign principal, and the taxable amount of whose income is assessed under s. 23 at five per cent. of the total amount received for such sales, is not entitled to deduct from the sum so ascertained any of the deductions provided for in s. 28.

SPECIAL CASE stated by the Court of Review under the Land and Income Tax Assessment Act, 1895.

This was an appeal from the Court of Review by W. Cooper, the agent, attorney and manager in New South Wales for Messrs. Cadbury Brothers, a firm whose principal place of business was outside the colony, and whose goods Cooper sold in the colony on commission. The Judge of the Court of Review held (1) that Cooper was assessable under the provisions of s. 23, and (2) that from the taxable amount of his income as ascertained upon the basis provided in s. 23 (*i.e.*, five per cent. on the gross proceeds of sales in the colony) he was not entitled to make any of the deductions provided for in s. 28.

It was admitted for the purposes of the appeal that the appellant was liable to taxation under the provisions of s. 23, and the only question for the determination of the Court was whether he was entitled to any deductions from the taxable amount of his income, ascertained upon the basis provided in that section.

Wise and *Bavin*, for the appellant. The appellant, as the agent for a principal permanently absent from the colony, is primarily liable to taxation under s. 18. Sect. 23 makes further and special provisions for such cases, but it cannot be contended that agents are not entitled to deductions. The expression used in s. 23, "taxable amount of the income," does not exclude the allowance of deductions. The sum on which tax is paid is, both in the Taxing Act and the Assessment Act, called "income chargeable." "The taxable amount" is a different sum altogether,

and is ascertained as provided in s. 27, and from that taxable
amount the deductions provided in s. 28 are made in order to
ascertain the "income chargeable." Therefore, from the taxable
amount in the present case, *i.e.*, the five per cent. on gross sales,
we are entitled to make deductions for losses, outgoings and
expenses, in order to arrive at the sum on which we have to pay
tax. Sect. 31 (3) distinguishes between taxable amount and
income chargeable. There is no reason for holding that s. 23
contains the only exception in the Act from the right to make
deductions. Sections 27 and 28 are of general application to all
assessments.

Sir *Julian Salomons*, Q.C., and *J. L. Campbell*, for the Commissioners, were not heard.

THE CHIEF JUSTICE. We are not called upon to decide
whether the case of Cadbury & Co. falls within the provisions of
s. 23 or not. We are to assume that it does, and that the
appellant carries on business in this colony for a principal who
is out of the colony, and sells goods in this colony for his
principal. Sect. 23 provides how the income of the agent is to
be assessed, and the question we have to decide is whether he is
entitled to the deductions allowed by ss. 27 and 28.

Looking at the general purview of the Act it seems to me that
the Legislature provided in the earlier portions of Part IV. of
the Act as to what incomes should be liable to taxation, *i.e.*, of
an individual, of a company, of a person absent from the colony,
of trustees, and so on. Then comes s. 23, which deals with a
distinct state of things, *i.e.*, the case of an agent who, on behalf
of a principal, whether a person or corporation, outside the
colony, sells goods in New South Wales. The section provides
that "the taxable amount of the income derived therefrom by
the principal shall be assessed at an amount equal to five pounds
per centum upon the total amount received for such goods," and
that for the purposes of the Act that income is to be treated as
if it were the income of the agent.

Mr. *Wise* has argued that the Act of Parliament which creates
the tax on incomes (59 Vic. No. 17), imposes it on the "amount
of all incomes chargeable" under the Assessment Act, that

1898.

W. Cooper
v.
Commission-
ers of
Taxation.

The C.J.

under the latter Act the "income chargeable" is an expression used to designate the "taxable amount" less the deductions authorised by the Act, and that, therefore, the expression "taxable amount" in s. 23 does not mean the ultimate sum on which tax is payable, but that from that taxable amount, i.e., five per cent. on the total receipts, the appellant is entitled to deduct the amounts referred to in ss. 27 and 28.

Looking at sections 27 and 28 it seems to me that these are again sections which stand by themselves, and that they read into each other. Sect. 27 provides that for the purpose of ascertaining the sum *hereinafter* termed the taxable amount, on which income tax is payable, certain directions shall be observed. Sect. 28 provides that from the taxable amount *so* ascertained certain deductions shall be allowed, and s. 28 appears, therefore, to me to refer expressly to s. 27, and not to any other part of the Act. The words "taxable amount" in s. 23, which is the first place where they occur, have no relation to the expression as used in ss. 27 and 28.

The taxable amount, or rather the sum on which income tax is payable under s. 23, is the five per cent. on the total receipts for goods sold, and I can see very good reasons why the Legislature should see fit to make an exception in this particular class of cases, and fix an arbitrary amount as the taxable amount. It would frequently be almost impossible to ascertain what deductions should be allowed in respect of cost of production, cost of importation, apportionment of losses incurred in business, and so on. I therefore think that the sum of five per cent. on the gross receipts was arbitrarily fixed as a sum which might fairly be taken to represent the profits.

For these reasons I am of opinion that the appellant has no right to the deductions, and that the question submitted to us should be answered in favour of the respondents.

Owen, J.   I am also of opinion that s. 23 is an exceptional section, and has nothing to do with the general provisions of the Act. No doubt in many cases of this sort the profits would be very largely in excess of five per cent. of the total amount received in payment for the goods, and in fixing such a low percentage I have no doubt the Legislature intended the net income, and to prevent the taxpayer making the usual deductions.

The expression "taxable amount" in the proper and ordinary grammatical sense attachable to the words, means, and can only mean, the amount upon which tax is payable; and if we attach their ordinary grammatical meaning to the words, then the five per cent. on the total of sales is the amount upon which the tax is payable. No doubt in ss. 27 and 28 a somewhat extended meaning is given to the same words, but that meaning cannot, in my opinion, attach to the expression as it is used in s. 23, because it is confined to the expression "as hereinafter used."

COHEN, J., concurred.

                                        Appeal dismissed.

Attorneys for the appellant: *Johnson, Minter, Simpson & Co.*

1898.

W. COOPER
        v.
COMMISSION-
   ERS OF
TAXATION.

Owen J.

AUSTRALIAN GASLIGHT CO. *v.* COMMISSIONERS OF TAXATION.

1898.
November 18.

The C.J.
Owen J.
and
Walker J.

Land and Income Tax Assessment Act, s. 68—Unimproved value—Reclaimed land.

The unimproved value of reclaimed land is the capital sum for which it would sell under reasonable conditions, assuming the actual improvements on it other than the reclamation had not been made, deducting from such sum the cost of such reclamation.

SPECIAL CASE stated by the Court of Review (*Murray*, D.C.J.) :—

" 1. As required by the above-mentioned Act the appellants made a return, in which they declared the value of a certain piece of land situate in Jenkins-street, Sydney, to be 60,000*l.* for the purposes of taxation.

" 2. The respondents assessed the land for the said purposes at the value of 123,000*l.*

" 3. The land has a foreshore frontage to the waters of Port Jackson, and the whole of such foreshore, to a varying depth back from such frontage, consists of land reclaimed from the harbour. It is admitted for the purposes of this special case that the whole of the remainder of such land over and above that reclaimed from the harbour has been made fit for building purposes by levelling, quarrying, the erection of retaining walls, and similar operations and works.

" 4. It is admitted for the purposes of this special case that the lands come within the proviso to the clause interpreting 'unimproved value' in s. 68 of the Land and Income Tax Assessment Act, and that they must be assessed for taxation purposes according to the terms of and in compliance with that proviso.

" 5. The appellants contended that the 'unimproved value' of the land for the purposes of taxation under the Act is the capital sum for which the land with all buildings, erections, fixtures and improvements thereon would sell under reasonable conditions, deducting from such sum, not only the cost of the reclamation or making, but also the cost of all improvements other than such reclamation or making.

"6. The respondents, on the other hand, contended that the "unimproved value" of the land is the capital sum for which the land would sell, under reasonable conditions, assuming the actual improvements, if any, other than the reclamation or making, had not been made, deducting from such sum the cost of such reclamation or making only ; or, in the alternative, that the sum to be deducted, within the meaning of the section, if deducted from the improved value, is the cost of the reclamation or making, added to the present value of all other improvements.

"7. I held that the construction of the section contended for by the respondents was correct, being of opinion that the word 'cost' was not intended to be read into the last· clause of the sentence.

"The question for the determination of the Supreme Court is whether I was right as a matter of law in holding as I did."

Pilcher, Q.C., and *Scholes*, for the appellants.   In valuing land which has been reclaimed the method of arriving at the un-improved value is by deducting from the capital sum for which the land would sell " the cost of reclamation or making as well as all other improvements " (see s. 68).   You do not, as in the case of land not reclaimed, treat it as if the improvements do not exist. That is the way the Commissioners valued the land in question, and which the Court of Review held to be the right way.   The words " cost of " must be read as applying to " all other improve-ments," otherwise the section would be nonsense, because you cannot deduct improvements from the capital sum ; you can only deduct the cost of the improvements.   Where land has been reclaimed, you have to value it as it stands and then deduct from that value the cost of reclamation and the cost of the improve-ments.

[THE CHIEF JUSTICE.   What the Legislature intended was that land which had been reclaimed should be valued in the ordinary way after deducting the cost of reclamation ; that is as if the improvements had not been there.]

The Legislature has not said that.   The Legislature has said that it is to be valued with the improvements on it, and that

1898.

AUSTRALIAN
GASLIGHT CO.
v.
COMMISSION-
ERS OF
TAXATION.

then the cost of reclamation and *the costs* of the improvements must be deducted.

Sir *Julian Salomons*, Q.C., and *J. L. Campbell*, for the respondents, were not called upon.

THE CHIEF JUSTICE. Sect. 68 of the Land and Income Tax Assessment Act is the definition clause of the Act ; the last definition in the section is that of the words " unimproved value," and this definition appears to me to be divisible into two parts. The first part deals with land generally, and the second part deals with land which has been reclaimed, or made fit for building purposes by levelling, quarrying, etc. In the first part the value of the land is arrived at by assuming that the improvements have not been made. Some expert valuers might be able to arrive at the value of the land by considering that the improvements had never existed, but others would take the value of the land as it exists with the improvements on it, and then would value the improvements, and by deducting the latter from the former would arrive at the value of the land without the improvements on it. I confess it seems to me almost impossible to arrive with any degree of certainty at the unimproved value of improved land. When the proviso to the clause is considered it is clear that the intention of the Legislature was that where land has been made fit for building purposes by reclamation, the cost of the reclamation should be deducted from the sum for which the fee simple would sell assuming that the improvements had not been made. There can be no difference in arriving at the unimproved value of land which has been reclaimed, and land which has not. In each case you have to treat the land as not carrying improve- ments. In this clause the word "deduct" means two things. It must be read as applying to the " cost of reclamation " in its ordinary sense ; and as applying to " improvements," it means that the land is to be taken as bare of improvements. I see no reason why a different principle should be adopted in arriving at the unimproved value of land which has been reclaimed, and land which has not. For these reasons I think that the appeal should be dismissed.

OWEN. J.   I cannot conceive any reason why the principle of arriving at the unimproved value of land which has been reclaimed should be different from the principle of arriving at the unimproved value of land which has not been reclaimed, except that in the former case the cost of reclaiming the land should be deducted.   When once land has been made fit for building purposes by reclamation and the cost of reclamation deducted, there is no reason why it should not be treated just as land in George-street, or in any of the suburbs.   The proper way to read the word "deduct" in s. 68 is by giving it its ordinary meaning when applied to the "cost of reclamation," and when applied to "improvements" reading it as meaning "omit."

WALKER, J.   I quite agree.   In arriving at the value of land containing improvements you value the land as it stands with the improvements on it and then you deduct the value of the improvements, and that gives you the unimproved value.

Appeal dismissed with costs.

Attorneys for the appellants: *Allen, Allen, & Hemsley.*

1898.

AUSTRALIAN GASLIGHT Co.
v.
COMMISSION-ERS OF TAXATION.

1898.

October 28.

The C.J.
Owen J.
and
Cohen J.

FINN *v.* LONDON BANK OF AUSTRALIA.

Mortgagor and mortgagee—Mortgagee in possession—Real Property Act, s. 58—
Tenant holding over.

A mortgagee in possession under a mortgage under the Real Property Act
has power to lease the land until redemption, and if the tenant hold over
against the mortgagor after redemption, the mortgagee is not responsible to the
mortgagor for the act of the tenant in so holding over.

THIS was a special case stated for the opinion of the Full
Court.

On the 19th Oct., 1888, the plaintiff executed a mortgage,
under the Real Property Act, to the defendants, including,
amongst other properties, an hotel at Broken Hill. There was
no provision in the mortgage enabling the defendants to lease
the hotel. The plaintiff having made default on the 15th July,
1892, the defendants entered into possession of the hotel.

On the 18th September, 1890, the plaintiff leased the hotel for
the term of three years. At the expiration of that lease the
defendants let the hotel for a further period of three years
in pursuance of an agreement, in which there was the
following clause:—" The bank's title to the land is that of a
mortgagee in possession by virtue of a mortgage under and
registered in accordance with the provisions of the Real Property
Act which mortgage does not contain any power to the bank to
lease and it is expressly stipulated that the bank does not and
shall not be required to covenant for quiet possession and that in
the event of the mortgagor redeeming the said mortgage this
agreement or any lease executed in pursuance hereof shall cease
and determine and the lessee shall deliver up to the mortgagor
quiet possession of the premises and shall have no claim against
the bank for damages or otherwise."

On the 26th Feb., 1896, the plaintiff paid off the money secured
by the mortgage, and obtained a discharge of the mortgage from
the defendants, and the defendants thereupon gave their tenant,
who was still in possession, notice that his tenancy had deter-

mined. The tenant, however, refused to give up possession of the premises to the plaintiff.

The plaintiff thereupon brought an action of ejectment in April, 1896, and obtained a verdict, and recovered possession of the premises on the 6th May, 1896. The plaintiff was unable to recover the costs of that action from the tenant.

The plaintiff contended that he was entitled to recover as damages from the defendants, as they were guilty of a breach of duty in not delivering up possession of the premises on the discharge of the mortgage, the following amounts :—

For loss of rent, from 24th February to 6th May	£62 0 0	
Costs of the ejectment action	85 5 7	
Costs incurred by the plaintiff in repair of hotel by reason of tenant not repairing according to his lease	30 0 0	
	£177 5 7	

The question for the opinion of the Court was, whether the plaintiff was entitled to the said damages, or any part thereof, from the defendants.

If the Court should be of opinion in the affirmative, then judgment was to be entered for the plaintiff for such sum as the Court should hold the plaintiff entitled to recover, with costs.

If the Court should be of opinion in the negative, then judgment should be entered up for the defendants, with costs.

Sly, for the plaintiff. When the money due under the mortgage was paid off, the mortgagee was bound to deliver up possession to the mortgagor, just as in the case of landlord and tenant. In *Woodfall* (13th. Ed., p. 740) the law is thus laid down : "If the tenant has let the premises to a sub-tenant, who is in possession at the time of the termination of the term, he must get him out, otherwise he will not be in a situation to render that complete possession to which the landlord is entitled."

[THE CHIEF JUSTICE. Is the mortgagee in the same position as a tenant ?]

Yes. When the mortgage is paid off the mortgagor is entitled to possession just as the landlord is at the expiration of the

1898.

FINN
v.
LONDON
BANK OF
AUSTRALIA.

tenancy. As to the right of a landlord, see *Henderson* v. *Squire* (1); *Ibbs* v. *Richardson* (2). This was a mortgage under the Real Property Act; no power is given by the mortgage to lease, and the Act does not give a mortgagee in possession power to lease, and, therefore, the defendants had no power to grant this lease.

[THE CHIEF JUSTICE. Does not the power in s. 58, to receive the rents and profits, imply a power to lease?]

That section gives him power to go into possession, but not to grant a lease.

Pilcher, Q.C., and *Lamb*, for the defendants. There is no analogy between the case of landlord and tenant and mortgagor and mortgagee. When a mortgagee goes into possession he is accountable to the mortgagor for the rents and profits, and he is bound to lease the property if he can get a tenant, otherwise he would be liable for wilful neglect and default. It is to the interest of the mortgagor that the property should be leased. The mortgagee in possession has, clearly, power at common law to grant a lease, and under the Act he is entitled to enter into possession by receiving the rents and profits. If that does not imply the power to lease it would be meaningless. If the mortgagee had to eject a tenant before the mortgage was paid off, he would be entitled to deduct the costs of the ejectment action from the rents and profits, and would only have to account for the balance to the mortgagor. After the mortgage was paid off the defendants could not have taken any proceedings against the tenant to eject him, because their title to the land had expired. The defendants were, therefore, not in any way bound to do anything more than they did do to deliver up possession, and are, therefore, not liable in any way for the amount now claimed by the plaintiff.

Sly in reply.

THE CHIEF JUSTICE. In this case it appears that the plaintiff was the proprietor of a public-house at Broken Hill, which he mortgaged to the London Bank of Australia. The land being

(1) L.R. 4 Q.B. 170.   (2) 9 A. & E. 849.

under the Real Property Act, the mortgage fell within the provisions of that Act. The plaintiff made default, and the bank
entered into possession, etc., under the provisions of s. 58.   During
the period that the bank was in possession, a lease of the premises,
which had previously been granted by the plaintiff, fell in, and it
became necessary to grant a fresh lease to some person, and accordingly the bank granted a lease to one Pearce. That lease was for
a term of three years, and contained the following clause:—
"The bank's title to the land is that of a mortgagee in
possession by virtue of a mortgage under and registered in
accordance with the provisions of the Real Property Act, which
mortgage does not contain any power to the bank to lease, and it
is expressly stipulated that the bank does not, and shall not, be
required to covenant for quiet possession, and that in the event
of the mortgagor redeeming the said mortgage this agreement, or
any lease executed in pursuance hereof, shall cease and determine,
and the lessee shall deliver up to the mortgagor quiet possession
of the premises, and shall have no claim against the bank for
damages or otherwise." During the existence of that lease the
plaintiff redeemed and called for possession of the property. The
bank gave notice to Pearce that the mortgage had been paid off,
and that the lease to him had determined. Pearce, however,
refused to give up possession of the property, and thereupon the
plaintiff brought an action of ejectment against him. In that
action the plaintiff was successful, and Pearce was turned out of
possession; but, Pearce being a man of straw, the plaintiff was
unable to recover the costs of that action from him, or the rent
for the time during which he held possession of the premises
against him. Being unable to recover from Pearce, he has now
brought an action against the bank to recover those amounts,
and also the costs incurred by him in the repair of the hotel by
reason of Pearce not repairing the premises according to the
terms of the lease. The question for us to determine is whether
the defendants are liable to pay that sum or any portion of it.
It has been argued that the defendants are in the same position
as if they had taken a lease from the plaintiff, and that, as in the
case of landlord and tenant, the tenant is bound to deliver up
possession of the premises at the expiration of the lease, and is

CASES AT LAW. [N. S. W. R.

1898.

FINN
v.
LONDON
BANK OF
AUSTRALIA.

The C.J.

responsible for an under-tenant holding over as against the landlord, so in this case as between mortgagee and mortgagor the mortgagee is liable after redemption for any person holding over as against the mortgagor. I am utterly unable to see that the law which is applicable between landlord and tenant in any way applies between mortgagee and mortgagor. The position is entirely different. When a mortgagee enters into possession he is bound to make the best use of the property, and he must act as a prudent owner would act, always considering the interests of the mortgagor. It is said that under s. 58, the mortgagee in possession has no power to lease. That section gives the mortgagee, on default, power to enter into possession of the mortgaged land by receiving the rents and profits thereof in the same manner as if the principal sum were secured to him by a conveyance of the legal estate. That section therefore leaves him in the position he would be at common law, and, therefore, enables him to make a lease. It may be that under that section he would have power to make a lease for years. It is, however, unnecessary for me to express any opinion upon that point, because it is clear that a mortgagee in possession can grant a lease of the premises until redemption. It appears to me that under the circumstances the defendants did what they were clearly entitled to do, and that they were in no way responsible for Pearce's action in not delivering up the premises to the plaintiff.

OWEN, J. I am of the same opinion. The case made for the plaintiff depends upon the question whether, when he paid off the mortgage, the defendants were bound to deliver up possession of the premises to him. The answer to that question depends upon whether the bank as mortgagees in possession had power to grant a lease. I am clearly of opinion that they had. The power to grant a lease necessarily flows from the power given in s. 58 to enter into possession and receive the rents and profits. In *Maxwell on Statutes*, at p. 502, it is laid down:—" When powers, privileges, or property are granted by statute everything indispensable to their exercise or enjoyment is impliedly granted also, as it would be in a grant between private persons." The power to grant a lease must necessarily be implied from the power to receive the rents and profits. Upon the mortgagor **making default** it is necessary for the mortgagee to go into possession, and if there were no power to grant a lease in a case where a lease of the premises had just run out when he went into possession, his whole security would be destroyed. Where a mortgagee goes into possession he is liable for wilful neglect and default, and he must deal with the property in the most beneficial way. In *Coote on Mortgages*, p. 1202 (5th Ed.), it is said "the mortgagee is liable if he refuse or remove a sufficient tenant." It seems to me absurd to say that a mortgagee may enter into possession of the land by receiving the rents and profits, and yet that he cannot grant a lease. There may be some question as to what length of lease he can grant. He is entitled to grant a lease, with the consent of the mortgagor, for any period, and he is also entitled to grant a lease for as long as he remains in possession; as to whether he can go further and grant a lease for a longer period, I express no opinion. When the mortgagor has redeemed, the mortgagee is not bound to turn the tenant out, as it was just as much for the benefit of the mortgagor as for the mortgagee that the tenant was put in.

COHEN, J., concurred.

Judgment for the defendants.

Attorney for the plaintiff: *W. H. Pigott*, agent for *J. R. Edwards* (Broken Hill).

Attorneys for the defendants: *Macnamara & Smith.*

1898.

FINN
v.
LONDON
BANK OF
AUSTRALIA.

Owen J.

1898.

August 22.
November 18.

The C.J.
Cohen J.
and
A. H. Simpson J.

Ex parte BOURKE.

Small Debts Court—Jurisdiction—Balance of account.

The plaintiff brought an action in the Small Debts Court to recover the sum of 9*l.* 12*s.*, and obtained a verdict for that amount. The accounts filed with the plaint shewed that 141*l.* was due to the plaintiff for wages less 131*l.* 8*s.* paid to him. *Held,* on a motion for a prohibition that as there was evidence before the Small Debts Court that the balance of account had been admitted, the Full Court could not grant a prohibition.

PROHIBITION.

This was a motion to make absolute a rule *nisi* calling upon T. H. Wilkinson, P.M., Mudgee, the Registrar of the Small Debts Court, Cobbora, and H. Robinson, to shew cause why a writ of prohibition should not issue to restrain them from further proceeding upon a judgment recovered in the Small Debts Court, Cobbora, wherein H. Robinson was the plaintiff, and W. Bourke was the defendant. The ground upon which the rule *nisi* was granted was that the said Small Debts Court had no jurisdiction to adjudicate in the said case, as the amount of the plaintiff's demand exceeded 30*l.*, and involved the investigation of a claim which exceeded that amount.

The plaint was as follows :—

" H. Robinson complains of W. Bourke that he is indebted in the sum of 9*l.* 12*s.* for wages due and payable from the said W. Bourke to the said H. Robinson . . ."

Particulars filed with the plaint were as follows :—

3rd June, 1895
to
16th Feb., 1898.

To 141 weeks wages at £1 per week	...	£141	0	0
To cash drawn	...	...	...	...	131	8	0
To balance due	...	...	...	...	9	12	0

The affidavit of the applicant set out :—

" I am a grazier residing at Upper Bromley, in the Mudgee district, and I had in my employ H. Robinson at a salary of 1*l.* per week.

said H. Robinson remained in my service from the
the year 1895 to about the month of February, 1898,
; this period he had received goods and cash to a large

the conclusion of his service I made up his account, and
then due to him a balance of a few pounds, which I
him, and he left the station perfectly satisfied with the
; made with him."

er stated that he was laid up in St. Vincent's Hospital,
vhen he received the Small Debts summons. He
a medical certificate, and forwarded it to the Small
urt with a request for an adjournment. The Police
a did not, however, adjourn the case, and gave a verdict
uintiff for the amount claimed. Bourke then applied for
il, and that was refused.

le amount credited in the said account as for cash drawn
· been assented to by me, nor was any such amount
on between H. Robinson and myself as being the amount
:h his account was to be debited.

am not indebted to H. Robinson in any sum whatever,
id him all that was due after he left my service."

spondent filed an affidavit in which he stated that he
an account of all moneys paid to him, and he shewed
nt to Bourke and asked for a settlement; that Bourke then
r admitted" that the amounts that he shewed to him as
en paid had been paid, and promised to pay him the
a few days; and that these facts were given in evidence
e Police Magistrate. The Police Magistrate filed an
in which he said that the claim of the plaintiff was
lly admitted."

re, for the applicant.

OURT called upon

mson, for the respondent. The payments were admitted
efendant previously to the action being brought. The
rs in this case were the same as in *In re Alp* (1). In
Wedderburn (2) *Windeyer*, J., says: "Where there is a

8 W.N. 57.   (2) 15 N.S.W. L.R. 482; 11 W.N. 82.

1898.

Ex parte
BOURKE.

large claim, and that claim is reduced by a payment which the defendant admits, then that Court has jurisdiction."

The Magistrate had jurisdiction to enquire into the fact whether the set-off had been admitted, and he has found as a fact that the set-off was. If there was evidence before him on that point, this Court will not interfere by prohibition.

If there is a conflict of evidence as to whether the balance of account was admitted, this Court will not review the finding of the Magistrate on that point.

He also rererred to *Kimpton* v. *Willey* (1); *Ex parte Guzzard* (2); *Ex parte Roberts* (3); *Ex parte Ashe* (4); *Ex parte Nelson* (5); *Ex parte Heggie* (6).

McIntyre in reply. The action here was not on accounts stated. If it had been, and the Magistrate had found that accounts had been stated, this Court no doubt would not interfere. This was an action for wages: *Ex parte McMillan* (7).

[COHEN, J. I do not think that we should apply the strict rules of pleading to this Court, and, therefore, the form of action would be immaterial.]

There was no evidence before the Magistrate on which he could find that the balance had been struck between the parties, and was due to the plaintiff. On the contrary, in the letter written by the defendant he says that he paid the plaintiff in full.

The distinction between *In re Alp* and *Ex parte Guzzard* is pointed out by *Windeyer*, J., in the latter case, where he says: " This case is not on all fours with *Alp's Case*, because in that case there was a claim which the defendant admitted had been reduced by payment." There was no evidence of any admission here, and the Magistrate could not give himself jurisdiction by finding that there was such an admission.

C.A.V.

November 18. On the 18th November,

THE CHIEF JUSTICE. This was an application at common law for a prohibition directed to the plaintiff in an action in the Small

---

(1) 19 L.J. C P. 269.　　　　　(4) 13 W.N. 76.
(2) 15 N.S.W.L.R. 394; 11 W.N. 21.　(5) *Wilk. Aust. Mag.*, 5th Ed., 750.
(3) 15 N.S.W.L.R. 294 ; 11 W.N. 16.　(6) 9 W.N. 100.
(7) 14 W.N. 32.

Debts Court, and to Mr. T. H. Wilkinson, Police Magistrate, to restrain them from proceeding upon a judgment in the plaintiff's favour, upon the ground that the Court had no jurisdiction to adjudicate in the case, as the amount of the plaintiff's demand exceeded 30*l.*, and involved the investigation of a claim which exceeded that amount.

It appeared that the plaintiff in the Court below had been in the defendant's employment for a considerable time before the month of February this year, when on leaving the employment a settlement took place between them, leaving, according to the plaintiff's case, an admitted balance of 9*l.* 12*s.*, and for this sum the plaintiff sued the defendant. There can be no question, that had this balance been admitted the Court had jurisdiction.

It appears that although the alleged settlement took place in February last, no proceedings to recover the balance alleged to be due were taken until three months afterwards, when the defendant, who was a resident of the Mudgee district, was at the time an inmate of St. Vincent's Hospital in Sydney, and unable to attend the Court. Notwithstanding this fact appeared before the Magistrate, and an adjournment was applied for, the Magistrate, in the defendant's absence, upon evidence which was eminently unsatisfactory, as appears from the affidavit of the Magistrate, and also from the affidavit of the plaintiff, refused the adjournment, and found a verdict for the plaintiff.

The plaintiff in his affidavit does not speak of any actual admission; he says: Bourke "then virtually admitted." The Magistrate in his affidavit says that the claim of the plaintiff was "practically admitted," and the reason he gives for this is, that when the unfortunate defendant applied to the Bench by letter for an adjournment he stated that he had paid the plaintiff in full. It is upon such evidence and for such reasons as this that the Magistrate found a verdict for the plaintiff.

I believe the verdict, so far as it is based upon the fact of an admitted balance, to be absolutely wrong, but unfortunately the Court is powerless to set the matter right. This is not a Court of Appeal from the Magistrate, and as he found a balance admitted, the verdict, no matter how erroneous and unjust it may happen to be, must stand.

I think it is greatly to be regretted that the Magistrate, under the circumstances of this case, did not grant a postponement. The proceedings were not taken for three months after the alleged settlement, and at a time when the plaintiff probably knew that the defendant could not attend. Then when a new trial was asked for, this matter was set down for a date when again the defendant through illness could not attend; he applied for a postponement, and the Magistrate, addressing a letter to him at St. Vincent's Hospital, says "If Robinson's costs were paid the application for postponement of case might be considered a fair one." The defendant paid the plaintiff's costs, and thereupon the Magistrate refuses to postpone the case, and for a second time determines the matter in the defendant's absence.

Although the defendant has grave cause of complaint, yet these matters, being within the discretion of the Magistrate, and, although I think that discretion to be wrongly exercised, I cannot say that the rule should be made absolute upon the grounds that the proceedings were contrary to natural justice.

I am of opinion, therefore, that the rule must be discharged, but, seeing the very unsatisfactory way in which the case has been dealt with in the Magistrate's Court, without costs.

COHEN, J.   This is an application for a prohibition to the Small Debts Court for want of jurisdiction, on the ground that the plaintiff's demand exceeded 30*l.*, and involved the investigation of a claim which exceeded that amount. The plaint stated that the defendant Bourke was indebted to the plaintiff Robinson in the sum of 9*l.* 12*s.*, for wages payable by Bourke to Robinson for his services as a servant of Bourke, and the particulars filed were as follows :—

June 3, 1895,
   to
Feb. 16, 1898.
William Bourke,
   Grazier, Broomley,   Dr. to H. Robinson.
     Cobbora.

	£	s.	d.
141 weeks wages at £1 per week	141	0	0
To cash drawn	131	8	0
To balance due	9	12	0

At the hearing Bourke was not present, as he was laid up at St. Vincent's Hospital, Sydney; but he had forwarded to the Bench a medical certificate of his inability to attend, and requested an adjournment, which was refused. Bourke thereafter applied for a new trial, but through apparent inability to attend at the application, it was not granted, and hence the present motion.

According to the cases of *Ex parte Gazzard* (1) and *Evans* v. *Wedderburn* (2), the judgment of this Court must depend upon whether or not there was evidence before the Magistrate that the defendant had admitted the sum sued for as the amount due by him to Robinson, because if there was such evidence a prohibition will not lie. Now Bourke in his affidavit of August 2nd, paragraph 3, says: "At the conclusion of his service I made up his account, and there was then due to him a balance of a few pounds, which I duly paid him, and he left the station perfectly satisfied with the settlement made with him." Now this shews that a balance of what was due to Robinson had been struck, though the fact of payment of that balance being in dispute, necessarily led to the action; and although this statement was not before the Magistrate, it confirms Robinson's statement in Court that a *balance* had been struck between him and Bourke. Then Robinson, in his affidavit of August 16th, paragraph 4, states: "An account of all such moneys (that is, moneys paid to him by Bourke) was kept by me, and when I left his employment I shewed him such account and asked for a settlement. The said William Bourke then virtually admitted that the amounts which I shewed to him as having been paid had been paid, and promised to pay the balance in a few days." Robinson further says that the facts so stated in his affidavit were sworn to in Court, and the Police Magistrate in his affidavit substantially corroborates Robinson. In the face of this, greatly as I may regret that Bourke was unable to be present at the hearing, and to tender evidence, and that the case was heard *ex parte*, I cannot see how this prohibition can be granted.

As to whether the Police Magistrate is to be censured, I express no opinion, for whilst it may, and no doubt does, seem unjust,

(1) 15 N.S.W. L.R. 394.   (2) *Idem.* 482.

that under the circumstances Bourke should not have been allowed the opportunity of being present at the hearing, both of the action and the application for a new trial, there may have been considerations presented to the Magistrate which pointed to an injustice to the plaintiff if the adjournment had been allowed.

A. H. SIMPSON, J.   This is an application for a prohibition against T. H. Wilkinson, P.M., Mudgee, the Registrar of the Small Debts Court, Cobbora, and Robinson, on the ground that the Small Debts Court had no jurisdiction to adjudicate in the case of *Robinson* v. *Bourke*, as the amount of the plaintiff's demand exceeded 30*l.*, and involved the investigation of a claim which exceeded that amount.

The plaint was for 9*l.* 12*s.* for wages, which the particulars shewed to be made up as follows :—

141 weeks wages at £1 per week	...	...	£141	0	0
To cash drawn ...	...	...	...	131	8	0
To balance due	...	...	...	£9	12	0

The plaintiff is bound under s. 20, Small Debts Recovery Act, to set forth shortly and in substance his cause of action, and it seems to me that his particulars comply with this condition.

In *Ex parte Gazzard* (1) the particulars shewed goods supplied to the value of 25*l.* 1*s.* 6*d.*, less value of goods credited 15*l.* 9*s.* 1*d.*; balance 9*l.* 12*s.* 5*d.* The only evidence that the value of the goods credited had been accepted as payment was an entry in the plaintiff's books. The Court held that this was not admissible as evidence, and the prohibition was granted ; but *Stephen*, J., held that if there had been evidence to the effect above-mentioned the decision would have been different.

In *Evans* v. *Wedderburn* (2) the particulars were in similar form, except the items on the credit side were cash.   On the rule *nisi* for prohibition being served on him the plaintiff discontinued the action.   *Windeyer*, J., said (p. 487) if the case had gone to a hearing it would have been competent for the Small Debts Court to see whether the amount for which the plaintiff gave the defendant credit had been admitted, and whether a

(1) 15 N.S.W. L.R 394.   (2) 15 N.S.W. L.R. 482.

balance had been struck by the parties. In this case it seems
to me impossible to say there was no evidence of admission by
the defendant as to 131*l*. (see Robinson's affidavit, paragraph 4,
and T. H. Wilkinson's affidavit). If so, this Court cannot
interfere by prohibition, however unsatisfactory the Court may
think the decision. The cases cited on the construction of the
District Courts Act, s. 7, do not throw any light on this case, as
the wording of that section is entirely different from the wording
of s. 4 of the Small Debts Court Act.

The real wrong in the case has been caused by the Magistrate
refusing to postpone the hearing, although he had a medical
certificate that the defendant was laid up in a hospital, and then
deciding on *ex parte* evidence of the most flimsy character that
the plaintiff was entitled to succeed. When Bourke applied for
a new trial he received a letter signed by the Magistrate, stating
that the application was set down for 21st July, and that if
Robinson's costs were paid, the application for a postponement of
the case might be considered a fair one. Bourke paid these costs,
but the application for a new trial was refused. If the case had
not been heard behind Bourke's back, it seems clear that it must,
or ought, to have failed. Though the conduct of the Magistrate
is, in my opinion, open to grave question, it does not afford ground
for a prohibition.

Rule discharged without costs.

Attorneys for the applicant : *Wallace & Son.*

Attorneys for the respondent : *Lee, Colquhoun, & Bassett.*

1898.

Ex parte
BOURKE.

A.H.Simpson J.

1898.   *Ex parte* HALES.

October 26, 28.   *Public Vehicle Regulation Acts—Transit Commissioners—By-laws—Unreasonable.*

The C.J.   *Prohibition—Justices—Affidavit.*

Owen J.   A by-law (by-law 57) which makes it an offence for a driver of a public vehicle
and   to arrive late at any public stand, no matter from what cause, *held* unreasonable
Cohen J.   and *ultra vires.*

An information for an offence against the by-laws of the Transit Commissioners,
cannot be laid by an inspector unless he has received a complaint under by-law 74.

On an application for a prohibition against a Magistrate he should not make an
affidavit.

PROHIBITION.

This was a motion to make absolute a rule *nisi* calling upon
G. H. Smithers, S.M., and A. Edward, Inspector of Licensed
Vehicles, to shew cause why a writ of prohibition should not be
issued to restrain them from proceeding further in the matter of
an information laid by A. Edward against W. Hales, and on the
hearing of which W. Hales was fined 20*s.* and costs.

The information charged Hales that he "being the driver of a
public vehicle, to wit, an omnibus plying for hire, did not run
the said omnibus in strict accordance with the time table, that he
was due at the Railway Bridge, George-street, Sydney, at 7.48,
and did not arrive until 7.51, and was three minutes late,
contrary to by-law 57."

The grounds upon which the rule *nisi* was granted were :—

1. That the Magistrate had no jurisdiction, as there was no
evidence that there was any person aggrieved, or that the
Inspector had received a complaint from any person aggrieved.

2. That by-law 57 is unreasonable and *ultra vires.*

3. That there was no evidence to support the conviction.

The evidence as appeared in the depositions was as follows:—

Beare, a transit officer, said, "On the 9th inst., I was on duty
in George-street. At 7.51 I saw defendant driving 'bus No. 134
plying for hire . . . .   He was due to arrive at the Railway

Bridge at 7.48 . . . . I stopped him and told him, and
asked him what kept him; he said he could not get along."

A. Edward, Inspector of Licensed Vehicles, said, " . . . .
I produce a copy of the Government Gazette containing the by-
laws relating to licensed vehicles. . . . . I also produce the
register of licensed owner, drivers, and conductors of licensed
vehicles. . . . ."

Nothing appeared in the depositions to shew that the time
table was produced before the Magistrate, but in an affidavit
sworn by him he said that A. Edward produced a time table.

A. Edward, in his affidavit, said, "At the conclusion of the
evidence of W. Beare in support of my case, I asked the defendant whether he would admit the by-laws and the time table,
and on such admission being refused I was duly sworn, and
holding the said time table, the Government Gazette containing
the said by-laws, and register of licenses in my hand whilst
giving evidence, I gave the evidence as appears in my deposition."

The part of by-law 57 under which the applicant was prosecuted was as follows:—

"Every driver who shall start or arrive at any public stand or place, otherwise
than in strict accordance with such time table, shall be guilty of an offence
against this by-law."

By-law 74 was as follows:—

"It shall be lawful for the Inspector on receiving a complaint from the owner,
driver, or conductor of any public vehicle, or from any person using or intending
to use, or hiring or intending to hire any such vehicle, or other person aggrieved,
that any of these by-laws have been disobeyed, to cause the person against whom
the said complaint shall have been made to be summoned to appear before any
Stipendiary Magistrate or Court of Petty Sessions."

Hamilton, for the applicant. By-law 57 is unreasonable.
Under this by-law a driver is liable even if he is late from no
cause of his own.

[THE CHIEF JUSTICE. If a horse in the omnibus were to fall
and the driver was in consequence late, he could be fined under
this by-law ?]

Yes. That shews how unreasonable the by-law is; if it made
the driver liable if he was wilfully late, then it might be good.

EE 2

Secondly, the time table was not produced in evidence, and, therefore, there was no evidence of the time at which the driver should have arrived.

[*Edmunds.* The Magistrate says that it was.

THE CHIEF JUSTICE. It does not appear on the depositions that the time table was before the Magistrate, and the depositions cannot be supplemented by an affidavit.]

Though the Magistrate says it was produced, Edward only says that he had it in his hand.

[THE CHIEF JUSTICE (to *Edmunds*). Do you appear for the Magistrate ?]

Edmunds. No.

.THE CHIEF JUSTICE. Then the Magistrate should not have made an affidavit.

COHEN, J. I do not agree with *The Chief Justice* on that point, because a Magistrate's affidavit has been received over and over again, to shew what took place before him.]

The third point is taken under by-law 74. It is only where the Inspector receives a complaint from some person that he can lay an information.

He was stopped.

Edmunds, for the respondent (Edward). It is within the powers of the Commissioners to make a by-law such as 57 (see s. 16 of 36 Vic. No. 14). The by-law was passed to regulate the traffic and prevent a driver loitering to pick up fares or racing. I admit that the by-law is unreasonable if it means that a driver is liable no matter what the cause of the delay may be, but I submit it does not mean that. It means that he is liable if he is wilfully late. It must be limited to mean late through his own act or default, or if he has no reasonable excuse.

He referred to *Kruse* v. *Johnson* (1).

As to the second point, I submit that the evidence shews that the time table was before the Magistrate.

Thirdly. By-law 74 does not prohibit an Inspector from laying an information if the by-laws have been infringed; it

(1) [1898] 2 Q.B. 91.

only empowers him to lay an information where he has not seen
the offence committed, without getting instructions from the
Commissioners to do so.   Suppose an Inspector were to see an
offence committed, such as the overcrowding of an omnibus, it
would be absurd to say that he must wait and receive a complaint
before he could lay an information.

[OWEN, J.   Where is there anything in the Act to enable the
Commissioners to authorise any officer to take proceedings ?]

There is nothing in the Act which enables them to do that.

[THE CHIEF JUSTICE.   Then the Commissioners would have
to take proceedings and call one of their officers to prove that
the offence had been committed.]

There is nothing to prevent an Inspector or anyone else who
knows that an offence has been committed from laying an information.

THE CHIEF JUSTICE.   I am clearly of opinion that the prohibition should go, and on all the points taken.   I will deal first
with the second ground taken in the rule *nisi*, that the by-law
in question is unreasonable.   That portion of by-law 57 which
says that " Every driver who shall start or arrive at any public
stand or place, otherwise than in strict accordance with such
time table, shall be guilty of an offence against this by-law," is
entirely unreasonable, and is, therefore, *ultra vires*.   The meaning
of that portion of the by-law is simply this, that no matter what
may be the cause of the delay if the driver is half a minute late
he commits a breach of the by-law, and is liable to no less a
penalty than 10*l*.   The schedule to these by-laws prescribes the
time for each portion of the journey, coming down as low in one
instance to three minutes.   If a horse falls or casts a shoe, or
anything occurs arising from no fault of the driver, and he be late
on any portion of the journey, nevertheless he becomes amenable to
that by-law.   That is so monstrously and flagrantly unreasonable
that it cannot stand.   It is quite right that the omnibus traffic
should be under strict control and that the drivers should not be
allowed to loiter; but the by-law dealing with that matter should
be so worded as to enable the driver to offer a reasonable
excuse for apparent default; of course, the by-law could be so

framed that the onus of shewing that should be on the driver. But as the by-law is at present, a man may have a perfect excuse and, nevertheless, he commits an offence and is liable to a severe penalty.

The first ground taken turns upon by-law 74; that by-law provides that the Inspector may lay an information " on receiving a complaint from the owner, driver, or conductor of any public vehicle, or from any person using or intending to use, or hiring or intending to hire any such vehicle, or other person aggrieved, that any of the by-laws have been disobeyed." In this case the Inspector received no complaint from any one of those persons, and, therefore, the Inspector had no power to lay the information. If it was necessary to lay an information in this case, it should have been laid by the Transit Commissioners themselves through their proper officer.

I am also of opinion that there was no evidence to prove the case. The Magistrate was induced to make an affidavit in the matter. When a Magistrate has decided a case his duty is at an end, and it is no part of his duty to maintain his judgment. If he makes an affidavit for one side or the other he puts himself in the invidious position of being considered a partizan. That is a position in which no Judge, whether high or low, should allow himself to be placed. The Magistrate made a very grave, though no doubt a perfectly innocent, mistake when he says that the time table was produced. In Edward's evidence he says, "I produce a copy of the Government Gazette containing the by-laws relating to licensed vehicles. . . . I also produce the register of licensed owner, drivers, and conductors. . . ." but he does not say one word about producing the time table, and in his affidavit all he says is that he held the time table in his hand whilst giving evidence. The Magistrate, however, says it was produced, and has made a very grave mistake. This only shews how unfortunate it is for a Magistrate to place himself in the invidious position of swearing an affidavit to support his own ruling. I hope that a case of this kind will not occur again.

OWEN, J. I am also of opinion that the by-law is *ultra vires*. In *Kruse* v. *Johnson* (1), Lord *Russell*, C.J., in considering the

(1) [1898] 2 Q.B. 99.

question of how far by-laws may be said to be unreasonable, says, " If for instance they were found to be partial and unequal in their operation as between different classes; if they were manifestly unjust; if they disclosed bad faith; if they involved such oppressive or gratuitous interference with the rights of those subject to them as could find no justification in the minds of reasonable men, the Court might well say ' Parliament never intended to give authority to make such rules, they are unreasonable and *ultra vires*.' But it is in this sense, and in this sense only, as I conceive, that the question of unreasonableness can properly be regarded. A by-law is not unreasonable merely because particular Judges may think that it goes further than is prudent or necessary, or convenient, or because it is not accompanied by a qualification or an exception which some Judges may think ought to be there." That lays down the law very clearly as to when the Court can say that a by-law is unreasonable and *ultra vires*. The by-law in question is manifestly unjust, and is an oppressive interference with the rights of those who are subject to them. It is a cast-iron by-law which gives a driver no opportunity of explaining why it was he happened to be late. I think it is very desirable that the Transit Commissioners should have full power to control the traffic, and prevent the drivers of omnibuses from loitering or racing. A by-law could be easily framed to meet those cases which would work no injustice, and which would give the driver an opportunity of explaining why he was late at his destination.

I also agree in thinking that a Magistrate should not make an affidavit as to what takes place before him. By so doing he puts himself in an unseemly position, and one of apparent antagonism to one side or the other.

COHEN, J. I am also of opinion that the by-law is unreasonable, and that the Inspector cannot lay an information except under by-law 74.

With regard to Magistrates making affidavits, on the whole, I am prepared to agree in thinking that it is an undesirable thing for a Magistrate to do. But in justification of the Magistrate's conduct in this case, I desire to say that it has been the rule where there has been a conflict of testimony as to what took

1808.

Ex parte
HALES.

Cohen J.

place before a Magistrate, to take the affidavit of the Magistrate on the subject. In this year there were two cases at least before the Court in which Magistrates made affidavits. I refer to *Ex parte Mylecharane* (1), and *Ex parte Bourke*, which is now awaiting judgment (since reported *ante*, p. 370). In those cases no exception was taken to the Magistrates making affidavits. I merely mention those cases as a justification of the Magistrate in this case, but I agree that it is a much more wholesome rule that Magistrates should not make affidavits at all, and if further evidence is required the Court could refer the matter to the Magistrate for a report.

Rule absolute with costs.

Attorney for the applicant: *A. Muddle.*
Attorneys for the respondent: *Waldron & Dawson.*

(1) 19 N.S.W. L.R. 7; 14 W.N. 125.

R. *v.* ALICE SHORT.

Criminal law—Special case—Error on the record—Jury improperly sworn.

On the trial of a prisoner one of the jurymen was taken ill and the remaining jurymen were discharged but did not leave the box. Another juryman was then called and sworn, but the other eleven jurymen were not re-sworn. *Held*, the point could not be raised by special case under s. 422 of the Criminal Law Amendment Act, but should have been raised by way of error on the record. *Held*, on a motion to reverse the judgment for error on the record, that the remaining eleven jurymen should have been re-sworn, and, therefore, the trial had taken place before an improperly constituted tribunal, and judgment was reversed. *Semble*, that the prisoner could not consent to being tried by a jury which had not been properly sworn.

1898:

August 18.
October 27.

The C.J.
Stephen J.
Owen J.
and
Cohen J.

CROWN CASE RESERVED.

The following special case was stated by *G. B. Simpson*, J.:—

"The prisoner was convicted of manslaughter before me on August 5th last, and was sentenced to five years' penal servitude. During the opening of the Crown Prosecutor one of the jurors was taken ill. He was seen by Dr. Jamieson, who informed me that the juror was not, in his opinion, fit to sit in the case. I asked the Crown Prosecutor what was to be done? He said: 'I suppose the case will have to stand over until the next sittings.' Hereupon, as I understood, a consultation or conversation took place between the Crown Prosecutor and Mr. *Levien*, the prisoner's attorney, and in order that the trial might proceed, the prisoner, after being advised by her attorney, consented to the eleven jurors being considered *as discharged and recalled, and said she did not wish to challenge any of them.* As there was no other case for trial on the 5th August, I had discharged the remainder of the jury, and a difficulty suggested itself about obtaining the services of a juror in the place of the one who had been taken ill. The deputy sheriff reported to me that two or three jurors were still within the precincts of the Court, and I asked Mr. *Levien* if he would accept the first person whose name should be called by the associate. He said he 'would like to hear the name called first.' This was done, and the person whose name was first called took his place in the jury box, and was sworn without any objection. The prisoner was then given in charge to the jury. Nothing was said about the remaining eleven jurors being re-sworn. They were not re-sworn. The eleven jurymen had never left the box after having been originally sworn.

"After the jury had found the prisoner guilty, Mr. *Levien* addressed me as follows :—' After the jury were sworn one of the jurymen became ill, and was unable to act, and was withdrawn. Another juryman was sworn. The indictment was then read over to the twelve jurors, and prisoner given in charge again. The remaining jurymen ought to have been re-sworn. I want reserved for the consideration of the Full Court the question whether the eleven jurymen who were discharged, should not have been re-sworn, and whether there has not been a mis-trial?'

" I reserve for the consideration of the Supreme Court the question whether, under the circumstances above stated, the eleven jurors should have been re-sworn, and whether as they were not re-sworn, there has been a mis-trial ? "

Wade, for the Crown, objected that the special case could not be heard. The point is that the tribunal was not properly constituted to try the prisoner. If the Court are of opinion that there has been a mis-trial, the proper order to be granted is a *venire de novo*. But a decision upon a special case under s. 422 is final, and if the prisoner be discharged, the Crown cannot put her on her trial again. The proper way, therefore, to bring this point before the Court, is by writ of error under s. 427, when the Court may order a *venire de novo*: *R.* v. *Mellor* (1), *R.* v. *O'Keefe* (2).

Gannon and *Mack*, for the prisoner.

THE CHIEF JUSTICE. I am of opinion that Mr. *Wade's* contention is correct, and that we must refuse to hear this special case. But the record may still be made up, and the matter brought before us under s. 427. Then if we are of opinion that the prisoner has suffered any substantial wrong, we shall declare that there has been no trial.

STEPHEN and COHEN, JJ., concurred.

Objection sustained.

(1) Dear. & Bell, *per Channell, B.,*   (2) 15 N.S.W. L.R. 1 ; 10 W.N.
     at 519.   194.

Wade. Will the Court affirm the judgment of the Court below ? I see that was the order made in *Mellor's Case.*

THE CHIEF JUSTICE. No, we merely say that we do not entertain the special case.

On the 27th October, a motion was made on behalf of the prisoner to reverse the judgment herein for error on the record.

The record was as follows :—

"Be it remembered at the Supreme Court holden at Sydney in the colony of New South Wales on the 25th July before the Hon. *G. B. Simpson* a Judge of the said Supreme Court which same Court is duly continued and adjourned by the said Judge until the 5th August an indictment was duly presented and filed in the said Court by *C. G. Wade* Barrister at Law being the officer duly appointed to prosecute for Her Majesty in this behalf being present in the said Supreme Court at Sydney aforesaid on the said 5th August charges that Alice Short on the 10th July 1898 at North Sydney in the colony aforesaid did feloniously and maliciously murder M. S. Gettens whereupon on this 5th August 1898 before the said Hon. *G. B. Simpson* a Judge of the said Supreme Court aforesaid come as well the said *C. G. Wade* Esq. Barrister at Law being the officer duly appointed as aforesaid as the said Alice Short in her proper person and having had hearing of the said indictment the said Alice Short was instantly to speak in this Court how she would acquit herself of the premises aforesaid above charged and imposed upon her who saith that she is not guilty of the felony aforesaid in the indictment aforesaid above alleged against her and therefore of the good and evil thereof doth put herself upon the country. And the said *C. G. Wade* Esq. Barrister at Law being the officer duly appointed as aforesaid doth follow for our said Lady the Queen doth so likewise and thereupon before the said Hon. *G. B. Simpson* a Judge of the said Court come as well the said *C. G. Wade* Esq. Barrister at Law being the officer duly appointed as aforesaid as the said Alice Short in her proper person and the jurors of the jury by C. E. B. Maybury Esq. sheriff of the said colony on this behalf empanelled and returned being called come who being chosen tried and sworn to speak the truth of and upon the premises in the indictment aforesaid above specified are unable to speak the truth of and upon the premises in the indictment aforesaid above specified by reason of one of the jurors so called chosen tried and sworn to speak the truth as aforesaid by name J. Gibson being ill and unfit to try and determine the premises aforesaid. And whereas the said Alice Short being advised by her attorney so to do consents to the eleven remaining jurors so called as aforesaid being considered as discharged and recalled and the said Alice Short saith she does not wish to challenge any of the said eleven jurors so called as aforesaid. And whereas it is reported to the said Hon. *G. B. Simpson* a Judge of the said Supreme Court as aforesaid that two or three of the jurors so empanelled and returned by the Sheriff of the said colony as aforesaid are still within the precincts of the said Supreme Court the Hon. *G. B. Simpson* a Judge of the said Supreme Court as aforesaid asks the said attorney for the said Alice Short if he will accept the first person whose name shall be called by the Associate to the said Hon. *G. B. Simpson* as such Judge as aforesaid whereupon the said attorney for the said Alice Short makes answer that he would like to hear the name of the said juror called first whereupon the name of Richard Cozens one of the jurors so empanelled and returned as aforesaid is called by the said Associate and the said R. Cozens takes his place in the jury box and is without any objection by the said Alice Short sworn to speak the truth of and upon the premises in the indictment aforesaid above specified And whereas the eleven remaining jurymen as aforesaid have not left the jury box after having been first sworn and they are not re-sworn And whereas the said Alice Short is upon the said premises in the indictment above specified given in charge to the said jury and the said jury do say that the said Alice Short is guilty of manslaughter Therefore it is considered by the Court here that the said Alice Short shall be kept to penal servitude for the period of 5 years."

The error assigned was " that by the said record it appears that the said jury was not duly sworn to try the issue raised upon the said trial, and that the judgment against her upon the verdict of the said jury at the said trial given is void."

Mack (*Gannon* with him), for the prisoner. When one of the jurymen was taken ill the jury was discharged, and, therefore, the eleven jurymen who remained in the box should have been re-sworn when another juryman was called: *R.* v. *Edwards* (1); *R.* v. *Scalbert* (2). It may be contended by the Crown that the prisoner gave her consent to be tried in this way. In the first place I submit that she did not give her consent to this course. Secondly, even assuming that she did, I submit that she had no power to consent to be tried before a jury which had not been sworn : *R.* v. *Bertrand* (3).

Wade, for the Crown. Although I admit that it is usual to re-swear the jury where a juryman is taken ill and another jury-man has to be called, I submit that it is not necessary. In the case of *R.* v. *Joyce*, referred to in the note to *R.* v. *Scalbert* (2), where, on a juryman becoming ill, another juryman was sworn, the remaining eleven were not re-sworn.

He also referred to *Hale's Pleas of the Crown*, vol. II. 296, on this point.

Secondly, assuming that the jury should have been re-sworn then I submit that it was a mere irregularity, and that the prisoner, having consented to it, is bound by the consent (s. 470).

[OWEN, J. Can a prisoner consent to being tried by a jury that has not been sworn ?]

A prisoner can give any consent which might lawfully be given in a civil case. *R.* v. *Bertrand* (3) was decided before s.

(1) 4 Taunt. 311.　　　　　(2) 2 Leach 620.
(3) L.R. 1 P.C. 520.

470 was passed. That section was passed to meet such a difficulty as occurred in that case.

[OWEN, J. Could a party to a civil action consent to have his
case tried before a jury which had not been sworn ?]

If there was an informality in the swearing of a jury, and the
party consented, he could not afterwards raise the point. The
Court had jurisdiction to try the prisoner, and, therefore, not
swearing the jury was nothing more than an irregularity ; it was
not a question of jurisdiction.

[STEPHEN, J. The record does not say that the prisoner consented to being tried by a jury which had not been sworn.]

It no doubt does not appear in the record, but the record could
be amended. Under s. 427 no judgment shall be reversed for
error on the record, unless some substantial wrong appears to
have been done, or some other miscarriage of justice occasioned.
Here the irregularity did not do any substantial wrong, or
occasion any miscarriage of justice.

STEPHEN, J. We ought not to allow the slightest doubt to
exist as to this point. The question we have to determine is,
whether the prisoner was tried by a properly constituted tribunal?
It appears that twelve jurymen were sworn to try the case, and
that, owing to the illness of one of them, they were discharged.
I take it that they were discharged from their oath, though they
did not physically leave the box. Another juror was then called
and sworn, but the remaining jurors were not re-sworn. If that
is a proper course to take, they might just as well have left the
box and gone to their lunch, and coming back again started to
try the prisoner without being sworn. It is quite clear on the
authorities that the remaining eleven jurymen should have been
re-sworn.

Then it is said that, if the jury were not properly sworn, the
conviction should not be set aside, because the prisoner consented
to the course which was taken. I do not think that it is necessary to consider that point, because it does not appear on the
record that the prisoner did consent. I may, however, say, so
that no wrong impression shall exist, that I do not think that a

1898.

R.
v.
ALICE SHORT.

prisoner could give his consent in such a case. It is said that a prisoner can, under s. 470, with the advice of his counsel, give any consent which might be given in a civil case. Even in a civil case I should not hold that the parties could consent to the trial of a case before a jury who were not properly sworn. In a civil case parties might consent to a matter being referred to arbitration, but would it for a moment be contended that the prisoner could give his consent to his trial taking place before any tribunal other than that appointed by law? The question was not whether the Court had jurisdiction, but whether the prisoner was tried before a properly constituted tribunal. In my opinion it is just as if there had been no trial at all, the prisoner having been tried by a jury who had not been sworn. The judgment must, therefore, be reversed for error on the record.

OWEN, J. I am also clearly of opinion that the prisoner has never been tried at all, inasmuch as the trial took place before a tribunal which is not recognised at law—a jury which had not been sworn. When the jury was discharged, the eleven jurors were in exactly the same position as the other members of the panel who had not been sworn in the case, and were simply members of the public in Court. They had no duty to perform in respect to the prisoner or the evidence before them.

The proper and only course to pursue was to re-swear the whole of the jury just as if a fresh jury had been drawn from the panel. In *Archbold's Criminal Cases*, 19th Ed., 182. it is laid down, "If one of the jury die before the delivery of the verdict, the remaining eleven will be discharged, and a new jury may be at once sworn, or a new juror added to the eleven . . . So also if one of the jurors be taken so ill that he is not able to proceed with the trial. In case another juror is so added to the eleven, they must be sworn anew, and the prisoner must again have his challenges." Then it is said that the prisoner consented to being tried in this way. I am clearly of opinion that she had no power to consent to being tried by such a *quasi* tribunal as this, and further than that, I do not think that this matter was brought under her notice, and that she did in fact consent to being tried by eleven jurymen who had not been sworn in the case.

COHEN, J. I agree. In my opinion there has been no trial before a properly constituted tribunal. When the eleven jurymen were discharged, they were discharged from their oaths, and the trial, therefore, took place before eleven jurymen who were not sworn to try the case. On the other point, I am also of opinion that the prisoner had no power to give her consent to being tried before jurymen who had not been sworn.

1898.

R.
v.
ALICE SHORT.

> *Prisoner discharged.   Judgment reversed for error on the record.*

Attorney for the prisoner: *R. H. Levien.*

REGINA *v.* KERMOND.

1898.

October 27.

The C.J.
Owen J.
and
Cohen J.

*Criminal law—Perjury – Judicial proceedings—Enquiry before Court of Petty
Sessions— Indictable offence.*

A proceeding before a Court of Petty Sessions to commit a prisoner to take his
trial for an indictable offence is a judicial proceeding, and, therefore, any person
endeavouring to persuade another to make a false statement on oath before such
Court may be convicted under s. 296 of the Criminal Law Amendment Act.

CROWN CASE RESERVED.

SPECIAL CASE stated by *Stephen*, J.

" This prisoner was convicted before me at the last Mudgee
Assizes, under s. 296 of the Criminal Law Amendment Act, of
endeavouring to persuade or induce one James Ernest Spradbrow
to make a false statement on oath in a judicial proceeding then
pending in the Court of Petty Sessions holden at Mudgee, &c.

" It appears that one James Ryan had been brought before a
Police Court on the 7th May last on a warrant charging him with
stealing a heifer. The case was adjourned by the presiding
Justice until the 16th of that month, when Ryan was committed
for trial. It was during the interval that the prisoner committed
the alleged offence in respect whereof he was convicted, by
endeavouring to persuade Spradbrow to give false evidence at
the adjourned hearing of the case against Ryan. The point I
am about to submit was not taken by the prisoner's advocate,
but I reserved it for the opinion of the Court.

" The question for the decision of the Court is whether I ought
not to have directed an acquittal on the ground that the
proceeding above-mentioned was not a judicial one within the
meaning of the section 296.

" I sentenced the prisoner, but allowed him to enter into
recognizances to surrender himself in execution."

Watt, for the prisoner. Under s. 296, under which the prisoner
was convicted in this case, it is only a person who endeavours
to persuade another to make a false statement on oath in a
judicial proceeding who can be convicted. I submit that

preliminary proceedings in the case of an indictable offence before Justices are not "*judicial*" proceedings, because the Justices have no power to finally determine the matter one way or the other. The Justices can only dismiss the case or commit the prisoner to take his trial. In the former case that does not finally determine the matter, because the Attorney-General could still file a bill. In the latter case it is clear that the Justices do not finally determine the matter. The Justices do not act as a Court of Justice: *Cox* v. *Coleridge* (1). It is only where the Justices have summary jurisdiction that the proceedings before them can be said to be judicial proceedings: *R.* v. *Webster* (2). The enquiry before Justices in the case of an indictable offence is a ministerial proceeding, and can no more be said to be a judicial proceeding than the arrest by a constable. It is a necessary attribute to judicial power that the person exercising that power can pass sentence: *R.* v. *Tomlinson* (3).

[*Wade* referred to *Kimber* v. *The Press Association* (4).]

In that case the Justices had power to finally determine whether or not a summons should issue. The test of whether a proceeding is judicial or not, is whether the Justices have power to finally determine the matter or not.

Wade, for the Crown, was not called upon.

THE CHIEF JUSTICE. In this case the prisoner was indicted under s. 296, for " endeavouring to persuade one Spradbrow to make a false statement on oath in a judicial proceeding then pending in the Court of Petty Sessions." It appeared that one Ryan had been brought before the Court of Petty Sessions on a warrant charging him with stealing a heifer. After certain evidence had been given the case was remanded. During the interval the prisoner saw Spradbrow, and endeavoured to persuade him to give false evidence before the Magistrate. Now the point is taken that these proceedings before the Magistrate were not judicial proceedings. I am of opinion that, although

(1) 1 B. & C. 37.   (3) C.C. R. 49.
(2) 1 N.S.W. L.R. 325.   (4) [1893] 1 Q. B. 65.

these proceedings were of a preliminary nature, they were judicial proceedings. To hold otherwise would be to bring about a dangerous state of things, for it would enable persons with impunity to endeavour to persuade others to give false evidence in order to induce Magistrates not to commit accused persons to take their trial. The view we now take is the same as the view taken by Lord *Esher,* in *Kimber* v. *The Press Association* (1), where he says, ' That being so, it is necessary to consider whether the proceedings on the application for the issue of a summons in the present case, were proceedings which must end in a final decision. Now, if the Magistrates refused to allow the summons to be issued, that would be a final decision of the matter. If they issued the summons there must be a further inquiry and the matter might go on to trial." And, at p. 70, Lord *Esher* says, referring to s. 19, which gives the Magistrates discretion to hold the enquiry in open Court : " As I have already said, s. 19 has no application to the case of an application for the issue of a summons. You have, therefore, only to consider the first section of the statute, which provides that ' in all cases it shall be lawful for such Justice or Justices to whom such charge or complaint shall be preferred, if they or he shall so think fit, instead of issuing in the first instance his or their warrant to apprehend the person so charged or complained against, to issue his or their summons directed to such person, requiring him to appear before the said Justice or Justices, etc., therefore, under that section, the Justices are acting judicially in a judicial proceeding, in considering the application for the issue of a summons, and by the law of England the proceeding must be in open Court." Lord *Esher* is there referring to the very Act (11 & 12 Vic. c. 42) under which the proceedings were taken in this case.

I am, therefore, clearly of opinion that the prisoner was rightly convicted.

OWEN, J., and COHEN, J., concurred.

Conviction sustained.

Attorney for the prisoner : *J. A. Gorrick,* agent for *G. Davidson* (Mudgee).

(1) [1893] 1 Q.B. 65.

BOROUGH OF RANDWICK *v.* DANGAR.

Privy Council, appeal to—Appealable amount.

1898.
—
November 18.
—
The C.J.
Owen J.
and
A.H.Simpson J.

The plaintiff borough on a special case stated for the opinion of the Full Court obtained judgment for 289*l.* 13*s.* 9*d.*, being municipal rates due from the defendant for 1897. The defendant moved in Chambers for leave to appeal to the Privy Council from this judgment on an affidavit shewing that the plaintiffs also claimed a further sum of 289*l.* 13*s.* 9*d.*, being the rates due for 1898, and *Cohen*, J., granted leave to appeal. *Held*, that leave to appeal should not have been granted.

THIS was an application to confirm an order made by Mr Justice *Cohen*, granting the defendant leave to appeal to the Privy Council (15 W.N. 56).

The plaintiffs sued the defendant, as nominal defendant for the Australian Jockey Club, to recover the sum of 289*l.* 13*s.* 4*d.* alleged to be due for rates on Randwick Racecourse, and on a special case the Court ordered a verdict to be entered for the plaintiffs for that amount. In the affidavits filed in support of the application for leave to appeal to the Privy Council from that judgment, it appeared that the plaintiffs claimed, not only the sum of 289*l.* 13*s.* 4*d.*, which were rates due for the year 1897, but also a further sum of 289*l.* 13*s.* 4*d.* due for the year 1898.

Pring, for the defendant.

Pilcher, Q.C., and *Browning*, for the plaintiffs.

THE COURT called upon

Pring. The amount in dispute between the parties is over 500*l.*

[THE CHIEF JUSTICE. How do you get over the case of the *Municipality of Gundagai* v. *Norton** (1)].

---

* In that case there was a petition by the defendant to the Privy Council to rescind the order of the Full Court giving the plaintiffs leave to appeal to the Privy Council, and the Privy Council rescinded that order ; but it is not clear exactly on what grounds that order was rescinded, because, as far as can be ascertained, no reasons for their judgment were given.

(1) 15 N.S.W. L R. 459; 11 W.N. 91.

FF 2

No report of that case before the Privy Council has been published, and after the appeal went home an Act of Parliament was passed validating the incorporation of the municipality, and, therefore, there was no more than 18*l.* in dispute between the parties, and the plaintiffs were not prejudiced by the judgment to any extent beyond 18*l.* Here there is more than 500*l.* at issue.

[THE CHIEF JUSTICE. In the case of *In re Tindal* (1) the Court refused leave to appeal.]

In that case there was nothing to shew that Tindal's income would continue, and, therefore, it was not shewn that more than 250*l.* was involved between the parties. Here the Australian Jockey Club have a lease of this land for 14 or 15 years, and, therefore, the rates will be payable on the land for those years if this judgment is not reversed. In *Peacock* v. *Powell* (2) this Court granted leave to appeal in a similar case to this. Here there is more than 500*l.* in dispute *between the same parties.* That is the distinction pointed out in the cases of the *Wavertree Sailing Ship Co.* v. *Love* (3), and *In re Bonang G. M. Co.* (4).

[THE CHIEF JUSTICE. If there is any doubt about our power to grant leave to appeal, it would be safer in the interests of the defendant to apply direct to the Privy Council for leave to appeal.]

If the Court will grant leave to appeal the defendant is quite willing to take the risk.

THE CHIEF JUSTICE. I cannot distinguish this case from *In re Tindal.* It is far better for the parties, if there is any doubt about it, for the defendant to apply direct to the Privy Council for leave to appeal. I have no hesitation in saying that the Privy Council will grant leave to appeal in such a case as this.

This application must be refused with costs.

OWEN, J., and A. H. SIMPSON, J., concurred.

Application refused with costs.

Attorneys for the plaintiffs: *Laurence & McLachlan.*

Attorneys for the defendant: *Macnamara & Smith.*

(1) 14 W.N. 134.   (3) 12 W.N. 62.
(2) 2 W.N. 108.   (4) 4 B.C. 47.

SIMPSON v. BANK OF NEW ZEALAND.

Contract—Construction—Latent ambiguity—Extrinsic evidence.

In an action by the plaintiff, who was a railway engineer, to recover commission alleged to be due for the construction of a railway line for the defendants, he put in evidence a letter which contained the following passage:—"Provided that I should be allowed another 1½ per cent. on the estimate of 35,000l., in the event of my being able to reduce the total cost of the works below 30,000l." The defendants tendered evidence, which was admitted, to shew that in the 35,000l. mentioned in the letter there was included not only the cost of construction, but also the cost of the land and the engineer's fees, and it was admitted that if those sums were included the "cost of the works" was not reduced below 30,000l. *Held*, that the evidence should have been rejected. The words "cost of the works" could not with legal certainty be applicable to both the total cost of the works and also to the total costs of the works plus the cost of the land and the engineer's fees, and unless the words were applicable to both, extrinsic evidence could not be adduced to shew that the latter was the intention of the contracting parties, and not the former.

NEW TRIAL MOTION.

This was an action to recover the sum of 576l. 9s., commission alleged to be due to the plaintiff, a railway engineer, by the defendants, who had employed him to prepare plans, etc., and supervise the construction of a railway from Rosehill to Dural.

The plaintiff wrote a letter to the defendants, in which he stated what his charges would be, and then followed this passage: "Provided that I should be allowed another 1½ per cent. on the estimate of 35,000l., in the event of my being able to reduce the total cost of the works below 30,000l.," and those terms were agreed to by the defendants.

The actual cost of the construction of the railway fell below 30,000l., and the plaintiff brought this action, claiming 1½ per cent. on the cost of construction. At the trial the defendants tendered evidence to shew that the sum of 35,000l. included the cost of land and the plaintiff's fees, and if those amounts were added to the cost of construction, the cost of the railway was over 30,000l. The Judge admitted that evidence, and the jury found a verdict for the defendants. The plaintiff now moved to

1898.

SIMPSON
v.
BANK OF N.Z.

set that verdict aside, upon the ground *(inter alia)* that his Honour was in error in ruling that extrinsic evidence was admissible to explain the words " total cost of works " in the said agreement and in admitting such evidence.

Pilcher, Q.C., and *Garland*, for the plaintiff, in support of the rule. The letter written by Simpson to the defendants was clear and unambiguous, and, therefore, no extrinsic evidence should have been admitted to explain it. There was neither a patent nor a latent ambiguity in the letter. The meaning of the word " works " is perfectly clear. The Judge admitted evidence to shew that the " cost of works " included the cost of the land and the engineer's commission.

They referred to *Chichester* v. *Oxenden* (1); *Grant* v. *Grant* (2); *Anson on Contracts* (8th Edit., 319).

Heydon, Q.C., and *J. L. Campbell*, for the defendants, shewed cause. The evidence was rightly admitted. There were two ambiguities in the letter. In order to construe this letter it was necessary first to shew what was included in the sum of 35,000l., and secondly, what was included in the sum of 30,000l. You can only find out what the 35,000l. included by extrinsic evidence. According to the evidence given for the defendants that amount included the cost of the land and the plaintiff's commission. The land and the commission together came to more than 5000l., and, therefore, if you deduct that from the 35,000l., there was no reduction to be made to entitle the plaintiff to commission.

They referred to *Taylor on Evidence* (§ 194).

Pilcher, Q.C. The meaning of the word " works " is plain. They cannot create an ambiguity by extrinsic evidence and then explain it. They want to read the word " works " as if it meant works plus land and fees.

[OWEN, J. The difficulty to my mind is this : when the plaintiff was in the witness box he gave evidence to shew that the 35,000l. mentioned in the letter included nothing but the actual cost of construction, and did not include land and fees. That evidence having been given, why should not the defendants have been at liberty to contradict it ?|

(1) 3 Taunt. 147 ; 12 R.R. 619.   (2) L.R. 5 C.P. 727.

The fact of the plaintiff giving evidence, which was inadmissible, without objection, did not entitle the defendants to give inadmissible evidence which was objected to.

C.A.V.

On the 18th November the judgment of the Court (THE CHIEF JUSTICE, OWEN, J., and G. B. SIMPSON, J.) was delivered by

THE CHIEF JUSTICE.   This was an action to recover the sum of 576*l.* 9*s*, being in respect of commission alleged to be due to the plaintiff, a railway engineer, by the defendants, who had employed the plaintiff to prepare plans, etc., and to supervise the construction of a certain railway from Rosehill to Dural, in the construction of which the defendants were interested.   It would appear that an interview had taken place between the plaintiff and a Mr. Chapman, acting for the defendants, at which the question of the amount of commission to be paid the plaintiff for services had been one of the matters for discussion, and thereupon the plaintiff upon the 23rd January, 1894, wrote a letter to Mr. Chapman in the words and figures following :—

113 Phillip Street,
Sydney, N.S.W.
January 23rd, 1894.

To
  J. Chapman, Esq.,
    Manager of the Bank of New Zealand Estates Co.,
      Ltd., Pitt-street, Sydney.

Dear Sir,—

In reply to your enquiry as to the engineering expenses of the construction of the first section of the Pennant Hills and Dural Railway, I beg to inform you that I am prepared to undertake the work on the following terms, which shall include the payment of all necessary professional assistants and inspectors.

For contract, specification and drawing	...	...	$2\frac{1}{2}$ per cent. on £35,000			
For supervision of work	...	...	...	...	5	,, ,, ,,
For measurement of work	...	...	...	...	1	,, ,, ,,

Provided that I should be allowed another $1\frac{1}{2}$ per cent on the estimate of £35,000, in the event of my being able to reduce the total cost of the works below £20,000.   I propose to effect this saving by extra labour in making comparative drawings of works for the sake of economy, and not by sacrificing the character of the work, and for this reason I do not recommend the adoption of any rail under $71\frac{1}{2}$lbs., as this is the weight recommended by the Engineer-in-Chief for Existing Lines, and as it is most probable that this line will be taken over by the Railway Commissioners, it is undesirable that any obstacle should be raised to such an arrangement by the adoption of material which is, in their opinion. insufficient.

I shall be glad to hear from you in reply to the terms contained therein.

Yours very truly,
B. C. SIMPSON.

It turned out that the actual cost of the construction of the railway fell below the sum of 30,000l.; the defendants did not dispute this fact, whereupon the plaintiff claimed the additional 1½ per cent., and this action was brought for the purpose of recovering it. The defendants, on the other hand, contended that the 35,000l. mentioned, and upon which sum the commission was based, included, not only the construction of the railway, but also the purchase money of the land over which the railway ran. and the fees paid by way of commission to the plaintiff, and that unless the total cost of making the railway, including the cost of the land and the fees paid by way of commission, fell below the sum of 30,000l., the plaintiff was not entitled to succeed.

The solution of the difficulty which has arisen between the parties depends upon the construction to be placed upon the letter from the plaintiff upon the 23rd of January. The plaintiff, on the one hand, contends that its terms are clear and unambiguous, that it was for the Judge to decide that the words "the total cost of the works" meant the total cost of the works, in other words, the total cost of the construction of the railway, and accordingly contends that he is entitled to recover the amount sued for.

The defendants, on the other hand, contend that in the words "the total cost of the works" lies a latent ambiguity, and they were therefore entitled to adduce extrinsic evidence to explain this latent ambiguity, and shew that these words included not only the construction of the line, but the purchase money of the land, &c.

The learned Judge refused to construe the contract, and admitted the extrinsic evidence. The jury having this extrinsic evidence before them, found a verdict for the defendants.

We are of opinion that the learned Judge took an erroneous view of the contract contained in this letter, and ought to have held that the clear meaning of the words "the total cost of the works" were the total cost of the construction of the railway, and accordingly should have excluded the extrinsic evidence objected to.

We think the word "works" coming from the pen of a railway engineer, has a clear and defined meaning. It is the word used in the Railway Clauses Consolidation Act, 1845, to indicate the thing which is to be constructed. The definition of the word "Railway," in that Act, is "the railway and works by the Special Act authorised to be constructed," and was held to include the construction of stations, and such other works as might be proper for the purposes of the railway: see *Cotton* v. *The Midland Railway Co.* (1).

Now, extrinsic evidence to explain a latent ambiguity is only admissible "where in a written instrument the description of the person or thing is applicable, *with legal certainty*, to each of several subjects," [*per* Lord *Chelmsford, Charter* v. *Charter* (2)].

In *Hiscocks* v. *Hiscocks* (3), when the terms of a will were in question, Lord *Abinger*, at p. 368, thus lays down the law: "Now there is but one case in which it appears to us that this sort of evidence of intention can properly be admitted, and that is when the meaning of the testator's words is neither ambiguous nor obscure, and when the devise is, on the face of it, perfect and intelligible, but from some of the circumstances admitted in proof an ambiguity arises as to which of the two or more things, or which of the two or more purposes (*each answering the words in the will*), the testator intended to express."

Upon this case, and others to the same effect, Sir *James Wigram*, in his work on *Extrinsic Evidence*, par. 184, deduces the following principle : "When the description in the will of the person or thing intended *is applicable with legal certainty to each of several subjects*, extrinsic evidence is admissible to prove which of such subjects was intended by the testator."

The law so clearly laid down with regard to wills is equally applicable to written contracts.

Now if in this case the defendants were about to have two railways constructed, the words "the total cost of the works" might be applicable to railway A or to railway B, if on the face of the contract there was nothing to indicate which railway was intended, then inasmuch as the word "works" would be applicable with legal certainty to both railways, extrinsic evidence would be admissible to shew which railway was intended.

(1) 2 Ph. 469.   (2) 7 H.L. 370

(3) 5 M. & W. 363.

Thus in *Macdonald* v. *Longbottom* (1), a man having wool
shorn from his own sheep and also wool bought from other
people, accepted a contract which described the wool as " Your
wool." Now as these words were applicable with legal certainty
either to the wool shorn from the vendor's sheep, or to all the
wool he was possessed of, extrinsic evidence was admissible to
shew that what was sold was, in fact, the whole of the wool he
was in possession of.

It is to us quite obvious that the principle so established cannot be applied to this case so as to admit of extrinsic evidence
being adduced. The words "the total costs of the works" cannot with legal certainty be applicable to both the total cost of
the works, and also to the total cost of the works plus the cost of
the land, plus the engineer's commission, and unless the words
be so applicable to both, you cannot have extrinsic evidence
adduced to shew that the latter was the intention of the contracting parties, and not the former.

Independently of the above, we are of opinion that the whole
tone and tenor of the letter shews that it was the work only
which was under consideration. The letter begins : " In reply to
your enquiry as to the engineering expenses of the construction
of the first section." Now, this clearly relates to the commission
which the engineer was to earn in and about the construction of
the line ; this has no reference to the price of land. Again, " I
beg to inform you that I am prepared to undertake the work on
the following terms." What work ? Why the engineering work
of the construction of the line. Again the work the engineer is
to do is specifications and drawings, supervision of work, and
measurement of work. Then the contemplated saving is to be
effected " by extra labour in making comparative drawings of
works for the sake of economy, and not by sacrificing the
character of the work." It is evident to us that the construction
of the work, and the payment therefor, was the only matter in
the mind of the plaintiff when he wrote this letter, nor can we
understand any person receiving it, after due consideration,
being misled by its terms.

(1) 1 E. & E. 977.

Upon the whole, we are quite clearly of opinion that the plaintiff is upon the admitted and undisputed facts entitled to recover this additional $1\frac{1}{2}$ per cent., and that so the jury should be instructed when this case goes down for a new trial.

1898.

SIMPSON
v.
BANK OF N.Z.

The verdict must be set aside, and there must be a rule absolute for a new trial granted with costs.

The C.J.

Rule absolute with costs.

Attorneys for the plaintiff: *Macnamara & Smith.*

Attorneys for the defendants: *Johnson, Minter, Simpson & Co.*

1898.

November 7.

The C.J,
G B. Simpson J.
and
Cohen J.

In re MUNICIPAL DISTRICT OF LAMBTON ; *Ex parte* THE
COMMERCIAL BANK OF AUSTRALIA.

*Municipalities—Loans to—Consideration for loan—S. 191 of Municipalities
Act of 1867.*

Under s. 191 the council of any municipality may by deed wherein the consideration shall be truly stated mortgage all general and special rates, etc. The Municipal District of Lambton mortgaged their rates " in consideration of the sum of 7,000*l.* paid to us by the Commercial Bank of Australia." It appeared that the sum of 7,000*l.* was not at that time paid to the council, but the money was paid to them from time to time as they required it. It was contended on behalf of the council that as the consideration was not truly stated the mortgage was bad. *Held*, that as there was a collateral agreement that the money was not to be advanced all at once, and that the bank was only to charge interest on the money actually drawn, the consideration was sufficiently stated.

THIS was a motion on behalf of the Commercial Bank of
Australia, Ltd., to make absolute a rule *nisi* calling upon the
Municipal District of Lambton to shew cause why a receiver of
the rates and other revenues of the said municipal district should
not be appointed, and why it should not be referred to the
Prothonotary to take such steps as the Court should direct in
respect of such appointment.

On the 29th September, 1890, the Municipal District of
Lambton executed the following mortgage :—

" We the Council of the Municipal District of Lambton, in
consideration of the sum of 7,000*l.* paid to us by the Commercial
Bank of Australia, do assign unto the said bank all the interests
of the said council in all rates and assessments and endowments,
and other revenues of the said council coming or arising from any
cause whatsoever, and all the estate, right, title, and interest of
the said council to the same, to hold unto the said bank until the
said sum of 7,000*l.* be repaid together with interest for the same
at the rate of 7*l.* 10*s.* for every 100*l.* per annum, the said
principal and interest to be paid on demand."

It appeared from the accounts that the sum of 7,000*l.* was not
advanced in one sum on that day, but that on the 4th October
2,000*l.* was advanced, on the 20th November 2,500*l.*, on the 21st

March 1,956l. 1s. 9d., and various other sums from time to time as the council wanted the money.   Interest was only charged from time to time on the amount actually advanced.   Immediately on the execution of the mortgage the sum of 7,000l. was held at the disposal of the council, and could have been drawn at any time.   But it was arranged that the money should not be all drawn in one lump sum, but should be drawn by the council as they required it, and that interest should only be charged as the money was actually drawn.

On the 30th June, 1898, there was due to the bank 11,071l. 10s. 7d.   Demand was duly made for that amount, but it was not repaid.   On the 27th December, 1893, a demand was made for the repayment of the money then due under the mortgage, and default was thereupon made   On the 12th February, 1895, *The Chief Justice* discharged a rule *nisi* calling upon the council to shew cause why a receiver should not be appointed, and on appeal that decision was affirmed on the 28th July, 1896 : (see 17 N.S.W. L.R. 187 ; 13 W.N. 72); the Court holding that the council had no power to borrow the money, inasmuch as the money was borrowed for the purpose of paying off an existing liability, and not for purposes authorised by s. 190.

Since then the Municipal Loans Further Validation Act of 1897 was passed, and a proclamation was issued under that Act declaring that the Municipal District of Lambton should be subject to its provisions.   Certain debentures had been issued by the Municipal District of Lambton prior to the execution of the mortgage to the bank.

Knox and *Kent*, in support of the rule.   This matter came before the Court in July, 1896, when the Court held that the motion must be refused as the council had no power to borrow money to pay off an existing liability; since then the Municipality Loans Further Validation Act, 1897, has been passed.   That Act gets over the difficulty which arose in the previous application.

Rich, for the Municipal District of Lambton and the debenture-holders.

[THE CHIEF JUSTICE (to *Rich*).   On what ground do you now oppose this application ?]

1898.

In re
MUNICIPAL
DISTRICT OF
LAMBTON ;
Ex parte
COMMERCIAL
BANK OF
AUSTRALIA.

1898.

In re
MUNICIPAL
DISTRICT OF
LAMBTON;
Ex parte
COMMERCIAL
BANK OF
AUSTRALIA.

Rich. I submit that the mortgage is bad because it does not truly state the consideration. Under s. 191 the consideration must be truly stated. The Validating Act makes no reference to that section, it merely cures any defects which may have arisen by reason of the non-compliance with the provisions of s 190.

Knox. The consideration is truly stated. The mortgage deed says, "in consideration of the sum of 7,000*l.* paid to us " by the bank, etc. They admit that the bank actually advanced 7,000*l.*, but they say that because it was not advanced in one lump sum the consideration is not truly stated. It was not necessary that the money should all be advanced at once. The moment the mortgage was executed the bank could have been compelled to pay that sum, and the money was held at the disposal of the council from that time; advancing the money from time to time us the council required the money was merely a matter of convenience to the council, and saved them interest, because interest was only charged on the money actually drawn.

Rich. The consideration was not truly stated. When the mortgage was executed the sum of 7,000*l.* was not paid to the council.

[G. B. SIMPSON, J. It was paid subsequently.]

But it was not paid at the time.

[THE CHIEF JUSTICE. How do you say the consideration should have been stated ?]

This mortgage was to secure an overdraft, and the consideration should have been stated in this form—" In consideration of the bank allowing the council an overdraft up to 7,000*l.*"

[COHEN, J. The consideration would be sufficiently stated if the true legal or business effect of what actually took place is stated: *In re Johnson* (1)].

I submit that the consideration is not truly stated, either according to its legal or business effect. Under s. 8 of the

(1) 26 Ch. D. 338.

English Bills of Sale Act (41 & 42 Vic. c. 81) the consideration for a bill of sale must be truly set forth, otherwise the deed is void. Under that section a number of cases have been decided. In *Ex parte Rolph* (1) a bill of sale was given "in consideration of 50*l*. paid at or before the execution hereof." In fact only 21*l*. 10*s*. was paid to the assignor, 3*l*. 10*s*. was retained by the assignee for the expenses of the deed, and 25*l*. was subsequently paid at the request of the assignor to a third party. There it was held that the consideration was not truly set forth, and the bill of sale was held void.

1898.

In re
MUNICIPAL
DISTRICT OF
LAMBTON ;
Ex parte
COMMERCIAL
BANK OF
AUSTRALIA.

He also referred to *Yate Lee* (3rd Ed. 835), and *Darlow* v. *Bland* (2) on this point.

A further question arises as to the priority of the debentures over the mortgage. There is a dispute between the mortgagees and the debenture-holders in the case of certain debentures which were renewed. Sect. 1 of the Municipal Loans Further Validation Act, 1897, provides that the validated securities are to rank in the order of the date of their creation. Some of the debentures which were given before the mortgage were renewed after it. The mortgagees contend that the mortgage takes priority of those, but we contend that it does not.

[THE CHIEF JUSTICE. We do not think that the facts are fully before us now to determine that point. If we direct that a receiver be appointed, the Master will, in the first instance, have to determine what are the priorities existing between the bank and the debenture-holders.]

Thirdly, we contend that the bank cannot charge the council compound interest.

[*Knox*. We admit that we cannot charge compound interest.]

In taking the accounts it will be found that payments have been made from time to time by the council. Those payments not having been appropriated in any way by the bank the payments should go to wipe off the more burdensome debt : *Clayton's Case* (3).

(1) 19 Ch. D. 98.   (2) [1897] 1 Q.B. 125.
(3) 1 Merivale 608.

1898.

In re
MUNICIPAL
DISTRICT OF
LAMBTON ;
Ex parte
COMMERCIAL
BANK OF
AUSTRALIA.

[THE CHIEF JUSTICE. The bank struck a balance every half year; was not that an appropriation ?]

Clayton's Case was a case of a banking account.

[THE CHIEF JUSTICE. That is a matter which we need not go into now. It will be a matter for the Master to decide in the first instance when he is taking accounts.]

Knox in reply. The consideration was truly stated in the mortgage. Immediately on the execution of the mortgage the sum of 7,000*l*. was available and could have been drawn by the council, and therefore it is just the same as if 7,000*l*. had been placed to their credit in the books of the bank. If that had been the transaction, how could it be said that the consideration was not truly stated? There is no difference between that transaction and what actually took place here.

Suppose this had been a case between two private individuals and when the mortgagee brought the money to the mortgagor that latter had said, " I do not want the money all at once, keep it for me and I will draw it as I want it." Could it then have been contended that the consideration was not truly stated ?

He referred to *Yate Lee*, 3rd Ed. p. 833 ; *Ex parte Boland* (1); *Credit Co.* v. *Pott* (2); *Hamlyn* v. *Betteley* (3).

THE CHIEF JUSTICE. I felt a good deal of difficulty at one time in coming to a determination, but I have now come to the conclusion pretty clearly that this deed does set out the consideration truly within the meaning of this section.

It appears that the Municipality of Lambton were desirous of borrowing the sum of 7,000*l*. for the purpose of paying off a liability which had been incurred by the municipality in the erection of certain electric lighting works. They determined to raise the money by way of mortgage on the rates, etc. They then went through the form, or rather I should say, they thought they had gone through the form, prescribed by s. 190, and got permission of the Governor to borrow that sum. And they borrowed that sum from the

(1) 21 Ch. D. 543.   (2) 6 Q.B.D. 295.
                    (3) 5 C.P.D. 327.

bank and executed the mortgage in question.   Default was made, and the bank applied to this Court to appoint a receiver.   That application was opposed on the ground that the municipality had no power under the Act to borrow money to pay off a past debt, and the Court dismissed the application.

The Legislature, by the Municipal Loans Further Validation Act, 1897, saw fit to validate loans in which the requirements of s. 190 had not been complied with   That Act having been passed, the bank again makes an application to the Court for the appointment of a receiver under s. 191.   Now the bank is met with the objection that, although the mortgage may have been validated by that Act so far as s. 190 is concerned, it is bad under s. 191, because the consideration in it is not truly stated.

It seems to me that it is very right that the Legislature should require that the consideration should be truly stated in order to prevent frauds from being practised on the ratepayers, and I think that unless the consideration be truly stated the mortgage is not valid.   The question then arises whether the consideration in this deed is truly stated.   It is thus stated, " in consideration of the sum of 7,000l. paid to us by the Commercial Bank of Australia," etc.   It is said that in point of fact if the accounts are looked at it will be seen that the 7,000l. was not then advanced, and that the first advance was made on the 4th October, some five days after the mortgage was executed, when 2,000l. was advanced.   And that the next advance was on the 20th November, when 2,500l. was advanced, and then on the 21st March 1,951l. 1s. 9d. was advanced, and various other advances were made from time to time.   These advances were to pay Messrs. Kingsbury & Co., who were the contractors for the erection of the electric lighting works.

On behalf of the municipality it is contended that the consideration has not been truly stated, and possibly if the matter stood there that contention should prevail.   But when we look into the accounts and apply our minds to the business transaction, we are driven to this irresistible inference.   The municipality wanted 7,000l. to pay off this liability, but they did not want the money all at once : some was to be paid in October, some in November,

1898.

In re
MUNICIPAL
DISTRICT OF
LAMBTON ;
Ex parte
COMMERCIAL
BANK OF
AUSTRALIA.

The C.J.

1898.

In re
MUNICIPAL
DISTRICT OF
LAMBTON;
Ex parte
COMMERCIAL
BANK OF
AUSTRALIA.

The C.J.

and some in March, and so on, and they entered into the arrangement that they were not to be charged interest except on the money drawn by them. The position, then, is the same as if the bank had handed them 7,000*l.*, and they had handed it back to the bank, and the arrangement was made that they were only to be charged interest on the money actually drawn. If that was the arrangement, and the inference is irresistible that it was, then it seems to me that the consideration was truly stated. The case of *Ex parte National Mercantile Bank* (1) bears out exactly what I have said.

(His Honour, after referring to the facts of the case, continued.) In his judgment, *James*, L.J., says, " In my opinion the consideration for the bill of sale in the present case was really the advance of 2,050*l.* which was lent by the bank to the grantor. Mr. *Rowland Williams*, in his very able argument, contended that any collateral stipulations as to the application of the consideration ought to be set forth as part of the consideration, that there should be recitals of the intended application of the consideration." That is exactly what Mr. *Rich* has argued in this case. His Lordship then continues, " I cannot see that recitals of the motive and object of the advance are required by the Act. The motive of the lender, as it seems to me, is no part of the consideration for the deed, though it may be a collateral inducement to him to make the advance. Suppose that, instead of there having been bills due by the grantor to the bank, there had been outstanding in the hands of some other bank bills upon which the lenders were liable, and that they had said to the grantor you must take up those bills ; or suppose a loan were made upon the security of farming stock and the lender said, ' You must pay the rent which is due to your landlord, or my security will be seriously prejudiced.' Stipulations of that kind would be part of the bargain between the parties, but they would be no part of the consideration, which is intended by the Act to be set forth. The Act requires the real, the actual consideration to be set forth, but it does not require that any bargain between the parties relating to it should be stated." So here they did not advance all the money at once, because there was a collateral

(1) 15 Ch. Div. 42.

agreement which was for the benefit of the municipality that the
money was to be advanced as they required it, and the bank was
not to charge interest except on the money actually advanced.
The case of *Ex parte Rolph* (1) has no application to this case.

I am, therefore, of opinion that this motion should be successful.

G. B. SIMPSON, J. I am of the same opinion. At one time I
was under the impression, against my inclination, that we were
bound by the decision in *Ex parte Rolph* (1), but I am now quite
satisfied that substantially there was an understanding that the
payment of the 7,000l. should be delayed. That makes the
difference between the present case and *Ex parte Rolph*, because
in that case the *Master of the Rolls* at p. 102 points out "that
there was no independent contract that the payment should be
delayed." I gather from what his Lordship there says that if
there had been such an independent contract the Court would
have held that the consideration was truly stated. The consideration for the mortgage was providing 7,000l. for the council. If
the money had been actually handed over to the council and the
money had then been handed back by the council and drawn out
as required the consideration would undoubtedly have been truly
stated, and that I think was substantially what took place.

I do not say that my mind is altogether free from doubt, but
on the whole I am willing to agree with their Honours.

COHEN, J. There can be no doubt that the matter is not free from
difficulty. There has always been a tendency of Courts to uphold
honest transactions, and in these cases Judges endeavour to place
themselves in the position of business men and construe documents as far as possible in that light. In *Ex parte Johnson* (2),
Bowen, L.J., 348, says—"Now who are going to be affected by
this bill of sale or to act on it? It is drawn up for present
purposes, it is not for posterity. It is intended, not for special
pleaders, or conveyancing counsel of the Court of Chancery, or
for the ingenious lawyers in the Court of Bankruptcy. It is
drawn up for business purposes and business men, for traders,
bankers, and people who lend money—in fact for the world at

(1) 19 Ch. Div. 98.   _(2) 26 Ch. Div. 338._

1898.

In re
MUNICIPAL
DISTRICT OF
LAMBTON ;
Ex parte
COMMERCIAL
BANK OF
AUSTRALIA.

The C.J.

1898.

In re
MUNICIPAL
DISTRICT OF
LAMBTON ;
Ex parte
COMMERCIAL
BANK OF
AUSTRALIA.

Cohen J.

large.' If that is so, I cannot help thinking that the Courts have taken the true point of view when they have said, 'you must take a broad and business view of the transaction, and not look at it with that minute accuracy which persons would use who were examining into it after the event in a Court of justice.'" Looking at this transaction from a business point of view, when this 7,000*l.* was held by the bank at the disposal of the municipality it was tantamount to the payment of 7,000*l.* I therefore think that the consideration was truly stated.

The order was as follows :—

> "*It is ordered that it be referred to the Master in Equity of this Honorable Court to appoint some fit and proper person to receive, collect, and get in the rates (whether accrued or to accrue due), and other revenues of the above-named Municipal District of Lambton, and it is further ordered that the said Master in Equity do fix the security to be given by such Receiver, and the remuneration to be paid to or retained by him for his services as such Receiver, and it is further ordered that the said Receiver when so appointed do receive, get in, and collect all rates and other revenues due, or accruing, or to accrue due to the said Municipal District. And it is further ordered that the ratepayers, tenants, and other debtors of the said Municipal District do pay to the said Receiver, when so appointed, the amounts of the rates, rents, and debts respectively due, or accruing, or to accrue due by them until this Honorable Court shall further or otherwise order. And it is further ordered that notice of the appointment of such Receiver be given to the said ratepayers, tenants, and other debtors of the said Municipal District in such manner as the said Master in Equity shall direct. And it is further ordered that the said Master in Equity do inquire and report to this Honorable Court what is the amount due by the said Municipal District to the said Bank, and what are the amounts (if any) due by the said Municipal District to the said Debenture-holders and whether the debentures are valid and binding charges on the rates and revenues comprised therein respectively. And*

also what are the priorities existing between the said bank and
the said respective debenture-holders. And it is further
ordered that the further consideration of this matter, and
all questions with reference to the costs thereof, be adjourned,
and any of the parties hereto are to be at liberty to apply to
this Honorable Court as they may be advised."

1898.

In re
MUNICIPAL
DISTRICT OF
LAMBTON ;
Ex parte
COMMERCIAL
BANK OF
AUSTRALIA.

Attorneys for the applicants: *Johnson, Minter, Simpson &*
Co.

Attorney for the respondents: *A. W. E. Weaver.*

DENHAM AND ANOTHER *v.* FOLEY AND ANOTHER.

1898.

April 26,
27, 28.
May 4.
August 9.
October 25.
November 4.

The C.J.
Stephen J.
and
Cohen J.

Bankruptcy Act, s. 4 (1) (h)—Notice of suspension of payment—Bill of sale—Bankruptcy Acts Amendment Act, 1896, s. 33—Bill of sale—Covenant for title—" Party or privy to act"—Notice of an act of bankruptcy—Estoppel—Judgment of Bankruptcy Court—Bankruptcy—Order and disposition—Possession of second bill of sale holder—New trial—Practice—Two issues—5 Vic. No. 9, s. 42.

A debtor in the course of conversation with one of his creditors said, "I will have to file." *Held,* that the creditor had notice that the debtor was about to suspend payment of his debts.

Sect. 33 of the Bankruptcy Act Amendment Act, 1896, is not retrospective, and does not apply to bills of sale given before the passing of the Act.

The defendants held a bill of sale over certain goods of G. On the 29th December they had notice that G. had committed an act of bankruptcy. On the 30th December they seized the goods under the bill of sale. On the 4th January they assigned the goods absolutely to the plaintiffs. In the deed of assignment they covenanted that they had not been "party or privy to any act" whereby they were prevented from assigning the goods absolutely to the plaintiffs. On the 13th January G. became bankrupt, and the goods were subsequently claimed by G.'s official assignee. *Held,* that the defendants having notice of the act of bankruptcy, were party or privy to an act whereby they were prevented from assigning the goods, and had therefore committed a breach of the covenant.

The defendants assigned to the plaintiffs the goods comprised in a bill of sale given by G. to them. These goods were claimed by the official assignee of G.'s estate, and on a motion under s. 130 of the Bankruptcy Act, 1887, the plaintiffs (in which they set up the title to the goods through the defendants) were ordered to pay the value of them to the official assignee. *Held,* that the judgment of the Bankruptcy Court did not prevent the defendants from setting up that they had a good title to the goods, when they transferred them to the plaintiffs in an action brought by the plaintiffs against them for breach of the covenant for title, inasmuch as they were not parties to the bankruptcy proceedings.

G. gave a bill of sale over certain goods to the defendants, and subsequently gave a second bill of sale over the same goods to the plaintiffs. The defendants seized the goods with notice of an available act of bankruptcy committed by G., and afterwards assigned the goods to the plaintiffs. In an action brought by the plaintiffs against the defendants for breach of covenant for title, the defendants in order to shew that the goods were not in the order and disposition of the bankrupt when they had notice of the act of bankruptcy, sought to give in evidence the plaintiffs' bill of sale and to give evidence that at that time the goods were not in the order and disposition of the bankrupt, because the plaintiffs had previously seized under their bill of sale without notice of an available act of bankruptcy, and this evidence was rejected. *Held,* that the evidence should have been admitted. The possession of a second bill of sale holder who seizes without notice of an available act of bankruptcy may enure for the benefit of the first bill of sale holder.

Where two issues were involved in a case on a new trial motion, and one was
decided in favour of the plaintiffs and one in favour of the defendants, the Court,
under the powers conferred on it by s. 42 of 5 Vic. No. 9, in granting a new trial
on the motion of the defendants, ordered the defendants to make an admission as
to the former issue so as to prevent that issue being tried again.

1898.

DENHAM
v.
FOLEY.

NEW TRIAL MOTION.

The declaration was as follows :—

1. For that the defendants at the time of the breach hereinafter complained of were the creditors of one Geoghegan and
were the holders of a bill of sale dated the 8th August, 1895, over
certain property of the said Geoghegan, and the said Geoghegan
having made default in payment of the moneys due under the
said bill of sale, the defendants took possession of the said
property, and previously to taking possession the defendants had
notice that the said Geoghegan had committed an act of
bankruptcy whereby the property comprised in the said bill of
sale in the event of the estate of the said Geoghegan being
sequestrated within a period of six months from the date of the
said act of bankruptcy would become the property of the official
assignee of the estate of the said Geoghegan, and within six
months of such act of bankruptcy the defendants by deed purported to assign to the plaintiff the property comprised in the said
bill of sale and thereby covenanted that at the time of making
the said assignment the defendants had not been party or privy
to any act, deed, matter or thing whereby the said property was,
could, or might be in any wise encumbered, or whereby they (the
defendants) were prevented from assigning and transferring the
same, yet the defendants had been party and were privy to
certain acts, &c., and the defendants had at the date of making
the said covenant notice that the said Geoghegan had committed
an available act of bankruptcy, and the said Geoghegan within
six months of the said act of bankruptcy and of the execution of
the said deed became a bankrupt, and the official assignee of the
estate of the said Geoghegan recovered by due process of law
from the plaintiffs the said property comprised in the said bill of
sale and so assigned as aforesaid on the ground that the same
was the property of the said official assignee at the date of the
said assignment, whereby the plaintiffs were deprived of the

same and lost the use and profits of the same and the price which they paid to the defendants for the same, and were put to great expense in defending their title to the same.

2. For that the defendants by warranting that they then had lawful right and title to sell and dispose of certain property, to wit, property comprised in a bill of sale given by Geoghegan to the defendants   .   .   .   sold the said property to the plaintiffs, yet the defendants had no lawful right and title to sell and dispose of the said property, and the plaintiffs were obliged to deliver up the said property to the official assignee of the estate of the said Geoghegan, who had the lawful right and title to the said property, whereby the plaintiffs were deprived of the same, &c.

3. Common money count.

Pleas :—

1. To first count, *non est factum.*

2. To first count, traverse of the alleged breaches.

3. To second count, *non assumpserunt.*

4. To second count, denial of breaches.

5. To third count, never indebted.

On the 8th August, 1895, Geoghegan gave a bill of sale to the defendants over certain property, and it was duly registered. On the 8th July, 1896, Geoghegan gave a bill of sale to the plaintiffs over the same property.

On the 30th December the defendants entered into possession, default having been made under their bill of sale. It was alleged by the plaintiffs that the defendants had notice of an act of bankruptcy committed by Geoghegan on the 29th December. The evidence on this point was as follows:—Geoghegan said: "I remember 29th December last; I was in Sydney then; I returned to Nowra the same day; I went down by 5.30 p.m. train; I saw Michael Foley (one of the defendants) just as the train was leaving—at the train; I was walking along the platform towards the carriage, having just jumped out of a vehicle; he said, 'How are you getting along'? I said, 'Not too well'; he said, 'Nothing wrong, I hope'? I said, 'Things are a bit bad'; he said, 'Why, what is up'? I said, 'I will have to file'; he then said, 'You will do nothing until you see me again'; I then said,

'No'; I was then in the carriage; he said again, 'On your honour you won't do anything till I see you again'? I said 'No, I will be up on Tuesday and give you particulars'; the train then left."

An affidavit, which had been prepared for Foley to sign, was put in evidence. It was prepared by the solicitor who was acting for the official assignee of Geoghegan's estate to be used on a motion under s. 130 of the Bankruptcy Act against the plaintiffs, and it was altered at Foley's instigation. The material parts were as follows :—

" 3. Prior to and during the month of December I had several interviews with the above-named bankrupt relative to his financial position, and from what I was informed by the bankrupt, ascertained that he was practically insolvent.

" 4. Hearing that the bankrupt was in Sydney on the 28th and 29th December last, and being anxious to see him, I endeavoured without success to do so, but ascertained that he intended returning to Bomaderry by the train leaving Sydney at 5 o'clock on the evening of the 29th December last, and accordingly attended at the Redfern railway station, where I met the above-named bankrupt, who then informed me that he had come up to Sydney with the view of laying his financial position before his creditors, and he said he had seen Denham Bros., and that Mr. Barlow, their clerk, would call in the morning and explain matters in reference to his financial arrangements. I thereupon, on the said 29th December last, requested the said bankrupt to let me know what he intended to do, meaning thereby whether he intended to file his schedule. To that he replied before anything was done he would let my said firm know. My object in so doing was to obtain sufficient time to get into possession before he filed his schedule."

On the 4th January, 1897, the defendants assigned everything comprised in the bill of sale of the 8th August, 1895, to the plaintiffs in the following terms :—" They the assignors do . . . . hereby grant bargain sell assign transfer and set over unto the assignees . . . . all and singular the machinery goods chattels credits book debts and all other effects whatsoever comprised in and assigned to them under and by virtue of the said recited indenture of the 8th August, 1895. . . . To have and hold receive take and enjoy the said machinery . . . . unto and by the said assignees . . . . absolutely freed and absolutely discharged from all right or equity of redemption therein and the said assignors . . . . covenant with the said assignees that they . . . have not done or knowingly permitted or suffered or been party or privy to any act deed matter or thing whereby the said machinery . . . is can or may be in anywise encumbered or whereby they are prevented from assigning and transferring the same in manner aforesaid."

On the 13th January Geoghegan's estate was sequestrated.

On the 16th June, 1897, on a motion by the official assignee of Geoghegan's estate, in which the plaintiffs were the respondents, it was ordered that it be referred to the Registrar in Bankruptcy to ascertain the nature and value on the 29th December, 1896, of all machinery, &c., seized or taken possession of by the plaintiffs under their bill of sale dated the 8th July, 1896, and under the defendant's bill of sale dated the 8th August, 1895, and the assignment of the 4th January, 1897, by the defendants to the plaintiffs, and that the said value when so ascertained be paid by the plaintiffs to the official assignee. [See *Re Geoghegan* (1).]

At the trial, before *Owen*, J., the jury found a verdict for the plaintiffs, and leave was reserved to the defendants to move the Full Court to enter a nonsuit or verdict for them. At the trial the defendants tendered evidence to shew that prior to the 29th December the plaintiffs were in possession of the goods. This evidence was objected to and rejected.

The defendants also tendered in evidence the bill of sale given by Geoghegan to the plaintiffs. This was objected to and rejected.

The defendants also tendered evidence to shew the plaintiffs' want of knowledge prior to the 29th December, 1896, or the 4th January, 1897, of an available act of bankruptcy having been committed by Geoghegan. This evidence was objected to and rejected.

(1) 18 N.S.W. L.R. B. & P. 26 ; 7 B.C. 82.

The defendants now moved to make absolute a rule *nisi* to enter a nonsuit or a verdict for them, or for a new trial, upon the following grounds :—

1898.

DENHAM
v.
FOLEY.

1. That the facts deposed to at the trial did not disclose that the defendants had at the time of taking possession under the bill of sale notice of any available act of bankruptcy having been committed by Geoghegan.

2. That even if the defendants had notice prior to the 28th December, 1896, that an available act of bankruptcy had been committed by Geoghegan they were not party or privy to any act, deed, matter or thing whereby the property comprised in the said bill of sale was, could, or might be encumbered, or whereby the defendants were prevented from assigning or transferring the same.

3. That inasmuch as the defendants complied with the requirements of 60 Vic. No. 29 with respect to the registration of their bill of sale of the 8th August, 1895, the goods therein comprised are protected by s. 33 of that Act.

4. That his Honour was in error in refusing to admit in evidence the bill of sale given by Geoghegan to the plaintiffs.

5. That his Honour was in error in rejecting evidence of the entering into possession by the plaintiffs of the goods, the subject of the plaintiff's bill of sale, from Geoghegan prior to the 29th December, 1896.

6. That his Honour was in error in rejecting evidence of the plaintiffs' want of knowledge prior to the 29th December, 1896, or the 4th January, 1897, of an available act of bankruptcy having been committed by Geoghegan.

Sly (*Want*, Q.C., and *Gordon*) appeared for the defendants in support of the rule.

Wise and *Broomfield* (Sir *Julian Salomons*, Q.C., and *Pilcher*, Q.C., with them), for the plaintiffs, shewed cause.

It was admitted that, if either of the first two grounds in the rule were decided in favour of the defendants, it would become unnecessary to decide the other points in the case, and it was therefore arranged that they should be first argued.

Sly. 1st ground. The conversation which took place between Foley and Geoghegan did not amount to an act of bankruptcy. It was merely a casual conversation. It was not a formal and deliberate notice that he was about to suspend payment of his debts: *Ex parte Oastler* (1). The conversation which took place goes to shew that there was no absolute intention on the part of Geoghegan to file his schedule. In order to constitute an act of bankruptcy under s. 4 (1) (h) there must be an absolute statement that the debtor intends to suspend payment. Here Geoghegan said that he would do nothing until he saw Foley again.

Wise. 1st ground. When Geoghegan said to Foley, "I will have to file," he clearly gave notice to him that he was about to suspend payment of his debts: *Crook v. Morley* (2); *In re Lamb* (3); *Re Missen* (4); *Re Davenport* (5); *In re Simonson* (6).

Sly in reply. *1st ground.* The question to be considered is whether Geoghegan intended to give notice that he was about to suspend payment. I submit he did not. *Re Pike* (7).

[THE CHIEF JUSTICE. The facts there are very different to the facts in this case.]

But that case decides that a statement to amount to a notice must not be mere casual conversation, but must be something formal and deliberate on the part of the debtor. In *Crook* v. *Morley* a circular was sent to all the creditors stating that the debtor was unable to meet his engagements; so also in *In re Lamb.* In *In re Thorold* (8) the debtor came down from the country specially to lay his financial position before his chief creditor. There must be an absolute and unqualified notice.

[THE CHIEF JUSTICE. Geoghegan said, "I will have to file"; could there have been anything stronger or more definite than that?]

But that is qualified by what he says immediately afterwards, that he would do nothing until he saw Foley again.

(1) 13 Q.B.D. 471.   (5) 1 B.C. 51.
(2) [1891] A.C. 316.   (6) [1894] 1 Q.B. 433.
(3) 4 Mor. 25.   (7) 17 N.S.W. L.R. B. & P. 34.
(4) 14 N.S.W. L.R. B. & P. 24;   (8) 11 N.S.W. L.R. 331.
    3 B.C. 112.

1898.

DENHAM
v.
FOLEY.

[COHEN, J., referred to *In re Johns* (1).]

In that case there was a deliberate notice.

Sly. 2nd ground. Assuming that the defendants had notice of an act of bankruptcy, when they went into possession they were not party or privy to any act whereby they were prevented from assigning the property to the plaintiffs on the 4th January. At the time the defendants made the covenant they were the only persons who had any title to the goods. If bankruptcy had not supervened, the fact that they had notice of an act of bankruptcy would not have affected their title; on the 4th January no other person had any title to the goods.

[THE CHIEF JUSTICE. But when a man becomes bankrupt the title of the official assignee dates back to the act of bankruptcy.]

The possibility or contingency of the man becoming bankrupt could not be a breach of the covenant. This covenant means that the defendants had not mortgaged the goods or sold them.

[THE CHIEF JUSTICE. May it not be said that they were "party or privy to an act whereby they were prevented from assigning," &c. ?]

"Act" there means some act done by the defendants. Here the defendants had done no act whereby they were prevented from assigning the goods. At the time they did assign there was nothing to prevent them from assigning.

[COHEN, J., referred to *Hobson* v. *Middleton* (2); where it was held that a covenant, that the covenantor has not knowingly permitted, or suffered any act, was not broken by assenting to an act which the covenantor could not prevent.

Wise. Under that case in *Dart on Vendors and Purchasers* (3), it is said, " but of course in such a case the covenant would have been broken had it proceeded in the usual form, ' or been party or privy to.' "

COHEN, J. Does not being "party or privy" mean assenting to something being done ?]

(1) 10 Mor. 190.   (2) 6 B. & C. 295.
              (3) 5th Ed. 785.

That is what I submit it does.

[*Wise.* "Privy" means having knowledge.

STEPHEN, J. Even assuming that it does, had the defendants knowledge of anything which at that time prevented them assigning the goods?]

At that time there was clearly nothing to prevent them assigning the goods.

[STEPHEN, J. The plaintiffs must read the covenant as if after the words "transferring the same," these words were inserted, "or whereby the conveyance may hereafter be in any way invalidated."]

Yes. That is what their contention amounts to.

Wise. 2nd ground. The assignment of the 4th January was not merely an assignment of the defendants' right, title and interest, but was an absolute assignment of the property. The words "transferring the same in manner aforesaid," mean transferring the property absolutely. Foley was privy to an act whereby he was prevented from transferring these goods absolutely. On the 30th December, Foley knew that an act of bankruptcy had been committed. He knew, therefore, if bankruptcy supervened, that he had no title to the goods. There was, therefore, a contingent defect in his title. "Privy" is defined in *Webster's Dictionary* to mean "admitted to knowledge of a secret transaction; secretly cognisant; privately knowing."

He referred to *Clifford* v. *Hoare* (1).

[STEPHEN, J. The words in the covenant are stronger than in this, because the words there are "is or *may be* impeached."]

He also contended that the plaintiffs were entitled to recover on the common money count. If a man pays for goods and they are afterwards taken from him through no fault of his own, he is entitled to recover his money back.

In view of the decision of the Court on the second ground it became unnecessary to consider this point.

(1) L. R. 9 C. P. 362.

Sly in reply. *2nd ground*. Being "party or privy" to an act does not mean having mere knowledge of the act. There must be some concert on his part, and some participation in the act. No act on their part in any way invalidated their title.

THE CHIEF JUSTICE. It appears that one Geoghegan gave a bill of sale over certain property to the defendants. That bill of sale was dated August, 1895. The defendants were carrying on the business of produce merchants in Sydney, and Geoghegan was carrying on the business of a bacon curer at Bomaderry. He gave this bill of sale over certain machinery and his stock in trade. Having given this bill of sale in August, 1895, he appears to have made default, and in December, 1896, having got into some difficulties, he came to Sydney with a view to seeing his creditors, and making some arrangement with them. At this time the money under the bill of sale was due to the defendants. Geoghegan also had an open account with the defendants, but so far as that account was concerned he does not appear to have owed them any money. When he came to Sydney he appears to have seen the plaintiffs, who were also creditors of his, but he did not call upon the defendants. The defendants, however, knew that he was in Sydney, and one of the defendants, no doubt as a man of business, and not understanding why Geoghegan did not call upon him, went to Redfern railway station to see him, and just before the train started an interview took place. It is said that this was a mere casual interview. I cannot see that it was. It was an interview sought by the defendant as a business man for the purpose of ascertaining the position of his debtor. The interview which then took place was as follows (as described by Geoghegan in his evidence):—" He said, ' How are you getting along ' ? I said, ' Not too well '; he said, ' Nothing wrong, I hope ' ? I said, ' Things are a bit bad '; he said, ' Why, what is up ' ? I said, ' I will have to file '; he then said, ' You will do nothing till you see me again '; I then said, ' No '; I was then in the carriage; he then said, ' On your honour you won't do anything till I see you again '; I said, ' No, I will be up on Tuesday and give you particulars.' "

This was not a mere casual conversation. Being in Sydney for the purpose of seeing his creditors, he informed a man who

1898.

DENHAM
v.
FOLEY.

1898.

DENHAM
v.
FOLEY.

The C.J.

had a right to enquire into his affairs, that he was about to file his schedule, the meaning of that was, that he was about to become bankrupt. We must take it that that was his intention at that time, and that must have been the impression which it left on the mind of Foley. For what do we find that he does? He goes by the first train next morning to Bomaderry, and on that very day seizes the property contained in the bill of sale. It is perfectly clear what was in his mind. He had been informed that Geoghegan was about to file his schedule, and he thought that he would put himself in the best position he could and get possession of the goods before the official assignee. Now the question arises whether that intimation, "I will have to file my schedule," was a notice that he was about to suspend payment of his debts within s. 4 (1), sub-s. (h). That sub-section is as follows :—" If the debtor gives notice to any of his creditors that he has suspended, or that he is about to suspend payment of his debts." I am of opinion that this statement was a notice within the meaning of that sub-section. We were referred to a number of cases on this section, some decided in England and others decided in this colony. I do not think that the law can be more clearly laid down than it is laid down by Lord Justice *Bowen* in *In re Lamb* (1). He points out that all these decisions are decisions on questions of fact, and that in each case we have to see whether there was a notice given by the debtor that he was about to suspend payment of his debts. His Lordship says at p. 32 :—" I hope we are not going in the construction of this statute to be encumbered in the future with a mass of cases which are really decisions on fact. The first thing which we have to decide is what the statute means. The statute provides that if a debtor gives notice to any of his creditors that he has suspended, or that he is about to suspend payment of his debts, that is an act of bankruptcy. Suspension of payment is a business term usually applied to traders, and in the present case we have to apply it. It seems to me that it means not meeting your engagements, and paying your debts in the ordinary course of business as they become due and as you are called upon to pay them. What, therefore, is the question that arises when we are presented with a statement of a debtor, and are asked to consider

(1) 4 Mor. 25.

that it falls within the mischief at which this provision of the statute strikes ? We have in each case to ask ourselves and in each case to answer the question, what is the reasonable construction which those who receive this statement of the debtor would have a right under the circumstances of the debtor's case to assume, and would assume, to be his meaning as to what he intends to do with respect to paying or suspending payment of his debts." We know what effect the statement made by Geoghegan had on Foley, and what construction he put upon it. We know that from his own action, his following this man down to Bomaderry next morning and seizing the goods. We also know it from what appears in the affidavit which was amended at his own instigation. He says there, " Hearing that the bankrupt was in Sydney, and being anxious to see him, I endeavoured without success to do so, but ascertained that he intended returning to Bomaderry by the train leaving Sydney at 5 o,clock on the evening of the 29th December last, and accordingly attended at the Redfern railway station, where I met the above-named bankrupt, who then informed me that he had come up to Sydney with the view of laying his financial position before his creditors, and he said he had seen Denham Brothers, and that Mr. Barlow, their clerk, would call in the morning and explain matters in reference to his financial arrangements. I thereupon, on the said 29th December last, requested the said bankrupt to let me know what he intended to do, meaning thereby whether he intended to file his schedule. To that he replied, before anything was done he would let my said firm know. My object in so doing was to obtain sufficient time to get into possession before he filed his schedule." And Geoghegan states in his evidence that he told him distinctly that he would have to file his schedule. The case of *In re Lamb* (1) was commented upon and approved in *Crook* v. *Morley* (2). Lord *Selborne* there says, " I will only refer to the words of Lord Justice *Bowen* in the case of *In re Lamb* (1), where he asks the question, ' what effect would the circular produce on the mind of a creditor receiving it as to the intention of

(1) 4 Mor. 25.   (2) [1891] A.C. 316.

the debtor with regard to his creditors?' That is the true test."
We know the effect this conversation had on Foley. If that
be the true test, then it is perfectly clear that he had, on the 30th
December, when he seized the goods, notice of an act of bankruptcy.

Having disposed of that part of the case, the question then
arises whether there was a breach of the covenant in the deed of
assignment of the 4th January. This deed recites the bill of
sale from Geoghegan to the defendants and then transfers to the
plaintiffs the property contained in the bill of sale in these terms,
"the assignors do . . . hereby grant bargain sell assign
transfer and set over unto the assignees . . . all and singular
the machinery &c. comprised in and assigned to them under and
by virtue of the said recited indenture of the 8th August, 1895,
to have and hold receive take and enjoy the said machinery, &c.
unto and by the said assignees freed and absolutely discharged
from all right or equity of redemption therein." That is an
absolute assignment to the plaintiffs. What is the covenant for
title ? It is in these terms, "The said assignors do and each of
them doth hereby for themselves and himself . . . covenant
with the said assignees that the said assignors have not done or
knowingly permitted or suffered or been party or privy to any
act deed matter or thing whereby the said machinery goods &c.
are is can or may be in anywise encumbered or whereby they are
prevented from assigning or transferring the same in manner
aforesaid." The words " in manner aforesaid " mean that they
had the absolute right to assign these goods at that time. But
at that time an act of bankruptcy had been committed. They
had, therefore, a defeasible title. At the moment this man
became bankrupt this property vested in his official assignee.
So that an act of bankruptcy having been committed, the assignment was an assignment of property which they had not an
absolute right to assign. They had been privy to the act
of bankruptcy, and were, therefore, in the terms of the covenant
privy to an act, whereby they were prevented from assigning and
transferring the property absolutely. Seeing that the assignment
was an assignment of property absolutely, and that they knew
that an act of bankruptcy had been committed, they must be

taken to have known that they could not transfer the property absolutely. I am therefore of opinion that an act of bankruptcy was committed, and secondly, that there was a breach of the covenant for title in the deed of assignment.

STEPHEN, J. I agree. My impression on the second ground was at first in favour of the defendants, but I am now clearly of opinion that the view taken by *The Chief Justice* is the correct one.

COHEN, J., concurred.

Sly. 3rd ground. The goods comprised in Foley's bill of sale were not in the order and disposition of the bankrupt within the meaning of s. 52 of the Bankruptcy Act of 1887, because the bill of sale was duly registered. Sect. 33 of the Bankruptcy Acts Amendment Act, 1896, provides that " the goods comprised in a bill of sale in respect of which the provisions of this Act have been duly complied with shall be exempt from the provisions of a. 52 (3) of the Principal Act." The provisions of the Act which have to be complied with are contained in s. 31. First, it provides that the bill of sale must be registered. This bill of sale was registered. Secondly, the registration must be renewed every twelve months. The time for renewal had not arrived because the Act had not been passed for twelve months when Geoghegan became bankrupt.

Wise was not called upon.

THE COURT held that s. 33 of the Bankruptcy Acts Amendment Act, 1896, was not retrospective, and did not apply to a bill of sale given prior to the passing of the Act.

Sly. Grounds, 4, 5, and 6. The Judge was in error in rejecting the evidence that Denham was in possession of the goods prior to the 29th December, when Foley had notice of an act of bankruptcy. If Denham was in possession, then the goods were not in the order and disposition of the bankrupt on that date, and, therefore, there was no breach of the covenant, because the official assignee had no claim to the goods.

[THE CHIEF JUSTICE. What you wanted to shew was that Denham had possession of these goods prior to the 29th December. Had he any right to the possession of them?]

Yes, as against Geoghegan.

[THE CHIEF JUSTICE. If the goods are in the hands of a wrong-doer, does that defeat the title of the official assignee?]

But we submit that Denham was not a wrong-doer as against Geoghegan. As between the mortgagor and the second mortgagee the possession of the second mortgagee is not wrongful as against the mortgagor. In *Robson on Bankruptcy* (1), citing *Fletcher* v. *Manning* (2), and *Ex parte Foss* (3), it is said, "If the bankrupt's possession has been lawfully interrupted adversely, although not by the true owner, such interruption will be sufficient to exclude the bankrupt's reputed ownership." Geoghegan being in possession at the time that he gave Denham the bill of sale, under s. 25 of the Trust Property Act, he had a good title at law notwithstanding Foley's bill of sale.

[THE CHIEF JUSTICE *Ex parte Edey* (4) seems in conflict with the passage quoted from *Robson*.]

In that case there was a wrongful possession as against the mortgagees, but here Denham's possession would not be wrongful against Foley until after the latter had demanded possession. But it is doubtful whether that case is good law [see *Williams on Bankruptcy* (5).]

[THE CHIEF JUSTICE. The question we have to consider is whether Denham's possession was wrongful as against Foley.]

If that be the question, we submit it was not, but we submit that the real question is whether his possession was wrongful against Geoghegan, and whether his possession took the goods out of the order and disposition of Geoghegan. *Ex parte Foss* (6).

[THE CHIEF JUSTICE. *Barrow* v. *Bell* (7) seems to be a very strong authority against you.]

(1) 6th Ed., p. 502.   (4) L.R. 19 Eq. 264.
(2) 12 M. & W. 576.   (5) 7th Ed. 213.
(3) 2 De G. & J. 230.   (6) 2 De G. & J. 230.
            (7) 5 El. & Bl. 540.

The possession of the sheriff was at most constructive, and the case shews that he did not in fact take possession of the plaintiffs' goods, and his possession was clearly wrongful.

[THE CHIEF JUSTICE. The whole question in this case was the possession of Denham legal or illegal. If legal the goods were not in the order and disposition of the bankrupt; but if his possession was illegal, then the goods were not taken out of his order and disposition.]

If Denham had constructive possession, it would be material to consider whether his possession was legal or not, but if he had possession in fact, then it would be immaterial. In the case of a wrong-doer, actual possession would take the goods out of the order and disposition of the bankrupt. But in the case of a second mortgagee who rightfully takes possession, then, whether the possession was actual or constructive, it would be sufficient.

Gordon followed. The defendants are not bound by the order of the Court made against Denham in the bankruptcy proceedings. They were not parties to those proceedings.

He referred to *In re Gordon* (1); *Davidson* v. *Dennis* (2); *Ex parte Saffery* (3).

Sir *Julian Salomons*, Q.C. The defendants sold to the plaintiffs property, to which they had no title, and therefore, whether the official assignee claimed it or not, the plaintiffs were entitled to recover their money back.

Gomperty v. *Bartlett* (4); *Gurney* v. *Womersley* (5); *Scurfield* v. *Gowland* (6).

[THE CHIEF JUSTICE. The defendants contend that the goods were not in the order and disposition of the bankrupt at the commencement of the bankruptcy, and that, therefore, they had a good title to the goods.]

But the Court has already held there was a breach of the covenant because they had no title.

(1) 6 Mor. 152 ; 61 L.T. 299.   (4) 2 El. & Bl. 849.
(2) 8 N.S.W. L.R. 282.   (5) 4 El. & Bl. 133.
(3) 16 Ch. D. 668.   (6) 6 East 240.

1898.

DENHAM
v.
FOLEY.

[THE CHIEF JUSTICE. But that judgment proceeded on the assumption that the goods were in the order and disposition of the bankrupt when Foley had notice of an act of bankruptcy.]

The Bankruptcy Court having decided that Denham had no title through Foley, Foley cannot now be heard to say that he had a good title, and, therefore, the point they want to raise is not open to them. The official assignee claimed these goods and Denham set up Foley's title and was defeated; it is not competent for Foley to say as against his assignee that that decision is wrong. That decision may have been wrong on the facts or the law, and if so. Foley's remedy is against the official assignee, and not against Denham.

[COHEN, J. Would Foley have had any *locus standi* to appear in those proceedings, and if not, why should he be bound by them ? *Re Von Weissenfeld* (1); *Re Doyle* (2).]

Even if Foley had no *locus standi* to appear, Denham was his assignee, and he set up Foley's title, and the case was decided against him: *Re Geoghegan* (3).

On this point he referred to *Smith* v. *Compton* (4); *Huggins* v. *Coates* (5); *Jones* v. *Williams* (6).

THE COURT held that the defendants were not bound by the judgment of the Bankruptcy Court in *Re Geoghegan*.

Sir *Julian Salomons*, Q.C., continued. If Denham seized the goods as Foley alleges, then I submit that he was a mere wrong-doer, and his possession would not take the goods out of the order and disposition of the bankrupt. Where there are two mortgages of personal property, the second mortgagee takes nothing at all, because the first mortgage is a transfer of the property, and puts the property out of the mortgagor, and there is no estate left in him. If the second mortgagee has no title, his possession cannot defeat the order and disposition clause in the Bankruptcy Act.

THE CHIEF JUSTICE. We do not want to hear you, Dr. *Sly*, in reply, but we will reserve our judgment.

(1) 9 Mor. 30.   (4) 3 B. & Ad. 407.
(2) 2 B.C. 64.   (5) 5 Q.B. 433.
(3) 18 N.S.W.L. R. B. & P. 26.   · (6) 7 M. & W. 493.

On the 9th August, the matter again came before the Court.

THE CHIEF JUSTICE. This case has been put in the list for further argument. Last term, when the Court reserved judgment, we intimated to Dr. *Sly* that we did not want to hear him in reply. My difficulty is this. The Court has already decided that the defendants were liable on the covenant, assuming that they took possession from Geoghegan with notice of an act of bankruptcy, and the Court thought that the jury were right in finding that the defendants had notice of an act of bankruptcy. Then it was contended that Denham had taken possession of these goods prior to the 29th December, and that, therefore, Denham's possession enured for the benefit of Foley. During vacation, whilst preparing my judgment, and when I came to read the evidence closely, it struck me that in point of fact Denham was not in possession when Foley entered.

Sly. The defendants wanted to shew that Denham was in possession, and that evidence was shut out; our contention was that Steel was in possession on behalf of Denham, and when I asked Foley the question whether Steel was there when he took possession, that question was rejected. When I tendered Denham's bill of sale, that was rejected also. It is clear from the evidence that Denham was in possession before Foley, but it is sufficient for us now to shew that the evidence tending to shew that Denham was in possession was rejected.

                                              C. A. V.

On the 25th October, the reserved judgment of the Court was delivered by

COHEN, J. The material circumstances of this case are as follow:—One Geoghegan was the proprietor of a bacon factory at Bomaderry, and he used to consign the products of his factory to the plaintiffs and defendants for sale, they being produce agents carrying on their business in Sydney. Geoghegan being indebted to the defendants, in August, 1895, gave them a bill of sale over certain goods, and in July, 1896, he also gave to the plaintiffs a bill of sale, both of which, it is said, included the goods in question in this action. Geoghegan having got into financial difficulties, the defendants on December 29th, 1896,

1898.

DENHAM
v.
FOLEY.

August 9.

October 25.

according to the finding of the jury, which this Court has
upheld, had notice of an available act of bankruptcy committed
by Geoghegan, and on December 30th they took possession of
the goods comprised in their bill of sale. On January 4th, 1897,
the defendants by deed assigned the goods comprised in their bill
of sale to the plaintiffs, and therein the defendants covenanted
with the plaintiffs "that the defendants had not been party or
privy to any act, deed, matter or thing whereby the said
property was, could, or might be in any wise encumbered,
or whereby they were prevented from assigning and transferring
the same," but the defendants did not disclose to the plaintiffs
that they had notice of an available act of bankruptcy.

On January 13th, 1897, Geoghegan was made bankrupt. The
goods so assigned were, it is said, taken possession of by the
plaintiffs, and the official assignee in Geoghegan's estate subsequently took proceedings against the plaintiffs under s. 130 of
the Bankruptcy Act to recover them, or their value, and
succeeded. To these proceedings the defendants were not made
parties, and although one of the defendants' firm gave evidence
in them, this Court, in the course of the present appeal, decided
that the defendants were not bound by the judgment in that
matter: see *Re Doyle* (1), and *Re Von Weissenfeld* (2).

The plaintiffs then brought this action to recover from the defendants the amount they had to pay Geoghegan's official assignee
as the value of the goods and the costs of defending the bankruptcy proceedings. The declaration contained three counts—
(1) for breach of the covenant hereinbefore set out ; (2) on
a warranty of title ; (3) for money had and received. At the
trial the defendants tendered evidence to shew that before the
act of bankruptcy on the 29th December, 1896, the plaintiffs
without notice of an available act of bankruptcy, had taken
possession of the goods in dispute and had taken them out of the
"order and disposition" of the bankrupt; but the presiding
Judge rejected the evidence, holding that evidence that the
plaintiffs so took possession of the goods was inadmissible, notice
or no notice. The jury, by a majority, found a verdict for the
plaintiffs, and hence this appeal.

(1) 2 B.C. 64.   (2) 9 Mor. 30.

During the argument counsel for the defendants contended that the fact of their having had notice of an act of bankruptcy prior to the date of the assignment did not make them "party or privy to any act, deed, matter or thing whereby, &c.," but the Court held that they were, upon the assumption that nothing had intervened to prevent the goods passing to the official assignee. Whether anything did so intervene was the question sought to be raised by the rejected evidence, for it is contended by the defendants' counsel that if the plaintiffs, acting under their bill of sale, and without notice of an available act of bankruptcy, took possession of the goods assigned to them by the defendants, before the act of bankruptcy of which the defendants had notice, the goods were not at the commencement of the bankruptcy in the order and disposition of the bankrupt, and the foundation of the official assignee's title therefore fails, and that this being so, the goods so assigned were not in fact encumbered, the defendants were not in fact or in law prevented from assigning and transferring them, and the plaintiffs thus having a good title the action must fail.

Various authorities were cited for this statement of the law, but having fully considered them, there are only two from which we can gather any material assistance in elucidating this somewhat difficult question.

In *Ex parte Foss* (1), Edward Baldwin on the 20th February, 1853, mortgaged to Foss certain plant, machinery, and other goods and chattels, and subsequently on the 7th May, 1856, mortgaged part of the same plant, &c., to Charles Baldwin subject to the mortgage to Foss. In May, 1856, Edward Baldwin was in difficulties, but by arrangement with some of his creditors, of whom the abovementioned mortgagees were two, on the 16th February, 1857, an execution was levied upon the chattels of Edward Baldwin, covered by the beforementioned mortgages. On the 17th February, 1857, Charles Baldwin (the second mortgagee) served notice of his security and required the sheriff to withdraw, and on the 18th February, 1857, Edward Baldwin was adjudged bankrupt. The mortgagees then presented their petitions to establish their mortgages, but the Commissioner

(1) [1858] 2 De G. & J. 230.

1858.

DENHAM
v.
FOLEY.

Cohen J.

held that they were invalid as against the assignees in bankruptcy on the ground of reputed ownership, and from this
decision the mortgagees appealed and appealed successfully.
Knight Bruce, L.J., in his judgment at p. 237 says, "As to the
tangible property in question upon these petitions, included in
the respective securities of the petitioners, which was seized by
the sheriff before the bankruptcy, and in his possession down to
the bankruptcy, I am of opinion that at the time of the bankruptcy it was not in the order, disposition and reputed ownership of the bankrupt with the consent of both or either of the
petitioners. The notice served on the bailiff before the bankruptcy on behalf in effect of the two petitioners, although
mentioning the security of the petitioner Mr. Baldwin only, was,
I conceive, available for both the petitioners, according to their
respective titles, and so for Mr. Foss as the prior mortgagee.
Thus far, therefore, I differ from the learned Commissioner."
And at p. 243 *Turner*, L.J., says : "Now how does this case
stand ? The sheriff takes possession of the plant. One of the
mortgagees gives him notice to withdraw. There is no pretence
for saying that the possession afterwards was in any sense the
possession of the bankrupt, or that the bankrupt continued in
possession, after the execution by the sheriff, in the same mode
as he had been in possession prior to the execution levied. This
state of circumstances, I think, brings the case distinctly within
the doctrine of *Fletcher* v. *Manning* (1), which is in conformity
with a long train of previous decisions to be found in *Jones* v.
Dwyer (2), and *Arbouin* v. *Williams* (3), and in *Ex parte Smith*
(4), and *Robinson* v. *McDonnell* (5)." *Payne* v. *Cales* (6),
although not so definite upon the point as *Ex parte Foss*, tends
in the same direction. There one Coleman, an innkeeper, on the
30th March, 1876, gave a bill of sale over his effects to the plaintiff, which was not registered. On the 21st June, 1877, Coleman
executed a bill of sale to the defendants over the same property,
which was registered. On the following day the defendants took
possession under their bill of sale, and thus took the goods out of

(1) 12 M. & W. 571.   (4) Buck. 149.
(2) 15 East 21.   (5) 2 B. & Ald. 134.
(3) Ry. & Moo. 72.   (6) [1878] 38 L.T.N.S. 355.

the order and disposition of the mortgagor, and on the 10th July
they sold the goods comprised in it. Between the seizure and
sale, viz., on the 25th June, the mortgagor was made bankrupt.
Out of the proceeds of the sale the defendants paid themselves
40*l.* in satisfaction of their debt, and handed the balance to the
trustee in bankruptcy. The plaintiff then brought his action
against the defendants to recover 17*l.* due to him by Coleman.
In the course of the argument it was in effect contended on
behalf of the defendants that, inasmuch as the goods comprised
in the plaintiff's bill of sale were at the time of the bankruptcy
of the mortgagor in the order and disposition of the bankrupt,
because his bill of sale was unregistered, the plaintiff could not
be allowed to say otherwise, and therefore, so far as he was concerned, the moneys received by the defendants belonged to the
trustee. It was held, however, that the plaintiff's bill of sale held
good against the defendants, and that the defendants were liable
for the seizure on June 22nd, which was tortious as against the
plaintiff.

It was generally argued on behalf of the plaintiffs in the
present case that the possession by a second mortgagee cannot
enure for the benefit of a first mortgagee, but we do not think
that general contention should prevail, for it might entail considerable hardship and injustice. Assume a first mortgagee
living a considerable distance from the place where the mortgagor
resides, that the mortgagor, without any knowledge in the first
mortgagee, is in financial extremities, which makes it necessary
for the mortgagee, in his own protection, to take possession
before the mortgagor's bankruptcy, and that there is a second
mortgagee near at hand who does take possession under his
security, why in justice such possession by the second mortgagee
should not enure for the benefit of the first mortgagee, so far as
the law sanctions the priority, we cannot understand. Inasmuch
as the title of the trustee in bankruptcy, so far as it depends
upon reputed ownership, depends upon the goods being in the
order and disposition of the bankrupt with the consent of the
true owner, at the commencement of the bankruptcy, and a
second mortgagee may be a true owner, we cannot discover any
injustice to the trustee if that order and disposition is determined

1898.   by the act of the second and not of the first mortgagee, or why,
DENHAM   if the order and disposition is so determined, the first mortgagee
v.   should not be allowed the preference which the law may attach
FOLEY.   to his security.

Cohen J.   But it was further submitted that the possession of a second
mortgagee cannot enure for the benefit of a first mortgagee who
has notice of an available act of bankruptcy.   But we do not see
why it should not.   If the asserted title of the official assignee
has never arisen because of the second mortgagee taking possession, and the title of the first mortgagee who has not taken
possession is defeasible only at the instance of and as against the
official assignee upon the assumption that the goods in question
remain in the order and disposition of the bankrupt at the commencement of the bankruptcy, why should not the first mortgagee, who has transferred his security to the second mortgagee,
be entitled to say to the second mortgagee, "although the official
assignee and he alone might have impeached my title to the
goods, if you had not taken timely possession, and so anticipated
any claim he might otherwise have set up, yet having taken such
possession, your title is good against him, against me, and against
the mortgagor personally, and with that complete title you have
all that I bargained to sell you."   The authorities cited, as well as
the reason of the thing, it seems to us, support this contention.

Considering that the doctrine of reputed ownership, to use a
somewhat familiar expression, involves the taking of one man's
goods to pay another man's debts, we are not disposed to extend
its operation beyond what the clear law compels or real justice
requires.   Inasmuch as we do not see that the clear law compels
us to hold that the possession by the second mortgagee cannot
enure for the benefit of the first, even where the first has notice
of an available act of bankruptcy, and as we do not now see under
the circumstances thus far disclosed in evidence that the real
justice of the case requires us so to hold, we are of opinion that
the rule *nisi* for a new trial should be made absolute with costs,
the costs of the first trial to abide the event of the second.

Wise. The new trial should be limited to the one point, as to
whether or not Denham was in possession without notice of an

1898
DENHAM
v.
FOLEY.

available act of bankruptcy when Foley took possession, because on the decision of the Court that is the only matter in dispute between the parties.

THE CHIEF JUSTICE. We cannot limit the new trial in that way. The only power we have is to grant a new trial generally.

Rule absolute, with costs; costs of the first trial to abide the event.

On November 4th, during the same term,

Wise, for the plaintiffs, moved to vary the order of the 25th October granting a new trial generally. Since the case was argued I have discovered that it is provided by s. 42 of 5 Vic. No. 9 (*Pilcher* 1535) that in granting a new trial the Court shall have power to direct the parties to make admissions for the purposes of such new trial, or to grant the new trial upon some particular point or points only. The jury found that the defendants seized with notice of an act of bankruptcy, and the Court held that they were right in so finding. I therefore ask the Court to amend its former order by limiting the new trial to the other issue—as to whether or not Denham was in possession without notice of an act of bankruptcy when Foley took possession—or by directing the defendants to admit that they seized with notice of an act of bankruptcy.

Sly, contra. The Court cannot limit the new trial where the ground is the improper rejection of evidence.

THE CHIEF JUSTICE. There were two issues before the jury in this case—first, whether the defendants seized Geoghegan's goods with knowledge of an act of bankruptcy committed by him, and upon this point the jury found in the plaintiffs' favour —that is to say, that the defendants had notice of an act of bankruptcy, and the Court has held that they properly so found. The second issue was whether, assuming the defendants to have had such notice, the plaintiffs had not themselves taken possession of the goods in question under their own bill of sale before the act of bankruptcy, of which the defendants had notice, and without notice of any other available act of bankruptcy, and that accordingly the goods were taken out of the order and disposition of the bankrupt; the effect of this latter issue being, if found in the defendants' favour, to defeat the action by shewing a good title to the goods in the plaintiffs. This issue was also found by the jury in favour of the plaintiffs, but owing to the rejection of certain evidence the Court held that the jury were not in a position properly to determine it, and sent the case down for a new trial. The case, therefore, stands in this position: that one issue has been properly tried and decided at the first trial, but the other issue has not been so tried and decided.

Under these circumstances, now that the provisions of s. 42 of 5 Vic. No. 9 have been brought to my notice, I am of opinion that the case should be sent down for a new trial with this condition attached, that the defendants must admit that they took possession of the goods under their bill of sale on the 30th December with notice of an act of bankruptcy commited by Geoghegan.

I must confess that until the present moment I have been entirely unaware of the provisions of s. 42. During all my experience I have never known it to be acted upon, and it is curious that the possession of such very valuable powers should so long have escaped the notice of the Court.

I think the best course will be to take out a rider to the order granting a new trial. The costs of this application will be costs in the cause to both parties. The order as to costs made on the rule absolute will stand as it is.

STEPHEN, J. I concur. I am also astonished that the provisions of s. 42 have till now escaped the notice of the profession. I certainly did not know of it myself.

COHEN, J. I concur.

*Order accordingly.**

The rule absolute dated the 25th October was as follows:—
"'It is ordered that the verdict entered herein for the plaintiffs be and the same is hereby set aside and that a new trial of the issues joined herein be had between the parties."

*NOTE.—In *Conlon* v. *M'Guigan* (5 N.S.W. L.R. 205) an application was made for an order under s. 42 of 5 Vic. No. 9.

On the 4th November the following order was made :—

"Upon hearing Mr. *Wise* of counsel for the above-named plaintiffs and Dr. *Sly* of counsel for the above-named defendants it is ordered that on the hearing of the new trial granted herein the defendants do admit that when they took possession of the goods on the 30th December 1896 they had previously to such taking possession notice of an available act of bankruptcy committed by Laurence Geoghegan. And it is further ordered that the costs of the day of this application to speak to the rule absolute granted herein on the 25th October last be costs in the cause to both parties And it is lastly ordered that this supplementary rule be read as a rider to the said rule."

Attorney for the plaintiffs: *James Baker.*

Attorney for the defendants: *H. A. Lyons.*

Ex parte TEWKESBURY.

1898.
———
November 8.

Owen J.
and
Cohen J.

Practice—Full Court—Power to rescind order—Affidavits in opposition to rule nisi —Reg.-Gen. 5th July, 1858—Municipalities Act, 1897, ss. 9, 109—Ouster of alderman—Rescission of order.

The Full Court has power to rescind its own order, even though the order be made in a previous term, and even though the power to make the order is conferred on it by statute. But it will only do so where it is clear that the order then made was made improvidently, or on materials which are clearly shewn to be false.

The Court has power to rescind an order made under s. 109 of the Municipalities Act, 1897, ousting an alderman of his office.

Semble. The effect of the rescission of such an order is to reinstate the alderman ousted. If an alderman has been elected in the place of the alderman ousted, on the rescission of the order he ceases to act as alderman, and s. 9 validates anything done by the council whilst he was in office.

Affidavits in opposition to a rule *nisi* can only be filed up to one o'clock on the day preceding the day on which the rule is returnable, unless a Judge allows further time.

THIS was a motion to make absolute a rule *nisi*, calling upon A. J. Long to shew cause why the rule of this Court made on the 3rd August, whereby A. R. Tewkesbury was ousted from the office of alderman of the Borough of Temora, should not be rescinded.

The rule *nisi* was granted upon the ground that the rule made on the 3rd August was made in pursuance of a rule *nisi* granted on the 5th May on the application of A. J. Long, calling upon A. R. Tewkesbury to shew cause why he should not be ousted of the office of alderman of the Borough of Temora, and that the said rule *nisi* was not served upon him.

Before the affidavits were read,

Kelynack, for the respondent, took the preliminary objection that the Court had no power to rescind its own order. The Court having made an order, it cannot be rescinded except during the same term : *Tierney* v. *Loxton* (1).

[COHEN, J., referred to *Jones* v. *Hill* (2).]

(1) 12 N.S.W. L.R. 308.   (2) 7 N.S.W. L.R. 369.

If the Court has general jurisdiction to set aside its own order, it cannot set aside an order made under s. 109 of the Municipalities Act, 1897. No provision is made under that section for the Court rescinding its own order. When a rule is made absolute under that section the alderman "is deemed to be ousted of such office," and an extraordinary vacancy occurs, which must under s. 69 be filled within 24 days. If this order is rescinded that will not reinstate Tewkesbury—or if it does reinstate him, what is to become of the alderman elected in his place? If the person now elected was not an alderman, then possibly the council has acted without having a quorum, and its acts would be invalid.

He also referred to *Ex parte Adams* (1).

Brissenden, for the applicant. This Court has clearly power to rescind its own order.

[OWEN, J. The Court may have the power, but will it exercise that power in a case of this kind?]

It is not shewn here that any inconvenience will arise such as is suggested. It does not appear that any person has been elected in the place of Tewkesbury, nor is it shewn that any acts of the council will be invalidated (if it is a fact that a new alderman has been elected) by reason of his acting in the council. But if there be any defect in his election, s. 9 validates the acts of the council whilst the person wrongly elected acts, and, therefore, no inconvenience such as is suggested could possibly arise.

Kelynack in reply. Sect. 9 would not apply, because that section can only apply to some defect in an election properly held. Here if the order of the Court is rescinded there was no vacancy, and no election could have been held to fill it up. The applicant can only suggest that difficulties might arise if this order be rescinded. He is not in a position to shew that difficulties will arise, because he cannot know what contracts the council has entered into, or what acts have been done by the council. A Court has not inherent jurisdiction to vary or rescind its own order. If a Court has that power, why was it necessary

(1) 10 N.S.W. L.R. 22.

Margin notes:

to insert a section in the Bankruptcy Act Amendment Act, 1896, g,v.ng the Bankruptcy Court that power (see s. 29)? No case has been cited to shew that where the Court is given power to make an order under a statute, and that statute does not give it power to rescind its order, it has such power.

OWEN, J. This is an application to the Court to rescind an order made by the Court on the 3rd August last. The preliminary objection has been taken that this order having been made in the preceding term, this Court has no power to rescind it. I am of opinion that the Court has that power, and must of necessity have that power if the Court see that the order was improperly obtained or granted by the Court improvidently, otherwise the Court would have to hold its hand even in the case of the grossest injustice—it may be in a case where the order of the Court was obtained on the suppression of material facts or on a forged document. It appears to me that the Court must have inherent power to rescind its own orders generally, not only in a case where the order was made at common law, but also where the order was made under a statute, though no doubt the Court would be very slow to act on that power. The only direct authority I can find on the point is *Todd* v. *Jeffery* (1). That was a case where a rule had been granted the previous term, and the Court was asked to rescind that rule. Lord *Denman*, C.J., there says: "This Court will alter its own rules" ["rules" there mean orders] "where there had been a plain misconception." And *Patteson*, J., says that the rule could not be altered after the term in which it was made "unless there had been some palpable mistake." That case, therefore, shews that where there has been some palpable mistake, the Court has power to rescind its order.

Then it is said that the Court would not rescind an order made under s. 109 of the Municipalities Act, 1897, because of the consequences which would flow; and it is said that the effect of making an order under s. 109 is to create a vacancy in the council, and the extraordinary vacancy thus created has to be filled under s. 69, and that possibly there might be two

(1) 7 A. & E. 519.

aldermen, the one which had been ousted, and the one elected under s. 69. I cannot see that any difficulty will arise, because if the Court rescinds the order the former alderman is re-instated, and the order ousting him is treated as if it had never been made. If that is so, there has been no vacancy in the council, and anyone elected to fill the vacancy has never been elected at all, and he would pass out of the council, and the former alderman would be re-instated. Then s. 9 renders valid all proceedings, although there has been some defect in the election. Mr. *Kelynack* has contended that a "defect" there means that there has been a good election under the Act, but that it has been improperly carried out. That would be a very narrow interpretation of the section, and would only cure part of the defects in elections. It appears to me that this section is intended to cure all defects, whatever they may have been. In this case the defect was that there was no vacancy, and that an election took place when there was no vacancy. Therefore no difficulty could arise from the actions of the alderman who was elected to fill the vacancy, and, therefore, it seems to me that no injurious consequences could flow from the Court rescinding its former order. For these reasons I am of opinion that the preliminary objection should be overruled.

COHEN, J. I am of the same opinion. With regard to the general power of the Court to rescind its own order, the only case in our own Court which I know of is *Jones* v. *Hill* (1). There an order was rescinded which had been made the previous term. The Court having that general power, I cannot see that it is deprived of that power by s. 109 of the Municipalities Act.

Preliminary objection overruled.

The affidavits were then read. Two rules *nisi* were granted on the same day on the motion of Long by the Court, one calling upon Tewkesbury to shew cause why he should not be ousted of the office of alderman ; and the other calling upon one Donnelly to shew cause why he should not be ousted. The applicant

(1) 7 N.S.W. L.R. 369.

II 2

(margin)
1898.

Ex parte
TEWKESBURY

Owen J.

swore that the rule in Donnelly's case was by some mistake served on him. He did not, however, swear that he did not know of the rule having been granted in his case, and from the affidavits filed on the other side it was clear that he did not know of it. The applicant's wife said that she saw the bailiff who served the rule *nisi* hand her husband some papers, and that she was then standing in the hall of her house, and that her husband came down the passage and shewed her the rule *nisi*, which was the rule in Donnelly's case. Tewkesbury's solicitor swore that Tewkesbury had brought him the rule *nisi* which had been served upon him, and that it was the rule in Donnelly's case. And he also swore that the bailiff had admitted to him that in serving the rule absolute on Donnelly he made a mistake in serving him with Tewkesbury's rule; and that when Donnelly pointed out the mistake to him, he had served him with the right rule. And he further swore that when he had interviewed him with reference to the service of the rule *nisi* he said that he could not positively swear that he had served the right rule on Tewkesbury.

The bailiff in an affidavit sworn on behalf of the respondent, denied that he had made any mistake in the service of the rules *nisi*, and he denied that he had admitted to the applicant's solicitor that he had made any mistake.

Kelynack proposed to read certain affidavits which were filed after the return day of this rule.

Brissenden objected to them on the ground that they were filed out of time.

Kelynack. Under R.G. 5th July, 1858 (*Pilcher*, 344), any affidavit can be filed in opposition to a rule up to one o'clock on the day preceding the day on which the motion is made to make the rule absolute.

OWEN, J. I think the day referred to in that rule is the day on which the rule *nisi* is returnable, and not the day on which the matter comes on to be heard. These affidavits are, therefore, filed too late, and cannot be read.

COHEN, J. Agreed.

Brissenden. It is clear from the affidavits that the rule *nisi* was never served. If the rule was not personally served, the Court had no jurisdiction to make the order against Tewkesbury, because there was nothing to bring him before the Court.

[OWEN, J. Do you admit that if the rule had been served, the order of the Court would have been right, and that Tewkesbury's election was invalid ?]

Yes. The applicant bases his right to have the order rescinded on the ground that he was never served with the rule *nisi.*

[OWEN, J. Did he not know that the matter was coming before the Court ?]

It is immaterial whether he knew or not. He was entitled to be served with the rule, and if not served the Court could make no order against him. His knowledge that a rule had been granted cannot avail the other side any more than in the case of a writ of summons: *Hudson* v. *Wilkinson* (1).

Kelynack was not called upon.

OWEN, J. I am satisfied that the Court ought not to rescind the order which was made by the Court on the 3rd August. It appears that upon the materials which were then before the Court the order was right. It is not disputed that the election was void for the reasons then assigned by the Court, and at that time there was an affidavit that the rule *nisi* had been personally served. Now the matter comes before us and we are asked to rescind that order, not on the ground that the election was valid, or that the Court was wrong in holding that the election was invalid, but upon the ground that the rule *nisi* was not served. A number of affidavits have been filed upon that point, and they are very conflicting, and it is impossible on these affidavits to say positively that the rule was not served. The Court will only rescind its own order made during the previous term, when it is clear that the order then made was made improvidently, or on materials which are clearly shewn to be false. I confess that I have very little compunction in making this order, because it is clear that Tewkesbury knew that the application was being made

(1) 6 W.N. 114.

1898.

Ex parte
TEWKESBURY

1898.

Ex parte
EWKESBURY

Owen J.

against him. That may not be a ground for the Court refusing this application; but he has nobody but himself to blame in the matter, and it is perfectly clear that if he had appeared the Court would still have made the order which it did.

COHEN, J., concurred.

Rule discharged with costs.

Attorney for the applicant: *L. L. Cohen*, agent for *E. A. P. Walsh* (Temora).

Attorneys for the respondent: *Chenhall & . Eddie*, agents for *R. Driscoll* (Temora).

Ex parte DONNELLY.

1898.
Nov. 8.

Owen J.
and
Cohen J.

In this case a similar application was made to the Court as in the last case.

The counsel were the same.

Brissenden. I understand the Court to hold that if the applicant knew of the rule *nisi* having been granted, although the rule had not been served, the Court would not rescind the order.

OWEN, J. The Court did not hold anything of the kind. Are the facts in this case the same as in the previous case?

Brissenden. They are the same except that there is an affidavit made by Donnelly in which he swears that the bailiff served Tewkesbury's rule on him.

OWEN, J. There is no doubt that the applicant in this case makes a stronger case than the applicant in the previous case; but I cannot see that the matter is free from doubt, and, therefore, we will make the same order as was made in that case.

COHEN, J., concurred.

Rule discharged with costs.

Attorney for the applicant: *F. R. Cowper*, agent for *R. C. Dibbs* (Temora).

Attorneys for the respondent: *Chenhall & Eddie*, agents for *R. Driscoll* (Temora).

C A S E S

DETERMINED BY THE

SUPREME COURT OF NEW SOUTH WALES

IN ITS

Equitable Jurisdiction,

AND BY THE

PRIVY COUNCIL ON APPEAL THEREFROM DURING 1898.

COOPER v. THE COMMISSIONERS OF TAXATION (1).

Land tax—59 Vic. No. 15 (Land and Income Tax Assessment Act), ss. 30, 40, 47, 54, 68—59 Vic. No. 16—Completion of Assessment Book—Land tax, how made a charge on the land taxed—Issue of Gazette notice—Construction of taxing statutes. .

The Court of Equity has jurisdiction to determine whether the steps to make the land tax payable have been legally carried out.

The land tax payable under 59 Vic. No. 15 and 59 Vic. No. 16 does not become a charge on the land taxed until the amount is due and payable, nor does it become due and payable until the assessment book contemplated by the Act is "complete" and a notice has subsequently thereto been issued in the *Gazette* under s. 47 of the Act 59 Vic. No. 15.

Whatever may be the meaning of the term assessment book in the Act 59 Vic. No. 15, it cannot be said to be complete when particulars of the assessment of only half the taxable land in the colony have been entered, but, *semble*, if the book were substantially complete that would be a sufficient compliance with the Act.

Consideration of what is meant by the term "assessment book" in the Act 59 Vic. No. 15.

If in a taxing Act the Court sees that a burden is clearly imposed, it will, so far as the mere machinery is concerned, be astute to carry out the clear intention of raising revenue for the Crown.

HEARING OF SUIT.

This was a suit by John Cooper for a declaration that the assessment of his land for the purposes of land tax was invalid

1897.

_____

June 14, 17, 21, 23, 28, 29.

July 22.

_____

C.J. Eq.

---

(1) See now the Land and Income Tax Amendment Act (No. 21, 1897).

and that there was no charge created on his lands, and for an injunction.

The facts are fully stated in the judgment of the Court.

The main points argued were (1) whether the tax became a charge on the land before it was due and payable; (2) what steps were necessary to make the tax due and payable; (3) the jurisdiction of the Court to entertain the suit.

Pilcher, Q.C., *Heydon*, Q.C., and *Lingen*, for the plaintiff. The land tax does not become a charge upon the land until it is payable; it is not payable until assessment notices have been sent out; and the notices are not to be sent out until the assessment book has been completed. There are six steps to be taken under the Act before the tax is payable :—(1) a return by the landowner or some person nominated by the Commissioners in the case of default by the owner; (2) a valuation of the land by the assessors; (3) the determination by the Commissioners of the proper assessment; (4) the complete record of these assessments in a book; (5) the publication in the *Gazette* of a notice when the tax is due under s. 47; and (6) the notice of the assessment to the individual taxpayer under s. 42; and all these must be done within the year. There was no difficulty in preparing the assessment book within the year. The *Gazette* notice of 21st Feb., 1896, required all landowners to furnish their returns by the 27th March following. In case of default on that date the Commissioners had ample powers under s. 30, sub-s. (IV), and under ss. 38, 39, to obtain the necessary materials for the assessment book. The Act does not make it the Commissioners' duty to find the owner, only to fix an assessment for all the land. The Act evidently contemplates some book being kept, capable of inspection under s. 40, and it must be complete before the *Gazette* notice is published under s. 47, or the assessment notices sent out under s. 42; both sections use the words " on completion of the assessment book." The taxing Act (59 Vic. No. 16), s. 1, clearly contemplates the assessments at all events all being completed within each year; the tax is for each year and is required by Government in each year; s. 42 says notice is to be sent to *every* taxpayer, not merely to those who have been assessed. If the

Commissioners can postpone any of the assessments for 1896 till 1897, they could postpone the whole of the assessments until the end of the first quinquennial period and so on for every period of five years.

If the plaintiff's set of papers is the book it is admitted no *Gazette* notice has been published since those papers were completed.

The Commissioners' interpretation puts the person who fails to make a return into a better position than the person who does send in a return; the latter has to pay within 60 days of the *Gazette* notice, the former can wait until the Commissioners have determined his assessment themselves.

Sir *Julian Salomons*, Q.C., and *W. Gregory Walker*, Q.C. (*J. L. Campbell* with them), for the Commissioners of Taxation. The plaintiff has no equity to come to the Court; the pleader has evidently felt this difficulty, and so far as can be gathered from the statement of claim he relies upon an allegation that the Commissioners contend that the assessment notice creates a charge upon the land and may enforce their powers. In the first place, the Commissioners never contended that the notice created a charge; the charge is created by the Act of Parliament to the extent of one penny in the £ on the first day of each year; the land then and there becomes charged with an amount to be subsequently ascertained and made payable by the owner.

The mere allegation of fears that the Commissioners may enforce their powers is no ground for coming to the Court; the plaintiff must allege and prove that the defendant "threatens and intends:" *Stannard* v. *Vestry of Camberwell* (1); *Proctor* v. *Bayley* (2); *Barrett* v. *Day* (3).

The intention to tax all the owners of land beyond a certain value is clear in the Acts; the Court will be astute to interpret the mere machinery provisions so as to give effect to that intention: *Coltness Iron Co.* v. *Black* (4). The Court will also consider the convenience or inconvenience of competitive constructions: *Queen* v. *Inghall* (5).

(1) 20 Ch. D. 195.	(3) 43 Ch. D. 450.
(2) 42 Ch. D. 399.	(4) 6 A.C. 330.

(5) 2 Q.B.D. 207.

A 2

The directions as to the completion of the books are only intended to be directory; the Legislature cannot have intended the tax to be defeated because the whole of the returns were not entered up in a book before the notices are sent out. At most, if the Legislature did require the particulars to be complete, it is sufficient if they are complete as regards the individual to whom a notice is sent; the set of papers referring to each individual are the book so far as he is concerned. The word book as applied to loose sheets subsequently to be bound up in a book is well known in Government offices here, *e.g.*, the Registry of Deeds. Put at their highest, however, all the objections of the plaintiff only go to the time when the tax is payable; they do not touch the time when the tax becomes a charge. The tax is *debitum in praesenti solvendum in futuro.* The plaintiff is only entitled to succeed in this suit if the tax is not yet a charge on his land; if it is only not payable, that will be an answer when he is sued for the amount. Sect. 2 of the taxing Act does not impose a tax on individuals, but upon all the alienated lands in the colony, and by s. 54, sub-s. (I), it immediately becomes a first charge on the land until payment. The details as to valuation and assessment only concern the individuals who have to pay the tax, who have certain exemptions which they can claim, and so forth; we contend that on the first day of every year a new charge attaches to all the land which may be discharged subsequently when the assessments, deductions, and exemptions have been ascertained. It is suggested that it is a hardship on landowners to have a charge on their land which they cannot get rid of, but there is the same difficulty even if a notice of assessment has to precede the creation of the charge; the tax then becomes a charge on the land and takes precedence under s. 54, sub-s. 1, over all prior charges and attaches to the land whether the taxpayer still remains the owner or not, provided he was owner at the commencement of the year.

[They cited *Liverpool Borough Bank* v. *Turner* (1); *Howard* v. *Boddington* (2); *Smith* v. *Jones* (3), on the construction of taxing statutes].

(1) 2 De G. F. & J. 502.　　　　(2) 2 P.D. 211.
(3) 1 B. & Ad. 328.

Pilcher in reply. The tax must be payable before it is a charge; "land tax" is defined in s. 68 as "the land tax imposed as such by any Act in force for the time being *as assessed* under this Act." The land tax only becomes a tax after assessment.

He also cited *Commissioner for Income Tax* v *Pemsel* (1).

1897.

COOPER
v.
COMMISSION-
ERS OF
TAXATION

Cur. adv. vult.

On the 22nd July the following judgment was read by

July 22.

MANNING, C.J. in Eq.   The plaintiff, John Cooper, is an owner of land within the meaning of the Land Tax and the Land and Income Tax Assessments Acts of 1895, and the defendants are the commissioners appointed under these Acts to assess and levy the land tax provided for.

The suit was instituted to have it declared that the assessment of the plaintiff's lands was not valid, and that no charge on his lands was created thereby, and for an injunction to restrain the defendants from taking any proceeding to sue for or raise the amount of the assessment made, and from letting, selling, or otherwise prejudicially dealing with the plaintiff's land.   At the time of filing the statement of claim no Court of Review to deal with appeals in terms of the Act had been appointed, and this led to the insertion in the statement of claim of a number of allegations for the protection of the plaintiff, who was bound to appeal within 30 days if he desired to dispute the amount, as he most unquestionably did in this case.   A Court of Review was, however, appointed shortly after this suit was commenced, and an appeal in due form was lodged, so that at the hearing many of the allegations had become irrelevant, and those relating to the Court of Review are material only for the purposes of one ground for the relief prayed, *i.e.*, by reason of the delay in the appointment of such Court.

The plaintiff has in his statement of claim, as it seems to me, somewhat confused the assessment with the notice of assessment, but this is quite pardonable, as the Act itself uses the word "assessment" as applied to three different stages or positions. At all events no prejudice can arise to the plaintiff therefrom, as

(1) [1891] A.C. 531.

1897.

COOPER
v.
COMMISSION-
ERS OF
TAXATION

C.J. Eq.

all proper amendments must be taken to have been made to allow of a decision on the real merits of the case as argued before me, which may be shortly stated as follows, viz. :—That whatever was done by the commissioners in this case in and about the assessment, no valid charge on the land exists under the circumstances, and that they must be restrained from taking any step for the enforcement of the charge or payment of the tax, such as they would be entitled to take if, as they assert and maintain, the charge were in existence or the tax due and payable.

The plaintiff set out in his statement of claim certain grounds entitling him to relief, viz., that the assessment was issued (1) before any Court of Review was appointed, and (2) before the assessment books had been completed or notified as completed, and (3) before any tables for calculation of values had been issued; and in the 19th paragraph of the statement of claim he also claims that in consequence of s. 67 of the Act he was unable to raise the question of the validity of the assessment except in the Equity Court. It is not quite apparent why the pleader departed from the usual custom in setting out grounds for relief in the prayer, especially as on the whole purview of the statement of claim and under the prayer for relief he was entitled to, and did in fact rely on, many other grounds as affecting his position before the Court; but he cannot and must not be held to be bound thereby; and here again, if necessary, all proper amendments must be taken as made to enable the case to be considered as hereinbefore stated by me.

The defendants objected that this Court had no jurisdiction to hear the case, and grant the relief prayed, on the ground that the Act prescribed the only method open to any dissatisfied landowner, i.e., by means of the Court of Review, and that the jurisdiction of this Court was thereby ousted if it could otherwise have been invoked; and also that the plaintiff could have set up the same case either in the Court of Review or when sued for the amount of the tax; or that at all events he should have waited to approach the Court until some step was actually taken to enforce the charge.

It was also argued that this Court had no jurisdiction to remove a charge created by an Act of Parliament, but that argument was clearly a confusion of ideas between the right to approach the Court and the right to succeed, for the plaintiff's contention is that no valid charge exists or no charge capable of being enforced, so that any claim founded on the charge or supposed charge is a *brutum fulmen*, and a cloud on his title; it was never contended that a valid existing charge could be removed.

As to the other grounds, I would say, first, that the words in the Act must be very clear to deprive the subject of his right to call to his aid the jurisdiction of the Supreme Court, and especially this branch, and it is manifest that there is no such restrictive language here. The Act merely provides in s. 44, sub-s. I., that "any taxpayer (*i.e.*, any person chargeable with land tax) may appeal from any notice of assessment to the Court of Review on the ground that he is not liable for the tax or for any part thereof, or that the amount of the assessment is excessive," and by s. 9 the Court of Review may be either the Land Court, a District Court Judge, or a Police Magistrate, as appointed, and the whole matter is to be treated on the lines of cases before the Land Court, the Court of Review being bound, if required, to state a case for the decision of the Supreme Court as to any question of law which may have arisen. That section clearly refers to cases of a valid assessment, which can be enforced against someone, but in respect of which the appellant contends that he is not the proper person to pay or that the amount is excessive, and that Court would not in my opinion be entitled to go into the question of the validity of the tax itself, when as here the plaintiff admits that he is the right person to pay, but that there is no legal tax in existence which he can be called on to pay.

Then it was said that the case made here could be set up as a defence in an action for the tax. Assuming that the case of the *Municipal District of Gundagai* v. *Norton* (1) is an authority for this position, how can that oust the jurisdiction of this Court? I have never before heard it contended that a man with an equity was bound to wait until legal steps were taken against him? If there is a cloud on anyone's title he is entitled to come to the Court of Equity at once to have it removed. In the present case time is

1897.

Cooper
v.
Commission-
ers of
Taxation

C.J. Eq.

(1) 15 N.S.W. L.R. 365.

1897.

COOPER
v.
COMMISSION-
ERS OF
TAXATION

C.J. Eq.

of especial importance, as the plaintiff's tenants are under a liability to recoup him as to portion of the tax, and if the plaintiff had to wait till the commissioners took steps to enforce their asserted position, he might be affected most prejudicially by reason of the inability of the tenants to pay their quota at one and the same time for three, four, or five years, or whenever it suited the convenience of the commissioners. Again, consider the tribunal which might have to consider such a point as this. Imagine the Court of Petty Sessions having to deal with the case in the first instance, and then having to state a case on appeal. Manifestly the Court of Equity is the proper Court to deal with the matter, even if it is not the only one, and it is unnecessary for me to consider whether or not the provisions of s. 67 would be fatal to the plaintiff in an action at law, as was contended.

I must, therefore, overrule all objections to the jurisdiction, and deal with the case on its merits.

The Land Tax Acts, which for convenience were referred to in the argument as the Taxing Act and the Machinery Act respectively, and which nomenclature I will adopt, though the latter term is a misnomer as to many of its provisions, were passed in December, 1895, on the same day, the separation having only taken place to get over the Parliamentary difficulty of the Legislative Council's power to amend a taxation bill. The commissioners promptly took steps to call for returns from all landowners under s. 30, sub-s. I., and a very large number of returns were duly sent in, roughly speaking with reference to about 90 per cent. of the whole of the alienated lands in the colony. Assessors, i.e., valuators, were appointed, and by October, 1896 (the material date for consideration), the valuators had sent in their valuation of all alienated lands in the colony, i.e., of all the lands liable to taxation. The work of the commissioners as assessors then was to go through the returns in connection with their own valuators' reports, and come to a conclusion as to the proper value for assessment purposes. Here, no doubt, difficulties would and did arise in consequence of subdivisions and sales of which the valuers were unaware; and it was, of course, quite possible that, in case of, say, Blackacre, A sent in his return for a portion only, and B., the purchaser of the balance, had made no return, or had to be searched for in another return; but though it might take an indefinite time to find the true owner for every piece of land in the colony, such a difficulty was clearly provided for in the Act, which allowed any amount of alterations and amendment after the "assessment books" were made up—see s. 32; but the commissioners were also given extraordinary powers, which could only have been done with a view to enable them to get through their assessments and make up their assessment books within a reasonable time and for a certain necessary purpose.

1897.

COOPER
v.
COMMISSION-
ERS OF
TAXATION

C.J. Eq.

By sub-s. (IV.) of s. 30 they could, in the case of any person failing to make a return (which under the earlier sub-sections he was bound to do within a prescribed time), appoint a stranger to make such return, which when made was to be, "for all the purposes of this Act, the return of the person liable to make the return." Further, they were entitled, under s. 39, in case of such default, or in the case of their not being satisfied with any return, to make their own assessment of the value or amount which ought to be charged, "and the tax shall be paid accordingly." Again, by section 38, which deals with the "assessment books," they were authorised to enter any land therein by the name of "the owner," where, "after due enquiry," the name of an owner of land could not be found. There was a good deal of argument on the words "after due enquiry," but surely these must be read with reference to the circumstances of each case, and especially to the time available, and that the commissioners took this view themselves is shewn by regulation 35 on the same point, which says: "So far as such name, address, and occupation can readily be ascertained." Bearing in mind that notice of assessment had to be sent out, and that each alleged taxpayer had 30 days therefrom to appeal, and that full power of amendment and alteration of the "assessment books" existed, there can be little doubt that what the Legislature had in mind was the necessity of an early preparation and completion of such books, and the intention was to put the commissioners in a position to meet possible difficulties as suggested and enable them to be able to complete the books as early as possible, with a view to the issue of the *Gazette* notice, upon which alone the tax came into life by "becoming due and payable."

1897.

Cooper
v.
Commission-
ers of
Taxation

C.J. Eq.

Such being the powers of the commissioners, let us consider their position, and what course they adopted. Mr. Lockyer, the first commissioner, who has been most closely associated with the Land Tax Department, stated that the total acreage of the alienated lands in the colony exceeded 45,000,000 acres ; that up to the 20th October, 1896 (he said the 30th October, but I will take it that his evidence applies to the 20th), separate returns had been received from 123,000 persons, which were estimated to cover 90 per cent. of the total acreage—that 60,000 of these returns had been dealt with, and the lands found to be exempt under the Act—that of the balance, 21,400, had then been dealt with and assessed as taxpayers. That left 41,600 returns in hand not then dealt with, and it was at that time unascertained whether they were taxpayers or not. Since then 15,300 of that balance have been assessed as taxpayers, the remainder being exempt. Very few returns have since been received of the additional 10 per cent. Of the 15,300 which have been assessed since the 20th October, 1896, 7000 were assessed and issued in the year 1896, but after the 30th October, and 8000 odd were for the first time assessed in 1897 for 1896. In the case before me the assessment was made on the 30th October, 1896, and the notice was issued the same day, and reached the plaintiff's agent on the 31st in the course of post, though the notice itself (exhibit H.) contained the words in print " Dated this 23rd day of October, 1896," as did also exhibit L, which is the document which indicates the assessment by the commissioners, and which the commissioners put forward as constituting a complete book of assessment within the meaning of ss. 42 and 47 of the Act.

I should here mention that exhibit L consists of a sheet of white paper of a flimsy nature, partly printed, available for each individual assessment, with a number of sheets of blue and easily destructible paper attached, forming a schedule of different properties, rendered necessary by the insufficiency of the space available on the white paper, but every word and figure both on the white and blue papers, which identify the papers with the individual case, are written with an ordinary lead pencil, except the figures on the white paper, 14,500, indicating the number of the register. Exhibit L is to be taken as typical of all other such assessment papers, or books, as they are called.

The notice Exhibit H contains in print the following notices
inter alia:—"For neglect to pay within 60 days *of the date
hereof* (the *italics* are my own) taxpayers will incur a fine
of 2*s*. in the *l.* on the tax. They may also be sued for the
amount," and "If you desire to appeal or object you must do so
within 30 days *from the giving of this notice* (the *italics*
again are mine) in the manner provided by regulations 27 and
30." The distinction will be noticed—the tax is said to be
due and payable on the date named, *i.e.*, 23rd October, 1896, or
in other words seven days before the plaintiff's lands were assessed,
while the time for appealing (which does not affect the time of
payment, see s. 46) runs from 30th October, the date of issue of
the notice. This is instructive, if only as shewing what was the
view taken by the commissioners at the time of preparing the
notices for the printers of the meaning of s. 47, *i.e.*, that it was
left to them on the happening of a certain event therein named,
"the completion of the assessment books," to fix a day on which
"such land tax," that is the land tax for the whole colony, was
to be due and payable. In no other way could they justify
sending notices, such as Exhibit H in this case and all others
assessed subsequently to 23rd October, 1896. If the commissioners' contention is correct that they could issue notices in
batches when assessed according to their own fancy or convenience,
but would be compelled to issue fresh *Gazette* notices under s. 47
for later cases, then I think that the expression I used during the
argument that the notice would be a trifling with the truth
correctly describes the position, the more especially if they relied
on such a paper as Exhibit L (as it was said they could) as conclusive evidence under s. 67 of all the contents of the document.
I go further, and say that on such a contention the plaintiff had
a distinct equity to come to the Court to have Exhibit H and L
altered to be in accordance with fact, or to have a fresh notice
issued. Mr. Lockyer, however, himself said that the date, 23rd
October, 1896, on the notice only indicated the prescribed date of
payment under the Act, and I am quite sure that neither he nor
his brother commissioners would ever have knowingly attempted
to work the Act in any way to the prejudice of an individual.
Indeed the fault, if any, has been the result of an earnest desire

1897.

COOPER
v.
COMMISSION-
ERS OF
TAXATION

C.J. Eq.

1897.
Cooper
v.
Commission-
ers of
Taxation

C.J Eq.

to treat every taxpayer fairly, without prejudice to the revenue.
The sole question is whether they have carried out the law as it
stands.

To resume the facts: The commissioners, on the 20th October,
1896, caused a notice to be issued in the *Gazette* as follows:—
"Sydney, 16th October, 1896.   Land and Income Tax Assessment
Act of 1895.   Day of payment of land tax.—Notice is hereby
given in pursuance of s. 47 of the Land and Income Tax Assessment Act of 1895, that the land tax for the year 1896, enforced
by the Land Tax Act of 1895, shall be due and payable at this
office on the 23rd October, 1896."   No further or other similar
Gazette notice has been published.   It is a peculiarity of these
Acts that the Act itself does not, as in England or in Victoria, fix
the due date of the tax.   In both of these countries there is a
provision made for delaying the first due date of payment in
certain cases, that is, in Victoria, until the publication in the
Gazette of the classification of any land which had not been
classified before the date mentioned in the Act, and in England
until the particular assessment had been signed.   After classification the Victorian Act works, so to speak, automatically, the
values being fixed by the Act.   Here, however, the date on which
the whole land tax is to be due and payable is left to the commissioners to fix "on completion of the assessment books," and
unless the assessment books were complete, within the meaning
of the Act, before the date of the *Gazette* notice, or at least before
the date fixed, that notice is wholly bad and of no effect, and no
land tax is due or payable up to the present time.

Sir *Julian Salomons* contended that this was immaterial, so far
as the charge on the land was concerned, that the tax, whatever
might afterwards be settled as to the amount by assessment,
became a charge immediately on the passing of the Act, and this
date he fixed as the necessary *terminus a quo*.   The Land Tax
Act provides that "from and after the 1st day of January, 1896,
there shall be annually assessed, levied, and paid, under the provisions of and subject to the exemptions and deductions enacted
in the Land and Income Tax Assessment Act of 1895, and in the
manner therein prescribed, a land tax of one penny in the *l.* of
the unimproved value of all lands as in the said Act specified."

That Act "declares and enacts" the rate referred to in s. 10 of the
other Act. The argument *ad rem* was as follows:—Mr. Cooper
is the owner of taxable land; by the Act his land stands taxed
at the rate of one penny in the *l.* of the unimproved value. The
amount payable is a matter of assessment; but the tax, though
it may not be assessed for years, is by virtue of s. 54 a charge and
a first charge on his land, and can only be got rid of by payment.
I would merely remark in passing, that if this argument is sound,
it affords the strongest possible argument in favour of the contention of the plaintiff (which I shall presently deal with) that
the tax, to be good at all, must be assessed during the year in
respect of which it is payable. If it is sound, then a man who
wants to sell his land, and is called on to remove the statutory
charge, cannot do so even by payment, because the commissioners
would not, until they had assessed the land, accept any sum in
full discharge. On the plaintiff's side it was contended that the
charge did not take effect until the tax was recoverable, that is
until it was payable, and that, if for any reason the commissioners
were not in a position to enforce the tax, no charge was created.

Before dealing with these opposite contentions, it would be
well to consider briefly the principles or rules applicable to the
construction of taxation or revenue Acts. In *Gilbertson* v.
Fergusson (1) (an income tax case) *Cotton*, L.J., at p. 572, says:
"I quite agree that we ought not to put a strained construction
upon the section in order to make liable to taxation that which
would not otherwise be liable; but I think it is now settled that
in construing the revenue Acts, as well as other Acts, we ought
to give a fair and reasonable construction, and not to lean in
favour of one side or other on the ground that it is a tax imposed
on the subject, and, therefore, ought not to be enforced unless it
comes clearly within the words. That is the rule which has been
laid down by the House of Lords in regard to Succession Duty
Acts, and I think it is the correct rule." The case referred to was
Partington v. *The Attorney General* (2), in which Lord *Cairns*
said, at p. 122: "As I understand the principle of all fiscal legislation it is this: If the person sought to be taxed comes within the

1897.

COOPER
v.
COMMISSION-
ERS OF
TAXATION

C.J. Eq.

(1) 7 Q.B.D. 562.   2) L.R. 4 H.L. 100.

1897.

COOPER
v.
COMMISSION-
ERS OF
TAXATION

C.J. Eq.

letter of the law, he must be taxed, however great the hardship may appear to the judicial mind to be. On the other hand, if the Crown seeking to recover the tax cannot bring the subject within the letter of the law, the subject is free, however apparently within the spirit of the law the case might otherwise appear to be." Again, in *Coltness Iron Company, Limited* v. *Black* (1), Lord *Blackburn*, at p. 330, says: " No tax can be imposed on the subject without words in an Act of Parliament clearly shewing an intention to lay a burden on him. But when an intention is sufficiently shewn, it is, I think, vain to speculate on what would be the fairest and most equitable mode of levying that tax. The object of those framing a taxing Act is to grant to Her Majesty a revenue. No doubt they would prefer, if it were possible, to raise that revenue equally from all, and, as that cannot be done, to raise it from those on whom the tax falls with as little trouble and annoyance, and as equally as can be contrived, and when any enactment for the purpose can bear two interpretations, it is reasonable to put that construction on them which will produce these effects. But the object is to grant a revenue at all events, even though a possible nearer approximation to equality may be sacrificed in order more easily and certainly to raise the revenue, and I think the only safe rule is to look at the words of the enactments and see what is the intention expressed by those words," and these remarks of Lord *Blackburn* are referred to with approval in the House of Lords in *Colquhoun* v. *Brooks* (2). But though the Courts will not put what is technically known as an equitable construction on such Acts, they will and must look for clear words imposing the burden, and in case of doubt put that construction which will be equitable and just—an inherent incident of all taxation—and not that which is inequitable or unjust; and if words construed in their technical sense would produce inequality, and construed in their popular sense would produce equality, you are to choose the latter, per Lord *Halsbury*, L.C., in *Commissioner for Income Tax* v. *Punch* (3), and they will in these, and in all other Acts, look at the Act as a whole in considering the meaning of any particular section. If, however,

(1) 6 App. Cas. 315.   (2) 14 A.C. 505.
(3) [1891] A.C. 548.

the burden is clearly imposed, the Courts will probably be astute, so far as mere machinery is concerned, to bring about the clear intention of raising revenue for Her Majesty.

The charging section here is sub-s. 54, and reads—" The land tax shall until payment be a first charge on the land taxed in priority," &c., and the interpretation clause, section 68, gives the meaning of the land tax unless the context otherwise requires as " the land tax imposed as such by any Act . . . as assessed under this Act." The tax, then, which is to be a charge, is not simply the tax " as imposed," but also " as assessed," and it is not a tax of one penny in the £ on the unimproved value of all lands, but is subject to exemptions and deductions which cannot be properly estimated until the final assessment. Until, therefore, the tax is assessed it is hard to see how there is anything definite to make a charge of. But to create a valid, living, enforceable tax, it must be also due and payable, and if this point is taken as the *terminus a quo* we then have all we expect to see in a charge complete. The tax as assessed fixes the amount which remains a charge from the time it is due until it is paid. That this is a proper construction, that it is just and right and free from the objections I stated before, is, I think, shewn by the very next sub-section, which provides for the courses given for enforcing the tax as against the land. " Whenever any land tax payable in respect of any land shall be unpaid for a space of two years," then, on giving certain notice, the power is given to the commissioners without any leave from the Court to let the land for a term of three years, or with the leave of the Court to sell the land. Clearly, then, the charge cannot be enforced until the tax is payable, and yet I am asked to read this section in such a way as to leave a cloud on the title, not only of the owner, but of persons who may have had a bona-fide mortgage charge or lien thereon for years previously, when there are no means open to such persons of getting it removed by payment or of the commissioners enforcing it. Read in the words " from the time it is due and payable," and all hardship and difficulties and injustice at once disappear. Then there is a tax which can either be sued for, in which case, of course, only the equity of redemption could be sold on a *fi. fa.*, or if it remains unpaid for two years the land

1897.

COOPER
v.
COMMISSION-
ERS OF
TAXATION

C.J. Eq.

1897.

COOPER
v.
COMMISSION-
ERS OF
TAXATION

C.J. Eq.

can be dealt with adversely to the encumbrancers after certain preliminaries.

For these reasons I am satisfied that the charge referred to in s. 54 does not come into operation until the tax is due and payable. In answer to a question from me, I understood Sir *Julian Salomons* to admit that a separate and new *Gazette* notice under s. 47 would be necessary to make any assessment due and payable which was not included in the batch of assessments complete at the time of the original *Gazette* notice, but whether he made any such admission or not the matter is for me to decide, and I have no doubt that if his theory of batches is correct there must be another *Gazette* notice to cover subsequent assessments, and inasmuch as clearly here the assessment was made on the 30th October, 1896, and there has been no subsequent notification, it would follow as a consequence on my previous view that in this case the tax is not yet due and payable, and that consequently no charge exists, and there is no debt to Her Majesty which can be sued for.

That alone would entitle the plaintiff to succeed in this suit. and entitle him to a temporary injunction at all events; but as the commissioners could put themselves right any day by a *Gazette* notice, it would not be proper for me to deal with the case on such ground, the more especially as it would appear to countenance the contention that the correct meaning of the words "completion of the assessment books" was as put forward by the defendants' counsel.

The next points, then, for consideration are the meaning of the words "assessment books" and "completion." As to the former, the following admission was made by the defendants: "We had at the time of the issue of the notices of assessment to the plaintiff (*i.e.*, 30th October, 1896) a very large quantity of sets of papers such as exhibit H, except as to the special notices affixed thereto, referring to all lands then assessed. Such sets were not bound together, but were kept distinct from other papers in the office, and so form what we call the assessment book or books under the Act, and beyond that we have no assessment book or books. There were at that time (apart from errors) thousands of persons who held lands liable to assessment with regard to some of which we had no returns, and with respect to all of which no

1897

COOPER
v.
COMMISSION-
ERS OF
TAXATION

C.J. Eq.

assessment had then been made." This was made in answer to Mr. *Pilcher's* demand for production of the assessment books, but subsequently exhibit L, which I have already described with some detail, was produced, so that the admission should more properly refer to exhibit L than exhibit H, which was the notice of assessment sent out. Subsequently also, on the evidence of Mr. Lockyer, the figures were approximately ascertained, which I had better here state again. The sets of papers referred to numbered 21,400. They had returns then in from 15,800 not then assessed, who have since been assessed as taxpayers. These figures are exclusive of cases in which no return has been made, which in a similar proportion of exemptions would leave over 4,100 liable to taxation, or, in other words, only a little over one-half of the taxpayers were assessed and called on to pay the tax when the *Gazette* notice was issued on the 20th October, 1896. These figures rather go to the question of completion, but it seemed more convenient to insert them here in explanation of the admission.

Coming then to what is meant by the word " book," I think that any person reading the Act with an ordinary knowledge of the English language, and not looking for any necessity to give words a meaning with special reference to the construction of a portion of the Act, could not fail to come to the conclusion that what was intended by the draughtsman was a book or books in the ordinary acceptation of the word; and it is a curious thing that the draughtsman goes out of his way in s. 34 to coin the very same words "assessment book" when he is referring to what is called in the Municipalities Act a "rate book." That would seem to shew that what was intended was a book of a similar nature to such rate book, *i.e.*, a book or books containing entries with reference to all taxpayers, which any taxpayer has a right to inspect, see s. 40 (in spite of regulation 35, sub-regulation 2, which is clearly *ultra vires*), but one would expect something of even a more lasting and permanent nature than the municipal rate book, because it is to be open to a vastly larger number of persons, and it is to stand as of record and the basis of taxation

1897.

COOPER
v.
COMMISSION-
ERS OF
TAXATION

C.J. Eq.

for five years: see s. 31. Not only so, but looking at an Act in *pari materia* such as the English Act of 1842, we have a guide as to the character of the book intended, and it was clearly contemplated that there would be, as in England, books for separate districts: see s. 44, sub-s. (VII.), of our Act.

If Sir *Julian Salomons* is correct that each set of papers is one of the books contemplated, what is meant by that sub-section: "The assessment book so altered or corrected shall be the assessment book for the district to which it relates?" How could the alteration of the plaintiff's assessment paper make it a book for a district of the whole colony? By s. 32, in the passage which occurs between sub-ss. (III.) and (IV.), the words "assessment book" and "assessment," which means such a paper as exhibit L, are placed in contradistinction, and the same may be said of the proviso to s. 31, at the commencement thereof. Moreover, all through the Act provisions are made as to alterations, additions, substitutions, and so on being made in or on the "books," which could not by any reasonable intendment be done in or on such papers as exhibit L. And this will equally apply to s. 67, which makes an "extract" from the book evidence. I am by no means prepared to say that the books should be bound. On the contrary, I should think it would be quite sufficient if they were capable of being bound, provided that when bound they would constitute the "book" required by the Act. No doubt it appears at first sight somewhat extraordinary that the practical validity, that is, the power to get in a tax solemnly imposed by the Legislature, should depend upon the question of compilation of assessment books, and it was suggested that the preparation of such books was directory, and not mandatory, so that this case would fall within *R.* v. *Ingall* (1), and if we were dealing only with s. 31, and with the question whether, if the tax were due and payable on a certain day under the Act, any taxpayer could resist payment on the ground that the preparation of such books was a condition precedent, I should be strongly inclined to that view, but here (unfortunately, perhaps) the Legislature has departed from the English system, which fixes a due date in the Act, and provides for the books being made up afterwards; it has been distinctly provided here that the

(1) 2 Q.B.D. 199.

tax is not to be due till the books are complete, so that the
Courts are bound to see that the Act has been complied with in
this behalf.

I cannot myself see how papers such as I have referred to can
be considered as pages of such a book as is contemplated, but,
assuming that they may be so treated, so that s. 47 may be read,
"On completion of the materials for making up the assessment
books," there remains the word "completion" to be dealt with.
By the Taxation Act the tax is to be annually assessed, levied,
and paid, which, however you may restrict the words, must at
least mean that the tax imposed, *i.e.*, on all landowners, is required
for the service of the year; and we know that the Treasurer
bases his estimate of revenue upon the right to receive a certain
sum from a particular tax. It is quite probable that the Legislature, which is concerned in making the incidence of taxation as
equal and just as possible, foresaw the difficulties that might arise
and have arisen with reference to this particular tax—viz., that
the commissioners would not be in a position to enforce the tax
against more than half the taxpayers for, at all events, some considerable time; it is possible they intended to prevent the chance
of a section only of the taxable community being called on to pay
the tax, and had the evil day postponed for years, or for ever,
by insisting upon provision being made that there should be one
date in each year for all, and that no one should be called upon
to put his hands in his pocket until he could be assured by the
commissioners, or, if he so desired, ascertain for himself by inspection, that the commissioners were in a position to enforce the tax
against all the lands and against all and sundry, however great
delay might be caused in ascertaining who were the proper
persons to sue in respect of any particular portion. The word
"completion" must, of course, have a liberal construction. It
cannot mean "perfected," and the words "errors and omissions
excepted" must, of course, be added, and it may be that the actual
definition of the word might depend upon special facts and
circumstances; but it passes my comprehension how anyone could
say that the assessment of the taxable lands of the colony was
complete when, as a matter of fact, barely more than a half were

1897.

COOPER
v.
COMMISSION-
ERS OF
TAXATION

C.J. Eq.

B 2

1897.

COOPER
v.
COMMISSION-
ERS OF
TAXATION

C.J. Eq.

assessed, and only a proportion of seven to five of those for which returns had been made.

In support of the view that s. 47 contemplated more than one *Gazette* notice for the land tax in each year of taxation, the words "from time to time" were strongly relied on. To my mind there is no weaker argument than that which depends upon redundant words in an Act of Parliament, and this particular phrase is a very common offender. It is rendered quite unnecessary by our own Acts Shortening Acts, but so is the use of the plural with reference to the word "day," which occurs in the same section. If an Act of Parliament were the finished work of an accomplished equity draughtsman or conveyancer, there might be something in such arguments; but an Act of Parliament passes through many hands, and those who would rather have the words in, though they may be unnecessary, are legion. Bearing in mind that the section applies to two different annual taxes under Acts of a permanent character, it is quite clear that what was intended to be made clear by the words in question, was that the day or days were not to be fixed once for every year, but that days were to be fixed from time to time in every year as the due dates with respect to those years, and, in fact, the words "in every year" immediately follow the words "from time to time."

There remains, then, only the argument *ab inconvenienti* or *impossibilitate*, and for this purpose I admitted the evidence of Mr. Lockyer and Mr. Sievers on this point contrary to my own judgment, but in order that the facts in support of such argument might be before any Court considering the case. The argument appears to me to be of no avail. If, by the use of very plain words, the Legislature have imposed a condition which in working is fatal to the tax, so much the better for that class of taxpayer, as it would have been so much the worse if the use of certain words had included a man unjustly. It is not a question of machinery in any sense, as I have already pointed out. It is a condition precedent to the tax being due, and no one ever heard of a condition precedent being got rid of because it was found impossible of performance through no fault of the person to be charged. It is, however, more than doubtful whether the performance was impossible, and whether the so-called impossi-

bilities are not the result of, to some extent at all events, the
action of the commissioners and not of the Act. I have already
pointed out that the commissioners had in their knowledge all
the lands of the colony and their value as assessed by valuators,
and for nine-tenths of these they had received returns. All these
they could have assessed at once, leaving alterations and correc-
tions to be dealt with afterwards, while as for the remaining one-
tenth they could either have appointed strangers to make returns
and accepted or altered their valuations, or they could have assessed
them without any return at all, and if they were not able to
ascertain any owner's name they could simply enter "owner" if
that were necessary for the completion of the books. No doubt
the books would have been very imperfect, but they would have
been complete, for every piece of taxable land in the colony
would have been assessed, and where no deductions were claimed
none would have been considered beyond the 240l. limit. If one
looks at sub-section (VIII.) of section 31, all that is provided is that
"the assessment books in respect of land tax shall contain
particulars (arranged in the prescribed manner) of all lands
liable to land tax." That sounds simple enough, but what the
commissioners did was to call into existence regulation 35 (which
can be got rid of any day), and prescribes a manner which raises
all sorts of difficulties. It is very probable that the course
adopted by the commissioners was on the whole kind and humane,
and it may be that they have by their conduct cut the Gordian
knot of a legal impossibility, but this is a process unknown to
the law, which requires knots to be untied or left alone. The
commissioners have in my opinion transgressed the law in issuing
the *Gazette* notice of the 20th October, 1896, in issuing the
notice of assessment in this case, and especially so with the date
of the 23rd October, 1896, thereon, and in claiming that they
have any rights at all (up to the present time at all events)
against the plaintiff.

There remains the question as to whether the defect is curable.
I do not say practically, but legally, and that depends upon
whether a tax for 1896 can be assessed and levied after the
expiration of that year. Mr. *Pilcher* contended that it could
not be done, basing his argument on the ground that the Taxing

1897.

COOPER
v.
COMMISSION-
ERS OF
TAXATION

C.J. Eq.

1897.

COOPER
v.
COMMISSION-
ERS OF
TAXATION

C.J. Eq.

Act itself, in using the word " annually," meant by that " in and
during each year," coupled with the fact that the tax was
manifestly one for the services of the year, and supporting the
position by the injustice of the incidence or possible incidence of
the tax if his contention was not correct ; and he pressed the
latter consideration the more strongly, as the Act affected others
than landowners, that is to say prior bona-fide encumbrancers.
Thus, as he said, a tax might be assessed for the first time in 1900,
and be levied then for the preceding five years, involving an amount
which the landowner might not be able to pay, and which might
sweep away the whole value of the security, whereas the owner
might and would have provided for annual payments. He also
suggested the possible case of a landlord being unable in such a
case to recover his statutory rights from a tenant. Such
arguments cannot, of course, prevail against clear words, but they
must be of great weight where the language is doubtful, and they
have caused me much fluctuation of mind ; nor can I say that I
am at the present time wholly free from doubt.

In the first place it seems to me that " annual " or " annually"
may mean " for the year " as well as " in the year," and that the
former is the fair construction in an Act of a permanent character
providing for a yearly tax.   Otherwise one would have expected
to find the words " in each and every year," especially as these
very words occur in the Machinery Act. Not only so, but in
s. 31, sub-s. (I.), it would seem as if a distinction were especially
drawn between the first and subsequent preparation of assessment
books of the land tax, though the language with reference to the
income tax in the same section might bear a different interpretation, and the distinction may well have been drawn with a view
to the great difficulties likely to occur in the initiation of a land
tax, which would have no application to an income tax. Thus
we find it said in s. 31, sub-s. (I.) (omitting unnecessary words):
" The commissioners shall ' as soon as may be ' cause separate
assessment books to be prepared in respect of land tax and
income tax." So far the two taxes are in the same class, but the
section proceeds: " And like assessment books shall thereafter
be prepared in respect of land tax ' in every fifth year ' after the
year 1895, and in respect of income tax in each and every

successive year after such last-mentioned year." I think one
would naturally gather that latitude was intended to be allowed
with reference to land tax certainly, and possibly also with
reference to income tax, as to the first assessment, though the
last few words create a difficulty as to income tax, as the next
successive year to 1895 is 1896; but with that I am not concerned.
It is, however, clear that the second assessment of land must be
in 1900, and could not be made in 1901 for the subsequent quin-
quennium, but that the income tax must be assessed in each and
every year, and if not so assessed cannot be recovered. In Sir
Robert Peel's Act of 1842, Schedule E to s. 146 provides that
"the said duties shall be annually charged," and yet in s. 176 I
find "every assessment to be made under this Act within the
year appointed for making the same shall be deemed to be for
the current year, and shall be in force for such year, and every
assessment made after the expiration of any year in which the
same ought to have been made shall be deemed to be for the
whole of the year current when such assessment ought to have
been made." This section was not referred to in argument, and
it may be that section is to be read as impliedly giving a power
to assess in a subsequent year which would not otherwise have
existed, but it shews, at all events, that the word "annually" in
the charge can stand with a power of subsequent assessment;
and it shews, further, that, so far as we are dealing with owners
alone as distinct from encumbrancers, the Legislature did not
think it unjust to allow an assessment after the year for which
the tax was required. It is of course only fair to admit that,
though the Act of 1842 dealt with assessment of land, it is only
for the purpose of income tax, and that the rights of innocent
third parties were not thereby affected. Still, on the whole, I
feel on safer ground in holding that, under the words of s. 31,
sub-s. (I.), before referred to, a first assessment of land for the
purpose of making up the assessment book would not be necessarily bad because made after the expiration of the year for
which the tax was assessed, and that consequently it is legally
possible that the defect in this case may be cured with reference
to the tax for 1896, with which alone I am concerned.

1897.

COOPER
v.
COMMISSION-
ERS OF
TAXATION

C.J. Eq.

1897.

COOPER
v.
COMMISSION-
ERS OF
TAXATION

C.J. Eq.

The plaintiff also relied as a ground for relief on the fact of the delay in the appointment of a Court of Review, and as success on that point would entitle him to wider relief than I am inclined to give I must deal with the contention. The commissioners have nothing to do with the appointment of a Court of Review, the power in that behalf being by s. 9 vested in the Governor-in-Council. The notice of assessment was, as before stated, issued to the plaintiff's agent on 30th October, and received by him on the 31st, and the plaintiff had, therefore, under sub-s. (I.) of s. 44, 30 days from the latter date within which he could appeal to the Court appointed—that is to say, he would have had to have lodged his appeal under Regulation 30 with the Registrar of such Court on or before the 30th November, 1896, and up to the time of the filing the statement of claim no such Court or Registrar was in existence. This Court was, however, duly appointed on 18th November, 1896, and, as a matter of fact, the plaintiff entered his appeal on the 27th November following, so that really the delay cannot amount to more than a matter of prejudice, which could be covered by damages and which could not be an answer to a proper assessment. Apart, too, from the direct appeal to the Court of Review, a process was provided by Regulations 27 and 28, which were dated 12th February, 1896, for an appeal by way of objection lodged with the commissioners in the first instance, which was to be treated as a notice of appeal, and to be forwarded by the commissioners to the Court of Review if no agreement thereon was come to. Of course, if no Court of Appeal had been provided within the 30 days, and thereby the right of appeal was lost, the matter might have been different, but it is idle to discuss such a question now.

As to the question of non-publication of the tables of calculation of values referred to in s. 13, that omission is clearly only a matter of prejudice, which would be covered by damages.

The conclusions I have come to are:—1. That there are no assessment books in existence as contemplated by the Act. 2. That in any case such books are not complete within the meaning of ss. 42 and 47 of the Act. 3. That the completion of such books is a condition precedent to the power of the commissioners to—(a) fix and notify the due date of the tax in the *Gazette*; (b)

issue notices of assessment; and consequently—4. That the act
of the commissioners in notifying the land tax as due on the 23rd
October, 1896, and in issuing the notice to the plaintiff under s.
42, is in both cases illegal. 5. That the provisions of s. 47 not
having been complied with, no land tax is as yet due and payable.
6. That there is, therefore, no charge on the plaintiff's land
in respect of the land tax for 1896, and that there is no debt due
from him to Her Majesty in respect thereof which he can be
called on to pay.   The plaintiff, therefore, is entitled to a declaration that there is no existing charge on his lands in respect of
the land tax for the year 1896, and that the notice of assessment
mentioned in the pleadings is wholly void and inoperative, and
that no such land tax as assessed is due and payable by him, and
that the defendants should be restrained from taking any proceedings to sue for or raise the amount stated in the said notice
of assessment, or of any other amount in respect of the land tax
for the year 1896, and from letting, selling, or otherwise prejudicially dealing with the plaintiff's land in question in this suit
until the said land tax shall have become due and payable as provided for in the Acts 59 Vic. Nos. 15 and 16, and the defendants
must pay the costs of this suit; and I decree accordingly.

Solicitors for the plaintiff: *Norton & Co.*

Solicitor for the defendants: *Crown Solicitor.*

1897.

COOPER
v.
COMMISSION-
ERS OF
TAXATION

C.J. Eq.

1897.   PARSONS AND OTHERS *v.* GILLESPIE AND OTHERS.

November 18.   *Trade name—Term of ordinary description—Name denoting the goods of a par-*
December 15.   *ticular manufacturer—Conclusiveness of the trade mark—Trade Marks Act of*
                 1865 (28 Vic. No. 9), s. 7—Suit instituted to try the right of any person to have
   J. C.*   *trade mark registered.*

A trader is entitled to take appropriate words of ordinary description to indicate
an article which he sells and makes, although the words form part of the trade
mark of a rival trader, provided his action is not calculated to pass off his manufacture as that of his rival, and is not proved in point of fact to have done so.

P. was the registered owner of a trade mark which consisted in part of the
words "Flaked Oatmeal," and was used by him for a preparation of oats. G.
five years afterwards placed a preparation of oats on the market under the name
of "G.'s Flaked Oatmeal," thereby accurately describing his preparation. P.
sought to restrain the user by G. of the words "Flaked Oatmeal," alleging that
the words were his trade mark, and also a trade name designating to the trade
and public his own commodity, and that G.'s preparation was put on the market
in order to get the benefit of P.'s trade, or was at all events calculated to do so.
G. denied that the words were P.'s trade mark, or that they denoted exclusively
P.'s preparation, and claimed that they were merely descriptive of his own preparation.

Held (overruling OWEN, C.J. in Eq.), that in a suit so constituted the trade
mark was conclusive of P.'s right thereto.

Held, also (affirming OWEN, C.J. in Eq.), that though the words formed part of
P.'s trade mark, G. was entitled to use the words as accurately descriptive of his
preparation, provided he did so bonâ fide, and sufficiently distinguished his use
of the words from P.'s user. *Reddaway* v. *Banham* (1) followed and applied.

THIS was an appeal to the Privy Council direct from the
decision of *Owen*, C.J. in Eq., reported in 17 N.S.W.R. Eq. 227 ;
in his Honour's judgment the facts will be found stated in detail.
They are also summarised in the decision of the Privy Council.
The Chief Judge in Equity held that in substance the suit was
instituted to try the plaintiff's right to have had his trade mark
registered, and that, therefore, the certificate of the trade mark
was not conclusive evidence of the plaintiff's right to the trade
mark.   The Privy Council, however, treated the certificate as
conclusive in the suit, holding that upon the pleadings the suit
was not framed to try the plaintiff's right.

   * Present : Lord WATSON, Lord HOBHOUSE, Lord DAVEY, Sir RICHARD COUCH.

                         (1) [1896] A.C. 199.

The statement of claim alleged that whereas prior to 1890 porridge made from oats in this colony was only made from oatmeal, about that year a new preparation was invented for the purpose, the oats being rolled or crushed by various processes instead of being ground. The plaintiffs, having discovered one of these processes, invented the fancy term or designation "Flaked Oatmeal" for their commodity which was placed on the market in March, 1890. On the 27th June, 1891, the plaintiffs procured the trade-mark certificate, which is described in the judgment of the Privy Council. The plaintiffs further charged that the fancy term "Flaked Oatmeal" was not only the plaintiffs' trade mark, but had also become a trade name exclusively denoting their commodity, so that persons ordering "Flaked Oatmeal" intended and expected to get the plaintiffs' commodity. The pleadings set out some correspondence which took place in 1895 between the parties and the Registrar-General with reference to an application by the defendants for the registration of a design bearing the words "Gillespie's Flaked Oatmeal"; this application was refused by the Registrar.

The statement of claim further alleged that on the 28th April, 1896, the plaintiffs ascertained that the defendants had placed on the market a preparation bearing the words "Flaked Oatmeal." There was then set out some correspondence between the parties in 1896, the plaintiffs demanding that the defendants should discontinue doing so, and the defendants claiming the right to do so on the ground that the words were merely descriptive, and that the plaintiffs' trade mark had been wrongly registered, and would not be upheld in a Court of Equity. The plaintiffs charged and it was the fact that the said term "Flaked Oatmeal" as applied to any preparation of oats for porridge was absolutely unknown prior to the plaintiffs using the same to designate their preparation, and prior to the plaintiffs' use of the said term the same would have conveyed no meaning to any agricultural chemist, miller or dealer in food products. The statement of claim concluded with an allegation of damage. The prayers of the statement of claim were :—(1) For an injunction restraining the defendants from applying to any preparation not being of the plaintiffs' manufacture the term "Flaked Oatmeal,"

1897.

PARSONS
v.
GILLESPIE.

or from selling as "Flaked Oatmeal" any preparation not being of the plaintiffs' manufacture ; (2) an account of profits ; (3) or in the alternative an account of damages.

The statement of defence, so far as it is material to be stated, denied that "Flaked Oatmeal" was the trade mark of the plaintiffs, or a fancy term invented by the plaintiffs, and submitted that the word "Flaked" was an ordinary adjective descriptive of the commodity sold ; it denied that persons ordering "Flaked Oatmeal" expected to get the plaintiffs' commodity ; the defendants denied having adopted the name to secure the benefit of the plaintiffs' trade, or that their preparation was intended or calculated to deceive the public ; they denied having attempted to pass off their goods as the plaintiffs' ; they submitted that the term "Flaked" as applied to oatmeal was an ordinary descriptive adjective not capable of being registered as a fancy term or designation, and that the expression "Flaked Oatmeal" was, previously to the registration of the plaintiffs' trade mark, *publici juris* ; and, finally, after describing their process, they submitted that the words "Flaked Oatmeal" were truly descriptive of their commodity.

The plaintiffs thereupon joined issue with the defendants.

Fletcher Moulton, Q.C., and *Sebastian*, appeared for the plaintiffs.

C. E. E. Jenkins, *Walter* and *Easton*, appeared for the defendants.

December 15.　　On the 15th December, 1897, the judgment of their Lordships was delivered by

LORD HOBHOUSE.　The question raised in this suit is whether a trade mark or a trade name which the plaintiffs (now appellants) claim as their own, has been wrongly used by the defendants who are respondents in this appeal.　It appears that until within the last few years the only method used in this colony of preparing oats for making porridge was by grinding them into fine meal or powder ; but that shortly before the year 1890 new processes were introduced by which the oats were not ground into powder but were crushed or flattened between rollers.　In the month of

1897.

PARSONS
v.
GILLESPIE.

Lord
Hobhouse.

March, 1890, the plaintiffs perfected one of these processes and called the product "flaked oatmeal." Exhibit A is a specimen of this product. In the month of June, 1890, the plaintiffs obtained the registration of a trade mark which in the Registrar's certificate is thus described :—

"A lion rampant against a sheaf of corn, the background being filled with a landscape and a pair of balance scales; below the lion is a scroll upon which are the Latin words '*Justus Esto Et Non Metue.*' The trade-mark is surrounded with a double line in the form of a circle. Above the circle are tho words 'Use Parsons,'' and below the circle are the words 'Finest Flaked Oatmeal.'"

That trade-mark has ever since been used by the plaintiffs, and the commodity so marked has met with a large sale.

From 1890 to 1896 several preparations of crushed or flattened oats more or less resembling that of the plaintiffs were put upon the market. Most of them were called "rolled oats" either simply or with some addition indicative of the maker. One was called "Oat Flakes," one "Wafer Oatmeal." None was called by the precise name of "Flaked Oatmeal."

In the year 1894 the defendants produced a preparation of rolled or crushed oats which they called "Rolled Oatmeal." Exhibit C is a specimen of it. This process was not satisfactory to them, and very soon they adopted another by which the oats were first ground small and then the meal so obtained was steamed and passed through rollers to be flattened or flaked. Exhibits B and L are specimens of this process. The right of the defendants to use this or any other process as against the plaintiffs is not questioned, and the nature of the process is only important in its bearing on their use of the name "Flaked Oatmeal," which is questioned.

In December, 1894, the defendants applied to register a trademark for their then manufacture. The device they chose is something entirely different from that of the plaintiffs; but they inscribed it with the words "Gillespie's Flaked Oatmeal"; the two latter words standing by themselves below the device. The plaintiffs raised objection to this, and the Registrar-General informed the defendants that they could not use the term

"Flaked Oatmeal" as a prominent feature in their trade-mark, and that the plaintiffs by their registration in 1890 had acquired the right to use those words. The defendants did not press for registration any further, but they put their goods on the market labelled with the same device and inscription or some slight variation of it.

In May, 1896, the plaintiffs instituted this suit against the defendants for an injunction, and an account of profits, and damages. They rested their case not on the possession of the trade-mark but on the right to the exclusive use of the term "Flaked Oatmeal." They prayed as follows :—

"That the defendants, their servants, and agents may be restrained by the order and injunction of this Court from applying to any preparation not being of the plaintiffs' manufacture the term 'Flaked Oatmeal' or from selling as 'Flaked Oatmeal' any preparation not being of the plaintiffs' manufacture."

An interlocutory injunction was granted in those terms; but at the hearing before *The Chief Judge in Equity* the Court dismissed the suit with costs, and directed an inquiry as to the damages sustained by the defendants by reason of the injunction. That is the decree from which this appeal is brought.

There is nothing in the decree to prejudice the plaintiffs' right to their trade-mark. Neither in their statements nor in their prayer do the plaintiffs rest their case on the trade-mark, and the mere dismissal of their suit does not deny their right. But in his judgment the learned Judge goes beyond the dismissal of the suit. He says that the suit is instituted to try the right of the plaintiffs to the trade-mark. And he expresses an opinion that the words "Flaked Oatmeal" ought not to have formed part of that mark. The appellants point out that the register is conclusive until altered in the way prescribed by statute—*i.e.*, by a suit framed for the purpose. Their Lordships are not in a position to know what may have taken place in Court to give to the litigation a character which the pleadings do not give to it. They confine themselves to the decree appealed from, and they express no opinion on the question whether the plaintiffs may or may not use the term "Flaked Oatmeal" as part of their trade-mark in conjunction with a number of other matters.

With these remarks their Lordships pass by the subject of trade-mark. The plaintiffs have no case, indeed they do not put forward a case, for complaint against the defendants on the score of the trade-mark unless by virtue of the registration they have acquired an exclusive right to that portion of it which consists of the term " Flaked Oatmeal." The defendants' trade-mark bears no resemblance to that of the plaintiffs as a whole. The question whether the defendants can use the term " Flaked Oatmeal" does not depend upon the trade-mark, but is part of the wider question whether the plaintiffs have by user identified the term with their goods so intimately that the use of it by another person has the effect of passing off his goods as the goods of the plaintiffs. That is the substantial ground on which the case of the plaintiffs has been argued at this bar.

1897.

PARSONS
v.
GILLESPIE.

Lord
Hobhouse.

It will be convenient here to state the principles of law by which the contention of the plaintiffs must be tested ; and that cannot be done better than was done by the learned Judge below in quoting the language used by Lord *Herschell* in *Reddaway* v. *Banham* (1). Lord *Herschell* there said :—

" The name of a person or words forming part of the common stock of language may become so far associated with the goods of a particular maker that it is capable of proof that the use of them by themselves without explanation or qualification by another manufacturer would deceive the purchaser into the belief that he was getting the goods of A. when he was really getting the goods of B. In a case of this description the mere ' proof by the plaintiff that the defendant was using a name, word or device which he had adopted to distinguish his goods would not entitle him to any relief.' He could only obtain it by proving further that the defendant was using it under such circumstances and in such manner as to put off his goods as the goods of the plaintiff."

The plaintiffs then must shew either that the term " Flaked Oatmeal " is not part of the common stock of language in the sense that it is not a term of description but is of an arbitrary or fanciful nature invented by the plaintiffs which the inventors may claim to have appropriated ; or they must shew that the

(1) [1896] A.C. 199.

term, being originally a description of the article itself, has come in practice to denote goods made by the plaintiffs. To both these points the plaintiffs have carefully addressed themselves. They maintain that the expression "Flaked Oatmeal" does not properly describe their own goods or those of the defendants, but is an artificial expression fit for appropriation by anyone who has hit upon it.

Now nobody can look at exhibit A without seeing that the word "Flaked" is a correct description. The oats have been only partially reduced to powder, and are presented in small flattened morsels like flakes of snow. The term is one in common use for food grains or other vegetable substances so treated by rolling or crushing; such as "flaked rice," "flaked barley," "flaked tapioca," "flaked cocoa," and so forth. But then it is said that the article is not "meal" because it is not ground to powder. Whether the word "meal" would by etymology or in the very strictest use of language be applicable to that which has passed through the mill but is only partially reduced to powder, is a point as to which their Lordships think that no nice enquiry need be made. It is a natural and obvious term to use for oats so treated; one which everybody would accept at once as appropriate enough; and probably everybody who breakfasted off porridge made from such a material would think and say that he was eating oatmeal porridge.

Then it is contended that the product of the defendants is not oatmeal; and that their adoption of an inappropriate name shews an intention of trading on the reputation acquired by the plaintiffs. It seems to their Lordships that the name as applied to the defendants' product is strictly appropriate; for they do reduce the oats to powder, which is afterwards steamed, rolled, and so flaked. The plaintiffs have been reduced to contend on this point that because the defendants take away some five per cent. of the finest powder the rest is not oatmeal; and, further, that to roll or flake oatmeal is impossible. To support these two contentions they brought several witnesses in the Court below; but the Court rightly gave no weight to the evidence, which has been little insisted on here.

1897.

PARSONS
v.
GILLESPIE.

Lord
Hobhouse.

Then has there been any such secondary use of the term as to identify it with the plaintiffs' manufacture ?   To prove that there has been, the plaintiffs call a number of grocers, who say that when customers asked for "Flaked Oatmeal" they supplied the plaintiffs' goods.   That was a matter of course during the five or six years for which nobody except the plaintiffs purported to sell goods under that name.   One witness, a miller, says in terms that between 1892 and the beginning of 1896 the words "Flaked Oatmeal" had got to mean the plaintiffs' manufacture.   That seems to their Lordships somewhat slender evidence to prove such a general association of the name of the product with the producer as to entitle the plaintiffs to say that the use of the name by another is an encroachment on their rights.

But supposing the evidence sufficient on this point, it falls far short of shewing that the proceedings of the defendants are such as to cause confusion between their goods and those of the plaintiffs.   There is no evidence that any buyer has got the defendants' goods when he desired to have those of the plaintiffs' ; nor that any seller has made confusion between the two.   As for external resemblance of the packages or labels, it has been shewn before with reference to the trade-mark that there is nothing of the kind except in the use of the two disputed words.   In fact the defendants could hardly have done more to shew that the articles came from different makers.

The result is that in their Lordships' judgment the defendants have done no more than they had a right to do in taking appropriate words of ordinary description to indicate the article which they make and sell, and that their action is not calculated to pass off their manufacture as that of the plaintiffs, and is not proved in point of fact to have done so.   Their Lordships will humbly advise Her Majesty that this appeal should be dismissed.   The appellants must pay the costs.

Solicitors for the appellants : *Walker, Martineau & Co.*, agents for *A. DeLissa.*

Solicitors for the respondents : *Snow, Snow & Fox*, agents for *Sly & Russell.*

CURTIS v. ALLIBAND.

1898.

Will—Construction—Annuities—Whether payable from the testator's death.

March 4, 10.

An annuity given out of residue is payable from the testator's death; *dictum* to the contrary in *Storer* v. *Prestage* (1) held overruled.

A.H. Simpson J.

THIS was a friendly suit for the construction of a will. Among other questions decided was the point whether all the annuities given by the will were payable from the testator's death. Several annuities were given both by will and codicil out of residue; the annuities given by the codicil were expressly directed to be paid from the testator's death; the residue after providing for the annuities was devoted to various charitable purposes.

Street, for the annuitants under the will, contended that there was nothing in the will to cut down the ordinary rule that annuities are payable from the testator's death. The *dictum* in *Storer* v. *Prestage* (1) that a gift of annuities out of residue postpones the payment for a year is inconsistent with *Leach*, V.C.'s, own decision in *Houghton* v. *Franklin* (2). The express direction in the codicil is not the expression of a contrary intention with respect to the annuities in the will: *Williams* v. *Wilson* (3).

Kelynack, for the annuitants under the codicil, contended that the special direction as to the payment of those annuities shewed that the testator did not mean the annuities under the will to be paid concurrently with them: *Irvin* v. *Ironmonger* (4).

L. Owen, for the Attorney-General representing the charities, followed in the same interest. The *dictum* in *Storer* v. *Prestage* (1) is cited without remark in the last edition of *Williams on Executors* (5), but acting for the Attorney-General, I conceive it to be my duty to point out that the *dictum* appears to be based

(1) 3 Madd. 167.   (3) 5 N.R. 267.
(2) 1 S. & S. 390.   (4) 2 R. & M. 531.
                    (5) 9th Edit. 1242.

on the *Vice-Chancellor's* own decision in *Stott* v. *Hollingworth* 1898.
(1) in the same volume, which has since been overruled: *Anger-*   Curtis
stein v. *Martin* (2); *Macpherson* v. *Macpherson* (3).   v.
                                                                      Alliband.

The express direction in the codicil is an indication of the
testator's intention sufficient to displace the rule; the point was *A.H. Simpson J.*
not argued in *Williams* v. *Wilson* (4).

Lingen, for the plaintiffs, trustees, did not argue the point.

A. H. SIMPSON, J.   I think that the annuities are in all cases
payable from the testator's death; that is the usual and well
settled rule in the absence of any indication of a contrary intention.

It is contended that two such indications are to be found in
the present will; first, from the fact that the testator in some
instances expressly directs that the annuities are to commence
from his death.   But that does not appear to me to afford
any argument against the other annuities commencing from
the same period; it is merely expressing in clear language
what the law implies in the other cases.   The second indication, which at first I thought more open to argument, is found
in the direction that the annuities are payable out of residue,
and it is suggested, therefore, that they are not payable
until the end of the first year, when the residue is ascertained.
This contention is based upon a *dictum* of Sir *John Leach*, V.C.,
in *Storer* v. *Prestage* (5).   But it is only a *dictum,* as there were
directions in that case shewing that the first payment was to be
made on the first quarter day after the testator's death, and the
dictum itself, as Mr. *Owen* candidly admitted, was based upon a
view of the position of the tenant for life of residue, which
has since been overruled.

Solicitors: *Norton & Co.; Langley; Crown Solicitor.*

(1) 1 Madd. 161.   (3) 16 Jur. 847.
(2) T. & R. 241.   (4) 5 N.R. 267.
            (5) 3 Madd. 167.

In re THE BERRIMA DISTRICT FARM AND DAIRY CO., Limited.

1898.

March 8.

A.H. Simpson J.

Company—Companies Act, 1874 (37 *Vic. No.* 19), *ss.* 33, 57—*Paid-up shares—Rectification of register—Shares for which the memorandum of association has been subscribed—Practice.*

A company went into liquidation for the purpose of transferring its business to a new company formed for the purpose. Immediately after the formation of the new company, a contract was entered into between the new company and the liquidator of the old company as trustee for the members of the old company, in accordance with which paid-up shares in the new company were allotted to shareholders in the old company. The contract, however, was not registered.

Upon motion to rectify the register of the new company by striking out the names of all the allottees of shares allotted to the members of the old company, and for a re-allotment of shares after the due registration of the contract—*Held*, that no order could be made in respect of the shares for which the memorandum had been subscribed.

THE Berrima District Farm and Dairy Company, Limited, was formed for the purpose of taking over the business of a former company. Immediately after the incorporation of the new company, a contract was entered into between the new company and the liquidator of the old company, as trustee for the members of the old company, which, however, was never registered; partially paid-up shares in the new company, however, were allotted to the members of the old company in accordance with the terms of the contract.

The shareholders, to whom such allotment was made, were not aware, at the time of receiving their shares, that the contract had not been registered, but were under the impression that all necessary formalities had been complied with.

Upon discovery of the omission to register the contract, these proceedings were immediately taken to rectify the register. Certain of the allottees had signed the memorandum of association of the new company for one share each.

Cullen, for the company, in support of the motion : I ask that all the shares allotted to members of the old company be cancelled, including those for which the memorandum was signed.

1898.

In re.
BERRIMA
DISTRICT
FARM AND
DAIRY CO.,
LTD.

[A. H. SIMPSON, J. I have upon two occasions refused to interfere with shares signed for in the memorandum.]

The memorandum states that the object of the new company is to take over the business of the old company on certain terms, and refers to the contract intended to be entered into ; one of its expressed objects is to carry out that contract.

A. H. SIMPSON, J. I do not think the clause in the memorandum of association referred to makes any difference. A contract made with a trustee for a proposed company, or with the proposed company itself before its actual creation, is of no effect as against the company until it has adopted such contract ; and that it can only do after the memorandum has been registered.

But the registration of the memorandum *ipso facto* imposes a statutory obligation on the signatories to pay in cash for the shares for which they sign—*Dalton Time Lock* v. *Dalton* (1)—as the shares are then issued before a contract otherwise determining the payment has been registered.

I have no power, therefore, to cancel the issue of the shares in respect of which the memorandum is signed.

With this exception I am willing to grant the application as asked.

Solicitor for the company : *T. Marshall.*

(1) 66 L.T. 704.

KEMP and Another v. PALMER and Another.

Advertising rights—Lease or license.

1898.

March 11.

A.H. Simpson J.
The lessee of an hotel "leased to A., his executors, administrators, and assigns, the privilege of attaching advertisement boards to the hotel balcony, and of affixing advertisements on a hoarding erected on the premises, with the sole right to erect hoardings for advertising purposes as yearly tenants from the 1st January, 1897, at an annual rental of 57l., payable quarterly, with right to remove all such hoardings."

Held, that this was a lease, not a license, and that the advertising rights were not put an end to by the lessee surrendering his lease to the landlord.

MOTION FOR INJUNCTION.

This was a motion for an injunction to the hearing, restraining the defendants from interfering with the plaintiffs' advertising rights.

The plaintiffs as trustees of the estate of Isaac Roff, deceased, carried on the business of bill posters, and the uncontradicted evidence was that in the course of such business they "obtained from one Samuel Thomas the privilege of attaching advertisement boards to the balcony of the Captain Cook Hotel, and of affixing advertisements on the hoarding erected by the plaintiffs along or upon the boundary line of the said hotel property in Oatly and Flinders streets."

On the 29th December, 1896, Samuel Thomas executed the following document:—

1 have this day leased to the trustees of the estate of Isaac Roff, deceased, of 80 Goulburn-street, Sydney, their executors, administrators, and assigns, the advertising privilege as heretofore enjoyed by them on my hotel premises and balcony, with the sole right to erect hoardings for advertising purposes as yearly tenants from the 1st day of January, 1897, at an annual rental of 57l., payable quarterly in advance, with right to remove all such hoardings and erections.

SAMUEL THOMAS.

Samuel Thomas was at the time lessee of the Captain Cook Hotel. In September, 1897, he surrendered his lease to his

1898.

KEMP
v.
PALMER.

landlord, who, on the 26th October, 1897, granted a fresh lease to the defendant Palmer. Palmer, in February, 1898, let to the defendant Eedy the sole right of advertising on the premises of the Captain Cook Hotel, and Eedy had accordingly painted advertisements over the advertisements of the plaintiffs. Both the defendants had notice of the rights that had been granted by Thomas to the plaintiffs.

Lingen, for the plaintiffs, moved for an injunction to the hearing. Whether the document of the 29th December, 1896, is a lease or license is immaterial. A contract was made with reference to the land, and equity will enforce that contract against any person taking the land with notice: *Catt* v. *Tourle* (1); *Kerrison* v. *Smith* (2).

[A. H. SIMPSON, J. The plaintiffs may have a right of action against Thomas, but unless they have a lease how can they restrain the defendant ?]

This is a lease, not a license: *Holmes* v. *The Eastern Counties Railway Co.* (3); *Taylor & Co.* v. *Overseers of Pendleton* (4). The latter case is almost a direct authority on the point. Palmer calls it a lease in the receipt given by him for the quarter's rent in 1897.

Cullen, for the defendants. This is a license, as the document of December, 1896, gives no exclusive right to any portion of the premises, nor is there an exclusive right to erect advertisements anywhere on the premises. The plaintiffs would have no right of action, for example, against anyone who put clothes to dry over the balcony. The decision in *Taylor* v. *Overseers of Pendleton* (4) was only a decision whether or not the advertiser had a sufficient interest in the land for rating purposes. He referred to *Taylor* v. *Caldwell* (5); *Hancock* v. *Austin* (6); *Coleman* v. *Foster* (7); *Rendell* v. *Romer* (8); *Wood* v. *Leadbitter* (9).

(1) 4 Ch. 654.   (5) 32 L.J.Q.B. 164; 3 B. & S. 826.
(2) [1897] 2 Q.B. 445.   (6) 32 L.J.C.P. 252; 14 C.B.N.S. 634.
(3) 3 K. & J. 675.   (7) 1 H. & N. 37.
(4) 19 Q.B.D. 288.   (8) 9 Times L.R. 192.
            (9) 14 L.J. Exch. 161; 13 M. & W. 838.

If it is a license it is revoked by Thomas' surrender of his lease, and his contract does not bind the land in the hands of a new lessee, who takes from the landlord.

If it is a lease it is revocable by six months' notice.

Without calling on the plaintiffs' counsel in reply,

A. H. SIMPSON, J. (After stating the facts his Honour continued):—I think the question I have to decide really turns upon the true construction to be placed upon the document of the 29th December, 1896, taken in conjunction with the circumstances existing at the time. No doubt the previous advertising privileges as stated in the statement of claim are a little vague, but I gather that the plaintiffs had erected boards on the boundary of the land, and that they had the right given them to put up advertisements there. Then the document of the 29th December, 1896, was signed in order more accurately to define the plaintiffs' rights. That document, in my opinion, is a lease conveying an interest, and not a mere license. The parties used the word "lease," the rights are given to the plaintiffs, "their executors, administrators, and assigns," and the plaintiffs are spoken of as "yearly tenants" paying an "annual rental." I think there was a clear intention to grant a lease, and I cannot see why it should not operate as such. It is a lease of the front of the balcony railing, and also a lease of the hoarding erected on the land. That hoarding, while erected, was an interest in the land, and a right to put advertisements on the hoarding is a right to put advertisements on so much of the land as the hoarding is erected on: see *Francis* v. *Hayward* (1).

That being so there is an end of the question. Thomas could not, by surrendering his lease, affect the rights of his sub-lessee.

The lease cannot be put an end to before the end of 1898, and then only by giving six months' notice. That appears to me to be a sufficiently long period for which to grant an injunction, and on the balance of convenience I see no reason why I should not grant an injunction to the hearing; either party may suffer damage from the order, but as the matter stands at present, I think the plaintiffs are in the right. Costs in the cause.

[This suit was subsequently settled before coming to a hearing.]

(1) 22 Ch. D. 177.

In re LODER AND THE MINISTER FOR PUBLIC WORKS,

Ex parte SINGLETON.

1898.
___
March 18, 22.
___
A. H. *Simpson* J

Resumption of land—Lands for Public Purposes Acquisition Act, s. 12—Public Works Act, 1888, ss. 23, 69, 70, 71—Claim by possession—Payment of resumption money into Court—Statute of Limitations (3 & 4 Will. IV.), c. 27.

L., who was in possession of land at the date of its resumption by the Crown, had not obtained a title by possession for 20 years. S., the owner by documentary title, sent in a claim to the Minister under s. 12 of the Lands for Public Purposes Acquisition Act before the period of 20 years had expired. The compensation money was paid into Court, as a title to the land was not made out, and S. petitioned for payment out after the period of 20 years had elapsed. *Held*, that the claim by S. prevented L.'s title by possession from maturing.

A claim under s. 12 of the Lands for Public Purposes Acquisition Act is analogous to the first step in a suit to recover land.

THE facts agreed upon for the purpose of the application were stated by his Honour as follows :—

On the 1st November, 1895, the respondent, Loder, had been in possession of land without a documentary title for a period somewhat less than 20 years, and it was admitted that if the land had not been resumed by the Government, and Loder had remained on in possession, the title of the petitioner, Singleton, the documentary owner, would have been barred by the Statute of Limitations. On the 1st November, 1895, a notification was published in the *Gazette* resuming the land under the provisions of the Lands for Public Purposes Acquisition Act, and thereupon the entire fee simple of the land became vested in the Minister for Public Works on behalf of the Crown, and the rights of the owners converted into claims for compensation under s. 10. On the 29th November, 1895, Singleton sent in his claim for compensation in accordance with s. 12, which date was before the expiration of the 20 years. Loder also sent in a claim as owner in fee, and by separate agreements between the Minister and Singleton, and the Minister and Loder, and the Minister and a third claimant, the value of the fee simple was agreed on as being 217*l.* 16*s.* As the alleged owners failed to make out a title to the satisfaction of the Minister in accordance with s. 69 of the

1898.

In re
LODER
AND
MINISTER FOR
PUBLIC
WORKS;

Ex parte
SINGLETON.

Public Works Act, which is to be taken as embodied in the Lands for Public Purposes Acquisition Act, the money was paid into Court under the provisions in that behalf of the Public Works Act so taken to be embodied in the Lands for Public Purposes Acquisition Act, on the 18th October, 1897, at which time the period of 20 years had expired. And, on the 2nd December following, this petition was presented by Singleton for payment out of the said sum to him.

L. Owen, for the petitioner. The Statute of Limitations ceases to run when a claim is made. The Lands Clauses Consolidation Act in England does not vest the land absolutely in the constructing authority, whoever the owner may be ; the local Act does. The money is to be paid to the owner, and Loder never was owner. The claim under s. 12 of the Lands for Public Purposes Acquisition Act is "an institution of proceedings."

He referred to *Ex parte Winder* (1); *Cripps on Compensation* (2); *Re Hollingsworth* (3); *Re Evans* (4); *Douglas* v. *L. & N. W. Ry. Co.* (5); *Trustees and Agency Co.* v. *Shortt* (6).

Cullen, for the respondent, Loder. The procedure laid down by the Act only applies for the purpose of settling claims between a particular claimant and the Minister. If the Crown had paid the compensation money to Loder before the time had elapsed, the true owner could have come in again and claimed compensation. Sect. 15 directs an issue as to value only, and not as to title. A declaratory decree in equity alone can settle questions of title. Resumption does not stop the statute running: *Chamberlain's Case* (7). The statute is only stopped by something in the nature of a judicial proceeding. The Crown is merely a trustee of the money, and notice to the trustee does not stop the statute: *Re Perry* (8). The Crown cannot settle the rights of the parties: *Re Stead* (9); *In re Stephens* (10).

Owen in reply. Any actions as to value against the Crown would be consolidated by the Court. The only way to proceed is that laid down by the Act. The petition is a distribution of the fund after the amount is decided. *Re Stead* (1) decides only that a petition stops the statute.

1898.

In re
LODER
AND
MINISTER FOR
PUBLIC
WORKS;
Ex parte
SINGLETON.

A. H. SIMPSON, J. (After stating the facts.) If the Statute of Limitations, which had been started running by Loder's entry into possession, continued running up to the presentation of the petition, notwithstanding the resumption, and notwithstanding the sending in of Singleton's claim, it is admitted that Singleton's case fails. I do not think the mere resumption of the land can stop the statute running; it is an Act done *in invitos* vesting the land absolutely in the Minister, but not in any way altering the rights of the parties *inter se.* Until the compensation money is paid over, the Minister holds it as trustee for the parties who may ultimately turn out to be entitled, and if the money were paid into Court and the income paid without adverse claim to the person with a possessory title for a period sufficiently long to give him a statutory title, I can see no reason why his title should be prevented from maturing, merely because the land has been converted by a paramount right into money. The cases *Re Perry's Estate* (2); *Re Evans* (3); and the observations of *Hall*, V.C., in *Ex parte Winder* (4), at the bottom of page 703, amply support this view.

When, however, an adverse claim is made within the twenty years, the matter seems to me to stand on an entirely different footing.

In this case the different claimants of the fee simple interest have agreed with the Minister as to the value of such fee simple, and it is unnecessary, therefore, to consider how the case would have stood if each claimant had sent in a claim for a different amount.

The sections which are material to consider are ss. 69, 70, and 71 of the Public Works Act, 1888, which are to be taken as embodied in the Lands for Public Purposes Acquisition Act. Those sections are taken from ss. 76, 78 and 79 of the Lands Clauses Consolidation Act (8 Vic. c. 18).

(1) 2 Ch. Div. 713.   (3) 42 L.J. Ch. 357.
(2) 1 Jur. N.S. 917.   (4) 6 Ch. D. 696.

1898.

In re
LODER
AND
MINISTER FOR
PUBLIC
WORKS;
Ex parte
SINGLETON.

A.H. Simpson J.

In *Douglas* v. *London and N.W.R. Co.* (1), *Wood*, V.C., held that a person who had merely a possessory title, which was not proved to have matured under the Statute of Limitations into a good title, was not an "owner" within s. 76; and this was approved by *Fry*, J., in *Wells* v. *Chelmsford Board of Health* (2). In *In re Hollingsworth* (3), the petitioner had been in possession for nearly twenty years, when the land was taken by a railway company and the purchase money paid into Court. After the expiration of twenty years without any adverse claim being made by Wright, the documentary owner, who, in fact, had not been heard of, the petitioners applied for payment out to them as "owners." *Stuart*, V.C., refused this on the ground that the petitioners had a mere "inchoate" right by "possession," and had failed to shew that Wright's title was barred.

This case came on again in 1877, before *Hall*, V.C., under the name of *Ex parte Winder* (4), in the presence of the representatives of Wright. The *Vice-Chancellor* held that the railway company had not taken the steps which they might have taken under the Lands Clauses Consolidation Act, to fix a binding value for the fee simple, but had merely paid into Court the purchase money of claimants' interests, and that there was nothing to prevent Wright or his representatives from recovering the value of the fee simple from the railway company if the title was made out. Under these circumstances the money was, of course, paid out to the claimants. None of these cases touch the exact point whether the sending in by Singleton of his claim to the Minister prevents the Statute of Limitations running against him, but it seems to me, on principle, that it should so prevent the statute running.

The Lands for Public Purposes Acquisition Act provides machinery for persons whose land is taken obtaining compensation from the Crown. The first step is to send in a claim under s. 12, and if the claimant and the Minister cannot agree, the claimant is then at liberty to institute proceedings in the Supreme Court in the form of an action for compensation against the Minister as nominal defendant under s. 14, and the amount of

(1) 3 K. & J. 173.   (3) 24 L.T. 347; 19 W.R. 580.
(2) 15 Ch. D. 108.   (4) 6 Ch. D. 696.

the verdict is then payable out of the consolidated revenue fund under s. 16.

The sending in a claim therefore is the first step in the proceedings prescribed by the statute for recovering compensation, and is, in my opinion, analogous to the first step in a suit to recover land or money, just as in *In re Stead* (1) the presentation of a petition for payment of money out of Court was held analogous to a suit.

It was contended by Dr. *Cullen* that the only way in which Singleton could prevent the statute continuing to run against him was by instituting a suit in equity against all the claimants for a declaration of right, and that the party then held to be entitled should send in his claim; but it is obvious that the equity suit would be merely a preliminary step to the statutory proceedings which are the real means of recovering the compensation. Previously to the year 1852 a merely declaratory decree could not be obtained, and before that date, therefore, the course suggested was not open. It can hardly be that in such a case the claimant had no means of preserving his rights.

I must, therefore, hold on the facts as assumed before me that Singleton's right is not barred.   Costs reserved.

Solicitors for the petitioner, Singleton: *Thompson & Ash.*

Solicitors for the respondent, Loder: *Gould & Shaw.*

(1) 2 Ch. D. 713.

1898.

In re
LODER
AND
MINISTER FOR
PUBLIC
WORKS;
Ex parte
SINGLETON.

A.H. Simpson J.

DAVIES v. FROST AND ANOTHER.

1898.
Feb. 18, 23.
A. H. Simpson J.

Practice—Production of documents—Affidavit of documents—Objection to produce
—Allegation of immateriality—Documents in which two or more are interested.

If a deponent in his affidavit of documents admits that he has documents
relating to the case, he is not relieved from producing them by alleging that they
are immaterial to, and do not support the case of the opposite side, nor impeach
his own case.

It is no answer in an application for production of a document, of which one
person is in sole legal possession, to say that another person, against whom discovery could not be obtained, has an interest in it, and may be injured by its
production.

SUMMONS.

This was an application by the plaintiffs for discovery of the
documents referred to in the second part of the first schedule to
the affidavit of discovery of the defendant Elizabeth Jane Frost.

The statement of claim in the suit prayed for a declaration
that the infant defendant, Maud Frost, was not the child of
Thomas James Frost, deceased; it asked to set aside an order of
the Court directing the rents of certain property to be paid to
the defendant, Elizabeth Jane Frost, as guardian of Maud Frost;
and for a declaration that Elizabeth Jane Frost was trustee for
the plaintiffs of the rents and profits of the property. The allegations in the statement of claim were practically to the effect that
Elizabeth Jane Frost had falsely and fraudulently represented
the defendant Maud Frost to be the child of herself and the
deceased Thomas James Frost, in order to get for the child a
benefit under the deceased's will.

The affidavit of discovery of the defendant, Elizabeth Jane
Frost, so far as material, was in the following terms:—

1. I say that I have in my possession or power the documents
relating to the matters in question in this suit, set forth in the
first and second part of the first schedule hereto.

2. I further say that I object to produce the said documents
set forth in the second part of the said first schedule hereto.

3. I further say that the documents, correspondence, and papers
marked L., and numbered 1-49 inclusive, are immaterial to the

relief prayed by the plaintiffs in this suit, and that they contain no matters supporting or forming the title or case of the plaintiffs, and they do not, to the best of my knowledge, information and belief, contain anything impeaching the case of the said defendants. (There was a similar statement with reference to the documents marked M., and numbered 1-50.) With regard to bundle of letters marked with the letter N. and numbered 1-19, I further say that they are immaterial to the relief prayed for by the plaintiffs in this suit, and are merely letters in relation to private matters, not in connection with the relief prayed for by the plaintiffs.

1898.

DAVIES
v.
FROST.

SCHEDULE I., PART II.

1. Documents, correspondence, and papers in connection with transmission application, No. 6401, marked L., and numbered 1-49.

2. Documents and correspondence in connection with assurance of Maud Frost, marked M., numbered 1-50.

3. Bundle of letters and replies thereto from Mrs. E. J. Frost, marked N., numbered 1-19.

Lingen, for the plaintiffs, in support of the summons.

Rich (*Harris* with him), for the defendant, E. J. Frost.

Rich, for the infant defendant, Maud Frost, took a preliminary objection on her behalf that the plaintiffs were asking Mrs. Frost, the first-named defendant, to give discovery of documents legally belonging to her, which were only in the physical possession of Mrs. Frost.

The Court will make no order for discovery against an infant: *Curtis* v. *Monday* (1). Possession for purposes of production must be legal possession: *Kearsley* v. *Phillips* (2).

Lingen referred to *Mansell* v. *Feeney* (3); *Plumley* v. *Horrell* (4); *Greenwood* v. *Greenwood* (5). The affidavit is inconsistent, and the plaintiffs can, therefore, look at the documents themselves: *Compagnie Financiere, &c.* v. *Peruvian Guano Co.* (6);

(1) [1892] 2 Q.B. 192.	(4) W.N. [1868] 240.
(2) 10 Q.B.D. 36.	(5) 6 W.R. 119.
(3) 2 J. & H. 320.	(6) 11 Q.B.D. 55.

1898.

DAVIES
v.
FROST.

Bray on Discovery (1); *Hutchinson* v. *Glover* (2). No privilege is claimed for the documents: *Ricketson* v. *Smith* (3).

Rich. We might have omitted these documents from our affidavit altogether as being immaterial to the suit; what we have done is the same in effect, we say that they are immaterial although they do refer to some of the matters mentioned in the suit. That is the only way we can expressly take the point that the documents are immaterial. The affidavit is in the prescribed form: see Schedule D. to the Reg. Gen. of 1891. It is not merely a question of privilege, but also of inability to produce the documents; other persons are interested in them: *Kettlewell* v. *Barstow* (4).

A. H. SIMPSON, J. I think this case is covered by authority, and that the three sets of documents marked L., M. and N. ought to be produced. It seems to me, as stated by *Blackburn, J.,* in *Hutchinson* v. *Glover* (5), that " everything which will throw light on the case is *prima facie* subject to inspection."

In this case Mrs. Frost has filed an affidavit, in which she says she has in her possession certain documents *relating to the matters in question* in this suit, and among them the documents of which production is now sought. The meaning of the words *relating to* is much discussed in the case of *Compagnie Financiere et Commerciale du Pacifique* v. *The Peruvian Guano Company* (6), in which *Brett,* L.J., as he then was, lays it down, that a wide meaning should be given to the expression. " The party swearing the affidavit," he says " is bound to set out all documents in his possession or under his control relating to any matters in question in the action. Then comes this difficulty : What is the meaning of that definition ? What are the documents which are documents relating to any matter in question in the action ? In *Jones* v. *Monte Video Gas Co.* (7), the Court stated its desire to make the rule as to the affidavit of documents as elastic as was possible. And I think that that is the view of the Court, both as to the

(1) Pp. 186, 187, 482, 215, 59.   (4) 7 Ch. 686.
(2) 1 Q.B.D. 138.   (5) 1 Q.B.D. 138.
(3) 17 N.S.W. R. Eq. 203.   (6) 11 Q.B.D. 55.
           (7) 5 Q.B.D. 556.

sources from which the information can be derived, and as to the nature of the documents. We desire to make the rule as large as we can with due regard to propriety; and, therefore, I desire to give as large an interpretation as I can to the words of the rule, 'a document relating to any matter in question in the action.'" He then shews that the rule is not confined to documents which would be evidence to prove or disprove the party's case, and on the succeeding page he says:—"Every document relates to the matters in question in the action, which would not only be evidence upon any issue, but also which, it is reasonable to suppose, contains information which *may*, not which *must*, either directly or indirectly enable the party requiring the affidavit either to advance his own case, or to damage the case of his adversary. I have put in the words 'either directly or indirectly,' because, as it seems to me, a document can properly be said to contain information which may enable the party requiring the affidavit either to advance his own case or to damage the case of his adversary, if it is a document which may fairly lead him to a train of enquiry, which may have either of these two consequences."

Mr. *Rich* admits that he would have to produce the documents if his affidavit had stopped at the end of the first paragraph which I have referred to, but contends that its effect is got rid of, because afterwards the deponent says the documents are immaterial. This contention appears to me to be met by the decisions in *Mansell* v. *Feeney* (1), and *Greenwood* v. *Greenwood* (2), in which cases it was laid down that when a party has once admitted a document to be relevant, his saying it is immaterial has no effect, as it is the right of the other party to decide this for himself. If we take the meaning of the words *relating to* from *Brett*, L.J., there appears to be a clear admission by Mrs. Frost that these documents are relevant to the suit, and Mrs. Frost's subsequent expression of opinion that they are immaterial to the relief prayed by the plaintiffs, is absolutely worthless. It is impossible for her to say that any of the documents might not put the plaintiff on to the track of some enquiry which might enable him to complete his chain of evidence, or that they might not contain

(1) 2 J. & H. 320.   (2) 6 W.R. 119.

1898.

DAVIES
v.
FROST.

A. H. Simpson J.

evidence which, if not directly in support of the plaintiff's case, might at any rate have the effect of damaging that of the defendant.

The second objection taken is that the documents really belong to the infant, and that the Court will not allow the documents to be produced to her injury, when they are really hers, simply because they happen to be in Mrs. Frost's physical possession.

Now, there is no affidavit on the part of Mrs. Frost that they really belong to the infant, and I do not think they do so belong, though it may be she has an interest in them. If so, it affords no answer where one person is in sole legal possession of a document, to say that another person has an interest in it, and may be injured by its production.

For these reasons the documents must be produced, and the application must be granted with costs.

Solicitors for the plaintiffs: *Norton, Smith & Co.*

Solicitors for the defendants: *Fitzhardinge, Son & Houston.*

In re the claim of CAROLINE MOORE AND OTHERS,

AND

In the matter of THE LANDS FOR PUBLIC PURPOSES ACQUISITION ACT.

Public Works Act of 1888, *s.* 72—*Resumption of land—Payment out of compensa-*
tion moneys—Costs payable by the constructing authority.

Where compensation moneys for resumed land are paid into Court by the constructing authority in consequence of the persons beneficially entitled thereto
being under age, the constructing authority is liable to pay the costs of the
separate applications for payment out made by each beneficiary as he comes of
age, although the compensation moneys have subsequently to the payment in
been carried to separate accounts in the same matter in the name of each beneficiary. Carrying the money to the separate accounts is not payment to the
person entitled within the meaning of s. 72 of the Public Works Act.

1898.

March 1.

A.H. *Simpson* J.

SUMMONS.

This was an application by Arthur Barrington Moore for payment out to him of the moneys standing to his credit in an
account in the above matter.

The compensation money was originally paid in by the Minister
for land resumed under the Lands for Public Purposes Acquisition
Act in 1882. In 1887 there were nine persons entitled to this
fund, of whom six were under age, and by an order of the Court
dated the 12th December, 1887, three-ninths of the fund was
ordered to be paid out to the three adults, and the balance was
ordered to be carried to separate accounts in the name of the six
infants respectively, of whom the present applicant was one.
This was accordingly done. In 1889, 1892, 1893 and 1895 as
four of these infants respectively came of age they severally
applied for their shares, and the costs of the several applications
were paid by the Minister.

A. Thompson, for the applicant Arthur Barrington Moore, now
applied for his one-ninth share, and asked for costs against the
Minister.

Canaway, for the Minister for Public Works. The Minister
has already paid the costs of five applications for payment out,

and there is still one more application to be made. He submits that he is not liable to pay costs under the circumstances. When a fund is transferred from one account to another, there is constructive payment within the meaning of s. 72 of the Public Works Act : *Melling* v. *Bird* (1), *Prescott* v. *Wood* (2).

[A. H. SIMPSON, J. The money is still standing to the credit of the same matter : see *Cripps on Compensation* (3).]

The money was the money of the trustees ; when they arranged with the beneficiaries to split it up into separate funds they exercised acts of ownership over the moneys, and the moneys were constructively paid.

A. H. SIMPSON, J. I think the Minister must pay the costs of this application. I do not think the cases cited support Mr. *Canaway's* contention. In some cases, no doubt, transfer from one account to another may amount to payment so as to relieve the Minister from his liability for costs ; but in all the cases to which I have been referred the transfer was, so far as appears, from one matter in which reference was made to the special Act, or the Land Clauses Act, under which the land had been taken into an account in another matter making no reference to the special Act, or to the promoters. In *Cripps on Compensation* (3) it is said :—" Transfer of the fund in Court to an account not referring to the Land Clauses Acts or the special Act has been in some cases held equivalent to payment out of Court so as to exempt the promoters from paying any costs of subsequent dealings with the fund. But where the promoters' names are included in the title of the account it has been held that the change of title does not affect their liability to pay costs." I have looked at all the cases referred to by Mr. Cripps, and they appear to bear out his statement, that, wherever the promoters were held not liable to pay costs, the fund had been transferred to another account in another matter bearing a different title.

In the latest of the cases cited, that of *Drake* v. *Greaves* (4), a fund had been transferred to the credit of an administration suit, but though no mention of the special Act or of the Land

(1) 17 Jur. 155.
(2) 37 L.J. Ch. 691.
(3) 3rd Edit. p. 285.
(4) 33 Ch. D. 609.

Clauses Act was made in the title of the account, it was still entitled "*Ex parte* the Metropolitan Board of Works," who were the undertakers. *North*, J., held that the undertakers were liable to pay the costs of an application for re-investment of the fund; he says, "it has been the practice for many years to draw up orders transferring funds in such cases as the present to accounts without reference to the special Act or the Land Clauses Act, and the registrar has produced orders for re-investment when, although the funds stand to the credit of accounts which had no reference to any special Act or the Land Clauses Acts, the undertakers have been required to pay the costs of re-investment."

That decision seems to be applicable to the present case, where the fund is still standing to an account entitled in the original matter in which the Minister paid the money into Court; in such a case the Minister must pay the proper costs of applications for payment out to the persons entitled.

Solicitors for the applicant : *Shipway & Berne.*

Solicitor for the Minister for Works : *Crown Solicitor.*

1898.

In re
CAROLINE
MOORE.

A.H Simpson

1897.   IRVING v. COMMERCIAL BANKING COMPANY OF SYDNEY.

Nov. 3, 4, 19. *Mortgagor and mortgagee—Mortgagee selling on terms under special power of sale*
              —Form of account—Practice—Purchase of equity of redemption from Sheriff
C.J. Eq.   *—5 Vic. No. 9, s. 31—22 Vic. No. 1, s. 3.*

                     Where the power of sale in a mortgage authorises a sale for cash or on terms,
                   and the mortgagee sells on terms by which the payment of the purchase money is
1898.   spread over a number of years, the mortgagee is not bound to credit the mortgagor
February 21.   with the whole of the purchase money as received on the day of the sale, but only
                   with the instalments as they are received. *Hickey* v. *Heydon* (1) overruled on
The C.J.   this point.
Stephen J.   Whether the conveyance to the purchaser of an equity of redemption from the
and
A.H. Simpson J. Sheriff must be registered in order to perfect the purchaser's title, *quære.*

THIS was a suit for an account against the defendant bank as
mortgagee by a purchaser of the equity of redemption. The bank,
as mortgagee, had exercised its power of sale, which was in the
following terms :—" to sell the said lands and premises hereby
conveyed or any part thereof for cash or on credit either together
or in lots, and either by public auction or private contract, and
either with or without special conditions or stipulations as to
title, mode, and time of payment of purchase money or otherwise,"
with power to buy in, or rescind and re-sell, &c. The mortgaged
premises were sold in March, 1894, for 400*l.*, payable 200*l.* in cash,
and the balance by two promissory notes of 100*l.* each, due in six
and twelve months respectively.

The plaintiff, after purchasing the equity of redemption at a
Sheriff's sale, gave notice of his purchase to the bank, and after
the sale had been effected by the bank, he wrote asking for an
account. The bank ultimately furnished an account after the
second promissory note had been met, shewing a balance of 54*l.*
odd due from them ; this sum it said it was willing to pay to the
plaintiff if he shewed the bank his title to the equity of redemption. The plaintiff contended that the account was inaccurate,
inasmuch as the bank had charged against the purchase moneys
costs which it was contended it had no right to charge. The

(1) 16 N.S.W. R. Eq. 49.

bank, however, insisted upon the correctness of its account, and always stated its willingness to pay the sum mentioned if the plaintiff would shew his title.

As a matter of fact, the plaintiff's conveyance of the equity of redemption from the Sheriff was not registered until the first day of the hearing of this suit.

At the hearing two questions only were raised, (1) by the bank, that as the plaintiff had not registered his conveyance until after suit brought, and had not shewn his title to the bank, the suit must be dismissed without prejudice to another suit, or the plaintiff must pay the costs up to and including the hearing in any event; (2) by the plaintiff, that in the account the bank must credit the plaintiff with the whole of the purchase money as on the day of sale.

Knox and *Harvey*, for the plaintiff, contended that s. 3 of the Titles to Land Act (22 Vic. No. 1) had repealed the provisions as to registration in s. 31 of 5 Vic. No. 9.

On the form of the account they cited *Hickey* v. *Heydon* (1).

Lingen, for the defendant bank, contended that it was the duty of the assignee of the equity of redemption to produce his title : *James* v. *Biou* (2) ; *Tasker* v. *Small* (3) ; *Evans* v. *Bagshaw* (4). The plaintiff had no title when the suit was brought, as he had not registered his conveyance from the Sheriff: 22 Vic. No. 1, s. 3; he had only a conditional title: *Hurst* v. *Hurst* (5).

The form of account in *Hickey* v. *Heydon* (6) was wrong: see *Dart's Vendors and Purchasers* (p. 89); the power of sale is a special power: *Fenton* v. *Blackwood* (7) ; *Sugden's Vendors and Purchasers* (p. 66); *Thurlow* v. *Mackeson* (8).

Knox in reply. The demand to see the plaintiff's title was always coupled with an offer of 54*l.*, which we regard as insufficient. The special power of sale enables the mortgagee to sell and take a mortgage back for part of the purchase money by the same transaction : see *Dart's Vendors and Purchasers* (p. 90).

Cur. adv. vult.

(1) 16 N.S.W.R. Eq. 49.	(5) 9 Ch. 762.
(2) 3 Swans. 234.	(6) 16 N.S.W.R. Eq. 49.
(3) 3 M. & Cr. 63.	(7) 1 V.R. Eq. 124.
(4) 5 Ch. 340.	(8) L.R. 4 Q.B. 97.

1897.   On the 19th November, the following judgment was read by

IRVING
v.   MANNING, C.J. in Eq. This was a suit by a purchaser of an
COMMERCIAL   equity of redemption against the mortgagee for an account after
BANKING Co.
OF SYDNEY.   sale, claiming that the mortgagee had been overpaid. This was

November 19.   not, in fact, denied by the defendant bank, but the dispute was
               as to how the account was to be taken, the plaintiff contending
               that the defendants must be charged in the account with the
               whole amount receivable under the contract as if the sale had
               been for cash, on the authority of *Hickey* v. *Heydon* (1). For the
               defendants it was contended that the said case was contrary to
               law and should not be followed, and secondly, that there was a
               distinction in the powers of sale in the two cases which would
               compel a different decision in this case in any event.

                   I stated at an early stage of the argument my intention to
               follow *Hickey* v. *Heydon* (1), unless it could be distinguished, as
               I considered it very undesirable on a matter of such importance
               to conveyancers and the public that there should be divergent
               decisions of Judges of the first instance, unless, of course, it was
               clear beyond a shadow of doubt that the first decision was wrong.

                   The judgment in *Hickey* v. *Heydon* (1) was not reserved, but
               it was delivered after the day's adjournment without hearing the
               plaintiff's counsel in reply, and his Honour expressed himself as
               being quite clear on the subject.

                   Whatever view I might be inclined to take were the matter a
               res integra, it would, I think, ill become me to assume the posi-
               tion of a Court of Appeal in treating as wrong the clearly
               expressed and decided opinion of so able a Judge as the late
               Chief Judge in Equity, and though I am prepared to admit that
               there is a great deal to be said in favour of the defendants' con-
               tention, I think I ought as a Judge of the first instance to con-
               sider myself bound by *Hickey* v. *Heydon* (1).

                   What I understand his Honour to have held is that a power of
               sale in a mortgage is an enunciation of the mortgagee's title in
               selling, and that when the power is taken in such full terms it is
               to place beyond doubt his right to sell in such a way as he thinks
               will lead to the realisation of his security in the simplest,

                            (1) 16 N.S.W.R. Eq. 49.

quickest, and most advantageous manner to him; but that is a
question of title only, and if he desires to treat it as other than
a cash sale, so far as the mortgagor is concerned, special provisions
must be inserted to that effect.

1897.

IRVING
v.
COMMERCIAL
BANKING Co.
OF SYDNEY.

C. J. Eq.

As I am quite unable to see that the additional words "for
cash or credit" make any difference between the power of sale
in this case and in *Hickey* v. *Heydon* (1), so far as to affect the
grounds upon which the judgment in the latter case was founded,
I must hold that the account of the mortgagor must be credited
with the full amount of the purchase money, not, I think, from
the date of the contract, because some time must always be
allowed for inspection of title and completion, but from the day
on which the first cash payment was credited.

On the pleadings the title of the plaintiff was put in issue, the
defendant properly insisting on his right to see that the right
person was asking for an account.

In proof of his title the plaintiff put in his conveyance from the
Sheriff, but though everything else was regular it appeared that the
deed had not been registered. This defect was cured at once
during the midday adjournment, but the defendants objected
that the plaintiff's title was not complete until registration, and
that as he had commenced his suit without perfecting the title
he must, at all events, be ordered to pay all costs up to the time
of such perfecting, if indeed the whole suit should not be dismissed with costs, and certain cases were cited which in the view
I take it is unnecessary for me to refer to.

The first question is, whether registration is now necessary at
all?

By the Act 5 Vic. No. 9, under which sales of equities of
redemption were provided for for the first time, a number of
precautions were required to be taken. The proviso to s. 31 runs
as follows: "Provided that where any such equity or equitable
interest shall relate to real estate, a deed of bargain and sale
thereof, or of such defendants' right and title to and interest
therein, shall be executed by such Sheriff to such purchaser and
be by him duly registered within one calendar month next after
such sale." By the Titles to Land Act, 22 Vic. No. 1, a number

(1) 16 N.S.W.R. Eq. 49.

1897.

IRVING
v.
COMMERCIAL
BANKING Co.
OF SYDNEY.

C.J. Eq.

of restrictions were removed, and s. 3 ends thus, "and no such deed shall be deemed invalid by reason only of non-registration within one calendar month as now prescribed by law."

It seems to me that these words are quite capable of being read either as doing away with registration altogether, as a condition precedent to the title, or as removing only the necessity for registration within one calendar month. Possibly the latter reading would strike most minds as the more likely one, but the question would still remain whether the proviso as to registration would not then become directory only. If time ceased to be of the essence, what necessity can there be for registration at all as a matter of title, for the deed can be registered at any moment by the purchaser, though, of course, his priority may be affected? It cannot have reference to notice, for it has been decided that registration is no notice.

But, whatever may be the true legal position, I am clear that it is immaterial, so far as this suit is concerned, whether the final crown was put on the title by registration before suit or not. Had there been no other question between the parties but one of title, this matter might possibly have been different, but, in such a case as this, it is quite sufficient if the plaintiff can shew a good title to have an account taken before his case is closed, because, beyond all question, the real question that the parties came to the Court to determine was the way in which the accounts were to be taken. Test the matter in this way: Had there been no question at all as to the amount for which the mortgagee was liable to the mortgagor or his assignee, the plaintiff would naturally have had to produce his "bargain and sale" before he could get the money. If the objection as to non-registration were taken, that would be put right in five minutes and another demand made. Here the defendants never offered to pay the proper amount according to the plaintiff's contention. If, eventually, it turns out that the amount actually offered by the defendant was correct, then the whole question of costs can be dealt with, but not, in my opinion, till then.

I must, therefore, direct an account with a declaration that the defendant is to be charged with the full amount of the purchase money in his accounts as on April 12th, 1894, and I reserve all further directions and all costs, and leave open all questions that may be raised on taking the accounts.

After the judgment had been delivered as above, and before the decree was drawn up, the plaintiff's solicitor informed the defendants that the plaintiff would not insist upon his rights under that portion of the judgment that declared that the purchase money must be given credit for *in toto* on the 12th April, 1894, and that he was willing that the costs, if any, incurred by the defendants in consequence of his contention at the hearing on that point should be deducted from the costs which the defendants would be ultimately ordered to pay to the plaintiff; or that the question of costs should be determined on further consideration when the whole costs of the suit would be dealt with; the decree would be drawn up as pronounced, but the plaintiff undertook unreservedly to have the accounts taken as contended for by the defendants. The defendants replied that as the decree would have to be drawn up as pronounced the plaintiff's offer was insufficient; they accordingly instituted an appeal upon the following grounds :—

1. The sale by the bank was in strict pursuance of the power contained in the mortgage given by the plaintiff's predecessors in title.

2. Such sale was therefore made with the authority of the mortgagor, and, therefore, it cannot be said that the sale was made behind the mortgagor's back, or that he had nothing to do with it.

3. The power of sale was a special and not general power.

4. A mortgagee selling under a power can only be charged with the moneys arising on the sale as and when they are paid to the mortgagee.

5. The mortgagee is not the *del credere* agent of the mortgagor in the exercise of the power of sale.

6. The interest payable by the mortgagor to the mortgagee bears no relation to the interest paid by the purchaser to the mortgagee. The first is a payment for the use of the mortgagee's money, the second is a payment for the use of the mortgagor's land until the purchase money is fully paid, and is in the nature of rent.

Sir *Julian Salomons*, Q.C., and *Lingen*, appeared in support of the appeal ; no fresh cases were cited.

1898.

IRVING
v.
COMMERCIAL
BANKING CO.
OF SYDNEY.

Knox and *Harvey*, for the plaintiff, did not oppose the substance of the appeal, but contended that the appellants were not entitled to their costs of the appeal after the plaintiff's submission.

Without calling on the appellant's counsel to reply,

THE CHIEF JUSTICE. The plaintiff in this case was the purchaser from the Sheriff of the equity of redemption of certain land, which was mortgaged to the defendant bank. The power of sale in that mortgage is of a very special kind, not found, so far as I am aware, in any English precedents, but peculiar to this colony, and possibly to the other colonies; it was in the following terms :—(His Honour read the power of sale and continued).

In the year 1895, the case of *Hickey* v. *Heydon* (1) came before Mr. Justice *Owen*, who was then *Chief Judge in Equity*, arising out of a mortgage containing a power of sale, not exactly in the same terms as the power in the present case, but one that certainly gave the mortgagee power to sell on cash or credit, though not in such express terms as the present power. From the judgment delivered in that case, it does not appear that his Honour's attention was pointedly called to the express terms of that power; his Honour, however, seems to have felt himself bound by certain English authorities, and by a passage in Lord *St. Leonards'* work on *Vendors and Purchasers*; and he held that, though the mortgagee had sold on terms, he must be taken to have received into his hands the whole of his purchase money as and from the date of the contract for the sale, and that he would have to account to the mortgagor as and from that date, although the payments might have been spread over several years. In the present case, Mr. Justice *Manning*, as a Judge of first instance, did not feel called upon to overrule the decision of another Judge of the first instance, and one of such experience in such matters as Mr. Justice *Owen*, though it is clear and manifest to me from the terms of the judgment now appealed against that he felt some difficulty with respect to the judgment in *Hickey* v. *Heydon* (1); he, however, thought it better to leave it to this Court to decide whether that case was to be taken as a binding authority or not, in reference to a power of sale couched in such terms as that in this case.

(1) 16 N.S.W.R. Eq. 49.

With the utmost respect for any decision given by Mr. Justice *Owen*, particularly in a matter of equity, I am clearly of opinion that the law as laid down in *Hickey* v. *Heydon* (1) is not applicable to a mortgage containing such a power of sale as the present. I am of opinion that under such a power the mortgagee is entitled, not merely as between himself and the purchaser, but as between himself and the mortgagor, to sell on credit according to the terms of his agreement with the mortgagor; and so long as he sells honestly and bona fide on credit on the best terms reasonably obtainable, he is only bound to give credit to the mortgagor in his account as and when he receives the money, and is not liable for the whole purchase money from the date of sale. It might be that he would never receive the outstanding balance of the purchase money from the purchaser; it might be that the mortgagee sold at a time when the land was very high in value, and before the period of credit had expired it might become so depreciated as not to be worth the amount remaining due upon it, seeing which the purchaser, not being in a position to pay anything, might abandon his contract. Nevertheless, according to the argument submitted, the mortgagee would be liable for the whole; which amounts to this, that the mortgagee selling on credit according to the terms of the mortgage nevertheless guarantees that the purchaser will carry out his contract.

I am of opinion that under such a covenant for sale as this the mortgagee is only bound to give credit for the purchase money as he receives it.

That does not, however, dispose altogether of this appeal. It appears that this matter was fully argued before Mr. Justice *Manning*, who reserved judgment, and sixteen days after the hearing gave the decision now appealed against. After the judgment the plaintiff, for the first time, discovered that to take the accounts on the basis of the whole purchase money being paid on the 12th April, 1894, instead of half then, and the balance in two instalments, was, under the circumstances of the case, rather less favourable to him, and, accordingly, after the decree had been pronounced, he gave notice to the defendants that he was willing to let the matter go before the Master, and to have the account

1898.

IRVING
v.
COMMERCIAL
BANKING Co.
OF SYDNEY.

The C.J.

(1) 16 N.S.W.R. Eq. 49.

IRVING
v.
COMMERCIAL
BANKING CO.
OF SYDNEY.

The C.J.

taken as the defendants had contended. A long correspondence ensued, the upshot of which was that the defendants filed their appeal in order to get the law determined whether they were bound by the decision in *Hickey* v. *Heydon* (1), and whether the decree in this case following that decision is right.

It is now contended that under the circumstances, although we may grant the appeal, the plaintiff ought not to be ordered to pay the costs, indeed that the defendants should be ordered to pay them. Well, my opinion is that the defendants are entitled to their costs; costs are not given against a party as a punishment, but as compensation to the successful party. Someone must bear the costs, and although it may be a hard matter on the plaintiff, it would be harder still on the defendants if they were deprived of the fruits of their success in this case. The plaintiff is not entitled to say to the defendants:—"You ought not to have appealed in this case when we undertook to go before the Master and submit to your view of taking the account; you ought not to have appealed to have that decision set right, and you ought to have allowed that decision to stand as a record of the Court for all time, and as a decision against you." And unless the plaintiff can say that, I do not see how he can successfully contend that he should not pay the defendants' costs.

I am of opinion, therefore, that this appeal should be allowed with costs.

STEPHEN, J. On the main point I cordially agree with his Honour *The Chief Justice.*

On the question of costs, it appears that the plaintiff in the Court below consistently opposed the contention of the defendants as to the basis of the account, and even now I do not gather that he admits the defendants are right, he merely says he will not argue that they are wrong. He now seeks to deprive the defendants of their costs of shewing that there should no longer appear on the records of this Court a decree which says in this particular matter that the defendants were wrong. It appears to me, in the absence of any authority to the contrary, that the defendants must have a right to have it on

(1) 16 N.S.W.R. Eq. 49.

record that in this particular transaction they have acted in accordance with the law.

1898.

IRVING
v.
COMMERCIAL
BANKING Co.
OF SYDNEY.

Stephen J.

The position which the plaintiff would place us in, if not in this case, in some other, would be that this Court upon an appeal would have to discuss the bearing of possibly a voluminous correspondence to determine on its construction how far the appellant is bound by the respondent's offer, whether a binding agreement is disclosed in the letters, and so forth. I do not think that is a position into which this Court should be put. I certainly see it is a hardship on the plaintiff if he was willing to do what the defendants wanted. However that may be, it is a novel point, and the plaintiff has not satisfied me, as he was bound to do, that the defendants should be deprived of their right of appeal, and having been successful that they should be deprived of their costs.

A. H. SIMPSON, J. I entirely concur on the main point, which seems to have been actually decided in *Bank of N.S.W.* v. *Taylor* (1). I have some doubt on the question of costs, and if the matter rested with me alone, I should have preferred to consider my judgment on the point; I do not, however, feel inclined to differ from their Honours. The main point that weighs with me is, that immediately after the decree is made, the plaintiff's solicitors write saying that they have taken the trouble to analyse the accounts and find the defendants' contention is really in their favour, and they are therefore willing to have the accounts taken as the defendants contend.

Under these circumstances, as the plaintiff is really responsible for the making of the erroneous decree, which has to be set right, it appears to me only fair that he should pay the costs of so doing.

Solicitors for the plaintiff: *Johnson, Minter, Simpson & Co.*

Solicitors for the defendants: *Cape, Kent & Gaden.*

(1) 2 N.S.W. L.R. 118.

ATTORNEY-GENERAL *v.* WALTERS AND OTHERS.

1898.

March 9, 10.

April 1.

J. C.*

Crown lands—Crown Lands Act of 1884 (48 Vic. No. 18), ss. 13, 14, 20, 39—
Reference as to question of forfeiture.

Questions of "lapse," "voidance," and "forfeiture," which the Minister may refer to the Land Board under s. 20 of the Crown Lands Act of 1884, are questions of fact to be determined by the Board after a trial under s. 14. Upon the questions of fact being determined by the Board, the responsibility of determining whether the land shall be forfeited for non-compliance with conditions rests with the Minister ; and this whether the land has been taken up prior to the Crown Lands Act of 1884, or not. Decision of the Full Court (THE CHIEF JUSTICE and COHEN, J. ; MANNING, J., *dissentiente*) reversed ; decree of OWEN, C.J. in Eq., restored.

THIS was an appeal from the decision of the Full Court, which is reported in 17 N.S.W.R. Eq. 105. The main points in dispute were, whether an informal reference from the Minister for Lands to the Land Board directing an enquiry as to fulfilment of conditions as to improvements, was a reference under s. 13 or s. 20 of the Crown Lands Act of 1884 ; and also as to power of the Minister to declare a forfeiture. The facts will be found set out in detail in the report in 17 N.S.W.R. Eq. 105, and are also summarised in the judgment of the Privy Council.

Vaughan Hawkins (*Cozens Hardy*, Q.C., with him), for the Attorney-General, the appellant.

The respondent Black did not appear.

April 1.

Judgment was, on the 1st April, delivered by

LORD MACNAGHTEN. The Crown in this case seeks to recover certain lands in the parish of Cumbertine in the county of Camden, which were the subject of two conditional purchases— an original conditional purchase of 400 acres on the 21st of June, 1883, and an additional conditional purchase of 44½ acres on the 28th of February, 1884. The contention of the Crown is that the lands became liable to forfeiture and have been duly forfeited

* Present : THE LORD CHANCELLOR (Lord HALSBURY), Lord HERSCHELL, Lord MACNAGHTEN, Lord MORRIS and Sir RICHARD COUCH.

for non-compliance with the statutory conditions in regard to improvements. The original selector or conditional purchaser was one Moore. In 1888 he transferred his purchases to one Walters, apparently by way of mortgage. In December, 1890, he conveyed the equity of redemption to the respondent Black. Moore and Walters have both been disposed of. The respondent Black, who is in possession of the land, resists the claim of the Crown on the ground that the proceedings on the part of the Crown were unauthorised and irregular, and that the alleged forfeiture was therefore invalid. In the Courts below some question was raised or suggested as to the position of the respondent Black. But for the purposes of this case it may be assumed that he duly became entitled to Moore's conditional purchases subject to the statutory conditions attached thereto.

1898.

ATTORNEY
GENERAL
v.
WALTERS.

Lord
Macnaghten.

The conditional purchases having been made before the 1st of January, 1885, when the Crown Lands Act of 1884 came into force, the conditions with regard to improvements applicable to the case under the combined operation of the Crown Lands (Alienation) Act of 1861, and the amending Acts of 1875 and 1880, were that the lands should be improved to the value of 6s. per acre within three years, and of 10s. per acre within five years after the purchase; but the Act of 1875, s. 17, provided that the period of three years might be held to commence from the date of the survey of the lands conditionally purchased.

Sect. 18 of the Act of 1861 declared that on default of a compliance with the requirements of that section, which included a condition as to improvements to some extent varied by subsequent enactments, the land conditionally purchased should " revert to Her Majesty," an expression which in the Act of 1880 and in subsequent Acts is treated as equivalent to the expression "become liable to forfeiture." The Act of 1861 provided no machinery for determining or investigating any question between a conditional purchaser and the Minister in charge of Crown lands. By the Act of 1861, as amended by the Act of 1875, the requirements of s. 18 of the former Act were to be held to have been complied with on a statutory declaration being made as therein prescribed, and " on the Minister being satisfied," and

1898.

ATTORNEY
GENERAL
v.
WALTERS.

Lord
Macnaghten.

thereupon on payment of the balance of the purchase money the grant in fee was to issue.

By the Act of 1875, s. 25, the Governor in Council was empowered to appoint a commissioner to whom should, in case of dispute or question, and might in every case, be referred by the Minister the claim of a conditional purchaser to a grant, and complaints by any person that a conditional purchaser had not fulfilled, or was not fulfilling, the condition as to improvements. The commissioner was to hear evidence in open Court and report to the Minister. The Act, however, did not contain any provision making the commissioner's report final as between the parties, or in any way binding upon the Minister. Both before and after the Act of 1875 it was held that the action of the Minister in declaring a forfeiture for non-compliance with statutory conditions, might be questioned at law, and that if it were so questioned it was incumbent on the Minister to prove that the forfeiture was justified.

The Act of 1884 repealed the previous Acts, but it contained a provision (s. 2B) to the effect that notwithstanding such repeal all rights accrued and obligations incurred and imposed under or by virtue of any of the repealed enactments should, subject to any express provisions of that Act in relation thereto, remain unaffected by such repeal.

The Act then proceeded to re-enact the repealed code of land legislation with various modifications and amendments. In place of the provisions relating to the appointment of a commissioner under the Act of 1875, it contained a group of sections (ss. 11-20) providing for the establishment of Local Land Boards, and defining their duties, mode of procedure, and powers. Sect. 13 provided that in addition to the matters thereinafter "required or permitted to be made the subject of adjudication . . . inquiry or report by Local Land Boards," it should be the duty of every Land Board to hear, examine, and report to the Minister upon (among other things) :—

"(II.) Any complaint or question as to the non-fulfilment of any condition of residence or improvement by a conditional purchaser under any of the said repealed Acts."

Then followed provisions regulating procedure. Every Local Land Board was to hear and determine all complaints and other matters brought before it, and was to conduct all inquiries sitting as in open Court, with power to take evidence on oath, and to compel attendance of witnesses, the procedure being the same as the procedure before a Court of Petty Sessions. The decision of the Board was to be given in open Court, and immediately after adjudication or decision upon any case, the chairman of the Board was to forward all papers connected with the case, together with any report required thereon to the Minister. Sects. 18 and 19 provided for an appeal to the Minister. But these two sections were repealed by the Act of 1889, which established a Land Court for the hearing of appeals, and for other purposes. Sect. 20 of the Act of 1884, on which the question in this case mainly depends, is in the following terms:—

" 20. Any question of lapse, voidance, or forfeiture, whether arising under this Act or any of the said repealed Acts, may be by the Minister referred to the Local Land Board, and the decision thereon of the said Court shall, unless appealed from in the prescribed manner, be final."

Sect. 136 provided that every forfeiture of land conditionally purchased whether under that Act or any of the said repealed Acts should be deemed to operate as a forfeiture of all additional conditional purchases held in virtue of such first mentioned lands, and that whenever any land should be forfeited under that Act such land should become Crown land and might be dealt with as such, but no forfeiture of any purchase under that Act, or any Act thereby repealed, was to take effect until the expiration of thirty clear days after notification of such forfeiture in the Gazette.

In 1887, the Minister for Lands directed that the period of three years within which improvements to the value of six shillings per acre were to be made on the lands comprised in Moore's conditional purchases should be held to commence from the date of the survey which had been finally approved on the 26th of February, 1885.

On the 18th of June, 1888, at the instance of the Minister, the Local Land Board held an inquiry, and having taken evidence

1898.

ATTORNEY GENERAL *v.* WALTERS.

Lord Macnaghten.

1898.

ATTORNEY
GENERAL
v.
WALTERS.

Lord
Macnaghten

found that improvements to the value of six shillings an acre had
been placed upon the land within three years from the date of
the acceptance of the survey by the Surveyor General. It is
common ground that this inquiry was held under s. 20 of the
Act of 1884, and that the decision upon it became final under
that section.

On the 4th of August, 1891, the period of five years allowed
for completion of the improvements having expired since the
former proceedings, the Minister further referred to the Local
Land Board, in addition to certain questions which are not now
material, the question whether the condition of improvements to
the value of ten shillings per acre had been fulfilled or not.
Notice to appear on the investigation before the Land Board was
duly served upon the respondent Black. He appeared by a solicitor, and objected to the proceedings.

The inquiry by the Land Board took place on the 28th of
October, 1891, and four subsequent days. On the 14th of
December, 1891, the Local Land Board gave their decision as
follows :—"Having taken evidence and inquired into the said
matter 'we find that 400 acres contained in C. P. 83, 11 ' (the
original conditional purchase) 'never was improved to the value
of 200l., and that 44½ acres contained in C.P. 84, 7 ' (the additional
conditional purchase) 'never was improved,'" and they reported
to the Minister accordingly.

Walters appealed against the finding of the Local Land Board.
The respondent Black was served with notice of the appeal, but
did not appear. On the 10th of June, 1892, the Land Court
dismissed the appeal.

On the 10th of August, 1892, the then Minister for Lands
approved of the forfeiture of Moore's conditional purchases.
Notice of forfeiture appeared in the Government Gazette of the
21st of September, 1892.

On the 8th of August, 1894, the Attorney-General filed an
information in equity in the Supreme Court against the respondents Walters and Black, and the respondent Coffill, a caretaker.
in possession on behalf of Black, praying that the title of the
Crown to the land in question might be established and that
Black and Coffill might be ordered to deliver up possession.

Walters appeared and submitted to such decree as the Court should think fit to make. Coffill disclaimed. The respondent Black filed a statement of defence, claiming to be entitled to the land as purchaser for value. He denied that the Local Land Board duly investigated the questions referred to it as alleged in the information.

1898.

ATTORNEY
GENERAL
v.
WALTERS.

*Lord
Macnaghten.*

On the 13th of December, 1895, the *Chief Judge in Equity* made a decree in accordance with the prayer of the information.

The respondent Black appealed to the Full Court. On the 3rd of July, 1896, the Full Court (*Darley*, C.J., *Cohen*, J.; *Manning*, J., dissenting) reversed the decree as against Black and dismissed the information. *The Chief Justice* held that the power of the Minister to declare a forfeiture has been, since the repeal of s. 18 of the Act of 1884, by the Act of 1889, "completely swept away." He thought that the finding of the Local Land Board of the 14th of December, 1891, was a finding upon a reference under s. 13, and not under s. 20 of the Act of 1884, and that, being under s. 13, it bound no one. His view was that the Minister, if he pleased, might have disregarded it altogether, but that if he still thought that the case was one that justified a forfeiture, the only course open to him was to refer the question of forfeiture to the Land Board, "which tribunal may," he said, "in their judicial discretion refuse to decide in favour of a forfeiture, notwithstanding that they had already reported according to the fact that the condition of improvements had not been complied with."

Their Lordships are unable to accept the conclusions of the Full Court. They agree in the opinion of the *Chief Judge in Equity*, and in the very able and careful judgment of *Manning*, J. They think that the reference which resulted in the findings of the 14th December, 1891, must be taken to have been made under the provisions of s. 20 of the Act of 1884. They are unable to agree with *The Chief Justice* in thinking that the power of the Minister to declare a forfeiture has been swept away, nor can they agree in his view that a judicial discretion to refuse to decide in favour of a forfeiture has been committed to the Land Board.

The reference to the Local Land Board was certainly not made in that precise and careful way in which one would expect an

1898.

ATTORNEY
GENERAL
v.
WALTERS.

Lord
Macnaghten.

important Government Department to conduct its business. But there can be no doubt as to the meaning of the reference. The Local Land Board had adjudicated under s. 20 on the question whether the required improvements had been made within the period of three years. Their decision on that point was final. The period of five years had expired, and the time had come for completing the investigation. The papers were sent back in a somewhat slovenly fashion, but with an intimation to the Land Board of the issues on which their opinion was desired. The matter on which the Minister required their report fell properly under s. 20. An inquiry without the element of finality would have been idle, and might have been a great hardship on the conditional purchaser. The Land Board conducted the investigation in a regular and formal manner, and they reported to the Minister the decision at which they arrived. The Act of 1884 does not prescribe any particular form of reference under s. 20. There seems to be no reason why a decision upon a reference framed in the words of sub-s. II. of s. 13, though not containing anything pointing directly and in terms to s. 20, should not be final under the provisions of that section if the question is really a question of forfeiture, that is, an issue of fact, which, if determined against the conditional purchaser, would render the purchase " liable to forfeiture."

Questions of " lapse," " voidance," and " forfeiture," which may be referred to the Land Board under s. 20, are, in their Lordships' opinion, questions of fact to be determined by the Board after a trial held in manner prescribed by s. 14. " Voidance," to give an example, would include a case where the Legislature has declared that in a certain event the purchase " shall become void," as, for instance, under s. 7 of the Act of 1875, in the case of a false statement as to the age of the applicant for a conditional purchase. " Lapse " applies to cases where the conditional purchase has been abandoned as mentioned in s. 17 of the Act of 1875. In both these cases the determination of the Land Board, as Manning, J., observes, must be simply a determination on a question of fact. Why should it be otherwise in the case of forfeiture ? The Local Land Board have simply to determine whether the statutory requirements have been complied with or not. If those requirements are found to have been complied with, the power of the Minister to declare a forfeiture for non-compliance is at an end. If the finding is the other way, the discretionary power of declaring a forfeiture with all responsibility rests with the Minister. It must be so as *Manning, J.*, points out in cases of forfeiture of conditional purchases under the Act of 1884. For s. 39 of the Act of 1884, which applies to conditional purchases under that Act, declares that if the Local Land Board shall report to the Minister that after due enquiry held by such Board, the conditions prescribed have not been duly fulfilled, "it shall be lawful" for such Minister to declare the conditional purchase to be forfeited. The discretion by that section is given to the Minister, and to no one else. In the absence of any distinct provision making a difference between conditional purchases under the Act of 1884, and those under the earlier Acts, it is difficult to suppose that the Legislature could have intended that in the one case the discretion should rest with the Land Board, and in the other with the Minister.

Their Lordships are of opinion that the judgment under appeal should be reversed, and the appeal to the Full Court dismissed with costs, and the judgment of the *Chief Judge in Equity* restored, and they will humbly advise Her Majesty accordingly.

As the difficulty in this case is mainly due to the carelessness of the Lands Department, their Lordships think that the appellants should bear their own costs of this appeal.

1898.

ATTORNEY
GENERAL
v.
WALTERS.

*Lord
Macnaghten.*

FLOWER and Others v. OWEN and Others.

1898.

June 14,
15, 16.

C.J. Eq.

Constructive notice—Notice of breach of trust from recital in title deed—Money subject to a settlement authorised to be laid out in the purchase of land—Erection of house on land subject to the setttlement—Payment of purchase moneys to nominee of trustee vendor.

Where in the recitals of one of the title deeds to land facts are disclosed which point to a possible breach of trust having been committed, a purchaser who omits to enquire has constructive notice of such facts as it is reasonable to suppose he would have learnt upon enquiry, but not of such facts as it is possible he might have learnt.

A purchaser from a trustee is justified in paying the purchase money to the trustee's nominee, provided he obtains a receipt from the trustee.

THIS was a suit brought by the children of Margaret Mary Flower against Percy Owen, James Thómpson and Margaret Mary Flower, for a declaration that a conveyance dated 30th June, 1885, by the trustee of a settlement made by Mrs. Flower on the 3rd December, 1869, might be declared fraudulent and void, or in the alternative that the defendants might be ordered to reconvey the lands comprised in such conveyance to trustees upon the trusts of the settlement free from all incumbrances so far as regarded the rights of the plaintiffs.

The facts were as follows :—

The defendant, Mrs. Flower, was entitled under the will of her father to certain real estate situated at Watson's Bay, and also in Crown-street, in the city of Sydney.   On the 3rd December, 1869, Mrs. Flower and her husband made a post-nuptial settlement of this real estate, by which it was conveyed to William McEachern upon trust for Mrs. Flower for life with remainder to her children.

The settlement also declared " that it should be lawful for the trustees or trustee for the time being of these presents at any time with the consent of the said Margaret Mary Flower during her life   .   .   .   to sell and absolutely dispose of any portion of the trust property in such manner and upon such terms as they shall think fit, and the receipt of the trustees shall discharge the purchaser or purchasers from all liability to see to the application of the purchase money, and to invest the net purchase moneys in Government securities or in the purchase or on mortgage of real or leasehold estate, etc."

Subsequently to this settlement, in the year 1881 or 1882, Mrs. Cameron, the mother of Mrs. Flower, advanced to her daughter the sum of 550*l.*, which sum was expended in building two houses on one of the allotments at Watson's Bay.

On the 30th June, 1885, a conveyance of the same land on which these two houses were built was executed by the then trustees William McEachern and Mrs. Flower to Mrs. Cameron.

The conveyance contained the following recitals: " And whereas the said Margaret Cameron some years ago at the request of the said Margaret Mary Flower and with the consent of the said William McEachern paid and advanced to the said Margaret Mary Flower the sum of 550*l.* for the purpose of building on or otherwise improving the said land and hereditaments " (viz., the whole of the settled land) " in consideration that the said William McEachern would convey, release or otherwise assure to her the said Margaret Cameron the lands and hereditaments hereinafter described and intended to be hereby conveyed, released or otherwise assured for an estate in fee simple which the said William McEachern agreed to do, and whereas no conveyance of the said land and hereditaments has yet been executed to the said Margaret Cameron."

The receipt clause was as follows :—

"Received as above-mentioned the sum of 550*l.* from the within-named Margaret Cameron, being the consideration money herein expressed to be paid by her to me.

W. McEACHERN."

Mrs. Flower said in her evidence that the recital in the conveyance was false, that her mother gave her the money, and that there was never any agreement to repay it, nor was it treated as purchase money for any part of the estate.

Shortly after this conveyance the land was made the subject of an equitable mortgage by Mrs. Cameron and Mrs. Flower to the Commercial Bank to secure advances made to J. W. C. Flower, the husband of Mrs. Flower, for his own use.   On March 7th,

1888, the land was again mortgaged to secure an advance of 350l., which sum was received by J. W. C. Flower.

These sums were in course of time paid off, and on the 12th May, 1894, the land was mortgaged to the defendants Owen and Thompson, Mrs. Flower making a statutory declaration to the effect that she knew of no claims against the land.

Mrs. Cameron died on the 11th February, 1898, leaving Mrs. Flower sole legatee and executrix under her will.

William McEachern died in 1895, leaving no property in New South Wales. No new trustee was appointed in his place.

In November, 1897, the interest on the mortgage being in arrear, the defendants Owen and Thompson threatened to sell the land.

The plaintiffs alleged that the conveyance of June 30th, 1885, was executed in pursuance of a scheme to enable J. W. C. Flower to borrow money on the security of the land so conveyed to Mrs. Cameron.

They also charged that the defendants Owen and Thompson had notice that the conveyance of 30th June, 1885, was a breach of trust, and submitted that they were entitled to a decree as above mentioned.

L. Owen (*Kelynack* with him), for the plaintiffs. The defendants Owen and Thompson had constructive notice of the breach of trust committed. The words in the recital " or otherwise improving the said lands and hereditaments " shewed that a breach of trust had been contemplated : *Drake* v. *Trefusis* (1), *Vine* v. *Raleigh* (2).

A reasonable purchaser would requisition whether any of the purchase money was spent on the land conveyed. The consideration was a past debt, and that in itself is a suspicious circumstance which should cause a purchaser to make careful enquiry. The consideration money was paid to the tenant for life and not to the trustee ; a purchaser has no right to pay purchase moneys to a trustee's nominee—he must pay it to the trustee; the receipt clause only acknowledges the receipt " as above mentioned." If the title deeds disclose suspicious circumstances, a purchaser is

(1) 10 Ch. 364.   (2) [1891] 2 Ch. 13.

bound to enquire what is the true transaction, and if he does not do so he is bound as if he had done so.

He referred to *Dart on Vendors and Purchasers* (1); *Hope* v. *Liddle* (2); *Re Bellamy* (3); *Jones* v. *Smith* (4); *Attorney-General* v. *Purgeter* (5); *Kerr* v. *Lord Dungannon* (6); *Douglass* v. *Bank of Australasia* (7); *Robinson* v. *Briggs* (8).

H. P. Owen, for the defendants Owen and Thompson. It is not correct to say that the conveyance was executed for a past consideration. The land was sold when the money was paid, the conveyance being merely postponed. It was really a case of misapplication of the purchase money.

The defendants were entitled to assume that the recital in the deed as to there being an agreement was correct. There is nothing on the face of the deed calling for enquiry. A person cannot be held to have had constructive notice of some fact that he might have discovered if he had made enquiry unless there is gross and culpable negligence on his part: *Ware* v. *Lord Egmont* (9); *Bailey* v. *Barnes* (10). All the cases cited for the plaintiffs are cases in which on the face of the deed there was something that disclosed an inherent defect in the title. Here the recital is that the purchase money was expended in building on some part of the settled land; and no one in his senses would have imagined that the houses were erected on the conveyed land. If a recital will bear an innocent interpretation the Court will so interpret it in favour of a purchaser for value: *Kenny* v. *Brown* (11); *Sugden's Vendors and Purchasers* (12). Defendants were entitled to assume that the trustee had satisfied himself the money had been properly expended when he executed the conveyance.

He also referred to *Hope* v. *Liddle* (13); *Robertson* v. *Armstrong* (14); *Locke* v. *Lomas* (15); *Lewin on Trusts* (16); *Dart on*

(1) 6th Edit., pp. 685, 986.	(9) 4 De G. M. & G. 460.
(2) 21 Beav. 183.	(10) [1894] 1 Ch. 25.
(3) 24 Ch. Div. 387.	(11) 3 Ridg. P.C. 462, 511.
(4) 1 Hare 43 at p. 55.	(12) 14th Ed., p. 779.
(5) 6 Beav. 150.	(13) 21 Beav. 183.
(6) 1 Dru. & W. 409.	(14) 28 Beav. 123, 127.
(7) 12 N.S W.R. Eq. 227.	(15) 5 De G. & Sm. 326.
(8) 1 Sm. & G. 188.	(16) 9th Ed., p. 523.

Vendors and Purchasers (1); *Jones* v. *Smith* (2); *Re A. W. Hall & Co., Ltd.* (3); *Gainsborough* v. *Watcombe* (4); *In re Rector of Claypole* (5); *In re Leslie's Trusts* (6); *In re Speer's Trusts* (7).

Loxton, for Mrs. Flower, submitted that she was not a trustee for those in remainder, and had no duty cast upon her to consider them.

L. Owen in reply. He referred to *Brunskill* v. *Caird* (8); *Lewin on Trusts* (9). The case of *Ware* v. *Lord Egmont* is qualified by that of *Montefiore* v. *Brown* (10). The reference to the land in the recital was in itself a suspicious circumstance enough to cause a purchaser to make enquiry.

MANNING, C.J., in Eq.* The defendant, Margaret Mary Flower, was entitled under the will of her father to certain real estate situated at Watson's Bay, and also in Crown-street in the city of Sydney; and on the 3rd December, 1869, she and her husband made a settlement of the land by which she took an estate for her life with remainder to her children.

In the settlement there was reserved a power of sale by the trustees with the consent in her lifetime of Mrs. Flower, and power was given to invest the proceeds in the purchase of real estate or Government securities. Subsequently, in the year 1881 or 1882, Mrs. Cameron, the mother of Mrs. Flower, advanced to her daughter the sum of 550*l*., which sum was expended in building two houses on one of the allotments at Watson's Bay. Mrs. Flower now says that her mother gave her the money, and that there was never any agreement that the money should be repaid, nor that it should be treated as purchase money of any part of the estate. But in an indenture of 30th June, 1885, the land, the subject of this suit, which is the land on which the two houses were built, was conveyed to Mrs. Cameron in pursuance of an agreement recited as having been made previously, and as having remained unexecuted up to that time.

(1) 6th Ed., p. 986.	(6) 2 Ch. Div. 185.
(2) 1 Phill. 244.	(7) 3 Ch. Div. 262.
(3) 37 Ch. Div. 712.	(8) 16 Eq. 493.
(4) 54 L J. Ch. 991.	(9) 9th Ed., p. 508.
(5) 16 Eq. 574.	(10) 7 H.L.C. 241.

* This judgment was not revised by the late *Chief Judge in Equity*.

The conveyance recited the settlement of the whole of the land, and then continued :—"And whereas the said Margaret Cameron some years ago at the request of the said Margaret Mary Flower and with the consent of the said William McEachern (the trustee) paid and advanced to the said Margaret Mary Flower the sum of 550l. for the purpose of building on or otherwise improving the said land and hereditaments in consideration of the conveyance to Mrs. Cameron of the land now in question." Then followed the operative part of the deed. Mrs. Flower was a party to this deed, so that she solemnly attested to the truth of what she now says is untrue. Some years afterwards Mrs. Flower negotiated a loan through the office of Messrs. Stephen, Jaques & Stephen on the security of this very property. That loan was paid off in 1894, and she afterwards negotiated a further loan on the same property from the defendants Thompson and Owen, acting as trustees of another estate.

These gentlemen having been in communication with Mrs. Flower, and having obtained a declaration from her that there were no claims against the estate, were satisfied with the title and advanced their money upon the security.

Subsequently Mrs. Flower, being anxious to pay off the mortgage, consulted Mr. Heydon's managing clerk, Mr. Austin, whether she could not sell other portions of the property to pay off the mortgage. He advised her, and very properly so, that she could not, as the only power in the settlement was to sell out and out, in which case the proceeds must be invested in accordance with the terms of the settlement. Thereupon all the transactions came to light, and, acting on Mr. Heydon's advice, this suit was instituted by the children to set aside the whole transaction—both the sale to Mrs. Cameron and also the mortgage to Thompson and Owen. I am not now concerned with the original sale to Mrs Cameron, as if that were the only matter I should have very little difficulty in dealing with it; anything more extraordinary than that transaction it is difficult to conceive, and, as it appears to me, Mrs. Flower could hardly be advised by anyone to come into Court and support it; she would be claiming under an agreement to sell the very land on which the purchase money was laid out.

The mortgagees, however, are in a very different position; they are beyond all question purchasers for valuable consideration without actual notice. They had no idea that this tale was untrue, or what was the nature of this transaction that took place. All they knew was what was disclosed in the documents, and what they heard on enquiry from Mrs. Flower.

Now it is said they must lose their mortgage because they had constructive notice of these transactions; that is, that the documents themselves on their face disclose a defect in the title so as to put them on enquiry, and if they had made such enquiry they would have found out the truth of the transaction.

In dealing with the case, I will first refer to what was said by Lord *Cranworth* in the case of *Ware* v. *Lord Egmont* (1), protesting against any extension of the doctrine of constructive notice. He says:—"Where a person has actual notice of any matter of fact there can be no danger of doing injustice he is held to be bound by all the consequences of that which he was to exist. But where he has not actual notice he ought not treated as if he had notice, unless the circumstances are su enable the Court to say not only that he might have acqui but also that he ought to have acquired the notice with whic is sought to affect him—that he would have acquired it but his gross negligence in the conduct of the business in questio The question where it is sought to affect a purchaser with con structive notice is not whether he had the means of obtaining and might by prudent caution have obtained, the knowledge in question, but whether the not obtaining it was an act of gross o culpable negligence. It is obvious that no definite rule as to what will amount to gross or culpable negligence so as to mee every case can possibly be laid down."

That passage is cited with approval by *Lindley, L.J.*, as late as 1893, in the case of *Bailey* v. *Barnes* (2), but he then adds what is practically to be collected from the language of Lord *Cranworth*, and what Lord *Cranworth* himself indicated the case of *Montefiore* v. *Brown* (3), namely, that gross an culpable negligence does not necessarily mean the breach of so

(1) 4 De G. M. & G. 473.   (2) [1894] 1 Ch. 25.
(3) 7 H.L.C. 241.

legal duty, "for a purchaser of property is under no legal obligation to investigate his vendor's title. But in dealing with real
property, as in other matters of business, regard is had to the
usual course of business, and a purchaser who wilfully departs
from it in order to avoid acquiring a knowledge of his vendor's
title is not allowed to derive any advantage from his wilful
ignorance of defects which would have come to his knowledge if
he had transacted his business in the ordinary way. In the
celebrated judgment of Vice-Chancellor *Wigram*, in *Jones* v.
Smith, the cases of constructive notice are reduced to two classes:
the first comprises cases in which a purchaser has actual notice
of some defect, inquiry into which would disclose others; and
the second comprises cases in which a purchaser has purposely
abstained from making inquiries for fear he should discover
something wrong."

That case quite explains what Lord *Cranworth* meant by
"gross and culpable negligence," and it also shews the classes
one of which a person must be brought before he can be
to have had constructive notice.

this case the defendants clearly cannot be brought into the
class, as there is no question of wilful abstention from
enquiries. Therefore, the question arises: can the
ants be brought within the first class? Which naturally
ise to the further question, what sort of defect is it that
e disclosed? It appears to me it must be one going to the
the matter indicating the existence of an equity to set
he transaction. If the defect only arises in connection with
bsequent application of the purchase money, it appears to
t would not be enough. Was there then anything disclosed
itle which would suggest to a purchaser that any person
uity to set aside the whole transaction? Clearly there
int of fact, an equity, but that is not the point; what
consider is, did the documents on their face disclose it?
ering this matter, first of all, one must look at all the
s; secondly, at the position of the parties making the
and thirdly, what other facts and circumstances the
r had before him in addition to the documents.

] 1 Ch. 25.   G 2

1898.

FLOWER
v.
OWEN.

C.J. Eq.

I understand the plaintiff's counsel to contend that four grounds for suspicion are disclosed : first, they say the recited transaction of itself would arouse suspicion ; secondly, they rely on the fact that the money is recited to have been advanced for the purpose, not only of building, but of otherwise improving the land and hereditaments ; thirdly, they point to the jumble of the language of the deed, which uses the expression " the land and hereditaments " as applying to the whole settled estate as well as to the particular property conveyed ; this they say would put a reasonable man on enquiry ; and fourthly, they rely on the fact that it was disclosed that the money was paid, not to the trustee, but to Mrs. Flower.

With regard to the first point, I am of opinion that the transaction itself, as recited in the deed, would not raise a suspicion that it was not bona fide ; I confess that I cannot see why it should. No doubt it is a clumsy recital, but it only amounts to this, that Mrs. Flower wanted money to build on trust estate, and she applied to her mother, who, in effect, said " I will give you 550*l.* for a certain allotment, and then you can lay out the money in building as you want." The trustee knew of the proposal, he knew of their agreement and approved of it, and under the settlement he had a power of sale, with the consent of Mrs. Flower during her lifetime. This transaction was not perfected by conveyance at the time, but two or three years later Mrs. Cameron called upon the trustee and her daughter to convey. He then being satisfied that all was right, and apparently with the approval of Mrs. Flower, for she joined in executing the deed, conveyed the land to Mrs. Cameron. I cannot see myself any cause for suspicion; just as there are persons with an unnaturally keen nose for a nuisance, so there are persons who will suspect a flaw in the most innocent-looking transaction ; but the ordinary purchaser is not expected to scent out irregularities where none appear. There was nothing in the position of these gentlemen which would make them anxious to close with the bargain, or ready to overlook any possible flaw in the title. They were mere mortgagees, not anxious purchasers; if one security for their money was not safe, they would have no difficulty in finding another; all they wanted was to be satisfied it was all right.

All they would gather from this recital was that there was an
out and out agreement to sell for 550*l.*, part of the estate, the
money to be laid out on the estate, and the agreement was carried
out some years after. There is nothing in that to put these
gentlemen on enquiry.

Passing from that point, I have next to consider the objection
as to the money being recited as having been used, not merely
for building on, but also for "otherwise improving" the estate.
The purchase money for any land sold was required by the settlement to be laid out in a certain way, *i.e.*, in the purchase of real
estate. Now this was not laid out in the purchase of real estate,
but in building and otherwise improving the settled land. In
Drake v. *Trefusis* (1), it was held that where there is a power to
invest in the purchase of real estate, such power can be properly
exercised by investing in building on other land subject to the
same trusts, that being equivalent to the purchase of a house.
But in that case it was also clearly laid down that that rule does
not apply to ordinary improvements, such as draining or fencing
the land, repairing cottages, etc. It is said that when Thompson
found out that in the inception the money was advanced for
building and improvements, he should have assumed that
apparently a breach of trust was contemplated, and he should,
therefore, have made enquiries ; at all events it is contended
there was notice that there might be difficulties in the matter,
and a prudent man would have made enquiries: and if any
enquiry had been made, the whole story would have come out.
Now I confess this is a matter of very great nicety, and a terribly
small reef on which to wreck a bona fide purchaser. But if the law
says that such conduct is negligence, it is no business of mine ;
if the mere fact of these words being in the document indicates
that there was a defect in the sale, and makes a purchaser bound
to enquire into the circumstances, and upon enquiry it is reasonable to suppose that the true circumstances would have been discovered, this Court has no option but to set aside the mortgage.

Here we have people who, as I said before, are not anxious
purchasers, they are mortgagees, and can retire from the negotia-
tion at any time up to the last moment before the contract is

(1) 10 Ch. 364,

1898.

FLOWER
v.
OWEN.

C.J. Eq.

1898.

FLOWER
v.
OWEN.

C.J. Eq.

completed, as no mortgagee is bound to advance the money until
it is signed. All they require is simply a security for their money.
They find out that the person who is negotiating the loan is Mrs.
Flower, and if any question of doubt had arisen on the construction of the documents, she would have been approached. She
was asking for the money, and she did, in fact, represent to them
that she knew of no reason why an advance should not be made.
She was a party to the deed, and is bound by the recital in it,
and she came to borrow money on this land. No questions are,
as a matter of fact, asked. The mortgagees knew that she had
had the money before from somebody else and had paid it off,
and she made a declaration that there were no claims against the
land. They also found that the trustee conveyed the land four
years after the transaction. Were they not, therefore, justified
in thinking that the trustee, when he executed the document,
had satisfied himself that the money, which had been advanced
partly for a legal, but possibly also for an illegal object, had been
properly laid out ? All these things he should have considered,
and the trustee, after careful consideration, has conveyed. Suppose that a breach of trust had been committed by spending 50l.
out of the 550l. on laying out a garden, then the transaction
could not have been set aside as to 500l.; the only result would
be to make the trustee, who had admitted the receipt of 550l.,
liable for the improper use of 50l. If the nature of the land,
suburban lots near Sydney, is considered, nobody could ever
suppose that all the purchase money would be expended in
draining or similar improvements. They were small building
allotments, on which the main improvements must be buildings,
and a garden might have cost a few pounds. If they had in fact
been informed that some part of the money had not been spent
in building, as to which there is no evidence, it would not have
gone to the whole transaction, but there would have been a breach
of trust only as to the application of part of the purchase money.

It appears to me that this recital as to other improvements is
only indicative of a possible improper outlay of portion of the
money; there is no evidence that in fact any of it was spent
otherwise than in building, and in fact, as I said, the trustee who
is responsible was prepared to convey away the property four

1898.

FLOWER
v.
OWEN.

C.J. Eq.

years after. Had they enquired they would naturally have
asked whether any portion of the money was expended in
improvements as distinct from building; and if they had made
enquiry they would naturally have been told that the money
had been spent in building and not in other improvements. I
think it is very improbable that they would have been told that
it was spent on the particular buildings on this particular land.
I feel little doubt that those cases which say that a purchaser
bound to enquire has imputed notice of any answer which he
might have received are not now law, and that the mortgagees
only had constructive notice of what answer they were reasonably likely to get if they had asked the question; in this case I
think the answer the mortgagees would have got to the question
how the money was expended would have been that it was all
expended in building.

I now turn to the third point, that from the conveyance the
mortgagees ought to have suspected that the money was laid out
on the land conveyed. I think the very monstrosity of the
transaction itself is an answer to the suggestion that it was a
breach of duty in not making enquiry whether the money was
so expended or not. No man in his senses could possibly suppose
that a piece of land was to be conveyed in consideration of a sum
of money which was to be expended on the land. The manifest
absurdity of the transaction is its own contradiction. There
then only remains the fourth and last objection as to the payment
of the purchase money to Mrs. Flower. It appears to me in the
first place that is simply a matter of the application of the
purchase money. It certainly appears from the cases that the
purchaser was under no compulsion to pay the money to Mrs.
Flower, although the trustee might so direct. But there is a
receipt in the document by the trustee himself; no doubt that
receipt clause contains the words "received as aforesaid," viz., by
payment to the tenant for life, but that appears to me to be
exactly the same as if the money had been paid to the trustee
himself. In one case it is said that a person may insist on all
the trustees being present to receive purchase money, or he may
insist on a joint receipt. I can see no distinction between that
and the trustee saying "Pay the purchase money to A.B. and I

1898.

FLOWER
v.
OWEN.

C.J. Eq.

give you the receipt for it." Possibly the trustees might be liable to the *cestuis que trustent*, but I do not see how the purchaser would be liable, provided he got a receipt from the trustee. But even if he were, that would be no ground for setting aside the transaction, which is the only matter I have to consider; at most it would only give the *cestuis que trustent* a remedy against the trustees and the purchaser for so much of the purchase money as was not forthcoming.

For all these reasons I am of opinion that the mortgagees had not constructive notice of such breaches of trust as will enable the plaintiffs to get the sale set aside.

Solicitor for plaintiffs : *L. F. Heydon.*

Solicitor for Owen and Thompson : *J. A. Thompson.*

Solicitor for M. M. Flower : *J. E. Murphy.*

SHAND v. ROBINSON AND OTHERS.

Will—Construction—Wills Act, s. 29—" In default of issue"—Estate tail—Trust for sale of land and distribution of proceeds where portion of the land sold before date of will—Whether the unpaid purchase moneys secured on mortgage pass under the trust.

1898.

April 24,
May 5.

C.J. Eq.

A testator devised an estate of 151 acres to a trustee on trust to sell and to pay the proceeds to H. Before the date of the will the testator had sold portion of the estate and received part of the purchase money, the balance being secured by mortgage of the portion sold and being unpaid at the testator's death. *Held*, that A. was not entitled to the unpaid balance of the purchase moneys.

A devise to H. for life and after his death to his heirs and in default of issue over gives A. an estate tail.

THIS was a friendly suit to determine a number of questions under the will of the late William Robinson, of Colyton.

By his will, dated the 23rd April, 1894, the testator, after payment of all his just debts, funeral and testamentary expenses, gave, devised and bequeathed to the plaintiff as executor all his real and personal estate upon the trusts following:—From and out of the 147 acres of land at Colyton, he directed that 7 acres should be conveyed to and vested in his daughter the defendant Mary Anne Robinson for her separate use for her life. And in the event of her dying and leaving issue then to her issue in fee simple, but in case she should die without issue then the said land should vest in his youngest son in fee simple, and he directed that the remaining 140 acres of the said land should be conveyed to and vested in his youngest son the defendant Alexander Robinson for life and after his death to his heirs, and in default of issue to the testator's lawful heirs in fee simple. And he further directed that the 151 acres adjoining Dr. M'Kay's land and known as Minchinberry should be sold, and the proceeds to be equally divided between the defendants Mary Anne Robinson and Alexander Robinson. And he also further directed that his funeral and testamentary expenses and his just debts should be paid and discharged out of the proceeds of the sale of the said 151 acres.

The testator died on the 4th May, 1896, leaving four children, including the two named in the will.

Prior to the making of his will the testator had sold and transferred 100 acres out of the 151 acres mentioned in his will. Some of the purchasers had paid their purchase money in full to the testator, who had mixed the same with his other moneys; two of the purchasers had not paid the whole of their purchase money, and had mortgaged back their respective purchases to the testator to secure their unpaid balances. These mortgages were dated in 1891 and 1892. One of these mortgages was paid off to the testator in April, 1897, and the amount received paid by him to the defendants Mary Anne Robinson and Alexander Robinson; the other was paid off to the plaintiff in 1897.

The testator left real and personal estate not disposed of by will.

The defendants Mary Anne Robinson and Alexander Robinson had barred their estates tail (if any) taken by them under the will. Alexander Robinson had also mortgaged his interest in Colyton.

It was stated to the Court that the 151 acres mentioned in the will was not named "Minchinberry" as appeared to be stated in the will; "Minchinberry" was the name of Dr. M'Kay's land adjoining the testator's 151 acres.

Rich, for the plaintiff, the executor of the will, stated the questions to the Court.

Knox, for the defendant Alexander Robinson. I submit that the interest taken by Alexander Robinson in Colyton is an estate tail : *Jarman on Wills*, p. 1173. The case is not within s. 29 of the Wills Act. The gift of the proceeds of sale of the 151 acres passes the moneys secured on mortgage; the testator must have meant Alexander Robinson and Mary Anne Robinson to take a beneficial interest in the whole 151 acres, because they could not take the legal estate owing to the provisions of the Probate Act, 1890, which passes the legal estate to the executor: *Re Clowes* (1). There is an evident intention to benefit only the two children

(1) [1893] 1 Ch. 214.

named in the will. The Court will lean against holding that he died intestate as to the mortgage moneys.

Street, for the mortgagee of the interest of Alexander Robinson, also contended that he took an estate tail in Colyton, citing *Morgan* v. *Morgan* (1); *Dawson* v. *Small* (2); *Jarman on Wills*, pp. 328, 532, 1174 and 1321.

R. K. Manning, for Mary Anne Robinson, contended that the devise of 7 acres in trust for Mary Anne Robinson gave her an estate in fee with an executory devise over in the event of death without children, citing *Woodhouse* v. *Meredith* (3).

This was uncontested by the other parties.

S. A. Thompson, for the children not mentioned in the will. The estate taken by Alexander Robinson was an estate in fee with an executory devise over in the event of death without leaving issue. Sect. 29 of the Wills Act applies, and the words in default of issue must be interpreted to mean in default of issue at his death; they are words which are capable of meaning that, and, therefore, the section applies: *Jarman on Wills*, p. 132; *Re Edwards* (4).

The devise of the 151 acres only passes the unconverted part of the estate; the direction to sell shews an intention only to pass what was unsold: *Morgan* v. *Thomas* (5); *Gale* v. *Gale* (6); *Blake* v. *Blake* (7); *Harrison* v. *Jackson* (8). There is no such difficulty about the devolution of the estate as was suggested in *Re Clowes;* there is no gift to the beneficiaries except of the proceeds after sale.

Knox in reply.

MANNING, C.J. in Eq.* As to the nature of the estate taken by Alexander Robinson, I hold a firm opinion that the legal effect of the words used is to give him an estate tail. In the first place, the words " in default of issue " do not occur in s. 29 of the Wills

(1) 10 Eq. 99.	(5) 6 Ch. D. 176.
(2) 9 Ch. 651.	(6) 21 Beav. 349.
(3) 1 Mer. 450.	(7) 15 Ch. D. 481.
(4) [1894] 3 Ch. 644.	(8) 7 Ch. D. 339.

* This judgment was not revised by the late *Chief Judge in Equity*.

1898.

SHAND
v.
ROBINSON.

C.J. Eq.

Act, so that if that section is to apply those words must in themselves be ambiguous, and import either an indefinite failure of
issue or a failure at the death of the tenant for life. I do not
think they are ambiguous; there never was any doubt as to
their meaning—that is, that they imported an indefinite failure
of issue, for there is nothing in the words to point to failure at
the death; and it is, to say the least of it, strange that since
1837 there is no case in which the words have been held to mean
failure at death, if they really are ambiguous, as Mr. *Thompson*
contends. And, apart from that, comparing the limitations in
the devise to Mary Anne Robinson with the limitations in this
devise, there is a marked contrast in the terms used; for whereas
in this case the words are " in default of issue," in the other they
are " die leaving issue," and " die without issue." Whoever drew
this will must, I think, have meant something different from the
use of these different expressions; and this is borne out by the
difference of the gifts over in the two cases, shewing clearly to
my mind an intention to create estates of different natures.

That brings me to what is to my mind the really difficult point
in this will; it is one of those cases in which it is only possible to
say confidently that the will has received its correct interpretation
when it has been interpreted by an ultimate Court of Appeal.

The testator devises and bequeaths all his real and personal
property to his executors; he then devises these interests in
favour of Mary Anne Robinson and Alexander Robinson, which
I have already dealt with, and then purports to dispose of a
certain estate which, it appears, is not itself named Minchinberry,
but adjoins an estate so named. At the date of the will the
testator had sold portion of this estate; part of the purchase
money he had himself received and mixed with his own moneys.
Some portion of the purchase money was left outstanding on the
security of the respective parts of the estate which had been sold.

This was what the testator knew at the time he made his will;
notwithstanding that, he speaks of this estate as if it was still
intact, he directs it to be sold, that is by his executors in whom the
estate is vested, and the proceeds to be divided between his
youngest son and daughter. There was no direct devise of the
land to the beneficiary in this case, so that the complication of

trusts suggested at the end of Lord Justice *Lindley's* judgment
in *In re Clowes* (1) does not apply. All that the beneficiaries
get is the procee ls of the land when sold, so that the devolution
of the estate is simple ; it passes to the executors with a power
of sale, coupled with a trust as to the proceeds.

It is contended that, because the testator mentions the whole
150 acres of which the estate originally consisted, the gift to his
children is equivalent to a gift of the proceeds of the whole of
the land, whether arising from a sale by the executors or by
himself. It is impossible, however, that they should get the
proceeds of the whole of the land, because portion was received
by the testator in his lifetime, and mixed with his own moneys ;
and, indeed, it is not contended by Mr. *Knox* that his clients
could get from the testator's estate that portion of the purchase
money. They can, therefore, only be entitled to the proceeds of
something less than the 150 acres which the testator mentions,
and the only question is of how much less. Mr. *Knox* contends
that they are entitled to the proceeds of the land still remaining
unsold, and so much of the proceeds of what has been sold as can
still be traced. I think they are only entitled to the proceeds of
the unsold portion. I am really in the same difficulty as the
Master of the Rolls in *Blake* v. *Blake* (2). He says :—" I must
read the will assuming that he still remembered so recent and
important a transaction, and what do I find ? He knew perfectly
well that a moiety of the settled estate had been conveyed to
such uses as he should appoint, and then he made a gift of that
same moiety to uses, including a term, and subject to the term,
to his son, in fee. Would it not be a straining of language to
say that that gift included the purchase money of a part of the
estate which had been sold ? The case of *falsa demonstratio* has
really no direct bearing on the subject, because, although in one
sense there is not anything to answer the description, in another
sense there is the same moiety of land remaining, although not
the same moiety of all the land ; and it can hardly be assumed
that a man who knew that part of the property had been sold
intended to give the proceeds by such words as these."

(1) [1893] 1 Ch. at 218..   (2) 15 Ch. D. 481 at 488.

That appears to me to be the only safe construction; putting myself so far as I can in the position of the testator as I am bound to do, knowing that the testator when he made this will had recently sold portion of this estate, and himself received portion of the purchase money, I feel that I am at any rate proceeding on a reasonable and safe principle in holding that the testator, in devising the estate to his executors and directing them how to deal with the proceeds of a sale which was to be effected by them, can only have meant them to take under the devise such portion of the estate as they could sell, viz., the unsold balance of the estate. That being so, the mortgages of those portions of the estate which the testator himself sold pass as part of his residuary personal estate. If no portion of the land had been left for the executors to sell, different considerations possibly might arise; it is not necessary now to discuss that question.

I was pressed with the well-known principle that the Court in construing wills leans against an intestacy, but I do not feel that that principle applies with much force to this will, where, whatever construction I put on this devise, I cannot altogether avoid holding that there is an intestacy as to the residuary personal estate.

For all these reasons, I hold that the devise to the executors in trust for Alexander Robinson and Mary Anne Robinson only applies to the unsold portion of the estate.

Costs of all parties will come out of the estate as between solicitor and client.

Solicitors: *S. J. Bull; C. Bull; Dowling & Taylor; Joseph Thompson.*

EVANS *v.* TORPY AND OTHERS.

1898.

March 31,
April 22.

A. H. Simpson J.

*Will—Construction—Forfeiture upon marriage with certain persons—Payment of
share upon giving bond to comply with condition.*

A testator devised and bequeathed certain interests under his will upon trust
for his children to vest when the youngest attained twenty-one years; but the
share of any child who intermarried with a Roman Catholic was immediately to
divest from him, and go to the others; each child was empowered to sell his
expectant share to another child, and thereupon the purchaser should be "entitled
to receive the share so purchased as if the share had been devised to him, the
purchaser."

Held, that the forfeiture clause was good, and applied to subsequent marriages,
and not merely to a first marriage; that, upon the sale by one child to another of
his share, that share became freed altogether from the forfeiture clause; that the
trustees might pay over the shares to the married children upon receiving bonds
from them to comply with the condition, and to the unmarried children upon a
similar bond from them and one surety.

THIS was a friendly suit to determine certain questions arising
under the will of the late Alexander Montgomery.

The testator, after making certain bequests, devised his estate
to trustees upon trust to hold and be possessed of his real estate
and the residue of his personal estate upon trust for all the
testator's children (except one) in equal shares, share and
share alike, to vest as and when the youngest or youngest survivor of his said children should have attained the age of twenty-
one years. The will then continued: " I further declare that any
child of mine except as aforesaid may sell his or her expectant
share to any other child or children of mine who may purchase
the expectant share or shares of any other child or children of
mine for a fair and reasonable price Upon such sale and purchase
the child or children so purchasing shall be entitled to receive the
share or shares so purchased as if the same had been legally
devised to him her or them the purchaser or purchasers thereof
· · · · and knowing by experience the misery and discord in

1898.

EVANS
v.
TORPY.

families caused by mixed marriages I declare that if any child of mine . . . . shall marry any Roman Catholic or member of the Church of Rome, then and immediately upon any such marriage such child shall absolutely cease to have any interest under this my will and any interest which any child of mine . . . shall become entitled to or shall have been actually received shall upon the happening of any such marriage become forfeited and shall fall into and become part of my said real and residuary personal estate and be distributable accordingly among the others or other of my said children entitled under this my will such distribution in the event of any such marriage taking place after vesting of any share as aforesaid to take place as if the person so marrying had not become entitled thereto under this my will and as if such share had not become vested in accordance with the terms of my will." One of the testator's children was insane; one son was unmarried; the other children were all married to persons not Roman Catholics. The plaintiff was one of the beneficiaries under the will, and the statement of claim prayed that the following questions might among others mentioned be determined by the Court:—

(c) Whether any child of the said testator on marrying a Roman Catholic forfeits his or her share of the said estate?

(d) Whether the aforesaid restriction as to marriage applies to second and subsequent marriages or only to a first marriage?

(e) Whether, in the event of one child of the testator purchasing the share of another child in the said estate, the said share is forfeited on either the vendor or purchaser thereof marrying a Roman Catholic?

(f) Whether, having regard to the aforesaid restriction, the trustees of the said estate will be justified in paying or handing over the share of any child of the testator in the corpus in the said estate until after the death of such child?

L. Owen, for the plaintiff, referred to the following cases upon the several questions referred to the Court. As to the validity of the forfeiture clause: *Hodgson* v. *Halford* (1); *Wainwright* v.

(1) 11 Ch. D. 959.

Miller (1). As to the period of time over which the forfeiture extended, he cited *Osborn* v. *Brown* (2), *In re Niebel's Will* (3), and *Knapp* v. *Noyes* (4). He contended that if the testator intended to attach the proviso for forfeiture to a purchased share upon the marriage of the purchaser with a Roman Catholic, the law would not allow it, and that upon a sale the share became absolutely freed from the forfeiture: *Gill* v. *Pearson* (5); *Ludlow* v. *Bunbury* (6); *In re Porter* (7); 2 *Jarman on Wills*, p. 858. The beneficiaries were all desirous of receiving their shares without giving any security: *Aston* v. *Aston* (8); *Griffith* v. *Smith* (9); *Faulkes* v. *Gray* (10).

Rich, for the trustees.

W. Hubert Manning and *Macarthur,* for two classes of defendant beneficiaries.

A. H. SIMPSON, J. I am quite clear that the provisions of this will declaring that upon any child marrying a member of the church of Rome his 'or her interest under the will is to be forfeited, are perfectly valid provisions, and that any vested share is liable to become divested in the event of such a marriage: see *Hodgson* v. *Halford* (11). Nor do I see any reason why the forfeiture should not apply quite as much to a second or subsequent marriage as well as to a first marriage; if authority is needed to shew that it does so apply, it is to be found in *In re Niebel's Will* (3), a decision of Mr. Justice *Owen's.* The case of *Osborn* v. *Brown* (2) appears to me clearly distinguishable, because of the express direction in the will that the legacy to the testator's daughter was to be paid twelve months after the testator's death. Lord *Rosslyn,* in consequence of that direction, held that the event upon which the bequest was revoked was to be referred to the twelve months during which the payment was suspended.

(1) [1897] 2 Ch. 255.	(6) 35 Beav. 36.
(2) 5 Ves. 527.	(7) [1892] 3 Ch. 481.
(3) 13 N.S.W.R. Eq. 161.	(8) 2 Vern. 452.
(4) Ambl. 661.	(9) 1 Ves. Jun. 97.
(5) 6 East 173.	(10) 18 Ves. 131.
(11) 11 Ch. D. 659.	

1898.

EVANS
v.
TORPY.

A.H. Simpson J.

   Since the matter was last before me I have given some consideration to the question asked in paragraph (e) of the prayer, and I cannot see any reason why the testator, having imposed a condition in a certain event, should not be able to provide that that condition should be removed in the event of the beneficiary disposing of his share ; and that the forfeiture clause, which would have attached to the share upon the marriage of the vendor with a Roman Catholic, should not attach to it in the hands of the purchaser. I do not, however, see, on principle, how the testator can attach another condition to that share in the hands of the purchaser, so that upon the purchaser marrying a Roman Catholic he should forfeit the share he had purchased. Accordingly, I hold that the children's shares are no longer liable to forfeiture after sale, whether the purchaser or the vendor intermarries with a Roman Catholic.

   Whether the Court will require a security to be given for the repayment of the shares in the event of the forfeiture clause coming into operation, seems from the cases to be a matter very largely of discretion, according to the probability of the case, and the likelihood of the anticipated event happening. The cases are collected in *Roper on Legacies* (3rd Edit. p. 752). I think that in this case the trustees may pay over the shares of those children who have intermarried with persons not Roman Catholics, without requiring any security from them other than a bond by each of the children; that the share of the child who is insane may be paid over to the Master in Lunacy without security ; and that the share of that son who is still unmarried may be paid to him upon the security of a bond by himself and one surety.

   Solicitors : *Myers* ; *Laurence & Rich* (for *Pilcher*, Orange); *Asher* ; *Street & Paterson*.

In the matter of the MOUNT DAVID GOLD MINING COMPANY

(No LIABILITY).

No Liability Mining Companies Act, 1896 (60 *Vic. No.* 15), *s.* 35—*Trustee Act* (17 *Vic. No.* 4), *s.* 6—*Rectification of register — Equitable owners of shares, rights of.*

1898.

March 24, 28, 29.

April 1.

A.H. Simpson J.

A transferee of shares of a company, until such transfer has been registered, is merely equitable owner of the shares, and, as such, liable to be postponed to those having prior equities.

Under a partnership agreement G. became entitled to certain shares, which stood in his partner's name. A doubt arose as to the number of shares to which G. was entitled, and a suit was brought by him on February 15th, 1897, to ascertain his rights, and a decree was pronounced on August 27th, 1897. In March and November, 1897, transfers of the shares to which G. had been declared entitled, were executed by G.'s partner to C. and R. respectively, and lodged by them with the company for registration. *Held,* that G.'s partner being a constructive trustee for G., it was no negligence in G. to allow the shares to remain in his name, and that G.'s equity being prior in date prevailed over that of C. and R.

Shropshire Union Railway Co. v. *The Queen* (1) applied.

THIS was an application to rectify the register of the Mount David Gold Mining Co., No Liability, by placing the name of W. F. Gale on the register in place of the name of James Maguire. The facts and nature of the application; as stated by his Honour in his judgment, were as follows :—

On the 8th April, 1896, Maguire had contracted to purchase a mine from Messrs. Crozier for 1,000*l.*, and, by an agreement of that date with Gale, in consideration of 500*l.* paid by Gale to Maguire, Gale and Maguire were to be joint owners and partners in the mine, which was to be re-sold, and the purchase money due to Messrs. Crozier paid out of the proceeds of sale, and the surplus divided equally between them. In July, 1896, this agreement was varied by the partners agreeing that, in lieu of his half-share, Gale should be paid 750*l.* on the sale of the mine, and receive one twenty-fifth interest in fully paid-up shares in the company to be formed to buy the mine. The company was formed, being the Mount David Gold Mining Co., and Maguire received a sum in cash and 15,000 fully paid-up shares.

(1) L.R. 7 H.L. 496.

H 2

1898.

In the Matter
of
THE MOUNT
DAVID GOLD
MINING CO.
(No
LIABILITY).

A dispute arose between Gale and Maguire, whether Gale was
to receive from Maguire one twenty-fifth of the shares allotted
to Maguire or one twenty-fifth of the whole of the shares in the
company, numbering 120,000. On the 15th February, 1897, the suit
of *Gale* v. *Maguire* was instituted to determine the question, and on
the same day an *ex parte* order was obtained restraining the defendant until the 19th February (among other things) from dealing
with the scrip or certificates of his 15,000 shares, so as to prejudice
Gale's right to receive 4,800 of the said shares. This order was
by consent continued till the 26th February, and on that day the
order, so far as the scrip or certificates were concerned, was
continued till the hearing.

On the 27th August, 1897, a decree was made at the hearing
by which it was declared that the plaintiff was entitled as against
the defendant to one twenty-fifth part of the whole number of
shares in the Mount David Gold Mining Co. fully paid up, that
was to say, to 4,800 fully paid-up shares and to an immediate
payment of 750*l.* out of the consideration for the sale of the mine,
and it was ordered that the defendant should forthwith do everything necessary for the purpose of having the scrip or certificates
for the said 4,800 shares transferred to the plaintiff. The decree
did not contain any injunction against the defendant dealing
with the shares, but on the 10th November, 1897, an order was
obtained restraining him from dealing with the 15,000 shares, so
as to reduce the number of fully paid-up shares in his name
below 4,800, and this injunction was afterwards continued till
further order, and is now in force. As Maguire refused or
neglected to transfer the 4,800 shares or any of them to Gale,
the latter, on the 18th January, 1898, obtained an order in
the suit vesting in himself the right to transfer the 4,800 shares
standing in Maguire's name. Gale accordingly executed transfers to himself, but, on his presenting them for registration
by the company, was informed the company could not do
this without an order of the Court, as there were only 4,800
shares standing in Maguire's name and transfers by Maguire
of 550 of these had previously been lodged by Crozier, and
transfers of 4,000 by the Reversionary Interest Finance Co.,
Limited. On the 29th January, 1898, a summons was taken out

by Gale under s. 35 of the No-Liability Mining Companies Act, 1898.
1896, for rectification of the register of shareholders by having *In the Matter of*
his name inserted as owner of 4,300 shares instead of Maguire, THE MOUNT DAVID GOLD
but the summons was only served on the Mount David Gold MINING CO. (No LIABILITY).
Mining Co.

When the summons came on for hearing,

A. H. Simpson, J., on the 15th February, 1898, decided that he could not deal with the application in the absence of the other claimants, and the summons was accordingly amended by making Crozier and the Reversionary Interest Finance Co. parties.

It appeared that on the 10th February, 1897, 15,000 fully paid-up shares were allotted to Maguire. From time to time he sold and transferred portion of them, but at the date of the decree he still had 9,450 in his name, a number sufficiently large to meet the claim of Gale, Crozier, and the Reversionary Interest Finance Co.

Immediately after the date of the decree he began transferring further shares until, on the 16th November, 1897, he had only 4,800 in his name. The transfers lodged by Crozier, executed by Maguire at some time in November, 1897, were handed to Crozier. The transfers lodged by the Reversionary Interest Finance Co. were executed in March, 1897, and handed to the Reversionary Company on the 17th and 18th March.

Both sets of transfers were endorsed on the respective certificates, and were executed by Maguire in blank.

It was admitted that these transfers did not pass any legal property in the shares which still remained vested in Maguire, and the contest was, therefore, between persons with equitable rights only.

W. G. Walker, Q.C. (*Mann* with him), for the applicant. I claim a lien on the whole of the 15,000 shares allotted to Maguire; *Shropshire Union Railway Co.* v. *The Queen* (1).

He was stopped by the Court.

Lingen, for the respondent Crozier.

(1) L. R. 7 H. L. 496.

1898.

In the Matter
of
THE MOUNT
DAVID GOLD
MINING CO.
(NO
LIABILITY).

The applicant has been guilty of such negligence as to distinguish his case from that of *Shropshire Union Railway Co.* v. *The Queen.* If the applicant had such a lien over the shares, he waived it on February 15th, 1897, when the *ex parte* injunction was obtained.

Maguire was as partner entitled to deal with the shares independently of the applicant.

I admit that Crozier was aware of the equity suit, but it was negligence to rely on the chance of a person obeying the order of the Court: *Union Bank of London* v. *Kent* (1).

A trustee has powers analogous to those of an agent, and he can give a good title to an innocent purchaser, even if he exceeds his authority.

[He referred to *Perry Herrick* v. *Attwood* (2); *Brocklesby* v. *Temperance Permanent Building Society* (3); and *Lloyd's Bank. Limited* v. *Bullock* (4).]

Rich, for the Reversionary Interest Company. In order that priority should give an advantage, the equities of parties must be in all other respects equal: *Farren* v. *Yorkshire Banking Co.* (5); *Société Générale* v. *Walker* (6). The applicant was negligent from the first in allowing the shares to be issued to Maguire.

At the date of the decree the share certificates should have been deposited in Court. Had the injunction been continued after the decree, Maguire would still have had sufficient shares without those mortgaged to the Reversionary Company to satisfy the decree of the Court.

Maguire transferred 4000 shares between August 27th, the date of the decree, and November 10th, the date on which the injunction was renewed.

The order of February 11th only restrained Maguire from dealing with 4,800 out of 15,000 shares, and he could, therefore, deal with the balance. It is a general principle that carelessness or negligence postpones an equitable mortgagee: *Wigram* v. *Buckley* (7). The Reversionary Company had possession of the

(1) 39 Ch. D. 238.   (4) [1896] 2 Ch. 192.
(2) 2 De G. & J. 21.   (5) 40 Ch. D. 188.
(3) [1895] A.C. 173.   (6) 11 App. Cas. 20.
                    (7) [1894] 3 Ch. 483.

scrip, and possession of deeds turns the balance in favour of the
person in possession of them. Scrip is analogous to deeds :
Laird v. *Moore* (1); *Spencer* v. *Clarke* (2).   The case of
Shropshire Union Railway Co. v. *The Queen* (3) must be confined to express trusts. At the best the applicant is only
entitled to one-third of the shares held by the Reversionary Co.

[He also referred to *National Prov. Bank* v. *Jackson* (4).]

Walker in reply.

The applicant is entitled to a lien over all the 15,000 shares,
which continues until 4,800 have been specifically allotted to him :
Lindley on Partnership (5).   The lien exists for the protection
of a partner until accounts have been settled, and a balance
struck.

Either the partnership still exists or it is in liquidation; and
if there was once a lien, such must still exist as between the
applicant and Maguire until the property is distributed.

The conversion of partnership property cannot affect the
rights of partners *inter se* : *Yeates* v. *Groves* (6).   Where there
is a charge on a larger sum for payment of a smaller, the latter
remains a charge until paid. If the respondents have a lien as
well as the applicant, the latter must succeed as being prior in
time. If the lien existed Maguire was a trustee for the applicant.

Shropshire Union Railway Co. v. *The Queen* (7) cannot be
limited to express trusts. The equity is the same in each case.
The gist of trusteeship is that a person has the legal ownership
to which he knows some other title attaches.

In *Union Bank of London* v. *Kent* (8) nothing was done,
but in this case the applicant prosecuted an equity suit to victory,
and there could not, therefore, have been negligence on his part
in the suit.

Knox, for the Mount David Gold Mining Co.

Cur. adv. vult.

1898.

In the Matter
of
THE MOUNT
DAVID GOLD
MINING CO.
(NO
LIABILITY).

(1) L.R. 4 Eq. 405.   (5) 5th Ed., p. 351.
(2) 9 Ch. D. 142.   (6) 1 Ves. Jun. 280.
(3) L.R. 7 H.L. 20.   (7) L.R. 7 H.L. 496.
(4) 33 Ch. D. 1.   (8) 39 Ch. D. 238.

1898.
In the Matter
of
THE MOUNT
DAVID GOLD
MINING CO.
(NO
LIABILITY).

April 1.

The following considered judgment was on April 1st delivered by,

A. H. SIMPSON, J. (after stating the facts as above set out, his Honour continued) :—The material points for consideration are, I think—(1) Had Gale a lien over the 15,000 shares ? ; (2) If he had, is he prevented by his negligence or otherwise from setting it up against the other claimants ?

(1) Gale's right in the shares accrued in July, 1896 ; the decree only declared and defined those rights. Under the original agreement Gale and Maguire were partners. Gale had a lien over the partnership property for the purpose of having it applied in discharge of partnership debts ; and a similar lien over the surplus assets, to have them applied in payment of what was due to him as partner : *Lindley on Partnership* (1).

This position he exchanged for a right to receive a sum of cash and 4,800 paid-up shares out of the proceeds of sale of the mine. This would, in my opinion, give him a lien over the proceeds of sale in Maguire's hands. An unpaid vendor, whether of real or personal property, has a lien over the property for unpaid purchase money, on the principle of equity that he who gets property under contract to pay its value, shall not keep it without payment : see *Macreth* v. *Simmons* (2). Here Maguire, with Gale's assistance, obtained shares under a contract to hand Gale part of them. On principle, therefore, Gale has a lien for the shares due to him. Again, a direction in a will to pay debts or legacies out of a fund has certainly been held to amount to a charge ; and in dealings *inter vivos* it was laid down by Lord Truro in *Rodick* v. *Gandell* (3) that the extent of the principle to be deduced from the cases is that " an agreement between a debtor and creditor that the debt owing shall be paid out of a specific fund coming to the debtor . . . . . will create a valid equitable charge on such fund." Numerous other instances will be found in the notes to *Ryall* v. *Rowles* (4).

The decree recognises and preserves Gale's right, and if this is so his rights are clearly prior in time to the other claimants, and being prior in time are, *prima facie* at any rate, better in law.

(1) p. 352, 5th ed.   (3) 1 D.M. & G. 763 p. 777.
(2) 15 Ves. 328.   (4) Wh. & Tud. L.C. 7th Ed. I., 96.

(2) Has then Gale done anything to prejudice his prior right ?

It was contended on various grounds that he had done so, and *In the Matter of* firstly that the case was within the class of cases of which *Lloyd's* THE MOUNT *Bank* v. *Bullock* (1) is a recent example, where an agent, DAVID GOLD intrusted by his principal with property for the purpose of raising (No LIABILITY). a certain sum on it, exceeds that authority, and raises a larger sum. In that case, no doubt, the lender's equity is better than *A. H. Simpson J.* that of the principal; but such a case bears no resemblance to this. Maguire was not an agent with any authority of any kind to deal with Gale's share.

Next it was contended that Gale was negligent in allowing the shares to be in Maguire's name, with possession of the certificates. The judgment of Lord *Cairns* in *Shropshire Union Railway Co.* v. *The Queen* (2) seems to me a conclusive answer to this, and I need not quote it at length. It was further contended that Gale ought to have mistrusted Maguire, and obtained at the hearing a continuation of the injunction against him; as it was during the lapse of the injunction the shares in Maguire's name were reduced from 9,450 to 4,800. If, however, there was no negligence in allowing the shares to be in Maguire's name, as the last cited case shews, there would have been no negligence in not instituting a suit at all. Indeed, the suit was instituted, not on account of any distrust of Maguire, but because the parties differed as to the meaning of their agreement. Gale was in no way bound at the hearing to regard Maguire as a knave, and indeed if he had obtained a continuation of the injunction, I do not know that it would have bettered his position if Maguire had chosen to disregard it : see the remarks of *Davey*, L.J., in *Wigram* v. *Buckley* (3).

In *The Union Bank of London* v. *Kent* (4) a company held land under a building agreement from the corporation of London, under which separate leases of the houses were to be granted as they were built. The company borrowed money from the plaintiff bank, and covenanted to mortgage the houses to them when the leases were granted, and that in the meantime the premises comprised in the building agreement should be a security to the

(1) [1896] 2 Ch. 193.   (3) [1894] 3 Ch. 483 p. 497.
(2) L.R. 7. H.L. 496.   (4) 39 Ch. D. 238.

1898.

*In the Matter
of*
THE MOUNT
DAVID GOLD
M'N'NG CO.
(NO
LIABILITY.)

A. H. Simpson J.

plaintiffs. The building agreement was handed to the bank, but they gave no notice to the corporation, the lessors. Subsequently, leases of two houses were granted to the company, who thereupon raised money upon them by equitable mortgage from a person who had no notice of the plaintiff's rights. It was held by the Court of Appeal that although giving notice to the lessors would probably have prevented the leases being handed to the company, as notice was not requisite to complete a security on real estate, the omission to give such notice was no ground for postponing the plaintiff's equity. It was said by *Fry,* L.J. (p. 247), that there were two sets of circumstances, that at first looked very similar—one class was where a mortgagee knew that a mortgagor had not fulfilled his obligations, and yet did nothing; the other was where he knew of no such failure, but only knew of obligations which in the future the mortgagor might fail to fulfil. After giving instances of the first class, he says with reference to the second (p. 248): "I know of no decided case in which the mortgagee has been postponed on the ground that he did not take precautions against a future fraud by the mortgagor, and I do not know of any general rule which obliges you to assume that every person with whom you are dealing is likely to be a knave." Previously to the decree there was no failure on the part of Maguire to fulfil his obligations, and the case, therefore, falls within the second class. The above reasoning applies to both Crozier and the Reversionary Interest Finance Co.; but the former is in a worse position than the Reversionary Interest Finance Co., as his equity did not arise till November, 1897, when, as is admitted, he had notice of the equity suit, *i.e.,* of the plaintiff's rights.

I order the register to be rectified by placing the 4,800 shares in the name of Gale. Gale's costs of taking out the summons and the affidavits filed by him in support, and his costs incurred after 15th February last must be paid by respondents, Crozier and the Reversionary Interest Finance Co. The costs of the Mount David Gold Mining Co. must be paid by the applicant, and he may recover against the other respondents so much of the Mount David Gold Mining Co.'s costs as were incurred after 15th February.

Solicitors for the applicant: *Thompson & Nott.*
Solicitors for Crozier: *White & Wolstenholme.*
Solicitor for the Reversionary Interest Finance Co., Ltd.: *W. Sands.*
Solicitor for the Mount David Gold Mining Co.: *W. G. Parish.*

FARNELL *v.* COX AND OTHERS.

Breach of trust—Trustee borrowing trust funds—Deposit of security—Further advances—Redemption of the security.

1898.

June 22, 24.

A.H. Simpson J.

C., a trustee, borrowed 1,500*l.* of the trust moneys in September, 1897. As security for the loan he deposited with the solicitors to the trust estate certain title deeds, together with a letter, in which he undertook to repay the loan in 1902, and to pay interest at 5 per cent., and gave a power of sale in case of default.

Held, that the deeds so deposited must be held as security, not merely for the 1,500*l.* and interest, but also for sums subsequently borrowed by C. from the trust estate, but not for sums borrowed prior to September, 1897.

SUMMONS.

This suit was instituted by one beneficiary in the estate of H. R. Cox, senior, against the trustees and the other beneficiaries, alleging breaches of trust, and asking for the usual accounts, enquiries, and directions, and, so far as necessary, administration by the Court.

This was a summons by Henry Robert Cox, junior, a defendant trustee, "for directions as to whether the Perpetual Trustee Company, the receiver herein, is justified in retaining title deeds relating to property belonging to the said H. R. Cox, and not in any way connected with the trusts of the will of the testator in the pleadings mentioned or whether the said company ought not to deliver up the same to the said H. R. Cox, or to whom he may appoint on his paying the principal, interest and costs due thereon under the circumstances and on the grounds set out in the affidavits filed."

The facts, which are fully set out by his Honour in his judgment, may be shortly stated as follows :—In October, 1897, the defendant, H. R. Cox, borrowed 1,500*l.* in breach of trust from the trust estate. He deposited as security title deeds of property valued at 5,000*l.* It was alleged that previously he had obtained other sums in breach of trust from the estate. He was also alleged to have obtained further sums subsequently to the deposit of the deeds from the trust estate. He now offered to redeem, and the question was whether the receivers appointed in the suit were entitled to a lien over the deeds so deposited, and which had come into their custody as receivers, for all sums irregularly obtained from the trust estate, and if not, for which of such sums.

W. Gregory Walker, Q.C. (*Mann* with him), for the plaintiff, the Perpetual Trustee Company (the receiver), and the infants Farnell, took the preliminary point that the Court could not try the case on a summons for direction, but that the applicant must bring a redemption suit.

Lingen, for the applicant.

The Court has jurisdiction to deal with this application on summons. He referred to *Kerr on Receivers,* p. 131.

[His Honour decided that he had jurisdiction.]

The investment is irregular, and as some of the beneficiaries demand restitution, the applicant must repay the money; the refusal of other beneficiaries to request payment is immaterial. Upon payment of the 1,500*l.* and interest secured by the deposit of the deeds, the applicant is entitled to receive back the deeds.

Walker, Q.C. Before the deeds are given up the plaintiff is entitled to the enquiries—(1) What sum is due under the security beyond the sum of 1,500*l.* ? (2) Whether the applicant has derived from the sum of 1,500*l.* and from any other sums due any profit above five per cent., and if so, how much ?

The maxim, "He who comes into equity must do equity," is applicable, and the applicant having come to the Court to obtain his deeds must do equity. He is therefore bound to make good all his deficiencies, whether prior to the deposit of the deeds or otherwise. He is not entitled to the deeds until this has been done.

Rich and *Noble* appeared for other parties to submit.

Lingen in reply.

There is no authority for plaintiff's contention, which would make it an advantage not to deposit security, and, therefore, be a premium on dishonesty.

1898.

FARNELL
v.
Cox.

The maxim " He who comes into equity must do equity," does not enable the Court to impose arbitrary conditions. The conditions must be referable to the subject matter of the suit, the equity to be done must be an equity in the matter in dispute. The deeds cannot be impounded to answer other matters than those in reference to which the applicant deposited them : *Hanson* v. *Keating* (1). The *cestuis que trustent* cannot approbate and reprobate the security ; they must either accept its terms or refuse it altogether. The deeds can only be retained in respect of the advances actually made on the security of them.

[A. H. SIMPSON, J. Can the applicant be heard to say that he did not intend to take the further advances on the faith of this security ? How can the Court go into the question whether a person has made a mental communication to himself ?]

A person cannot be bound except upon a declaration, and there was none here.

[A. H. SIMPSON, J. Cannot a person be a constructive trustee without a declaration?]

No doubt ; but there is no case here to make the applicant a constructive trustee. There is an express declaration in writing which cannot be extended by mere subsequent actions without further declarations.

In so far as the beneficiary gets interest against the trustee under the declaration, he is limited to the terms of the declaration.

No doubt he has other rights arising from the mere relationship of trustee and *cestui que trust;* but that is altogether outside the declaration, and the terms of the declaration cannot be extended so as to include other matters.

[A. H. SIMPSON, J. May not the Court say you deposited deeds to cover an improper loan of 1,500*l.*, and you cannot get those deeds back until you repay the 1,500*l.* with such interest as the Court says you must pay ?]

No; the deeds must be returned upon the applicant paying the 1,500*l.* and the interest stipulated to be paid. They cannot be retained to secure the payment of excessive interest which the Court might order to be paid.

(1) 4 Hare 5.

[A. H. SIMPSON, J. Could the applicant refuse to repay the loan until 1902, in accordance with the terms of the mortgage?]

No; he could not refuse to repay the money directly it is asked for under the ordinary remedies arising from the relationship of trustee and *cestui que trust*; but the beneficiaries could if they chose retain the security until the money was paid with the interest contracted to be paid.

Cur. adv. vult.

June 24.   On June 24, the following judgment was read by

A. H. SIMPSON, J. H. R. Cox, senior, the testator in the cause, died on the 8th October, 1885, having by his will given all his real and residuary personal estate to his trustees on trust to pay his wife an annuity mentioned in the will, and to allow her to occupy one of his houses for life, and another annuity to a sister-in-law, and subject thereto on trust for his children for their respective lives, with remainder to their children *per stirpes*. The present trustees are Mrs. Eliza Cox the widow, and H. R. Cox a son of the testator. On the 2nd December, 1897, a statement of claim was filed by Mrs. Farnell, one of the testator's eight children, against the trustees and the other beneficiaries, alleging grave breaches of trust, and asking for the usual accounts, enquiries, and directions, and so far as might be necessary for administration of the estate by the Court. No mention was made of the advance of 1,500*l.* hereafter referred to, as it does not appear to have been known at that time to the plaintiff. On the 14th December, 1897, the Perpetual Trustee Company was appointed receiver.

In September last, Mrs. Eliza Cox was in England, having appointed H. P. Ellis her attorney under power of attorney. It appeared that H. P. Ellis was employed by H. R. Cox to keep the trust accounts, and he was apparently willing to act as H. R. Cox wished. At all events, on the 16th September, 1897, a sum of 1,500*l.* trust money was advanced to H. R. Cox in clear breach of trust, for at that time the trust account was overdrawn at the Bank of New South Wales to the amount of about 1,100*l.*, on which six per cent. compound interest was being charged; had the 1,500*l.* been paid into the trust account, as it should have been, this would have placed the account in credit. In October, 1897, the title deeds of land at Brisbane Water, belonging to H. R. Cox, and valued at about 5,000l., were deposited with Messrs. Shipway & Berne, the solicitors of the trust estate, by H. R. Cox's directions, and by a letter dated October, 1897, but said to have been written on the 16th October, H. R. Cox informed them that they were to hold the deeds by way of equitable mortgage until he had repaid to the trustees the sum of 1,500l., and interest and costs, charges, and expenses in connection therewith; he then referred to the advance of 1,500l. to himself by the trustees, and promised to repay it on the 16th September, 1902, with interest at five per cent.; the letter contained a proviso for redemption on the 16th September, 1902, and gave a power of sale on default of payment of principal and interest. It appears from H. P. Ellis's affidavit that H. R. Cox's title deeds were mortgaged to his own bank to secure his overdrawn account, and part of the 1,500l. was expended in paying off the overdraft and thereby releasing the deeds. When the Perpetual Trustee Company was appointed receiver, the deeds were handed to them.

In March last, H. R. Cox, wishing to recover his deeds, offered to pay off the 1,500l., with five per cent. interest and costs. The Perpetual Trustee Company declined to hand them over except under the direction of the Court, and a summons was taken out by H. R. Cox to obtain such directions or leave to institute a redemption suit against the receiver. The matter came before me, the plaintiff being the only beneficiary who was made a party to the application. On the 31st March last, I held that I could only deal with the matter in the presence of all the beneficiaries, and dismissed the summons, but gave leave to H. R. Cox to institute any proceedings for redemption which he might be advised against the Trustee Company and others.

The present summons was thereupon taken out, to which all the beneficiaries are parties, asking for redemption of the deeds on payment of 1,500l., interest, and costs. The plaintiff, Mrs. Farnell, opposes the giving up of the deeds; the infants submit to any order the Court thinks right. An objection was taken that the Court had no jurisdiction on summons to try the question raised, but in a suit for administration, when all the parties are before it,

1898.

FARNELL
v.
COX.

A. H. Simpson J.

I am unable to see why the Court cannot do so, and I ought not,
in my opinion, to put the parties to the unnecessary expense and
delay of instituting a redemption suit.   The only other fact to
which it is necessary to refer is that in April, 1898, the trustees
received a letter signed by three adult and two infant beneficiaries,
requesting them to at once call in the said 1,500l. and interest.

Mr. *Walker*, for the plaintiff, contends that the deeds ought not
to be handed to H. R. Cox till the accounts have been taken in
the suit, and it is seen whether he is indebted to the estate for
alleged breaches of trust, and that if it turns out he is so
indebted, the beneficiaries have a lien on the deeds for the amount;
he also claims that if H. R. Cox has obtained from the user of
the 1,500l. a greater profit than five per cent., the beneficiaries
are entitled to this profit, and he asks for an enquiry on this
point. Mr. *Lingen*, on the other hand, contends that the beneficiaries cannot approbate and reprobate, that they must take the
deeds on the terms of the letter of October, and cannot impose
any other or further terms.

So far as the beneficiaries claim a lien in respect of breaches of
trust committed prior to the 16th September, 1897, that is,
breaches of trust in no way connected with the subject matter of
this application, I think the claim is not maintainable.   The
maxim "He who comes into equity must do equity" does not, as
Wigram, V.C., pointed out in *Hanson* v. *Keating* (1), enable the
Court to impose arbitrary conditions on a party because he
happens to be plaintiff. "It is only to the one matter which is
the subject of a given suit that the rule applies, and not to
distinct matters pending between the same parties." "A party,
in short, does not, by becoming plaintiff in equity, give up any of
his rights, or submit those rights to the arbitrary disposition of
the Court. He submits only to give the defendant his rights in
respect of the subject matter of the suit, on condition of the
plaintiff obtaining his own."

Advances, however (if any), made subsequently to the advance
of the 1,500l. stand, in my opinion, on a different footing. If a
person borrows money from a trustee on a deposit of title deeds,

(1) 4 Hare, at pp. 5 and 6.

and subsequently applies for a further loan, it would obviously
be the duty of the trustee to stipulate that the security should
cover the further advance.   When borrower and lender are one
person, the Court would presume he had acted honestly, or rather
would not allow him to set up that he had acted dishonestly, that
is, would not allow him to say the further advance was not
covered by the security. It seems to me a fallacy to treat the letter
of October, 1897, as a contract ; it is really merely a declaration
by H. R. Cox, and if so the Court may well regard it as binding
on him so far as it imposes on him obligations, but disregard it
so far as it purports to confer on him rights, for a man may, by
his own statement, impose on himself liabilities, but cannot give
himself rights against third persons.   H. R. Cox must be treated
as if he had paid into the trust account at the Bank of New
South Wales the sum of 1,500*l.*, as it was his obvious duty to do.
The account would then have been in credit some 400*l.*   He must
then be treated as overdrawing the account by lending to himself
1,500*l.*, depositing as a security for the advance certain title
deeds, accompanied by a memorandum by which he promised to
repay the loan on the 16th September, 1902, with five per cent.
interest in the meantime.

It is contended, as I understand the argument, that although
the overdrawn account may be carrying eight or nine per cent.
compound interest, the beneficiaries cannot insist on the trustee
paying more than 5 per cent. simple interest under the security ;
it would follow, it seems to me, that they could not call in the
money till 1902, without in effect giving up their security.   The
answer, in my opinion, is that the Court will treat the trustee as
doing the best he could to repair or neutralise his breach of trust
by depositing the deeds to meet the liability he has incurred, and
will consider the deposited deeds as a security for the repayment
of all money borrowed at the time the deposit was made
or subsequently, with such interest or profit as the Court
may hold the trustee liable to pay, and it will not allow the
trustee to set up that by agreement with himself the security is
only to cover part of the liability.

1898.

FARNELL
v.
COX.

A.H. Simpson J.

There must be—(1) an account of what is due to the trust estate under the equitable mortgage including any sums advanced to H. R. Cox subsequently to 16th October, 1897 ; (2) an enquiry whether H. R. Cox has derived from the sums so advanced any interest or profit beyond 5 per cent. per annum, and if so, what ; (3) an enquiry what loss the trust estate has sustained by the trustee making such advances to himself. Further consideration and costs reserved. Subject to the above accounts and enquiries being satisfied, it seems to me Mr. Cox is entitled to have the deeds delivered to him.

Solicitors for the plaintiff, The Perpetual Trustee Company, and the infants Farnell : *Holdsworth & Son.*

Solicitors for the defendant infants Cox : *Sullivan Bros.*

Solicitor for the defendant Edward C. Cox : *W. S. Gray.*

Solicitors for the defendant H. R. Cox : *Norton, Smith & Co.*

CRAMPTON v. FOSTER AND OTHERS.

Vendor and purchaser—Specific performance against vendor and a subsequent
purchaser with notice—Damages for breach of contract—Right of vendor to
deduct amount of damage from the balance of purchase moneys due from him to
the vendor.

1898.

April 30.

A.H. Simpson J.

A purchaser obtained a decree for specific performance against a vendor and a
subsequent purchaser who had purchased with notice of the prior contract ; and
also a decree for damages for breach of contract against the vendor.

Held, that although the subsequent purchaser was entitled to the balance of the
purchase moneys due from the prior purchaser, and, although he was not liable to
the prior purchaser for the damages, the prior purchaser was entitled to deduct
from the balance the amount of the damages due to him from the vendor.

THIS was the further consideration of a suit, the hearing of
which is reported in 18 N.S.W.R. Eq. 136. The suit was
instituted to obtain specific performance of a contract for the sale
of land entered into between Crampton and the defendant
Foster, on the 17th November, 1896. Subsequently to that date
Foster had entered into a second contract for the sale of the
same land to the other defendants, who were the executors of the
estate of Major West. West's executors purchased, with notice
of the prior contract with Crampton, but they contended that at
the time of that sale Foster was so intoxicated that he was not
aware what he was doing.

At the hearing a decree was made for specific performance, and
for an enquiry as to damages in addition. Pending the enquiry
as to damages the plaintiff paid into Court the balance of the
purchase money which was due from him. The plaintiff now
filed short minutes of decree on further consideration, whereby
he proposed that the amount of the balance in Court, less the
assessed damages and costs, should be paid to Foster, and that the
amount of damages and costs should be paid to himself out of the
moneys in Court.

Knox, for the plaintiff. We only look to Foster, we have no
privity with West's executors; Foster's is the hand to which we
have to pay the purchase money, and any sums which we may

I 2

deduct as against him may be taken out of the purchase moneys.
There is no authority on the point, but on principle I submit the
second purchaser with notice takes subject to all equities between
the prior purchaser and the vendor.

W. Gregory-Walker, Q.C., for West's executors. The plaintiff's
argument is based upon a supposed right of set-off. But the
relief by way of damages is only to be obtained against Foster,
and the damages are Foster's debt. The second purchase by us
was an equitable assignment to us of Foster's balance of the
purchase moneys. Crampton received notice of that assignment
at once, and from that date the purchase moneys became, in the
eyes of the Court, our moneys. The plaintiff is not entitled to
set off Foster's debt against our moneys.

[A. H. SIMPSON, J. Are not damages, in effect, compensation
for being kept out of possession, and, as such, liable to be deducted
from the purchase moneys ?]

No. A purchaser has no charge on the land or lien on the
purchase moneys for possible damages of this sort. Unless the
plaintiff can put his case as high as a lien on the purchase moneys
he must fail. At the very highest, the plaintiff's right was only
a possible right, and my contention is, we take the purchase
money subject only to then existing equities, not subject to all
possible deductions in the future.

Russell (Solicitor), for the defendant Foster, did not contest
the point, but consented to the purchase moneys being paid to his
co-defendants.

Without calling on the plaintiff's counsel in reply,

A. H. SIMPSON, J. I think the point is a nice one, but on
principle I do not see why the purchaser should not have the
right to make the deduction he claims. Take the case where a
vendor enters into a contract to convey a certain area of land at
a certain price ; suppose the area is short, and the vendor is
unable to convey all he contracted to convey, there can be no
doubt—in fact, I understood Mr. *Walker* to admit it—that the
purchaser would be entitled to deduct from the purchase money
any compensation for the deficiency that might be assessed by the
Court.

This is, no doubt, not exactly that case, but is there really any substantial distinction between them? Here the vendor has delayed completing the contract, and the plaintiff has suffered loss through not acquiring the land on the date when, by the contract, he was entitled to it. In such a case as this the damages payable for the delay appear to me as much in the nature of compensation as the deduction for the deficiency in area in the other supposed case. Possibly it would be incorrect to speak of the purchaser's right as a lien on the purchase moneys; it is rather an inchoate right, which may or may not ripen into a complete right to make the deduction after the amount of compensation has been assessed.

The contract made by the second purchaser amounts to this : I will take the land if you can give it me; if you cannot, I will take your interest in the land, including your right to receive the purchase money.   But such a sale must be subject to all equities, actual or inchoate, existing between the vendor and the prior purchaser, and if the prior purchaser is entitled to deduct a certain sum of money in a certain event, the second purchaser takes subject to that right; he only takes such sums as the vendor is entitled to receive.

For these reasons I think the plaintiff is entitled to deduct the amount of damages and of his costs from the moneys in Court; the balance, by consent of the defendant Foster, will be paid out to West's executors.

Solicitors: *Chenhall & Eddie; Curtiss & Barry; Russell & Russell.*

1898.

CRAMPTON
v.
FOSTER.

A.H. Simpson J.

1898.

July 25, 26,
28.

August 2.

C.J. Eq.

In re J. B. SCOTT'S PATENT.

Patents Law Amendment Act, 1895 (60 *Vic. No.* 39), *s.* 5, *sub-s.* iv. (c), (d), (e)
—*Revocation of patent—Petition for —" Author and designer "—" True and
first inventor."*

A person obtaining a patent for an invention in respect of which a patent has
already been granted to another, cannot for that reason alone petition under s. 5
iv (d) of the Patents Law Amendment Act, 1895. Under s. 5 iv (c), (d), (e),
persons claiming rights prior to those of a patentee may petition for their own
protection for revocation of the patent, without the fiat of the Attorney-General,
and before proceedings for infringement are taken by the patentee.

THIS was a proceeding by way of petition under "The Patents
Law Amendment Act, 1895," for the revocation of letter of registration granted to one J. B. Scott, in respect of an invention for
starting races, and now by assignment the property of the
respondent Alexander Gray.

The facts appear fully stated in his Honour's judgment.

The petitioner Miller, who had patented a machine having a
similar object, claimed in his patent—(1) Apparatus for starting
races, consisting of a bearing or a swinging blind mounted therein,
horizon, tally, rubber cords for throwing the blind open, and
trigger gear for unlatching the blind; (2) In apparatus for the
purpose set forth, having a blind swinging about a horizontal
axis overhead operating such blind through a lever mounted or
in a carrier.

Scott in his patent claimed—(1) Improved mechanical contrivance for use in starting races, consisting essentially of the
various parts constructed, arranged and operating substantially
as and for the purposes herein described and explained.

(2) In mechanical contrivances for use in starting races, a
frame having tapes stretched across the lower ends and mounted
upon a pivot; so that said tapes can be swung forwardly and
upwardly into their raised positions.

(3) In mechanical contrivances for use in starting races, the
combination with a pivotted frame of a pivotted catch.

1898.

In re
SCOTT'S
PATENT.

(4) In mechanical contrivances for use in starting races, the combination with a pivotted frame mounted upon rigid supports of two flat springs having their upper ends curved outwardly.

Scott's patent was granted on October 25th, 1893, and Miller's patent on October 28th, 1894.

Flannery, for the petitioner. Scott's claim is a claim for the principle of the forward and upward movement so far as it can be claimed. His second claim is the apt form of his claim, and that is a claim for a principle and a mode of carrying it into effect. He referred to *Househill C. & I. Coy.* v. *Neilsen* (1), *Easterbrook* v. *G. W. R.* (2), *Tupe* v. *Pratt* (3).

The words "author and designer," in sub-s. iv (d) of s. 5 of the Patents Law Amendment Act of 1895, include the real inventor as distinguished from the person who has obtained the patent.

Petitioner's claim is included in Scott's patent.

Knox, for the respondent A. Gray. The petitioner is really claiming an improvement on his patent, which as patented will not work.

The respondent does not claim the forward and upward movement. The essential part of his patent is the barrier of tape, or other light material. Petitioner has not brought himself within the section under which he asks for relief.

Flannery in reply.

                                        Cur. adv. vult.

On the 2nd August the following written judgment was delivered by

MANNING, C.J. in Eq. This is a proceeding by way of petition under 60 Vic. No. 39, by Richard Miller, for the revocation of letters of registration granted to J. B. Scott, in respect of an invention for starting races, on the 25th October, 1893, and now by assignment the property of Alexander Gray. This proceeding is substituted for the old form of a *scire facias*, but whereas that could only have been instituted in the name of the Attorney-General, the above-mentioned Act allows a petition for revocation to be presented by five different classes of persons, and the petitioner herein claims to come under class (d), sub-s. (iv) of s. 5, "any

(1) 1 Webst. P.C. 673.   (2) 2 R.P.C. 207.
(3) 1 Webst. P.C. 144.

K 2

person alleging that he . . . was the author or designer of any invention or improvement included in the claim of the patentee."

Before the petitioner can be heard to impeach the patent it is necessary for him to prove his *locus standi* by shewing that he comes within the designated class.

This involves the proof of two matters:—

(1) That he is the author or designer of an invention.

(2) That the invention is included in the patent sought to be impeached.

The words "author or designer" were substituted in our Letters of Registration Act of 1852 for the words "true and first inventor," which had been the apt words used in the United Kingdom before the Monopolies Act, in that Act, and in every Act with reference to patents since, and this is probably the only English-speaking country in which this departure has been made.

What was intended by the change I have always been at a loss to discover, and have never found anyone able to throw any light on the subject, and so far as I know there has never been a judicial decision on the subject, but one would naturally suppose that some reason existed, and that owing to the distance of the colony from the centres of trade and invention, it was thought desirable to in some way extend the right. It has, however, been held that a person who is not the true and first inventor, as a matter of fact, may import the invention and patent it here.

That, however, was the law in England by the common law, and was so decided under the Monopolies Act, and although Sir *G. Jessel*, in *Marsden* v. *Saville Street Foundry* (1), protested that it rested on no principle, he felt bound to treat the matter as settled law.

This communication from a foreign country does not, however, include one from another person in the United Kingdom, and the person acting on such information does not become entitled to a patent as the "true and first inventor."

Neither is a man the true and first inventor who has first thought out and conceived the idea, unless he has in some way

(1) 3 Ex. D. 203.

1898.

In re
SCOTT'S
PATENT.

C.J. Eq.

made it public property, either, for instance, by experiments in public or by application for a patent, and if another person subsequently conceives the idea and makes it known, he is the " true and first inventor," and his patent therefore cannot be interfered with, provided, of course, that he has not obtained the idea from the person who was actually first in ,time. The language used by the learned editor in the notes on the *Househill C. & I. Company* v. *Neilsen* (1) clearly expresses the law, "the terms (true and first inventor) are applicable to that person only who shall have invented, published, and introduced into or put in use a complete, perfect, and finished invention."

From this it would follow that the man who first conceived the idea, and only publishes it by taking out a subsequent patent, cannot put himself forward as the " true and first inventor."

I have dwelt on the position under the English words because whatever "author or designer" means, that person cannot put his case higher than the "true and first inventor" could. No doubt, in the sub-section under consideration, the words of our earlier Act were substituted for the words "true and first inventor," which appear in the corresponding section of the adopted English Act, because of the verbiage already employed ; but if our words mean something different from the English words it may be found difficult to apply the section, and in any case I do not see how it can be applied to a person who rests his right to an invention on his subsequent patent, and not on a claim to prior rights to the patentee he attacks.

In other words, a person cannot bring himself within the section simply because he chooses to make a claim to and succeeds in getting a patent for something for which patent rights have already been given to another.

That this is so would seem to be clear from a consideration of the position of the persons named, who are entitled to interfere without the sanction of the Attorney-General, who, of course, would consider only public and not private rights. Sub-sect (c) refers to a person alleging the patent was obtained in fraud of his rights, *i.e.*, rights existing before the grant of the patent.

(1) 1 Webst. P.C. 720.

Sub-sect. (e) refers to the case of a person alleging that he had publicly manufactured, used, or sold within the colony, *before the date of the patent,* anything claimed by the patentee as his invention or improvement, *i.e.,* to protect prior user.

So surely must it be with sub-s. (d), which I have been considering, and the three sub-sections mean that any person who claims rights prior to the patentee may take steps for his own protection, and not wait to defend a suit for infringement, which may seriously injure his trade or rights, and without any occasion to seek the fiat of the Attorney-General.

In this case the petitioner sought to give evidence of his own knowledge and ideas on the matter prior to J. B. Scott's patent, but as it was admitted that this was not communicated to the patentee or made public in any way, the evidence was excluded, as it could not affect the position of the patentee as having thought out the matter for himself.

The petitioner's case rests, therefore, on his position under his own patent, and if my previous reasoning is correct, then admitting that the claims in the two patents are identical, it seems to me that the petitioner must fail through not having proved that he was the "author and designer," whatever those words mean, and even if they are equivalent to the words " true and first inventor."

Assuming, however, that this view is incorrect, I am of opinion that the petitioner fails in proving his second position, *i.e.,* that his claim is *included* in the prior patent.

It is difficult to see how a claim for a combination (as I shall shew the petitioner's is), which may include an integer specifically claimed as such by a prior patentee, can be said to be "included" in the prior claim, although the converse may be fairly clear.

If A. claims a gate made in a certain way, and B. subsequently claims a mechanical contrivance for opening a gate of that description, how is B.'s claim included in A.'s. The argument is that my contrivance involves the use of your gate, and is useless for any other kind of gate, and, therefore. I can say, not that my invention includes your gate, but that your gate includes my invention.

The use of this very word "include" is, to my mind, another argument to support my prior position that sub-s. (d) only refers to the invasion of prior rights, which would naturally be included in the confederated patent.

Coming now to the consideration of what is actually claimed by the petitioner and respondent, attention must be confined to claims 1 and 2 in Miller's patent, and to claim 2 in Scott's patent. Mr. *Flannery* admitted that he could not succeed unless Scott's claim 2 were read as practically a claim for the principle of a forward and upward swinging movement of a blind, so as to give Scott the right to restrain the use of any blind, gate, or barrier, however constructed. If so, he argued that as his invention necessarily involved the use of a blind with a similar movement, it must be held to be included in Scott's and that he had therefore brought himself within the sub-section.

There is no doubt that Miller's invention does include the use of a blind or barrier as a necessary part of any apparatus of the kind, and that his invention is carried out by such blind or barrier swinging outwardly and upwardly, but his claim 1 is distinctly for a special combination, and his claim 2 is entirely governed by the word " operating " as a claim for a special mode of operation, which is quite distinct from that claimed by the respondent, just as the blind he describes in his claim and specification is manifestly distinct from that claimed and specified by Scott.

Coming now to the consideration of Scott's 2nd claim, the language seems to me to be very simple and clear : " a frame having tapes stretched across its lower end and mounted on a pivot so that (or in such a way that) the said tapes can be swung forwardly and upwardly into their raised positions substantially as specified." That seems to me to be a claim for a certain description of frame, blind, or barrier pivotted in such a way as to be capable of being worked in a well-known way as described. In other words, it is a claim for a pivotted frame of a certain description, and that this must be so is shewn by claims 3 and 4, which both claim certain combinations with a pivotted frame."

Turning to the specification, we find, after a general statement of the invention, that the very first thing that is claimed as the " main feature of the invention " is the frame, which is there described as pivotally supported, and as having two or more lengths of tape or webbing stretched tightly across the lower ends.

1898.

In re
SCOTT'S
PATENT.

C.J. Eq.

1898.

In re
SCOTT'S
PATENT.

C.J. Eq.

That is followed by a description of the pivotted catch referred to in claim 3, and that again by the flat springs mentioned in claim 4. Coming now to the *modus operandi*, we find " a barrier of tapes will now extend from side to side of the course, having the appearance of a fence. The horses about to take part in the race are then brought into line immediately below this barrier."

Bearing in mind that what is required is something that the horses will recognise as a barrier (and what better than one which has the appearance of a fence?), and yet something that will give way easily and not injure or encumber the horses in case of an accident, one can easily see why a great point is made of the specified construction of the barrier, and this is the more apparent when one sees the sort of barrier that was provided by certain inventions of Forbes and O'Sullivan in the United States of a prior date.

Both these patents, which were known of in the colony long before Scott's patent, provide for a forward and upward movement in connection with these barriers and their *modus operandi*, and it is, therefore, most improbable that anyone would seek to get patent rights for such a movement, if it were possible, while abundant reason is shewn for claiming protection for a barrier made according to Scott's description.

The claim, in my opinion, is for a blind of a certain specified description, but pivotted as described so as to be capable of being operated on, and moved with a forward and upward swinging movement. The petitioner's barrier or blind, as claimed in his specification and plans, is of an entirely different description, and, moreover, could not be used upon a wide course, such as Randwick, without a considerable amount of additional strengthening.

The apparatus which he used, which is the one the respondent threatened proceedings about, I have nothing to do with, beyond saying that the barrier used is manifestly not the one claimed and described in his patent.

Coming as I do to the conclusion that the petitioner has not shewn himself to be an author or designer within the meaning of sub-s. (d), and that his claimed invention is not included in Scott's claim, I have no course open to me but to dismiss this petition with costs, leaving it open to Mr. Miller to set the Attorney-General in motion on the question of the validity of the respondent's patent, or to get his leave to proceed, in either of which cases he will be free from the initial difficulties which have proved fatal in this matter.

On the 8th August Mr. Justice *Manning* died, after the order made on this petition had been settled, but before approval.   On a subsequent date

Knox, for the respondent, mentioned the matter to *A. H. Simpson,* C.J. in Eq., and asked the Court for directions as to the course to be adopted.

A. H SIMPSON, C.J. in Eq., directed that the matter should be put in the list again to be mentioned on notice to the other side; his Honour then made a *pro forma* order similar in terms to that made by Mr. Justice *Manning.*

Solicitor for the petitioner : *P. J. O'Donnell.*

Solicitors for the respondent : *Alfred Shaw & Jagelmann.*

OATLEY *v.* OATLEY AND OTHERS.

1898.

August 31.
Sept. 1, 5.

C.J. Eq.

Partition—Sale—Partition Act (41 Vic. No. 17)—*Over-riding trust—Power—*
Jurisdiction—Equitable estate.

A testator bequeathed and devised to his trustees the whole of his real and
personal estate ; he gave his trustees power to sell, lease, or mortgage any part of
his estate, and after payment of debts and legacies to stand seized and possessed
of all the residue of the estate "upon trust to divide the same equally share and
share alike between" three beneficiaries.

Held, that the trust to divide the estate equally did not oust the operation of
the Partition Act, but that a majority of the beneficiaries could insist upon a sale
unless good cause was shewn to the contrary ; nor was it material that the estate
did not wholly consist of realty.

MOTION FOR DECREE ON ADMISSIONS.

The following statement of facts is taken from his Honour's
judgment :—

The late Edward Flood, by his will dated 1st September, 1888,
appointed his son the late J. W. Flood, the plaintiff Ernest
Oatley and the defendant F. A. Oatley, since deceased, his executors and trustees, and gave to them all his real and personal
estate.

He directed his trustees to get in moneys owing to him, and to
sell so much of the estate as should be necessary for the payment
of debts and legacies, and he authorised and empowered his
trustees to sell any part of his estate, to lease, to raise money by
mortgage, to carry on and manage all or any part of the testator's
stations, to allow any investment to remain as invested at his
death, and to invest in the securities in the will mentioned. He
then directed the trustees to stand seized and possessed of his
real and personal estate on trust to pay debts and general expenses
and certain legacies, and out of the income to pay certain
annuities, and to stand seized and possessed of all the residue of
the estate after payment of his debts and the legacies mentioned
in two schedules upon trust to divide the same equally share and
share alike between the said J. W. Flood, Ernest Oatley and F.
A. Oatley.

The debts and legacies were all paid, and the annuities
released except one of 250*l.* to an annuitant of 65 years of age.

The estate consisted of stations and valuable pieces of land estimated as worth over 262,000l., and personal estate worth over 14,000l., with liabilities amounting to only about 1,800l. The shares of the three beneficiaries had from time to time been mortgaged.

In April, 1893, Ernest Oatley instituted the present suit for administration of the estate. The representatives of J. W. Flood and of F. A. Oatley, who died since the institution of the suit, the trustees of the will and the various mortgagees and sub-mortgagees of the respective shares, were parties to the suit.

The prayer of the statement of claim was as follows :—

1. That the trusts of the said will may be administered and a division effected of the testator's residuary estate amongst the persons representing the three residuary legatees and devisees under his will, the plaintiff undertaking upon a decree for such division being made to pay off the amount found due from him to the defendants Frederick Augustus Oatley, Florence Adelaide Flood and John M'Pherson under his said securities.

2. That a partition or sale under the Partition Act may be ordered. And for the usual consequential relief.

This motion was for an order in terms of the first prayer.

Sir *J. E. Salomons*, Q.C., and *Lingen*, for the plaintiff. The whole question is, whether the plaintiff is entitled to a division of the property, or whether the estate is subject to the provisions of the Partition Act ?

The plaintiff submits that he is entitled to a division of the estate both real and personal, and that the defendants are not at liberty to avail themselves of the provisions of the Partition Act, because there is personalty involved as well as realty.

The Partition Act is limited to these cases where before the Act the Court of Equity would have made an order for partition.

The words in the will " I authorise and empower my said trustees to sell and absolutely dispose of all or any part of my real and personal estate " . . . . give the trustees a power to sell both real and personal estate only. But the words " my said trustees shall stand seized and possessed of all the residue and remainder of my estate . . . *upon trust to divide the same* equally share and share alike between my son, Joseph Washington Flood, and the said Edwin Ernest Allen Oatley and Frederick Augustus Oatley" are an ultimate trust to divide both realty and personalty between the three persons mentioned. Consequently the trustees are bound to divide to carry out the trusts.

No authority can be cited to shew that the Court will grant a sale in lieu of partition where the testator has himself left a trust to divide both realty and personalty. Such an order would amount to an alteration of the will by the Court.

The Partition Act is limited to land only, and no Court of Equity will take the realty out of the will, and divide it, leaving the personalty undivided. The Court has no power to separate the realty from the personalty where the two are left together as a blended fund.

No person has an absolute right to the property, as the trustees can divide as they see fit, and have an absolute power to do so equally : *Biggs* v. *Peacock* (1). The trust in this will is to divide the property equally ; that the trustees can do after valuation of the several parts of the estate.

There is no difficulty in arriving at an equal division without selling the property. The trustees are given a trust to divide equally, and consequently can arrive at the value themselves, and provided they act without fraud or negligence, no one has any control over them. The power to assess the value is implied in the trust to divide equally.

A decree for partition of the realty would amount to an administration of the trusts separately contrary to the authority of *Taylor* v. *Grange* (2), which says that the whole of the property in its entirety must be left in the hands of the trustees.

They also referred to *Lees* v. *Lees* (3) ; *Sinclair* v. *James* (4); *Cooper* v. *Cooper* (5).

Knox (*M'Arthur* with him), for the representatives of J. W. Flood and F. A. Oatley and for the trustees of the will. The

(1) 22 Ch. D. 284.   (3) 15 Eq. 151.
(2) 15 Ch. D. 165.   (4) [1894] 3 Ch. 554.
                    (5) L.R. 7 H.L. 53.

gift in the will is an ordinary gift to three persons as tenants in common. It is argued that because the testator uses the words "on trust to divide," he did not give the beneficiaries the ordinary rights of tenants in common.

If the testator had intended the property to be divided in specie, he would have said so; the books of precedents contain apt forms for the purpose. The word "equally" is conclusive against the plaintiff. Money alone is susceptible of an absolutely equal division, and land cannot be.

If the contention of the plaintiff is correct, then one person out of a number could insist on a division, although it might ruin the estate. The object of the Partition Act was to prevent this: *Pemberton* v. *Barnes* (1). In the case of *Boyd* v. *Allen* (2), there was an open power of sale and a mixed devise, the will being in the same terms as the will in this case, and it was held that the right to partition was not taken away by a discretionary power of sale in the trustees.

If the beneficiaries agreed, they could divide amongst themselves as they liked, independently of the trustees. This is a residuary gift which the beneficiaries are entitled to receive in money.

There is nothing in this will to deprive these tenants in common of their right to partition or sale. The first prayer is an attempt to evade the provisions of the Partition Act.

The trustees have no power at their own pleasure to force a division *in invitos* upon the majority of the beneficiaries.

L. Owen, for the Commercial Banking Co. of Sydney, mortgagees of the defendant beneficiaries. The security of the bank will be prejudiced if the Court grants the plaintiff's prayer.

This application is premature, as there is no allegation that the trustees have ever been asked to divide, or that they have refused.

[A. H. SIMPSON, C.J. in Eq. Any beneficiary has a right to administration, subject to his liability for costs.]

Lys v. *Lys* (3) and *Stones* v. *Heurtly* (4) were also referred to.

(1) 6 Ch. 685 at p. 691.   (3) 7 Eq. 126.
(2) 24 Ch. D. 622 ; 48 L.T. 628.   (4) 1 Ves. Sen. 164.

J. W. Allen, for C. W. Westbrook, and *Gordon*, for the Bank of New South Wales, consented to the application without prejudice to their rights under existing mortgages.

Salomons in reply. The testator has vested the power to divide in certain persons, and they alone have the right to do so. The Court will not allow any one of the beneficiaries to come in and get the Court practically to make a new will.

[A. H. SIMPSON, C.J. in Eq., referred to *Lewin on Trusts*, 9th Edit., pp. 667, 668.]

The word "irregular" species of property there mentioned means "unauthorised."

Cur. adv. vult.

On September 1st, the following written judgment was delivered by

A. H. SIMPSON, C.J. in Eq. (after stating the facts as above set out his Honour continued :—)

It seems to me clear that, as the learned pleader himself sets out in paragraph 3 of the statement of claim, the three residuary devisees were (subject to the charges on the estate and to the powers conferred on the trustees) tenants in common in equity of the estate, and any one of such tenants in common would be *prima facie* entitled to ask for a partition by the Court. This right, however, may be displaced if it is inconsistent with, or over-rides the trusts of the will.

"The right of partition which is an incident to the property in an undivided share is not taken away by a discretionary power of sale given to trustees," per *Fry*, J., in *Boyd* v. *Allen* (1). It is, however, taken away by a trust for sale, for that converts the property in view of a Court of Equity into personalty. To ask for a partition is to treat the property as realty, and this reconversion can only be effected if all the beneficiaries concur: *Biggs* v. *Peacock* (2).

Similarly if the testator has fixed a time for the sale, it would be inconsistent with the sale to have the property partitioned beforehand : *Swaine* v. *Denby* (3).

(1) 24 Ch. D. 622, 633.   (2) 22 Ch. D. 284.
(3) 14 Ch. D. 326.

In *Taylor* v. *Grange* (1), which was affirmed by the Court of
Appeal (2), under a will two of the children of the testator were
equally entitled for life with remainder to their children and
issue. The property was vested in trustees who were directed to
make a quarry on the estate and had powers of making roads,
and depositing earth and refuse, etc., for the purpose of making
the quarry. It was held by *Fry*, J., and by the Court of Appeal,
that the active trust of making the quarry would be stopped if
the estate were partitioned, and the trusts were, therefore, inconsistent with a right to have the estate partitioned.

Is there then anything in this will inconsistent with the right
to a partition? It is contended that the trust to divide the
estate is so: that as there is considerable personal estate the
testator intended the estate to be divided as a whole, and that
the trustees might allot among the beneficiaries any portion of
land at such values as they might fix, using the personal
estate for owelty of partition. Assuming that the trust for
division clothes the trustees with the very wide powers mentioned,
there is, in my opinion, no inconsistency between that trust and
the right to have the real estate partitioned by the Court, or
rather by the trustees under the direction of the Court which has
power in making partition to allot money for owelty of partition:
See the notes to *Agar* v. *Fairfax* (3).

Of course it may be a matter of considerable practical importance whether the division is made by the trustees or the Court,
but every *cestui que trust* has a right to have the trusts of any
deed or will administered by the Court, and in this case the
plaintiff himself asks that the trusts may be administered, and a
division of the residuary estate effected, which must, of course,
mean by the Court.

A sale is, no doubt, inconsistent with a trust to divide in specie,
but this is immaterial if the Partition Act attaches to the right to
call for a division a right to call in certain cases for a sale.

In the cases cited on behalf of the plaintiff, the trusts were
inconsistent with the right to call for a partition, and, therefore,
the Partition Act did not apply. I must, therefore, hold that the

(1) 13 Ch. D. 223.   (2) 15 Ch. D. 165.
                (3) 1 Wh. & T. L.C. 181.

beneficial owners of two-thirds of the real estate are entitled to call for a sale in lieu of partition unless the Court sees good reason to the contrary (see the Partition Act, s. 5).

It must not be taken that I concur in the view that a trust to divide real and personal estate among beneficiaries authorises trustees to allot land to a beneficiary at a valuation in part satisfaction of his share. It may be done with personal estate which has a market value, because the executors could sell and hand over the money to the legatees, who could at once reinvest it : the handing over of the property in specie, therefore, merely saves the double brokerage : see *Re Richardson* (1).

Transferring land, however, at a valuation is a very different matter. The practice among conveyancers has always been, according to my experience, to insert special powers when it was desired to enable a trustee to do this. No authority was cited for the proposition that a trust to divide real and personal estate authorises the trustee to allot land to a beneficiary at a valuation, and, in my opinion, such a trust only authorises a division of real estate with the consent of the beneficiaries or under the direction of the Court. It is, in fact, a gift to trustees in trust for certain persons in equal shares as tenants in common ; if the Court orders a sale any practical hardship will be removed by giving each beneficiary a right to bid.

Solicitors for the plaintiff: *MacNamara & Smith.*

Solicitors for the executors of J. W. Flood and F. A. Oatley, and for the trustees of the will : *Johnson, Minter, Simpson & Co.*

Solicitors for C. Westbrook and the Bank of New South Wales: *Allen, Allen & Hemsley.*

Solicitors for the Commercial Banking Company of Sydney : *Dibbs, Gibson & Parker.*

(1) [1896] 2 Ch. 512 p. 516.

OATLEY v. OATLEY and OTHERS.

Partition—Practice—Mortgage by one tenant in common to another—Partition against the consent of mortgagee of an undivided interest—Conditional offer to redeem.

1898.

September 12.

C.J. Eq.

A tenant in common who has mortgaged his undivided interest must, before he can sue for partition, offer to redeem unconditionally, and must satisfy the Court that the mortgage will be paid off at once; and it is immaterial that the mortgagee is a co-tenant in common.

THIS was a motion by the defendants, Florence Adelaide Flood, J. Macpherson, Edward B. McKenny, J. Johns, and F. S. Willis, who were the representatives of J. W. Flood and F. A. Oatley, for an order that the suit do stand dismissed with costs, upon the ground that the plaintiff having executed mortgages over his undivided share or interest under the will of Edward Flood, deceased, is not entitled to maintain a suit for partition or sale of the real estate devised by the said will against the will or without the consent of the mortgagees of his said share or interest, except upon the terms of first paying off the mortgages held by such of the said mortgagees as do not consent to such sale or partition; and upon the further ground that the plaintiff has not paid off the mortgage debt due to the said defendants upon the security of his said share or interest; and that the said defendants do not consent to the plaintiff suing for partition or sale of the said real estate.

To the facts stated in the report of a previous motion (*ante*, p. 122) it is only necessary to add the following:—

Ernest Oatley, the plaintiff, had mortgaged his undivided share in the residuary estate of the testator, and such mortgage was now vested in the representatives of his co-devisees, who had obtained a decree for foreclosure, whereby the plaintiff had until October 28th to redeem. The plaintiff had then brought this suit for partition pursuant to leave reserved by the decree for foreclosure, which had been made without prejudice to the plain-

tiff's right to sue for partition.   The present suit was opposed by
the defendants upon the grounds appearing in the notice of motion.
The plaintiff in his statement of claim offered to redeem, but only
made such offer in the event of the Court making a decree for
partition instead of for sale.

The defendants were the owners of two third undivided shares
of the estate, and they had mortgaged their beneficial interests
to the Commercial Banking Company of Sydney.

Knox, for the defendant co-devisees.

Three of my clients are trustees of the will as well as co-
devisees and mortgagees of the plaintiff. This motion is by them
in their capacity as mortgagees, and it is argued upon the basis
of the offer to redeem by the plaintiff in the statement of claim.

This offer by the plaintiff to redeem is only made conditionally
on the Court making a decree for partition.   He has, first of all, to
shew the Court that there is good reason to the contrary why
there should be partition instead of a sale.   If he cannot do this,
and get a decree for partition, then he makes no offer.

A mortgagor cannot sue for partition unless his mortgagee
consents: *Watkins* v. *Williams* (1); *Agar* v. *Fairfax* (2). If
the estate *as a whole* is mortgaged, one mortgagor can, subject to
the rights of the mortgagees, sue for partition, but if an undivided
interest is mortgaged, the mortgagor cannot sue for partition
without the consent of the mortgagee.

The defendants must not be taken as anxious for a sale, but
they say if the plaintiff is entitled to sue for partition then they
ask for a sale in lieu of partition.

The plaintiff must redeem before he can bring this suit: *Gibbs*
v. *Haydon* (3); *Sinclair* v. *James* (4).

The plaintiff is attempting to put the defendants, who are his
mortgagees, in such a position that they must defend a partition
suit, and incur heavy costs.   They, as mortgagees, are entitled to
be redeemed before he can do this.   If the plaintiff owned two-
thirds instead of the defendants, then the onus of shewing that a
sale was beneficial to the parties would be upon them, although

(1) 3 Mac. & G. 622.   (3) 30 W.R. 726 ; 47 L.T. 184.
(2) 1 W. & T. L.C. p. 200, 7th Ed.   (4) [1894] 3 Ch. 554.

they were mortgagees, if the plaintiff's contention is correct. The

plaintiff's offer to redeem must be unconditional.

L. Owen, for the Commercial Banking Company, did not consent to a partition.

Sir *Julian Salomons*, Q.C., and *Lingen*, for the plaintiff.

The only interest the defendants have as mortgagees is to be paid, and if a decree for partition is made the plaintiff undertakes to pay the money at once.

The defendants, as mortgagees, are attempting to defeat the rights of the plaintiff as a co-devisee. In the case of *Sinclair* v. *James* (1) Brewis was a mortgagee only.

The nature of the property subject to the mortgage would not be altered by a decree, as the plaintiff has undertaken to pay the money before the division is made, and *Gibbs* v. *Haydon* (2) is, therefore, in plaintiff's favour. The moment the decree for partition is made the plaintiff is prepared to redeem the mortgage.

Any costs of the partition suit would be incurred by the defendants, not as mortgagees, but in their capacity as co-devisees.

They might be able to add to their mortgage debt any extra costs of the suit incurred by them owing to their dual position, if there were any such costs.

[*Knox.* The defendants took a transfer from the Commercial Banking Company of their mortgage over the plaintiff's share, and claim through the bank, and have the same rights as the bank had.]

[A. H. SIMPSON, C.J. in Eq. Supposing after a long enquiry the Court orders a sale; in that event the plaintiff makes no offer.]

In *Sinclair* v. *James* (1) the mortgagee and co-owner were different persons, but here they are the same persons. The plaintiff can give security for the costs. A mortgagor can discuss his rights with his mortgagee before payment, provided he offers to redeem.

(1) [1894] 3 Ch. 554.   (2) 30 W.R. 726; 47 L.T. 184.

1898.
OATLEY
v.
OATLEY.

The mere fact of the Commercial Banking Co. not being interested in all matters is not fatal to the plaintiff. Sect. 11 of the Equity Act is borrowed from Ord. 16, R. 4, and the defendant is justified in asking for the decree in its present form: *Cox* v. *Barker* (1).

The decree in *Swan* v. *Swan* (2) is really conditional.

They also referred to *Dalton* v. *Hayter* (3), *Hickey* v. *Heydon* (4).

J. W. Allen, for C. W. Westbrook and the Bank of New South Wales, submitted.

Knox was not called on to reply.

A. H. SIMPSON, C.J. in Eq. The question in this case seems to me to be amply covered by authority. I have listened very carefully to what was said by Sir *Julian Salomons* and Mr. *Lingen* on behalf of their client, and it may be that I have not properly apprehended the force of their arguments, but it appears to me that the case of *Gibbs* v. *Haydon* (5) very clearly decided what are the rights of a mortgagee of an undivided share in property. In that case *Fry*, J., in his judgment stated that the question to be determined was whether or not the plaintiff had lost his right to have a partition, and that, in his judgment, by the execution of the mortgage he had done so.

Mr. Justice *Fry* could not have there meant that the plaintiff had absolutely lost his right. That is not, to my mind, a fair meaning to put upon his remarks, but what I think is clear he did mean was, that the plaintiff had lost the right for the time being, or, in other words, that it was suspended, and his Lordship added, "As a general rule a mortgagor cannot enforce any rights against his mortgagee unless he is at the same time prepared to redeem the mortgage. It is, therefore, wrong that the character of the property in the hands of the mortgagee should, upon the application of the mortgagor, be altered, and the mortgagee not paid off."

(1) 3 Ch. D. 359.   (3) 7 Beav. 313.
(2) 8 Price 518.   (4) 15 N.S.W. L.R. Eq. 167.
                 (5) 30 W.R. 726 ; 47 L.T. 184.

That case is cited with approval by *North*, J., in *Sinclair* v.

James (1), where he says, "I think the case of *Gibbs* v. *Haydon* before Mr. Justice *Fry* is clearly in point, a case in which the decision was justified by the cases referred to in it, and which has been taken as settled law ever since. Then it was said there was a mistake in the pleadings, and I am asked to allow an amendment by the addition of a claim for redemption. If there were merely a slip, and the action would be right when amended, I should allow an amendment; but this is not so, for I do not think that a plaintiff mortgagor can combine in the same action a claim against his own mortgagee to redeem him with a claim for partition against another defendant."

Now, the case before me is complicated by the fact that the original mortgagee has transferred his mortgage to the co-devisees.

But supposing this had not been done, then the original mortgagee would have had a right to say to the plaintiff, you cannot infringe or interfere with my rights unless you pay me off.

But in this case the plaintiff says, I will pay you off conditionally, that is only if, as a result of the enquiry under the Partition Act, a decree for partition is made. If, on the other hand, an order for sale is made by the Court (and the defendants, representing two-thirds of the beneficial interest under the will, are *prima facie* entitled to a sale), then I make no offer to redeem your mortgage.

Now, for the plaintiff to do that would clearly be an infringement of the rights of the defendants as mortgagees, and I therefore think that any such offer on those terms is unavailing.

Then it was contended that although this right may have belonged to the Banking Company, it did not attach to their transferees because the transferees were also co-devisees with the plaintiff under the will. But the case of *Gibbs* v. *Haydon* seems to me to be an answer to that contention, as in that case the mortgagee was a co-devisee, and the Court held there that it could not disturb the rights of the defendant as mortgagee, and the plaintiff could not succeed unless he could shew that he was prepared to redeem.

(1) [1894] 3 Ch. 554.

1898.

OATLEY
v.
OATLEY.

C.J. Eq.

As the first prayer asks for administration of the testator's estate, it seems to me that I cannot dismiss the suit because the plaintiff is entitled to administration as a matter of right, subject, however, to his liability to pay costs. I therefore declare that the plaintiff is not entitled to enforce his right to partition unless he first of all pays off, or satisfies the Court that he is prepared to pay off, the mortgagees of his undivided share in any event.

The plaintiff thereupon consented to an order that if he did not redeem the mortgage on or before the 28th October next, or such further time, if any, as the Court should allow for redemption, the suit should stand dismissed.

Solicitors for the applicants: *Johnson, Minter, Simpson & Co.*

Solicitors for the plaintiff: *MacNamara & Smith.*

Solicitors for the Commercial Banking Co. of Sydney: *Dibbs, Gibson & Parker.*

Solicitors for the Bank of New South Wales and C. W. West-brook: *Allen, Allen & Hemsley.*

BOULTER *v.* BOULTER AND OTHERS.

1898.

August 29.
September 1.

C.J. Eq.

*Tenancy in common—Landlord and tenant—Ordinary repairs—Improvements—
 Expenditure by one tenant in common in remainder on permanent improvements
 —Contribution—Partition—Use and occupation.*

The rule that one of several tenants in common of real estate is entitled, when
the property is sold, to receive out of the purchase money the increased price
obtained in consequence of permanent improvements effected by himself applies in
suits for administration as well as suits for partition. *Lee* v. *Dickinson* (15 Q.B.D.
60) explained.

The rule also applies whether the improvements are effected while the estate of
the tenant in common is only an estate in remainder as well as where his estate is
an estate in possession.

MOTION.

This was an application by Frederick Lassetter, one of the
defendants in the suit, for an order for a reference to the Master
in Equity to take an account to ascertain what moneys were
expended by the said defendant in permanent improvements on
allotment 13, s. 26, City of Sydney, or any part thereof, and being
portion of the property the subject matter of this suit, and to
enquire and certify by what amount the value of the said property
was increased at the date of the sale thereof by reason of such
improvements, and for such further or other order as this
honourable Court may think fit to make, upon the grounds
appearing in the affidavits.

The facts, as stated by his Honour in his judgment, were as
follows :—Under the will of Mrs. Boulter, dated the 4th of
February, 1858, the whole of her property was vested in John
Greer, as trustee upon trust for the testatrix's son Uriah Boulter
for life, and at his death to be equally divided amongst his wife
and children. Uriah Boulter had nine children, so that on his
death on the 28th December, 1896, the property, which comprised
a block of land in George-street, Sydney, became divisible into
ten shares. By a lease dated the 27th of November, 1875, the
trustee, Uriah Boulter and his wife, joined in leasing the block of

land to James Beaumont for a term of 21 years from the 28th October, 1874, at a rental of 258l., till the 28th October, 1881, and afterwards at a rental of 312l.; and the lessee covenanted among other things that unless prevented by fire or other inevitable accident he would keep the demised premises in ordinary and reasonable tenantable repair. On the 26th March, 1878, in consideration of 1000l., James Beaumont sublet the demised premises or part of them to Frederick Lassetter for the remainder of the term at a rental of 200l. till the 28th October, 1881, and afterwards at a rental of 260l.; and the underlease contained a covenant by the underlessee to repair similar to that in the head lease. In October and November, 1878, the defendant Lassetter purchased from three of the children of Uriah Boulter their three-tenths interests in the said property. During the course of his tenancy he expended a considerable sum of money, said to be 3,500l., in repairing and improving the demised premises. In July, 1897, this suit was instituted in equity by the trustee of Mrs. Boulter's will against the beneficiaries, stating among other things that parties interested collectively to the extent of more than a moiety in the lands passing under Mrs. Boulter's will desired a sale, and that in any case it would be desirable and for the benefit of all parties interested that the land should be sold and asking for an administration decree. On the 22nd October, 1897, an administration decree was made in the usual form, and the real estate of the testatrix was ordered to be sold, and the block of land in George-street was purchased by the defendant Lassetter for 23,000l.

Lingen (*Gordon* and *H. P. Owen* with him), for the defendant Lassetter, the applicant. This case is covered by authority: *Re Jones* (1), and the rule is not confined to partition suits: *Re Cooke's Mortgage* (2); *Watson* v. *Gass* (3).

Knox, for the defendant Eliz. Boulter, *contra*. Lassetter executed these repairs as lessee; he had no right to be in possession except as lessee; he went in before purchasing any of the interests; Lassetter was bound by his lease to repair.

(1) [1893] 2 Ch. 461, at 475.   (2) [1896] 1 Ch. 923.
(3) 45 L.T. 583.

Leigh v. *Dickinson* (1) is of superior authority to *Re Cooke's Mortgage.*

Rolin, for the Suttons. Lassetter has got the benefit of his expenditure by not paying an increased rent to the tenant for life: *Pascoe* v. *Swan* (2); *Scott* v. *Guernsey* (3).

L. Owen and *Macmanamey*, for the plaintiff.

Harvey, Todd and *H. P. Owen*, for the other parties on the record.

C.A.V.

On the 1st September, the following judgment was read by   *September* 1.

A. H. SIMPSON, C.J. in Eq. (After stating the facts as above set out his Honour continued): Where an owner of an undivided interest in land spends money in improving the property so that on a sale under the Partition Act it fetches an enhanced price, a Court of Equity in dividing the proceeds of sale will not allow the other co-owners to take their shares of the increased price without making an allowance for what has been expended to obtain that increased value: *Leigh* v. *Dickinson* (4). This course of action cannot inflict any injustice on the other co-owners, for it takes nothing out of their pockets, it only prevents them putting into their pockets moneys obtained by the expenditure of another person, unless they recoup him such expenditure. In no case can the co-owner who has improved the property obtain more than his outlay, though such outlay may have trebled the value of the property. And, on the other hand, the increase in the price obtained is the limit of what he can receive, though his actual outlay may be far larger.

It was not, I understand, contended on behalf of Mr. Lassetter that he could take into account moneys expended by him on repairs which his lease bound him to carry out, but his claim as to other sums expended on the property was opposed on two grounds :—

(1) That the equity above referred to was strictly confined to partition suits, and reliance was placed on the language of *Cotton,*

(1) 15 Q.B.D. 60.   (3) 48 N.Y. 106, cited in 62 Amer. Dec. 486.
(2) 27 B. 508.   (4) 15 Q.B.D. 60, at p. 67.

1898.

BOULTER
v.
BOULTER.

C.J. Eq.

L.J., in *Leigh* v. *Dickinson*, p. 67—"The procedure is confined to suits for partition." This seems to me being a slave to the letter of the words used and neglecting their spirit. In that case the plaintiff sued his co-owners for contribution in respect of moneys spent on repairs. The Court held he could not recover, but *Cotton*, L.J., pointed out that if a Court of Equity were dividing the proceeds of sale his equity to contribution would be recognised. This seems to me the fair meaning of his language. He never, in my opinion, meant to say that the equity was confined to partition suits technically so called, and that if the Court were dividing proceeds of sale in a partition suit, it would recognise the equity, but would disregard it if the division were in an administration suit; and *North*, J., so in fact decided in *Re Cooke's Mortgage* (1). This ground therefore fails.

(2) It was contended that the expenditure was made by Mr. Lassetter in his character of lessee, and ought not to be taken into account against the co-owners, but I am unable to see on principle why that should be so, and it is opposed to the principle on which *Re Jones* (2) was decided, where expenditure by the tenant for life of the entirety, who was also owner in fee of a moiety in remainder, was allowed to be taken into account against the co-owner in dividing the proceeds of sale after the death of the tenant for life.

(3) It was contended that if Mr. Lassetter is allowed his expenditure on improvements to the extent above-mentioned, he ought to be charged with an occupation rent to the extent to which an increased rental might have been obtained in consequence of the improvements, if he had let the property, and the case of *Teesdale* v. *Sanderson* (3) was relied on in support of the contention.

For the period up to the death of the tenant for life, 28th December, 1896, that case does not apply. No occupation rent could possibly be payable during that time to any one except the tenant for life, or persons claiming under him, and it was immaterial to the co-owners in remainder whether the tenant for life chose to receive an inadequate rent or none at all. For the

(1) [1896] 1 Ch. 923.   (2) [1893] 2 Ch. 461.
          (3) 33 Beav. 534.

subsequent period I think the contention also fails. *Teesdale* v.
Sanderson was explained in *Re Jones* (1), as deciding that where a
co-owner who has been in sole occupation of the property asks for
the assistance of the Court to get his expenditure on improvements
repaid out of proceeds of sale, the Court will impose on him the
terms of being charged with an occupation rent.   Here Mr.
Lassetter has paid what was apparently a full rent for the
property as it stood when leased to him, but it is said that an
increased rental might have been obtained after his improvements
were made, and, therefore, he must be taken to have recouped
himself for his outlay on improvements to the extent of such
increase since the 28th December, 1896.   The question seems
rather an academic one, as it appears unlikely that there could
be any such increase as to affect any sum that Mr. Lassetter is
likely to recover, but as it has been raised I must deal with it.
It must be borne in mind that Mr. Lassetter's equity to be
recouped anything can only be enforced because the Court is
distributing the proceeds of sale, and is practically therefore an
equity to be recouped out of the proceeds of a sale.   I cannot see
how the right can be affected by the co-owners saying, your
improvements have brought you a certain advantage that you
might have commuted into money.   Possibly, if he had done
so, the case might be different, but on this I express no opinion.
As the facts stand, the claim is to charge Mr. Lassetter with rent
on his own outlay.

The costs had better be reserved till the result of the inquiry
is known ; it may be it will turn out that the selling price was
not increased.

The order will be for an account of Mr. Lassetter's expenditure
on the property beyond moneys required to be expended by the
lease to him, and to what amount the price obtained was increased
by such expenditure.

Solicitor for the plaintiff: *Murray-White.*

Solicitor for the defendant Lassetter : *W. M. Barker.*

Solicitors for the other defendants: *Rolin & Gilder; M. A.
Williamson.*

(1) [1893] 2 Ch. 477.

1898.

BOULTER
v.
BOULTER.

C.J. Eq.

In re FELIX WILSON'S SETTLED ESTATE.

1898.
August 29.

C.J. Eq.

Settled Estates Act, ss. 19, 23, 24—Opposition of majority of beneficiaries to petition under the Act.

The Court is bound to respect the wishes of the beneficiaries interested in a settled estate, and if a vast majority of them oppose the exercise by the Court of its powers under the Settled Estates Act the Court is bound to refuse to exercise them.

THIS was a petition under the Settled Estates Act by the Perpetual Trustee Company to sanction a lease of certain land of which they were seized as trustees. The land was held on trust to receive the rents and profits until the youngest of the children of William Coker came of age, when it was to be sold, and the proceeds divided between the surviving children; in the meantime the rents and profits were to be applied for the benefit of the children in such manner as the trustees thought fit. There were five children, two of whom were of age; the petition was served on one of the adult children and the three infants; it was not known where the other adult child was.

H. P. Owen, for the adult child served and for the guardian under the Act of the three infant children, opposed the petition, and contended that under those circumstances the Court had no power to make the order: ss. 19, 23, 24 of the Settled Estates Act; *Taylor* v. *Taylor* (1); *Re Redman* (2); *Ex parte Bellamy* (3); *In re Merry* (4). The Court in the absence of any evidence of *mala fides*, must assume that the expressed opinion of the guardian represents what is most beneficial for the infants: *In re Birchall* (5).

L. Owen, for the petitioning company. The Court has jurisdiction and it is really a matter of discretion; in *Ex parte Bellamy* the dictum of *Jessel*, M.R., in *Taylor* v. *Taylor* is dissented from. None of the respondents have any absolute

(1) 1 Ch. D. 426 ; 3 Ch. D. 145.   (3) 11 N.S.W. R. Eq. 187.
(2) 11 N.S.W. R. Eq. 324.   (4) 15 W.R. 307.
(5) 16 Ch. D. 41.

right to the income of the land; the trustees have a discretion.
The Court will itself consider the advisability of the matter for
the three infants.

1898.

In re
FELIX
WILSON'S
SETTLED
ESTATE.

[SIMPSON, C.J. in Eq. There is no suggestion of *mala fides*
against their guardian, and *In re Birchall* appears to shew that
his wishes must be regarded.]

At all events the petition will not be dismissed with costs.

SIMPSON, C.J. in Eq. On the authority of the cases cited I
cannot see any alternative but to dismiss this petition   *Ex
parte Bellamy* certainly went a very long way, but that case was
explained and very much cut down in *Re Redman*, as being a
decision under somewhat special circumstances.   In the last mentioned case Mr. Justice *Owen* adopts the language of *Jessel*, M.R.,
in *Taylor* v. *Taylor*, and held that the Court cannot ignore the
opposition of a vast majority of the beneficiaries.   Possibly the
respondents are unreasonable, and taking a foolish view of the
desirability of this lease, but if they are, which I cannot assume,
it is to their own detriment.   The petition must be dismissed
with costs.

Solicitors for the petitioners : *Shaw and Jagelmann.*

Solicitor for the respondents : *Baker.*

FARNELL v. COX.

Trustee—Breach of trust—Interest—Profits gained by use of trust fund.

1898.
_____
September 7.

C.J. Eq.

A trustee in breach of trust borrowed trust funds and paid them into his overdrawn account with a bank on which the trustee was paying seven per cent. interest; the account remained overdrawn in varying amounts up till the hearing of the suit. *Held*, that the trustee must repay the trust funds with seven per cent. interest.

FURTHER CONSIDERATION OF SUMMONS.

This was the further consideration of the summons, the hearing of which is reported *ante*, p. 103. The Master reported that the trustee, H. R. Cox, had not borrowed any further trust funds beyond the sum borrowed at the time of the deposit of the deeds. The Master also reported the facts as to the position of H. R. Cox's account with the bank which appear in his Honour's judgment. The Master, at the request of the parties, left it to the Court to decide whether H. R. Cox· had under the circumstances made a profit of seven per cent. on the trust fund.

Lingen, for H. R. Cox, applied for the return of his title deeds upon his paying back the moneys with five per cent. interest. Interest is not punitive; more than five per cent. is not ordered unless the trustee has actually received more; the relief from a liability is not a profit within the meaning of this principle. Where a trustee has used trust funds in his business he is never ordered to pay more than five per cent. unless his business shews a larger profit: an enquiry has never been directed whether the trustee by use of the trust funds has been relieved from a liability, and has therefore made a constructive profit. Suppose a trustee ten years ago owed money to a money-lender and the debt carried interest at fifty per cent., if he then paid it off with trust funds must he to-day restore the trust fund with ten years' interest at fifty per cent. ? There is no precedent for charging a trustee with what he has escaped paying, but only with profits which he has actually put into his pocket: *Vyse v.*

Foster (1); *Whitney* v. *Smith* (2). To charge a trustee in this way assumes that without the accommodation from the trust funds he would have continued to owe the principal and pay the interest to the bank up to the present time.

Mann (*Heydon*, Q.C., with him), for certain of the defendants. The case is determined by the application of the general maxim that a trustee cannot make a profit from his trust: *Robinson* v. *Pett* (3); the rule that a trustee must repay trusts funds with profits earned thereby is only a particular form of the general maxim: *Forbes* v. *Ross* (4); *In re Hilliard* (5); *Bray* v. *Ford* (6).

Rich and *Noble*, for other parties submitted.

Lingen in reply.

SIMPSON, C.J. in Eq. The defendant, H. R. Cox, was one of the trustees of the will of his father, and was permitted by his co-trustee to have in his hands the control of the trust funds. In breach of his trust, though with a perfectly bona fide motive, he lent himself the sum of 1,800*l.* upon an equitable mortgage on which he agreed to pay interest at 5*l.* per cent. This sum was paid by Mr. Cox into his account with the Bank of New South Wales on the 23rd September, 1897, the account being then overdrawn to the extent of 1,133*l.*; by this transaction the overdraft was converted into a credit balance. Mr. Cox continued to operate upon this account, and as his withdrawals exceeded the amounts he paid in, the account was on the 8th November again overdrawn; and it continued overdrawn from that time onwards, the amount of the overdraft on the 30th June, 1898, being 924*l.* 19*s.* 10*d.* It is admitted that the bank has been charging seven per cent. interest on the overdraft. No case at all like this in its facts has been cited, and I have therefore to deal with the question on principle. Two principles appear to me to be applicable: the first is the principle to be found in *Forbes* v. *Ross* (4), and numbers of other cases, that a trustee cannot bargain with himself so as to reap a benefit for himself out of the estate; the

---

(1) L.R. 7 H.L. 318; 44 L.J. (N.S.) 37.   (2) 4 Ch. 513.
(3) 2 Wh. & Tud., 7th Edit. 606.   (4) 2 Cox 113.
(5) 1 Ves. Jun. 90.   (6) [1896] A.C. 44.

second is the principle that no man can take advantage of his own wrong.

The general principle to be considered in determining what advantage a trustee has gained for which he ought to account is laid down in *Attorney-General* v. *Alford* (1). In that case Lord *Cranworth*, at p. 851, states that this Court ought not to proceed *in poenam* against a trustee :—" What the Court ought to do, I think, is to charge him only with the interest which he has received, or which it is justly entitled to say he ought to have received, or which it is so fairly to be presumed that he did receive that he is estopped from saying he did not receive it." The same principle is to be found expressed by *Page-Wood*, V.C., in *Penny* v. *Avison* (2), where it is observed that there are three cases where the Court charges more than four per cent. upon balances in the hands of a trustee :—Where he ought to have received more, where he has actually received more, and where he must be presumed to have received more. His Honour gives instances of each class, giving as an instance of the third class the use by the trustee of his trust fund in his trade.

Does this case fall within the principle of those cases ? Had the trustee done what he ought to have done in this case, it is clear he ought not to have paid this money into his account at all, and, *a fortiori*, he ought not to have paid it into an overdrawn account; if the money was paid into the bank at all, it should have been paid into a separate account entitled as a trust account so as to prevent the bank from setting off the sum paid in against his private account. Had he done so, and had he then represented to the bank that it was hard that he should be charged with interest at seven per cent. on his overdraft while there was a balance to his credit on the trust account not bearing any interest, the bank conceivably might have recognised the hardship, and arranged to credit his trust account with interest at seven per cent. so as in effect to set the one off against the other; the trustee could not possibly under these circumstances have claimed for himself any portion of the interest so credited to the trust fund. Such a transaction would be exactly the same in effect as what Mr. Cox did in the present case, but carried out in a legiti-

(1) 4 De G. M. & G. 843.   (2) 3 Jur. N.S. 62.

mate way. I cannot see how Mr. Cox can claim to be in any better position because he carried out the same arrangement, but in an improper manner. To allow such a claim would be to permit him to take advantage of his own wrong. I think, therefore, that as Mr. Cox has benefited from the use of the trust fund to the extent of seven per cent. he must be charged on that footing.

I thought at one time that the fact that Mr. Cox deposited ample security for his loan might affect the rate of interest payable, but on more mature consideration I feel no doubt that it makes no difference.

Solicitors: *Norton, Smith & Co.; Holdsworth & Son; Sullivan Bros.; W. S. Grey.*

1898.

Sept. 18, 19,
20, 21.

C.J. Eq.

MOSS AND OTHERS *v.* MOSS AND OTHERS.

Further consideration — Breach of trust—Trust for accumulation - Compound interest—Locke King's Act (19 Vic. No. 1, s. 1 ; [1898] No. 17, s. 109)—Exoneration of mortgaged property—" Contrary or other intention "—Direction to pay debts out of estate generally.

A testator devised the whole of his real and personal estate except certain specific chattels to his trustees subject to the payment of debts (with payment of which except his mortgage debts he primarily charged his personal estate) upon certain trusts :—as to Property A upon certain specific trusts : as to Property B on trust to sell, and out of the proceeds in the first place to pay off a mortgage on Property A, and to invest the balance of the proceeds of sale.

Held, that A was not exonerated from payment of the mortgage debt except to the extent of the proceeds of sale of B, and these proceeds being insufficient the balance of the debt must be charged on A.

Woolstencroft v. *Woolstencroft* (1) and *Brownson* v. *Lawrance* (2) followed : *Eno* v *Tatham* (3) and *Stone* v. *Parker* (4) distinguished.

A trustee, who fails to carry out a trust to invest a sum of money and accumulate the income, must repay the principal with compound interest for the period allowed by law for the accumulation and thereafter at simple interest.   This rule applies whether the principal sum has been actually or only constructively received by the trustee sought to be charged : *Byrne* v. *Norcott* (5) and *In re Hulkes* (6) followed.

A trustee is chargeable with interest, although interest is not asked for by the statement of claim.

THIS was the further consideration of a suit which had been instituted for the construction of the will of William Moss, who died on the 11th March, 1873, for the appointment of the Permanent Trustee Company as trustee of the will in the place of George Collins (deceased) and Stephen Josiah Bryen, who consented to retire, for an account of the real and personal estate of the testator come to the hands of Bryen and Collins, or either of them, and of their dealings therewith, and for an account of the trust funds misappropriated by Collins or lost to the estate by reason of his conduct, and that Bryen might be ordered to repay such moneys, with interest, and for administration so far as might be necessary.

(1) 2 De G. F. & J. 347.	(4) 1 Dr. & Sm. 212.
(2) 6 Eq. 1.	(5) 13 Beav. 336.
(3) 3 De G. J. & S. 451.	(6) 33 Ch. D. 552.

The testator's will was, so far as is material, in the following terms:—"I appoint Stephen Josiah Bryen and George Collins trustees and executors of my will   I devise and bequeath all my real and personal estate which shall belong to me at my decease (except that portion of my personal estate hereinafter otherwise bequeathed) subject to the payment of my just debts funeral and testamentary expenses (with payment of which except my mortgage debts I primarily charge my said personal estate) unto and to the use of my said trustees upon the trusts following : upon trust to let for terms not exceeding three years in possession all or any part of my real estate and out of the rents to pay my wife Bridget Moss the sum of 3*l.* per week and as to the balance of such rents I direct that the same after payment of any interest due or accruing due on mortgages shall be invested or shall accumulate for the benefit of my children hereinafter named in manner hereinafter expressed   And from and immediately after the death or marrying again of my wife I direct that my said trustees shall hold my said real and personal estate upon trust as to (property A.) for my son William George Moss for life with remainder to the children of my said son (as directed) [There then followed similar trusts of two other properties in favour of the testator's daughters Selina Clarke and Emily McDaid and their children. The testator then directed his trustees to sell a property in Parramatta Street] and out of the clear proceeds thereof to pay off in the first place the mortgage now owing on (property A.) and to invest or accumulate the balance as hereinafter mentioned   And I direct my said trustees to sell and convert into cash when they shall see fit my vacant allotment of land in Regent Street and also all such parts of my personal estate as shall not consist of cash (except my secretaire which I hereby bequeath to my said son William George and the family pictures glass cases and all the household furniture and effects about any dwelling occupied by me at my death which I hereby give and bequeath to my said wife Bridget) and out of the proceeds in the first place to pay (a debt of £400) and then either to accumulate the balance of such moneys together with the surplus rents and the balance proceeds of my Parramatta

M 2

Street property or at their discretion to invest the same as directed and I declare that this direction to accumulate or invest shall extend to the unapplied income of such investments And I empower and direct my trustees out of the capital of such accumulations to assign to my daughters Mrs. Hyde Mrs. Mackenzie and Mrs. Ryan on their respective marriages the sum of 200l. or such proportionate part thereof as my trustees shall think my estate able to bear and the balance of such accumulations and investments shall upon the death of my said wife or her marrying again be equally divided between and among my daughters Mrs. Hyde Mrs. Mackenzie and Mrs. Ryan or such of them as shall then be living and the lawful issue of such of them as may be deceased the issue taking the parent's share as tenants in common.   Shares of daughters to be their separate estate.

The testator died on the 11th March, 1873, leaving a widow and eight children, viz., two besides the six mentioned in the will who were the wives respectively of Edward Smith and William Smith.

There was an allegation in the statement of claim that, from the death of the testator until April, 1886, Bryen left the entire management of the trust estate to his co-trustee Collins, and that Collins misappropriated the rents and profits received by him.

At the hearing of the suit the principal matters dealt with were the effect of a forfeiture clause in the will, and how far the beneficiaries under the will had brought themselves within it. The testator's widow was still alive, but at the hearing the Court held that the trust for accumulation was not valid beyond the 11th March, 1894.

Before the suit came on for hearing Bryen admitted his liability to pay the capital sums misappropriated by Collins, but disputed his liability to pay interest; he accordingly paid 898l. 16s. 3d. into Court, which, he alleged, was sufficient to meet those defalcations, and also the trust moneys which he had himself received, and had in hand.

By the decree at the hearing the following enquiries were directed to be taken by the Master: (1) An account of the trust funds received by or on behalf of Collins and Bryen or either of them ; (2) An account of the rents and profits received by or on behalf of Collins and Bryen or either of them; (3) An account of Collins' misappropriations, and in what manner those appropriations were made; (4) An account of the state of the trust funds at the end of 21 years from the testator's death.

The Master certified that certain balances were or should have been in Bryen's hands from time to time, and that with certain small exceptions no portion of the capital nor of the rents and profits had been invested; that Bryen had paid into Court all the principal moneys due from him including the amount of Collins' defalcations. As to the manner in which Collins had appropriated the rents and profits the Master reported in the following terms:—
(3) The said George Thomas Collins and the defendant Stephen Josiah Bryen as executors and trustees of the will of the said testator opened and kept a trust account at the Bank of New South Wales, Southern Branch, Sydney, into which all trust moneys were or ought to have been paid. (4) All cheques operating on this account were signed by both trustees, and the defendant Stephen Josiah Bryen signed cheques in blank, leaving the same for the said George Thomas Collins to fill up and sign as co-trustees when such cheques were required. (5) The defendant Stephen Josiah Bryen kept a cash book in which he, with a few exceptions of entries made by the said George Thomas Collins, made all entries from the date of the death of the testator up to the 24th day of June, 1881. (6) Such entries appear to have been made by the defendant Stephen Josiah Bryen on instructions obtained from the said George Thomas Collins, and not from personal information. (7) Save as aforesaid the said George Thomas Collins between the year 1875 and the time of his departure from the colony of New South Wales in the ship "Flora" on or about the 20th day of October, 1886, assumed the financial control and sole management of the money matters of the said trust estate with the knowledge and consent of the defendant Stephen Josiah Bryen. (8) Between the dates mentioned in the next preceding sub-paragraph, the said George Thomas Collins collected all the rents from the said trust estate, and appropriated the same to the extent of 460l. 13s. 1d. to his own use; with the exception of the said sum of 460l. 13s. 1d., all rents collected were paid into the said trust. The said George

Thomas Collins concealed this misappropriation from the defendant Stephen Josiah Bryen, who did not become aware of the same until after the departure of the said George Thomas Collins from the said colony as aforesaid. (9) Save as aforesaid the defendant Stephen Josiah Bryen did not, between the said dates, participate in the management of the said trust estate owing to the death of his father John Bryen, who died on or about the 13th day of June, 1877, and who was at the time of his death possessed of a large amount of real and personal estate, the management of which devolved upon the defendant Stephen Josiah Bryen. (10) Save as aforesaid the defendant did not, between the said dates, in fact, receive any moneys arising from or deal with the said trust estate in any way; but between the said dates the said George Thomas Collins had the sole management thereof, and received all moneys arising from the said trust estate, and his defalcations were entirely unknown and unsuspected by the defendant Stephen Josiah Bryen until after the said George Thomas Collins departed from the said colony as before mentioned in sub-paragraph 7 of this paragraph.

It also appeared that the net proceeds of sale from the Parramatta Street property amounted only to 827l., and that the mortgage on " Property A " amounted to 1200l. A sum of 373l. was, therefore, paid to the mortgagee by the trustees out of the accumulations of rents and profits. The first question submitted to the Court was, whether this sum of 373l. should have been raised out of the mortgaged property or out of the general estate.

L. Owen, for the plaintiffs, contended that the mortgaged property was exonerated, and that Locke King's Act (19 Vic. No. 1) did not apply. The amending Acts passed in England have not been passed here; the law is, therefore, in the same condition as it was after the passing of the original Act : *Stone* v. *Parker* (1); *Allen* v. *Allen* (2) ; *Rodhouse* v. *Mold* (3) ; *Jarman on Wills,* p. 649 ; *Maxwell* v. *Hyslop* (4). A direction to pay debts is a contrary or other intention.

H. P. Owen, for the defendant Selina Clarke. This is a charge of debts on the whole estate; it is, therefore, not a contrary or

(1) 1 Dr. & Sm. 212.   (3) 12 L.T.N.S. 629.
(2) 30 Beav. 395.   (4) 4 Eq. 407.

other intention: *Woolstencroft* v. *Woolstencroft* (1); *Theobald on Wills*, 4th Edit., p. 140; *Brownson* v. *Lawrance* (2).

(He was stopped by the Court).

SIMPSON, C.J. in Eq. This question really turns upon whether the testator has in his will expressed an intention contrary to that which the Legislature has declared shall be the usual rule in the administration of estates, viz., that mortgage debts are to be paid out of the real estate subject to the mortgage.

As is pointed out by *Jessel*, M.R., in *Gull* v. *Fenwick* (3), most of the early decisions on the Act appear to have proceeded on the principle of giving as little effect as possible to its provisions, and it was thought advisable by the Imperial Parliament to get rid of the effect of these decisions, and two amending Acts have consequently been passed ; since those Acts were passed the Courts have shewn themselves more disposed to assist in carrying into effect the spirit of this series of statutes.

Our Legislature has not seen fit to follow in the footsteps of the English Parliament, and in consequence to the extent that those earlier decisions may be taken to have established a rule, I assume that I am bound by them, but only to that extent; I do not feel called upon to go one jot further than the decided cases compel me to go.

Taking into consideration all the cases cited by Mr. *Langer Owen*, and treating them as correctly decided, it appears to me possible to distinguish them from the present case. The cases really appear roughly to be grouped into two classes : one in which the testator has directed his debts to be paid out of a particular part of his estate, such part not including the mortgaged land, e.g., his personal estate, as in *Eno* v. *Tatham* (4), and *Moore* v. *Moore* (5); or the residue of his real and personal estate, not including the mortgaged property, as in *Stone* v. *Parker* (6), and *Allen* v. *Allen* (7); the other class being those where the testator has made his debts a charge on his whole estate, and therefore on the mortgaged property concurrently with

(1) 2 De G. F. & J. 347.
(2) 6 Eq. 1.
(3) 43 L.J. Ch. 179.

(4) 3 De G. J. & S. 451.
(5) 1 De G. J. & S. 602.
(6) 1 Dr. & Sm. 212.

(7) 30 Beav. 395.

the rest of the estate ; such cases are *Woolstencroft* v. *Woolsten-croft* (1), and *Brownson* v. *Lawrance* (2), where the direction was a general one to pay debts out of the estate. The present case appears to me to fall within the second class ; the testator here uses the words :—"I devise and bequeath all the real and personal estate which shall belong to me at my decease (except that portion of my personal estate hereinafter otherwise bequeathed) subject to the payment of my just debts, funeral and testamentary expenses (with payment of which, except my mortgage debts, I primarily charge my said personal estate), unto and to the use of my trustees," &c. I think that these provisions are indistinguishable in principle from those cases where a direction to pay debts out of the estate generally has been held not to be a contrary intention within the meaning of the Act.

Besides this, however, the testator later on in his will sets apart a specific fund, out of which this mortgage debt is to be paid, and from the terms in which that fund is spoken of it is clear the testator contemplated that it would be more than sufficient for the purpose, as the trustees are directed, "in the first place," to pay the mortgage debt out of the fund, and to invest and accumulate "the balance." That clearly is the first fund applicable for payment of the debt, but as to the deficiency recourse must be had to the general law, which says that it must be paid out of the mortgaged property in the absence of a contrary intention. In the words of the *Lord Chancellor* in *Woolstencroft* v. *Woolstencroft* : " I am not judicially satisfied of the testator's intention, by any language he has used in his will, to exempt his devisee of the land in question from the charge of the mortgage debt," except to the extent of the fund specifically directed to be applied in payment of the debt. So much of the debt, therefore, as was paid out of the accumulations of rents and profits, must be raised by a charge upon the mortgaged land and repaid to the accumulations.

Among the other questions submitted to the Court was the question whether the trustee Bryen was liable to pay interest on the trust moneys in his hands, and if so, at what rate ?

(1) 2 De G. F. & J. 347.   (2) 6 Eq. 1.

Lingen (*G. Harris* with him), for the defendant Bryen, took the preliminary objection that no interest was asked for by the prayer of the statement of claim except as to Collins' defalcations, and that there had been no direction to the Master to ascertain what sum was improperly retained by Bryen in his hands from time to time.

L. Owen, for the plaintiffs. It is immaterial that there is no prayer for interest; interest is given as a matter of course: *Turner* v. *Turner* (1); *Stafford* v. *Fiddon* (2); *Hollingsworth* v. *Shakeshaft* (3). In *Plomley* v. *Shepherd* (4) there was no prayer for interest. A trustee is always liable *prima facie* on balances which are or ought to be in his hands: *In re Hulkes* (5).

Rich, for the defendant Smith, followed in the same interest, and cited *Daniel Ch. Pr.*, p. 1231; *Johnson* v. *Prendergast* (6); *Goodyear* v. *Lake* (7); *Pattendon* v. *Hobson* (8).

A. H. SIMPSON, C.J. in Eq. I think, subject to what Mr. *Lingen* may say, that a trustee is liable for interest on balances improperly in his hands, or which must be taken to be improperly in his hands, and it is immaterial that there is no prayer for interest in the statement of claim; but here there has been no direction to the Master to ascertain what balances were improperly in the hands of the trustee from time to time. No doubt the Master finds that no investments were made by the trustees, and that certain sums must be taken to have been in Mr. Bryen's hands from time to time; but *non constat* they were not properly retained, at all events some portion of them. Of course Collins' defalcations are a separate matter altogether; that matter I think I am in a position to decide finally now. I understand Mr. Bryen has paid in the principal, and, as at present advised, I think he is liable to interest.

Lingen. Yes, I admit he must pay simple interest on that sum.

(1) 1 J. & W. 39.	(5) 33 Ch. D. 552, at 558.
(2) 23 Beav. 286.	(6) 28 Beav. 480.
(3) 14 Beav. 492.	(7) Ambl. 584.
(4) 18 N.S.W.R. Eq. 5.	(8) 17 Jur. 406.

L. Owen. Bryen is liable to pay compound interest, as there is a trust for accumulation: *Lewin on Trusts,* pp. 379, 380; *Raphael* v. *Boehm* (1); *Feltham* v. *Turner* (2).

Sir *Julian Salomons,* Q.C. (*S. A. Thompson* with him), for the defendants W. G. Moss and Mrs. McDaid. Trustees are bound to pay interest if they are liable for the capital, as otherwise they do not indemnify the estate for their breach of trust: *Attorney-General* v. *Köhler* (3). And it is immaterial whether the trust funds have actually or only constructively come into their hands. The principle must be the same: *Dornford* v. *Dornford* (4).

[*Lingen.* It is shewn in *Tebbs* v. *Carpenter* (5) that the report of *Dornford* v. *Dornford* is inaccurate as to compound interest being charged.]

The whole question in *Dornford* v. *Dornford* was whether simple or compound interest was payable. In *Byrne* v. *Norcott* (6) the moneys were only constructively received. So also in *Gilroy* v. *Stevens* (7). The case of *Amiss* v. *Hall* (8) is practically overruled by *In re Emmett's Trusts* (9).

Lingen. I have admitted my liability for simple interest on this sum. The distinction between actual and constructive receipt of moneys is a substantial one. In *Byrne* v. *Norcott* the money had got into the joint names of the trustees; here it was intercepted before it reached the trustees' banking account. Had the money once got into the banking account, it may be Bryen would have had to pay compound interest. At all events only simple interest must be paid since 1894, viz., 21 years after the testator's death: *Wilson* v. *Peake* (10). As to the balances apart from the defalcations, I submit the trustee is only liable for balances improperly retained and actually retained. Here the Master has treated money as being in the trustee's hands which he had expended on improvements to the property. The Master disallowed the expenditure in Bryen's accounts as not coming

(1) 11 Ves. 92.   (6) 13 Beav. 336.
(2) 23 L.T.N.S. 345.   (7) 51 L.J. Ch. 834.
(3) 9 H.L.C. 654.   (8) 3 Jur. N.S. 584.
(4) 12 Ves. 129.   (9) 17 Ch. D. 142 at 148.
(5) 1 Madd. 290.   (10) 3 Jur. N.S. 155.

within the definition of "salvage." There are also other sums which Bryen expended, but was disallowed because he could not produce vouchers: *Saltmarsh* v. *Bennett* (1).

[A. H. SIMPSON, C.J. in Eq. That case is hardly law now, I think; it was dissented from in *In re Hulkes* (2), which latter case was approved in *In re Sharpe* (3).]

At all events, there must be an enquiry what balances were improperly retained; a trustee would be wrong if he invested every penny of trust money as it came into his hands, when he had the management of a large trust property.

Harvey Browne, for Selina Clarke.

Newham, for Mrs. Mackenzie.

Harvey, for the administrator *ad litem* of the estates of Mrs. Ryan and Mrs. Hyde.

Loxton, for Daniel James Hyde, the only child of Mrs. Hyde.

Watt, for the testator's widow.

SIMPSON, C.J. in Eq. I think that in this case I must order the trustee to pay compound interest, although I make the order with great reluctance. In the ordinary run of cases the Court looks on simple interest as a sufficient compensation for the *cestuis que trustent*, but in certain cases it does allow compound interest. One of the cases for compound interest is where there is an express trust for accumulation, and the trustee disregarding the trust does not accumulate and retains the trust fund. It appears to be suggested in *Lewin on Trusts*, 9th Edit., p. 380, that this rule only applies in those cases of trusts for accumulation where the money has actually come to the hands of the trustee sought to be charged; and in the course of the argument I asked more than once whether counsel could refer me to any case where compound interest was charged against a trustee who had not actually had the handling of the trust moneys. At first they were unable to do so, but further research has enabled them to discover two, and they appear to me to govern this case. At the same time I do not feel inclined to go further than those cases compel me.

(1) 31 Beav. 349.　　　　　　(2) 33 Ch. D. 558.
(3) [1892] 1 Ch. 170.

1898.

Moss
v.
Moss.

C.J. Eq.

I am unable to distinguish this case from *Byrne* v. *Norcott* (1) and *Gilroy* v. *Stevens* (2) ; in neither case was the receipt by the trustee of the fund more than constructive.   In *Byrne* v. *Norcott* (1) the trust moneys were in the hands of the trustees' agent in India, who was asked by the trustees to invest the fund, and accumulate the proceeds.   The agent disobeyed his instructions, and the trustees were held liable to replace the money with compound interest, that is to say, they were made liable for such accumulations as the money would have made if the trust in the will had been complied with.   In the other case of *Gilroy* v. *Stevens*, the dividends from the trust fund had been received by the solicitor for the trustee, and retained by him ; the trustee was held liable for three per cent. interest with half-yearly rests.

Mr. *Lingen* endeavoured to distinguish *Byrne* v. *Norcott* (1) by saying that the trustees adopted the custody of their agent as their own custody, and, therefore, had in law actually received the fund ; but I do not think that is really any distinction.   In one sense no doubt they did adopt his custody, but not his custody of the funds in an uninvested condition, for they expressly instructed him to invest them ; therefore, they did not in any way acquiesce in his mode of dealing with the fund. Here the Master finds that Collins assumed sole control of the affairs of the trust with the knowledge and consent of Mr. Bryen, and that by this means he appropriated 465*l.* of the rents.   That amounts, in my opinion, to a ·finding that Collins as agent for himself and his co-trustee collected the rents, and, therefore, that the money came into his hands as agent for both trustees.

I must therefore hold that Mr. Bryen must replace this money with four per cent. with annual rests ; the parties do not press for more than that, but under the terms of this will, which authorises investments in bank deposits, I do not think they would be entitled to any higher rate of interest or to half-yearly rests.

With regard to the other sums of money which the Master has found were or ought to have been balances in his hands from time to time, I think it follows from the cases I have already referred to that the trustee is also chargeable with compound

(1) 13 Beav. 336.   (2) 51 L J. Ch. 834.

interest, so far, of course, as they were improperly in his hands. At the present time, however, I cannot say on what amounts this interest is to be paid, because in an estate of this nature the trustee would clearly not have been bound to invest every penny that came into his hands. A special enquiry will be necessary (unless the parties can agree upon a sum) to enquire whether any, and if so what, portion of these balances, which I must take were from time to time retained by Mr. Bryen uninvested, were improperly so retained; on these sums I think the trustee must pay interest at the same rate as on the other sum. Of course, in calculating these balances the defalcations must be put aside altogether, as they have been separately dealt with, and the trustee is not liable to pay compound interest on that sum twice over.

Compound interest on these sums is only payable up to the 11th March, 1894, when the period for accumulation expired; from that date the trustee must pay simple interest at four per cent.

Solicitors: *Heydon; Davenport; Lenehan & Pratt; Salwey; Fitzhardinge, Son & Houston; Parry.*

1898.

Moss
v.
Moss.

C.J. Eq.

BRAITHWAITE AND ANOTHER *v.* W. & A. McARTHUR, LIMITED.

Company—Debenture issued by English company—Registration as bill of sale.

A debenture issued by an English company is valid in this colony without the necessity of registration in the colony as a bill of sale.

1898.
November 25.
December 1.

C.J. Eq.

DEMURRER.

The question raised was whether a debenture issued by an English company must be registered as a bill of sale in this colony. It was admitted that the debenture could not now be registered, the thirty days limited by the statute having expired.

Gordon and *Knox*, for the defendant company. Mortgages and charges over personalty, registration of which is required by the Companies Acts, are not within the mischief of the Bills of Sale Act, 1878 : *In re Standard Manufacturing Company* (1); nor are debentures bills of sale : *Read* v. *Joannon* (2).

The language of s. 4, sub-s. 1 (*e, i*), 2 (*a*), of the Act No. 10 of 1898 is inconsistent with the idea of a corporation ; no mention is made of the official liquidator, and to speak of the residence and occupation of a corporation is absurd. It makes no difference that the company is English.

It is true that there is no provision in this colony for register-ing the charges of an English company, but the real mischief aimed at by the Bills of Sale Act is secrecy, and there can be no secrecy about debentures. They have, at all events, to be regis-tered in England The register of charges in any case is no protection to intending creditors. The case of *The G.N.R. Com-pany* v. *Coal Co-operative Society* (3) is reconcilable, but even if it is not so, the cases before cited are binding in this Court. In *Lee* v. *Roundwood Colliery Company* (4), *A. L. Smith*, L.J., reads the judgment of the Court of Appeal in *In re Standard Manu-facturing Company* (1) as shewing that the debentures of a com-pany are not within the scope of the legislation dealing with bills of sale.

(1) [1891] 1 Ch. 627.   (3) [1896] 1 Ch. 187.
(2) 25 Q.B.D. 300.   (4) [1897] 1 Ch. 373 at p. 395.

Lingen, for the plaintiffs.

1898.

BRAITHWAITE
v.
W. & A.
McARTHUR
LTD.

The decision in *In re Standard Manufacturing Company* is really based on the fact that the Legislature had provided specially for the registration of debentures of a company in the Companies Acts. The statements as to the purview of and mischief aimed at by the Bills of Sale Acts are mere *dicta* which *Vaughan Williams*, J., disregarded in the *G.N.R. Company* v. *Coal Co-operative Company* (1). The colonial Legislature in passing the Bills of Sale Acts cannot be taken to have had in contemplation foreign legislation, and the Courts of this colony can only consider the local law. There is no provision of which the Court can take cognizance for registration of these debentures. This Court must treat the provisions of the English Companies Acts as mere private regulations. The decision in *The G.N.R. Company* v. *Coal Co-operative Society* (1), therefore, applies.

The case of *Read* v. *Joannon* only decides that the debentures of a limited company registered under the English Companies Acts are not bills of sale within the meaning of the English Bills of Sale Act; otherwise the elaborate judgment of *Bowen*, L.J., in *In re Standard Manufacturing Company* (2), would not have been necessary.

Knox in reply.

Cur. adv. vult.

The following considered judgment was, on December 1st, delivered by

December 1.

SIMPSON, C.J. in Eq. The defendants are a limited company registered in England under the Companies Acts, but with a branch office here. The plaintiffs have advanced and agreed to advance large sums to the defendant company on the security of a charge as a floating security over the real and personal property of the company, and proper deeds and debentures have been executed in England and sent to the colony for carrying out this object. They cannot, however, be registered in this colony within the time required by the Bills of Sale Act of 1898, and the plaintiffs contend that, as this cannot be done, the debenture-

(1) [1896] 1 Ch. 187.   (2) [1891] 1 Ch. 627.

O 2

1898.
Braithwaite
v.
W. & A.
McArthur,
Ltd.

C.J. Eq.

holders will not be protected so far as personal chattels are concerned against execution creditors.

The demurrer raises the point whether this contention is sound. Previous to the year 1890 it was generally assumed that debentures of a company, so far as they charged personal chattels, were within the provisions of the Bills of Sale Acts; and the decision of *Read* v. *Joannon* (1), that such debentures were not within the provisions of the Bills of Sale Act, 1878, came, it is said as a surprise on the profession. This decision was emphatically upheld in *In re The Standard Manufacturing Company* (2), where *Bowen*, L.J., delivered the reserved judgment of the Court of Appeal. It was pointed out that the objects of the Bills of Sale Acts of 1854 and 1878 were to strike at the frauds perpetrated upon creditors by secret bills of sale, and that having regard to the provision made by the Companies Act for the registration by companies of the mortgages and charges affecting their property, such documents could not be described as secret, or as belonging to the class of documents by which frauds were perpetrated on creditors by secret bills of sale. They were, therefore, not within the mischief of the Bills of Sale Act, 1878. In summarising their view at the close of the judgment, the Court based their decision " on the ground that the mortgages or charges of any incorporated company for the registration of which other provisions have been made by the Companies Clauses Act, 1845, or the Companies Act, 1862, are not within the Bills of Sale Act of 1878." This decision has been followed on several subsequent occasions, the last being *Davey and Co.* v. *Williamson and Co.* (3).

In *The Great Northern Railway Co.* v. *The Coal Co-operative Society* (4), the point arose whether debentures issued by a society registered under the Industrial and Provident Society Acts and charging the personal chattels of the society by way of security for money borrowed required registration as bills of sale. After carefully considering the previous cases, especially *The Standard Manufacturing Company* (2), *Vaughan Williams*, J., held that the question was left open whether the Bills of Sale Acts applied to securities of companies in the case of which no provision had

(1) 25 Q.B.D. 300.   (3) [1898] 2 Q.B. 194.
(2) [1891] 1 Ch. 627.   (4) [1896] 1 Ch. 187.

been made for registration of securities—as was the case with the society before him—and he decided that such securities required registration under the Bills of Sale Acts. I apprehend that s. 75 of our Companies Act, which requires the registration of securities given by companies only applies to companies registered in New South Wales; and the question I have to decide is whether the corresponding provisions of the English Act are sufficient to bring the case within the principle laid down in *The Standard Manufacturing Company*. A person supplying an English company carrying on business in New South Wales with goods or labour on credit, may fairly be held bound to enquire whether the company has issued debentures. The mere fact that such debentures have to be registered, presumably though not necessarily in London, prevents, in my opinion, these documents being in any sense secret, and is sufficient to take them out of the provisions of the Bills of Sale Act of 1855 or 1898.

I must, therefore, allow the demurrer.

Whether registration as bills of sale would be necessary in the case of a foreign company, not being an English company, carrying on business here, is a matter on which I express no opinion.

Solicitors for the plaintiff: *Pigott & Stinson.*

Solicitors for the defendant company: *Allen, Allen & Hemsley.*

1898.

BRAITHWAITE

v.

W. & A. McARTHUR, LTD.

C.J. Eq.

1898.

Dec. 7, 14.

C.J. Eq.

ELLIOTT v. ELLIOTT.

Incomplete voluntary assignment—Assignment of choses in action—Shares in companies—Bank deposits—Mortgage debts—Power of attorney.

' A settlor voluntarily assigned to a trustee for his wife certain mortgage debts with the benefit of the mortgagor's covenants with power to sue for the debts; he also granted and released to the trustee the mortgaged lands ; he also assigned to the trustee all the moneys held by certain banks on fixed deposit in his name and also all shares in certain limited companies with power to sue and give receipts for the same. *Held,* that there was a complete gift of the mortgaged land and the mortgage debts ; that the settlor having done all that lay in his power to assign the fixed deposits at the date of the settlement they also passed ; but that the shares did not pass as the settlor had not transferred them in the manner provided for by the constitutions of the companies. *Quære,* whether the Court of Equity would have enforced the assignment of the shares if the settlement had contained an irrevocable power of attorney to the trustee.

HEARING OF SUIT.

This was a suit by the trustee under a voluntary settlement against the settlor seeking to enforce the settlement ; the plaintiff asked that the settlement and all title deeds and documents, scrip and other writings relating to the land and personal property, the subject of the settlement, might be delivered to him, and for an injunction against any dealing with the property by the defendant.

By an indenture, dated the 17th August, 1896, made between the defendant of the first part, Elizabeth Elliott, his wife, of the second part, and the plaintiff as trustee of the third part, after reciting that the defendant, in consideration of natural love and affection to his said wife and children and for other good causes, was desirous of making the conveyance and assignment in the indenture now in statement afterwards contained, it was witnessed that the defendant granted and released unto the said trustee, his heirs and assigns, the lands and hereditaments described in the first schedule thereto, and it was further witnessed that the defendant assigned and transferred to the said trustee a mortgage debt for 500*l.* and a mortgage debt for

150*l.* in the same indenture mentioned, and the full benefit of
the covenants entered into by the respective mortgagors and all
other securities for the premises comprised in the said mortgages,
and all the estate and interest of the defendant in the premises, with
power to the said trustee to sue and give receipts for the said respective sums of 500*l.* and 150*l.* with interest due and to accrue due with
respect to the said mortgage debts in the name or names of the
defendant, his executors or administrators, and the defendant
thereby granted and released to the said trustee, his heirs and
assigns, the lands and hereditaments comprised in the respective
mortgages to hold unto and to the use of the said trustee, his
heirs and assigns subject to the respective equities of redemption
affecting the same; and the indenture now in statement further
witnessed that the defendant assigned to the said trustee all the
moneys held by the English, Scottish and Australian Bank,
Limited, and the Commercial Banking Company, Limited, upon
fixed deposit in the name of the defendant, and also all shares in
the Kangaroo Valley Dairying Company and in the Intercolonial
Land and Investment Company as specified in the third schedule
thereto, to have, receive and take the same unto the said trustee,
his executors, administrators and assigns, and all interest due
and to accrue due in respect of the same with power to the said
trustee to sue and give receipts for the same, and it was declared
that the said trustee should stand seized and possessed of the
said hereditaments and of the said mortgage debts, deposits,
shares and other real and personal property in trust for the said
Elizabeth Elliott for her life, and from and immediately after
her death upon trust for all the children of the defendant and
the said Elizabeth Elliott in equal shares as tenants in common.
The said indenture contained no covenant for further assurance.
Beyond executing this indenture the settlor had done nothing to
convey or transfer the settled property to the trustee.

Langer Owen, for the plaintiff. The trustee has done all in
his power to pass the property to the trustee, and that is sufficient;
the mere intention to declare trusts in the hands of a trustee is
sufficient: *Airy* v. *Hall* (1); trusts being declared, the settlor

(1) 3 Sm. & G. 315.

cannot keep the property; this Court will interfere, though it will not when there has been an incomplete direct assignment to a beneficiary: *Parnell* v. *Hingston* (1). The power of attorney is sufficient: *Wheatley* v. *Purr* (2). The Court will imply a covenant by the assignor not to derogate from his assignment: *In re Patrick* (3).

[He also referred to *Ellison* v. *Ellison* (4); *Milroy* v. *Lord* (5).]

Cullen, for the defendant. The plaintiff's remedy for the deeds is not in this Court; he should bring an action of detinue at law.

In *Airy* v. *Hall*, the trustees had received the property; here the settlor has not completely assigned the property: *Dillon* v. *Coppin* (6); *May on Fraudulent Conveyances*, p. 405.

Owen in reply.

Cur. adv. vult.

December 14. On the 14th December, the following judgment was delivered by

SIMPSON, C.J. in Eq. The suit is instituted by the trustee of a voluntary settlement asking the Court that the defendant may be directed to hand over to him the settlement and all title deeds and documents, scrip and other writings relating to the land and personal property the subject of the settlement, and that the defendant may be restrained from alienating or dealing with the same or any of them. The defence set up is that when the defendant executed the settlement he believed his wife to be faithful to him, but after the execution of the settlement he discovered that she had been for a considerable time living in adultery, and it was urged that this case ought to stand over until the proceedings which he has instituted in the Divorce Court for a divorce have been heard. This I declined to allow. No evidence was offered to shew that the wife had been guilty of misconduct; the case, therefore, resolves itself into a matter of law as to how far the settlement is a complete gift.

Questions of this kind tempt one to concur in the well-known observation of Lord *Westbury* that he heartily wished that there

(1) 3 Sm. & G. 337.
(2) 1 K. 551.
(3) [1891] 1 Ch. 82.
(4) II Wh. & Tud. 835.
(5) 4 De G.F. & J. 274.
(6) 4 M. & C. 647.

were no reported cases. The cases on this subject are very
numerous, some of them conflicting, and others turning on refined
distinctions and qualifications, not always easy to follow. The
classification given in May's well-known book on Voluntary
Conveyances at p. 405 affords some clue through the labyrinth.
He specifies three classes: (1) cases in which the donor is both
legal and equitable owner, and intends to make a complete
transfer of his interest to the donees direct or to trustees for
them; (2) cases in which the donor only intends to confer on
his donees his equitable interest; (3) cases in which the donor
wishes to give his donees the benefit of property belonging to
him which is of a legal nature, but is not assignable at law. The
second class of cases may be left out of consideration, as it is
clear that the settlor in this case intended to transfer the legal
interest. The cases of *Milroy* v. *Lord* (1) and *Richards* v.
Delbridge (2) may be regarded as the leading cases of this class.
They shew that, if the settlement is intended to take effect by
transfer, the Court will not hold the intended transfer to operate
as a declaration of trust; for then every imperfect instrument
would be made effectual by being converted into a declaration of
trust; as it was put by Sir *George Jessel*, "for a man to make
himself a trustee there must be an expression of intention to
become a trustee, whereas words of present gift shew an intention
to give over property to another, and not retain it in the donor's
hands for any purpose, fiduciary or otherwise." It is well settled
that the Court of Equity will not compel a settlor to complete an
imperfect gift, but in this case there is a complete gift of the
land and the mortgage debts.

The bank deposits and the shares in companies present greater
difficulties, and stand on different footings. The bank deposits
were at the date of the settlement choses in action not transfer-
able at law, and with reference to this class the question is this:—
Has the donor done all that he could to make the gift complete as
between himself and the donee; if so, the Court will support the
assignment as a declaration of trust just as if it had been a
transfer or assignment of an equitable interest. The case of

1898.

ELLIOTT
v.
ELLIOTT.

C.J. Eq.

(1) 4 D.F. & J. 274.   (2) 18 Eq. 11.

1898.

ELLIOTT
v.
ELLIOTT.

C.J Eq.

Blakely v. *Brady* (1) may be taken as an illustration of this class
of cases. I am unable to see what further step the settlor could
have taken to transfer the deposits at the date of the settlement,
and I must, therefore, hold that the trustee is entitled. The
shares in the companies are on a different footing. Here the
settlor could have done something more, viz., transfer the shares
in the way provided by the constitutions of the respective
companies, and I am unable to distinguish this case from *Dillon*
v. *Coppin* (2). Reliance was placed on the fact that in the deed
the assignor gives to the trustee power to sue and give receipts
for the shares. In several cases in which an irrevocable power
of attorney was given the Court has regarded the assignment as
complete, but there was nothing in this settlement to prevent
the settlor from revoking the power of attorney, as by his
conduct he has, in my opinion, done. There was a very full
power of attorney given in the case of *Dillon* v. *Coppin*, and if
there is any conflict between that and the other cases I think
that I ought to follow that case, and to hold that the gift of the
shares was incomplete.

It was then contended that in some cases an assignment has
been held to imply a covenant by the assignor not to do anything
to prevent the assignee from having the full benefit of the
assignment, and in the cases of *Deering* v. *Farringdon* (3);
Aulton v. *Atkins* (4); *Gerard* v. *Lewis* (5); and *In re Patrick*
(6), were relied on. In the first three of these cases the assignment was apparently for valuable consideration. The last case
was not a decision, but *Lindley*, L.J., pointed out that, if the
settlor could be sued at law by the trustee for the amount of the
debts got in by him, it followed that his estate was liable in
equity for the same amount, and he referred to the case of
Fletcher v. *Fletcher* (7). This, however, is no new doctrine, as it
has long been established that if there is a complete legal liability
under a voluntary instrument, the Court will enforce it: See
the cases collected, *May*, p. 398. I am not aware, however, of

(1) 2 D. & Wal. 311.   (4) 18 C.B. 249.
(2) 4 M. & C. 647.   (5) L.R. 2 C.P. 305.
(3) 1 Mod. 113.   (6) [1891] 1 Chan. 82.
(7) 4 Hare 67.

any case in which a Court of Law or Equity has held that such
a covenant as above-mentioned ought to be implied in cases of
voluntary assignment, and to imply such a covenant in this case
would go far to overturn the well-established doctrine of the
Court of Equity on the subject of incomplete gifts.

I think that the plaintiff is entitled to the relief prayed in
respect of the land, mortgage debts and bank deposits, but not as
to the shares in companies. The defendant must pay the general
costs of suit except so far as the plaintiff's costs have been
increased by including the shares in the companies; as to the
defendant's costs, additional costs incurred in consequence of the
shares being included, must be paid by the plaintiff.

Solicitors for the plaintiff: *McDonnell and Moffitt.*
Solicitor for the defendant: *T. Marshall.*

1898.

ELLIOTT
v.
ELLIOTT.

C.J. Eq.

1898.

MACDOUGALL AND OTHERS v. SMITH.

Nov. 7, 8, 10. *Building Society—Investing members, withdrawal of—Breach of trust by director.*

C.J. Eq. Where a director, who is also a shareholder of a building society, withdraws the amount of his shares, having at the time knowledge of prior notices of withdrawal, and that the liabilities of the society exceeded its assets—*Held*, that he committed a breach of trust for which not only the prior withdrawing members, but also the society itself could sue.

THIS was a suit by the trustees of the Grafton Building, Land and Investment Society to obtain a transfer from the defendant Smith, of certain securities, originally given by one Young to the society, upon the society rescinding the cancellation of thirty-nine shares formerly held by the defendant Smith, and for a declaration that the arrangement by which Young's security had been transferred to Smith, and Smith's shares had been cancelled, was a breach of trust.

The Grafton Building, Land and Investment Society was a society carrying on business in Grafton, and was registered in 1884, under the Friendly Societies Act of 1873.

The following rules of the society were material :—

PAYMENT OF SUBSCRIPTIONS.

12.—Every person taking shares in the society shall, in addition to the entrance fee before named, pay on the first Saturday in each month (or on such other day as may be substituted for it by the Board), *as subscription, on each investing share* the sum of two shillings and sixpence in advance, such payments to be made at the office of the society until the subscription, interest, and bonus, as further provided for in these rules, have accumulated to twenty-five pounds for each share, when the payment shall cease and the amount of £25 shall be paid to the shareholder, and his connection with the society, so far as such share is concerned, shall cease and determine ; or he may convert the same *into a fully paid-up share.*

INTEREST ON INVESTING SHARES.

16.—A general account of the affairs of the society shall be prepared at the end of every financial year, shewing the gross receipts, expenditure, assets and liabilities of the society, and eight per cent. interest shall then be added *to the balance due to each investing shareholder* at the close of the preceding year, and interest also at the same rate per annum upon the subscriptions paid during the current year on such shares as have been held by the members for upwards of six months, and the remaining portion of the profits of the society shall be set aside as a reserve fund for the purpose of meeting future contingencies.

19.—*Investing shareholders* shall, after holding any share or shares for upwards MACDOUGALL
of twelve months, be allowed to withdraw the same on giving written notice to   *v.*
the secretary, and shall be entitled to receive, at the end of one month from the SMITH.
receipt by the secretary of such notice the full amount of his contributions (exclusive of entrance fees) together with such interest as by the books of the society
may appear to be due on such share at the time of the last preceding annual
balance, but in no case shall the Board be compelled to apply more than one-half
of the monthly receipts in payment to withdrawing members ; and it is further
provided that in the event of two or more shareholders giving notice at or about
the same time they shall be paid in rotation according to priority of notice, all
subscriptions and fines ceasing, however, after the first subscription night subsequent to the receipt of such notice, *and the society being liable in eight per cent. per
annum interest from the time of the sum becoming due until paid* ; in all cases such
member or members shall before being entitled to receive the value of his or their
shares, deliver up to the secretary the scrip for cancellation.

POWER OF TRUSTEES, &C.

26.—The trustees shall have full power under the direction of the Board for the
time being, to sell and dispose of all property belonging to the society, whether
the then present trustees are the same whose names are inserted in the deeds
and writings relating to such property or not : and all receipts given by the trustees,
for the time being, shall be good and sufficient discharges to any purchaser or purchasers of any hereditaments and premises, which shall be sold pursuant to the
rules of the society, or otherwise howsoever ; and any conveyance by the trustees,
for the time being, of property vested in any former trustee or trustees, shall be
sufficient both at law and in equity, to transfer and vest the whole estate and
interest of such former trustee or trustees, therein as effectually as if the trustee
or trustees, for the time being, were the parties to whom such security had been
originally given.

PERIODICAL INVESTIGATIONS.

35.—Immediately preceding the close of every fifth year of the society, or at the
close of each year, or at such other time as may be determined, the Board may, if
they deem it desirable, cause a survey to be made of any of the properties they
hold as security for advances and obtain a report of the then value of the same,
for which survey and report such fee shall be paid as the Board may decide. At
the end of every five years or oftener, at the discretion of the Board, an actuary
may be appointed by the Board, and paid out of the funds of the society (nothing
herein contained being construed as contrary to the appointment of one of the
members of the Board, if duly qualified), who shall investigate the affairs of the
society, the profits then made, and after all losses and anticipated losses have been
provided for, the profit over and above the interest which has accrued on the
investing shares, as provided for in rule 13, shall be apportioned equitably to the
investing and borrowing members. The interest or profits thus ascertained to be
due to members shall be allowed to remain and accumulate, forming part of the
general funds of the society until, in the case of the investing members, such
accumulated profits, together with the subscription money paid by them and the
8 per cent. interest added from year to year, shall make up the sum total of
twenty-five pounds, then all payments to the society as far as such share is concerned shall cease and determine, and the amount of twenty-five pounds for such
share shall be paid by the Board to the shareholder, or he may convert the amount

into a fully paid-up share ; and in the case of the borrowing members, the surplus profit apportioned to the shares held by them and advanced on by the society, shall be applied according to an equitable scale to the reduction of the future payments, either in number or amount at the option of each member.

PAID-UP SHARES.

46.—The Board may from time to time as often as they may think it conducive to the interest of the society, issue paid-up shares of the value of twenty-five pounds ; such shares shall bear interest at the rate of eight per cent. per annum, payable yearly. Members holding paid-up shares for twelve months will in addition to the interest be entitled to receive the bonus payable at the annual division of profits. The Board shall fix the entrance fee payable from time to time upon such shares.

BALLOT FOR WITHDRAWAL OF INVESTING SHARES.

47.—It shall be lawful for the Board when there is no demand for the society's funds, to appoint a ballot to take place to determine what investing shares shall be withdrawn, notice of such ballot to be given by advertisement. The member on whom the lot shall fall shall be obliged to accept repayment of his subscriptions and full profits as at last balance on one share, if the number he holds unadvanced does not exceed five—on two shares if that number does not exceed ten—on three shares if that number does not exceed fifteen—and on four shares on any number above fifteen—but shall not have his name put again into the box until every member holding unadvanced shares shall have had a portion withdrawn by this process ; and in the event of any member upon whom a share or shares shall be ballotted failing to withdraw such share or shares from the society, then all interest or profits upon such share or shares shall cease and determine.

For some years the society apparently prospered, but when times of depression came they were in difficulties, and since the end of 1892 they were only carrying on in liquidation, though the society was not formally being wound up.

The defendant was a director from 1893 up to and after 3rd August, 1895, the date of the transaction complained of. On 6th October, 1894, he gave notice of withdrawal of 40 fully paid-up shares held by him in the society. Some months previous to that time four other holders of fully paid shares had given notice of withdrawal, and none of these four had at the date of the suit been paid.

On the 3rd August, 1895, the following arrangement was come to by the defendant with the other directors, viz., that the society should hand to the defendant cheques for 1,017l. as the withdrawal money due on his shares, and that these should be cancelled ; that the defendant should then hand the cheques back to the society in discharge of a mortgage for 1,000l. held by the society, from John Young, and interest, and that John Young, on getting this mortgage released, should execute a fresh mortgage to the defendant for 1,000*l.* At this time the society was practically insolvent; it had an overdraft at the bank of 196*l.*, and owed a depositor 900*l.* The overdraft had since been paid, but the 900*l.* was still owing. It appeared from the report and balance sheet for the year ending 31st March, 1895, that in reckoning the value of assets against liabilities there was a debit balance of 168*l.* 0*s.* 3*d.*, and that on the income account for the year there was a balance owing of 422*l.* 11*s.* 7*d.* The report for the year ending 31st March, 1896, shewed that in reckoning the values of assets against liabilities, the debit balance was 135*l.*, but no balance sheet of income and expenditure for the year was attached.

1898.

MACDOUGALL
v.
SMITH.

L. Owen (*R. K. Manning* with him), for the plaintiff. The rules distinguished between holders of fully paid-up shares and ordinary investing members. R. 19 providing for withdrawals, is limited to investing members properly so called, and therefore the defendant had no right to withdraw.

At all events Smith as a director knew the financial position of the company when he effected this transaction: *In re Ambition Society* (1).

The effect of the transaction was to postpone investing members who had given notice of withdrawal before Smith.

Lingen and *Cullen*, for the defendant. The transaction was bona fide and authorised by the rules, a paid-up member being an investing member: *In re Norwich Provident Insurance Society* (2); *Hirsche* v. *Sims* (3). The trustees have full power under rule 26 to dispose of any of the society's property.

So far as the case depends on priority the injury is individual, and the person injured must sue: *Pulbrook* v. *Richmond Mining Company* (4)

Without calling on the plaintiff's counsel to reply,

SIMPSON, C.J. in Eq. (After referring to the facts of the case as above set out his Honour continued):—When the facts are once stated, it is clear that if Young's mortgage is taken as a good security for the amount due under it, as I must assume it to be

(1) [1896] 1 Ch. 89.   (3) [1894] A.C. 654 at p. 660.
(2) 8 Ch. D. 334.   (4) 9 Ch. D. 610.

1898.

MACDOUGALL
v.
SMITH.

C.J. Eq.

in the absence of evidence to the contrary, the defendant has been paid off the value of his shares in full, and that such payment was a clear breach of trust, both as against outside creditors [*Re Ambition Building Society* (1); and *Strand* v. *Permanent Mutual Building Society* (2)], and shareholders who had given earlier notices of withdrawal: *Botten* v. *City and Suburban Land Society* (3).

It was contended that the only persons who had a right to complain were the shareholders who had been deprived of their priority, but the fact that a wrong has been done to them, for which they might sue, does not shew that a wrong has not also been done to the society, for which the plaintiffs are the proper persons to sue: see *Pulbrook* v. *Richmond Mining Company* (4). Under these circumstances it is immaterial to consider whether, if the shareholders in question had been plaintiffs, they would have been barred by acquiescence; but I see no sufficient evidence to support such a contention.

It is also immaterial to consider whether, having regard to rules 12, 16, 19, 35, 46 and 47, fully paid-up shareholders have a right to withdraw at all under rule 19, but my impression is they have no such right.

The transaction must be set aside by the society rescinding the cancellation of the defendant's paid-up shares, and issuing to him fresh certificates for them, and by the defendant transferring to the society the mortgage from Young to himself. The defendant must pay the costs.

Order accordingly.

Solicitor for the plaintiff: *Everingham* (Grafton), by *G. E. R. Jones.*

Solicitors for the defendant: *Norrie & McGuren.*

(1) [1896] 1 Ch. 89   (3) 72 L.T. 87.
(2) 18 N.S.W. Eq. 194, 203, seq.   (4) 9 Ch. D. 610, p. 613.

LOGAN *v.* RAPER AND OTHERS.

Trustee—Breach of trust—Investment—Real or personal securities—Fixed   1898.
deposits—Building society.   ———
                                                                             Nov. 15, 21.
Trustees were authorised to invest trust funds "in good real or personal   ———
securities ;" they invested in fixed deposits with a building society.   C.J. Eq.
Held, that the investment was authorised by the power.

HEARING OF SUIT.

By a marriage settlement made in 1873 upon the marriage of
John Logan to Jane Margaret Raper, the sum of 2000*l.* was
assigned to the trustees upon trust to invest the same " in their
names in good real or personal securities " in trust for Mrs. Logan
during her life or, in the event of her husband's decease, *durante
viduitate*, and, after her decease or second marriage, for the issue
of the marriage.   There was one child, a daughter, the plaintiff
in this suit.   Mrs. Logan, after her husband's death, had remarried.
The trustees had invested 1,000*l.* of the trust fund on fixed deposit
with the Federal Building Society and the other 1,000*l.* with the
St. Joseph's Building Society, both being societies registered
under the Friendly Societies Act.   The Federal Building Society
was now in liquidation, and the St. Joseph's Building Society
had adopted a scheme of reconstruction.   The result was that
the fixed deposit receipts were worth considerably less than their
face value.   It was admitted that, provided this form of investment was open to the trustees, they had not been guilty of any
want of prudence or caution in depositing or leaving this money
with the societies; the sole question was whether fixed deposits
of this nature were within the class of securities authorised.

Gordon and *Harriott*, for the plaintiff. . Fixed deposits are not
a security at all ; the receipts are merely evidence of a simple
contract debt. To have a " security " there must be something
bound to be answerable for the debt, or at all events there must

1898.

LOGAN
v.
RAPER.

be something which makes the debt more secure, more easy to recover: *Hopkins* v. *Abbott* (1); *Manning* v. *Purcell* (2); *Ryder* v. *Bickerton* (3); *Pickard* v. *Anderson* (4); *Langston* v. *Ollivant* (5). The security of a company is worse even than that of an individual, as the liability of the members is limited. A deposit receipt is no better than an I.O.U., it is simply evidence of a debt; to recover, the depositor has to sue on the debt, not on the deposit receipt.

Piddington (*Waddy* with him), for the defendant. It has been held that a promissory note or a bill of exchange is a security: *Barry* v. *Harding* (6); and a deposit receipt is as good.

(He was stopped by the Court.)

SIMPSON, C.J. in Eq. The only question that I have to decide in this case is whether the power of investment contained in Mrs. Logan's marriage settlement authorised an investment on fixed deposit with companies of this nature. If it did, no question is raised as to the prudence of the trustees in making the investment.

Apart altogether from authority I should have thought that, whatever the words "personal security" might mean standing by themselves, when coupled with the words "real security" the expression would mean on security of real or personal property. And I find that that view is taken by the learned author of *Underhill's Law of Trusts*, 3rd Edit. 257 :—" It has been held," he says, "that, where trustees were authorised to invest on real or personal security, they might permit money to remain merely on the security of a personal promise or bond; but it is humbly submitted that, however this might be, if the expression 'personal security' stood alone, its juxtaposition in this case with the alternative 'real security' ought to have restricted its meaning to 'the security of personal property,' and that to enlarge it so as to cover the security of a personal promise was scarcely justified." I must say that I should have thought that that contention was a sound one.

(1) 19 Eq. 222.	(4) 13 Eq. 608.
(2) 2 Sm. & G. 284 ; 7 D. M. & G. 55.	(5) Coop. 33.
(3) 3 Swans. 80.	(6) 1 J. & Lat. 483.

There are, however, at least three cases which practically amount to decisions to the contrary. The first is the case of *Forbes* v. *Ross* (1), where trustees were directed to lay out the trust fund on "heritable or personal security." The trustees agreed that one of them should retain the money in his hands at 4*l.* per cent. interest. The *Lord Chancellor* was of opinion that the trustee could not make a profit out of his trust, and directed that he must pay 5*l.* per cent.; but if the investment were altogether unauthorised, the *Lord Chancellor* must have ordered him to refund the principal instead of allowing it to remain in his hands on a mere undertaking to pay an increased rate of interest.

Similarly in *Langston* v. *Ollivant* (2), the trustees had power to lend the trust fund upon "real or personal security." The trustees lent the money to the husband of the *cestui que trust*, he being at the time in good credit and circumstances. Sir *William Grant*, M.R., ordered the money to be refunded, on the ground that the trustees had been induced to accommodate the husband from relationship, and that the loan was not a bona fide investment, but an accommodation. Had his Honour thought they were not authorised to lend the money at all in that way, it would have been sufficient to say so and order it to be refunded; all evidence as to the object of and reasons for the loan would have been superfluous. That case, therefore, by implication appears to me to be an authority to the same effect as *Forbes* v. *Ross* (1).

So in *Pickard* v. *Anderson* (3), the trustees of a marriage settlement were empowered to invest the funds on such security, either real or personal, as they should think proper. Part of the trust fund was left outstanding on the note of hand of the husband. The trustees applied to the Court to ascertain whether this was authorised, and Sir *James Bacon*, V.C., thought the husband should execute a bond, but left the money outstanding in the husband's hands.

It is then contended that a deposit receipt is not a security at all, but is on exactly the same footing as an I.O.U., and in support

1898.

LOGAN
v.
RAPER.

C.J. Eq.

(1) 2 Bro. C.C. 430.   (2) G. Coop. 33.
(3) 13 Eq. 608.

of that contention a number of cases on the construction of bequests of securities in wills have been cited to me. Where there is a bequest of securities in a will, it may very well be that the Court must construe very strictly the words used to see what the testator intended to pass to the donee under the name of securities, where there are conflicting claims to decide between. But, to my mind, it would be lamentable if this Court were forced to apply a similar strictness in construing a power of investment, and to hold that trustees were guilty or innocent of a breach of trust according to the mere form into which the parties threw the security, the security itself in each case being identically the same. Whether the borrower gives a promissory note or an I.O.U., the money is equally outstanding on a personal promise or undertaking; it would, I think, be difficult to make the ordinary layman appreciate the distinction that if he takes a promissory note, viz., an express promise to repay, he is safe; but that if he takes an I.O.U. and relies on the promise of repayment which the law implies, he is guilty of a breach of trust

The cases shewing that the security of a personal promise to repay is within the power, I do not feel constrained by the other authorities cited to hold that a deposit receipt is not a personal security within the meaning of the power.

I therefore dismiss this suit with costs.

Solicitors for the plaintiff: *Abbott, Vindin & Littlejohn.*
Solicitors for the defendants: *White & Wolstenholme.*

THE PERPETUAL TRUSTEE COMPANY, LIMITED *v.* A'BECKETT AND OTHERS.

Club—Personal liability of members—Ratification—Principal and agent—Contribution—Liability of members to indemnify trustee for liabilities incurred in excess of their authority—Class suit—Form of decree—Costs.

1898.
———
September 26,
27, 28.
Oct. 10, 11,
12, 13, 27.

C.J. Eq.

Members of a club may by acquiescence waive compliance with the provisions of the rules of the club.

A person, joining a club, paying subscriptions, and using the club premises, does not thereby become liable on previous contracts of the committee.

At a meeting of a club held in December at which a quorum was not present, the meeting purported to pass a resolution appointing trustees and empowering them to lease premises on behalf of the club. At the following meeting of the club in January, which was duly convened and held, the minutes of the December meeting were read and confirmed. The trustees, in their own names, entered into a ten years' lease of premises for the club, which was shortly afterwards dissolved.

Held, that the members present at the January meeting were bound to indemnify the trustees against their liability under the lease, but that existing members who were not present were not so bound in the absence of conduct amounting to ratification; ratification was implied by members who knew of the existence of the lease, and discussed the indemnification of the trustees and the disposal of the lease, and generally treated the lease as an asset of the club.

HEARING.

In 1886 a number of persons agreed to form a club in Sydney to be known as the Cercle Français, with premises in Wynyard Square. In January, 1887, rules were adopted in the French language for the government and management of the club, and of these it is only necessary to set out the following as translated :—

3. Any person desiring to become a member must be proposed by two active members and be elected by a majority of the committee.

Apparently the practice of the club was subsequently altered as to this; members were elected at general meetings by ballot.

4. No candidate will be allowed to enjoy the advantage of the club until he has paid his entrance fee and one-fourth of the yearly subscription, which must be paid within a fortnight of the notification of his admission.

12. The administration of the affairs of the club is entrusted to a committee elected at the first general meeting in each year. The duties of the committee are purely honorary.

17. . . . . The committee disposes of the funds of the society, and has full power to take all measures for the internal management which it may deem necessary.

18. General meetings are held four times a year in the first fortnight of January, April, July and October.

The secretary will give members notice of the meetings several days in advance by means of postal card and by a notice in the principal newspaper in Sydney. Members who by reason of some neglect may not receive an invitation must regard the announcement in the newspaper as sufficient notice.

19. One-sixth of the members of the club must be present at any general meeting in order to validate any decision arrived at in such meeting. If in any general meeting one-sixth of the members are not present the meeting must be adjourned for a week; the decisions arrived at in this second meeting will be valid whatever number of members may be present. Before taking part in any deliberations members are obliged (the French word is "tenu") to sign an attendance sheet and must have paid their subscription for the last quarter. Members absent from general meetings are held bound by decisions arrived at in such meeting.

At what purported to be a general meeting held on the 14th January, 1887, at which sixteen persons were present in person, and the defendant A'Beckett was present by proxy, a committee was elected.

At what purported to be an extraordinary general meeting held on the 31st August, 1887, at which fourteen members were present, including the defendant A'Beckett, the defendant J. J. Lauchaume, as president of the club, invited the meeting to discuss a proposal for enlarging the club, and pointed out that the present premises were too small for the requirements of the club. The meeting decided that they recognised the necessity for enlarging the club, and authorised the committee to insert for a week advertisements in *The Sydney Morning Herald*, calling for suitable premises in the centre of the city. If such were not forthcoming, they were authorised to expend 10*l.* in the preparation of a plan, and estimate of repairs to be carried out in the house behind the then present premises, the improvements to include a billiard room, dining room, and from eight to ten bedrooms. Mr. Morell, an architect and a member of the club, was to be entrusted with the preparation of the plans from instructions furnished by the committee. The advertisement was inserted, but no answer was received.

At what purported to be a general meeting held on the 14th October, 1887, at which eleven members were present, after

1898.

PERPETUAL
TRUSTEE Co.,
LTD.

v.

A'BECKETT.

examination of the plans and discussions the president put to the meeting the following questions: " Do the members here present recognise the necessity for enlarging the club?" Answered unanimously "Yes." " Are the committee authorised to treat with the architect and owners of the premises for the purpose of making the changes and repairs specified in the plans and estimate submitted to the meeting this evening?" Answered unanimously " Yes."

On the 28th October, 1887, the defendant Burne became a member of the club.

At what purported to be an extraordinary general meeting held on the 9th December, 1887, at which the defendant A'Beckett and six other persons, not including the defendant Burne, were present, the defendant W. J. Fesq, after being proposed and seconded, was unanimously elected to the club. The minute of the meeting, which was stated to contain a correct account of what took place, continues :—" Several propositions were made with regard to the lease of the new premises of the club, and the matter was left in the hands of the president to make the best arrangement in the interests of the club. Messieurs J. J. Lauchaume, W. H. Paling, E. Doublet and Van de Velde were nominated trustees, and have accepted. Mr. A'Beckett was asked to give his opinion upon the several contracts to be made and to lend the president his assistance."

At what purported to be a general meeting held on the 13th January, 1888, at which fourteen persons were present, including the defendant A'Beckett and the defendant Fesq, the secretary read the minutes of the last meeting, which were unanimously adopted or confirmed. On the 12th July, 1888, the lease of the additional premises was made to Messrs. Lauchaume, Paling, Van de Velde and Doublet for a term of ten years from the 9th July, 1888, at a yearly rental of 555l., and possession was taken of the new premises by the club.

Under the lease the trustees covenanted jointly and severally to pay the rent agreed upon, all rates and taxes, and to effect all necessary repairs, etc., during the term.

In the same month, but subsequently to the execution of the lease, the old rules were repealed, and new rules adopted by the club. Of these the following only are material :—

14. The affairs of the club shall be under the management of the following office-bearers, viz., a President, a Vice-President, four Trustees, a Committee and a Treasurer.

15. All purchases, investments, leases, conveyances, securities, or contracts by, to or on behalf of the club shall be made, taken or entered into in the names of the trustees. All the real and personal property of the club shall be vested in, and shall be held by them upon trust for the members for the time being, and shall (except as to the real property) be subject to the disposition of the committee whose order certified in writing, under the hand of the chairman of the day and attested by the secretary, shall be obligatory upon, and a justification to the trustees as to making, taking or entering into any such purchase, investment, lease, conveyance, security or contract, or any disposal of any personal property vested in them as such trustees. And the orders of the committee certified in like manner as to any purchases necessary for carrying on the internal management of the club shall also be obligatory upon, and a justification to the trustees for making the same. The real property of the club shall not be dealt with except by the resolution of a general or special general meeting of the members of the club.

21. The committee shall hold when practicable an ordinary meeting within one week after the Annual General Meeting and at least once every week thereafter and the President, or Vice-President, or any three members thereof may cause a special meeting to be held at any time, by giving to every member at least twenty-four hours' notice thereof in writing, specifying the day and hour when, and the business for which it is to be held.

26. The committee may at any time cause a special general meeting of the members of the club to be held for any purpose . . . .

27. Every such special general meeting shall be called in pursuance of a resolution of the committee, to be passed at least eight days before the day to be appointed for holding the same and specifying the day and hour when, and the business for which it is to be held; upon the passing of which resolution the secretary shall call such special general meeting by exhibiting in the club house for at least seven consecutive days immediately before the day appointed for holding the same, notice thereof in writing signed by him, specifying the day and hour when, and the business for which the same is to be held.

38. Any member intending to withdraw from the club must signify his intention to do so in writing to the committee or secretary on or before the first day of January, April, July and October respectively, and in default of such notice he shall be liable to the payment of his subscription for the current quarter; but no such resignation shall relieve any member from the payment of any subscription or other liability due or payable by him at the time of such resignation.

60. All resolutions passed at meetings of the club shall be conclusive and binding on all the members of the club whether they shall be present at such meeting or not; provided that such meetings are held in conformity with the rules at present or which may hereafter be in force in the club.

Neither the rules of January, 1887, nor the rules of July, 1888, contained any reference to voting by proxy.

The club continued in possession of the premises until February, 1891, and during that time paid the rent, and fulfilled the covenants of the lease.

In February, 1891, the club went into liquidation, and the lease of the premises was in that month sublet by the trustees to the Cosmopolitan Club Company, Limited, for the residue of the term at the same rent and subject to the same covenants that the trustees were liable for. The Cosmopolitan Club continued in occupation of the premises, and fulfilled all the covenants of the lease, and paid all rent due until 4th January, 1894.

It was then wound up under the Companies Acts, leaving no assets with which to pay the rent, or fulfil the covenants of the sub-lease for the remainder of the term.

The trustees thereupon re-entered upon the premises and endeavoured to re-let them, but were unable to do so except for a very reduced rental.

They also sent notices to all persons who were members of the Cercle Français on 21st February, 1891, summoning a general meeting for the purpose of instructing and directing the trustees, but no one attended it. W. H. Paling was himself compelled to pay the rent, and fulfil the covenants in the lease.

W. H. Paling died about 27th August, 1895, and at his death he had expended over 925l. in excess of moneys received by him in respect of the premises. Probate of his will was granted to the plaintiffs, his executors, in October, 1895.

The plaintiffs, at the time of filing the statement of claim, had paid a sum of 764l. to the lessors, and estimated that they would be liable to pay a further sum of about 670l. in respect of the rent and covenants.

The plaintiffs accordingly, on 22nd April, 1897, commenced this suit against the defendants for a declaration "that all persons who were members of the said Cercle Français on the twelfth day of July in the year 1888, and all persons who became members of the said Cercle Français subsequent thereto, and the personal representatives of any of such persons respectively, who are now deceased, became and are jointly and severally liable to contribute to, and make good, and indemnify the plaintiffs and the estate of the said W. H. Paling against the rent paid and expenses incurred by the said W. H. Paling during his lifetime and by the plaintiffs since his death in respect of the said lease and the covenants thereof, and the future rent and expenses to which the plaintiffs, as executors of the said W. H. Paling, are or may become liable under the said lease and the covenants thereof, and that the defendants and all such other persons and representatives as respectively aforesaid may be jointly and severally decreed to repay to the plaintiffs, and indemnify them against all such rent and expenses with interest on the same at such rate as this Honourable Court shall direct and also to pay the plaintiffs' costs of suit, and for consequential relief."

The defendants were M. E. A'Beckett, W. J. Fesq, A. Burne, F. Woolcott Waley, J. Henderson, J. J. Lachaume, E. Doublet and C. Van de Velde. Of these the defendants Lachaume, Doublet and Van de Velde were co-trustees with W. H. Paling in taking the lease for the club.

The statement of claim contained the following paragraph :—

"40. The said Cercle Français, on the said 12th day of July in the year 1888, consisted of about 80 members, and 90 members or thereabouts joined the said Cercle Français subsequently to the said date. It is impossible to make so large a number of persons, defendants, without enormous expense and delay, and the plaintiffs submit that the said members are sufficiently represented by the defendants herein, and that any decree made against the present defendants ought to bind such of the said members as are not defendants."

It was then alleged that the several defendants were representatives of several classes of committee men and members of the club.

On the 25th May, 1897, on the plaintiffs' application the following order was made by *Manning*, C.J. in Eq. :—

" That the defendants be and they are hereby authorised and directed to defend in this suit on behalf and for the benefit of the following classes of defendants, that is to say, the defendant, M. E. A'Beckett, on behalf and for the benefit of the members of the committee of the Cercle Français at the time of the making of the lease in the statement of claim mentioned. The defendant, W. J. Fesq, on behalf and for the benefit of the members of the said Cercle Français present at the general

meeting thereof held on the 13th day of January, 1888. The
defendant, A. Burne, on behalf and for the benefit of the members
of the said Cercle Français at the time when the said lease was
made, but who did not attend the said meeting of the 13th day
of January, 1888. The defendant, F. Woolcott-Waley, on behalf
and for the benefit of the members of the committee of the said
Cercle Français who became members of such committee at a
date subsequent to the 12th day of July, 1888. The defendant,
J. Henderson, on behalf and for the benefit of the members of
the said Cercle Français who became members thereof at a date
subsequent to the said 12th day of July, 1888."

1898.

PERPETUAL
TRUSTEE CO.,
LTD.
v.
A'BECKETT.

The defendant W. J. Fesq resigned his membership of the
club in February, 1889.

The defendant Burne became a member of the committee on
21st June, 1889 ; house committee July 12th, 1889, and vice-
president in January. 1890. He attended a committee meeting
on 6th December, 1890, when the indemnity to the trustees was
discussed. On 22nd January, 1891, he moved a resolution
dealing with the lease, and in other ways treated the lease as
club property, as appears in his Honour's judgment. The facts
relating to the validity of the proceedings with regard to the
taking of the lease are also fully stated by his Honour.

At the hearing of the suit the liability of the defendants
Henderson and Woolcott-Waley was dealt with as a preliminary
point, it being admitted that they did not become members of
the club until after the lease had been made.

Pilcher, Q.C., and *Rich* (*Foster* with them), for the plaintiffs.
It is assumed for the purposes of this argument that the members
existing at the time the lease was taken expressly authorised the
trustees to do so. A person becoming a member after the lease
was taken is liable, because he takes the benefit of all contracts
then existing, and by joining the club he takes all burdens as
well as benefits. He is also liable by (1) Acquiescence ; (2) By
adopting the trustees as his trustees, and making a fresh contract.
On learning of the existence of the lease the new members
should have at once resigned ; by not doing so they elect to stand
in with the other members. The fact of allowing the rent to be

paid amounts to ratification of the contract, and an authority to pay the rent every year as it becomes due.

[A. H. SIMPSON, C.J. in Eq., referred to *Flemyng* v. *Hector* (1).]

A trustee is entitled apart from any express authority to be indemnified by his beneficiary against all loss: *Jervis* v. *Wolferstan* (2); *Balsh* v. *Hyham* (3). A new member takes an interest in the club property *cum onere*: *Richardson* v. *Hastings* (4). If the trustees had taken the lease for themselves they could have been sued by any member. New members when taking benefits cannot refuse to bear liabilities. The lease was taken for the benefit of all members, present and future, who, by joining the club, request the trustees to continue as such, and they thereby become liable: *Lewin on Trusts*, 9th Ed., p. 724; *Fraser* v. *Murdoch* (5).

Part of the contract of an incoming member arises from an implied request to the trustees to continue as such, and the term of admission is to pay the subscription, and take the liability. There is a contract between the candidate and the old members.

In Rule 15, the word "justification" means that the trustees are to be indemnified by the members for the time being. The rules must be known to the members, and assent to Rule 15 is a request to the trustees to hold the property, and that request makes the members liable to indemnify the trustees. The lease was the personal property of the club: *Brown* v. *Dale* (6).

They referred to *Austen* v. *Bays* (7); *Minnitt* v. *Lord Talbot* (8); *Parr* v. *Bradbury* (9); *Mount Cashel (Earl of)* v. *Barber* (10); *Lindley on Partnership*, 5th. Edit. 373, 374; *Toohey* v. *McCulla* (11); *Chippendale's Case* (12); *James* v. *May* (13).

L. Owen, for the defendant Woolcott-Waley and those whom he represented. The question of trustee and *cestui que trust* does not arise at all in this case; the real question being what

(1) 2 M. & W. 172.
(2) 18 Eq. 18.
(3) 2 P.W. 453.
(4) 11 Beav. 17.
(5) 6 A.C. 855.
(6) 9 Ch. D. 78.
(7) 27 L.J. Ch. 243; 2 De G. & J. 626; 24 Beav. 598.

(8) 1 Ir. L.R. Ch. Div. 143; 7 Ir. L.R. Ch. 409.
(9) 1 T.L.R. 285, 525.
(10) 23 L J. C.P. 43; 14 C.B. 53.
(11) 10 N.S.W.L R. Eq. 264.
(12) 4 De G. M. & G. 19, 43.
(13) 6 L.R. H. L. 328.

contract was made by the new member when joining the club. 1898.
The relation existing between the members and the committee is PERPETUAL
that of principal and agent only: *Flemyng* v. *Hector* (1); *Chis-* TRUSTEE Co.,
holm v. *Strickland* (2). There can be no question of ratification, LTD. v.
as the contract was made before Waley's class were in existence A'BECKETT.
as members: *Kellner* v. *Baxter* (3); *Scott* v. *Lord Ebury* (4);
Melhado v. *Porto Alegre R. Co.* (5); *In re The Empress
Engineering Co.* (6); *In re The Northumberland Avenue Hotel
Co.* (7); *Lindley on Partnership*, 5th Edit. p. 50.

Gordon (*S. A. Thompson* with him), for the defendant Henderson and those whom he represented, followed in the same interest.
The original liability arose by authorisation either direct or
indirect. There was no power to pledge the credit of the members
in any other way. The only ratification alleged is that of
frequenting the club premises. Henderson was no party to the
lease, and there is nothing in the rules to make new members
liable for burdens previously incurred. An agent must contract
for a principal in existence at the time: *Anson on Contracts* (5th
Edit. p. 339). The lessors could have no remedy against Henderson. The only liability of members is to pay a subscription, and
the committee have no authority to pledge their credit except by
express direction. In the case of *Minnitt* v. *Lord Talbot* (8), the
persons liable were limited to those who directly authorised or
assented to or subsequently ratified the contract.

Pilcher, Q.C., in reply. Although a company cannot ratify
contracts made before it came into existence, yet it can do so by
novation. Henderson is liable on a contract to indemnify, made
when he joined the club, and did not repudiate the lease. The
new members by their conduct requested the trustees to continue
the lease on their behalf. There was a tacit understanding
between the trustees and the new members that the new members
would indemnify the trustees, and that the trustees would not
sell the lease to protect themselves.

(1) 2 M. & W. 172	(5) L.R. 9 C.P. 503.
(2) 9 N.S.W.L.R. 395.	(6) 16 Ch. Div. 125.
(3) L.R. 2 C.P. 174.	(7) 33 Ch. Div. 16.
(4) L.R. 2 C P. 255.	(8) 1 Ir. L.R. Ch. 143; 7 Ir. L.R. Ch. 409.

A. H. SIMPSON, C.J. in Eq. I am of opinion that the plaintiffs'
contention on this point must fail. The law applicable to this
point is laid down in *Lindley on Partnership* (5th Edit. p. 50),
where he says : " It is a mere misuse of words to call such
associations partnerships, and if liabilities are to be fastened on
any of their members, it must be by reason of the acts of those
members themselves or by reason of the acts of their agents, and
the agency must be made out by the person who relies on it, for
none is implied by the mere fact of association." The law so laid
down is fully borne out by the case of *Flemyng* v. *Heaton* (1)
and the case of *Chisholm* v. *Strickland* (2) in our own Court.

In order, therefore, that the defendants Woolcott-Waley and
Henderson may be made liable, it must be shewn affirmatively
that they entered into a contract to share the liability incurred
by the trustees under the lease, and this is a question of fact which
the plaintiffs must prove. The plaintiffs contend that the mere
fact of these persons becoming members and using the club
premises is evidence that they entered into such a contract.

The first thing to ascertain in determining the liabilities of new
members is to see what the rules of the club themselves contain on
the subject of the members' liabilities. If the rules expressly
provided that new members were to indemnify the officers of the
club against all liabilities, both past and present, incurred on
behalf of the club, then of course new members would be liable
on this contract, but there is nothing in the rules dealing with
the matter. Had the rules disclosed the existence of this lease
and provided that each member, on becoming a member, became
liable to indemnify the trustees against the rent payable under
the lease, then there would be evidence that the members entered
into a contract with the trustees to indemnify them by the fact
of their becoming members. Or possibly, if there was no mention
of the lease in the rules, but the fact of the existence of the lease
had been brought to the notice of the members, and the lease had
been terminable at will, it might be that the silence of members
might be taken to be an implied request to the trustees to continue
the lease on their behalf. Here the lease was for ten years certain,
and the whole liability had been incurred before these persons

(1) 2 M. & W. 172.   (2) 9 N.S.W. L.R. 391.

became members.   It is not easy to see what their supposed
contract could have been: was it a contract to pay an aliquot
part of the rent? or a contract to become jointly and severally
liable with the trustees? or a contract to pay a share with solvent
members?   There is nothing in the rules to call attention to any
liability other than the payment of entrance fee and subscription specifically mentioned, and although it might have been
shewn that the members had in fact agreed to take a share of the
liability, no such case has been made on these pleadings, and I
do not think that there was any implied contract to take such a
liability.   It was ingeniously contended that there might be a
liability outside of contract arising from the relation of trustee
and *cestui que trust*, and the right of the trustees to be indemnified;
that as the members, in the event of the club being wound up,
and of there being surplus assets arising from the sale of the lease,
would be entitled to such surplus, so they would be liable for any
loss.   If that is so, then the liabilities of members *inter se* to
their own trustees must stand on a very different footing to that
of members to outside creditors, which is only one of principal
and agent.   That distinction was suggested but did not meet with
approval in the *St. James' Club Case* (1), where Lord *Leonards*,
L.C., said at p. 390: "It was also contended that, though not
liable to third persons, the members are liable *inter se*.   There is
the fallacy, they are not liable except to the extent to which they
have agreed to be so."   We therefore come back to the question
whether there was any agreement to take the liability, express or
implied.   How can the mere fact of using the club premises and
the payment of a subscription amount to an agreement to pay
rent?   It was contended that the liability would arise from an
equity outside of contract, and reliance was placed on the language
of *Owen*, C.J. in Eq., in the case of *Toohey* v. *McCulla* (2), where
he stated "that the doctrine of contribution does not depend upon
contract but upon general principles of equity, and is not an
incident of suretyship alone."

These words, if divorced from their context and pressed in their
literal sense, would give colour to such a contention.   But what
I think his Honour meant in that case was to distinguish

(1) 2 De G. M. & G. 383.   · (2) 10 N.S.W. L.R. Eq. 264.

1898.

PERPETUAL
TRUSTEE Co.,
LTD.
v.
A'BECKETT.

C.J. Eq.

between express and implied contracts. If the facts of that case
are considered, it will, I think, be seen that there was no express
contract of indemnity, but that from the conduct of the parties a
contract of indemnity was to be implied. Whether you call it
an implied contract or a liability arising on a general principle of
equity, independently of contract, seems to me a mere matter of
language. In that case a shareholder had, at a general meeting
of a company, moved the adoption of a report and balance sheet
containing a statement of liabilities, and it was held that he had
ratified the action of the directors and made himself liable. My
decision then is that the mere fact of these two members joining
the club and paying their subscriptions and using the club
premises, does not make them liable upon the previous contracts
of the committee. I therefore dismiss the suit with costs as against
these two defendants, but without prejudice to any right the
plaintiffs may have against members of these two classes other
than the two defendants on different facts.

Evidence was then taken as against the other defendants.

Pilcher, Q.C., and *Rich* (*Foster* with them), for the plaintiffs.
The plaintiffs have only to establish a certain state of facts, from
which the Court can draw inferences, and on those inferences
being drawn the law imposes the liability.

Notice of the meeting of 31st August, 1887, was sent to
members, and if that meeting was valid the resolutions then
passed bind the club: Rule 18. Advertisements are not necessary if notice is given. The resolutions passed on 14th October,
1887, are valid. Proxies are evidence of consent, by the person
giving them, to what was done at the meeting.

The meeting of the 9th December, 1887, was sufficient to bind
those present; no doubt a quorum was not present, but the
meeting of the 13th January, 1888, was a valid meeting, and
unanimously adopted the minutes of 9th December, 1887, which
is equivalent to going through the form of re-passing them: *In
re North Sydney Investment & Tramway Co. Ltd.* (1); *In re
Johannesburg Hotel Co.* (2). The club then made itself a party
to a contract to which it was not a party before. No lease had

(1) 16 N.S.W. L.R. Eq. 252.   (2) [1891] 1 Ch. 119.

been taken in January, and any member disapproving could have said so: *Ashurst* v. *Mason* (1); *Doubleday* v. *Muskett* (2).

A'Beckett directly took part in all the transactions, and Fesq, by adopting the resolutions of the 9th December, 1887, on 13th January, 1888, is in the same position as A'Beckett. Resignation does not get rid of the liability: *Parr* v. *Bradbury* (3): Rule 38 of July, 1888.

Burne is liable by ratification. He did, in fact, agree to indemnify, and made representations by acts and conduct that estop him from now saying the lease does not belong to the club: *Wolmershausen* v. *Gullick* (4); *Dering* v. *Earl of Winchelsea* (5); *Chippendale's Case* (6); *Balsh* v. *Hyham* (7).

The trustees are entitled to consider that existing members authorised them to take the lease. This is a different case from the defendant Henderson's, and falls within the principle of trustee and *cestui que trust.* There must be an inference that rooms were added to the club on some sort of tenure, and members would and must have known what the tenure was: *Whittaker* v. *Kershaw* (8); *In re St. James' Club* (9). All who concurred in expenditure might be liable, and Burne not only concurred but was a party to dealing with the lease: *De Launey* v. *Strickland* (10); *Cheeseborough* v. *Wright* (11); *Mount Cashel (Earl of)* v. *Barber* (12); *Spottiswood's Case* (13). Acts *ultra vires* director of companies can be assented to and ratified by the shareholders so as to validate them, and shareholders acting so as to make themselves liable may be estopped: *Everett & Strode*, p. 388; *Challis' Case* (14); *Irvine* v. *Union Bank of Australia* (15); *Lyell* v. *Kennedy* (16); *Bolton Partners* v. *Lambert* (17); *Ex parte Badman* and *Ex parte Bosanquet* (18).

(1) 20 Eq. 225.	(10) 2 Stark. 116.
(2) 7 Bing. 110.	(11) 28 Beav. 283.
(3) 1 T.L.R. 285.	(12) 14 C.B. 53; 23 L.J. C.P. 43.
(4) [1893] 2 Ch. 523.	(13) 6 De G. M. & G. 345.
(5) 1 Cox 318.	(14) 6 Ch. 266.
(6) 4 De G. M. & G. 19.	(15) 2 A.C. 366.
(7) 2 P.W. 453.	(16) 14 A.C. 437.
(8) 45 Ch. Div. 320.	(17) 41 Ch. Div. 295.
(9) 2 De G. M. & G. 389.	(18) 45 Ch. Div. 16.

They also referred to *Carr* v. *L. & N.W.R.* (1); *Raggett* v. *Musgrave* (2); *Toohey* v. *McCulla* (3); *Ex parte Ford* (4). The plaintiffs ask for a decree as in *Minnett* v. *Lord Talbot* (5).

Lingen, for the defendant A'Beckett and those whom he represented. A'Beckett personally knew of the lease, but he is sued as representing a class: Paragraphs 40, 41 of the statement of claim order of May 25th, 1897; *Commissioners of Sewers* v. *Gellatly* (6). Authority was given to Paling, not by A'Beckett as an individual, but as a member, and the plaintiffs, after suing A'Beckett as a member, now attempt to give evidence against him personally. The fact of being a committeeman imposes no liability, as the committee had no authority as such. The delegation was direct from the general meeting to Lauchaume.

If A'Beckett is held liable, costs should not be given against him personally. Paling neglected his rights, and by his negligence has increased defendants' liability if it exists. Costs should be dealt with as in an administration suit, or added to the debt.

Hanbury Davies, for the defendant Fesq and those whom he represented. Fesq is sued as a member of a class. Plaintiffs have not proved that the club authorised Paling to take the lease: *Flemyng* v. *Hector* (7). The club could only speak by general meeting, and if they were not properly convened Paling acted at his own risk. There was no advertisement. Rule 18: *Ashurst* v. *Mason* (8); *Cambrian Peat & Fuel Co., Limited* (9); *Ramskill* v. *Edwards* (10). Hearing minutes read is only notice of acts by six individuals, not acting as members, and Fesq could have disregarded them. No meeting of the club was called to acquaint members with the terms of the lease.

Knox, for the defendant Burne and those whom he represented. No evidence should have been admitted of anything that happened after 12th July, 1888. Even if Burne personally ratified

(1) 44 L.J. C.P. 113 ; L.R. 10   (5) L.R. Ir.7 Ch. 409.
    C.P. 307.   (6) 3 Ch. Div. 610.
(2) 2 C. & P. 556.   (7) 2 M. & W. 183.
(3) 10 N.S.W. L.R. Eq. 264.   (8) 20 Eq. 225.
(4) 16 Q.B.D. 305.   (9) 23 W.R. 405 ; 31 L.T. 773.
            (10) 31 Ch. Div. 100.

under seal, on the pleadings I claim to argue on behalf of anyone in the same class. The only ground on which it is sought to charge Burne is that he was a member on 12th July, 1888. He cannot now be charged as an individual. To prove ratification the plaintiffs must prove ratification by the club, and not by Burne personally, but as a member. The principal is the club, and not individual members. Burne's individual ratification does not make him liable unless the plaintiffs shew the club ratified. Lauchaume's appointment must be shewn to be ratified by the club: *Annual Practice* [1898] p. 354. Defendants must have a common interest. The order of 25th May, 1897, stands, and plaintiffs must admit that Burne has a common interest with all in his class. If he is liable, they must be. All evidence against Burne must be against his class. Personal acts cannot be admitted. Even if the evidence is admitted, it does not prove ratification by Burne, either individually or as representing a class, as Burne could not ratify in ignorance of material facts, and until this suit was instituted there was no evidence, and no one knew that the meetings were informal. He did not know that all the members of the club were not bound by the lease. To rely on Burne's acts of ratification, plaintiffs must prove that he knew the meetings were informal. Knowledge is necessary before ratification can exist : *Spackman* v. *Evans* (1); *Holdsworth* v. *Evans* (2). There is no evidence to shew that Burne knew the trustees were under a personal liability for the lease. What he did he did in ignorance of the fact that the trustees were not authorised by the club: *Evans on Principal and Agent*, p. 74. There was no consideration afterwards for Burne taking any liability whatsoever. The fact of alteration of the premises was not notice of the terms of the lease. Up to July 12th Burne had in no way authorised the lease, and on the pleadings he is charged as being liable by reason of membership on that date. It is also contended that resignation does not release from liability; if Burne had resigned on July 14th in consequence of the speeches at the banquet, he could still be liable if plaintiffs' contention is correct. The plaintiffs do not on the pleadings raise the question

1898.

PERPETUAL
TRUSTEE CO.,
LTD.
v.
A'BECKETT.

(1) L.R. 3 H.L. 171.   (2) L.R. 3 H.L. 263.

of previous authority or subsequent ratification, and the Court must deal with Burne as representing a class only.

Burne was not present on 13th January, and no authority has been cited to shew that the Court will not permit an absent member from taking the fullest advantage of any deviation from the rules. Confirmation of minutes is a recognition only by a subsequent meeting that the transactions of the previous meeting are correctly recorded in the minute book. The case of *Ashurst* v. *Mason* (1) decides that a person present at a meeting at which the minutes are read has notice of what was transacted at that meeting. It is not an authority to shew that the transactions of the second meeting validated those of the first meeting. If the proceedings of 13th January do not bind absent members, then they cannot be liable until July 13th, and all evidence after that date is inadmissible unless it is shewn that acts were done by members with the knowledge that by doing such acts they were taking a liability they had not before. *The St. James' Club Case* (2) shews that the only relation existing is that of principal and agent.

For the doctrine of estoppel to apply it must be shewn that Burne induced Paling to alter his position to his own detriment by false statements: *Carr* v. *L. & N. W. Railway* (3). Paling knew all the facts, and the doctrine of estoppel must fail. There is no evidence to shew that Burne induced Paling to alter his position. Paling must be presumed to know the rules: *Raggett* v. *Musgrave* (4). Burne never concurred in incurring the liability. Ratification must be by the principal, *i.e.*, all the members of the club. One member individually cannot ratify.

In the case of *Ramskill* v. *Edwards* (5) the defendant, by signing a cheque, adopted in deed what he protested against in words. He also referred to *Bowstead's Digest of Agency* (Articles 27, 28); *Chippendale's Case* (6); *Hallmarke's Case* (7); *Cornwell's Case* (8).

Pilcher in reply. The plaintiffs are entitled to prove Burne liable in any way they can, and any member of his class can apply

(1) 20 Eq. 225.   (5) 31 Ch. Div. 100.
(2) 2 De G. M. & G. 383.   (6) 4 De G. M. & G. 19.
(3) 44 L.J. C.P. 113; L. R. 10,C.P. 307.   (7) 9 Ch. Div. 329.
(4) 2 C. & P. 556.   (8) [1894] 2 Ch. 392.

1898.

PERPETUAL
TRUSTEE CO.,
LTD.
v.
A'BECKETT.

by summons: *Annual Practice* ([1898] 354); *Watson* v. *Cane* (1); *Fraser* v. *Cooper* (2); *May* v. *Newton* (3). Burne had the minute book before him and must have had knowledge: *Spackman* v. *Evans* (4); *Ashurst* v. *Mason* (5); *Phosphate of Lime Co.* v. *Green* (6); *Bruce* on *Ultra Vires* (3rd Edit. p. 33); *Sargent* v. *Webster* (7). The committee could not have appropriated the club funds for rent unless the premises had been legally taken for the club in accordance with the rules, or by the members adopting the transaction. The committee are not mere servants of general meetings. Fesq admits he was a member, and this can only be by the meeting of 13th January validating the proceedings of 9th December : *Ex parte Ford* (8).

Cur. ad. vult.

On 27th October the following judgment was delivered by   *Oct. 27.*

A. H. SIMPSON, C.J. in Eq. (After referring to the facts and rules already set out, his Honour continued). With regard to the validity of general meetings prior to the 12th July, 1888, Mr. Cornillon, who was managing secretary from May, 1887, to the 24th November, 1887, inclusive, and who left the club on the 1st January, 1888, but was acting secretary from the 29th September onwards, gave evidence that in every case of meetings held while he was secretary he posted notices to all members some days beforehand, stating the date of the meeting and the objects for which it was called. Mr. Van de Velde states that he was appointed secretary on the 18th November, 1887, and he sent out notices to all members of the club of the meeting of the 9th December, 1887, and that of the 13th January, 1888. There is also evidence that notices of meetings and all important resolutions passed by general meetings were posted up upon a notice board in a conspicuous position in the most frequented room in the club.

As regards the number of members of the club in the years 1887 and 1888, the book containing the list of the members has unfortunately been lost. Mr. Cornillon stated that in the year

(1) 17 Ch. Div. 19.
(2) 21 Ch. Div. 718.
(3) 34 Ch. Div. 349.
(4) L.R. 3, H.L. 221.
(5) 20 Eq. 225.
(6) L.R. 7 C.P. 43.
(7) 3 Meto. 497.
(8) 16 Q.B.D. 307.

1898.

PERPETUAL
TRUSTEE Co.,
LTD.
v.
A'BECKETT.

C.J. Eq.

1887 there were about sixty members, but he subsequently corrected this by saying that there were not more than fifty on the 31st August, 1887, not counting honorary members.

It appears from the evidence of Mr. Lauchaume that a meeting was held on the 3rd May, 1888, at which only ten members were present, and as they were not sufficient to form a quorum, the meeting was postponed for a week. There must, therefore, have been more than sixty members on the 3rd May, 1888. On the above evidence it appears to me there were sufficient members present to form a quorum at the meetings of the 31st August, 1887, the 14th October, 1887, and 13th January, 1888, but there was not a quorum at the meeting of the 9th December, 1887.

As regards the notices, I think the evidence shews that sufficient notices were sent of these meetings, though it does not appear that any advertisement was inserted as required by Rule 18. No objection, however, was taken to the absence of the advertisement, and I must now hold that this irregularity was cured by acquiescence.

In cases of partnership, however clear or stringent the provisions of the partnership deed may be, the parties may shew by their conduct that they have tacitly agreed to waive or alter them. A striking instance of this occurred in *Pilling* v. *Pilling* (1), and I see no reason why the same rule should not apply to members of a club.

Such being the position of things on the 12th July, 1888, when the lease was executed and possession taken, the next point to be considered is what is the law applicable to the subject? It is clear that a club is not a partnership, and if liabilities are to be fastened upon any of its members, it must be by reason of the acts of those members themselves or by reason of the acts of their agents, and the agency must be made out by the person who relies on it, for none is implied by the mere fact of association: *Lindley on Partnership* (5th Edit. p. 50). Where the rules were substantially the same as in this club, it was held that the committee had no power to pledge the credit of members: *Flemyng* v. *Hector* (2); unless they were authorised to do so: *Todd* v. *Emley* (3).

(1) 3 De G. J. & S. 162.   (2) 2 M. & W. 172.   ·
(3) 7 M. & W. 427.

1898.

PERPETUAL
TRUSTEE CO.,
LTD.
v.
A'BECKETT.

C.J. Eq.

Where the funds are insufficient to carry out the purposes of the club, the proper course is for the committee to call a general meeting and expose the state of the club, and call upon the society to support them. As pointed out by Lord *Abinger* in *Flemyng* v. *Hector* (1): " It is very well known that in many of these recent establishments great expense has been incurred by building, and though the committee may have signed the contracts for the buildings, yet it has always been done after a general meeting and the sense of the club has been taken upon it, for you cannot suppose that they would pledge their own credit to pay the builder's bill."

The real question therefore is : "Did the defendants authorise the trustees to enter into the lease?": *Todd* v. *Emley* (2). The authority may be expressed or implied from the acts of the parties sought to be charged, and may be given at the time or by subsequent ratification: *De Launey* v. *Strickland* (3); *Earl of Mount Cashel* v. *Barber* (4). The question therefore is really one of fact, and when the principle is once settled the citation of cases is not of much assistance. In the Common Law Courts the question usually arises in an action by the creditor against the alleged principal. In this case the creditors (the lessors) can only sue the lessees, the contract being under seal; but the right of the lessees to be indemnified by their principals is, I apprehend, the same as if the principals could be made directly liable to the creditors. In the *St. James' Club Case* (5) it was contended that although there might not be sufficient evidence to make the members directly liable to the creditors, they might be liable to indemnify the committee. On this, Lord *St. Leonard*, L.C., says at p. 390 :—" It was also contended that though not liable to third persons the members are liable *inter se:* They are not liable except to the extent to which they agreed to be so": see also *Earl of Mount Cashel* v. *Barber* (6).

In other cases the obligation to indemnify the agent or trustee is said to rest upon an equity outside the contract: *Ex*

(1) 2 M. & W. at p. 182.
(2) 8 M. & W. 505.
(3) 2 Stark. 416.
(4) 14 C.B. 53.
(5) 2 De G. M. & G. 383.
(6) 14 C.B. 69.

parte Chippendale (1); *Toohey* v. *McCulla* (2). The inconsistency between these two statements is apparent only. What the Judge in each case was pointing out was that the liability is not necessarily based on express contract, but may rest on the acts of the parties, and it seems to me to be merely a verbal difference, whether it is said to rest on an equity arising out of conduct or on an agreement to be implied from conduct. It is sufficient to adopt the words of *Jessel*, M.R., in *Jervis* v. *Wolfeston* (3), at p. 24 : " I take it to be a general rule that when persons accept a trust at the request of another, and that other is a *cestui que trust*, he is personally liable to indemnify the trustees from any loss accruing in the due execution of the trust."

It is immaterial to consider whether or not the meetings of the 31st August, 1887, and 14th October, 1887, were properly convened, as nothing was done at either of these meetings which, in my opinion, bound either the club or the members present to take the lease. The resolution passed at the first of those meetings did not commit the club to any liability beyond the expense of the advertisements, and the 10*l*. for the plan and estimates ; and I do not think I can treat the resolution passed at the meeting of the 14th October as doing more than giving authority to the committee to treat, but not authority to bind, the club by a contract. It is immaterial also whether the meeting of the 9th December was properly convened or not, as no quorum was present, but the meeting purported to pass the resolution entrusting the matter of the lease to trustees.

At the meeting of the 13th January, 1888, which seems to me to have been duly convened, fourteen persons were present, including the defendants A'Beckett and Fesq, and the secretary read the minutes of the last meeting, which were unanimously adopted or confirmed. I think that Mr. A'Beckett, and the other persons who were present at the meeting of the 9th December, 1887, are liable. I think that Mr. Fesq, who was present at the meeting of the 13th January, 1888, is also liable. As the minutes of the previous meeting were read, the members present must be taken to have known that there was no quorum at the meeting of the

9th December, 1887, consequently any resolution passed at that
meeting was of no effect. I can only interpret the adoption or
confirmation of the minutes as meaning that the meeting of the
13th January desired to validate what the meeting of the 9th
December purported to do. This seems to me borne out by the
fact that only in this way can Mr. Fesq be regarded as a duly
elected member of the club. I do not lay any stress on the word
"adopted," as I see that the French word *adopté* is apparently
used throughout, and is sometimes translated "adopted" and
sometimes "confirmed." At all events, Mr. Fesq must have
known on the 13th January, 1888, what the meeting of the 9th
December purported to do, and I think that his presence at the
meeting of the 13th January, taken in conjunction with his
subsequent conduct, is sufficient to bind him. After the 13th
January, 1888, he continued to use the club both before and
after the 12th July, 1888, and never raised any objection to the
trustees taking or holding the lease on behalf of the club. It is
true that he resigned in February or March, 1889, but such
resignation could not exonerate him from an existing liability.
The same reasoning would, of course, apply to all members who
were present and subsequently ratified in the same way what
was done at the meeting of the 13th January, 1888.

As regards Dr. Burne and the other members who were not
present at that meeting, I do not think I can hold them bound
by what took place at that meeting in the absence of subsequent
ratification. The erection of new buildings, or the taking a lease
of new buildings at a high rent, is a matter outside the ordinary
business of the club's affairs, and even if the notice of the meeting
stated that the meeting would be asked to adopt the resolution
informally carried at the previous meeting, and set out such
resolutions, which I cannot assume to be the case, I do not think
a majority at such meeting could commit absent members to
what might be a very large liability. The case against Dr.
Burne and the other members who were not present on the 13th
January, 1888, must therefore rest on subsequent ratification.
Up to the 12th July, 1888, there does not appear to be any
distinct evidence of ratification against Dr. Burne other than the
fact that he frequently used the club, and that he must have

1898.

PERPETUAL
TRUSTEE Co.,
LTD.
v.
A'BECKETT.

C.J. Eq.

been aware that additions were to be made to the club, and that these additions were being carried out. On the 21st June, 1889, Dr. Burne became a member of the committee, and on the 28th January, 1890, was elected vice-president.

It is quite clear from what took place at the general meetings of the 20th and the 27th June, 1890, and from the reports and balance sheets which have been put in evidence, that during the year 1890 Dr. Burne was fully aware of the financial position of the club, and the difficulty of meeting the rent of the club premises.

At the committee meeting of the 6th December, 1890, at which Dr. Burne was present, the indemnity to the trustees of the club was discussed.

At the general meeting of the 22nd January, 1891, at which Dr. Burne was present, an offer from Mr. Rowley was made to take over the lease, and after considerable discussion a resolution was carried that the trustees and the committee of the Cercle Français were thereby authorised to dispose of the furniture, stock, etc., in the club premises for the sum of 500*l.*, together with an assignment of the lease of the premises subject to the lessor's consent, and the meeting was adjourned until the 30th January.

At the adjourned meeting held on 30th January, 1891, Dr. Burne was chairman, and a resolution was carried that the words "or to sublet" should be added to Mr. Rowley's motion carried at the last meeting. At a committee meeting held on the 10th February, 1891, at which Dr. Burne was present, the chairman read a letter from Mr. Rowley, dated the 30th January, requesting the trustees and the committee of the club to put under offer the furniture and effects of the club for the sum of 500*l.*, and the lease of the premises occupied by the club at the same rental as then paid or thereafter to be paid. A resolution was carried that the assets of the club be put under offer for 14 days to Mr. Rowley for any company to be formed by him, for the sum of 500*l.*, and that the committee were thereby authorised to effect such sale and transfer and sign any documents, and that the trustees were authorised to sub-let the house and premises then held by them in trust for the club at the same rent to the said George Rowley

or the said company upon such terms and conditions as they
should think expedient, and to sign and execute all necessary
documents to effect the same.   The secretary was also instructed
to write to Mr. Rowley informing him of the effect of the above
resolution.

1898.

PERPETUAL
TRUSTEE CO.,
LTD.
v.
A'BECKETT.

C.J. Eq.

The club premises were subsequently sub-let to the Cosmopolitan Club at the existing rental, and the Cosmopolitan Club
remained in possession and paid rent up to 14th January, 1894.

From the above evidence I can only draw the inference that
Dr. Burne ratified the action of the trustees in taking the lease
on behalf of the club, and that he and all other members in the
same position as himself are liable to indemnify the trustees
against the rent of the lease.

The decree will contain a declaration similar to that in *Minnitt*
v. *Lord Talbot* (1), that the defendants A'Beckett, Fesq, and
Burne, and all other persons who were members of the club on
the 12th July, 1888, and who assented to or subsequently ratified
the action of the trustees in taking the lease of that date, are
bound to indemnify the late W. H. Paling and his estate against
the rent payable under the said lease.

I express no opinion as to what constitutes ratification, or
whether or not membership on the 12th July, 1888, taken alone
is sufficient to impose the liability.   The suit has been dismissed
with costs against the defendants Woolcott-Waley and Henderson;
as the other defendants represent classes, I think the plaintiffs'
costs, so far as not already dealt with, and those of the defendants
A'Beckett, Fesq, and Burne, should be treated as part of the club
debt, and taken as added to the amount against which the plaintiffs are entitled to be indemnified.

I direct a reference to the Master to ascertain the amount to
be raised, and what persons are liable to contribute on the basis
of the decree.   Time for appealing from the judgment on
demurrer to run as from to-day.

Reserve further consideration and further costs.

Solicitors for the plaintiffs : *Ickerson & Ebsworth.*
Solicitor for defendants A'Beckett and Fesq : *Alfred Horrocks.*
Solicitor for defendant Woolcott-Waley : *J. S. Thom.*
Solicitors for defendant Henderson : *Richardson & Thompson.*
Solicitor for the defendant Burne: *W. H. Piggott.*

(1) L.R. Ir. 7 Ch. D. 407.

BOARD *v.* WEEKES and Others.

Will—Restraint against anticipation—Reversionary interest—Trust to convey to A., coupled with a direction to trustee to retain and manage the property for payment of debts.

1898.
Dec. 6, 12.

C. J. Eq.

A testator by his will devised and bequeathed the whole of his realty and personalty to trustees. He directed them during such period as they should think fit to receive the rents and profits of the realty, and manage the same as if they were absolutely entitled; to invest the receipts and apply them in payment of his debts, including mortgage debts, and from and immediately after his debts should have been fully discharged to convey a certain freehold to the testator's daughter. The will contained a restraint against anticipation of all reversionary or expectant interests of any female under the will.

Held, that so long as the trustees were in receipt of the rents and profits for the payment of the debts, the daughter's interest in the freehold was a reversionary interest within the meaning of the restraint clause.

Semble : A mortgagee suing for foreclosure of a mortgage comprising both real and personal property can only recover six years' arrears of interest.

HEARING OF SUIT.

This was a suit for foreclosure of a mortgage dated 16th April, 1889, made between Phillip Weekes and the defendant Eliza Weekes, his wife, of one part, and the plaintiff of the other part, and duly acknowledged by the defendant, whereby Mr. and Mrs. Weekes mortgaged to the plaintiff the estate, right, title and interest of Mrs. Weekes of, in and to all the real and personal estate given to her under the will of her father, James Hogg, to secure payment of 500*l.* to the plaintiff on the 15th April, 1890, with interest at 10 per cent.

James Hogg died on the 31st August, 1886, having by his will appointed two of his sons and Andrew McGregor executors and trustees, and after giving to his two daughters, Mrs. Weekes and Mrs. Hay, his jewellery, furniture, and other household effects for their absolute use and benefit equally, he provided, that, in the event of his daughter, Mrs. Hay, dying in his lifetime without leaving lawful issue her surviving (which event happened), the share in the said household furniture and effects bequeathed to her should become the absolute property of the said Mrs. Weekes; and after a bequest to his son, John Hogg, of the goodwill of the business carried on by the testator in Sussex-street, Sydney,

and the assets and effects used or employed in connection with
the business, he gave all the real estate of every tenure and all the
personal estate and effects of which he might be seized or possessed,
or to which he should be entitled at the time of his decease in
possession, reversion, remainder, or expectancy, or over which he
might have a power of disposition by will, unto and to the use of
the trustees absolutely upon the trusts in the said will declared,
and after directing the sale and conversion of his residuary personal
estate, the testator directed that his trustees should during such
period as they should think fit, collect, get in, and receive the
rents and profits of the whole of his real estate, and manage the
same with the same powers in that behalf as if they were
absolutely entitled thereto, and after authorising his trustees to
carry on the business of lime merchant then carried on by him at
Marulan during such period as they should think fit, he directed
the trustees to invest the moneys to arise from the sale and conversion of his personal estate together with any ready money
which he might have at the time of his death, also all the rents
and profits of his said real estate, and the income to arise from
the carrying on of the said Marulan business, and he declared
that the trustees should stand possessed of the moneys directed
to be invested and apply the same in payment of his just debts,
funeral, and testamentary expenses (except the debts which
might be due in respect of his Sydney business), and in paying
off and discharging all principal and interest moneys which might
be due by him at the time of his death, or which might accrue
due after his decease to any persons under or by virtue of any
mortgage or other security whatsoever given or executed by him,
and upon such principal and interest moneys, together with all
costs and expenses properly incurred being paid off and discharged,
the said testator authorised his trustees to obtain proper
discharges of the said mortgages or securities; and from and
immediately after all such his debts secured or unsecured shall
have been fully paid, discharged and satisfied the testator gave
to two of his sons all the cattle and horses in the said will
mentioned equally between them, and made other specific bequests
and devises not material to be here mentioned. Among the said
specific devises was a gift of testator's freehold land situated in

1898.

BOARD
v.
WEEKES.

Woolloomooloo, on which were erected the houses known as 193 Palmer-street, and 10 and 12 Berwick-lane, upon trust to pay the rents and profits to his daughter, the defendant Mrs. Weekes, or permit her to receive the same during her life, and from and after her death in trust for all or any the child or children of the defendant, who, being a son or sons, should attain the age of 21 years, or being a daughter or daughters should attain that age or marry, if more than one in equal shares as tenants in common. As to other part of his freehold land situated at Woolloomooloo, on which were erected the houses known as 191 Palmer-street, and 21 and 22 Woods' Lane, upon trust to pay the rents and profits to his daughter, the said Mary Hay, or to permit her to receive the same during her life, and from and after her death in trust for any child or children of the said Mrs. Hay in the same manner in all respects as in the case of the children of the said Mrs. Weekes, and it was provided that in the event of the said Mrs. Hay dying in the testator's lifetime without leaving lawful issue her surviving (which event happened) the trustees should convey and assure the said premises unto and to the use of the said Mrs. Weekes for her sole and separate use, her heirs and assigns for ever; and the said testator directed his trustees to stand seized and possessed of all the residue of his real and personal property upon trust to convey and assure or to divide the same equally between all his children who should be living at the time of his death, their respective heirs, executors, administrators, and assigns absolutely. The will then contained the following proviso : " Provided always and I declare that every estate or interest whether in real or personal estate, and whether absolute or limited, hereby given to or in trust for any female shall be for her separate use independently of any husband and so that in the case of any estate or interest given to her for her life or any reversionary or expectant interest she shall not have power to anticipate the same."

The testator left no personal estate except furniture and household effects. These were handed to Mrs. Weekes, and sold by her husband, who received and applied to his own use the proceeds of sale. The estate was heavily indebted at the testator's death for a bank overdraft and on various mortgages. The trustees received the rents and profits in accordance with the provisions of the will until April, 1896, and applied them in paying off all debts, including mortgage debts, and from April, 1896, onwards they allowed the defendant to receive the rents of the properties devised to her.

1898.

BOARD
v.
WEEKES.

Phillip Weekes, the husband, died in January, 1897. The interest on the mortgage was at the date of the suit in arrear some 8 years.

Sheppard, for the plaintiff. The restraint against anticipation is limited to the interest devised to Mrs. Weekes directly, without the intervention of trustees.

The mortgage is at all events good as to 191 Palmer-street, and 21 and 22 Woods' Lane, which were equitable estates vested in fee in possession in Mrs. Weekes. There is a direction to convey these properties to Mrs. Weekes, which overrides the restraint : *In re Bown* (1) ; *In re Grey's Settlement* (2).

The mortgagees are not in possession of the property, they are entitled to the ordinary account against the mortgagor, and mere notice to pay rent to the mortgagee does not without more amount to taking possession : *Hickman* v. *Mackin* (3) ; *Towerson* v. *Jackson* (4). The plaintiff is entitled to more than six years' arrears of interest against the land ; the mortgage is a mortgage of a blended fund of realty and personalty : *Mellersh* v. *Brown* (5).

Lingen, for the defendant. Mrs. Weekes' interest under the will was wholly reversionary until the trustees had paid the debts, which was not done until long after the mortgage.

Sheppard in reply. The trust for payment of debts does not postpone the period of vesting ; *Caudel's Case* (6) ; *Manning's Case* (7) ; *Carter* v. *Barnardiston* (8). The words " estate in reversion or remainder on expectancy " are technical words, and must be so construed.

C.A.V.

(1) 27 Ch. D. 411.　　　　(5) 45 Ch. D. 225.
(2) 34 Ch. D. 712.　　　　(6) Cro. Eliz. 1, 316.
(3) 4 H. & N. 716.　　　　(7) 8 Coke 96.
(4) [1891] 2 Q.B. 484.　　　(8) 1 P.D. 505.

On the 12th December the following judgment was delivered by

SIMPSON, C.J. in Eq. (After stating the facts of the case as above set out his Honour continued)—

Three points were raised and argued :—

(1) At the date of making the mortgage was the defendant restrained from anticipation as to any of the land comprised in the mortgage ?

(2) If not, can the mortgagee recover against the land more than six years' arrears of interest ?

(3) Did the mortgagee go into possession of any part of the mortgaged property ?

The first point depends entirely on the meaning and effect of the will. It was contended on behalf of the plaintiff that, though the defendant took for her separate use all property "given to or in trust for" her, the restraint on anticipation was limited to the case of any estate or interest given to her for life or any reversionary or expectant interest that is given to her directly without the intervention of trustees. I do not think this argument is tenable : it seems to me an equitable estate or interest is an estate or interest given to her within the words of the proviso.

It was then contended that the property given to Mrs. Hay for life with remainder to her children, and given over to Mrs. Weekes in the event of Mrs. Hay dying in the testator's lifetime without issue was not either an estate for life or a reversionary or expectant interest. As the will is to be construed with reference to the real and personal estate comprised in it, to speak and take effect as if it had been executed immediately before the death of the testator, I think this contention is sound, so far as concerns the prior interest limited to Mrs. Hay and her children. It was, however, pointed out by Mr. *Lingen* that the interest given to Mrs. Weekes was reversionary in another way, inasmuch as Mrs. Weekes was not entitled to go into possession or receive rents until the debts had been paid off out of rents and income. As a matter of fact, the trustees received the rents for nearly ten years from the testator's death, and applied them in paying debts, and it was only in April, 1896, that Mrs. Weekes was allowed to receive the rents of the property given to her.

In answer to this, some venerable authorities were referred to by Mr. *Sheppard* shewing that the limitation of a term of years does not interfere with the immediate vesting in possession of the legal seisin of the freehold. Undoubtedly that is so, but it hardly affects this case. The legal fee simple in possession is vested in the trustees, the only question is whether the beneficial interest given to Mrs. Weekes was at the testator's death and at the time of giving the mortgage in possession or reversionary. One object of imposing the restraint on dealing with a reversionary interest was, I imagine, to protect female beneficiaries from borrowing at ruinous rates. The testator may well have thought that a married woman actually receiving rents could borrow on fair terms, but that if she were only entitled to receive rents in the future she could only borrow on money-lender's terms. If real estate is given unto and to the use of trustees in fee simple on trust to pay the rents to A. for ten years, and on the expiration of the ten years to convey the property to B., I think B.'s interest during the currency of the ten years may well be described as reversionary. I therefore hold that the restraint on anticipation applied at the date of the mortgage to all the land comprised in the mortgage.

In this view it becomes unnecessary to consider questions 2 and 3, but, in my opinion, a mortgagee suing for foreclosure cannot recover out of the land more than 6 years' arrears of interest (Statute of Limitations, s. 42), and it makes no difference in this respect that the mortgage comprises personal as well as real estate : *Cf. Charter* v. *Watson* (1).

As regards the third point, it is clear that mere giving notices by the mortgagee to the mortgagor's tenant to pay the rent to the mortgagee does not make the possession of the tenant the possession of the mortgagee : *Towerson* v. *Jackson* (2).

The plaintiff is entitled to the usual mortgagee's account and foreclosure against any personal estate which passed by the

(1) [1899] 1 Ch. 175.   (2) [1891] 2 Q.B. 484.

mortgage deed, which is practically nothing, and the costs of this part of the suit he can add to his debt.

As regards the costs of the rest of the suit, the defence is not a meritorious one. Mrs. Weekes has had the money, and when called on to repay sets up that she had no power to mortgage. As the terms of the testator's will are not quite as clear as they might be, I think there should be no order as to the remaining costs.

Solicitors for the plaintiff: *Deane & Deane.*

Solicitors for the defendants: *Stephen, Jaques, and Stephen; Langley.*

In re LORD'S TRUSTS.

1898.
Oct. 14, 21.

C.J. Eq.

Trustees—Power of sale—How far trustees must sell for the actual value in cash.

Trustees with a power of sale are not justified in selling portion of the settled land to a municipality in consideration of a nominal sum, and a covenant to erect buildings thereon which will have the effect of increasing the selling price of the rest of the land, although the benefit to the estate will be greater than the actual value of the land proposed to be sold.

PETITION FOR ADVICE.

George Lee Lord by his will devised all his real estate at or near Botany upon trust for his children and their heirs, and if all his children died under age and unmarried on trust for Herbert Edward Lord, one of his trustees. The will contained a power to his trustees to sell all or any part of his real estate by public auction or private contract at such time and upon such terms and conditions as they might think fit. The testator died on the 12th June, 1883, leaving one daughter, now an infant of the age of 15 years. The petition then continued: (4) Part of the land at or near Botany, so devised as aforesaid, consists of a block of land comprising 14 acres or thereabouts, having an extensive frontage to Botany Road, at the corner of Banksia-street. (5) The Borough of Botany is desirous of purchasing a small portion of the said 14 acres for the sum of 10*l.*, for the purpose of erecting thereon council chambers and a post and telegraph office at the cost of 2,000*l.* or upwards, and the said borough is willing to enter into a covenant with the trustees to erect the said buildings at the cost aforesaid within twelve months from the date of the contract of sale, and the trustees consider the proposal an advantageous one, and are willing to carry it out under the sanction of the Court.

It was also stated in the petition that the parcel proposed to be sold was 85 feet frontage, with a depth of 150 feet, and that Messrs. Richardson & Wrench estimated that the transaction with the borough would enhance the value of the remaining frontage to the extent of 250*l.*, and make the land sell more readily. The then present value of the piece of land which it was proposed to sell was 187*l.* 10*s.* In the opinion of Messrs. Richardson & Wrench the transaction would be an advantageous one to the estate. The municipality stipulated that the trustees must obtain the advice of the Court as to their power to carry out the transaction.

Lamb, for the trustees. The trustees have a general power of sale on such terms as they think best; from the petition it appears that the estate is benefiting to the extent of 260*l.* by the sale of land worth 187*l.*: *Re Stone's Settlement* (1).

A. H. SIMPSON, C.J. in Eq. The difficulty I feel is whether this is a sale at all, whether it is not a disguised gift. I fancy it has been held that trustees with a power of sale cannot dedicate land for a road, however beneficial it may be to the estate. But I will think the matter over.

Cur. adv. vult.

On October 21st,

A. H. SIMPSON, C.J. in Eq. This is a petition asking whether the trustees of the will of George Lee Lord are justified in selling a piece of land to the Botany Municipal Council in consideration of a nominal sum of money, and a covenant on their part to erect buildings of a certain value on the land.

Under the will of the testator his real estate was left to his trustees upon trust for his children equally, with a gift over, in the event of all his children dying under twenty-one and unmarried, to one of his trustees; the will also contained a power of sale in the usual form. It is stated in the petition that the selling value of this portion of the land is 187*l.*, but that it will be greatly for the benefit of the rest of the land if this portion, which is only a small part of the whole, is conveyed to the municipality for a nominal sum of 10*l.*, because the buildings which the council have agreed to erect on the land if sold to them will increase the value of the rest of the property to the extent of 250*l.*; in that way the net benefit to the estate is estimated at

(1) W.N. (1874) 4.

1898.

In re
LORD'S
TRUSTS.

C.J. Eq.

73*l.* There is only one child of the testator, a daughter of the age of 15, and the petitioner, Herbert Lee Lord, is entitled in the event of the gift over taking effect; under the circumstances, therefore, it is very unlikely that the transaction, if carried out, will be disturbed, but that is a matter which I can, of course, pay no regard to.

The question really turns upon whether the proposed arrangement is a valid exercise of the power of sale; if it is not, I cannot advise the trustees to carry it out, as, though my opinion might protect the trustees, it would not give the municipality a good title in the event of the daughter successfully contending hereafter that the transaction was not within the powers of the trustees.

In *Dart's Vendors and Purchasers*, p. 89, it is laid down that "trustees must sell for a gross sum of money unless any consideration be specially authorised; for instance, a sale in consideration of a rent charge or annuity is invalid." In *Read* v. *Shaw* (1) trustees sold to the purchaser for 1,700*l.*, and the purchaser in consideration of the like sum granted to the trustees a perpetual annuity of 73*l.* 16*s.* out of the estate, and covenanted to lay out 3000*l.* on building on the estate. That expenditure would, of course, have largely increased the value of the security for the rent charge, but it was held not to be a valid exercise of the power of sale.

If that is the law, the proposed transaction is not, in my opinion, within the power of sale; if the land were sold to the corporation simply in consideration of the building covenant it would clearly not be a sale, and I cannot see that the addition of a mere nominal sum of 10*l.* betters the matter to any extent. I must, therefore, advise the trustees that they are not justified in carrying out this arrangement. I do not say it is necessary that the trustees should receive absolutely the full price, but it must be something approximating to the full price.

Solicitors: *Holdsworth & Son.*

(1) Sug. Pow., 364, 953.

In re THE COLLAROY COMPANY, Ltd.

1898.

December 16.

Walker J.

Company—Reconstructed Companies Act, 1894 (57 *Vic. No.* 25), s 7.

The provisions of the Reconstructed Companies Act. 1894, will only be extended to companies reconstructing during such a financial crisis as existed in 1893 and 1894, and requiring assistance in the public interest.

THIS was a petition by the Collaroy Company, Ltd., for the recommendation of the Chief Judge in Equity that the Governor in Council should, under his hand, issue a proclamation, and publish the same in the Government Gazette, declaring that the provisions of the Reconstructed Companies Act, 1894, shall apply to the company from the 8th day of March, 1898.

From the petition and affidavits it appeared that a company named The Collaroy Co., Ltd. (the original company), was incorporated in England on the 20th July, 1881, for the purpose of sheep farming and grazing upon certain lands known as the Collaroy estate near Cassilis in this colony. The capital of the company was 200,000*l*. divided into 2,000 shares of 100*l*. each. By special resolution duly passed and confirmed in December, 1897, it was resolved *inter alia* that it was desirable to reconstruct the original-company, and, accordingly, that that company should be wound up voluntarily, and that the liquidator should consent to the registration of a new company to be named The Collaroy Company, Ltd., to be formed for the purpose of taking over the assets and liabilities of the original company. The new company was formed with the same objects and with the same shareholders as in the original company, but with an alteration in the nominal capital of the original company: it was incorporated in England on March 8th, 1898, with a capital of 300,000*l*. divided into 10,000 preference shares of 10*l*. each, and 20,000 ordinary shares of 10*l*. each.

It was subsequently agreed that the original company and its liquidator should transfer, and the new company should take over, the whole of the assets and liabilities of the original company.

It further appeared that the whole of the assets were situated in New South Wales, and that no transfer or assignment of the assets from the original company to the new company had been made.

L. Owen, for the petitioner.

WALKER, J.   This is an application under s. 7 of the Reconstructed Companies Act, 57 Vic. No. 25, asking me, as Judge in Equity, to recommend to the Governor in Council that the provisions of the Act should apply to The Collaroy Company, Ltd.

It appears that the company is an English company, and has been reconstructed in England, and, further, that it is perfectly solvent, and has been reconstructed solely for its own benefit. Under these circumstances the present application for my recommendation involves the consideration of the principles on which the discretion given to the Judge should be exercised.

The Act is intituled, " an Act to facilitate the carrying out the reconstruction schemes of certain companies," and the preamble recites the reconstruction of certain companies named in the schedule to the Act, some of them being Australian companies, and some having an English domicil ; and further recites that " it is expedient to facilitate the carrying out of the reconstruction of such companies and corporations in the way and to the extent hereinafter appearing." By s. 3 it is enacted that " immediately upon the passing of this Act all the property in New South Wales of each of the old companies mentioned in the schedule to this Act vested in or belonging to, or held in trust for or on behalf of such company at the date of the order of Court sanctioning its reconstruction not expressly excepted by such order from passing to the new company, and which shall not, previously to the passing of this Act, have been conveyed, transferred, released or otherwise assured by the old company, to which such property originally belonged, shall, without any conveyance, assignment, transfer, assurance, application, or other instrument, and without payment of any fees or duties whatsoever, vest in, pass to, and become absolutely the property of the new company." By s. 7 the Governor in Council may from time to time, on the recommendation of the Judge sitting in

Equity, by proclamation under his hand, and published in the New South Wales Government Gazette, declare that the provisions of the Act shall apply to any reconstructed company or corporation named in such proclamation from a date to be therein specified.

If I were to grant the present application, I do not know how I could refuse any application by a company to obtain the benefit of the Act, for here no special circumstances are alleged, but the application is based simply upon the fact that the company has been reconstructed.

If the Legislature had intended that the provisions of the Act should apply to all reconstructed companies, it could have said so in very few words ; but s. 7 is framed on quite other lines. That being so, in what cases is the Judge in the exercise of his discretion to make the recommendation ?

In my opinion the recommendation should be made only where the facts of the particular case resemble the facts which prevailed at the time when the Act was passed.

It is a matter of notoriety that the Act was a piece of panic legislation, that is, that at the time of the passing of the Act the colony was undergoing a very grave financial crisis, and it was considered of the utmost public importance that the scheduled companies (which comprised some of the largest banking institutions in the colony, and Goldsbrough, Mort & Co., Ltd., which had very large financial transactions here), should have assistance of a special character given to them in order to tide them over the crisis.   In order to prevent the collapse of the credit of the companies named, the Legislature passed the Act in question, and in effect declared that so great was the danger, and so great was the interest the public generally had in supporting these institutions, that they should be assisted and put on their feet at (in some measure) the public expense, and accordingly it was provided that they should be able to reconstruct themselves, and transfer their assets to a new company at slight expense, the property of the old company vesting in the new company under the Act without conveyances or transfers (which might cost very large amounts of money), and the transfers being effected without the usual toll in the form of stamp duty.

1898.

In re
COLLAROY
Co., LTD.

Coming now to s. 7, it seems to me that the Legislature saw that circumstances similar to those of 1894 might arise in the future, and that there might be cases in which assistance should in the public interest be given to companies not mentioned in the schedule, and that such companies should have the right to apply for the benefits conferred by the Act. If a company, therefore, applies under the section, and shews that it is in the public interest that assistance should be given to it, I think the recommendation should be made; but I do not see why exceptional legislation should be extended to a company merely because it has been reconstructed.

For these reasons I do not think that it was the intention of the Legislature that the Act should apply to such a case as this, and I must, therefore, refuse the application.

Order accordingly.

Solicitor for the petitioner: *Creagh.*

1897.

April 26,
27, 28, 29.

C.J. Eq.

THE AUSTRALASIAN INCANDESCENT GAS LIGHT COMPANY,
LTD. *v.* TURNER AND ANOTHER.

*Patent—Validity—Construction—Infringement—Construction of claim—Doctrine
of equivalents—Process—Substance of invention taken.*

The plaintiffs were the owners of a patent for the manufacture of an illuminant
cap or hood for gas and other burners. The specification stated that there was
employed in the manufacture of the hood a compound of oxide of lanthanum and
zirconium, or of these with oxide of yttrium : and that, instead of using oxide of
yttrium, ytterite earth, and instead of oxide of lanthanum cerite earth containing
no didymium, and but little cerium might be employed. These minerals were
at the time of the patent the less expensive " rarer earths," and it was then
known that the "rarer earths," if exposed to a gas flame, became incandescent:
the patent was the first successful application of this knowledge, so as to produce
an illuminant of a commercial value. The defendants adopted the plaintiffs'
process, but substituted thorium for the minerals named in the plaintiffs' patent.
The evidence shewed that "thorium" was a cerite earth.

Held, that it was an infringement of the plaintiffs' patent ; and that the plaintiffs' patent was really a patent for the use of the "rarer earths," equivalents of
those named in the specification.

THIS was a suit to restrain the defendants from manufacturing
or selling incandescent gas burners, which were an infringement
of the Letters of Registration belonging to the plaintiffs, and for
consequential relief.

The specification of the plaintiffs' patent was as follows:—
" My invention relates to the manufacture of an illuminant
appliance in the form of a cap or hood to be rendered incandescent by gas and other burners, so as to enhance their illuminating
powers. For this purpose, 1 employ a compound of oxide of
lanthanum and zirconium, or of these with oxide of yttrium,
which substances in a finely divided condition when they are
heated by a flame give out a full, large almost pure white light
without becoming volatilized, or producing scale or ash even
after being kept incandescent for many hours, but remain efficient without deterioration even when they are long exposed to
the air.

" The proportions in which the substances are compounded
may be varied within certain limits. I have found the following

proportions very suitable :—60 per cent. zirconia or oxide of 1897.
zirconium, 20 per cent. oxide of lanthanum, 20 per cent. oxide AUSTRAL-
of yttrium. The oxide of yttrium may be dispensed with, the ASIAN INCAN-
DESCENT
composition being then :—50 per cent. zirconia, 50 per cent. oxide GASLIGHT CO.
LTD.
of lanthanum. Instead of using the oxide of yttrium, ytterite v.
earth, and, instead of oxide of lanthanum, cerite earth contain- TURNER.
ing no didymium, and but little cerium may be employed.

"For part of the zirconia, a mixture of magnesia and zirconia
may be employed with a little loss of intensity of the light given
out.

"For applying the substances mentioned as an illuminant, I
use a fine fabric, preferably of cotton, previously cleansed by
washing with hydrochloric acid. I saturate this fabric with an
aqueous solution of nitrate or acetate of the oxide above-mentioned, and gently press it until it does not readily yield fluid, so
that, in stretching or opening out the fabric, the fluid does not
fill up its meshes. The fabric is then exposed to ammonia gas,
and when it has been dried it is cut into strips and folded into
plaits.

"In order to give the fabric thus prepared a suitable shape, a
fine platinum wire is drawn through the meshes of the net, and
bent to the form of a ring, so as to give the fabric the shape of a
tube, the edges of which are then sewn together with an
impregnated thread.

"The cap or hood thus formed can be supported on cross wires
in the chimney of the lamp, or the platinum ring may be attached
to a somewhat stronger platinum wire, serving as a supporting
stem by which the hood can be secured to a holder on the burner
tube, the platinum ring of the hood being thus held about an
inch or more above the burner.

"On igniting the flame, the fabric is quickly reduced to ashes,
the residuum of earthy matters nevertheless retaining the form
of a cap or hood.

"Obviously, fabrics of various forms or constructions may be
employed according to the character of the burner to which they
are applied.

"In order to protect the fabric, and prevent its rupture when
it is exposed to a strong current of gas, stronger threads can be

added to the fabric before it is converted into ashes. Also the

AUSTRAL-
ASIAN INCAN-
DESCENT
GASLIGHT CO.
LTD.
v.
TURNER.
fabric can be painted with, or dipped into a concentrated solution of the salts, so as to provide a fresh layer of the metallic salts, which become fully oxidized soon after the hood becomes incandescent. In order to strengthen the connection to the platinum wire, those parts of the fabric which are next the wire should be more fully impregnated with the solution employed, or with a solution of about equal parts of magnesium nitrate and aluminium nitrate.

"Having thus described the nature of this invention, and in what manner the same is to be performed, I claim :—

"An illuminant appliance for gas and other burners, consisting of a cap or hood made of fabric impregnated with the substances hereinbefore mentioned, and treated as hereinbefore described."

The plaintiffs alleged, in their statement of claim, that the defendants were selling hoods of the same or similar shape and material, and impregnated with the same chemicals as those of the plaintiffs', or with other salts of the rare earths equivalent thereof, and particularly that they contained quantities of thoria and ceria, which were respectively oxides of thorium and cerium.

The defendant Bakewell submitted to the decree of the Court.

The defendant Turner contended that the plaintiffs' patent had been anticipated by the English Patent No. 225 of 1882, which received provisional protection only, and which was known as the Stokes Williams' patent. He also contended that thorium, of which his mantles were made, was distinct from any of the substances mentioned in the plaintiffs' patent, and was a better illuminant than any of them.

An analysis of the constituents of mantles purchased from the defendant Turner by the plaintiffs shewed that they were mainly composed of thoria with a small percentage of ceria.

The rest of the facts appear fully in his Honour's judgment.

Lingen (*Leverrier* with him), for the plaintiffs. The case is governed by *The Incandescent Gas Light Co., Ltd.* v. *De Mare* (1), on both questions of want of novelty and infringement.

[MANNING, C.J. in Eq. I do not want to hear you on the question of validity.]

(1) [1896] 13 R.P.C. 301 & 559.

Welsbach saturated the mantle with oxides of rare earths, and clearly thorium was a rare earth. The plaintiffs' patent covers all rare earths; thorium is cerite earth.

He also referred to *Vadische's Patent*, (1) ; *The Incandescent Gas Light Co., Ltd.* v. *The Sunlight Gas Light Co.* (2).

1897.

AUSTRAL-
ASIAN INCAN-
DESCENT
GASLIGHT CO.
LTD.
v.
TURNER.

The defendant Turner, in person, contended that his mantles did not contain any of the ingredients of the plaintiffs' patent.

The plaintiffs were not called upon in reply.

MANNING, C.J. in Eq.   The solution of this case has been rendered comparatively simple to me by the trials with reference to this very patent which have already taken place in England. I have before me the judgments of *Wills*, J., in the *De Mare Case* and the *Sunlight Case.* I have also what is of vastly greater importance to me, the judgment of the Court of Appeal in the *De Mare Case*, because I am bound by it. In the *De Mare Case*, which is quite sufficient for my purposes, the patent was impeached on almost every possible ground.   Amongst the objections taken to the letters of registration was want of novelty, and under the Patents Act of 1883 particulars of the objections taken were set out.   The same course has been followed in this case, but in the course of the proceedings the defendant has dropped all objections except one, viz, the provisional specification of Mr. Stokes-Williams.   That objection was also taken in the *De Mare Case*.   I have not got the evidence before me that was taken in the *De Mare Case* or in the *Sunlight Case*, and if I had I would not be entitled to look at it, but I find from the judgment of *Wills*, J., that in the former case the specification of Mr. Stokes-Williams was fully gone into, and so far as I am able to give an opinion, or justified in giving an opinion, it seems to me that *Wills*, J., dealt with that specification very properly when he said that it was apparent from his specification that Mr. Stokes-Williams was a man of varied but superficial knowledge, and therefore these hints, or whatever he has given, were impracticable and of no value as indicating in any way the process ultimately adopted by Welsbach.   In addition to that, I have the evidence, taken upon commission in this case, of Professor Dewar, Mr. Swin-

(1) 24 Ch. D. 156.   (2) [1896]13 R.P.C. 333.

1897.

AUSTRAL-
ASIAN INCAN-
DESCENT
GASLIGHT CO.
LTD.
v.
TURNER.

C.J. Eq.

burne, and Sir Frederick Bramwell, three most eminent men, and the opinion of the English witnesses is that this specification is practically a conglomeration, and nothing can be done with it; in fact, they were utterly incapable of understanding it. Professor Threlfall, who deservedly has a very high reputation in this colony, and who is a man of singular intelligence, besides being a very clear thinker, also said that he could not understand this specification. He said that the first time he read it he hardly succeeded in getting through it, and he had to read it through three times before he could follow it. The only witness called on the other side, who gave evidence as to this specification, was Mr. Gross, but on cross-examination he was tested as to his knowledge of chemistry, and he failed to shew even an elementary knowledge of it. He said that upon reading the specification he would have no difficulty in forming exactly what Welsbach had done. Mr. Manfield Newton, who is a patent agent, was examined on this point, but I pointed out that it was very easy for anyone to be wise after the event, but it was very difficult for a man, who had the solution of a problem pointed out to him, to say whether or not he could have found it out if that solution had not been pointed out. The solution of such a problem seems so simple, and then when you are told of it you cannot believe that you could not have found it out if you had devoted a reasonable amount of intelligence to it.

I give Mr. Gross the benefit of the doubt, but I cannot accept his evidence in face of that given by these men of high standing. Mr. Gross is a consulting and mechanical engineer, but he is not a man who had risen to any eminence in that profession. I have, therefore, come to the conclusion that the evidence is really all one way, and I am exactly of the same opinion as *Wills,* J., with regard to this specification; even if the evidence before me had been evenly balanced, I should have felt it to be my duty to adopt the view of an English Judge of very considerable amateur knowledge in a matter of this kind, if only on the ground that the understanding of the patent law should be the same throughout all Her Majesty's dominions, so that all her Majesty's subjects should know exactly their position with regard to such an important matter. Upon the evidence before me I am

satisfied that the Stokes-Williams' specification constitutes no
anticipation of this patent, and that is the only tangible objection
which has been taken to its validity.

There still remains the point what the patent was for. The
construction of a patent is a matter of mixed law and fact;
mainly of law, and that has been dealt with by the Court of
Appeal in the *De Mare Case.* I must say that speaking under
the same difficulty as that I have referred to with regard to these
other gentlemen, if I had been without this instruction I should
have found it impossible to have come to any other conclusion;
but that is immaterial, because I am bound by the decision of
the Court of Appeal. *Kay*, L.J., points out that certain things
were well known before the Welsbach patent, viz., that, where
the rare earths were exposed to a gas flame, they gave off incandescent properties, and thereby the light was very much increased.
That was common knowledge, but, as far as we are concerned, it
was practically useless. That certain chemists knew this was no
advantage to me or any other member of the community. The
problem that Welsbach had to solve, as *Kay*, L.J., said, was how
to apply this; and it was Welsbach who produced an apparatus
for applying these substances, so as to produce this result. It
seems to me that that is exactly what the patent in this case
claims:—"An illuminating appliance for gas or other burners
consisting of a cap or hood made of a fabric impregnated with
the substance before mentioned and treated in the manner hereinbefore described."

I now turn to the judgment of *Wills*, J., in the *Sunlight
Case*, where he says that what was there done by the defendants
was not an infringement of the Welsbach patent. And this leads
me to remark that this judgment was delivered two months
before that of the Court of Appeal in the *De Mare Case. Wills*,
J., in this judgment, says:—"The case of the rare earths is
beyond all doubt the essence of Welsbach's invention." That is
sufficient for the present case; but supposing that there is anything in this last judgment inconsistent with that of the Court
of Appeal, that judgment will have to give way. What the
chemists wanted to do was to find out how the light could be
made available for the general public, and Welsbach shewed

1897.

AUSTRAL-
ASIAN INCAN-
DESCENT
GASLIGHT CO.
LTD.
v.
TURNER.

C.J. Eq.

1897.

AUSTRAL-
ASIAN INCAN-
DESCENT
GASLIGHT CO.
LTD.
v.
TURNER.

C.J. Eq.

exactly how that could be done by applying these rare earths to a fabric in such a way, that practically the rare earths could be substituted for the vegetable fabric; this fabric, when placed in connection with a gas burner, gave off the whole of their incandescent properties, thus producing a light greatly in excess of that which the public got without them.

In all these registrations of patents there is always a formula given, and it is very often put that " this may be done in certain ways, but I prefer such and such a way." In this case the patentee gives a certain formula, which he varies and afterwards very considerably extends.

Now let us look at what was done as to these rare earths. I need only look at those mentioned by Welsbach and thorium. The incandescent properties of thorium were very well known, but of all these rare earths thorium, which had the strongest incandescent power, was the rarest; so rare that the defendant Turner mentioned that he knew of as much as 420l. having been given for one pound of the oxide; a weight which I am informed can be now purchased for 2s. 6d. That value would shew that Professor Threlfall was perfectly correct when he said that this particular oxide was very rare indeed. Naturally, therefore, anyone who wanted to give a practical illustration of the way in which the work could be done would deal with those oxides which, while they might not give such an illuminating power, would be more easily within the reach of chemists. It seems to me it must have been a chemist who prepared this specification, for the invention mentions not all those known, but only the most easily obtainable. He then proceeds to say that for these might be substituted cerite earth. The Court of Appeal in *De Mare's Case*, and *Wills*, J., in the *Sunlight Case*, decided that the essence and substance of this patent was the use of the rare earths, and it seems to me that, on the application of either of those judgments to this case, as thorium is manifestly a rare earth, the use of it, either by itself or with a certain proportion of cerium, or anything else, as in this case, is an infringement of the plaintiffs' patent, because it is the use of a rare earth well known at the time the patent was taken out.

The evidence is really all one way that thorium comes amongst the cerite group, and there is ample evidence that it is found with cerium.   The defendant put several questions to Professor Threlfall with reference to this matter, and I allowed him to produce a book which was to confound the Professor and shew that thorium was a distinct thing and found by itself and not found with cerium, and that, therefore, it could not be called a cerite earth; but, unfortunately, on the very page shewn to Professor Threlfall, he pointed out an analysis in which thorium and cerium were found together.   The Professor said that from thorite you get thorium, and practically nothing else; but there are a number of chemicals from which, from processes known to chemists, you separate first the grosser oxides and afterwards the individual rarer oxides, and in this way you find thorium in the cerite earths. Unquestionably cerite earths are mentioned.   None of the English witnesses examined on commission were cross-examined, but there was no witness called here of any value against them and Professor Threlfall; and I am certainly right in saying that, upon the evidence before me, thorium is properly classed among the cerite earths, and is therefore within the patent.

But, supposing it is not, what the defendant does is simply arriving at the same result by the same process as that patented by the plaintiffs, but by the use of an equivalent, and, therefore, it is an infringement.   Although Mr. Turner was short in his address at the end, I heard a considerable number of arguments as to his position through the case, which were of considerable value, as they allowed me to see what was the point at issue. His position was simply that thorium gives a better light; therefore, by the use of thorium, those whom he represented were the first to call attention to it, and thereby conferred a great benefit on the public, and they should get the benefit and advantage arising from that.   The answer to that is, that if the use of thorium in this way was really an invention of theirs, and something distinct from the plaintiffs', they should have patented it as an improvement upon Welsbach's patent.   In which case, if it had been held that Welsbach's patent did not entitle him to use thorium, the public would not have been kept waiting for it

1897.

AUSTRAL-
ASIAN INCAN-
DESCENT
GASLIGHT CO.
LTD.
v.
TURNER.

C.J. Eq.

1897.

AUSTRAL-
ASIAN INCAN-
DESCENT
GASLIGHT Co.
LTD.
v.
TURNER.

C.J Eq.

for fourteen years, as he says, but some arrangement would certainly have been come to whereby the public would have got the benefit of it. Supposing that this had been in fact patented, the question would still have arisen whether they were entitled to use thorium, or whether it did not amount to an infringement. The case resolved itself into an appeal *ad misericordiam* as to what effect a decision of this kind would have in keeping the public out of the enjoyment of a valuable ingredient. To my mind, it is not keeping the public out of the use of a valuable ingredient, because, in my opinion, the plaintiffs' are entitled to use it. If, as suggested, a mantle of such permanent character is produced that it can be handled, and is not so fragile as that at present in use, there will be time enough for the Court to deal with the question whether or not it is an infringement, and I am not called upon to express an opinion. It may be that that would not be an infringement of the patent, and that it could only be dealt with as an improvement on the present patent. However, the fact that that might be an improvement cannot affect the value of the previous patent. That is an argument no Court could listen to. If a man discovers something, the contract between him and the Crown is this :—if, instead of hoarding up his discovery he can put it before the public in such a way that men can make use of it, then for a certain number of years he may have a monopoly of it. It is no part of the contract that because a man sees where an improvement will come in, which improvement might not have been known but for the discovery of another man, that he should be allowed to make use of that previous discovery.

I have to decide what is the meaning of this patent, and I hold that I am bound by the decision of the Court of Appeal in the *De Mare Case*, with which I fully agree. I am also satisfied that there was no anticipation by the Stokes-Williams specification. Therefore, the patent is good. The question whether or not there has been an infringement is one of fact, and I find that fact against the defendant for the reasons stated. I must therefore make the decree as asked.

I might add that if you strike out the word "erbium" in the judgment of the Court of Appeal, and insert "thorium" in its place, you have the decision in this case.

Solicitor for the plaintiff company : *V. Le Gay Brereton.*

Solicitors for the defendant Bakewell : *Billyard, Andrews & Moseley.*

Ex parte THE COMMISSIONERS FOR RAILWAYS ; *In re* THE CLAIM OF
SARAH WILLIAMS AND OTHERS.

Will—Construction—Substituted class—" In case of the death "—" Share to which
he would have been entitled "—Gift in remainder to persons living at the death
of the tenant for life.

A testator devised his real estate to his wife, and on her death on trust for
five persons by name, or such of them as should survive his wife and attain
twenty-one, and in case these five persons should all be living at his wife's
death and attain twenty-one he devised to them five several parcels of land,
one to each, for their respective lives, and he declared that in case of the death
of any of the before-mentioned persons, then he devised the share to which he
would have been entitled to the heir-general of such person so dying as aforesaid.

Held, by the Full Court, affirming the decision of *Walker*, J., that in the
event of any of the five persons predeceasing the testator's widow, the substitutory devise to the heir-general did not apply, but the survivors were entitled
in fee to the whole real estate.

1898.
———
September 8.
Walker J.

October 31.
December 13.

The C.J.
Owen J.
and
Cohen J.

James Williams died on the 25th December, 1857, having on
the 22nd March previous made a will in the following terms :—
"I appoint my wife Sarah Williams and Andrew Morton surgeon &c. of Queanbeyan executors and trustees of this my will
and I direct them so soon as conveniently may be after my
decease to collect get in and receive all moneys which may be
due and owing to me at my decease and to pay all my just debts
funeral and testamentary expenses. Next I give devise and
bequeath all my real estate unto my said wife for and during her
natural life and after her decease upon trust that my said
executors and trustees shall stand possessed thereof in trust for
William James Penny Francis Penny Thomas Penny and Henry
Penny sons of my said wife by a former marriage and my son
James Williams or such of them as shall be living at the time of
the decease of my said wife and who shall attain the age of
twenty-one years and in case my sons in law the sons of my said
wife by a former marriage that is to say William James Penny
Francis Penny Thomas Penny and Henry Penny and my son
James Williams shall all be living at the time of the decease

P 2

1898.

Ex parte
COMMISSION-
ERS FOR
RAILWAYS;
In re
CLAIM OF
SARAH
WILLIAMS.

of my said wife and who shall attain the age of twenty-one years then I give and bequeath unto William James Penny (property A describing it by metes and bounds) to the use of the said William James Penny and his assigns during his life."

The testator then made similar devises to the other step sons, and to James Williams, of four specific properties, describing them each by metes and bounds, and continued :—" And I declare that in case of the death of any of the before-mentioned persons then I give and devise the share to which he would have been entitled to the use of the person or persons who shall then answer to the description of heir-general to such person so dying as aforesaid his her or their heirs and assigns for ever if more than one as tenants in common and upon to or for no other trust intent or purpose whatsoever."

William James Penny died on the 20th September, 1872, leaving a wife and two children, James Penny and Amelia Penny.

Henry Penny died unmarried on the 21st July, 1882.

Sarah Williams, the testator's widow, died on the 13th June, 1898.

In 1885 the Commissioner for Railways resumed portion of the devised land. After paying to Sarah Williams the value of her life estate, the Commissioners paid into Court two sums of 382*l.* and 209*l.* as compensation for the interests in remainder. The former sum was for part of the land in the specific devise of James Williams; the latter was for part of the land included in the specific devises to Henry Penny and Thomas Penny.

Francis Penny and Thomas Penny now presented a petition praying that one-third of the fund in Court might be paid out to them. Before the petition came on for hearing Francis Penny became bankrupt, and N. F. Giblin was appointed his official assignee.

Cullen, for the petitioner Thomas Penny. As the five beneficiaries did not all survive the widow, the specific devises for life did not come into operation, nor the gift over to their respective heirs general; the petitioners, as two of the three who survived the widow, are entitled to two-thirds of the fund in Court.

1896.

Ex parte
COMMISSION-
ERS FOR
RAILWAYS;
In re
CLAIM OF
SARAH
WILLIAMS.

R. K. Manning, for N. F. Giblin, and *Gordon*, for the respondent James Williams, followed in the same interest.

Macmanamey, for James Penny. The gift over on the death of the beneficiaries applies generally to the preceding clauses in the will.

Canaway, for the Railway Commissioners. The Railway Commissioners are not liable for the costs of this petition; at all events they are only liable for one set of costs to the petitioners.

Cullen in reply.

WALKER, J. In this case James Williams by his will devised all his real estate to his wife during her life, and (1) after her decease upon trust that his trustees should stand possessed thereof in trust for five persons (naming them), or such of them as should be living *at the time of the decease of his said wife*, and who should attain the age of twenty-one years; (2) and in case the said five persons *should all be living* at the time of the decease of his said wife, and who should attain the age of twenty-one years, then he gave to W. J. Penny a certain parcel of land specifically described to the use of him and his assigns during his life—and other parcels of land specifically described to each of the others of the five for their respective lives in similar words; (3) and the testator declared that in case of the death of any of the before-mentioned persons, then he gave the share to which he would have been entitled to the use of the person or persons who should then answer to the description of the heir-general to such person *so dying as aforesaid*, his, her, or their heirs and assigns as tenants in common.

Three only of the five persons named were living at the death of the widow and attained twenty-one, viz., Thomas Penny, Francis Penny, and James Williams. In these circumstances Thomas Penny, James Williams, and Mr. Giblin, as official assignee of the bankrupt estate of Francis Penny, claim to be entitled in equal shares to the whole of the funds in Court, representing lands forming part of the testator's estate and taken under their powers by the Railway Commissioners. This view was contested by James Penny, son of William James Penny.

1898.

Ex parte
COMMISSION-
ERS FOR
RAILWAYS;
In re
CLAIM OF
SARAH
WILLIAMS.

Walker J.
.

W. J. Penny was a son of the testator who predeceased the testator's widow.

In my opinion only the three who were living at the death of the testator's widow and attained twenty-one are entitled to the money. They get their title under the plain words of that part of the will which, for convenience, I have numbered 1. Part 2 was only applicable in the event, which never happened, *of all* of the five surviving the widow; and part 3 was, in my judgment, never meant to apply to any part other than part 2. Parts 2 and 3, as I understand them, are closely connected, and confer life estates and remainders in fee, " in case of the death" meaning " on the death "; but they never came into operation, as they depended on a contingency which never happened. Mr. *Macmanamey*, on behalf of James Penny, contended that part 3 controls and qualifies part 1, and that " in case of the death " means " in case of the death before my said wife." But this seems to me a strained and violent construction, and one which is open to two further objections, viz. (a) the words " to which he would have been entitled " cannot, as the argument assumes, apply to a person predeceasing the widow, for such a person takes nothing under any part of the will; (b) if the words "in case of the death " are to be read as " in case of the death before my said wife," then, if the specific devises in part (2) had come into operation, in every case in which the tenant for life survived the testator's widow there would have been an intestacy as regarded the fee simple. For these reasons I think the view of the petitioners is the correct one, and I order the fund to be divided and paid out accordingly. The Commissioners will pay the costs of all parties, but I shall only allow one set of costs for the petitioners Thomas Penny and the official assignee of Francis Penny, and these costs are to be paid to Thomas Penny or his solicitor. After the petition had been presented by Thomas Penny and Francis Penny, Francis Penny became bankrupt, and his official assignee has appeared before me by separate solicitor and counsel. This is a course which I shall not encourage. In the absence of good reason to the contrary (no such reason is suggested), the official assignee ought to have adopted the petition and appeared by the same solicitor and counsel as his co-petitioner. A trifling amendment would have put the record into proper order, and costs would not then have been unnecessarily incurred. In making this special order as to costs I am following *Owen*, C.J. in Eq., in *Herbert* v. *Badgery* (1).

From this decision the respondent James Penny obtained leave to appeal *in forma pauperis*; the appeal came on for hearing on the 31st October.

Macmanamey and *Hogg*, for James Penny the appellant, cited *Price* v. *Lockley* (2); *Home* v. *Pillans* (3); *In re Merrick's Trusts* (4); *Keay* v. *Boulton* (5); *Galland* v. *Leonard* (6); *In re Hannan* (7); *In re Luddy* (8); *Da Costa's Case* (9); *Cumbridge* v. *Rouse* (10); *O'Mahoney* v. *Burdett* (11); *Theobald on Wills*, 3rd Edit., p. 459; *Jarman on Wills*, 4th Edit., p. 850.

Gordon, for James Williams, cited *Morrell* v. *Sutton* (12); *Roe* v. *Nevill* (13); *Carr* v. *Clinton* (14); *Re Willcock* (15); *Bibben's* v. *Potter* (16); *Anon.* (17).

Cullen, for Thomas Penny and N. F. Giblin, cited 2 *Jarm. on Wills*, 759.

Canaway, for the Railway Commissioners.

Macmanamey in reply.

Cur. adv. vult.

On the 13th December, the judgment of the Court (THE CHIEF JUSTICE, OWEN, J., and COHEN, J.) was delivered by

OWEN, J. This was an appeal from the decision of Mr. Justice *Walker*, whereby he directed a sum in Court to be paid out, one-third to Thomas Penny, one-third to Norman Frederick Giblin, and one-third to James Williams.

margin notes:

1898.

Ex parte
COMMISSIONERS FOR
RAILWAYS;
In re
CLAIM OF
SARAH
WILLIAMS.

Walker J.

December 13.

(1) 14 N.S.W. R. Eq. 328.
(2) 6 Beav. 180.
(3) 2 M. & K. 20.
(4) 1 Eq. 559.
(5) 25 Ch. D. 212.
(6) 1 Swanst. 161.
(7) [1897] 2 Ch. 39, at 43.
(8) 25 Ch. D. 394.
(9) 3 Russ. 360.
(10) 8 Ves. 12.
(11) L.R. 7 H.L. 388.
(12) 1 Phill 545.
(13) 11 Q.B. 466.
(14) 8 Eq. 462.
(15) [1898] 1 Ch. 95.
(16) 10 Ch. D. 733.
(17) Cro. Eliz. 9.

1898.

Ex parte
COMMISSION-
ERS FOR
RAILWAYS;
In re
CLAIM OF
SARAH
WILLIAMS.

Owen J.

The claim arose out of the will of James Williams, who devised his real estate to his wife, Sarah Williams, for life, and after her decease upon trust that his executors and trustees should stand possessed thereof in trust for William James Penny, Francis Penny, Thomas Penny, and Henry Penny (sons of his wife by a former marriage), and his son James Williams, or such of them as should be living at the time of the decease of his wife, and who should attain the age of 21 years. And in case they *all* should be living at the death of his wife, he devised to each of the five by name a separate portion of his land (describing it by metes and bounds) for life, and then made the following declaration :—" And I declare that in case of the death of any of the before-mentioned persons, then I give and devise the share to which he would have been entitled to the use of the person or persons who shall then answer to the description of heir-general to such person so dying as aforesaid, his, her, or their heirs and assigns for ever if more than one as tenants in common." Two of the sons predeceased the widow. The difficulty in construing this will arises out of this declaration.

The words " in case of the death " may be interpreted in three ways :—(1) As meaning "on the death " generally ; (2) " In case of the death during the lifetime of the widow "; or (3) "In case of the death after the decease of the widow." If the first meaning is given, then the devise may present the same difficulties as I shall point out in respect of the second meaning, in the event of the death occurring during the lifetime of the widow. If the second meaning is given, the declaration is not consistent with the first part of the devise, which is *to such* of the sons " as shall be living at the time of the decease of my said wife." The third construction makes the will consistent throughout, because the declaration would only come into force in the event of *all* the sons surviving the widow.

Adopting this construction the disposition of the real estate is that :—If any of the sons die in the lifetime of the testator's wife, the survivors only take an estate in fee ; if *all* the sons survive, then each son takes in severalty a separate portion of the estate, with remainder in fee to his heir. The only difficulty of this construction is that it does not give effect to the words in

the declaration " the share to which he would have been entitled,"
because after the death of the widow the share of the sons would
be vested in possession.   To give effect to those words the death
referred to in the declaration must refer to death in the lifetime
of the widow, and before the sons' shares became vested in
possession, and must be read in connection with the first part of
the will.   If so, it is inconsistent with the devise to the survivors
only, and, moreover, creates an intestacy as to the ultimate fee
in the event of *all* the sons surviving the widow.   We think,
therefore, that these words must be disregarded, and the third
construction we have mentioned adopted.

It is hard to understand why the testator should leave out of
his will the children of a son who has predeceased his widow,
when the children of the son who survives take an estate in
fee; but it is impossible to guess at a testator's reasons.   It is
enough if the Court can make a will grammatically and logically
consistent in its various provisions, without prying into the
ethical reasons for those provisions.

The view we have taken of the true construction of this will
is that adopted by his Honour Mr. Justice *Walker* in his judgment, and, therefore, we dismiss this appeal.   As to the costs of
this appeal, we are of opinion that they should be paid by the
appellants who have failed.   Under s. 56 of the Railways Act
the Commissioners have to pay the costs of getting moneys paid
out of Court, "except such as are occasioned by litigation between
adverse claimants."

Although Mr. Justice *Walker* was right in ordering the Commissioners to pay the costs of the petition before him, we think
the appeal comes within the exception, and the costs of the
appeal should not be borne by the Commissioners.

Solicitors: *Gould & Shaw; Sly & Russell; Howarth.*

1898.

Ex parte
COMMISSION-
ERS FOR
RAILWAYS;
In re
CLAIM OF
SARAH
WILLIAMS.

Owen J.

1898.

October 6.

Walker J.

In re THE MERCANTILE BUILDING, LAND AND INVESTMENT
COMPANY, LTD.

*Company—Municipal rates—Charge—Rights of Mortgagee—Municipalities Act,
1867 (31 Vic. No. 12), s. 176—Municipalities Act Amendment Act of 1892 (55
Vic. No. 33), s. 5.*

The charge created by the Municipalities Acts of 1867 and 1892 is a first charge
upon the property rated, and has priority over any mortgage over the same property, even with respect to rates which become due after the date of such mortgage.

THIS was a summons on behalf of the municipality of Hurstville for an order that the lands subject to the charge for certain
rates due to the municipality should be sold and the proceeds
applied, subject to payment of the costs of sale and other costs,
in the payment of such rates to the municipality, and that the
balance, if any, should be paid to the liquidators of the company.

It appears that in October, 1891, the company was wound-up
voluntarily, and in November in the same year such voluntary
winding-up was ordered to be continued under the supervision
of the Court. A further order was made on September 7th,
1894, that all further proceedings in the winding-up should be
taken before the Master in Equity.

The company had been, and still was, owner in fee of certain
allotments within the municipal district of Hurstville since
April 26th, 1887, and of certain other allotments within the
same district since April 13th, 1888.

A claim for rates due and payable by the company in respect
of these allotments was allowed by the Master at 431*l*. 18*s*. 5*d*.,
and the Master certified that all formalities and conditions
precedent necessary to charge the respective rates on the allotments, in respect of which they had been made, had been duly
performed and complied with.

Some of the lands mentioned were subject to a mortgage dated
September 10th, 1889, in favour of the City Bank of Sydney, as
part security for an advance made to the company.

Cullen, in support of the summons. The municipality is entitled to this order as being a creditor holding a charge. The charge is in substance preferential, as any sale of the property must be subject to it, the charge having to be paid off or the amount thereof deducted from the purchase money. A mortgagee is in no better position, but buys something loaded prospectively by the statute. The properties charged are those included in the assessments from year to year.

1898.

In re
MERCANTILE
B. L. & I. Co.,
LTD.

[WALKER, J. Are not different properties differently assessed?]

Yes; that is the only way of getting at their value.

[WALKER, J. Do you contend that the rates on one assessment can be recovered out of land under another assessment?]

No; I do not carry my argument as far as that, but the properties in one assessment must all bear the burden of the rates.

Knox, for the liquidator. The City Bank of Sydney is not represented, but it is the duty of the liquidator to put the whole matter before the Court. The Court will not assume an interference by the Legislature with the rights of secured creditors. A mere charge is given by the statute, and nothing is said as to priority. The case is different in the case of the Land and Income Tax Act, which expressly refers to the priority of the charge there mentioned.

The charge for rates made after the date of the mortgage to the bank must be *qua* those rates subject to the mortgage. Subsequent rates are in the same position as the debt of a second mortgagee.

[WALKER, J. Suppose a man takes a mortgage over property, all rates on it being then paid; he remains in possession and rates become due; can he sell the property free from those rates?]

No; but that does not shew that there is any priority, because upon sale the mortgage is at an end, and the purchase money is subject to the rates.

Cullen in reply.

WALKER, J. The question I am asked to decide in this case arises from the sections of the Municipalities Acts of 1867 and 1892, which make the rates a charge upon the property rated; the question being what is the meaning of a "charge"; does such charge constitute a first charge and give prior rights?

The case is one of the greatest importance, but there are no authorities on the point, and, therefore, nothing will be gained by my taking time to consider my decision.

I think that the "charge" given by the sections referred to means a first charge. Such a construction is in no way unreasonable, the Municipalities Acts having been passed to enable local taxation to be enforced for the benefit of local property; such is, at any rate, the theory of such statutes, if not literally true in practice.

That such a charge should be a first charge, even to the postponement of an existing mortgage, is not, in my opinion, unreasonable, because the mortgagee gets the benefit of the taxation. Another reason for my decision is this: it seems to me that a municipality, where property is mortgaged, must in respect of their charge be in the position either of first or second mortgagees; I put it to Mr. *Knox* whether in such a case the mortgagee could sell under his power of sale free from the charge given by the statute, and he admitted that the mortgagee could not do so. Now, in the ordinary case of first and second mortgagee, the first mortgagee selling under his power of sale can sell free from the second mortgagee, the second mortgagee only having recourse to the purchase money; the municipality is, therefore, not in the position of second mortgagee. The conclusion then is that the municipality has a charge which is that of first mortgagee; and, as I have said, such is a reasonable construction of the Acts, having regard to the object with which they were passed.

It is not disputed that the municipality must only have recourse in respect of any rate to the particular property rated in that assessment; I therefore say nothing on that point.

The order will be that in default of payment within three months the liquidator sell the property rated to enforce the rates, such sale to be approved by the Master.

The balance of purchase money will be dealt with in the liquidation in the ordinary way. The council will add their costs to their charge, and the liquidator will have his costs out of the assets.

1898.

In re
MERCANTILE
B. L. & I. Co.,
LTD.

Order accordingly.

Walker J.

Solicitors for the municipality: *Carruthers & McDonald.*

Solicitors for the liquidator: *Villeneuve-Smith & Dawes.*

CASES

DETERMINED BY THE

SUPREME COURT OF NEW SOUTH WALES

IN ITS

Bankruptcy and Probate Jurisdictions,

AND BY THE

PRIVY COUNCIL ON APPEAL THEREFROM DURING 1898.

Re WALTERS.

Ex parte THE OFFICIAL ASSIGNEE.

CURRIE, Respondent.

1898.
_____
March 16, 17, 21, 22, 23, 31.
_____
A. H. Simpson J

Bankruptcy—Unsuccessful motion to set aside sale by bankrupt—Costs.

On application by an official assignee to set aside a sale made by the bankrupt as fraudulent under the Statute 13 Eliz. c. 5—*Held*, that the official assignee, though unsuccessful, ought not, under the circumstances, to be ordered to pay the costs of the application notwithstanding that examinations of various witnesses, including the parties to the sale, had been held under s. 30 of the Bankruptcy Act, and that the official assignee had not been misled by the evidence given on such examination.

THIS was a motion by the official assignee of the estate of J. J. Walters to set aside, as fraudulent under the Statute 13 Eliz. c. 5, a sale by the bankrupt to the respondent Donald Currie.

Prior to the proceedings being taken, the bankrupt, the respondent and other witnesses had been examined by the official assignee under s. 30 of the Bankruptcy Act.

The evidence given by the respondent on such examination was substantially the same as that given on the hearing of this application.

Gordon (*R. K. Manning* with him), for the official assignee.

1898.

Re
WALTERS.
Ex parte
OFFICIAL
ASSIGNEE.
CURRIE,
Respondent.

Wise (*Bavin* with him), for the respondent. The transaction was not fraudulent, and the official assignee, if not successful, should not be relieved from having to pay costs as he had previously investigated the circumstances of the sale by examination under s. 30.

Gordon in reply. Owing to the suspicious nature of the transaction, the official assignee was justified in bringing this matter before the Court.

Cur. adv. vult.

March 31.   On March 31st,

A. H. SIMPSON, J. The question which I have to decide in this case is, whether a sale by the bankrupt to Currie in February or March, 1892, of a ½ share in the Farmers' and Dairymen's Refrigerating Co. is void against creditors under the statute 13 Eliz. c. 5. The sequestration order was made on 3rd July, 1896; there is, therefore, no suggestion that the transaction can be impeached under the bankruptcy laws. There is no difficulty as to the law. Where valuable consideration is given the deed is *prima facie* valid, but it may be shewn to be invalid by proving that both vendor and purchaser had a fraudulent intention of defeating or delaying creditors. A fraudulent intent on the part of the vendor is insufficient, it must be brought home to the purchaser. Whether this fraudulent intent can be brought home to both parties is a question of fact, and, of course, depends on the circumstances of each particular case. There are various indications of fraud, inadequacy of consideration, retention of possession by the vendor, secrecy, &c.; but in all cases the only question is, do the facts prove fraud? The law as above stated is practically taken from *Re Johnson* (1), affirmed by the Court of Appeal (2). When the law is clear, not much assistance can be derived by reference to other cases where the facts are different; to quote the language of Lord *Halsbury*, L.C., in *London J. S. Bank* v. *Simmons* (3): "I must make a protest that it is not a very profitable enquiry to consider whether one case resembles another in its facts."

(1) 20 Ch. D. 389.   (2) 51 L.J. Ch. 503.

(3) [1892] A.C. 201 at p. 210.

The material facts in this case are as follows :—

1898.

Re
WALTERS.

Ex parte
OFFICIAL
ASSIGNEE.
CURRIE,
Respondent.

A.H. Simpson J.

In July, 1890, the business in question was started by Kyle and Walters as partners in equal shares under the style of Sneddon and Co., a name which was afterwards changed to The Farmers' and Dairymen's Refrigerating Co. About April, 1891, Walters sold an interest in the business to Sneddon for 1000*l*., the interest being the right to get 300*l*. a year out of profits. Afterwards it was agreed between Walters and Sneddon that the latter was to have ¼ interest. On 1st January, 1892, a partnership deed was drawn up between Kyle and Sneddon, by which it appeared that Kyle held ¼ interest, and Sneddon ¾; Sneddon, however, being a trustee of ½ for Walters. At that time the profits were estimated at about 1200*l*. a year. At the beginning of 1892, Walters, being heavily in debt, and to use his own expression, " wanting money badly," endeavoured to sell his ½ share, and placed it in Mr. Way's hands for sale. Way placed the share in the hands of J. W. Cliff, but whether any real attempt was made to sell it does not appear. In February, 1892, Currie verbally agreed to purchase the ½ share and a piece of land at Picton belonging to Walters on the following terms : 300*l*. cash and 500*l*. in promissory notes, which Currie was not to be called on to pay, but which were to be payable out of the business. Currie was also to take on himself the liability on Walters' share, which was estimated as 3,200*l*. Currie was also to pay Walters 200*l*. a year for looking after his share in the business. As Currie had no property but his farm, the value of which was some 400*l*., he was unable to pay any cash, and accordingly it was arranged that Currie should mortgage his farm to Mrs. Walters, the mother of the bankrupt, an old lady over 70 and of no means. for 300*l*.; that she should transfer this mortgage to her bank, and thereby obtain an overdraft for 300*l*. This was done, and according to Walters' account he got cheques from his mother for various sums at different times, amounting to 300*l*.; the first payment being 60*l*. on 16th August, 1892. There was no deed or writing of any kind transferring the ½ share to Currie.

It was contended by Mr. *Gordon* that the transaction was clearly fraudulent on Walters' part, for the following reasons :—

1898.

Re
WALTERS.
Ex parte
OFFICIAL
ASSIGNEE.
CURRIE,
Respondent.

A. H. Simpson J.

(1) The sale was at a gross undervalue, and (2) Mrs. Walters' name was used as a blind, so that creditors might not know Walters had money at his command. It was further contended that Currie, who was a mere puppet in Walters' hands, must be taken to have been a party to the fraud. In the view I take, it is unnecessary to decide whether Waters was guilty of fraud. I, therefore, refrain from doing so, but I was not favourably impressed with him as a witness, and place little reliance on his testimony when uncorroborated. Assuming, however, that Walters was guilty of fraud, it must be shewn that Currie was a party to it, and of this I am not satisfied. It is extremely difficult to say what the value of the ½ share was in February or March, 1892. According to Mr. Fullwood the value was about 5,000*l.*, the ½ share of profits for the year 31st March, 1891, to 31st March, 1892, being 1,466*l.* Mr. Nathan said this was much too high, as some 800*l.*, an estimated amount for repairs, renewals and maintenance of plant, ought to have been deducted from the value of the plant as given by Fullwood, and charged in profit and loss account, also a further sum of 437*l.*, being 10 per cent. for depreciation ; this would reduce the ½ share of profits to 847*l.* I do not think it is possible on the evidence before me to say which of these views is right, though, as far as I can judge, Fullwood's valuation is excessive in charging no sum for depreciation. Assuming, however, Fullwood's valuation to be correct, the value of the plant is really not very important ; if the business failed, the plant would realise very little on sale. The materiality of the evidence lies in its bearing on the amount of profits. Taking then Fullwood's estimate of profits to be correct, I cannot say the sale was at an undervalue. The purchase was a purely speculative one ; the business had only been carried on for some 20 months, there was an apparent lack of working capital, and there was the chance of opposition. It was contended by Mr. *Gordon* that, except as to 300*l.*, the consideration was purely illusory, as the 500*l.* was to be paid out of profits only, and Currie's indemnity against the liabilities was worthless. From a purchaser's point of view, however, this would not be so. He would, of course, buy on the assumption the business would prosper ; and, if so, the 500*l.* and the amount of the liabilities on the ½ share would have to be paid

out of moneys received by him, and in Currie's case his interest would also be burdened by his agreement to pay Walters 200*l*. a year for looking after Currie's share in the business; Currie being of incapable of doing so himself.   Under these circumstances I do not think the price given (if inadequate at all) was so inadequate as to suggest to Currie any idea of fraud, even though the equity of redemption of land at Picton, which Walters estimates as worth some 200*l*. or 300*l*., was included.   Nor do I think the introduction of Mrs. Walters' name need have conveyed any idea of fraud to Currie, and I do not believe as a matter of fact that he had any fraudulent intent.   In his present condition it is difficult to say what amount of intelligence he possessed at the beginning of 1892, but I believe his wife's evidence that he never was a business man at all, and he no doubt relied to a very unwise extent on Walters.   Where the consideration was marriage, a false recital that the property settled was the wife's was held insufficient to bring home fraud to her: *Campion* v. *Cotton* (1).   So, in a later case, a false recital that the intended husband was indebted to the intended wife in 20,000*l*.: *Kevan* v. *Crawford* (2).

Under these circumstances, the case for setting aside the sale fails.   As Currie, for the purpose of this motion, admits that 120*l*. was owing by him to the bankrupt at the date of the sequestration order, there must be an order on him to pay this amount. I make no order as to costs.   The whole transaction was very suspicious, and Currie, practically by his conduct, brought the litigation on himself; (2) As to the alternative claim, he did not either tender or pay into Court any part of the 120*l*. owed by him.

Order accordingly.

Solicitors for the official assignee: *Allen, Allen & Hemsley.*
Solicitor for the respondent: *H. R. Way.*

(1) 17 Ves. 263.   (2) 6 Ch. D. 29.

1898

Re
WALTERS.
Ex parte
OFFICIAL
ASSIGNER.
CURRIE,
Respondent.

A. H. Simpson J.

1898.
June 13.

A.H. Simpson J.

Re BRADY; *Ex parte* THE OFFICIAL ASSIGNEE.

Bankruptcy Act, 1887 (51 *Vic. No.* 19), *s.* 4, *sub-s.* 1 (h)--*Amendment Act*, 1896,
s. 8—*Act of bankruptcy—Notice of suspension.*

Sub-sect. 1 (h) of s. 4 contemplates the case of a debtor dealing with his creditors as a body. To constitute an act of bankruptcy under that sub-section, a
mere declaration of insolvency is not enough, unless it be accompanied by some
words from which the intention of the debtor as to the future conduct of his
business can be gleaned.

THIS was an application by the official assignee of the estate of
the above-named bankrupt, for an order ante-dating the commencement of the bankruptcy to 14th September, 1897, when, it
was alleged, the bankrupt gave notice to Harry Elliott, one of
his creditors, that he (the bankrupt) had suspended, or was about
to suspend, payment of his debts.

The affidavit of the bankrupt stated that prior to his bankruptcy he was a 'bus proprietor ; that, on 13th April, 1897, he
borrowed from Harry Elliott the sum of 528*l.* 12*s.* upon the
security of all his 'buses, horses, harness, and household furniture,
by a sale note, with a hiring agreement back, whereby, *inter alia*,
the bankrupt was to pay a weekly sum of 4*l.* to Elliott ; that he
got in arrears in his weekly payments, and saw the said Harry
Elliott, and induced Elliott to give him (the bankrupt) a month's
grace, but, notwithstanding that, he was unable to pay Elliott.

" The said Harry Elliott took possession under his securities
on or before the 21st September last.   Before taking possession
the said Harry Elliott sent a man to me for a cheque for rent.
I then owed the said Harry Elliott two weeks' rent, and also 15*l.*
for repairs executed by him for me since the date of the security.
I told the man that I could not pay it ; but that if Mr. Elliott would
give me time I might be able to pay it.   He said that he must
have the money, and on my telling him that I had no money to
give him, he went away.   I afterwards saw the said Harry
Elliott in his yard, and referred to the conversation I had with
his man.   He said I must either pay him or he would take possession.   I said I had no money to give him.   I told him that I could

not pay the people I was getting the feed and stuff from, let
alone him.   I told him that if he could give me time I would try
and get on another run, and might be able to pay him.   He said he
could not give me any further time, that he must have his
money. . . . .   This conversation took place about a week
before the 21st September last."

Elliott, on examination under s. 30 of the Bankruptcy Act,
stated :—" He (the bankrupt) saw me about the 21st September
at my shop.   He owed me 15*l.* for repairs done since date of sale
note.   He was two months' in arrears with his payments under the
lease.   He said he could not pay the arrears, and he could not raise
the money.   He said it was no use trying to raise the money.   I
knew he had a man trying to raise a loan for him in a number
of places, but nobody would take the risk.   The bankrupt told
me the line was not paying well. . . .   He said he might be
able to pay 2*l.* per week under the lease, but I told him I could
not consent."

The estate of the bankrupt was voluntarily sequestrated on
October 6th last.

Gordon, for the official assignee, cited *Re Bacon* (1); *Re Pike*
(2); *Re Scott* (3); *Re Thorold* (4); *Crook* v. *Morley* (5).

Cur. adv. vult.

On June 13th,

A. H. SIMPSON, J.   The question which I have to decide is
whether or not Brady has given notice to any of his creditors
that he has suspended, or that he is about to suspend payment of
debts, within s. 4, sub-s. 1 (h), of the Bankruptcy Act.

Each case must, of course, stand on its own footing ; the Court
must take into account the circumstances under which the statement is made, and the true meaning of the statement so made.
As there is practically an infinite variety in the words used
in each case, and in the circumstances under which they are
used, it is obvious that the only object of citing cases is to establish the principles which are to guide the Court.   It may be that

(1) 6 B.C. 85.   (3) 3 Mans. 102.
(2) 17 N.S.W.L.R. B. & P. 34.   (4) 11 N.S.W.L.R. 331.
                (5) [1891] A.C. 322.

1898.

Re
BRADY.
Ex parte
OFFICIAL
ASSIGNEE.

A.H. Simpson J.

it is not easy to reconcile all the cases on the subject, and still less all the dicta which may be extracted from the cases, especially if taken apart from their context, but I concur in the statement of the law by *Manning*, J., in *Re Pike* (1).   After an examination of the previous cases, and after laying down that statements under s. 4, sub-s. 1 (h), must not be mere casual conversation, his Honour continues : " In every case the creditor who relied upon the expression used as an act of bankruptcy, must be in a position to say the man had his attention drawn to the question of his carrying on, and any reasonable man would imply from what he said that he did not intend to carry on.   An admission of insolvency, in fact, is not enough, unless it be accompanied by some words from which the intention of the debtor as to the future conduct of his business can be gleaned."   It is contended that this cannot be reconciled with the law as laid down by *Vaughan Williams*, L.J., in *In re Scott* (2).   That was the case of a non-trader, and it was unnecessary to the decision to consider what would be sufficient notice in the case of a trader ; but, in my opinion, there is no discrepancy between the two cases.   Mr. *Gordon* relies on the following passages at p. 105 : " The notice must be a notice of intention to suspend payment in ordinary course.   Now, in the case of a trader, payment in ordinary course is payment of all commercial debts when they are due and payable, and in such a case if a person calls at the debtor's place of business and demands payment, and receives in answer not only a refusal to pay, but a refusal to pay based upon inability to pay, I can well understand it being held that such a declaration of inability would amount to a notice of suspension or intention to suspend, because it is a notice of suspension or intention to suspend payment of debts by such trader in the ordinary way."   Taken by itself the passage, no doubt, affords a basis for the argument that a declaration by a trader of inability to pay his debts, amounts to a notice of suspension within sub-s. 1 (h) ; but on p. 106 the L.J. says : " I am convinced myself that what this clause contemplates is the case of a debtor dealing with his creditors as a body.   If a trader gives notice to any one of his creditors that the state of his finances is such that he cannot pay

(1) 17 N.S.W. B. & P. 34, p. 38.   (2) 3 Man. 102.

all his debts as they become due, and that consequently he proposes to deal with his creditors collectively, that is a case which falls within the clause; but I do not think that any case falls within the clause, whether the case of a trader or private individual, which does not shew that such a state of things has occurred, or is about to occur, as necessarily involves a dealing with his creditors as a body." Here an additional element is supplied to the declaration that the trader cannot pay all his debts as they become due, viz., that consequently he proposes to deal with his creditors collectively. This seems to me exactly in accordance with the law as stated in *Re Pike*. Is there then any statement in this case from which the intention of the debtor as to the future conduct of his business can be gleaned? I think not. There is a clear enough statement of inability to pay Elliott, and a statement that he could not pay the people from whom he was getting the feed and stuff for his horses, and that he could not raise the money to pay Elliott. No doubt, if a trader states that he has no money, and cannot raise any, the inevitable consequence must be stoppage if his creditors press him, but I can find nothing to shew that this alternative was present to Brady's mind, or that he had any intention either as to stopping or not stopping. In all the cases, so far as I am aware, in which the notice has been held to come within sub-s. 1 (h), there have been words from which the intention could be gleaned.

I have assumed, for the purposes of this case, that the debts due to Elliott were ordinary trade debts, but it seems to me extremely doubtful whether the money due for rent can be considered a trade debt, and open to some argument whether the debt for repairs was so. The application must be dismissed. The official assignee is to have his costs out of the estate.

Solicitor for the official assignee: *A. W. McCarthy.*

1898.

Re
BRADY.
Ex parte
OFFICIAL
ASSIGNEE.

A.H.'Simpson J.

1898.
_____
May 29.
A H. Simpson J.

In the Estate of T. MAHER (deceased).

Executor—Accounts—Application for—Want of interest—Laches.

An executor will not be ordered to file accounts on the application of a person who has no interest in the estate.

A testator, who died in 1860, by his will devised and bequeathed certain of his real and personal property to his daughter, but not to her separate use. In 1861 the daughter married ; and in 1898 applied for an order, directing the surviving executor to file accounts. *Held*, that she had no interest in the personal estate, and was not entitled to ask for accounts, and that the Court had no jurisdiction to order the executor to file accounts of the real estate.

THIS was an application by Ellen Kelly, the wife of Myles Kelly, for an order, directing Isaac Gorrick, the only surviving executor of the will of the deceased Thomas Maher, to file accounts in accordance with the provisions of the Charter of Justice. It appeared that the deceased died in August, 1860, that probate of his will was in November, 1860, granted to John Kingsmill, who died in 1869, and Isaac Gorrick.

By the will, one-sixth of the real and personal estate of the deceased was devised and bequeathed to the applicant (but not to her separate use), who married Myles Kelly in 1861.

In 1892, Kelly and his wife filed a bill in equity against Gorrick, asking that the usual administration accounts be taken. This suit was dismissed in 1892 for want of prosecution.

It further appeared that Gorrick had never acted in any way under the probate.

Watt, for applicant.

R. K. Manning, by way of preliminary objection. Under the Charter of Justice an executor was bound to file accounts of the personal estate only of the deceased. As to the real estate he was a trustee, and subject to the jurisdiction of the Equity Court only. On her marriage in 1861 the whole of the applicant's personal estate became the property of her husband, and consequently she has no interest in the estate, and is not entitled to ask for accounts.

Watt, in reply, cited *Sladen* v. *Sawther* (1); *Acaster* v. *Anderson* (2); *Ritchie* v. *Rees* (3).

A. H. SIMPSON, J.   In my opinion this motion must be dismissed.   So far as the real estate is concerned, I have no power to order accounts; and as regards the personalty, that, on the applicant's marriage, passed to her husband, who is not now before the Court; but even if he were, it seems to me there would be difficulties in his way, considering the time that has elapsed. The applicant, having no interest, is not entitled to an account, and I must, therefore, dismiss this motion with costs.

Order accordingly.

Solicitor for the applicant: *Whittel* (West Maitland), by *Gorrick.*
Solicitor for the respondent: *Prentice* (West Maitland), by *R. B. Asher.*

1898.

Re the Estate of
T. MAHER
(Deceased).

(1) 1 Phill. 245.   (2) 1 Rob. 672.
                    (3) 1 Add. 14.

Re MOONEY ;

Ex parte THE OFFICIAL ASSIGNEE ;

HILL, Respondent.

1898.

April 18, 19, *Bankruptcy Act Amendment Act, 1896, ss. 17, 18, sub-s. (e)—Sale by bankrupt—*
27.   *Intent to defeat or delay creditors—Bona fide advance.*

A. H. Simpson J.   " Bona fide " in s. 18, sub-s. (e), of the Bankruptcy Act Amendment Act, 1896,
means in good faith towards the other creditors of the bankrupt. A bankrupt,
with intent to defeat or delay certain of his creditors, sold his property to one of
his creditors in consideration of 153*l.*, of which 52*l.* were a past debt. The purchaser at the time of the transaction knew of, and was a party to the carrying out
of the bankrupt's intention.

   Held, that the transaction was void within the meaning of s. 17 of the Bankruptcy Act Amendment Act, 1896, and that the payment of the 101*l.* was not
bona-fide within the meaning of s. 18, sub-s. (e), of the Bankruptcy Act Amendment Act.

THIS was a motion by the official assignee of the estate of
Patrick Mooney to set aside a sale by the bankrupt to the respondent John Hill. The facts are fully set out in the considered
judgment of *A. H. Simpson,* J.

   Gordon (*R. K. Manning* with him), for the official assignee.
The sale was to the knowledge of the respondent made with
intent to defeat or delay the Oxleys, and is bad under s. 17 of
the Bankruptcy Act Amendment Act and ss. 58 and 4 (1b) of
the Bankruptcy Act. As to the 101*l.* paid by Hill, that is not
protected under s. 18, as it was not paid bona-fide.

   Wise (*Bavin* with him), for the respondent. Whatever the
intention of the bankrupt may have been, the transaction is protected under s. 18, as the respondent acted bona-fide, and without
notice of any act of bankruptcy.

   Gordon in reply.

Cur. adv. vult.

On April 27th,

   A. H. SIMPSON, J.   On the 10th December, 1897, the estate of
P. Mooney was sequestrated. On the 2nd October, Mooney sold
to the respondent Hill substantially the whole of his property in
consideration of a past debt of 52*l.* owing to Hill and a payment

of 101*l.* 13*s.* 8*d.*, making together 153*l.* 13*s.* 8*d.*, which I must take as the fair value of the property.   The law on the subject as laid down by *Manning*, J., in *Re Rogers* (1), is that where there is an actual preference accompanied by an intention on the part of the bankrupt to defeat or delay creditors or any of them, the transaction is an act of bankruptcy, and void, however innocent the other party may be, and that the question of intent is a question of fact.   If the intent is proved, the whole transaction is bad.   It is obvious that this might operate very hardly on an innocent creditor in many cases, and accordingly, by the Amending Act (60 Vic. No. 29), s. 18, which repeals and replaces s. 57 of the original Act, it is provided that nothing in the principal Act shall invalidate " any transaction to the extent of any present advance bona-fide made by any existing creditor."

There is practically no conflict as to the essential facts in this case.   On the 23rd September, 1897, the petitioning creditors, the Oxleys, issued a plaint in the District Court for moneys owing to them by Mooney, and on the 5th October obtained a verdict for 63*l.* 1*s.* 8*d.* and costs.

After the summons was issued, Mooney came to Hill in a great state, and said he did not owe the money, and could not pay ; that he had consulted a lawyer, who advised him a verdict would probably go against him, and he had better go insolvent.   This Mooney objected to do, and it was then arranged Hill should buy substantially all Mooney's property on the terms mentioned above. Mooney told Hill he would not pay the Oxleys' debt as it was an unjust claim, and Hill said he could not bear to see the man crushed.   Hill, in his evidence, says: " When I bought the property, it didn't matter to me about Oxley so long as I got my money."   He also says Mooney told him on Friday, 1st October, he had no defence.   In his deposition Hill says that he pressed for payment of his (Hill's) debt, and that Mooney told him he had not got it ; that Mooney said he did not owe the money to the petitioning creditors, it was an unjust claim, and he would not pay it.   Further on, Hill says: " I bought him out to secure my account; I knew bankrupt had no means to pay his debts, he was not able to pay me; I know now he was practically

1897.

Re

MOONEY.

Ex parte

OFFICIAL

ASSIGNEE.

HILL,

Respondent.

A. H. Simpson J.

(1) 1 B.C. 46.

1898.

Re
MOONEY.
Ex parte
OFFICIAL
ASSIGNEE.
HILL,
Respondent.

A. H. Simpson J.
insolvent at that time; Miles said he was sorry Mooney was pressed; Mooney said 'I would not like to go insolvent, but the solicitor (*Elliott*) wanted him to;' I said it was a bad thing to go insolvent." When he was recalled, Hill said, "I know now that the bankrupt was solvent when I made the purchase; it would be impossible for me to say that he was insolvent, as I did not know what he owed." Later on, he said, "What I meant in saying bankrupt was solvent was that he could pay his way; I do not mean out of his own moneys; he could not pay my debt unless he sold his stock; I knew that bankrupt was in debt when I bought him out; I mean that I supposed he owed some small accounts on the farm." Further on, Hill says that, when Mooney told him of Oxley's summons he pressed him for payment of the amount due to him (Hill) in full, as, seeing he had an action against him, he was anxious to have the account settled.

On this evidence it seems to me clear that Mooney was in insolvent circumstances at the time of the transaction in question, and that he had the intention of defeating or delaying the Oxleys' claim, and that Hill knew of and was a party to carrying out this intention. Under these circumstances the transaction must be set aside. It seems to me bad under the original Act, and the sum of 101*l.* paid to Mooney is not protected by s. 18 (e) of the Amending Act of 1896, as it was not made bona-fide.

It is unnecessary to consider the case of a sale for value accompanied by an intention on the part of the vendor to defeat his creditors, such intention being unknown to the purchaser. In England the sale could not be set aside by the official assignee and I am not aware of any decision in this colony which would lead the Court to set it aside here.

The respondent must pay to the official assignee the sum of 153*l.* 13*s.* 8*d.*, with costs.

Order accordingly.

Solicitor for the official assignee : *Oxley* (Bowral), by *G. E. Russell-Jones.*

Solicitor for the respondent : *Gale* (Moss Vale), by *McDonnell & Moffitt.*

Re KELLY ;   *Ex parte* THE CALEDONIAN COAL CO., LTD.

Bankruptcy Act, ss. 4, sub-ss. 1 (g), 3 ; 8, sub-s. 4—R. 95···Creditors' petition—
Objections to validity of bankruptcy notice.

Rule 95 of the Bankruptcy Rules of 1896, which provides that where the act of
bankruptcy relied on in a creditor's petition is non-compliance with a bankruptcy
notice, no objection to such bankruptcy notice shall be entertained at the hearing
of the petition if such objection could reasonably have been taken before the
expiration of the time specified in the endorsement on the bankruptcy notice for
that purpose is *intra vires.*

1898.

May 12.

A.H. Simpson J.

THIS was a petition for an order sequestrating the estate of the
above-named debtor Kelly.

The act of bankruptcy alleged in the petition was non-compliance with a bankruptcy notice.

No application was made to set aside the bankruptcy notice,
but on a petition being presented an objection was taken that the
judgment, in respect of which the notice had been issued, was not
a "final judgment."

The petition came on to be heard before the Registrar, and
counsel for the petitioning creditors submitted that no objection
could be taken to the validity of the bankruptcy notice, and
referred to R. 95. It was then contended on behalf of the debtor
that the rule was *ultra vires*, whereupon the matter was referred
to the Judge.

Rolin, for the debtor.   The Act makes no provision for setting
aside a bankruptcy notice. A debtor who thinks that a bad
notice has been issued may come in under s. 4, sub-s. 3, but there
is nothing in the Act to limit the time of the debtor. The Judges
have power to make rules for regulating matters under the Act
but as the Act does not limit the time within which objections to
the validity of the bankruptcy notice can be set up, so rules
could not be made regulating the time.

Gordon (*Pickburn* with him), for the petitioning creditors.
This is simply a matter of procedure.

Rolin in reply.

1898.

Re
KELLY.
Ex parte
CALEDONIAN
COAL CO.,
LTD.

A. H. SIMPSON, J. I have had an opportunity of considering this matter during the adjournment, and it seems to me that Rule 95 is not *ultra vires*. That rule is made under s. 119 of the Bankruptcy Act, which gives power to the Judges of the Supreme Court, or a majority of them, to make rules from time to time for the purpose of regulating any matter under the Act, and by that section it is provided that the rules, when made, are to be laid before both Houses of Parliament within a prescribed time.

The validity of rules made under an Act of Parliament was considered by the Privy Council in *Blackwood* v. *London Chartered Bank of Australia* (1), and it was there pointed out (at p. 108) that "security is taken, which is very usual in such cases, but neither usual nor necessary as to mere matters of form, that a copy of every such regulation shall be within a short limited time laid before both Houses of Parliament, that they may be advertised of the manner in which the persons to whom they have delegated this legislative power have exercised it, and if they disapprove of that manner may take the proper steps to interfere." There being this provision in the Bankruptcy Act, the Judges have power to make rules going beyond matters of form and dealing with questions of substance, provided those questions of substance are not going beyond the provisions of the Act.

By s. 4, sub-s. 1 (g), it is provided that a creditor can, under certain circumstances, issue a bankruptcy notice, and, so far as I know there is no actual provision in the Act expressly authorising a debtor to apply to set aside the notice, but such a provision, one would think, was not necessary.

Sect. 4, sub-s. 3, provides that "upon the debtor satisfying the Judge that such notice ought not to have been issued, the Judge may order the payment to him by the creditor applying for such notice of all the costs occasioned by the issue thereof," and this, I take it, clearly gives the Judge power to set the bankruptcy notice aside. Under the old rules a debtor could set up on the hearing of a petition for the sequestration of his estate any defence of which he gave notice under the old Rule 61, and

(1) L.R. 5 P.C. 92.

could, by simply disputing the allegation as to the act of bank- 1898.
ruptcy, set up any objection he wished to the validity of the *Re*
KELLY.
bankruptcy notice on which the petition was founded.

A.H. Simpson J.
Rule 95 of the Rules of 1896, no doubt, goes further than the
old Rule 61, and prevents him from setting up any defence to the
petition, unless he files a written notice of his objections, stating
specifically the grounds of defence relied on, and it is then provided that where the act of bankruptcy relied upon is non-compliance with a bankruptcy notice, no objection to such bankruptcy
notice shall be entertained at the hearing of the creditors' petition,
if such objection could reasonably have been taken before the
expiration of the time specified in the endorsement on the bankruptcy notice for that purpose; the rule says, in effect, that a
debtor shall not rely on a defence to the petition if he could have
relied on it as a substantive ground for setting aside the bankruptcy notice.

Is not that a question of procedure only, and is it not analogous
to the rule which prevents the Statute of Frauds being set up as
an answer to a bill in equity, unless it is specially pleaded in the
statement of defence ? see *Kennedy* v. *Currie* (1).   It is not inconsistent with but supplementing the Act.

For these reasons, I am of opinion that the rule is *intra vires*,
and remit the matter to the Registrar.

Order accordingly.

Solicitor for the petitioning creditor : *C. Bull.*
Solicitors for the debtor: *White & Wolstenholme.*

(1) 17 N.S.W. L.R. Eq. 28.

1898.

May 30.
June 8.

A.H. Simpson J.

In the Estate of DAVIS (deceased).

Probate Act, 1890 (54 *Vic. No.* 25), *ss.* 15, 19, 32, 34, 39—*Amendment Act*, 1893 (56 *Vic. No.* 30), *ss.* 20, 23—*Probate—Death of executor—Administration of the estate not administered, with will annexed—Title to real estate.*

On the death of an executor intestate who had partially administered his testator's estate, administration with the will annexed of the estate not administered was granted to the testator's widow. The estate unadministered consisted almost entirely of real estate. The Court refused under the circumstances on the application of the personal representative of the executor to set aside the administration with the will annexed of the estate not administered, notwithstanding that the real estate was vested in the personal representative of the executor.

THIS was an application under s. 30 of the Probate Act, by Rhoda Julia Kenyon, the administratrix of the estate of William Kenyon, deceased, for an order revoking the administration, with the will annexed, of the estate remaining unadministered of one Thomas Davis, deceased, granted to his widow Agnes Davis, now Agnes Bridge, and for an order, if necessary, granting administration with the will annexed of the personal estate, if any, not administered of the said William Davis.

It appeared from the affidavits filed that Thomas Davis died on December 11th, 1895, testate, and by his will William Kenyon and Joseph Millard were appointed executors of his will, and the testator's property, after payment of his debts, and subject to an annuity of £60 to be paid to his widow during widowhood, was left to the testator's two infant children.

Probate of the will was granted to William Kenyon, who subsequently died on September 18th, 1897, intestate. On the 29th November, 1897, administration of Kenyon's estate was granted to the present applicant, and on the same day administration of Davis' estate left unadministered with the will annexed was granted to his widow, who married on the following day one John Bridge.

The estate consisted almost entirely of rent-producing land; the personal estate was of little value. Mrs. Bridge had called on the tenants of the real estate to pay the rents to her, and had threatened to distrain for the same.

R. K. Manning, for the applicant.   Under s. 15 of the Probate

1898.

Act the real and personal estate of William Davis vested in his *In the estate of*
executor Kenyon, who, by s. 19, held such real estate according DAVIS
to the trusts and dispositions of the will. (Deceased.)

On his death intestate, and on the grant of administration to *A. U. Simpson J.*
the applicant, the real estate of Davis vested in the present applicant under s. 34, and she thereupon became trustee of these
lands.   The Court had no jurisdiction to grant to the respondent
administration of the real estate, which is already vested in the
applicant.   Sect. 34 is taken from s. 30 of the Conveyancing Act
(44 & 45 Vic. c. 41).   He referred to *Lewin on Trusts*, Ed. IX.,
pp. 233, 245 § 21, 534 § 34, and Probate Act, s. 32.

As to the personal estate, I submit that, in order to prevent
confusion and expense arising from having one person adminis-
tering the real estate and another person the personal estate,
administration with the will annexed should be granted to the
applicant.

Conroy, for the respondent, referred to the Probate Act
Amendment Act, ss. 20, 23.

Manning in reply.

Cur. adv. vult.

On June 1,

June 1.

A. H. SIMPSON, J.   This is an application to revoke adminis-
tration *cum testamento annexo de bonis non* of the estate of
Thomas Davis, and for grant of similar administration to Mrs.
Kenyon.

Thomas Davis died 11th December, 1895; and by his will
dated the 9th December, 1895, he appointed one William Kenyon
and another his executors, and subject to an annuity to be paid
to his widow during life or widowhood, he gave the whole of his
property, real and personal, to his two infant children.

Probate was granted to William Kenyon on 20th February,
1896, the other executor having renounced.   On the 18th
September, 1897, W. Kenyon died intestate, and on 29th
November, 1897, administration of his estate was granted to Mrs.
Kenyon, his widow.   On the same day administration *cum testa-
mento annexo de bonis non* of the estate of T. Davis was granted

1898.

In the estate of
DAVIS
(Deceased).

A. H. Simpson J.

to his widow, Mrs. Davis, now Mrs. Bridge, during the minority of her children. On the following day she married John Bridge. It is stated in the affidavit of Mrs. Kenyon that all the debts and funeral and testamentary expenses of T. Davis have been paid, except three instalments of 18*l.* each of purchase money for some land bought by the testator; and that the estate consists almost entirely of land, the personalty being valued at nothing. To this Mrs. Bridge replies that there is some furniture valued at 8*l.* to 10*l.*, a horse, and a sum of 3*l.* 3*s.* 8*d.* standing to the credit of W. Kenyon, as executor. It appears, therefore, that there is a small portion of the personal estate still unadministered. On her marriage, Mrs. Bridge ceased to have any interest in the estate of Thomas Davis, except that there was due to her the sum of 23*l.* for her annuity up to her marriage.

The Probate Act, 1890, provides that on the grant of probate the real estate of a deceased person, whether held beneficially or in trust, shall vest in his executor (s. 15), that in case of intestacy the real estate shall vest in the administrator, and in the case of partial intestacy in the executor or administrator, with the will annexed (s. 32). The Act omits to provide for the case of a will dealing with land, but appointing no executor, or the executor failing to take out probate. The Amending Act of 1893, in my opinion, supplies this defect above-mentioned in cases of death, after the commencement of that Act. Sect. 23 provides that from the death of any person dying testate, and until probate or administration *cum testamento annexo* is granted the real and personal estate is to vest as provided in s. 39 of the Probate Act, 1890, that is, in *The Chief Justice*. Sect. 20 provides as follows :—" When any real estate, not under the provisions of the Real Property Act is devised to any person by a will duly proved under the provisions of the Probate Act of 1890, the executor of the will or the administrator with the will annexed may, as such executor or administrator, instead of executing a conveyance, sign an acknowledgment in a form to be prescribed by rule of the Supreme Court hereby authorised to be made in that behalf, that the devisee is entitled to such real estate for the estate for which the same is devised to him, which acknowledgment may be registered under the Acts in force regulating the registration of deeds ; and upon registration of such acknowledgment as aforesaid such real estate shall vest in the devisee for such estate as aforesaid in the same way and subject to the same trusts and liabilities as if the executor or administrator had executed a conveyance of the same." This distinctly implies that land as to which a person dies testate vests in his administrator, with the will annexed, and on such administrator signing and registering an acknowledgment that such land, if not under the Real Property Act, vests in the devisee.   The implication, in my opinion, applies to land under the Real Property Act, as well as under the old system, though the acknowledgment can only be used for the latter.   The object of the Legislature clearly was to vest the real estate, as well as personal estate, of a deceased person in his executor or adminis-trator, with full powers of dealing with the real estate.   The Acts, however, do not provide for carrying out that intention in such a case as the present, where an executor is appointed and afterwards dies.   There is nothing, apparently, in such a case to prevent the operation of s. 34 of the Principal Act, by which the land held by W. Kenyon, as executor of T. Davis, would pass to Kenyon's administratrix.   The legal estate, therefore, in such land is, in my opinion, vested in Mrs. Kenyon, but such legal estate gives her no right to call for administration of Davis' estate.   The persons entitled to such administration are the persons who, under his will, are beneficially interested, that is, his two children ; but as they are infants of tender years, I think the proper person to be appointed during their minority is their mother.   It is true such appointment will not divest Mrs. Kenyon of the legal estate vested in her, but this defect is easily cured, either by Mrs. Kenyon executing a conveyance, or by Mrs. Bridge applying to the Court of Equity for a vesting order.

No suggestion has been made that Mrs. Bridge is not a fit and proper person to be appointed, and I must, therefore, dismiss the application with costs.

Order accordingly.

Proctor for the applicant : *Dickey* (Lismore), by *Gray*.

Proctor for the respondent : *Shorter* (Lismore), by *Poole*.

1898.

In the estate of
DAVIS
(Deceased.)

A. H. Simpson J.

Re NEVILE (deceased),

Ex parte THE OFFICIAL ASSIGNEE,

GARDINER AND ANOTHER, Respondents.

1898.

June 15.

A.H. Simpson J.

Bankruptcy—Policy of assurance—Waiver of protection by charge—Words creating charge—Parties — Trustees—Beneficiaries—Equity Act, 1880 (44 *Vic.* No.* 18), *s.* 7.

A protected policy loses its protection by an express charge for payment of debts, and such a charge is created by words in the will, "after payment of all my just debts, &c.," followed by a gift including the proceeds of the policy.

The question whether the beneficiaries, as well as the trustees, are proper parties to a suit concerning property vested in trustees under a will or settlement, is a matter entirely in the discretion of the Court: *Merry* v. *Pownall* (1) is not an authority to the contrary.

THIS was a motion on behalf of the official assignee to recover the sum of 188*l.* 3*s.* 10*d.*, being the net proceeds of a certain policy of assurance, coming within the statutory protection against liability for debts, which sum had been received by the respondents, and was still held by them. It appeared that the deceased died on June 16th, 1895, leaving a will, which was proved by the respondents, as executors, on September 12th, 1895; on February 8th, 1896, the executors voluntarily sequestrated the estate of the testator.

The will appointed the respondents executors and trustees, and continued in the following terms:—

"After payment of all my just debts funeral and testamentary expenses I bequeath and devise all my real and personal estate whatsoever and wheresoever situate unto my son . . . subject to the payment of the sum of one pound per week to . . . my mother during her life."

Mocatta, for the respondents, submitted whether the beneficiaries should not be joined as parties, and referred to *Re Worth* (2).

Gordon, for the official assignee, submitted that the beneficiaries were unnecessary parties, as the trustees were there as fighting

(1) [1898] 1 Ch. 306.   (2) 1 B.C. 68.

respondents ; and that it was unfair, in the event of the official assignee succeeding, that the trustees should be allowed costs of a fighting brief out of the fund, the beneficiaries being also parties ; he referred to *Merry* v. *Pownall* (1).

A. H. SIMPSON, J.   The matter is one entirely in the discretion of the Court, and I do not think that *Merry* v. *Pownall* (1) decides otherwise.   As the evidence is on affidavit, I will hear the affidavits, and shall then be in a position to see what course I will take as to adding parties or otherwise.

Gordon.   The statutory protection of a policy can be waived by the testator ; that has been done here by an express charge on the real and personal estate of the testator, which includes the policy ; *Re Adams* (2) ; *In the Will of Kesterton* (3).

[A. H. SIMPSON, J., referred to *Withers* v. *Kennedy* (4) and *Jarman on Wills* (5th Ed., p. 1390, *et seq.*, and cases there cited.)]

Mocatta.   There must be clear and distinct words to charge the policy.   In *Re Adams* (2) it was held that a mere direction to pay debts was not sufficient to create a charge, and the words "after payment of all my debts" carry the case no further. There is no express charge of the particular property.

Gordon was not called upon in reply.

A. H. SIMPSON, J.   I think this case is amply covered by authority.   It has been held over and over again that words in a will such as "after the payment of all my debts," "subject to the payment of my debts," create a charge on the property passing under the will, and I can only avoid holding that the proceeds of this policy are charged with payment of debts, by holding that the testator died intestate as to those proceeds ; that, however, is impossible in the case of a will by which the testator devises and bequeaths all his "real and personal estate whatsoever and wheresoever."

(1) [1898] 1 Ch. 306.	(3) 17 N.S.W. L.R. (Bky. & P.)
(2) 15 N.S.W. L.R. (Bky. & P.)	31 ; 6 B.C. 82.
135 ; 5 B.C. 38.	(4) 2 My. & K. 607.

1898.

Re
NEVILE
(Deceased.)
Ex parte
OFFICIAL
ASSIGNEE.
GARDINER
& ANOTHER,
Respondents.

1898.

Re
NEVILE
(Deceased.)

Ex parte
OFFICIAL
ASSIGNEE.

GARDINER
& ANOTHER,
Respondents.

A.H. Simpson J.

I must hold, therefore, that the policy moneys are expressly charged with payment of debts, and that the official assignee is entitled to them.

I order payment of the proceeds of the policy to the official assignee, the respondents, however, by consent, retaining 15 guineas in respect of their costs. The official assignee will have his costs as between solicitor and client out of the estate. Notice of this order must, under s. 7, Rule 6, of the Equity Act, be served on the beneficiaries, and may be served on the beneficiary who is out of the jurisdiction by registered letter. In serving both the beneficiaries, it should be pointed out to them that, as the order has been made in their absence, they are to be at liberty to apply to set the order aside if they so elect, but, of course, at their own risk as to costs.

Order accordingly.

Solicitors for the official assignee: *Allen, Allen, & Hemsley.*

Solicitor for the respondents: *Salenger* (Bourke), by *S. J. Bull.*

Re BRIERLEY ; *Ex parte* THE OFFICIAL ASSIGNEE.

Bankruptcy Act Amendment Act, 1896 (60 *Vic. No.* 29), *s.* 10—*Indemnifying creditors—Advantage over others.*

1898.
May 19.

A. H. Simpson J.

The Judge has power under s. 10 of the Bankruptcy Act Amendment Act, 1896, to order that the whole amount recovered by an official assignee be distributed amongst the creditors who have indemnified the official assignee against the costs of the litigation whereby the assets were recovered.

THIS was an application by the official assignee of the estate of the above-named bankrupt to approve a proposed scheme of distribution, whereby it was proposed to distribute the whole of the assets recovered by the official assignee in a motion under s. 130, amongst the creditors who had indemnified the official assignee against the costs of the litigation.

The amount recovered was 182*l.* 3*s.*, and was the only asset in the estate, and after payment of all the expenses in the bankruptcy there remained the sum of about 60*l.* available for distribution. The debts proved against the estate amounted to 323*l.* 9*s.* 2*d.*, of which 156*l.* 6*s.* 6*d.* were due to the indemnifying creditors. If the motion under s. 130 had been dismissed with costs, it appeared that the indemnifying creditors would have been liable to pay about 184*l.*, and if without costs the liability would have amounted to about 92*l.*,—the official assignee's costs of the motion.

The Official Assignee in person.

Kemp, for Brierley, a proved creditor, to oppose. The Court has no power to distribute the whole amount recovered amongst the indemnifying creditors. In any event, under the circumstances of this case, no such order will be made.

A. H. SIMPSON, J., held that he had power to distribute the whole amount recovered amongst the indemnifying creditors, and approved of the scheme.

Order accordingly.

Solicitor for Brierley : *Baker.*

Re KERLE, *Ex parte* SIMPSON.

1898.   *Bankruptcy Act*, 1887 (51 *Vic. No.* 19), *s.* 6, *sub-s.* (d)—*Creditor's Petition—*
May 26.   *Domicil—Proof of Judgment.*

A.H. Simpson J.   A creditor's petition was presented against the debtor resident at Perth, West
Australia, and described in the petition as "late of Sydney, but at present of
Perth." The alleged act of bankruptcy was non-compliance with a bankruptcy
notice served on the debtor's attorney here, W., under an order granting leave to
effect service out of the jurisdiction and substituted service on W. Certain
objections to the making of the sequestration order were taken on the hearing of
the petition, but no objection was taken that the Court had no power to order
service of the bankruptcy notice out of the jurisdiction. *Held*, on appeal (affirming the decision of *Henry*, R.), that in the absence of evidence to the contrary
there was, from the statutory affidavit verifying the petition and the order
granting leave to serve the bankruptcy notice out of the jurisdiction, sufficient
evidence of domicil in New South Wales, and that the order sequestrating the
estate of the debtor was rightly made.

THIS was an appeal against the decision of *Henry*, R., sequestrating the estate of one Walter Kerle. The petition described
Kerle as "late of Sydney, but at present of Perth," and alleged
as the act of bankruptcy relied on, that "the debtor has failed to
comply with the requirements of a bankruptcy notice duly served
on him on the 25th March last, in compliance with an order for
service made herein on the same day."

The debtor filed certain objections to the making of the order,
but did not object that the Court had no jurisdiction to make the
order in that the debtor was not domiciled in New South Wales.
The Registrar refused to allow evidence as to domicil to be given
by the debtor unless the objections were amended, and this not
being done, an order was made sequestrating the estate. The
bankruptcy notice had been served on Mr. White, of Messrs.
White & Wolstenholme, under an order granting leave to serve
the bankruptcy notice out of the jurisdiction, and substituted
service on Mr. White.

The further facts appear from the judgment.

Rolin, for the appellants. In the face of the decision in *Re
Kelly* (1), I cannot now argue that the bankruptcy notice was

(1) *Ante*, p. 15.

invalid. Apart from the rules, a creditor is not entitled to present a petition unless the requirements of the Act are complied with. Here it was not even alleged in the petition that Kerle was domiciled in Sydney. The description "late of Sydney" does not shew domicil in Sydney any more than "at present of Perth" shews a present domicil in West Australia, and further it does not appear that he was domiciled in New South Wales within a year.

There was no evidence of a judgment having been recovered. A certificate is not evidence. The proper evidence is the judgment roll or a certified copy under 13 Vic. No. 16, s. 1.

Gordon (*R. K. Manning* with him), for the petitioning creditor. There was sufficient evidence of domicil. If Kerle was not domiciled here, the bankruptcy notice could not have been served out of the jurisdiction.   Kerle did not move to set aside the bankruptcy notice or the order granting leave to serve out of jurisdiction. He cited *Ex parte Blain, In re Sawers* (1) and *In re Pearson* (2).

It was unnecessary to put in the certificate or a certified copy of the judgment, for the debt has been proved by the affidavit and oral evidence of the petitioning creditor, and further, the bankruptcy notice which was put in evidence shews that a judgment for the amount named in the petition was recovered, and as the bankruptcy notice was not set aside the debtor must be taken to have admitted that a judgment for that amount was recovered.

Rolin in reply.

A. H. SIMPSON, J. This is an appeal from an order of the Registrar, sequestrating the estate of Walter Kerle. It appears that Kerle is now resident at Perth, Western Australia, and is described in the petition as "late of Sydney." A judgment was obtained against him by the petitioning creditor on September 27th, 1897, for 91*l.* 16*s.* 9*d.*, which includes costs. On March 25th last, the judgment creditor filed a request for leave to issue and serve a bankruptcy notice for the amount of the judgment, and by an order made on the same day leave was given to effect

(1) 12 Ch. D. 522.   (2) [1892] 2 Q.B. 263.

service of the bankruptcy notice out of the jurisdiction, and substituted service on White was granted.

No application was made to set aside the bankruptcy notice, and on the 6th of April a petition was presented to which notice of objections was filed, stating that the debtor "intends to dispute the truth of the statements contained in paragraphs two, three and four of the petition filed herein, also to deny the petitioning creditor's debt, the act of bankruptcy alleged in the said petition and the service of the bankruptcy notice referred to in paragraph four of the said petition," or in other words, that he disputed that he was indebted to the petitioning creditor in the aggregate sum of 91*l*. 16*s*. 9*d*.; that the creditor held no security, and that the debtor had failed to comply with the requirements of a bankruptcy notice duly served on him on the 25th March last in compliance with an order for service made herein on the same day. At the hearing before the Registrar, objection was taken on behalf of Kerle that the Court had no jurisdiction to make the order, inasmuch as Kerle was not domiciled in New South Wales. The Registrar declined to consider the objection unless the notice of objections was amended, which Kerle refused to do.

To give the Court jurisdiction to make a sequestration order, either the debtor must have been domiciled here when an act of bankruptcy was committed, or must have committed an act of bankruptcy within the colony, for, as was pointed out in *Ex parte Blain, In re Sawers* (1), some restriction must be put on the word "debtor" in the beginning of s. 4, and the word must be limited to debtors subject to the jurisdiction of our Courts, namely, English subjects or foreigners who, by coming into the country, whether for a long or short time, have made themselves during that time subject to English jurisdiction.

Then s. 6 adds further requirements, and says that a creditor shall not be entitled to present a petition unless *inter alia* "the debtor is domiciled in New South Wales, or within a year before the date of the presentation of the petition has ordinarily resided, or had a dwelling-house or place of business in New South Wales;" in other words, that in the case of a foreigner who has committed

(1) 12 Ch. D. 522.

an act of bankruptcy within the jurisdiction, a petition may not
be presented against him unless he, within a year before the date
of the presentation of the petition, has ordinarily resided or had
a dwelling-house or place of business in this colony.

1898.

Re
KERLE;
Ex parte
SIMPSON.

A.H. Simpson J.

[See *Ex parte Blain, In re Sawers* (1) and *In re Pearson, Ex
parte Pearson* (2).]

In this case, as Kerle was out of the jurisdiction of the Court
when the bankruptcy notice was served, non-compliance with it
was not an act of bankruptcy within the jurisdiction, and it
follows that the Court would have jurisdiction to make the order
only in the case of his being domiciled here, and I, therefore, have
to consider what evidence there is here of domicil.

The petition speaks of Kerle as being "late of Sydney, but at
present of Perth," and although this is slight evidence of domicil
in Sydney, I think, in the absence of evidence to the contrary, it
was enough to turn the scale, and further, unless the debtor was
domiciled in New South Wales the Registrar ought not to have
allowed service of the bankruptcy notice out of the jurisdiction.
No doubt the order was made *ex parte*, but the debtor might
have moved to set it aside, and as he has not done so there is, I
think, in the absence of any evidence the other way, sufficient
evidence of domicil. In *Ex parte Barne, In re Barne* (3), the
Court of Appeal held that on the hearing of a petition the creditor
was not bound to go to the Court armed with a quantity of evidence of domicil unless he had reason to suppose the domicil would
be disputed. *Lindley, L.J*, on p. 525, says: "The burden of
proving the domicil of the debtor is on the petitioning creditor if
there is any dispute about it. No one expects that the petitioning
creditor should go into Court armed with evidence of the debtor's
domicil when there is no reason for supposing that his English
domicil will be disputed. If it is disputed, the burden of proof
is on the petitioning creditor."

For these reasons I think there was sufficient evidence of domicil,
and that, as the debtor declined to amend his notice of objections,
he is now precluded from setting up that he was not domiciled
here, but at the same time, I think that if the objection to the

(1) 12 Ch. D. 522.   (2) [1892] 2 Q.B. 263.
         (3) 16 Q.B.D. 522.

jurisdiction clearly appeared on the face of the petition, he could have taken the objection notwithstanding he had not taken it in his notice of objections.

With regard to the objection that there was no proof of the judgment in that a certificate that judgment had been recovered was not evidence, I think that, strictly speaking, this objection is well founded; but to this there appear to be three answers—(1) that in the objections it is not specifically stated that judgment had not been recovered for 91*l*. 16*s*. 9*d*.; (2) that the debt is proved by the oral evidence and affidavit of the petitioning creditor; and (3) that, if this were a defect, I should certainly allow the papers to be sent for in order to see whether there was a real debt, and would not set aside the order by reason of any such informality in the proof.

The appeal must, therefore, be dismissed, the costs of the petitioning creditor to be costs of his petition.

Order accordingly.

Solicitors for the appellant : *White & Wolstenholme.*

Solicitor for the respondent : *R. G. C. Roberts.*

Re TAYLOR ; *Ex parte* TAYLOR.

Bankruptcy Act, 1889 (51 *Vic. No.* 19), *s.* 43—*Annulment of sequestration order
—Payment in full.*

Payment in full in s. 43 of the Bankruptcy Act means payment of twenty shilling in the *l.*

Re Gale, Ex parte Gale (1), not followed.

1898.
_____
June 2, 28,

C.J Eq.

THIS was an application by the above-named bankrupt for an order annulling the sequestration order made on September 20th, 1897. The debts had not been paid in full, but the bankrupt had obtained a legal acquittance of the debts due by him to his creditors.

Stinson (solicitor), for the bankrupt.

Cowper (*Stephen, Jaques & Stephen*), for the A.J.S. Bank, Ltd., proved creditor, to assent.

Palmer (official assignee).   Payment in full in s. 43 means payment of 20s. in the *l.* In s. 35 a distinction is drawn between payment in full and obtaining a legal acquittance of debts.

He cited *In re Gyll* (2); *In re Leslie, Ex parte Leslie* (3); *In re Hester, Ex parte Hester* (4); *In re Burnell* (5).

Cur. adv. vult.

June 28th.   *June* 28.

MANNING, C.J. in Eq.   The bankrupt was so adjudicated on 20th Sept., 1897, on the petition of the A.J.S. Bank, Ltd., which subsequently proved in the estate for the sum of 1,646*l.* 6*s.* 11*d.* There was only one other creditor, for an amount of 15*l.*

Early in the year 1898, proceedings were taken in Queensland against the wife of the bankrupt, and while these were pending the said bankrupt entered into an agreement, whereby the bankrupt's wife was to pay into the hands of a third party the sum

(1) 17 N.S.W.L.R. B. & P. 18.   (3) 4 Mor. 75.
(2) 5 Mor. 272.   (4) 6 Mor. 85.
                        (5) 1 Man. 89.

of 800*l.*, of which 500*l.* was to be paid to the said bank at once, and the balance, if the bankrupt obtained an annulment of his bankruptcy, or the release of his estate, or if he did not proceed promptly to make application therefor. In consequence, the bank covenanted not to sue the bankrupt or his guarantor for the debt owing to them, and agreed that both might plead the deed of agreement in bar of any action. The other creditor was paid in full by the bankrupt's wife.

This was an application under s. 43 of the Bankruptcy Act, for an order annulling the adjudication, both creditors consenting, and as there was no question of commercial morality arising, the bankrupt claimed his right to an order in pursuance of a decision of mine in the case of *In re Gale* (1).

The official assignee, however, opposed the application, on the ground that the section required " payment in full," and that the Court could not, or would not, make the order upon any payment short of 20*s.* in the *l.*

If *In re Gale* (1) was rightly decided, the applicant must succeed ; but in that case I expressly reserved the right of reconsideration if the question was ever raised in a contested matter.

Now, having heard Mr. *Palmer's* very clear and concise argument contra, and having carefully examined this case, I am satisfied that my decision was wrong, and that an order cannot, or will not, be made, except on proof of payment by the bankrupt, or of some person on his behalf, of 20*s.* in the *l.* to his creditors.

I say cannot be made, out of deference to the opinion of that eminent Bankruptcy Judge, *Cave*, J., expressed in *In re Gyll* (2), that the Act of 1883 was a code of the bankruptcy laws, and that the general power of the Court to rescind, alter, or vary any of its decisions was curtailed as to annulment by the provisions of s. 35.

If, however, there be any doubt on this point, it is clear that the Court will look to this section, and act on it, and will not, therefore, exercise its general power.

(1) 17 N.S.W. L.R. Bcy. 18 ; 6 B.C. 42.   (2) 5 Mor. 272.

Before considering this case, I would point out there are four courses open to a man who wants to get clear of the Bankruptcy Court :

(1) He can apply under s. 43 for an order annulling the adjudication, on the ground that it ought not to have been made; or, on the ground that his creditors have been paid in full.

If he succeeds he goes scot free, and is as though he had never been in the Court at all ; and consequently, this order will never be made if any question of commercial morality is likely to arise. That is really all that was decided in *In re Gyll*, though *Cave*, J., several times expressed his opinion, incidentally, that there was no jurisdiction in the case to make the order.

(2) He may adopt the cumbrous method of obtaining the acceptance and approval of a scheme of composition, and then apply for a release under s. 34.

This is altered by the English s. 15, except that power is there given to annul instead of release.

(3) He may apply under s. 35 for a release on payment in full of all his creditors, or on his obtaining a legal acquittance of the debts due.

This useful section has no equivalent in the English Act. Whether the release be granted under s. 34 or 35, there would be no enquiry as to " commercial morality," because the bankrupt is not absolutely free of the Court till he has obtained his certificate of discharge, or an equivalent order, that the release shall so operate, and all such questions would arise on such application for the certificate.

(4) He may apply for a certificate of discharge in the ordinary way.

It will be seen that annulment under s. 43 is the highest form of relief open to a bankrupt, and it is easy to understand that the Legislature intended to reserve that for very exceptional cases.

Observe also, that though the words " pay in full " occur in s. 35, the bankrupt has the alternative to " obtain a legal acquittance of the debts due," and it would have been very easy to have added that alternative in s. 43 had it been thought right that that section should be applied in any case short of payment of 20*s*. in the *l*.

Reading the Act itself, without authority, I should be inclined to hold that what was intended was, that the power of annulment should be confined to cases where the order ought never to have been made, or where such a state of things existed between the bankrupt and his creditors as would have prevented the order for sequestration being made had they existed at the time, *i.e.,* that the bankrupt, or someone on his behalf, had paid his creditors in full, or in other words, 20*s*.in the *l*.

Such, indeed, was my view on a cursory consideration of the Act when I dealt with *Re Gale,* but the mistake I made was in thinking that *Levita's Case* (1) was an authority that the Court of Appeal had treated something short of payment in full, coupled with the consent of creditors, as an equivalent for payment in full; or that the Court would order an annulment on such grounds.

In that case, McHenry was adjudicated bankrupt in 1886, and the application was made in 1890, from which it would seem that the proceeding was under the Act of 1883; but, as a matter of fact, the adjudication was made under the Act of 1869, which contained no such section as the one under consideration; and it is, therefore, fully explained why *Re Gyll* was not cited.

Levita's Case (1), then, is valueless as an authority; but I go further, and I am clear that upon the cases cited by Mr. *Palmer,* it has been absolutely decided that to come within the section there must be payment in full.

In *Re Gyll,* the Court did not, in fact, decide that there was no jurisdiction to make the order; indeed, Lord *Coleridge,* C.J., expressly reserves his opinion on that point, the reason being that the Court was satisfied that, jurisdiction or no jurisdiction, no Court would annul a bankruptcy under such circumstances; but a close consideration of the case shews that the outstanding question of jurisdiction rested solely on the general power of the

(1) [1894] 1 Ch. 365.

Court, and not on the construction of s. 35 of the Act, and *Cave*, J., no less than three times expressed his opinion that there was no such jurisdiction.

The case of *Re Burnett* (1) puts the matter beyond doubt.

In that case debts were proved in Burnett's estate to the extent of 1,600*l.* A friend, Watson, bought all these debts up for 140*l.*, with the intention of assigning them back to the bankrupt. As they were advised that this would not enable Burnett to get an annulment, another friend paid 1,600*l.* on behalf of Burnett to Watson, who then, at the purchaser's request, re-assigned the debts to the bankrupt, and he therefore applied for an order of annulment.

During the course of the argument, *Wright*, J., asked the question : " If a bankrupt gets a release on payment of 10*s.* in the *l*, or ultimate payment in full "? And *Vaughan-Williams*, J., in his judgment, holds, first, that no order can be made except under s. 35 ; and after stating that this payment need not be necessary to the original creditor, he proceeds, "There yet remains the question, had or had not the debts been paid in full," and after stating the facts, he says, "It is to me perfectly obvious that the whole of these payments were made in the interests of, and on account of the bankrupt, and if we were to allow this adjudication to be annulled, the bankrupt would be really getting rid of his bankruptcy on the terms of paying a small composition to each of his creditors. In my opinion s. 35 has no application to such a case, and it is not pretended here that the order for annulment can be supported under any other section or any other principle of law."

And *Wright*, J., says, "There is no proof that the creditors have been paid anything in point of fact, and I very much doubt whether they have all been paid in full in law. When the original creditors were paid by Watson they were certainly not paid in full."

That seems to me to be a clear authority that with regard to applications under s. 35 of the English Act (the 43rd of our Act),

(1) Manson 89.

1898.

Re
TAYLOR ;
Ex parte
TAYLOR.

Manning J.

Re
TAYLOR ;
Ex parte
TAYLOR.

Manning J.

nothing short of a bona fide payment in full of 20*s*. in the *l*. will avail the applicant.

On the construction of our Act, and upon authority also, I think that this application must be dismissed, but under the circumstances, I think, without costs, and if Mr. *Palmer* has incurred any costs he must charge them against the estate.

Order accordingly.

Solicitors for the A J.S. Bank : *Stephen, Jaques & Stephen.*

Re HAYES;

Ex parte THE OFFICIAL ASSIGNEE;

HAYES AND ANOTHER, RESPONDENTS.

1898.

―――

Sept. 22, 23.

Walker J.

Bankruptcy Acts Amendment Act, 1896 (60 *Vic. No.* 29), *s.* 7—*Sequestration of estate of undischarged bankrupt—Right of second official assignee to impeach transaction by bankrupt—Property—Trustee—Costs.*

An undischarged bankrupt acquired assets, and voluntarily assigned them to his wife. His estate was shortly afterwards again sequestrated. *Held*, that the official assignee in the second bankruptcy was entitled to recover the assets so assigned.

A trustee of money claimed by two other persons was not allowed his costs of proceedings taken to recover the money, notwithstanding that he had entered an appearance submitting, where the trustee unduly assisted one of the persons claiming the money.

THIS was a motion by the official assignee of the estate of the above-named bankrupt, claiming as against one of the respondents, Mrs. Hayes, certain moneys voluntarily assigned by the bankrupt to her, and held by the respondent Adams as trustee.

The circumstances of the case appear fully from the judgment of *Walker*, J.

By s. 7 of the Bankruptcy Act Amendment Act of 1896, "s. 10, sub-s (1), of the Principal Act is hereby repealed, and in lieu thereof it is enacted that upon the making of a sequestration order, the property of the bankrupt shall vest in one of the official assignees, to be made in such order, and be divided among the creditors of the bankrupt, in accordance with the provisions of the Principal Act, and any Act amending the same. Upon the making of an order for the sequestration of the estate of an undischarged bankrupt or insolvent, the property of such bankrupt or insolvent possessed by him at the date of the second order of sequestration, shall, if the official assignee or trustee appointed under such prior order has not intervened, vest in the official assignee named in the subsequent order, and be divisible in the first instance among the creditors of the bankrupt in the subsequent bankruptcy."

Gordon (*R. K. Manning* with him), for the official assignee, referred to s. 7 of the Bankruptcy Act Amendment Act, 1896, and cited *In re Farnham* (1).

(1) [1895] 2 Ch. 799.

1898.

Re
HAYES ;
Ex parte
OFFICIAL
ASSIGNEE;
HAYES AND
ANOTHER,
Respondents.

Wise (*Kemp* with him), for Mrs. Hayes. The only person who can impeach the transaction is the first official assignee. The bankrupt was not "possessed" of the moneys claimed at the date of the second order of sequestration. He cited *Re Clarke, Ex parte Beardmore* (1).

Bavin, for Adams.

WALKER, J. I do not want to hear you, Mr. *Gordon*. The bankrupt, John Edwin Hayes, became bankrupt in 1894, and Mr. Palmer was appointed the official assignee in that bankruptcy. The bankrupt has never obtained his certificate in that bankruptcy. He became bankrupt again by a sequestration order on the 2nd June last, and in that bankruptcy Mr. Lloyd is his official assignee. His assets are nil, and his proved debts, if I remember right, amount to something over 300*l.*, there being other proofs of debt in abeyance pending investigation. Mr. Lloyd now moves the Court to set aside what he alleges to have been a disposition by the bankrupt of certain assets amounting to 333*l.* on the 31st March, 1898, and he makes that motion on various grounds, to which it is unnecessary for me to refer, because it was admitted by Mr. *Wise*, who appears as counsel for Mrs. Hayes, that if I find that the money in question ever belonged to the bankrupt, it belongs either to Mr. Palmer, the official assignee in the first bankruptcy, or to Mr. Lloyd, the official assignee in the second bankruptcy. That being so, I have only two points to consider. The first is an issue of fact, as to whether this money was ever the property of the bankrupt; and if I find that it was his property, then I must consider whether or not the present application is defeated by reason of the prior bankruptcy. On the issue of fact, the evidence is that one Gallagher, a manager of a mining company, who seems to combine with that position the avocation of a mining speculator, had a certain mine, known as the Mount Molloy Copper Mine, brought under his notice ; and he was minded to form a syndicate or company which would take over this mine, on, of course, the usual terms of profit resulting to the person who set that machinery in motion. The idea of forming a syndicate seems to have fallen through. The bankrupt then introduced to Mr. Gallagher a Mr. Adams, who as I read the evidence, purchased the mine, and resold it to a Melbourne syndicate at a profit of 1,500*l.* The official assignee says that the sum of 333*l.*, which is the subject matter of this motion, was

(1) [1894] 2 Q. B. D. 393.

money earned by the bankrupt in respect of his having so introduced the purchaser. That is denied on behalf of Mrs. Hayes, who alleges that the money is hers, having been handed to her as a gift or present by Mr. Gallagher. The document in which this sum is mentioned is dated 31st March, 1898, and is signed " H. J. Adams, by his attorney J. W. Birkenhead," and is addressed to Mrs. Hayes, the wife of the bankrupt. It is in these terms :—

1898.

Re
HAYES ;
Ex parte
OFFICIAL
ASSIGNEE;
HAYES AND
ANOTHER,
Respondents.

Walker J.

Re Mount Molloy Copper Mine.

"I have sold this mine to Mr. Keate Hall, of Melbourne, for the sum of seven thousand five hundred pounds (7,500*l*.) cash ; deposit 10 per cent., balance on completion of title or possession of property ; and have received 750*l*. (seven hundred and fifty pounds) as a deposit on same, 500*l*. of which I am remitting by wire to the vendors in Mr. A. A. Gallagher's name to-morrow. As soon as the sale is completed, and the money is paid to me, viz., the balance of 6,750*l*., I hereby undertake and agree to hand you the sum of three hundred and thirty-three pounds (333*l*.), less your proportion of expenses, and being your share of ½ of ⅔ in the total profit of fifteen hundred pounds (1,500*l*.)."

It is unnecessary for me to go into the evidence at length ; it is all recorded in the depositions, and it is available to any Court that may be asked to review my decision. It is enough for me to say that, as I read the evidence of Gallagher and of Adams, it shews that this sum of 333*l*. was agreed to be given by Gallagher to the bankrupt for services rendered in connection with the introduction to Gallagher of the person who ultimately purchased the mine. It is not necessary to say that this was an agreement for commission ; it is enough if it was a sum earned or agreed to be paid for services rendered. Gallagher admits that in all cases of this kind, it is usual that the person who introduces a purchaser should be allowed to " stand " in, that is, of course, to have a share in the profits made, and I have come to the conclusion upon the evidence given during the examination before the Registrar, that that was the arrangement come to in this case. I should have come to that conclusion upon the evidence of Gallagher and Adams if it stood alone, because when this matter was more fresh in their recollection, and when, it may be, that the importance of shaping the evidence one way or the other was not so apparent as it is now, they so stated what the nature of the transaction was. The reasonable construction to be placed upon the evidence which they gave is, that by virtue of an agreement

1898.

Re
HAYES ;
Ex parte
OFFICIAL
ASSIGNEE;
HAYES AND
ANOTHER,
Respondents.

Walker J.

between Gallagher and the bankrupt, the bankrupt was entitled to a share in the profit in respect of services rendered, by means of the introduction of Adams.   Mr. *Wise* said that the amount was uncertain, and no doubt on the evidence taken before the Registrar it is left in uncertainty, but it is made as certain as anything can be made certain, by the document of the 31st March, which is signed by Mr. Adams' attorney.   One has to bear in mind that in cases of this sort where a bankrupt is charged with putting property away from his creditors, it is very difficult to obtain full and explicit evidence, but that, of course, does not justify me in drawing upon my imagination, and imagining things that do not appear upon the evidence, or cannot be properly inferred.   I may, however, bear in mind the difficulty in obtaining direct evidence in drawing inferences from the facts that have been proved.   The letter is a fact in the case, and when I find that on the 31st March last Adams wrote this letter by direction of Gallagher, and the writer refers to this sum of 333*l.* as being the bankrupt's wife's share in the profit, less her proportion of the expenses, I think that the inference is a reasonable and proper one, that the actual agreement between the parties was not of a vague character as Mr. *Wise* contends it was; but that it was arranged that he should receive a specific portion of the profit, and that specific portion was set out in the letter of the 31st March. Though that is the first time that, so far as the evidence shews, it was put into writing, I consider that it had been arranged between the parties previous to that letter.   But the case does not rest upon the evidence of Gallagher and Adams alone.   The case for the official assignee is enormously strengthened by the fact that neither the bankrupt nor his wife, who are of all people best able to know the facts of the case, was put into the box.   That coupled with the evidence given before the Registrar convinces me that the case of the official assignee is true.   It is said that this money was given by Gallagher to Mrs. Hayes out of kindly feeling, but I am unable to come to that conclusion.   Having regard to who the persons were, their pecuniary position and the surrounding facts, that suggestion is one that I cannot accept, using my common sense.   I am, therefore, compelled to find that this was money earned by the bankrupt in respect of his share in this transaction.   That being so, it is admitted that I must make an order in favour of the official assignee, unless I hold that on the point of law raised by Mr. *Wise*, his title is ousted by the previous bankruptcy in which Mr. Palmer was the official assignee.   In support of that contention I have been referred to *Re Clarke, Ex parte Beardmore* (1). Assuming for a moment that the English law and the law of this colony are identical, this case decides no more than that in such a case, if the official assignee in the first bankruptcy were to claim this money, then it would go to him rather than to the official assignee in the second bankruptcy, but I have the evidence of Mr. Palmer that he was aware of the second sequestration order being made, and of the examinations which were held for the recovery of assets as well as of the present notice of motion, but he did not intervene or make any claim, because, rightly or wrongly, he could not, in his view of the law, make such a claim.   I am not concerned now whether Mr. Palmer is, or is not, justified as between himself and the creditors of the estate he is representing in taking up that position ; it is enough for me that he waived, and continues to waive, any rights he might otherwise have to claim this 333*l*.   But my attention has been drawn to s. 7 of the Bankruptcy Act Amendment Act, 1896, which is different from anything in the English statute.   A point was raised as to the meaning of the word "possessed."   It seems to me that the words "possessed by him" amount to no more than if they had been "which is his."   It cannot be that the word "possessed" is to be pressed or made to imply some particular mode of possession, because if that were so, as pointed out by Mr. *Gordon*, it would be easy in such a case as this for the bankrupt to entirely defeat the second bankruptcy by placing, however impudently it might be done, his assets in the hands of some other person, and then saying that it was not in his own "possession."   I must construe these words in view of the intention of the section, which is that property the bankrupt has at the date of the second sequestration, if there had been no intervention by the official assignee in the first sequestration, and must go to the official assignee in the second sequestration ;

1898.

Re
HAYES ;
Ex parte
OFFICIAL
ASSIGNEE ;
HAYES AND
ANOTHER,
Respondents.

Walker J.

(1) [1894] 2 Q.B.D. 393.

1898.

Re
HAYES ;
Ex parte
OFFICIAL
ASSIGNEE;
HAYES AND
ANOTHER,
Respondents.

therefore, the plea of *jus tertii* must fail. That being so, I must make an order in terms of the notice of motion declaring that this sum of 333*l.*, less the bankrupt's proportion of the expenses, is the property of the official assignee in the second sequestration, and I must order the respondent H. J. Adams to pay that sum to the official assignee.

On the statement made by Mr. Adams, and accepted by Mr. *Gordon*, that the proportionate expenses to be set off against the 333*l.* is the sum of 39*l.*, I order Mr. Adams to pay 294*l.* to the official assignee, that being the difference between the two sums. It has been suggested that I should allow Mr. Adams, before paying over the money, to deduct his costs. If this were a case in which I saw that the trustee had taken up a neutral position, and was not attempting unduly to assist either party, as a matter of course I should have given him his costs out of the fund, and if the matter had rested on the memorandum of submission, that is the course I should have pursued ; but he has been called as a witness, and I have to determine whether he has by his demeanour in the witness box shewn that he was not doing his best to assist the Court to come to a decision upon the real facts, or tried rather to assist Mrs. Hayes, and acted the part of a partizan. I have come to the conclusion that he was so acting. The evidence he gave before me was, to my mind, very unsatisfactory, and I am not at all satisfied with the manner in which he sought to give a colour to the evidence given by him before the Registrar during his examination under the section. Taking this in conjunction with his demeanour as a witness, I have come to the conclusion that he has been a partizan in this case of Mrs. Hayes. He seems to have been a sort of acquaintance of the bankrupt, but to have had very little knowledge of Mrs. Hayes. At all events she said she had no knowledge of him beyond having heard of his name. I am afraid the fact is that he is a friend of the bankrupt, and has been assisting him as far as he could in secreting the money from his creditors. I think I am not justified in making an order for costs against him, because that would be an extreme measure seeing that he has not placed himself in the position of a litigant, and the opinion I have formed of him has been deducible from his conduct in the witness box. I think, however, that under the circumstances it is impossible for me to give him his costs, and he must pay the whole of the 294*l.* to the official assignee.

I order that the respondent Mrs. Hayes pay the official assignee's costs out of her separate estate, if any.

I extend the time for Mrs. Hayes to appeal to 28 days, on the undertaking of Mr. *Bavin* that the 294*l.* will be paid into Court forthwith.

1898.

Re
HAYES ;

Ex parte
OFFICIAL
ASSIGNEE.

HAYES AND
ANOTHER,
Respondents.

Walker J.

Order accordingly.

Solicitor for the official assignee : *Mark Mitchell.*
Solicitors for the respondents : *Baker ; Ellis & Button.*

Re AIKEN,

Ex parte AIKEN,

THE OFFICIAL ASSIGNEE, *Respondent.*

1898.

October 6.

Walker J.

Bankruptcy Act, 1898 (No. 25), ss. 3, 10, sub-ss. 1, 7 ; 52 (c)—Personal injury
    —Unsatisfied judgment at date of sequestration order—Property.

In 1892, A. recovered a judgment in a District Court action for an assault. In August, 1898, the estate of A. was sequestrated. In September the amount of the judgment was paid into the District Court. *Held*, that the judgment debt passed to A.'s official assignee.

ON the 31st of October, 1892, Edward Imlay Aiken recovered judgment in an action which he had brought in the District Court against Thomas Cashman for an assault. On August 18th, 1898, Aiken voluntarily sequestrated his estate as bankrupt. The bankrupt, in his affidavit, stated that before he could obtain payment of the amount of the judgment, the defendant Cashman absconded from the colony, and so far as he (the bankrupt) was able to ascertain, did not return to this colony again until about the 26th September last, when the bankrupt ascertained Cashman was in Sydney. The bankrupt applied for, and obtained a writ of *capias ad satisfaciendum,* and Cashman was arrested thereunder on the 28th September, and on the 29th September paid the sum of 43*l.* 15*s.* 6*d.,* the amount of the judgment debt and costs, to the Registrar of the District Court, who subsequently paid the amount to the official assignee. The bankrupt thereupon filed a notice of motion asking that the sum of 43*l.* 15*s.* 6*d.* be paid to him by the official assignee.

R. K. Manning, for the bankrupt.

The damages recovered were in respect of a personal injury done to the bankrupt, and did not pass to the official assignee.

He referred to the Bankruptcy Act, 1898, ss. 3, 10, sub-ss. 1, 7 ; 52 (c): and cited *Howard* v. *Crowther* (1); *Ex parte Vine, In re Wilson* (2); and *Clarke* v. *Clarke* (3).

(1) 8 M. & W. 601.   (2) 8 Ch. Div. 364.
        (3) 18 N.S.W. L.R. Div. 5.

In order to recover the amount of the judgment, it was necessary to take some further proceeding after the making of the sequestration order, and, therefore, the case comes directly within the proviso to sub-s. 7 of s. 10.

Gordon, for the official assignee.

1898.

Re
AIKEN;
Ex parte
AIKEN;
OFFICIAL
ASSIGNEE,
Respondent.

The right of action having passed into a judgment, the judgment debt passed to the official assignee. The cases cited apply only to cases where judgment has been recovered during bankruptcy in respect of a personal injury done to a person during his bankruptcy.

The proviso to s. 10, sub-s. 7, applies to cases where judgment has not been recovered.

WALKER, J. It appears that in October, 1892, the bankrupt recovered judgment against one Thomas Cashman in an action for assault for 43*l.* 15*s.* 6*d.*, including costs. The estate of the bankrupt was sequestrated in August last, but owing, as is alleged, to the bankrupt being unable to discover the address of Cashman, the amount of the judgment was not actually recovered till September last, when it was paid into the District Court.

It has been argued on behalf of the bankrupt, that, as the action was one for a personal injury to the bankrupt, certain authorities cited require me to hold that the benefit of the judgment did not pass to the official assignee, but remained in the bankrupt to be disposed of as he thought proper.

The language of the Act vesting property of a bankrupt in the official assignee is in the widest possible terms, but it seems, from the cases cited, that a right of action for a personal injury done to a bankrupt during his bankruptcy does not pass to the official assignee, and that he is not entitled as against the bankrupt to the amount recovered.

It seems to me that if I were to hold that the principle laid down in those cases applied to the present case, I should be doing more than following those cases, I should be extending them. I do not see why, on principle, I should extend them to a case like this, where judgment had been recovered, and

1898.

Re
AIKEN ;
Ex parte
AIKEN ;
OFFICIAL
ASSIGNEE,
Respondent.

Walker J.

accordingly the right of action had been converted into ascer-tained damages before the bankruptcy.

I do not think that the proviso to s. 10, sub-s. 7, was intended to apply to such a case. I am not disposed to hold that it prevents the official assignee from recovering where the bankrupt, prior to his bankruptcy, recovered judgment, and that judgment remained unsatisfied at the date of the sequestration order. Up to judgment the proceedings were proceedings for a personal injury or wrong, and so were within the protection of the proviso ; any proceedings after judgment were not for a personal injury or wrong, but for enforcement of a debt, and if that debt accrued before sequestration, it passed, in my view, to the official assignee.

It is true that a reason is given by the bankrupt for not issuing execution before September last, but that does not, in my opinion, alter the case.

The matter is not free from difficulty, and I think that, on the authorities cited, there was much to be said in favour of the bankrupt's contention, and that, therefore, the motion is not a frivolous one. Unless costs are pressed for I think the motion should be dismissed without costs.

Order accordingly ; no order as to costs.

Solicitor for the applicant : *Baker.*

Solicitors for the official assignee : *Sullivan Bros.*

In the estate of GREAVES (deceased).

1898.

August 26.

A.H. Simpson J.

Probate Act (54 Vic. No. 25 [1890)], s. 6—Executor becoming Trustee—Payment into Court—Jurisdiction.

The Probate Court has no jurisdiction to order a person who has been appointed executor and trustee of an estate to pay money into Court where he has discharged all his duties as executor, and holds the estate as trustee only.

THIS was an application by the widow of the deceased for an order directing the respondent, the trustee of the estate, to pay certain moneys alleged to be owing by him to the estate into Court. By the testator's will, probate of which was granted in September, 1894, the testator, after payment of his debts, funeral and testamentary expenses, gave, devised, and bequeathed " unto my dear wife Selina Greaves as guardian of my two children of her body .   .   . without power of anticipation all my estate and effects both real and personal whatsoever or wheresoever and of what nature and quality soever for her use until my two children shall have attained the age of 25 years On their attaining the age of 25 years the income arising out of my estate shall be divided into two equal portions My wife to have one portion the other portion to be equally divided between my two children .   .   .   At the decease of my wife the estate shall be realised upon and shall be equally divided into equal portions between my two children." And the testator appointed the respondent and another (who renounced) " executors of this my will."

R. K. Manning, for the respondent. This Court has no jurisdiction over the respondent. He has paid all the debts, funeral and testamentary expenses, and has passed from an executor to a trustee : *Lewin on Trusts* (1)

Although the testator has appointed him an "executor," he clearly intended from the direction in the will to realise and

(1) 9th Ed. p. 757.

E 2

divide that the respondent should act as trustee as well. The
Probate Act has no application to trustees. He referred to ss.
15, 19, 56, 57, 58, 59, 61 of the Probate Act, and cited *In re James
Thomson* (1).

Freehill, solicitor, for the applicant.

Manning in reply.

A. H. SIMPSON, J.   In this matter the applicant asks for an
order directing the respondent to pay a certain sum of money
into Court, and to this it is objected that this Court had no jurisdiction to make the order asked for, in that the respondent is now
a trustee of the estate and not an executor, and that this Court
has no jurisdiction over trustees.   If he is an executor I certainly
have jurisdiction to make the order asked, but if he is a trustee,
then the Equity Court, and not this Court, has jurisdiction.

It appears that the respondent was appointed an executor of
the will, and that he has paid all the debts, funeral and testamentary expenses, and discharged his duties as executor.

If a trustee had been expressly appointed by the will I do not
think that the respondent could set up on the present application
that he was a trustee only, but on looking into the will it seems
to me that the testator intended the respondent to be not only an
executor, but a trustee also.   By the will the testator, after
directing payment of his debts, funeral and testamentary
expenses, gave, devised, and bequeathed unto his wife, as guardian
of his two children, without power of anticipation, all his estate
and effects, both real and personal, whatsoever and wheresoever,
for her use until his two children should have attained the age of
25 years, and on their each attaining the age of 25 years, the
income arising out of his estate was to be divided into two equal
portions, one to his wife, and the other to be equally divided
between the two children.   If the will had stopped there I would
think that Mrs. Greaves had been appointed trustee of the will,
but the will continues, "at the decease of my wife the estate
shall be realised upon and shall be equally divided between my
two children."

(1) 8 N.S.W. W.N. 13.

It is clear from this that the testator intended that some one should realise and divide his property after his wife's death, and he clearly could not have intended his wife to do this. The only persons shewn by the testator as being required to do this are, I think, the executors, and therefore I must come to the conclusion that the respondent here is a trustee of the will, and as he has ceased to be an executor I have no jurisdiction over him. I must therefore dismiss this application with costs.

1898.

In the estate of
GREAVES
(Deceased).

Order accordingly.

Proctor for the respondent : *Murphy.*

1898.
_____
October 26, 27.
Walker J.

Re HORTON ; *Ex parte* WILSON.

Bankruptcy Act, 1898, ss. 30, 31, 32—Examination of witness—Representation by solicitor or counsel—Prevarication—Evasion—Committal of witness—Several committals—Term of imprisonment—Practice.

A witness summoned for examination, under s. 30 of the Bankruptcy Act, 1898, is not entitled as a matter of absolute right to be represented on such examination by either solicitor or counsel.

Prevarication and evasion, as dealt with in s. 31 of the Act, are not contempts of Court, but special statutory offences created by the section.

A witness may be committed for prevarication or evasion at any time during the course of his examination under s. 30 for any term not exceeding 14 days, and the committal may be repeated in the case of the same witness from time to time.

THIS was an appeal from an order made by the Registrar, committing the appellant Wilson to Darlinghurst Gaol for a period of 14 days for evasion and prevarication.

The appellant had on a previous occasion during the same examination been committed for evasion and prevarication.

The facts of the case and the grounds of appeal are set out fully in the considered judgment of *Walker,* J.

Shand (A. Thompson with him), for the appellant, cited *Yate Lee & Wace on Bankruptcy,* 3rd Edit., p. 135 ; *In re Breech Loading Armoury Company* and *In re Merchants' Company* (1); *Ex parte Kemp* (2) ; *Ex parte Waddell, In re Lutscher* (3); *In re Grey's Brewery Company* (4) ; *In re Pennington* (5). Rule 5 *(f).*

Gordon (R. K. Manning with him) cited *In re Towsey* (6); *In re Norwich Equitable Fire Insurance Company* (7) ; *In re Walters, Ex parte Currie* (8); *Yate Lee & Wace on Bankruptcy,* 3rd Edit., p. 135 ; *Williams' Bankruptcy Practice,* 6th Edit., p. 83.

(1) L.R. 4 Eq. 453.
(2) 42 L.J.N.S. Bcy. 26.
(3) 6 Ch. Div. 328.
(4) 25 Ch. Div. 400.
(5) 5 Mor. 269.
(6) 9 L.T.N.S 613.
(7) 27 Ch. D. 515.
(8) 18 N.S.W. L.R. Bcy. & Pr. 51.

Shand in reply.   ·

1898.

WALKER, J. I must dismiss the appeal with costs, and will give my reasons in writing on a subsequent occasion.

Re
HORTON ;
Ex parte
WILSON.

On November 28th,

This was an appeal to me, under s. 32 of the Bankruptcy Act, 1898, from an order made by the Registrar on the 24th October last, whereby he committed Wilson to Darlinghurst Gaol for a period of fourteen days for evasion and prevarication, of which, in the opinion of the Registrar, Wilson had been guilty in the course of his examination under s. 30. When the matter was before me on the 26th and 27th October, the case was fully argued, and questions were raised as to the proper practice under ss. 30 and 31. I was satisfied at the conclusion of the argument that I must dismiss the appeal, and I dismissed it accordingly with costs ; but, inasmuch as the case involved important matters of practice, which ought to be laid down with clearness and precision, I reserved the expression of the reasons for my decision until I should have an opportunity of putting the same into writing.

The facts of the case when it was before the Registrar appear by an affidavit of the appellant Wilson filed on the 25th October, which (so far as material to this judgment, and in fact so far as I permitted the affidavit to be read) was in the following terms : —(2) "On the 24th day of October instant, I was under examination at the Bankruptcy Court as a witness in the matter, and at the conclusion of my said examination was committed to Darlinghurst Gaol for fourteen days for alleged evasion and prevarication. (3) My solicitor, Mr. P. W. Berne, was present in Court during the early part of my examination, but when Mr. Gordon, the counsel for Mr. W. H. Palmer, the official assignee of this estate, was examining me with reference to an action which I have pending against the Bank of New South Wales for the detention of a certain document of title to certain of my property, the said Mr. Gordon requested the Registrar of this honourable Court to issue an order clearing the Court, and the Registrar thereupon issued such order. My said solicitor, Mr. Berne, then applied to the Registrar to be allowed to remain in

1898.

Re
HORTON ;
Ex parte
WILSON.

Walker J.

the Court-room during my examination, but the said Registrar
refused to allow the said Mr. Berne to remain in the Court,
which was cleared in accordance with the order of the said
Registrar. . . . (7) My warrant of commitment bears the
following endorsement thereon by the Registrar of this honourable Court :—It is requested that no one may be allowed access
to the prisoner except by request of the official assignee. . . .
(9) Immediately upon the conclusion of my said examination,
and no order having been made declaring the Court open, the
said Mr. Gordon applied to the said Registrar for an order for
my committal, which was granted accordingly."

Wilson's grounds of appeal were as follows :—(1) That the
Registrar made the said order acting upon evidence that did not
justify him in coming to the conclusion that Wilson was guilty
of evasion and prevarication. (2) That the Registrar was not
justified in deciding that Wilson was guilty of evasion and prevarication. (3) That Wilson was not guilty of evasion and prevarication. (4) That the questions which Wilson was required
to answer were not put *bona fide* for the purpose of eliciting
information, as the official assignee and his counsel were admit-
tedly aware of the correct answers thereto. (5) That the Registrar was in error in allowing questions to be put to Wilson which
should not have been put and which were irrelevant and which
were not put for the purpose of obtaining information respecting
the bankrupt, his dealings and property. (6) That the Registrar
had no power or jurisdiction to order that no one be allowed
access to the said Edward Wilson except by request of the official
assignee. (7) That the application for the committal of Wilson
should have been made in open Court. (8) That the Registrar
was in error in not permitting the solicitor for Wilson to be
present in Court during the examination of Wilson. (9) That
the Registrar had no power to conduct the examination of Wilson,
or to make the said order of committal after an order had been
made by the said Registrar excluding the public from the Court,
and no order having been made declaring the Court open.

On the appeal being opened, Mr. *Gordon*, on behalf of the
official assignee, objected by way of demurrer that the grounds 6,
7, 8, and 9, were not really grounds of appeal, and ought not to

be entertained.   I declined at that stage to entertain the demurrer, 1898.
thinking it better to have the case fully argued, and I still think *Re*
Horton ;
it expedient to give no opinion on the demurrer, but rather to *Ex parte*
base my reasons for dismissing the appeal upon a consideration Wilson.
of the various matters raised in the notice of appeal.   I neither *Walker* J.
allow the demurrer, nor disallow it; I simply prefer to base my
judgment upon my view of the substantial points which have
been argued.

As to the 1st, 2nd, and 3rd of the grounds of appeal, it is
enough for me to say that the depositions of the witness have
been read to me, and I can see that the Registrar may have had
ample grounds for finding Wilson guilty of evasion and prevarication, and I am certainly not disposed to disturb his finding on
that question of fact.   In determining whether a witness is
evasive or a prevaricator the man's conduct and demeanour in the
box may in many cases count for much.   The advantage of
observing that conduct and demeanour was enjoyed by the
Registrar, and I see no reason for disturbing, or differing from,
the view he took.

The 4th and 5th grounds of the appeal are rather hard to
understand, even with the aid of Mr. *Shand's* argument.
Certainly the mere suggestion that Wilson was questioned not
bona fide, but for the purpose of entrapping the witness (I cannot
see any other meaning in these grounds of appeal), is one that
would have to be very strictly proved.   In this case no proof
was offered, the depositions do not afford it, and I must of course
disregard the unproved suggestion.

The 6th ground of appeal is based on a mistake of fact.   The
Registrar did not make any order limiting access to Wilson, but
merely requested the gaol authorities to limit that access.   The
request was one with which those authorities might comply, or
refuse to comply, the matter of the request being, I apprehend,
more or less governed by gaol regulations.   In any case I am of
opinion that the request, which was external to the Registrar's
order, and in no way a part of it, did not avoid or invalidate the
committal.

The 7th, 8th, and 9th grounds of appeal raise very important
matters of practice, which have had my serious attention.   I will

take the 8th ground first. If it is, as contended by Mr. *Shand.*
a matter of absolute right that a witness summoned for examination under s. 30, and against whom it is apparent from the course
of the examination that proceedings may be instituted, should be
represented by solicitor or counsel, then I apprehend that the
order for Wilson's committal in respect of an examination at
which that absolute right was denied to him, ought not to stand.
The Court must, therefore, enquire whether the absolute right
alleged exists.

It is singular that so little apposite authority on the point can
be found. In *Ex parte Parsons* (1), Lord *Hardwicke* said he
would not make any order that a person summoned for examination under the commission of bankruptcy in that case should be
at liberty to be attended by counsel upon her examination,
because it might be made a precedent in other commissions, and
he thought an inconvenience would arise if allowed in every case,
and therefore he only recommended it to the Commissioners in
that particular instance to indulge the witness with counsel, but
would make no order for that purpose.

It does not appear from the report whether in that case proceedings were contemplated or could be taken against the witness.

In *In re Towsey* (2), Mr. Commissioner *Goulburn* said that,
strictly speaking, a witness had no right to be attended by counsel
at all, but courtesy permitted it.

In the cases *In re Breech Loading Armoury Company*, and
In re Merchants' Company (3), the question was raised whether
a person summoned for examination under the Companies Act
of 1862, s. 115, and against whom it was plain that a hostile
application might subsequently be made, had a right to be
attended by solicitor and counsel. Lord *Romilly* held that he
was so entitled, stating that the cases on the practice in bankruptcy had no analogy. As far as one can collect from the
report, his Lordship considered that the practice in bankruptcy
was to exclude the solicitor and counsel of a witness, if their
presence was objected to, but he laid down a different rule under
the Companies Act.

(1) 1 Atkins 204.   (2) 9 L.T. N.S. 613.
(3) I. R. 4 Eq. 453.

In *Ex parte Kemp* (1), where the trustee in bankruptcy had examined under s. 96 of the Bankruptcy Act of 1869 (corresponding with the section in this case under which Wilson was examined), a person who had tendered a proof in the bankruptcy, with a view of eliciting facts to shew that the proof should be rejected, *Mellish*, L.J., said, " the trustee's proper course was to have proceeded originally under R 72 and required further evidence from him " (*i.e.*, the creditor who had been examined), " but in this instance as in others he appears to have tried to avoid litigation with the creditor, and, in order to obtain a decision on the matter, to have examined him under s. 96 of the Act. This was not a proper mode of procedure. The creditor was thereby treated as a mere witness in a strange litigation, whereas he was in fact the principal party, and was entitled to the assistance of counsel and solicitor."

If I rightly understand this observation of *The Lord Justice*, it is an expression of opinion by him directly adverse to the appellant in this case, the point of the observation being that, on a question of proving a claim, the claimant was entitled to the assistance of his counsel and solicitor, and that on a question of that kind the trustee had done wrong in summoning him for examination under the section, because on such an examination he would be deprived of that legal assistance which he ought to have. The judgment of the *Lord Justice* is somewhat shortly reported, but, taking the observation as I find it (and no other part of the judgment is material to the point I am considering), I can only see in it the meaning I have indicated.

The next case is *Ex parte Waddell, In re Lutscher* (2). There the point actually decided does not help one in the present matter, but *James*, L.J., in his judgment said, "This is not the case of a man who is charged with having property in his possession belonging to the bankrupt, and is summoned to give evidence in respect of it. In such a case it might possibly be said that there was litigation between him and the trustee, and that he was entitled to be protected by counsel." This, it will be observed, is in no sense a decision, nor indeed anything more

1898.

Re
HORTON ;
Ex parte
WILSON.

Walker J.

(1) **42** L.J.N.S. Bcy. 26.   (2) 6 Ch. D. 323.

than a statement that when such a case arose, the line of argument might be adopted which has been adopted before me.

In the case *In re Grey's Brewery Company* (1), the question was again one of practice under the Companies Act, and the matter submitted for decision has no bearing upon that which I have to decide, but in the course of his judgment *Chitty*, J. (at p. 404), says, "It turned out from what has taken place before me to be quite clear that the practice in bankruptcy is to allow a person who is under similar examination proper assistance," but, unfortunately, the report does not shew what had taken place before the learned Judge which made it clear to him what the practice in bankruptcy was. Again at p. 405 he said : "The practice in bankruptcy appears to be this, the party is allowed to have the professional assistance of counsel or solicitor."

These, I think, are all the cases having any bearing on the point before me. How do the text books treat the point ? In the 7th edition of *Williams' Bankruptcy Practice*, page 95, I find this statement :—"In practice a witness is allowed on examination to be represented by counsel and solicitor, but it does not seem very clear how far this is a matter of right. It would certainly seem to be a matter of right where the examination is really the first step in a litigation hostile to the witness—*e.g.*, an examination as to the circumstances under which a bill of sale was given to the witness." As authorities for this statement, the learned writer refers to *Ex parte Waddell*, which contains no decision, nor even, as I understand it, any expression of opinion upon the point ; and to *Ex parte Kemp*, in which, as I have already stated, the expression of opinion seems to have been the other way. In *Yate Lee's Bankruptcy Practice* (3rd edition, page 135) the learned author says :—"The witness may, if he wish, require the assistance of a solicitor and counsel on his behalf ; this if not strictly a right is now seldom refused."

In my opinion there is no absolute right, on the part of any witness, even if he be examined with a view to ulterior proceedings against him, to be represented on such examination by either solicitor or counsel. Doubtless on most occasions he has been, and will be, allowed to be attended by his legal advisers, and I

(1) 25 Ch. D. 400.

think it especially desirable in this colony, where the Registrar possesses the power of summary committal, that a witness should not be deprived of the assistance of those advisers, unless real necessity exists for their exclusion.   But it is plain that, if a witness has a right to be represented by solicitor or counsel he has a right to be represented by any solicitor or counsel whom he may select.   The result might be that, in bankruptcy, where serious grounds existed for suspecting a conspiracy between the bankrupt and his friends to secrete the assets of the bankrupt, and for the investigation of which it might be absolutely necessary that the witnesses should be examined apart from one another, all one after the other might be represented on their examination by the same solicitor.   If the object be to keep from a witness, who has yet to be examined, statements made by witnesses who have been examined already, it is clear that this object may be easily defeated by one solicitor acting for a series of witnesses, and retailing to each what the others have said. This danger was apprehended by *Goulburn*, Commissioner, in *Re Towsey*.   It is to my mind so plain that the whole purpose of an examination of witnesses under s. 30 may be defeated by holding it to be the absolute right of any witness to be represented by solicitor or counsel, that I should be most unwilling by any decision of mine to establish such an absolute right.   There is no authority, as I understand the cases, which requires me to decide in favour of the right alleged; indeed I think that the balance of such authority as exists is against the right, and I hold accordingly.   It is, no doubt, a plausible argument that in the case of a witness, who is being examined not merely as a witness, but with a view to proceedings being taken against him, that should be held to be a right, which (it is admitted) is not the right of a mere witness ; but I do not see why any distinction should for this purpose be drawn between the two classes of witnesses. The sole object of the examination is to elicit facts for the guidance of the official assignees, to enable them—as *Jessel*, M.R., said in *In re the Gold Company* (12 Ch. D. 85)—" to find out facts before they bring an action, so as to avoid the expense of some hundreds of pounds in bringing an unsuccessful action, when they might by examining a witness or two at a trifling expense have

1898.

Re
HORTON ;
Ex parte
WILSON.

Walker J.

discovered that the litigation could not succeed"; and *Chitty*, J., in the course of his judgment in *In re Grey's Brewery Co.*, before referred to, more than once expresses his view that the object of the examination is simply to get information for the use of the official assignee. But it is said that, if the legal advisers of a witness are excluded from the examination, the evidence, for want of re-examination, will be incomplete and misleading. To my mind the sufficient answer is, that that is a risk which the official assignee, for whose information the examination is held, takes upon himself, when he asks to have witness's counsel or solicitor excluded. He must know that in some cases at all events there will, on such exclusion, be a risk that the evidence given will, for want of completeness, be misleading. If the official assignee chooses to act on misleading evidence, that is his concern. I cannot see that the witness, even where it is plain that he is being examined with a view to proceedings being taken against him, will be prejudiced. If such proceedings are instituted, and any use is sought to be made against the witness of his depositions, he can shew that these depositions only represent a part of the truth, and it will not lie in the mouth of the official assignee to comment on the fact of the explanatory evidence being then given for the first time, inasmuch as he had himself, by the course he had pursued, prevented it from being earlier given.

On what I conceive, then, to be the balance of authority, and on a view of what is best calculated to give effect to the intention of examinations held under s. 30, and without, as I think, doing any injustice to witnesses, I hold that in no case has a witness an absolute right to be represented by counsel or solicitor, though I think that the power to exclude them should not be exercised without grave reason. Moreover, as Lord *Esher*, M.R., said in *In re Pennington* (1), it is the duty of the Registrar, if it is clear that the object of a question is to lead the witness to say something which he or she does not intend, to stop it and tell the witness not to answer.

It is too late to listen to attacks upon the inquisitorial nature of examinations held under the section, and nothing is gained by

(1) 5 Mor. 269.

allusions to the Star Chamber. The answer is that the Legislature have chosen to give these stringent powers to the Court because, as *Baggaley*, L.J., says in *In re Norwich Equitable Fire Insurance Co.* (1), "the exigencies of justice required it."

The 7th and 9th grounds of appeal raise another very important question of practice. Mr. *Shand* referred me to the 5th Bankruptcy Rule under which applications for the committal of any person to prison for contempt must be heard and determined in open Court, and he contended that this rule was fatal to the legality of the committal in the present case. In my opinion evasion and prevarication as dealt with in s. 31 are not contempt of Court, but a special statutory offence created by the section. As Mr. *Gordon* pointed out, if the matter be one of contempt of Court, the power of committing for 14 days, which is obviously introduced as conferring a new power upon the Court, would not confer a new power at all ; but, on the contrary, would limit the much larger power already possessed of dealing with contempts. Again it was laid down in *In re Walters* (2) that examinations under the section are of a private character, and, as a matter of strict right or power, the Registrar can, in my opinion, commit while he is sitting in private during the exclusion of the public. The section, as far as publicity or privacy goes, makes no distinction between the holding of an examination and the committal of a person for his conduct at such examination ; both are placed upon the same footing in this respect. If then the examination may be in private, so, as a matter of strict law, may the committal be. The committal, therefore, in the present case, is not invalidated by the fact of its having been made at a time when the public were excluded from the Registrar's Court. At the same time I wish, for the guidance of the Registrar, to state my very strong opinion that, though he has the power to commit in private, he should never do so. The idea of publicity is so happily associated with British notions of the administration of justice that nothing should be done without urgent necessity to weaken that association. The Legislature has for sufficient reasons declared that official assignees may subject persons coming within s. 30 to a rigorous examination held in private,

1898.

Re HORTON;
Ex parte WILSON.

Walker J.

(1) 17 Ch. D. 515.   (2) 18 N.S.W L.R. B. & P. 51.

and believing that provision to be a very wholesome one, I should be the last to do anything which would infringe upon the privacy which, in the case of many of these examinations, I believe to be essential to eliciting the truth; but I see no reason why the act of committal should be done in private, and every reason why so drastic an order should be pronounced, if it has to be pronounced, in the full light of day. I think the course for the Registrar to pursue, in any case where he has ordered his Court to be cleared, and has come to the conclusion that he ought to commit a witness who has been examined privately, is to open his Court by proclamation, and then to state—he need not reveal anything which the interests of justice require to be kept secret—that So-and-So has been examined before him under the section, that he has found him guilty of prevarication or evasion, or as may be, and that accordingly he commits him to prison for so many days. A proclamation of this kind may, or may not, result actually in greater publicity, but it is of the greatest importance, in my opinion, before committing a man to prison, to secure for that act at least as much publicity as in the circumstances is possible.

Mr. *Shand* further argued that a witness could not be committed until the end of the examination under s. 30, or at all events not until the end of the examination of the person committed; and that, however often in the course of his examination a witness might evade questions or prevaricate, he could only be committed for 14 days in all. So to hold would be to destroy the whole value of the provision. If the object of conferring on the Court this power of committal be, as I believe it to be, primarily for the purpose of eliciting facts, it is plain that that purpose would be to a large extent defeated, if no committal could take place until the examination was concluded. I do not know that, so long as a bankruptcy is open, such examination can ever be said to come to a conclusion, for a man may be recalled for examination as often as is thought desirable; but if there be such a conclusion, and the committal can only then take place, it is then too late to elicit the truth, and the primary object of the Legislature is defeated. If again only an aggregate term of 14 days' imprisonment can be pronounced upon any one prevaricating witness, then, if the witness is one whose examination will last, as it conceivably may, for many days, the Registrar will be placed in the absurd position of having to dole out imprisonment by driblets, so as not to exceed the maximum allowance, and yet retain something in hand. I cannot accept this construction. The section says " if any such person while under examination is guilty of prevarication, etc., the Court may commit him to prison for any term not exceeding 14 days." In my opinion, the clear meaning is that committal for not exceeding 14 days may be ordered at any time during the examination, and may be repeated in the case of the same witness *toties quoties*.

1898.

Re
HORTON ;
Ex parte
WILSON.

Walker J.

Appeal dismissed with costs.

Solicitors for the appellant : *Shipway & Berne.*

Solicitor for the official assignee : *M. Mitchell.*

1898.
September 13.
Walker J.

BROWN *v.* NEEN.

Wills, Probate and Administration Act, 1898, *s.* 143 — *Probate Suit—Fresh Evidence—Practice.*

An order granting probate of a will had been made but not drawn up in a suit brought to determine the validity of the will. *Held*, that the Court had power to grant a rehearing, but that under the circumstances a rehearing should not be directed.

Section 143 of the Wills, Probate and Administration Act explained.

THIS was an application by the defendant, Mrs. Neen, to the Probate Judge for an order directing a rehearing before him of a suit brought to determine the validity of the will of her husband.

The deceased entered the Liverpool Asylum in the end of December, 1897, and remained there up to the time of his death on March 5th, 1898. While in the Asylum Neen executed a will in favour of the plaintiff. The defendant had not seen or communicated with the deceased for many years, and she disputed the will on the grounds of testamentary incapacity and undue influence.

At the hearing of the suit evidence was given as to Neen's capacity during the time only that he was in the Asylum, and probate of the will was granted.

After the order had been made, but before it was taken out, statements were made to the defendant's proctors by several people who knew Neen immediately prior to his admission to the Asylum, which tended to shew that he was not then capable of making a will.

S. A. Thompson, for the applicant. The order has not been settled. The Court has absolute power over its own order, until the order has been passed and entered. He cited *In re Gray, Dresser* v. *Gray* (1); *The Perpetual Trustee Co., Ltd.* v. *Clarke* (2).

Gordon, for the plaintiff, referred to *Chitty's Archbold's Pr.*, XI. Ed., Vol II., p. 1516.

(1) 36 Ch. D. 205.   (2) 16 N.S.W. L.R. B. & P. 20.

Thompson in reply.

1898.

BROWN
v.
NEEN.

WALKER, J. In this matter I think I have jurisdiction to make an order as asked. The order granting probate of the will not having been drawn up, I have power to rectify it and to direct a rehearing, if I see that I have made an order *per incuriam*, or one that is unjust.

It is, no doubt, true that the Court before granting probate of a will must be satisfied that the will is that of a capable testator upon the evidence brought before it, and in the suit which has just been heard, if evidence had been given as to the testamentary capacity of Neen prior to his admission to the Liverpool Asylum, I should have given all due weight to such evidence; but the question now is, should I allow the matter to be reopened because such evidence can now be given, and could not have been given before ?

In the affidavits filed, it is stated that certain persons are able to give material evidence as to Neen's capacity before his admission to the Asylum, but no suggestion is made that any further evidence can be given as to his capacity during the time that he was in the Asylum, or as to undue influence. I must bear in mind that although there were certain circumstances of a suspicious nature given in evidence, I was satisfied beyond all doubt that the testator was capable of making a will, and there was not a tittle of evidence given as to any undue influence having been exercised by Brown, in whose favour the will was made.

So far as the affidavits now filed go, a rehearing would leave all the evidence already given untouched, but it is suggested that reading the present evidence with the evidence proposed to be given as to Neen's state of mind before he went to Liverpool, a different conclusion may be arrived at.

However strong the evidence may be as to his mental condition before he went to the Asylum, there is ample evidence of his capacity during the time he was there, and if that evidence remained unchallenged and if I believed the witnesses, which I do, evidence as to his state of mind at a prior date would have to be disregarded.

F

1898.

BROWN
v.
NEEN.

Walker J.

Sect. 143 of the Wills, Probate and Administration Act, 1898, to which I have been referred, was never intended to apply to such a case as this, but to a case where a difficult question of law arises, and the Judge desires the opinion of the Full Court to be taken, or where it is desired by the parties to get the matter before the Full Court as quickly as possible, and by consent a formal order is made and a rehearing directed.

I certainly could not grant a rehearing before the Full Court on further evidence. Any application for leave to adduce fresh evidence on such a rehearing would have to be to the Full Court itself.

I must, therefore, dismiss this application with costs.

Order accordingly.

Proctor for the applicant: *Boyd* (Inverell), by *Mackenzie & Mackenzie.*

Proctor for the respondent: *Marsden.*

Re RUSH,

Ex parte RUSH.

1898.

Nov. 1, 29.

Walker J.

Bankruptcy—Application for certificate of discharge—Right of official assignee to appear—Practice.

Upon an application to review the refusal of the Registrar to grant a certificate of discharge, it is the duty of the official assignee to appear where creditors are not otherwise represented. *In re Reed, Bowen & Co.* (1), discussed.

Though the Court has upon such application full power to consider questions of fact, as being a re-hearing, it will not lightly interfere with the discretion of the Registrar. *Re Goldstein* (2) followed.

THIS was an application by the bankrupt for an order reviewing the decision of the Registrar, whereby he refused to grant the bankrupt a certificate of discharge.

Wise, Q.C. (*Bavin* with him), for the bankrupt   I object to the official assignee appearing on this application.   The opposing creditors can appear, but not the official assignee, whose costs will come out of the estate : *In re Reed, Bowen & Co.* (3).

The Registrar was wrong in law in finding the bankrupt guilty of misdemeanours before his public examination had been concluded : *R.* v. *Walters* (4) ; and on the facts there was no evidence to support the finding that a misdemeanour had been committed.

Gordon, for the official assignee.   The creditors are not represented ; if the official assignee has no right to appear now, he had no right to appear on the original application, this application not being an appeal but a re-hearing.   This is an opposed application, and the official assignee represents, not only the creditors, but the public generally to defend the rights of commercial morality.   He referred to *Re Gibbs* (5).

Wise in reply.

Cur. adv. vult.

(1) 3 Morr. 90.
(2) 4 B.C. 18.
(3) 3 Morr. at p. 103, 104
(4) 5 C. & P. 138.
(5) 3 B.C. 24.

On November 29th the following considered judgment was delivered by

WALKER, J. In this case the bankrupt moved the Court to set aside an order of the Registrar, made on the 21st June last, refusing a certificate of discharge. Mr. *Wise*, who appeared for the bankrupt, submitted that Mr. *Gordon*, who represented the official assignee, ought not to be allowed to appear, and he referred me to *In re Reed, Bowen & Co.* (1), to *Ex parte Dixon* (2), and also to *Ex parte White* (3). I expressed the opinion (which I now confirm) that those cases did not go to the length of saying that the official assignee had no *locus standi* to appear on such an application as the present, or that, if he appeared, his costs would necessarily be disallowed. In those cases creditors or other interested persons appeared in their individual capacity to oppose the appeal, and in such a case I agree that the official assignee ought not to appear, his presence being superfluous ; but if in his opinion, the appeal ought to be opposed, and no individual creditor appears to oppose it, it is not only the right, but, I think, the duty of the official assignee to appear. An appeal on which the appellant only can be heard would be a startling anomaly, and, apart from other considerations, the Court is, in my opinion, entitled in the case I have put to the assistance of counsel for the official assignee.

Mr. *Wise* admitted that the bankrupt had committed breaches of the bankruptcy law, and that he could not expect to have his certificate granted unless the grant were coupled with some suspension or some condition ; but he argued that the Registrar was wrong in refusing the certificate absolutely, and insisted, as a matter of law, that the Registrar was premature in finding the bankrupt guilty of misdemeanours until his public examination had been concluded. In support of this contention he relied upon *R.* v. *Walters* (4). That was a case of indictment of a bankrupt for concealing account books. *Parke*, J., directed the jury to acquit the prisoner, saying " Even if the prisoner had concealed these books, I am of opinion that he is not indictable until after he has concluded his last examination ; till then he has a *locus*

(1) 3 Morr. 90.   (3) 14 Q.B.D. 600.
(2) 13 Q.B.D. 106.   (4) 5 C. & P. 138.

poenitentiæ. How do we know that when he comes to complete his last examination he will not deliver up all his books correctly ?" Such a ruling struck me as being so disastrous to the administration of justice in the bankruptcy jurisdiction, and it opened up such a vista of obstruction and deception of creditors by bankrupts, and gave such a broad hint to the latter that, for at least a considerable time, they could pursue these tactics without the risk of criminal consequences, that I doubt whether the directions given by *Parke,* J., to the jury were law, and I reserved my judgment that I might have an opportunity of looking into the matter. It now appears that *R.* v. *Walters,* the date of which was 1831, has been bad law for half a century. In *R.* v. *Hughes,* which came before the Supreme Court of this colony in 1848, and is reported in a note in 5 S.C.R. 69, the bankrupt had been charged with removing or concealing his effects, and *R.* v. *Walters* was relied upon on behalf of the prisoner, but the Court held that the offence existed at the moment of perpetration in and by the act itself. In *Courtivron* v. *Mennier* (1), *Parke,* C.B., had at the trial ruled in accordance with *R.* v. *Walters,* but on the case coming on, upon a motion to make absolute a motion for a new trial, the *Chief Baron* recanted, and held that there was no *locus poenitentiæ,* and *Parke, Alderson* and *Platt,* BB., concurred with the *Chief Baron* in holding that the ruling in *R.* v. *Walters* was not law. The point came again before this Court in *R.* v. *Harris* (2), where the prisoner had been indicted for fraudulent concealment, and *Stephen,* C.J., said, "I am of opinion that the prisoner has not the *locus poenitentiæ* which has been claimed on his behalf, and that any repentance after he has committed the offence is only a matter for the consideration of the Judge. It is clear that the subsequent disclosure could not make the previous concealment, which was, in fact, a removal less a fraud, although the disclosure, if for an honest purpose, may operate on the question of punishment," and with him the other Judges concurred. It is plain, then, that there was nothing in law to prevent the Registrar from coming to the conclusion that in this case Rush had committed the criminal offences of which he found him guilty.

But it was argued that, even so, the Registrar came to a wrong conclusion as to the alleged misdemeanours, and that I ought so

1898.

Re
RUSH ;
Ex parte
RUSH.

Walker J.

(1) 6 Ex. 74.   (2) 5 S.C.R. 66.

1898.

Re
RUSH :
Ex parte
RUSH.

Walker J.

to find, and accordingly vary his decision. There is no doubt
that I am not bound by the Registrar's findings upon issues of
fact. I am at liberty, and indeed bound, to investigate the
evidence for myself, and if I can see that the Registrar has come
to a wrong conclusion, it is my duty to reverse his finding. That
this is so is plain from Re Castle Mail Packet Co. (1), Coglan v.
Cumberland (2), and, no doubt, other cases, but at the same time
my power and duty of considering, and, if necessary, revising the
findings of the Registrar, have their limitation. I do not know
that these limitations can be better expressed than they were by
Manning, J., in Re Goldstein (3). There his Honour said, " The
Registrar in inquiring into the whole matter has had the advantage I have not had of seeing the bankrupt under examination
with reference to several matters . . . Had I heard the
application originally myself, having power to take the question
of conduct into consideration outside the filed objections, I should
have, at the least, imposed the penalty of a considerable suspension. . . . The Registrar has had all the facts before him,
and has thought he should go further and refuse the certificate.
This application is, no doubt, a re-hearing, and I am to exercise
my own discretion in fixing the penalty ; but, as I said in In re
Gibbs (4), the Judge will in no case lightly interfere with the discretion of the Registrar, especially in cases where the witnesses
have been partly or entirely examined before the Registrar.
These applications must be dealt with just in the same way as
equity appeals are dealt with by the Full Court, that is with no
light interference with the decisions of the Court below. Though
possibly I might not have absolutely refused the certificate
myself, yet I cannot see that the Registrar was so clearly wrong
in doing so, that I ought to interfere with his decision," and
accordingly his Honour dismissed the appeal.

In the present case I have considered very carefully the evidence
given by the bankrupt on his examination, and the affidavit
which he filed in answer to the report of the official assignee, and
I have also had before me the statement of affairs and the
accounts he filed. It is not necessary, in the view I take of the

(1) 18 Q.B.D. 156.   (3) 4 B.C. 18.
(2) [1898] 1 Ch. 784.   (4) 3 B.C. 24.

case, to review the circumstances disclosed in the evidence. It is enough for me to say that after listening attentively to the argument of Mr. *Wise*, and with an anxiety not to do an injustice to the bankrupt, I am quite unable to say that the Registrar was not perfectly justified in coming to the conclusion that Rush had committed the misdemeanours to which he referred in his judgment. I entirely agree with the finding of the Registrar, and think that fraudulent intent is amply shewn. Mr. *Wise* argued that subsequent disclosure by the bankrupt negatived any idea that the previous concealment had any fraudulent intent. I am unable to follow this suggestion, if it is thereby meant to lay down a general rule. No doubt the concealment may be followed so quickly and so spontaneously by disclosure as to make it difficult to think that the concealment was fraudulent, but each case must depend upon its own circumstances, and having regard to the circumstances of this case, I feel no doubt that the bankrupt had a fraudulent intent. The bankrupt sought to excuse himself from keeping back money from his official assignee by saying that he retained it "to keep himself going," and it was argued that that shewed there was no intention to defraud. I cannot yield to so dangerous a contention. The law does not allow a man to maintain himself out of the money of other people, however little money of his own he may have for maintenance. As I put it during the argument, a hungry man who takes a loaf from a baker's shop, takes it "to keep himself going," but I never heard that this excuse took his offence out of the category of crimes. Under all the circumstances of the case I must deal with this appeal as the appeal in *Re Goldstein* (1) was dealt with, and dismiss it with costs.

Order accordingly.

Solicitor for the official assignee : *M. Mitchell.*

Solicitors for the bankrupt: *Norrie & McGuren.*

(1) 4 B.C. 18.

1898.

Re
RUSH ;
Ex parte
RUSH.

Walker J.

CASES

DETERMINED BY THE

SUPREME COURT OF NEW SOUTH WALES

IN ITS

𝔇ivorce and 𝔐atrimonial Jurisdiction,

AND BY THE

PRIVY COUNCIL ON APPEAL THEREFROM DURING 1898.

HAWKSWORTH *v.* HAWKSWORTH.

Costs—Appeal—Assessment of costs—Wife's costs on appeal.

On an appeal from the Judge in Divorce on a question of costs the Full Court cannot interfere unless it sees that the discretion of the Judge has been erroneously exercised, or that the Judge has acted on a wrong principle.

The wife, if an unsuccessful appellant, is not entitled to her costs of the appeal.

A Judge has no power to assess the costs of an application except by the consent of the parties.

1898.
———
Feb. 21, 22.

The C.J.
Stephen J.
and
Cohen J.

THIS was an appeal from *G. B. Simpson,* J.

This was a suit for divorce by the husband. On the 27th Sept. the respondent (wife) filed a notice of motion for an order directing the petitioner to pay to the respondent or her solicitor such further sum of money as to his Honour might seem fit to meet the costs of the respondent incurred and to be incurred in this cause and the hearing thereof.

The affidavit in support of the motion stated that the costs of taking evidence on commission in England amounted to 52*l*. 10*s*. 8*d*., and that the costs of the solicitor in England, apart from the commission, amounted to 20*l*. The costs in this suit here, apart from the costs in respect of which special orders had been made, amounted to 20*l*. The respondent was entirely without means to pay such costs.

. The petitioner stated in reply that the costs in connection with the taking evidence on commission had not been taxed. The costs incurred here had not been taxed. He had already paid to the respondent's solicitors the sum of 60l. by way of the respondent's costs of suit, and the sum of 6l. 6s. the costs of the application. He had paid 58l. for alimony *pendente lite,* and 20l. the costs of the alimony application. He denied that the respondent was without means.

After various postponements the matter came before his Honour on 19th October, and was adjourned till the 26th October, when his Honour made an order directing the petitioner to pay the sum of 40l. to the respondent's solicitor, and ordered that no costs of and incidental to the motion and order be allowed to the respondent except the costs of the day, which costs were assessed at 2l. 2s.

The respondent now appealed from that portion of the order refusing to allow the costs of the motion except the sum of 2l. 2s., on the ground (*inter alia*) that his Honour was in error in refusing to allow the respondent her costs of and incidental to the order.

Ralston, for the appellant.

Whitfeld, for the respondent, took the preliminary objection that there was no appeal. The costs of interlocutory matters are entirely in the discretion of the Judge. The practice with regard to these interlocutory matters in divorce is the same as at common law (R. 79). At common law there is no appeal on a question of costs from a Judge in Chambers.

· [THE CHIEF JUSTICE referred to s. 41 of the Matrimonial Causes Act, the proviso to which was repealed by s. 1 of 42 Vic. No. 3.]

Sect. 41 deals with the question of costs at the hearing of the suit. There is no appeal on a question of costs in a matter in Chambers.

Ralston. This was not a Chamber application. It was a motion under R. 163. The repeal of the proviso to s. 41 expressly gives a party the right of appeal on the subject of costs. Here a proper application was made to the Court, and there was a proper affidavit in support of the application. The Judge granted the application and yet refused the costs of a successful application He must, therefore, have proceeded on a wrong principle. His Honour said that the solicitors of the respondent should have made a demand upon the petitioner before making the application. There is nothing in any of the rules to require that a demand should first be made. Here the application was successful, but even if the solicitor for the wife is unsuccessful, unless he is guilty of misconduct he is entitled to his costs : *Robertson* v. *Robertson* (1) ; *Flower* v. *Flower* (2) ; *Dorn* v. *Dorn* (3).

Whitfeld did not further argue the preliminary objection, and continued. It has not been shewn that the Judge acted on a wrong principle. The petitioner previous to this application had paid the respondent's solicitor 60*l.*, and the Judge was entitled to say "you must satisfy me that this money has been properly expended before I make a further order." The application was unnecessary, as a further sum might be applied for when the case was called on, or the application might have been saved by making a demand. That was a matter for his discretion. When it first came before his Honour, he was prepared to dismiss the application on the ground that it was not shewn that this money had been properly expended. The English bill of costs had not been taxed nor had the costs incurred in Sydney been taxed. But the matter was allowed to stand over to enable the petitioner to see these bills of costs, and to save the expense of a second application.

The costs of these interlocutory applications are on a different footing from costs of suit. There are many cases where the successful wife does not get the costs of the application : *Bacon* v. *Bacon* (4).

He also referred to *Glennie* v. *Bowles*(5); *Ash* v. *Ash*(6); *Thompson* v. *Thompson* (7) ; *Thompson* v. *Thompson* (8).

He was stopped.

(1) 6 P. D. 119.	(5) 3 Sw. & Tr. 109.
(2) 3 P. & D. 132.	(6) [1893] P. 222.
(3) 9 N.S.W.L.R.D. 17.	(7) 57 L.T. 374.
(4) L.R. 1 P. & D. 167.	(8) 2 Sw. & Tr. 402.

THE CHIEF JUSTICE. This was clearly a matter for the discretion of the Judge, and unless it is clear that he acted on a wrong principle, the Court cannot interfere.

Ralston. If the application was made in a proper way, and his Honour held that before the application was made a demand should have been made on the other side, when there is nothing in the rules which requires that a demand should be made, then I submit that he did act on a wrong principle. But I go further and contend that there is an appeal, even in a matter where a Judge exercises his discretion as to costs. If on an appeal on the subject of costs the appellant is to be met with the answer that the Judge exercised his discretion, and, therefore, there is no appeal, the repeal of the proviso to s. 41 is meaningless. In England, where the section as to appeals (s. 51 of 20 & 21 Vic. c. 85) is the same as s. 41 of our Act, it has been held that there is an appeal if a Judge exercises his discretion on a wrong principle, notwithstanding the proviso to that section : *Robertson* v. *Robertson* (1). The repeal of the proviso to s. 41 therefore gives this Court the right to interfere with the discretion of the Judge. Unless the solicitor for the wife is guilty of some misconduct in making the application he is entitled to his costs : *Aires* v. *Aires* (2). Even if the wife is unsuccessful in this appeal, she ought to get her costs. The appeal here was bona fide, and not made for the purpose of harassing the petitioner : *Te Kloot* v. *Te Kloot* (3).

[THE CHIEF JUSTICE. Is it not the rule that the wife if she is an unsuccessful appellant is not entitled to her costs ? : *Earnshaw* *Earnshaw* (4).]

In *Te Kloot* v. *Te Kloot* the wife, though an unsuccessful appellant, was allowed her costs.

THE CHIEF JUSTICE. I am not called upon to say what order I should have made in this case if the matter had come before me in the first instance, but a very strong case would have to be made out against an attorney before I should deprive him of his costs where he made a successful application. We had a consultation with Mr. Justice *G. B. Simpson* this morning, and he informed us that there were several reasons why he did not

(1) 6 P. D. 119.   (3) 15 N.S.W. L.R.D. 1 ; 11 W.N. 25.
(2) 65 L.T. 859.   (4) [1896] P. 160.

allow the costs of the application. He thought a demand should have been made to the other side before the application was made to the Court. Whether the demand would have been complied with if it had been made in this case I am not called upon to say, but I can see that there may be numbers of cases in which it would be utterly useless to make a demand. Another matter which weighed with his Honour was that the English bill of costs had not been taxed before the application was made. To say that the attorney has been guilty of misconduct in making the application is to use a term which has no application to this case, all that can be said is that before making the application there might have been more caution on his part.

But the Court can only interfere in a case of this kind, where it clearly sees that the discretion of the Judge has been erroneously exercised (and it rests with the appellant to shew that), or where the Judge has proceeded on a wrong principle. I am unable to see that the Judge has erroneously exercised his discretion, or has proceeded on a wrong principle, and I therefore think that the appeal should be disallowed. We say nothing about costs. It is quite clear that where the wife is the appellant, and is unsuccessful, she is not entitled to get her costs.

STEPHEN, J. I do not see that it necessarily follows that because an attorney makes a successful application he is entitled to his costs. We have seen Mr. Justice *Simpson*, and he seems to have considered that under all the circumstances of the case (which are really not before us), the attorney did not take certain steps which, in his opinion, should have been taken before making the application. That being his view, I am unable to say that he was wrong.

COHEN, J., concurred.

THE CHIEF JUSTICE. I see that the costs of the day were assessed at 2 guineas. I presume that the costs were assessed with the consent of the parties, otherwise I do not see what power his Honour had to assess them.

Appeal dismissed.

Solicitors for the appellant: *Johnson, Minter, Simpson & Co.*
Solicitors for the respondent: *Curtiss & Barry.*

1898.

HAWKS-
WORTH
v.
HAWKS-
WORTH.

The C.J.

1898.
February 21.

TAURO *v.* TAURO (RIZZO, Co-respondent).

Costs—Co-respondent—36 Vic. No. 9, ss. 31, 41—Appeal—Practice—Evidence in Court below—Moving party in contempt.

The C.J.
Stephen J.
and
Cohen J.

An order for costs of suit against a co-respondent can only be made at the hearing, and cannot be made on a specific motion after the hearing has determined.

On appeal to the Full Court, it is not necessary that the evidence taken in the Court below should be before it, if the point of law to be argued does not turn on the evidence.

The appellant, who has not complied with the order appealed against, and has not obtained a stay of proceedings, cannot be said to be in contempt of Court so as to preclude him from appealing.

THIS was an appeal from *G. B. Simpson,* J.

The husband petitioned for divorce on the ground that his wife had committed adultery with the co-respondent. The issue of adultery was found in favour of the petitioner, to whom the jury awarded 50*l.* as damages against the co-respondent. The Judge granted a decree *nisi* returnable in three months, for the dissolution of the marriage on the 17th June. No order for costs was asked for or made at the hearing, but the decree *nisi,* when drawn up, contained an order that the co-respondent should pay the petitioner's costs of suit. On the 24th September, on the application of the co-respondent, the decree, as drawn up, containing an order for costs, was set aside (see 14 W.N., p. 113). On the 10th September, a notice of motion was filed, and on the 19th October, *G. B. Simpson,* J., made an order directing the co-respondent to pay the petitioner's costs of suit. On the 10th November the decree *nisi* was made absolute.

The co-respondent now appealed against that order on the ground that the said order was not made on the hearing of the suit, within the meaning of s. 41 of the Matrimonial Causes Act (36 Vic. No. 9).

Brissenden, for the appellant.

Shand, for the respondent, took two preliminary objections. The order of the 19th October was made on an affidavit which has not been printed in accordance with R. 96. That rule

1898.

TAURO
v.
TAURO

(RIZZO,
Co-Respon-
dent).

requires that in all cases of appeal, the moving party shall, within 14 days after the filing of the notice of appeal, file with the Registrar four printed copies of the issues and *evidence.*

Brissenden. That rule only requires the evidence to be printed where it is necessary to read the evidence. It is not necessary to read the evidence to shew what the point of law is in this case, the whole question being whether an order for costs can be made under s. 41 after the hearing has determined. The decree has been printed, and the order appealed against has been printed. They are sufficient to shew the point of law raised.

THE COURT overruled that objection.

Shand. The second objection is that the appellant has not complied with the order of the Court directing him to pay the costs, and, therefore, is in contempt, and cannot make this application to the Court.

[THF CHIEF JUSTICE. Surely a party cannot be said to be in contempt, and be prevented from appealing because he has not paid money under an order against which he is appealing?]

The co-respondent should have applied to have the proceedings under that order stayed.

THE COURT overruled that objection.

Brissenden. Sect. 31 of the Matrimonial Causes Act gives the Court jurisdiction to award costs against the co-respondent. Sect. 41 provides when that order is to be made, *i.e., on the hearing.* The power given by s. 31 must be exercised under s. 41. Sect. 31 does not give the Court jurisdiction to make an order for costs at any time.

[THE CHIEF JUSTICE. I am inclined to think that the question really is, whether we can give an extended meaning to the words " on the hearing " in s. 41 ?]

Shand. Sect. 31 gives the Court power to award costs against a co-respondent at any time. That is a general section, and does not limit the time when the application can be made. Very often the decree *nisi* is not moved for until some time after the hearing, and the Court at that time invariably deals with the question of costs. Rule 166, which corresponds to the English

1898.

TAURO
v.
TAURO
(RIZZO,
Co-Respon-
dent).

Rule 201, clearly contemplates a specific application for costs after the decree *nisi* has been granted. If the contention of the appellant is right, that an order for costs can only be made at the hearing, what was the necessity for R. 165 ? I admit that it is the usual practice to make an order for costs at the hearing, because it is the most convenient course, but I submit that it is not necessary. If s. 31 does not bear the meaning that I contend for, what was the necessity for it, because under s. 41, the Court would clearly have jurisdiction to award costs against a co-respondent. There is no reason why s. 41 should be read as restraining the power given to the Court under s. 31. Secondly, " at the hearing " in s. 41 should not be given the limited meaning contended for. It only means that the application should be made within a reasonable time, and before the decree absolute.

[THE CHIEF JUSTICE. I do not see why this course should not have been adopted. When the application was made to set aside the decree, which was erroneously drawn up, why should not his Honour, when setting it aside, have made a decree *nunc pro tunc*, and ordered the co-respondent to pay the costs ?]

If the order could have been made then, the Judge had power to make it when he did. The whole object of s. 41 was that the application should be made while the facts were fresh in the mind of the Judge. If, when an application was made after the decree *nisi*, the facts were fresh in his mind, he would make the order, but if not he could refuse to make it. In this case all the facts were fresh in his mind when he made the order. His Honour said he would have made the order at the hearing had he been asked to do so : *Somerville* v. *Somerville* (1); *Woolley* v. *Whitby* (2).

Brissenden in reply.

THE CHIEF JUSTICE. This is an appeal from Mr. Justice *G. B. Simpson* sitting in Divorce. On the 19th October his Honour made an order giving the petitioner costs as against the co-respondent.

It appears that the case came on in June, and on the 17th June, the issues having been found in favour of the petitioner,

(1) 36 L.J.P. & M. 87.   (2) 2 B. & Cr. 580.

his Honour made a decree granting divorce. The co-respondent
having been found guilty of adultery, damages were awarded
against him. When that decree was moved for, no application
was made by the petitioner for costs.

1898.

TAURO
v.
TAURO
(RIZZO,
Co-respon-
dent).

The C.J.

At first it struck me that in Divorce an order should be made
for costs without any special application, just as in the Full
Court we make up our minds which party is to pay the costs,
and make the order, and we will not hear separate argument on
the question of costs. But in Divorce it is not so. It may be
that in some cases the petitioner exercises a wise discretion in
not asking for costs, because the Judge might in the exercise of
his discretion, in the place of giving him costs, make him pay the
costs himself. It is, therefore, the duty of the party, if he thinks
himself entitled to costs, to ask for them.

In this case, when the Judge granted the decree, he was not
asked to make any order as to the costs, though if he had been,
he would have ordered the co-respondent to pay the costs.
However, when the decree was drawn up, it directed the co-
respondent to pay the costs, an order which the Judge had never
made. Some time afterwards, in September, the co-respondent
became alive to the fact that the decree erroneously contained
this order, and applied to have it set aside. The decree was set
aside, and a fresh decree was drawn up. That decree was silent
as to costs. I need not now consider whether the Judge could
then have made a decree for costs *nunc pro tunc*. No application was made to him for that purpose.

On the 10th September a notice of motion was filed, and on
the 19th October this order, which is now appealed against, was
made, directing the co-respondent to pay the petitioner's costs.
The co-respondent appeals from that order on the ground that
under s. 41 of the Divorce Act, this order should have been made
at the hearing, and formed part of the decree, and could not be
made afterwards.

This objection to the order is met in two ways. First, it is
said that the order was made, not under s. 41, but under s. 31.
[His Honour read ss. 31 and 41.] It appears to me that s. 31 is
entirely ancillary to s. 41. Sect. 31 gives the Court jurisdiction
to make the co-respondent pay the whole or any part of the

1898.

TAURO
v.
TAURO.
(RIZZO,
Co-respon-
dent).

The C.J.

costs of the proceedings; but when has that order to be made?
Clearly, under s. 41, on the hearing of the suit; that is when the
Court must exercise the discretion vested in it under s. 31
That gets rid of the first objection to this appeal.

Then it is argued by Mr. *Shand* that the Court should not put
too limited a construction upon the words "on the hearing," in
s. 41, and that as long as an order for costs is made before the
decree absolute, it is made under s. 41, and made on the hearing.
I do not think this contention can be given effect to. We must
give this section its plain meaning, and hold that the order for
costs can only be made on the hearing. If there be any difficulty
in coming to a correct determination on this head the hearing
may be adjourned in order that certain information may be
brought before the Court to enable it to say which party should
pay the costs.

The case of *Wait* v. *Wait* (1) really determines this matter.
There, no doubt, the application was made after the decree
absolute, but the reasons in that case apply equally where the
application is made after the hearing and before the decree
absolute. In that case the Judge Ordinary, after referring to s.
51 of the English Act, which corresponds to s. 41 of our Act,
says: "In the very terms of the Act it is at *the hearing* that the
Court shall exercise its discretion, and it is the universal practice
of all Courts at the time of trial to determine what order ought
to be made as to costs. It is true that sometimes the final
decision is adjourned in order to allow of an application as to
costs; but in such a case the Court acts within the spirit of the
statute. Now in this case no application was made at the trial
to condemn the respondent in costs, nor was there any adjournment to allow such an application to be made." Now the reason
of it is this. If the application is made at the hearing, the
Judge then has the whole matter in his mind, and can exercise
his discretion whilst the facts are fresh in his memory, and
whilst there has been nothing intervening to take his mind off
the facts. Under s. 31 the Court can make the co-respondent
pay the whole or part of the costs. There are many cases in the

(1) 2 P. & D. 228.

books where the co-respondent has been made to pay only part
of the costs, and it is important in considering whether he should
be made to pay a part or the whole of the costs, that all the
facts of the case should be fresh in the mind of the Judge who
has to exercise his discretion. Those are the reasons why the
Legislature has provided that the order must be made "*on the
hearing.*" Those words in s. 41 should be given their ordinary
plain meaning. They do not mean that the order can be made
at some subsequent time.

In the case of *Somerville* v. *Somerville* (1) nothing was brought
to the attention of the Court, but the Rule of Court (the section
of the Act not being referred to), and the reasoning in the later
case of *Wait* v. *Wait* is directly opposed to it; we, therefore,
cannot follow it. This appeal must be allowed with costs.

STEPHEN, J. I agree. If our decision were otherwise the
question of costs would remain in abeyance for the whole time
between the hearing and the decree absolute.

COHEN, J., concurred.

Appeal allowed with costs.

Solicitor for the appellant : *R. G. C. Roberts.*

Solicitors for the respondent : *Aitken & Aitken.*

(1) 36 L.J.P. & M. 87.

1898.

TAURO
v.
TAURO.
(RIZZO,
Co-respon-
dent).

The C.J.

JONES v. JONES ; HIGGINS, Co-respondent.

1898.
_____
May 16, 18.

Matrimonial Causes Act, ss. 6, 7 – RR. 57, 98—Issues for trial—Adultery of co-respondent—Memorandum for new trial - Signature of counsel—Notice of appeal—Informality—Amendment.

The C.J.
Stephen J.
and
Cohen J.

In a suit for dissolution of marriage the issues on the record were—(1) Marriage; (2) Whether the respondent committed adultery with the co-respondent ; and (3) What amount of damages (if any) the petitioner is entitled to recover from the co-respondent in respect of the adultery (if any) committed by him with the respondent. The jury found upon ample evidence that the co-respondent had committed adultery with the respondent, and awarded damages. *Held*, that there was no issue on the record raising the question whether the co-respondent had committed adultery with the respondent, and that the jury were, therefore, not at liberty to consider that question or to award damages.

A memorandum for a new trial must be signed by counsel.

A notice of appeal asked for a new trial, or that the decree *nisi* might be set aside or varied, upon a number of grounds, some of which were grounds for granting a new trial, and some of appeal against the decree. The notice was informal as a memorandum for a new trial for non-compliance with the provisions of R. 98. The Court struck out the matter relating to a new trial, and entertained the application as one of appeal only.

DIVORCE APPEAL.

This was a suit by the husband for a dissolution of his marriage with the respondent on the ground of her adultery with the co-respondent, from whom the petitioner claimed damages. The issues for trial were settled before the Registrar in accordance with the usual practice, in the following form :

1. Whether Alfred Richard Jones (the petitioner) was married to Christina Jones (the respondent) on the 19th of February, 1896.

2. Whether the respondent, on or about the 9th day of February, 1897, committed adultery with George Albert Higgins, the co-respondent, at Wirroo, near Carinda, in the Colony of New South Wales.

1898.

JONES
v.
JONES;
HIGGINS,
Co-re-
spondent.

3. What amount of damages (if any) the petitioner is entitled to recover from the co-respondent in respect of the adultery (if any) committed by him with the respondent.

The suit was heard before the Judge in Divorce and a jury, on the 21st February, and 1st, 2nd, and 3rd March. Before counsel addressed the jury, the learned Judge suggested that it would be better if an issue were added, whether the co-respondent had committed adultery with the respondent. *Ralston*, for the co-respondent, objected to the amendment, and submitted that under the issues as they stood it was not open to the jury to find damages against the co-respondent. *Piddington*, for the petitioner, also objected to the proposed amendment, on the ground that the issues were in the usual form, and that under the third issue the question of damages was open to the jury. The case was therefore left to the jury under the issues as they stood, and the Judge directed the jury that they might assess damages against the co-respondent if they found that he had been guilty of adultery with the respondent.

The jury found the first and second issues in favour of the petitioner, and 400*l.* damages against the co-respondent on the third issue, and they specially found that the co-respondent did commit adultery with the respondent on a certain date.

The decree *nisi* was taken out on the 3rd March, stating the finding of the jury against the co-respondent, and ordering him to pay into Court the damages awarded, and the petitioner's costs when taxed. On the 16th March, by consent, the decree *nisi* was amended by striking out the allegation of the finding of the jury against the co-respondent, and the order that he should pay the damages into Court, and by a separate order made on the same day the co-respondent was ordered to pay the damages awarded against him into Court within twenty-eight days, to abide the further order of the Court.

On the 17th March, the co-respondent filed a notice of appeal asking that "the said decree *nisi* made herein be set aside, and that a new trial of the issues herein be granted, or that the said decree be set aside so far as it affects the said co-respondent, or that such other order be made, etc," upon the grounds (1) that

1898.

Jones
v.
Jones;
Higgins,
Co-re-
spondent.

there being no issue before the jury as to whether the co-respondent committed adultery with the respondent, his Honour was in
error in leaving the third issue as to the damages for their consideration. (2) That there being no valid finding that the co-
respondent had committed adultery with the respondent, his
Honour was in error in ordering the costs to be paid by the
co-respondent.

A number of other grounds were included, some of them being
grounds of appeal from the Judge, and some grounds for granting
a new trial, e.g., surprise.

The co-respondent also filed a notice of appeal against the
order of the 16th March requiring him to pay the damages into
Court, upon the ground, amongst others, that there having been
no issue before the jury whether the co-respondent committed
adultery with the respondent, the jury had no power to assess
the said damages, and his Honour had no power to make the
order appealed against.

Piddington and *Kelynack*, for the petitioner, took the preliminary objection that the first appeal being a motion for a new
trial under s. 9 of the Divorce Act, the provisions of Rule 98
had not been complied with. That rule provides that a memorandum shall be filed and a rule *nisi* obtained as at common law
under R. 5 of the Rules of 19th August, 1861 (*Pilcher Pr.* 609)
and R. 18 of the yearly Rules. Here no memorandum signed by
counsel has been filed, nor is the notice of appeal signed by
counsel, nor does it contain the necessary particulars as to date
of trial, verdict given, etc.

The Chief Justice. As to those particulars, could we not
amend under 12 Vic. No. 1, s. 3, and insert them ?

Piddington. Perhaps, but no rule *nisi* has been obtained.
However, the point as to the signature of counsel is fatal: see
Wakely v. *Quinn* (1), *Dennis* v. *Horsley* (2), *Wentworth* v. *Hill*
(3), *Jenkins* v. *Douglas* (4), *Cross* v. *Goode* (5).

(1) 2 W.N. 28.   (3) 7 W.N. 4.
(2) 2 W.N. 36.   (4) 7 W.N. 95.
            (5) 8 N.S.W. L.R. 255 ; 5 W.N. 100.

Pilcher, Q.C. We are not really moving for a new trial; all we want is to reverse the decree, and we are at liberty to move by way of appeal to reverse the decree upon any grounds, even though they involve matter affecting a new trial. Further, appeals and motions for new trials are perfectly distinct, and if the notice of appeal is bad as a memorandum for a new trial, it is still good as an appeal upon those grounds which are properly grounds of appeal.

THE CHIEF JUSTICE. Some of the grounds stated in the notice are purely grounds of appeal, as, for instance, grounds one and two, whilst others are as clearly grounds for granting a new trial. I do not think we can now consider those grounds which relate to a new trial, because there has been no memorandum filed, signed by counsel, and otherwise complying with the practice regulating new trial motions at common law as required by R. 98 of the Divorce Rules. But I am of opinion that if we are against Mr. *Piddington* upon the two first grounds, which are grounds of appeal, we can strike out of the notice all that relates to a new trial, and consider the matter as purely one of appeal.

STEPHEN and COHEN, JJ., concurred.

Pilcher, Q.C., *Ralston*, and *Whitfeld*, in support of the appeal. It was necessary, before the co-respondent could be cast in damages, that there should be a definite issue before the jury whether he had committed adultery with the respondent. It is well settled law that the wife may be found guilty of adultery with the co-respondent, whilst there is no evidence that the co-respondent has been guilty of adultery with the respondent: *Robinson* v. *Lane* (1), *Crawford* v. *Crawford* (2), *Ruck* v. *Ruck* (3); and the jury must find some damages against a co-respondent who does not appear, even though they find that the respondent has not committed adultery: *McGarry* v. *McGarry* (4). The question whether the co-respondent has committed adultery is entirely different, in its nature and results, from whether the respondent

(1) 1 Sw. & Tr. 362.   (3) [1896] P. 152.
(2) 11 P.D. 150.   (4) 8 N.S.W. L.R. D. 8; 3 W.N. 129.

1898.

JONES
v.
JONES;
HIGGINS,
Co-re-
spondent.

has committed adultery with the co-respondent, and before the jury can find any verdict against the co-respondent, there must be a definite and distinct issue upon that point before them. Here there was no such issue, and no such question is raised either by the second or third issue on the record. That being so, it does not matter whether there was or was not evidence to support the finding of the jury against the co-respondent; if there was evidence there was no issue for it to support.

Piddington. In the first place the question whether the co-respondent committed adultery with the respondent is contained in the third issue, which consists in reality of two questions; first, has the co-respondent committed adultery with the respondent, and if so, what damages is the petitioner entitled to recover. The sole ground of the right to recover damages is the co-respondent's adultery with the respondent, and the jury must find that fact, as they did in this case, before they can assess damages under the other portion of the issue. The main issue of the suit, the object of which is to obtain a dissolution of the marriage, is whether the respondent has been guilty of adultery, and it has therefore been hitherto thought sufficient to combine the issues as to the co-respondent in one.

Secondly, we have followed the practice which has always obtained in this Court since the Divorce Act was passed. The issues were settled in the usual way by the Registrar upon the direction of the Judge (RR. 54, 55, 57), and in accordance with the form prescribed (Form 7). *Browne & Powle* (6th Ed. 1897, p. 560) give the same form.

Pilcher, Q.C., in reply. The third issue does not contain the two issues; it refers solely to damages, and the only answer to it is £. s. d. The forms of issues in our rules are not exhaustive, and are intended merely as guides to an intelligent pleader. The form itself says : " Here set forth in the same form all the issues settled between the parties." *Oakley's Divorce Practice* (3rd Ed., 1892, p. 62) gives a form containing both issues separately stated; and see *Dixon on Divorce* (p. 299), and ss. 6 and 7 of the Divorce Act.

1898.

JONES
v.
JONES;
HIGGINS,
Co-re-
spondent.

The C.J.

THE CHIEF JUSTICE. This was a suit for dissolution of marriage upon the ground of the respondent's adultery with the co-respondent, which was heard before the Judge in Divorce and a jury. At the close of the evidence his Honour, seeing that there was no issue upon the record directly raising the question whether the co-respondent had committed adultery with the respondent, suggested that the record should be amended by adding such an issue. Mr. *Ralston*, counsel for the co-respondent, naturally objected to the issues being amended, and contended that, as there was no issue before the jury raising the question of the co-respondent's guilt, that matter could not be considered by them. Curiously enough, counsel for the petitioner also objected to the course his Honour proposed to pursue, and the case, therefore, went to the jury upon the issues as they were settled upon the record, *i.e*, (1) marriage, (2) whether the respondent had committed adultery with the co-respondent, and (3) what damages (if any) should be paid by the co-respondent. His Honour, however, left it open to the jury to find a verdict against the co-respondent, and they found that the co-respondent did commit adultery with the respondent, and assessed the damages at 400*l*. It is now argued that his Honour was right in leaving the case to the jury in that way, inasmuch as the third issue was before the jury, and it is said that that issue is so worded as to involve the question, was the co-respondent guilty of adultery with the respondent. If, however, the third issue does not involve that question, then it is clear there was no question touching the co-respondent before the jury.

To shew that the third issue does, or at all events, is intended to raise the question of the guilt of the co-respondent, we have been referred to what has hitherto been the practice, and to Form 7 of the forms appended to the Rules in Divorce. That form, however, is not compulsory, and need not be followed. It is a form merely for the guidance of practitioners, and when examined it is found that the form does not in any way provide for this particular question.

In the first place, it is necessary to look at the Act of Parliament to see how the questions raised in a suit are to be laid before the Court or the jury. Section 6 provides that questions

1898.

JONES
v.
JONES;
HIGGINS,
Co-re-
spondent.

The C.J.

of fact may be directed to be tried before the Court or before a jury. Section 7 provides that " when any such question shall be so ordered to be tried, *such question shall be reduced into writing* in such form as the Court shall direct, and at the trial the jury shall be sworn to try the question, and a true verdict to give thereon according to the evidence." That section is mandatory, that *the question* to be tried shall be reduced into writing. The reason is that in Divorce there are no pleadings, in the proper sense of the word, and the different questions of fact to be determined have to be gathered from the statements in the petition and answer ; accordingly, it is deemed necessary that the exact questions in issue should be distinctly stated in writing, in order that the Court or the jury may know what they are trying. Then section 9 provides that " it shall be lawful for the parties to apply for a new trial of any such question, or of any issue which under this Act may be tried before a jury." If the question is not on the record, how could a party apply for a new trial of it ?

Under the Rules we find that in defended cases the Judge directs what issues are to be tried, and R. 57 provides that "after the Judge has directed what are the issues to be tried, the same are to be briefly stated in writing by the petitioner (Form No. 7), and by him taken to the Registrar, who shall upon perusal of the pleadings and order of the Judge directing what are to be the issues, settle the same." Form No. 7 is, as I have already said, clearly intended to be nothing more than a guide, and is not exhaustive. For one thing, no form is given of an issue of marriage ; and then there is the direction, " Here set forth in the same form all the issues settled between the parties." After this comes the form for damages against a co-respondent, clearly referring to a preceding issue as to the adultery of the co-respondent, in a form similar to the one given as to the adultery of the respondent. In *Oakley's Divorce Practice,* a standard work by the Chief Clerk of the Divorce Registry in England, a form is given stating the issue in the precise way contended for by the co-respondent, and *Dixon on Divorce* states that where damages are asked for against a co-respondent the two questions are always separately involved: (1) did the respondent commit adultery with the co-respondent; and (2) did the co-respondent commit adultery with the respondent. There must be a distinct issue as to the adultery of the co-respondent, because there may be evidence sufficient to convict the respondent of adultery with the co-respondent, and yet no evidence against the co-respondent. The respondent and co-respondent are entirely distinct parties, and have no relation to each other on the record, and, therefore, there should be distinct issues on the record with regard to them.

I am, therefore, of opinion that before a co-respondent can be mulcted in damages, there must be before the jury a distinct and definite issue whether he committed adultery with the respondent, and as in the present case there was no such issue I am of opinion that it was not open to the jury to consider the question whether the co-respondent committed adultery with the respondent, or to find any verdict against him for damages. It is not a question of a new trial, because there is nothing to try between the petitioner and the co-respondent, but the first ground of the notice of appeal aptly states the point, and the appeal must be sustained upon that ground. As to the second ground, it follows that, the finding of the jury being nugatory, his Honour had no power to order the co-respondent to pay the costs.

As to the second appeal, it appears that the decree *nisi* having been drawn up dissolving the marriage, and ordering the co-respondent to pay the costs of the suit, a separate order was made, which, I think, is the proper practice to adopt, ordering the co-respondent to pay the damages into Court. That order has been appealed against upon a number of grounds, but the only one we need consider is that which takes the point we have just considered in the appeal against the decree *nisi*. The jury having had no power to award damages, it follows that the Judge had no power to make the order appealed against.

STEPHEN, J. I regret that I am constrained to concur with their Honours. I can quite understand the learned Judge in Divorce leaving the case to the jury as he did, because this particular form has been in constant use for many years, and

1898.

JONES
v.
JONES;
HIGGINS,
Co-re-
spondent.

The C.J.

1898.

JONES
v.
JONES;
HIGGINS,
Co-re-
spondent.

Stephen J.

under it the guilt of co-respondents has been constantly determined.   In the present case the whole of the evidence was given
without objection, and there is no doubt that the guilt of the
co-respondent was fully considered and found by the jury.

COHEN, J., concurred.

Appeal sustained with costs.

Solicitors for the petitioner : *Newman & Son* (Tamworth).

Solicitors for the co-respondent: *Abbott, Vindin & Littlejohn.*

ERSKINE *v.* ERSKINE.

Judicial separation— Wife's costs of suit—Liability of husband — Wife's separate estate.

On an application by a wife, petitioner in a suit for judicial separation, for an order that the respondent should pay into Court a sum of money for her costs incurred, and to be incurred in the suit —*Held*, that the fact that the wife has some separate estate will not relieve the respondent of his liability to supply her with money to prosecute the suit. The question is whether, having regard to the income necessary to maintain her suitably to her station, she has sufficient for the payment of her costs, as well as for her own support.

1898.

May 17.

The C.J.
Stephen J.
and
Cohen J.

DIVORCE APPEAL.

This was a suit for a judicial separation brought by the wife, and the petitioner applied to the Judge in Divorce for an order directing the respondent to lodge a sum of money with the Registrar, to meet the petitioner's costs of prosecuting the suit. The costs already incurred amounted to some 20*l.*, owing to an application for an order for substituted service arising out of the evasion of service by the respondent, and the costs of the trial were expected to be heavy, owing to the number of witnesses. The Judge refused to make any order, upon the ground that the wife was the possessor of separate estate, and he also refused to allow her the costs of the application. From the order dismissing the application, the petitioner appealed on the ground that under the circumstances disclosed by the affidavits the Judge was wrong in refusing the application, and in refusing the petitioner the costs of it.

L. Armstrong, for the appellant.

Ralston, for the respondent, took the preliminary objection that no security for the costs of the appeal had been given under s. 5 of the Divorce Act and R. 95.

THE CHIEF JUSTICE. That point really depends on the same question as the appeal itself, *i.e.*, whether the wife has separate property. We must hear the facts before we can decide it.

The affidavits were then read. It appeared that the petitioner had a life estate in ten houses which had been settled on her by the respondent, the gross value of which was about 5,000*l.*, and that after the trustees had paid ground rent and other expenses, the petitioner received the rents, and that at the present time she was receiving some 1*l.* 5*s.* per week. The respondent owned a terrace of houses and also the reversion in the houses settled on the petitioner, in one of which he was then living rent free. He admitted having a sum of 150*l.* to his credit in his bank, and he kept several carriages and horses and a groom, but he swore that his income, after all expenses, did not amount to 50*l.* a year.

Armstrong. The fact that the wife has enough to pay for her bare living does not make her the possessor of separate estate, so as to bar her from getting an order for her costs. The question is, if she has *sufficient* separate property to prevent the order being made, and here the petitioner is only in receipt of 1*l.* 5*s.* a week, which is not enough to support her in a manner proper for the wife of a man in the respondent's position. If the wife has *not more* than is sufficient for her to live on, she is entitled to an order: *Gronn* v. *Gronn* (1); *Belcher* v. *Belcher* (2); *Allen* v. *Allen* (3).

Ralston. It is a matter for the discretion of the Judge, and it has not been contended that the Judge exercised his discretion upon a wrong principle. See *Hawksworth* v. *Hawksworth* (4). His Honour had all the facts before him, and he was referred· to the case of *Allen* v. *Allen* (3), but considering the relative incomes of the parties, and that the petitioner's income is actually larger than the respondent's, he felt that it would be unjust to make any order. If a husband is a pauper or bankrupt, or clearly unable to comply with the order, the Judge may refuse to make it. Another matter which his Honour might take into consideration was, that this is a suit for a judicial separation, in which the wife is the petitioner, and in such cases, although this Court has in some cases departed from the strict rule, the wife is not entitled to the order, because in the Ecclesiastical Court

(1) 1 S.C.R. N.S. D. 8.   (3) [1894] P. 134.
(2) 1 Curt. 444.   (4) *Ante*, p. 1.

her costs were only taxed *de die in diem* when she was respon- 1898.

ERSKINE.
v.
ERSKINE.
dent in the suit. Here she is the moving party, and, if unsuccessful, will not be entitled to her costs; but once the money is
paid to her the respondent will never recover it, although he
succeeds. As to the costs of the application, his Honour has
made it a rule not to allow costs unless a demand has been made
before the application, and it was on that ground that he refused
them.

THE CHIEF JUSTICE. I am of opinion that the appeal should
be sustained. It seems that the petitioner, the wife of a man
who is apparently in a good position, and who owns carriages and
horses, is the possessor of separate estate from which she is
receiving twenty-five shillings a week, which is all she has to
live on. She has had to leave her home, and a woman in her
station of life cannot earn her own living. On the other hand,
I think it clearly appears that the husband is in a position to
pay both his own and his wife's costs. It is quite clear from
Belcher v. *Belcher* (1), that, when a wife has separate property, the
Court will take the amount of it into consideration, and notwithstanding its existence may make an order against the husband,
unless the property of the wife is sufficient both for her own support
and for the payment of her costs. In that case the husband was a
captain in the navy, and his income was 510*l.* a year, the wife having
an income of 236*l.*, and it was held that, although the wife had
sufficient to support herself, she had not enough to pay her costs,
and the husband was ordered to pay them.

Upon the facts of this case, I think it is clear that the discretion of the Judge below has been exercised erroneously, and that
the wife's application ought to have been granted. As to the
costs of the application, it may no doubt in many cases be desirable to enforce the rule that a demand shall have been made
before applying to the Court, but such a rule cannot be enforced
in a hard and fast manner. In the present case it would not
have been the least use to make a demand. For these reasons
I am of opinion that the preliminary objection as to security

(1) 1 Curt. 444.

taken by Mr. *Ralston* must be overruled, and that the appeal should be allowed with costs.

STEPHEN, J. I agree upon the ground that the position of the husband is better than that of the wife.

COHEN, J. I am of the same opinion. It is laid down in . *Allen* v. *Allen* (1), that the question for consideration, in such a case as this, is whether the wife has sufficient property to prevent the order being made, and that to arrive at a decision the relative incomes of the parties must be taken into consideration. Here the husband can raise money upon the property of which he has the fee simple in possession, whilst the wife cannot raise money upon her life estate, except perhaps, if she is a good life, by a policy of life insurance being added to the life estate.

> *Appeal sustained. 40l. to be paid by the respondent within a fortnight. Appellant to have her costs of the application and of this appeal.*

Solicitor for the petitioner : *Lewis Levy.*

Solicitors for the respondent : *Curtiss & Barry.*

(1) [1894] P. 134.

INDEX.

Common Law, Equity, Bankruptcy and Probate, and Divorce.

The defendants held a bill of sale over certain goods of G. On the 29th December they had notice that G. had committed an act of bankruptcy. On the 30th December they seized the goods under the bill of sale. On the 4th January they assigned the goods absolutely to the plaintiffs. In the deed of assignment they covenanted that they had not been "party or privy to any act" whereby they were prevented from assigning the goods absolutely to the plaintiffs. On the 13th January G. became bankrupt, and the goods were subsequently claimed by G.'s official assignee. *Held,* that the defendants having notice of the act of bankruptcy, were party or privy to an act whereby they were prevented from assigning the goods, and had therefore committed a breach of the covenant.

The defendants assigned to the plaintiffs the goods comprised in a bill of sale given by G. to them. These goods were claimed by the official assignee of G.'s estate, and on a motion under s. 130 of the Bankruptcy Act, 1887, the plaintiffs (in which they set up the title to the goods through the defendants) were ordered to pay the value of them to the official assignee. *Held,* that the judgment of the Bankruptcy Court did not prevent the defendants from setting up that they had a good title to the goods, when they transferred them to the plaintiffs in an action brought by the plaintiffs against them for breach of the covenant for title, inasmuch as they were not parties to the bankruptcy proceedings.

G. gave a bill of sale over certain goods to the defendants, and subsequently gave a second bill of sale over the same goods to the plaintiffs. The defendants seized the goods with notice of an available act of bankruptcy committed by G., and afterwards assigned the goods to the plaintiffs. In an action brought by the plaintiffs against the defendants for breach of covenant for title, the defendants in order to shew that the goods were not in the order and disposition of the bankrupt when they had notice of the act of bankruptcy, sought to give in evidence the plaintiffs' bill of sale and to give evidence that at that time the goods were not in the order and disposition of the bankrupt, because the plaintiffs had previously seized under their bill of sale without notice of an available act of bankruptcy, and this evidence was rejected. *Held,* that the evidence should have been admitted. The possession of a second bill of sale holder who seizes without

tax, how made a charge on the land taxed—Issue of Gazette notice—Construction of taxing statutes.]
The Court of Equity has jurisdiction to determine whether the steps to make the land tax payable have been legally carried out. The land tax payable under 59 Vic. No. 15 and 59 Vic. No. 16 does not become a charge on the land taxed until the amount is due and payable, nor does it become due and payable until the assessment book contemplated by the Act is "complete" and a notice has subsequently thereto been issued in the *Gazette* under s. 47 of the Act 59 Vic. No. 15. Whatever may be the meaning of the term assessment book in the Act 59 Vic. No. 15, it cannot be said to be complete when particulars of the assessment of only half the taxable land in the colony have been entered, but, *semble*, if the book were substantially complete that would be a sufficient compliance with the Act. Consideration of what is meant by the term "assessment book" in the Act 59 Vic. No. 15. If in a taxing Act the Court sees that a burden is clearly imposed, it will, so far as the mere machinery is concerned, be astute to carry out the clear intention of raising revenue for the Crown. COOPER *v.* COMMISSIONERS OF TAXATION - - - - - - - Eq. 1

LEASE—*Advertising rights—Lease or license.*]
The lessee of an hotel "leased to A., his executors, administrators, and assigns, the privilege of attaching advertising boards to the hotel balcony, and of affixing advertisements on a hoarding erected on the premises, with the sole right to erect hoardings for advertising purposes as yearly tenants from the 1st January, 1897, at an annual rental of 57l., payable quarterly, with right to remove all such hoardings." *Held*, that this was a lease, not a license, and that the advertising rights were not put an end to by the lessee surrendering his lease to the landlord. KEMP *v.* PALMER. - - - Eq. 38

LIEN—*See* ATTORNEY.

LIMITATIONS (STATUTES OF)—*Nullum Tempus Act, 9 Geo. III. c. 16—Construction of 9 Geo. IV. c. 83, s. 24—Application of English Statutes to New South Wales.*] *Held*, confirming the judgment of the Supreme Court, that the Imperial Nullum Tempus Act, 9 Geo. III. c. 16, is in force in New South Wales, and that it applies to lands which have never been dealt with by the Crown. The Act 9 Geo. IV. c. 83, s. 24, *prima facie* on its true construction applies the Nullum Tempus Act to the colony. Its operation to that effect cannot be restricted by confining the laws and statutes thereby applied to those relating to procedure, or by shewing that a specific exception in the applied Act preserving the Crown's right could not operate in the circumstances of the colony. ATTORNEY-GENERAL *v.* LOVE - - - 205

2.—— *Resumption of land—Lands for Public Purposes Acquisition Act, s. 12—Public Works Act, 1888, ss. 23, 69, 70, 71—Claim by possession —Payment of compensation money into Court— See* PUBLIC WORKS.

LOCKE KING'S ACT (19 Vic. No. 1, s. 1; [1896] No. 17, s. 109)—*Exoneration of mortgaged property—"Contrary or other intention"—Direction to pay debts out of estate generally.*] A testator devised the whole of his real and personal estate except certain specific chattels to his trustees subject to the payment of debts (with payment of which except his mortgage debts he primarily charged his personal estate) upon certain trusts :—as to Property A upon certain specific trusts: as to Property B on trust to sell, and out of the proceeds in the first place to pay off a mortgage on Property A, and to invest the balance of the proceeds of sale. *Held*, that A was not exonerated from payment of the mortgage debt except to the extent of the proceeds of sale of B, and these proceeds being insufficient the balance of the debt must be charged on A. MOSS *v.* MOSS - Eq. 146

MALICIOUS PROSECUTION. *See* BANKRUPTCY.

MARRIED WOMAN. *See* REGISTRATION OF DEEDS.

MASTER AND SERVANT—*Employers Liability Act (50 Vic. No. 8), s. 9—Workman—Miner—Manual labour—Work incidental to ordinary employment.*] M. was a miner employed in the defendants' coal mine, and ordinarily engaged as a hewer. The mine having been laid idle owing to the occurrence in the workings of a poisonous gas, the manager organised an exploring party, consisting partly of officials and partly of miners, to enter the mine and locate the origin of the gas. M. was sent for by the manager to make one of the party, and whilst down the mine died from the effects of the gas. The plaintiff, his administratrix, sued the defendants under the Employers Liability Act, alleging that his death was caused by the negligence of the manager in taking the exploring party into the mine without proper precautions. *Held*, that M. was a workman in the employment of the defendants within the meaning of the Employers Liability Act. If the real and substantial business of a person whose avocation is mentioned in the Act involves manual labour, and such workman is injured while carrying out some duty or work incidental to his real and substantial avocation, although the latter does not involve immediate manual labour, nevertheless he is within the purview of the Act. HOLLAND *v.* STOCKTON COAL CO. - - - 100

MATRIMONIAL CAUSES. *See* DIVORCE.

MINING—*Mining Act, 1874, s. 115—Reg. Gen. 18th Nov., 1875—Appeal—Special case—Signature of Judge—Notice of appeal—Form of appeal.*] A mining appeal was heard in the District Court before an acting Judge, and on an appeal from his decision to the Supreme Court, the acting Judge's commission having expired, the special case was signed by the then Judge of the District Court in which the appeal had been heard. *Held*, that the case was properly signed. The notice of appeal did not contain a statement of the determination or direction appealed from as required by Reg. Gen., 18th November, 1875, but contained instead a number of grounds of appeal. *Held*, that the notice of appeal was informal, but as the special case contained a statement of the final determination arrived at by the Judge below, the Court (COHEN, J., *dissentiente*) overruled the objection to the notice of appeal. *Semble*, an appeal under the Mining Act, s. 115, from the District Court to the Supreme Court, is not intended to take the form of a special case, but to be set down for argument, upon the notice of appeal and the statement signed by the Judge whose decision is appealed from, in the same way as special cases are set down for argument. LINDSAY *v.* HANSON · · · · · · **348**

2.——*Mining Act, 1874, s. 70—Reg. 3 of Practice Regulations—Warden's Court—Summons—Personal service—Substituted service—Discretion of Warden.*] Where a summons under s. 70 of the Mining Act, 1874, has not been personally served, the Warden may proceed with the case in the absence of the defendant if, in his opinion, there has been sufficient substituted service, either in the manner prescribed by R. 3 of the Rules of 21st July, 1874, or otherwise. *Ex parte* KELLY · · **201**

3.—— *Workman. See* MASTER AND SERVANT.

MOORE STREET IMPROVEMENT ACT, 54 *Vic. No.* 30—*Assessment—Nature of liability—Landlord and tenant—Covenant to pay rates, taxes, assessments, impositions and charges.*] The plaintiff, the owner of freehold property within the improvement area contemplated by the Moore Street Improvement Act, 54 Vic. No. 30, let to the defendants for ten years by a lease containing a covenant by the lessee to pay "all taxes, rates, assessments, impositions and charges, whether municipal, parochial, or otherwise, now and hereafter to be imposed, etc., excepting a Government property tax." The Moore Street Improvement Act came into force about two years after the date of the lease, and the plaintiff, having paid certain annual instalments of the amount thereby assessed in respect of the premises, now sued the defendants under the covenant to recover the amount. *Held*, that the liability imposed upon owners of property by the Moore Street Improvement Act is a personal liability upon such owners, and not a charge upon the land. *Held, further* (COHEN, J., *dissentiente*), that the liability imposed by the Act was not contemplated by the parties when executing the lease, and was not covered by the terms of the covenant. WRENCH *v.* RICHARDSON & WRENCH · · · **78**

MORTGAGE—*Mortgagor and mortgagee—Mortgagee in possession—Real Property Act, s. 58—Tenant holding over.*] A mortgagee in possession under a mortgage under the Real Property Act has power to lease the land until redemption, and if the tenant hold over against the mortgagor after redemption, the mortgagee is not responsible to the mortgagor for the act of

the tenant in so holding over. FINN *v.* LONDON BANK OF AUSTRALIA · · · · **364**

2.——*Mortgagor and mortgagee — Mortgagee selling on terms under special power of sale—Form of account—Practice.*] Where the power of sale in a mortgage authorises a sale for cash or on terms, and the mortgagee sells on terms by which the payment of the purchase money is spread over a number of years, the mortgagee is not bound to credit the mortgagor with the whole of the purchase money as received on the day of the sale, but only with the instalments as they are received. *Hickey* v. *Heydon* overruled on this point. IRVING *v.* COMMERCIAL BANKING CO. · · · · - Eq. **54**

MUNICIPALITIES—*Municipalities Act, s.* 165—*Rates—Lighting—"Property deriving benefit or advantage."*] If any portion of a property derives benefit or advantage from lighting the whole property is benefited, and lighting rates are payable in respect of the whole property (per THE CHIEF JUSTICE and COHEN, J.) *Quære* (per STEPHEN, J.), whether if in action to recover lighting rates it be found that some portion of the property is not benefited lighting rates can be recovered in respect of the whole property. BOROUGH OF WALLSEND *v.* NEWCASTLE WALLSEND COAL CO. · · · **263**

2.—— *Loans to—Consideration for loan—S. 191 of Municipalities Act of 1867.*] Under s. 191 the council of any municipality may by deed wherein the consideration shall be truly stated mortgage all general and special rates, etc. The Municipal District of Lambton mortgaged their rates " in consideration of the sum of 7,000*l.* paid to us by the Commercial Bank of Australia." It appeared that the sum of 7,000*l.* was not at that time paid to the council, but the money was paid to them from time to time as they required it. It was contended on behalf of the council that as the consideration was not truly stated the mortgage was bad. *Held*, that as there was a collateral agreement that the money was not to be advanced all at once, and that the bank was only to charge interest on the money actually drawn, the consideration was sufficiently stated. *In re* MUNICIPAL DISTRICT OF LAMBTON ; *Ex parte* COMMERCIAL BANK OF AUSTRALIA · · · · · · · **404**

3.—— *Rates — Charge — Rights of mortgagee —Municipalities Act, 1867* (31 *Vic. No.* 12), *s.* 176—*Municipalities Act Amendment Act of 1892* (55 *Vic. No.* 33), *s.* 5.] The charge created by the Municipalities Acts of 1867 and 1892 is a first charge upon the property rated, and has priority over any mortgage over the same property, even with respect to rates which become due after the date of such mortgage. *In re* THE MERCANTILE BUILDING L. & I. CO. · · · · · · · · · - Eq. **230**

4. —— *Ouster — Rescission of order — See* PRACTICE.

NEW TRIAL—*See* DISTRICT COURT—PRACTICE.

NOTICE—*Constructive notice—Notice of breach of trust from recital in title deed—Money subject to a settlement authorised to be laid out in the purchase of land—Erection of house on land subject to the settlement.*] Where in the recitals of one of the title deeds to land facts are disclosed which point to a possible breach of trust having been committed, a purchaser who omits to enquire has constructive notice of such facts as it is reasonable to suppose he would have learnt upon enquiry, but not of such facts as it is possible he might have learnt. FLOWER *v.* OWEN. - - - - - - Eq. 72

NULLUM TEMPUS ACT—*See* LIMITATIONS.

PARTITION—*Sale—Partition Act* (41 *Vic. No.* 17) — *Over-riding .trust—Power—Jurisdiction—Equitable estate.*] A testator bequeathed and devised to his trustees the whole of his real and personal estate ; he gave his trustees power to sell, lease, or mortgage any part of his estate, and after payment of debts and legacies to stand seized and possessed of all the residue of the estate "upon trust to divide the same equally share and share alike between" three beneficiaries. *Held,* that the trust to divide the estate equally did not oust the operation of the Partition Act, but that a majority of the beneficiaries could insist upon a sale unless good cause was shewn to the contrary ; nor was it material that the estate did not wholly consist of realty. OATLEY *v.* OATLEY - - Eq. 122

2.— *Practice—Mortgage by one tenant in common to another—Partition against the consent of mortgagee of an undivided interest - Conditional offer to redeem.*] A tenant in common who has mortgaged his undivided interest must before he can sue for partition offer to redeem unconditionally, and must satisfy the Court that the mortgage will be paid off at once ; and it is immaterial that the mortgagee is a co-tenant in common. OATLEY *v.* OATLEY - Eq. 129

3.— *Tenancy in common—Landlord and tenant - Ordinary repairs - Improvements—Expenditure by one tenant in common in remainder on permanent improvements—Contribution—Use and occupation.*] The rule that one of several tenants in common of real estate is entitled when the property is sold to receive out of the purchase money the increased price obtained in consequence of permanent improvements effected by himself applies to suits for administration as well as suits for partition. The rule also applies whether the improvements are effected while the estate of the tenant in common is only an estate in remainder as well as where his estate is an estate in possession. BOULTER *v.* BOULTER - - - - - - - - Eq. 135

PATENT—*Patent Law Amendment Act,* 1895 (60 *Vic. No.* 39), *s.* 5, *sub-s.* iv. (c), (d), (e)—*Revocation of patent - Petition for — " Author and Designer " — " True and first inventor."*] A person obtaining a patent for an invention in respect of which a patent has already been granted to another, cannot for that reason alone petition under s. 5 iv (d) of the Patent Law Amendment Act, 1895. Under s. 5 iv (c), (d), (e), persons claiming rights prior to those of a patentee may petition for their own protection for revocation of the patent, without the fiat of the Attorney-General, and before proceedings for infringement are taken by the patentee. *In re* SCOTT'S PATENT - - - Eq. 114

2.— *Validity—Construction—Infringement—Construction of claim—Doctrine of equivalents—Process—Substance of invention taken.*] The plaintiffs were the owners of a patent for the manufacture of an illuminant cap or hood for gas and other burners. The specification stated that there was employed in the manufacture of the hood a compound of oxide of lanthanum and zirconium, or of these with oxide of yttrium ; and that, instead of using oxide of yttrium, ytterite earth, and instead of oxide of lanthanum cerite earth containing no didymium, and but little cerium might be employed. These minerals were at the time of the patent the less expensive " rarer earths," and it was then known that the "rarer earths," if exposed to a gas flame, became incandescent; the patent was the first successful application of this knowledge, so as to produce an illuminant of a commercial value. The defendants adopted the plaintiffs' process, but substituted thorium for the minerals named in the plaintiffs' patent. The evidence shewed that " thorium " was a cerite earth. *Held,* that it was an infringement of the plaintiffs' patent : and that the plaintiffs' patent was really a patent for the use of the " rarer earths," equivalents of those named in the specification. THE AUSTRALASIAN INCANDESCENT GAS LIGHT CO. *v.* TURNER - - - - - Eq. 214

PRACTICE—4 *Vic. No.* 22, *s.* 27—*Confirmation of rule nisi.*] Where the rule *nisi* has been granted by a Judge in Chambers under 4 Vic. No. 22, s. 27, the respondent may not oppose the confirmation of the rule *nisi* by the Court. JONES *v.* JONES - - - - - - - 43

2.— *Attachment for contempt of Court—Contempts of criminal and civil nature—Affidavits sworn before J.P.—Matter pending—*37 *Vic. No.* 10.] An application by one party to a suit or action to attach another for contempt of Court in interfering with the due administration of justice, is an application in respect of a criminal offence, and is not a proceeding in the suit, and therefore, although the suit is still proceeding, there is no matter pending within the meaning of 37 Vic. No. 10, s. 1, so as to permit of the affidavits upon which the application is founded being sworn before a Justice of the Peace. Ib.

3.— *New trial — Two issues — Admission.*] Where two issues were involved in a case on a new trial motion, and one was decided in favour of the plaintiffs and one in favour of the defendants, the Court, under the powers conferred on it by s. 42 of 5 Vic. No. 9, in granting a new trial on the motion of the defendants, ordered the defendants to make an admission as to the

authority is liable to pay the costs of the separate applications for payment out made by each beneficiary as he comes of age, although the compensation moneys have subsequently to the payment in been carried to separate accounts in the same matter in the name of each beneficiary. Carrying the money to the separate accounts is not payment to the person entitled within the meaning of s. 72 of the Public Works Act. *In re* MOORE - - - - - - Eq. 51

RABBIT ACT (54 *Vic. No.* 29), *s.* 5—*Crown Lands Act of* 1889 (53 *Vic. No.* 21), *s.* 8, *sub-s.* 4—*Appeal from Land Appeal Court.*] Held (reversing the decision of the Full Court), that the Land Appeal Court, sitting under the Rabbit Act of 1890, has power at the request of a party to state a case for the opinion of the Supreme Court. HILL, CLARK & Co. *v.* DALGETY & Co. - - - - - - - - - 98

RATES. See MUNICIPALITIES.

REGISTRATION OF DEEDS ACT (7 *Vic. No.* 16, *s.* 16)—*Married woman—Acknowledgment—Power of appointment.*] It is not necessary for a deed made by a married woman executing a power of appointment to be acknowledged under s. 16 of the Registration of Deeds Act. HEATH *v.* COMMERCIAL B. & I. Co. - - - - 246

RESUMPTION OF LAND. See PUBLIC WORKS.

SETTLED ESTATES ACT, *ss.* 19, 23, 24—*Opposition of majority of beneficiaries to petition under the Act.*] The Court is bound to respect the wishes of the beneficiaries interested in a settled estate, and if a vast majority of them oppose the exercise by the Court of its powers under the Settled Estates Act the Court is bound to refuse to exercise them. *In re* WILSON's ESTATE - - - - - Eq. 140

SHERIFF—*Sheriff's sale*—5 *Vic. No.* 9, *s.* 31; 22 *Vic. No.* 1, *s.* 3—*Purchase of equity of redemption from sheriff.*] Whether the conveyance to the purchaser of an equity of redemption at a sheriff's sale must be registered in order to perfect the purchaser's title, *quære.* IRVING *v.* COMMERCIAL BANKING Co. Eq. 54

SMALL DEBTS RECOVERY ACT—*Jurisdiction—Balance of account.*] The plaintiff brought an action in the Small Debts Court to recover the sum of 9*l.* 12*s.*, and obtained a verdict for that amount. The accounts filed with the plaint shewed that 141*l.* was due to the plaintiff for wages less 131*l.* 8*s.* paid to him. Held, on a motion for a prohibition that as there was evidence before the Small Debts Court that the balance of account had been admitted, the Full Court could not grant a prohibition. *Ex parte* BOURKE - - - - - - 370

SPECIFIC PERFORMANCE — *Specific performance against vendor and a subsequent purchaser*

with notice—Damages for breach of contract—Right of vendor to deduct amount of damage from the balance of purchase moneys due from him to the vendor.] A purchaser obtained a decree for specific performance against a vendor and a subsequent purchaser who had purchased with notice of the prior contract; and also a decree for damages for breach of contract against the vendor. Held, that although the subsequent purchaser was entitled to the balance of the purchase moneys due from the prior purchaser, and, although he was not liable to the prior purchaser for the damages, the prior purchaser was entitled to deduct from the balance the amount of the damages due to him from the vendor. CRAMPTON *v.* FOSTER - Eq. 111

STAMP DUTIES—*Stamp Duties Act of* 1880, *ss.* 2, 53—*Settlement — Pecuniary consideration — Amount of duty payable.*] I. settled certain property which was mortgaged for 10,000*l.* upon trustees in consideration of their entering into a covenant to personally pay any balance that might be due to the mortgagees, if, upon the sale of the property, which was estimated to be worth 40,000*l.*, it did not realise 10,000*l.* Held, that the settlement was not made for bona fide pecuniary consideration within the meaning of s. 2. Semble, that the duty payable under s. 53 was on the full value of the property, 40,000*l.*, and not the value of the property less the amount due under the mortgage. The settlement had been stamped as a conveyance on sale, the consideration being taken as the amount due under the mortgage. Semble, that that duty was properly payable in addition to the duty payable on it as a settlement under s. 53. *In re* IRVING - - - - - - 269

STATUTE OF FRAUDS. See CONTRACT.

STREET. See PUBLIC WORKS.

SYDNEY CORPORATION. See PUBLIC WORKS.

TRADE MARK—See TRADE NAME.

TRADE NAME—*Term of ordinary description—Name denoting the goods of a particular manufacture—Conclusiveness of the trade mark—Trade Marks Act of* 1865 (28 *Vic. No.* 9), *s.* 7—*Suit instituted to try the right of any person to have trade mark registered.*] A trader is entitled to take appropriate words of ordinary description to indicate an article which he sells and makes, although the words form part of the trade mark of a rival trader, provided his action is not calculated to pass off his manufacture as that of his rival, and is not proved in point of fact to have done so. P. was the registered owner of a trade mark which consisted in part of the words "Flaked Oatmeal," and was used by him for a preparation of oats. G. five years afterwards placed a preparation of oats on the market under the name of "G.'s Flaked Oatmeal," thereby accurately describing his preparation. P. sought to restrain the user by G. of the words "Flaked Oatmeal," alleging that the words were his trade mark, and also a trade name designating to the trade and public his own commodity, and that G.'s preparation was put on the market in order to get the benefit of P.'s trade, or was at all events calculated to do so. G. denied that the words were P.'s trade mark, or that they denoted exclusively P.'s preparation, and claimed that they were merely descriptive of his own preparation. *Held* (overruling Owen, C.J. in Eq.), that in a suit so constituted the trade mark was conclusive of P.'s right thereto. *Held, also* (affirming Owen, C.J. in Eq.), that though the words formed part of P.'s trade mark, G. was entitled to use the words as accurately descriptive of his preparation, provided he did so bona fide, and sufficiently distinguished his use of the words from P.'s user. *Reddaway* v. *Banham* ([1896] A.C. 199) followed and applied. Parsons *v.* Gillespie - - - - - - - - - Eq. 26

TRUSTEE—*Breach of trust—Investment of trust funds—Trust to accumulate - Compound interest.*] A trustee who fails to carry out a trust to invest a sum of money and accumulate the income, must repay the principal with compound interest for the period allowed by law for the accumulation, and thereafter at simple interest. This rule applies whether the principal sum has been actually or only constructively received by the trustee sought to be charged : *Byrne* v. *Norcott* (13 Beav. 336) and *In re Holkes* (33 Ch. D. 552) followed. Moss *v.* Moss - Eq. 146

Practice—Suit for breach of trust—No prayer for interest.] A trustee is chargeable with interest, although interest is not asked for by the statement of claim - - - - Ib.

2. —— *Breach of trust — Investment — Real or personal securities — Fixed deposits — Building society.*] Trustees were authorised to invest trust funds "in good real or personal securities;" they invested in fixed deposits with a building society. *Held,* that the investment was authorised by the power. Logan *v.* Raper - - - - - - - - - Eq. 173

3. —— *Breach of trust — Interest — Profits gained by use of trust fund.*] A trustee in breach of trust borrowed trust funds and paid them into his overdrawn account with a bank on which the trustee was paying seven per cent. interest ; the account remained overdrawn in varying amounts up till the hearing of the suit *Held,* that the trustee must repay the trust funds with seven per cent. interest. Farnell *v.* Cox - - - - - - - Eq. 142

4. —— *Breach of trust—Constructive notice from recital in title deeds. See* Notice.

5. —— *Trustee vendor—Payment of purchase money to nominee—Receipt.*] A purchaser from a trustee is justified in paying the purchase money to the trustee's nominee provided he obtains a receipt from the trustee. Flower *v.* Owen - - - - - - - Eq. 72

6. —— *Breach of trust— Trustee borrowing trust funds—Deposit of security - Further advances—Redemption of the security.*] C., a trustee, borrowed 1,500*l.* of the trust moneys in September, 1897. As security for the loan he deposited with the solicitors to the trust estate certain title deeds, together with a letter, in which he undertook to repay the loan in 1902, and to pay interest at 5 per cent.. and gave a power of sale in case of default. *Held,* that the deeds so deposited must be held as security, not merely for the 1,500*l.* and interest, but also for sums subsequently borrowed by C. from the trust estate, but not for sums borrowed prior to September, 1897. Farnell *v.* Cox- Eq . 108

7. —— *Power of sale—How far trustees must sell for the actual value in cash.*] Trustees with a power of sale are not justified in selling portion of the settled land to a municipality in consideration of a nominal sum and a covenant to erect buildings thereon which will have the effect of increasing the selling price of the rest of the land, although the benefit to the estate will be greater than the actual value of the land proposed to be sold. *In re* Lord's Trusts - - - - - - - - - Eq. 207

VENDOR AND PURCHASER—*See* Specific Performance.

VOLUNTARY ASSIGNMENT—*Incomplete voluntary assignment—Assignment of choses in action —Shares in companies—Bank deposits—Mortgage debts—Power of attorney.*] A settlor voluntarily assigned to a trustee for his wife certain mortgage debts with the benefit of the mortgagor's covenants with power to sue for the debts ; he also granted and released to the trustee the mortgaged lands ; he also assigned to the trustee all the moneys held by certain banks on fixed deposit in his name, and also all shares in certain limited companies with power to sue and give receipts for the same. *Held,* that there was a complete gift of the mortgaged land and the mortgage debts ; that the settlor having done all that lay in his power to assign the fixed deposits at the date of the settlement they also passed : but that the shares did not pass as the settlor had not transferred them in the manner provided for by the constitutions of the companies. *Quære,* whether the Court of Equity would have enforced the assignment of the shares if the settlement had contained an irrevocable power of attorney to the trustee. Elliott *v.* Elliott - Eq. 162

WILL—*Construction—Wills Act, s. 29—"In default of issue"—Estate tail—Trust for sale of land and distribution of proceeds where portion of the land sold before date of will—Whether the unpaid purchase moneys secured on mortgage pass under the trust.*] A testator devised an estate of 151 acres to a trustee on trust to sell and to pay the proceeds to H. Before the date of the will the testator had sold portion of the estate and received part of the purchase money, the balance being secured by mortgage of the portion sold and being unpaid at the testator's death. *Held*, that A. was not entitled to the unpaid balance of the purchase moneys. A devise to H. for life and after his death to his heirs and in default of issue over gives A. an estate tail. SHAND *v.* ROBINSON - Eq. 85

2.—*Construction—Forfeiture upon marriage with certain persons—Payment of share upon giving bond to comply with conditions.*] A testator devised and bequeated certain interests under his will upon trust for his children to vest when the youngest attained twenty-one years; but the share of any child who inter-married with a Roman Catholic was immediately to divest from him, and go to the others; each child was empowered to sell his expectant share to another child, and thereupon the purchaser should be "entitled to receive the share so purchased as if the share had been devised to him, the purchaser." *Held*, that the forfeiture clause was good, and applied to subsequent marriages, and not merely to a first marriage; that, upon the sale by one child to another of his share, that share became freed altogether from the forfeiture clause; that the trustees might pay over the shares to the married children upon receiving bonds from them to comply with the condition, and to the unmarried children upon a similar bond from them and one surety. EVANS *v.* TORPY - - Eq. 91

3.—*Construction—Substituted class—"In case of the death"—"Share to which he would have been entitled"—Gift in remainder to persons living at the death of the tenant for life.*] A testator devised his real estate to his wife, and on her death on trust for five persons by name, or such of them as should survive his wife and attain twenty-one, and in case these five persons should all be living at his wife's death and attain twenty-one, he demised to them five several parcels of land, one to each, for their respective lives, and he declared that in case of the death of any of the before mentioned persons then he devised the share to which he would have been entitled to the heir general of such person so dying as aforesaid. *Held*, by the Full Court affirming the decision of *Walker*, J., that in the event of any of the five persons predeceasing testator's widow the substitutory devise to the heir general did not apply, but the survivors were entitled in fee to the whole real estate. *In re* WILLIAMS' CLAIM - - - Eq 223

4.—*Construction — Annuities —Whether payable from the testator's death.*] An annuity given out of residue is payable from the testator's death; *dictum* to contrary in *Storer* v. *Prestage* (1) held overruled. CURTIS *v.* ALLIBAND - - - - - - - Eq. 34

5.—*Restraint against anticipation--Reversionary interest—Trust to convey to* A., *coupled with a direction to trustee to retain and manage the property for payment of debts.*] A testator by his will devised and bequeated the whole of his realty and personalty to trustees. He directed them during such period as they should think fit to receive the rents and profits of the realty, and manage the same as if they were absolutely entitled; to invest the receipts and apply them in payment of his debts, including mortgage debts, and from and immediately after his debts should have been fully discharged to convey a certain freehold to the testator's daughter. The will contained a restraint against anticipation of all reversionary or expectant interests of any female under the will. *Held*, that so long as the trustees were in receipt of the rents and profits for the payment of the debts, the daughter's interests in the freehold was a reversionary interest within the meaning of the restraint clause. BOARD *v.* WEEKES Eq. 200

6.—*Insurance—Protected policy—See* PROBATE AND ADMINISTRATION.

WITNESS—*See* BANKRUPTCY.

Lightning Source UK Ltd.
Milton Keynes UK
UKHW020417090119
334943UK00009B/1334/P